CompTIA® Network+® Review Guide

Exam N10-008

Fifth Edition

Jon Buhagiar

I dedicate this book to my wife, Teresa, and my son, Joseph. I love you both.
—JAB

Acknowledgments

I would like to thank my wife, Teresa. She has had so much patience during the writing of this book. I would also like to thank the many people who made this book possible, including the following: Kenyon Brown at Wiley Publishing for giving me the opportunity to write this book; Kim Wimpsett, for working with me as the developmental editor and making the entire project seamless; Christine O'Connor, for helping with production editing; Buzz Murphy, for serving as technical reviewer to ensure I didn't miss any details; Judy Flynn, for her many edits that helped make this book a polished product; and Saravanan Dakshinamurthy, for helping make sure the content was perfect. Thank you to the many other people I've never met who worked behind the scenes to make this book a success.

About the Author

Jon Buhagiar, BS/ITM, MCSE, CCNA, is an information technology professional with two decades of experience in higher education and the private sector.

Jon currently serves as supervisor of network operations at Pittsburgh Technical College. In this role, he manages data center and network infrastructure operations and IT operations and is involved in project management of projects supporting the quality of education at the college. He also serves as an adjunct instructor in the college's School of Information Technology department, where he has taught courses for Microsoft and Cisco certification. Jon has been an instructor for 23+ years with several colleges in the Pittsburgh area, since the introduction of the Windows NT MCSE in 1998.

Jon earned a bachelor of science degree in Information Technology Management from Western Governors University. He also achieved an associate degree in Business Management from Pittsburgh Technical College. He has recently become a Windows Server 2016 Microsoft Certified Solutions Expert (MCSE) and earned the Cisco Certified Network Associate (CCNA) certification. Other certifications he holds include CompTIA Network+, CompTIA A+, and CompTIA Project+.

In addition to his professional and teaching roles, he has authored *CCNA Routing and Switching Practice Tests: Exam 100-105, Exam 200-105, and Exam 200-125*; *CompTIA Network+ Review Guide: Exam N10-007, Fourth Edition*; *CompTIA A+ Deluxe Study Guide: Exam 220-1002* (all Sybex, 2016); and *CCNA Certification Practice Tests: Exam 200-301, First Edition*. He has also served as the technical editor for the second edition of the *CompTIA Cloud+ Study Guide* (Sybex, 2016), *CCNA Security Study Guide: Exam 210-260* (Sybex, 2018), *CCNA Cloud Complete Study Guide: Exam 210-451 and Exam 210-455* (Sybex, 2018), *CCNP Enterprise Certification Study Guide: Implementing* (Sybex, 2018), and *CCNP Enterprise Certification Study Guide: Implementing and Operating Cisco Enterprise Network Core Technologies: Exam 350-401* (Sybex, 2020). He has spoken at several conferences about spam and email systems. He is an active radio electronics hobbyist and has held a ham radio license for the past 18 years, KB3KGS. He experiments with electronics and has a strong focus on the Internet of Things (IoT).

About the Technical Editor

George "Buzz" Murphy, CISSP, SSCP, CASP, is a public speaker, corporate trainer, author, and cybersecurity evangelist who has instructed thousands of cyber security professionals around the world over the past 25 years with courses, seminars, and consulting presentations on a variety of technical and cybersecurity topics. A former Dell technology training executive, he has addressed audiences at Comdex, Networld, and the National Computer Conference as well as major corporations and educational institutions such as Princeton University. Buzz has earned more than twenty-nine IT and cybersecurity certifications from such prestigious organizations as ISC², CompTIA, PMI, and Microsoft, and other industry certification organizations. He is an ISC² Authorized Instructor and recently served as technical editor for the ISC² *CCFP - Certified Cyber Forensics Professional Certification Guide* published by McGraw-Hill (2014). During the past year, he served as technical editor on five cybersecurity textbooks for both McGraw-Hill Education as well as Sybex an imprint of Wiley and Sons, which includes technical editor for the recent publication *CASP: CompTIA Advanced Security Practitioner Study Guide* by Michael Greg.

Having held a top-secret security clearance in both US and NATO intelligence, he has trained network and cybersecurity operators for the U.S. Army, various U.S. government security agencies, and foreign military personnel across CONUS and EMEA, and has been involved with facilitating such course subjects as Critical Site Nuclear EMP Hardening, International Cryptographic Methodology, and Computer Forensic Sciences, as well as cybersecurity topics. Buzz may be reached at buzz@buzzmurphy.com.

Contents at a Glance

Introduction   *xvii*

Chapter 1   Domain 1.0: Networking Fundamentals   1

Chapter 2   Domain 2.0: Network Implementations   169

Chapter 3   Domain 3.0: Network Operations   261

Chapter 4   Domain 4.0: Network Security   343

Chapter 5   Domain 5.0: Network Troubleshooting   421

Appendix   Answers to Review Questions   537

Index   *553*

Contents

Introduction   *xvii*

Chapter   1   **Domain 1.0: Networking Fundamentals**   **1**

1.1 Compare and contrast the Open Systems
Interconnection (OSI) model layers and encapsulation
concepts.   11
  OSI Model   12
  Protocol Data Units   21
  Data Encapsulation and Decapsulation   22
  Exam Essentials   26
1.2 Explain the characteristics of network topologies and
network types.   28
  Wired Topologies   28
  Types   33
  Service-Related Entry Point   39
  Virtualization   40
  Virtual Networking Components   40
  Service Type   43
  Service Delivery   48
  Exam Essentials   50
1.3 Summarize the types of cables and connectors and
explain which is the appropriate type for a solution.   51
  Media Types   51
  Connector Types   55
  Transceivers   60
  Media Converters   62
  Characteristics of Fiber Transceivers   63
  Termination Points   65
  Copper Cabling Standards   70
  Copper Termination Standards   73
  Ethernet Deployment Standards   76
  Exam Essentials   78
1.4 Given a scenario, configure a subnet and use appropriate
IP addressing schemes.   80
  Private vs. Public   80
  NAT/PAT   81
  IPv4 Concepts   84
  IPv6 Concepts   88

Address Assignments   93
Subnetting   99
Virtual IP (VIP)   107
Exam Essentials   108
1.5 Explain common ports and protocols, their application,
    and encrypted alternatives.   110
Protocols and Ports   110
IP Protocol Types   117
Connection-Oriented vs. Connectionless   121
Exam Essentials   122
1.6 Explain the use and purpose of network services.   123
DNS   123
DHCP Service   132
NTP   137
Exam Essentials   137
1.7 Explain basic corporate and datacenter network
    architecture.   139
Three-Tiered Model   139
Software-Defined Networking   140
Spine and Leaf   142
Traffic Flows   143
Host Locations   144
Network Storage Types   145
Connection Type   147
Exam Essentials   150
1.8 Summarize cloud concepts and connectivity options.   151
Characteristics of a Cloud   151
Cloud Delivery Models   152
Types of Services   155
Infrastructure as Code   157
Connectivity Methods   160
Multitenancy   161
Elasticity   161
Scalability   162
Security Implications/Considerations   162
Relationship Between Local and Cloud Resources   163
Exam Essentials   163
Review Questions   165

Chapter   2   Domain 2.0: Network Implementations   169

2.1 Compare and contrast various devices, their features,
    and their appropriate placement on the network.   173
Network Devices   173
Exam Essentials   203

2.2 Compare and contrast routing technologies and
   bandwidth management concepts.   204
      Routing   204
      Bandwidth Management   212
      Exam Essentials   215
2.3 Given a scenario, configure and deploy common
   Ethernet switching features.   216
      Characteristics of Ethernet and IP Communications   216
      Basic Switch Functions   220
      Segmentation and Interface Properties   227
      Switching Features   231
      Exam Essentials   234
2.4 Given a scenario, install and configure the appropriate
   wireless standards and technologies.   235
      802.11 Standards   235
      Frequencies   238
      Wireless Considerations   239
      Wireless Modes of Operation   245
      Wireless Security   248
      Cellular   252
      Exam Essentials   254
   Review Questions   256

Chapter   3   Domain 3.0: Network Operations   261

3.1 Given a scenario, use the appropriate statistics and
   sensors to ensure network availability.   265
      Performance Metrics   265
      SNMP   270
      Network Device Logs   274
      Interface Statistics/Status   279
      Interface Errors or Alerts   286
      Environmental Factors and Sensors   289
      Performance Baselines   291
      NetFlow Data   292
      Uptime/Downtime   293
      Exam Essentials   294
3.2 Explain the purpose of organizational documents
   and policies.   296
      Plans and Procedures   296
      Hardening and Security Policies   303
      Common Documentation   307
      Common Agreements   315
      Exam Essentials   316

3.3 Explain high availability and disaster recovery concepts
and summarize which is the best solution.   318
    Load Balancing   318
    Multipathing   318
    Network Interface Card (NIC) Teaming   320
    Redundant Hardware/Clusters   320
    Facilities and Infrastructure Support   326
    Redundancy and High Availability (HA) Concepts   330
    Backups   334
    Exam Essentials   336
Review Questions   338

Chapter   4   Domain 4.0: Network Security   343

4.1 Explain common security concepts.   348
    Confidentiality, Integrity, Availability (CIA)   348
    Threats   349
    Vulnerabilities   350
    Exploits   351
    Least Privilege   351
    Role-Based Access   352
    Zero Trust   352
    Defense in Depth   353
    Authentication Methods   357
    Security Assessments   364
    Security Information and Event Management (SIEM)   366
    Exam Essentials   366
4.2 Compare and contrast common types of attacks.   368
    Technology-Based   368
    Human and Environmental   378
    Exam Essentials   379
4.3 Given a scenario, apply network hardening techniques.   381
    Best Practices   381
    Wireless Security   390
    IOT Considerations   395
    Exam Essentials   396
4.4 Compare and contrast remote access methods and
security implications.   397
    VPN   397
    Remote Desktop Connection   400
    Remote Desktop Gateway   401
    SSH   401
    Virtual Network Computing (VNC)   402
    Virtual Desktop   402

Authentication and Authorization Considerations   403
In-Band vs. Out-of-Band Management   403
Exam Essentials   405
4.5 Explain the importance of physical security.   406
Detection Methods   407
Prevention Methods   410
Asset Disposal   413
Exam Essentials   415
Review Questions   416

Chapter   5   Domain 5.0: Network Troubleshooting   421

5.1 Explain the network troubleshooting methodology.   427
Identify the Problem   428
Establish a Theory of Probable Cause   430
Test the Theory to Determine the Cause   431
Establish a Plan of Action to Resolve the Problem
    and Identify Potential Effects   432
Implement the Solution or Escalate as Necessary   432
Verify Full System Functionality and, If Applicable,
    Implement Preventive Measures   433
Document Findings, Actions, Outcomes, and Lessons
    Learned   433
Exam Essentials   433
5.2 Given a scenario, troubleshoot common cable
connectivity issues and select the appropriate tools.   434
Specifications and Limitations   434
Cable Considerations   435
Cable Application   437
Common Issues   439
Common Tools   445
Exam Essentials   456
5.3 Given a scenario, use the appropriate network software
tools and commands.   458
Software Tools   458
Command-Line Tools   466
Basic Network Platform Commands   481
Exam Essentials   485
5.4 Given a scenario, troubleshoot common wireless
connectivity issues   486
Specifications and Limitations   486
Considerations   489
Common Issues   493
Exam Essentials   498

5.5 Given a scenario, troubleshoot general networking issues.   499
    Considerations   499
    Common Issues   501
    Exam Essentials   530
Review Questions   532

Appendix   **Answers to Review Questions**   **537**

Chapter 1: Domain 1.0: Networking Fundamentals   538
Chapter 2: Domain 2.0: Network Implementations   541
Chapter 3: Domain 3.0: Network Operations   544
Chapter 4: Domain 4.0: Network Security   547
Chapter 5: Domain 5.0: Network Troubleshooting   550

Index   553

Introduction

You may be new to the field of computer networking, or perhaps you are in pursuit of proving your knowledge and understanding of computer networking. In either case, the CompTIA Network+ certification exam is a great start to your professional development. The Network+ certification is considered by employers industry-wide to be proof of the knowledge of networking theory, skill, and systems. The Network+ certification is granted to those individuals who have attained this information and show a basic competency for meeting the needs of both personal and organizational computing environments.

The CompTIA Network+ objectives have changed with the introduction of the CompTIA Network+ N10-008 certification exam. This change in objectives and topics from the prior exam was necessary to keep up with the latest technologies used in networks today. The foundation of networking concepts has remained relatively similar, despite the introduction of more advanced technologies. This is one of the reasons the CompTIA Network+ exam is so widely valued by employers. As of this writing, the objectives are current for the Network+ N10-008 certification exam as stated by CompTIA (www.comptia.org).

What Is Network+ Certification?

The Computing Technology Industry Association (CompTIA) developed the Network+ certification to be vendor-neutral and recognized industry-wide. The Network+ certification is considered the benchmark of networking theory. Candidates who earn the Network+ certification have knowledge of the design, operation, maintenance, security, and troubleshooting of networks. Employers worldwide recognize Network+ certified individuals as having a basic vendor-agnostic networking theory that can be applied to any specific system.

The Network+ certification was originally sponsored by IT industry leaders like IBM, Microsoft, and Compaq, among others. The goal was to create a certification that would give recognition of individuals with a basic theory of networking. Today, more complex networking theory is required by employers, and Network+ has evolved into a comprehensive exam. The CompTIA Network+ Exam N10-008 tests five domains of network theory:

- Networking Fundamentals
- Network Implementations
- Network Operations
- Network Security
- Network Troubleshooting

For the latest pricing on the exam and updates to the registration procedures, go to www.vue.com. You can register online for the exam. If you have further questions about the scope of the exam or related CompTIA programs, refer to the CompTIA website at www.comptia.org.

Is This Book for You?

The *CompTIA Network+ Review Guide: Exam N10-008, Fifth Edition* is designed to be a complete, portable exam review guide that can be used either in conjunction with a more complete study program (such as Sybex's *CompTIA Network+ Study Guide: Exam N10-008, Fifth Edition*, computer-based training courseware, or a classroom/lab environment), or as an exam review for those who don't need more extensive test preparation. The goal of this book is to thoroughly cover those topics you can expect to be tested on.

Perhaps you've been working with information technologies for many years. The thought of paying lots of money for a specialized IT exam preparation course probably doesn't sound too appealing. What can they teach you that you don't already know, right? Be careful, though—many experienced network administrators have walked confidently into the test center only to walk sheepishly out of it after failing an IT exam. I've run across many of these network administrators throughout my 24 years of teaching networking. After you've finished reading this book, you should have a clear idea of how your understanding of networking technologies matches up with the expectations of the Network+ test writers.

 The goal of the Review Guide series is to help Network+ candidates brush up on the subjects that they can expect to be on the Network+ exam. For complete in-depth coverage of the technologies and topics involved, I recommend *CompTIA Network+ Study Guide* from Sybex.

How Is This Book Organized?

This book is organized according to the official objectives' list prepared by CompTIA for the Network+ exam N10-008. The chapters correspond to the five major domains of objective and topic groupings. The exam is weighted across these five domains:

- Domain 1.0 Networking Fundamentals (24 percent)
- Domain 2.0 Network Implementations (19 percent)
- Domain 3.0 Network Operations (16 percent)
- Domain 4.0 Network Security (19 percent)
- Domain 5.0 Network Troubleshooting (22 percent)

In each chapter, the top-level exam objective from each domain is addressed in turn. This discussion also contains an Exam Essentials section. Here you are given a short list of topics that you should explore fully before taking the test. Included in the Exam Essentials are notations on key pieces of information you should have gleaned from *CompTIA Network+ Review Guide: Exam N10-008, Fifth Edition*. At the end of each chapter you'll find the "Review Questions" section. These questions are designed to help you gauge your mastery of the content in the chapter.

Interactive Online Learning Environment and Test Bank

The interactive online learning environment that accompanies *CompTIA Network+ Review Guide: Exam N10-008, Fifth Edition* provides a test bank with study tools to help you prepare for the certification exam, and it increases your chances of passing it the first time. The test bank includes the following:

Sample Tests   All of the questions in this book are provided, including the chapter review tests at the end of each chapter. In addition, there are two practice exams. Use these questions to test your knowledge of the review guide material. The online test bank runs on multiple devices.

Flashcards   Flashcard questions are provided in digital flashcard format (a question followed by a single correct answer). You can use the flashcards to reinforce your learning and prepare last minute before the exam.

Other Study Tools   A glossary of key terms from this book and their definitions is available as a fully searchable PDF.

Go to http://www.wiley.com/go/netplustestprep to register and gain access to this interactive online learning environment and test bank with study tools.

Tips for Taking the Network+ Exam

Here are some general tips for taking your exams successfully:

- Bring two forms of ID with you. One must be a photo ID, such as a driver's license. The other can be a major credit card or a passport. Both forms must include a signature.

- Arrive early at the exam center so you can relax and review your study materials, particularly tables and lists of exam-related information.

- Read the questions carefully. Don't be tempted to jump to an early conclusion. Make sure you know exactly what the question is asking.

- Don't leave any unanswered questions. Unanswered questions give you no opportunity for guessing correctly and scoring more points.

- There will be questions with multiple correct responses. When there is more than one correct answer, a message on the screen will prompt you to either "Choose two" or "Choose all that apply." Be sure to read the messages displayed so that you know how many correct answers you must choose.

- Questions needing only a single correct answer will use radio buttons for selecting an answer, whereas those needing two or more answers will use check boxes.

- When answering multiple-choice questions you're not sure about, use a process of elimination to get rid of the obviously incorrect answers first. Doing so will improve your odds if you need to make an educated guess.

- On form-based tests (nonadaptive), because the hard questions will eat up the most time, save them for last. You can move forward and backward through the exam.

- For the latest pricing on the exams and updates to the registration procedures, visit CompTIA's website at www.comptia.org.

 With so many changes over the past year, Pearson VUE has introduced a change to its testing policies and procedures with the introduction of online exams. You can now schedule and take the Network+ exam online from the comfort and safety of your home. The instructions to prepare for an online exam can be found at https://www.comptia.org/testing/testing-options/take-online-exam.

How to Contact the Publisher

Sybex welcomes feedback on all of its titles. Visit the Sybex website at www.sybex.com for book updates and additional certification information. You'll also find forms you can use to submit comments or suggestions regarding this or any other Sybex titles.

The Exam Objectives

The following are the areas (referred to as domains by CompTIA) in which you must be proficient in order to pass the Network+ exam:

Domain 1.0: Networking Fundamentals   This domain begins with the descriptions of the OSI model layers and the specific function and purpose of each layer are then covered. The domain examines the various topologies of networks, the various network types and characteristics, virtual network concepts, and WAN connectivity. The domain explores the various cables and fiber-optic cables, connectors and overall solutions for connectivity, and Ethernet standards. IP addressing, subnetting, and VLSM are covered to support routing and efficient network design. The domain covers the various protocols that can be found at the upper layers of the OSI model. It then covers DHCP, DNS, and NTP and explores basic corporate network and data center network architecture, to include storage networks. The domain concludes by exploring cloud computing concepts.

Domain 2.0: Network Implementations   This domain covers the basic building blocks of network devices, such as firewalls, routers, switches, and more. It then covers more advanced network devices, such as VoIP, access control devices, and SCADA, just to mention a few. The domain also compares routing technologies and bandwidth management concepts. It concludes with the coverage of various wireless standards and cellular technologies.

Domain 3.0: Network Operations   This domain covers the various metrics and collection methods that can help administrators identify performance problems and outages. The domain examines the various log files that an administrator might use to identify a problem. it also covers the various counters on an interface that can help an administrator identify a problem. The domain examines the purpose of organizational documentation and the various policies. It concludes by examining high availability and disaster recovery concepts and solutions.

Domain 4.0: Network Security   This domain focuses on security for both the physical and nonphysical aspects of network design and operations. It covers the various detection and prevention methods of security and examines the various network attacks that you may encounter in a network. Wireless security is also covered to support secure wireless communications. The domain then covers hardening techniques and mitigation techniques so that security problems can be avoided. It concludes with remote access methods and their security implications.

Domain 5.0: Network Troubleshooting   This domain covers the various troubleshooting methodologies used to diagnose problems in a network. It then explores the various hardware and software tools that you will use to diagnose problems in both wired and wireless networks. The domain covers both wired and wireless connectivity issues and performance-related issues that you may encounter in your daily operations. It concludes with real-world application of the tools and troubleshooting methodologies used to diagnose problems in a network.

The Network+ Exam Objectives

At the beginning of each chapter, I have included a complete listing of the topics that will be covered in that chapter. These topic selections are developed straight from the test objectives listed on CompTIA's website. They are provided for easy reference and to assure you that you are on track with learning the objectives. Note that exam objectives are subject to change at any time without prior notice and at CompTIA's sole discretion. Please visit the Network+ Certification page of CompTIA's website at https://certification.comptia.org/certifications/network for the most current listing of exam objectives.

Chapter 1: Domain 1.0: Networking Fundamentals

1.1 Compare and contrast the Open Systems Interconnection (OSI) model layers and encapsulation concepts.

- OSI model
    - Layer 1 - Physical
    - Layer 2 - Data link
    - Layer 3 - Network
    - Layer 4 - Transport
    - Layer 5 - Session
    - Layer 6 - Presentation
    - Layer 7 - Application
- Data encapsulation and decapsulation within the OSI model context
    - Ethernet header
    - Internet Protocol (IP) header
    - Transmission Control Protocol (TCP)/User Datagram Protocol (UDP) headers
    - TCP flags
    - Payload
    - Maximum transmission unit (MTU)

1.2 Explain the characteristics of network topologies and network types.

- Mesh
- Star/hub-and-spoke
- Bus
- Ring
- Hybrid
- Network types and characteristics
    - Peer-to-peer
    - Client-server
    - Local area network (LAN)
    - Metropolitan area network (MAN)
    - Wide area network (WAN)
    - Wireless local area network (WLAN)
    - Personal area network (PAN)
    - Campus area network (CAN)

- Storage area network (SAN)
  - Software-defined wide area network (SDWAN)
  - Multiprotocol label switching (MPLS)
  - Multipoint generic routing encapsulation (mGRE)
- Service-related entry point
  - Demarcation point
  - Smartjack
- Virtual network concepts
  - vSwitch
  - Virtual network interface card (vNIC)
  - Network function virtualization (NFV)
  - Hypervisor
- Provider links
  - Satellite
  - Digital subscriber line (DSL)
  - Cable
  - Leased line
  - Metro-optical

1.3 Summarize the types of cables and connectors and explain which is the appropriate type for a solution.

- Copper
  - Twisted pair
  - Cat 5
  - Cat 5e
  - Cat 6
  - Cat 6a
  - Cat 7
  - Cat 8
- Coaxial/RG-6
- Twinaxial
- Termination standards
  - TIA/EIA-568A
  - TIA/EIA-568B

- Fiber
  - Single-mode
  - Multimode
- Connector types
  - Local connector (LC), straight tip (ST), subscriber connector (SC), mechanical transfer (MT), registered jack (RJ)
    - Angled physical contact (APC)
    - Ultra-physical contact (UPC)
  - RJ11
  - RJ45
  - F-type connector
  - Transceivers/media converters
  - Transceiver type
    - Small form-factor pluggable (SFP)
    - Enhanced form-factor pluggable (SFP+)
    - Quad small form-factor pluggable (QSFP)
    - Enhanced quad small form-factor pluggable (QSFP+)
- Cable management
  - Patch panel/patch bay
  - Fiber distribution panel
  - Punchdown block
    - 66
    - 110
    - Krone
    - Bix
- Ethernet standards
  - Copper
    - 10BASE-T
    - 100BASE-TX
    - 1000BASE-T
    - 10GBASE-T
    - 40GBASE-T

- Fiber
  - 100BASE-FX
  - 100BASE-SX
  - 1000BASE-SX
  - 1000BASE-LX
  - 10GBASE-SR
  - 10GBASE-LR
  - Coarse wavelength division multiplexing (CWDM)
  - Dense wavelength division multiplexing (DWDM)
  - Bidirectional wavelength division multiplexing (WDM)

1.4 Given a scenario, configure a subnet and use appropriate IP addressing schemes.

- Public vs. private
  - RFC1918
  - Network address translation (NAT)
  - Port address translation (PAT)
- IPv4 vs. IPv6
  - Automatic Private IP Addressing (APIPA)
  - Extended unique identifier (EUI-64)
  - Multicast
  - Unicast
  - Anycast
  - Broadcast
  - Link local
  - Loopback
  - Default gateway
- IPv4 subnetting
  - Classless (variable-length subnet mask)
  - Classful
    - A
    - B
    - C
    - D
    - E
  - Classless Inter-Domain Routing (CIDR) notation

- IPv6 concepts
  - Tunneling
  - Dual stack
  - Shorthand notation
  - Router advertisement
  - Stateless address autoconfiguration (SLAAC)
- Virtual IP (VIP)
- Subinterfaces

1.5 Explain common ports and protocols, their application, and encrypted alternatives.

- File Transfer Protocol (FTP) 20/21
- Secure Shell (SSH) 22
- Secure File Transfer Protocol (SFTP) 22
- Telnet 23
- Simple Mail Transfer Protocol (SMTP) 25
- Domain Name System (DNS) 53
- Dynamic Host Configuration Protocol (DHCP) 67/68
- Trivial File Transfer Protocol (TFTP) 69
- Hypertext Transfer Protocol (HTTP) 80
- Post Office Protocol v3 (POP3) 110
- Network Time Protocol (NTP) 123
- Internet Message Access Protocol (IMAP) 143
- Simple Network Management Protocol (SNMP) 161/162
- Lightweight Directory Access Protocol (LDAP) 389
- Hypertext Transfer Protocol Secure (HTTPS) [Secure Sockets Layer (SSL)] 443
- HTTPS [Transport Layer Security (TLS)] 443
- Server Message Block (SMB) 445
- Syslog 514
- SMTP TLS 587
- Lightweight Directory Access Protocol (over SSL) (LDAPS) 636
- IMAP over SSL 993
- POP3 over SSL 995
- Structured Query Language (SQL) Server 1433
- SQLnet 1521
- MySQL 3306

- Remote Desktop Protocol (RDP) 3389
- Session Initiation Protocol (SIP) 5060/5061
- IP protocol types
  - Internet Control Message Protocol (ICMP)
  - TCP
  - UDP
  - Generic Routing Encapsulation (GRE)
  - Internet Protocol Security (IPSec)
    - Authentication Header (AH)/Encapsulating Security Payload (ESP)
- Connectionless vs. connection-oriented

1.6 Explain the use and purpose of network services.

- DHCP
  - Scope
  - Exclusion ranges
  - Reservation
  - Dynamic assignment
  - Static assignment
  - Lease time
  - Scope options
  - Available leases
  - DHCP relay
  - IP helper/UDP forwarding
- DNS
  - Record types
    - Address (A)
    - Canonical name (CNAME)
    - Mail exchange (MX)
    - Authentication, authorization, accounting, auditing (AAAA)
    - Start of authority (SOA)
    - Pointer (PTR)
    - Text (TXT)
    - Service (SRV)
    - Name server (NS)

- Global hierarchy
  - Root DNS servers
  - Internal vs. external
  - Zone transfers
  - Authoritative name servers
  - Time to live (TTL)
  - DNS caching
  - Reverse DNS/reverse lookup/forward lookup
  - Recursive lookup/iterative lookup
- NTP
  - Stratum
  - Clients
  - Servers

1.7 Explain basic corporate and datacenter network architecture.

- Three-tiered
  - Core
  - Distribution/aggregation layer
  - Access/edge
- Software-defined networking
  - Application layer
  - Control layer
  - Infrastructure layer
  - Management plane
- Spine and leaf
  - Software-defined network
  - Top-of-rack switching
  - Backbone
- Traffic flows
  - North-South
  - East-West
- Branch office vs. on-premises datacenter vs. colocation
- Storage area networks

- Connection types
    - Fibre Channel over Ethernet (FCoE)
    - Fibre Channel
    - Internet Small Computer Systems Interface (iSCSI)

1.8 Summarize cloud concepts and connectivity options.

- Deployment models
    - Public
    - Private
    - Hybrid
    - Community
- Service models
    - Software as a service (SaaS)
    - Infrastructure as a service (IaaS)
    - Platform as a service (PaaS)
    - Desktop as a service (DaaS)
- Infrastructure as code
    - Automation/orchestration
- Connectivity options
    - Virtual private network (VPN)
    - Private-direct connection to cloud provider
- Multitenancy
- Elasticity
- Scalability
- Security implications

Chapter 2: Domain 2.0: Network Implementations

2.1 Compare and contrast various devices, their features, and their appropriate placement on the network.

- Networking devices
    - Layer 2 switch
    - Layer 3 capable switch
    - Router
    - Hub
    - Access point

- Bridge
- Wireless LAN controller
- Load balancer
- Proxy server
- Cable modem
- DSL modem
- Repeater
- Voice gateway
- Media converter
- Intrusion prevention system (IPS)/intrusion detection system (IDS) device
- Firewall
- VPN headend
- Networked devices
  - Voice over Internet Protocol (VoIP) phone
  - Printer
  - Physical access control devices
  - Cameras
  - Heating, ventilation, and air conditioning (HVAC) sensors
  - Internet of Things (IoT)
    - Refrigerator
    - Smart speakers
    - Smart thermostats
    - Smart doorbells
  - Industrial control systems/supervisory control and data acquisition (SCADA)

2.2 Compare and contrast routing technologies and bandwidth management concepts.

- Routing
  - Dynamic routing
    - Protocols [Routing Internet Protocol (RIP), Open Shortest Path First (OSPF), Enhanced Interior Gateway Routing Protocol (EIGRP), Border Gateway Protocol (BGP)]
    - Link state vs. distance vector vs. hybrid
  - Static routing
  - Default route

- Administrative distance
- Exterior vs. interior
- Time to live
- Bandwidth management
- Traffic shaping
- Quality of service (QoS)

2.3 Given a scenario, configure and deploy common Ethernet switching features.

- Data virtual local area network (VLAN)
- Voice VLAN
- Port configurations
  - Port tagging/802.1Q
  - Port aggregation
    - Link Aggregation Control Protocol (LACP)
  - Duplex
  - Speed
  - Flow control
  - Port mirroring
  - Port security
  - Jumbo frames
  - Auto-medium-dependent interface crossover (MDI-X)
- Media access control (MAC) address tables
- Power over Ethernet (PoE)/Power over Ethernet plus (PoE+)
- Spanning Tree Protocol
- Carrier-sense multiple access with collision detection (CSMA/CD)
- Address Resolution Protocol (ARP)
- Neighbor Discovery Protocol

2.4 Given a scenario, install and configure the appropriate wireless standards and technologies.

- 802.11 standards
  - a
  - b
  - g
  - n (WiFi 4)
  - ac (WiFi 5)
  - ax (WiFi 6)

- Frequencies and range
  - 2.4GHz
  - 5GHz
- Channels
  - Regulatory impacts
- Channel bonding
- Service set identifier (SSID)
  - Basic service set
  - Extended service set
  - Independent basic service set (Ad-hoc)
  - Roaming
- Antenna types
  - Omni
  - Directional
- Encryption standards
  - WiFi Protected Access (WPA)/ WPA2 Personal [Advanced Encryption Standard (AES)/ Temporal Key Integrity Protocol (TKIP)]
  - WPA/WPA2 Enterprise (AES/TKIP)
- Cellular technologies
  - Code-division multiple access (CDMA)
  - Global System for Mobile Communications (GSM)
  - Long-Term Evolution (LTE)
  - 3G, 4G, 5G
- Multiple input, multiple output (MIMO) and multi-user MIMO (MU-MIMO)

Chapter 3: Domain 3.0: Network Operations

3.1 Given a scenario, use the appropriate statistics and sensors to ensure network availability.

- Performance metrics/sensors
  - Device/chassis
    - Temperature
    - Central processing unit (CPU) usage
    - Memory

- Network metrics
  - Bandwidth
  - Latency
  - Jitter
- SNMP
  - Traps
  - Object identifiers (OIDs)
  - Management information bases (MIBs)
- Network device logs
  - Log reviews
    - Traffic logs
    - Audit logs
    - Syslog
  - Logging levels/severity levels
- Interface statistics/status
  - Link state (up/down)
  - Speed/duplex
  - Send/receive traffic
  - Cyclic redundancy checks (CRCs)
  - Protocol packet and byte counts
- Interface errors or alerts
  - CRC errors
  - Giants
  - Runts
  - Encapsulation errors
- Environmental factors and sensors
  - Temperature
  - Humidity
  - Electrical
  - Flooding
- Baselines
- NetFlow data
- Uptime/downtime

3.2 Explain the purpose of organizational documents and policies.

- Plans and procedures
  - Change management
  - Incident response plan
  - Disaster recovery plan
  - Business continuity plan
  - System life cycle
  - Standard operating procedures
- Hardening and security policies
  - Password policy
  - Acceptable use policy
  - Bring your own device (BYOD) policy
  - Remote access policy
  - Onboarding and offboarding policy
  - Security policy
  - Data loss prevention
- Common documentation
  - Physical network diagram
    - Floor plan
    - Rack diagram
    - Intermediate distribution frame (IDF)/main distribution frame (MDF) documentation
  - Logical network diagram
  - Wiring diagram
  - Site survey report
  - Audit and assessment report
  - Baseline configurations
- Common agreements
  - Non-disclosure agreement (NDA)
  - Service-level agreement (SLA)
  - Memorandum of understanding (MOU)

3.3 Explain high availability and disaster recovery concepts and summarize which is the best solution.

- Load balancing
- Multipathing

- Network interface card (NIC) teaming
- Redundant hardware/clusters
  - Switches
  - Routers
  - Firewalls
- Facilities and infrastructure support
  - Uninterruptible power supply (UPS)
  - Power distribution units (PDUs)
  - Generator
  - HVAC
  - Fire suppression
- Redundancy and high availability (HA) concepts
  - Cold site
  - Warm site
  - Hot site
  - Cloud site
  - Active-active vs. active-passive
    - Multiple Internet service providers (ISPs)/diverse paths
    - Virtual Router Redundancy Protocol (VRRP)/First Hop Redundancy Protocol (FHRP)
  - Mean time to repair (MTTR)
  - Mean time between failure (MTBF)
  - Recovery time objective (RTO)
  - Recovery point objective (RPO)
- Network device backup/restore
  - State
  - Configuration

Chapter 4: Domain 4.0: Network Security

4.1 Explain common security concepts.

- Confidentiality, integrity, availability (CIA)
- Threats
  - Internal
  - External

- Vulnerabilities
  - Common vulnerabilities and exposures (CVE)
  - Zero-day
- Exploits
- Least privilege
- Role-based access
- Zero Trust
- Defense in depth
  - Network segmentation enforcement
  - Screened subnet [previously known as demilitarized zone (DMZ)]
  - Separation of duties
  - Network access control
  - Honeypot
- Authentication methods
  - Multifactor
  - Terminal Access Controller AccessControl System Plus (TACACS+)
  - Single sign-on (SSO)
  - Remote Authentication Dialin User Service (RADIUS)
  - LDAP
  - Kerberos
  - Local authentication
  - 802.1X
  - Extensible Authentication Protocol (EAP)
- Security assessments
  - Vulnerability assessment
  - Penetration testing
  - Risk assessment
  - Posture assessment
- Security information and event management (SIEM)

4.2 Compare and contrast common types of attacks.

- Technology-based
  - Denial-of-service (DoS)/ distributed denial-of-service (DDoS)
    - Botnet/command and control
  - On-path attack (previously known as man-in-the-middle attack)

- DNS poisoning
- VLAN hopping
- ARP spoofing
- Rogue DHCP
- Rogue access point (AP)
- Evil twin
- Ransomware
- Password attacks
    - Brute-force
    - Dictionary
- MAC spoofing
- IP spoofing
- Deauthentication
- Malware
- Human and environmental
    - Social engineering
        - Phishing
        - Tailgating
        - Piggybacking
        - Shoulder surfing

4.3 Given a scenario, apply network hardening techniques.

- Best practices
    - Secure SNMP
    - Router Advertisement (RA) Guard
    - Port security
    - Dynamic ARP inspection
    - Control plane policing
    - Private VLANs
    - Disable unneeded switchports
    - Disable unneeded network services
    - Change default passwords
    - Password complexity/length
    - Enable DHCP snooping

- Change default VLAN
- Patch and firmware management
- Access control list
- Role-based access
- Firewall rules
  - Explicit deny
  - Implicit deny
- Wireless security
  - MAC filtering
  - Antenna placement
  - Power levels
  - Wireless client isolation
  - Guest network isolation
  - Preshared keys (PSKs)
  - EAP
  - Geofencing
  - Captive portal
- IoT access considerations

4.4 Compare and contrast remote access methods and security implications.

- Site-to-site VPN
- Client-to-site VPN
  - Clientless VPN
  - Split tunnel vs. full tunnel
- Remote desktop connection
- Remote desktop gateway
- SSH
- Virtual network computing (VNC)
- Virtual desktop
- Authentication and authorization considerations
- In-band vs. out-of-band management

4.5 Explain the importance of physical security.

- Detection methods
  - Camera
  - Motion detection

- Asset tags
- Tamper detection
- Prevention methods
  - Employee training
  - Access control hardware
    - Badge readers
    - Biometrics
  - Locking racks
  - Locking cabinets
  - Access control vestibule (previously known as a mantrap)
  - Smart lockers
- Asset disposal
  - Factory reset/wipe configuration
  - Sanitize devices for disposal

Chapter 5: Domain 5.0: Network Troubleshooting

5.1 Explain the network troubleshooting methodology.

- Identify the problem
  - Gather information
  - Question users
  - Identify symptoms
  - Determine if anything has changed
  - Duplicate the problem, if possible
  - Approach multiple problems individually
- Establish a theory of probable cause
  - Question the obvious
  - Consider multiple approaches
    - Top-to-bottom/bottom-to-top OSI model
    - Divide and conquer
- Test the theory to determine the cause
  - If the theory is confirmed, determine the next steps to resolve the problem
  - If the theory is not confirmed, reestablish a new theory or escalate
- Establish a plan of action to resolve the problem and identify potential effects
- Implement the solution or escalate as necessary

- Verify full system functionality and, if applicable, implement preventive measures
- Document findings, actions, outcomes, and lessons learned

5.2 Given a scenario, troubleshoot common cable connectivity issues and select the appropriate tools.

- Specifications and limitations
    - Throughput
    - Speed
    - Distance
- Cable considerations
    - Shielded and unshielded
    - Plenum and riser-rated
- Cable application
    - Rollover cable/console cable
    - Crossover cable
    - Power over Ethernet
- Common issues
    - Attenuation
    - Interference
    - Decibel (dB) loss
    - Incorrect pinout
    - Bad ports
    - Open/short
    - Light-emitting diode (LED) status indicators
    - Incorrect transceivers
    - Duplexing issues
    - Transmit and receive (TX/RX) reversed
    - Dirty optical cables
- Common tools
    - Cable crimper
    - Punchdown tool
    - Tone generator
    - Loopback adapter
    - Optical time-domain reflectometer (OTDR)
    - Multimeter
    - Cable tester

- Wire map
- Tap
- Fusion splicers
- Spectrum analyzers
- Snips/cutters
- Cable stripper
- Fiber light meter

5.3 Given a scenario, use the appropriate network software tools and commands.

- Software tools
  - WiFi analyzer
  - Protocol analyzer/packet capture
  - Bandwidth speed tester
  - Port scanner
  - iperf
  - NetFlow analyzers
  - Trivial File Transfer Protocol (TFTP) server
  - Terminal emulator
  - IP scanner
- Command line tool
  - ping
  - ipconfig/ifconfig/ip
  - nslookup/dig
  - traceroute/tracert
  - arp
  - netstat
  - hostname
  - route
  - telnet
  - tcpdump
  - nmap
- Basic network platform commands
  - show interface
  - show config
  - show route

5.4 Given a scenario, troubleshoot common wireless connectivity issues.

- Specifications and limitations
  - Throughput
  - Speed
  - Distance
  - Received signal strength indication (RSSI) signal strength
  - Effective isotropic radiated power (EIRP)/power settings
- Considerations
  - Antennas
    - Placement
    - Type
    - Polarization
  - Channel utilization
  - AP association time
  - Site survey
- Common issues
  - Interference
    - Channel overlap
  - Antenna cable attenuation/signal loss
  - RF attenuation/signal loss
  - Wrong SSID
  - Incorrect passphrase
  - Encryption protocol mismatch
  - Insufficient wireless coverage
  - Captive portal issues
  - Client disassociation issues

5.5 Given a scenario, troubleshoot general networking issues.

- Considerations
  - Device configuration review
  - Routing tables
  - Interface status
  - VLAN assignment
  - Network performance baselines

- Common issues
  - Collisions
  - Broadcast storm
  - Duplicate MAC address
  - Duplicate IP address
  - Multicast flooding
  - Asymmetrical routing
  - Switching loops
  - Routing loops
  - Rogue DHCP server
  - DHCP scope exhaustion
  - IP setting issues
    - Incorrect gateway
    - Incorrect subnet mask
    - Incorrect IP address
    - Incorrect DNS
- Missing route
- Low optical link budget
- Certificate issues
- Hardware failure
- Host-based/network-based firewall settings
- Blocked services, ports, or addresses
- Incorrect VLAN
- DNS issues
- NTP issues
- BYOD challenges
- Licensed feature issues
- Network performance issues

Objective Map

In case it's not clear, the following shows where you can find each objective covered in this book:

Objective	Chapter
Domain 1.0: Networking Fundamentals	1
Domain 2.0: Network Implementations	2
Domain 3.0: Network Operations	3
Domain 4.0: Network Security	4
Domain 5.0: Network Troubleshooting	5

Network+ Acronyms

Here are the acronyms of security terms that CompTIA deems important enough that they're included in the objectives list for the exam. We've repeated them here exactly as listed by CompTIA.

AAAA	Authentication, Authorization, Accounting and Auditing
AES	Advanced Encryption Standard
AH	Authentication Header
AP	Access Point
APC	Angle Polished Connector
APIPA	Automatic Private Internet Protocol Addressing
ARP	Address Resolution Protocol
BGP	Border Gateway Protocol
BYOD	Bring Your Own Device
CAN	Campus Area Network
CDMA	Code Division Multiple Access
CIA	Confidentiality, Integrity, and Availability
CIDR	Classless Inter-Domain Routing
CNAME	Canonical Name

CPU	Central Processing Unit
CRC	Cyclic Redundancy Checking
CSMA/CA	Carrier Sense Multiple Access/Collision Avoidance
CVE	Common Vulnerabilities and Exposures
CWDM	Course Wave Division Multiplexing
DaaS	Desktop as a Service
dB	Decibel
DDoS	Distributed Denial-of-Service
DHCP	Dynamic Host Configuration Protocol
DNS	Domain Name Service/Domain Name Server/Domain Name System
DoS	Denial-of-Service
DSL	Digital Subscriber Line
DSSS	Direct Sequence Spread Spectrum
DWDM	Dense Wavelength Division Multiplexing
EAP	Extensible Authentication Protocol
EIGRP	Enhanced Interior Gateway Routing Protocol
EIRP	Effective Isotropic Radiated Power
ESP	Encapsulated Security Payload
EUI	Extended Unique Identifier
FCoE	Fibre Channel over Ethernet
FHRP	First Hop Redundancy Protocol
FTP	File Transfer Protocol
GRE	Generic Routing Encapsulation
GSM	Global System for Mobile Communications
HA	High Availability
HTTP	Hypertext Transfer Protocol
HTTPS	Hypertext Transfer Protocol Secure
HVAC	Heating, Ventilation and Air Conditioning
IaaS	Infrastructure as a Service

ICMP	Internet Control Message Protocol
IDF	Intermediate Distribution Frame
IDS	Intrusion Detection System
IMAP	Internet Message Access Protocol
IoT	Internet of Things
IPS	Intrusion Prevention System
IPSec	Internet Protocol Security
IPv4	Internet Protocol version 4
IPv6	Internet Protocol version 6
iSCSI	Internet Small Computer Systems Interface
ISP	Internet Service Provider
LACP	Link Aggregation Control Protocol
LAN	Local Area Network
LC	Local Connector
LDAP	Lightweight Directory Access Protocol
LDAPS	Lightweight Directory Access Protocol (over SSL)
LED	Light Emitting Diode
LTE	Long Term Evolution
MAC	Media Access Control/Medium Access Control
MDF	Main Distribution Frame
MDIX	Media Dependent Interface Crossover
mGRE	Multipoint Generic Routing Encapsulation
MIB	Management Information Base
MIMO	Multiple Input, Multiple Output
MU-MIMO	Multiuser - Multiple Input, Multiple Output
MOU	Memorandum of Understanding
MPLS	Multiprotocol Label Switching
MTBF	Mean Time Between Failures
MT-RJ	Mechanical Transfer-Registered Jack

MTTR	Mean Time To Recovery
MTU	Maximum Transmission Unit
MX	Mail Exchanger
NAT	Network Address Translation
NDA	Non-Disclosure Agreement
NFV	Network Function Virtualization
NIC	Network Interface Card
NS	Name Server
NTP	Network Time Protocol
OID	Object Identifier
OSI	Open Systems Interconnect
OSPF	Open Shortest Path First
OTDR	Optical Time Domain Reflectometer
PaaS	Platform as a Service
PAN	Personal Area Network
PAT	Port Address Translation
PDU	Protocol Data Unit
PoE	Power over Ethernet
POP3	Post Office Protocol version 3
PSK	Pre-Shared Key
PTR	Pointer Record
QoS	Quality of Service
QSFP	Quad Small Form-Factor Pluggable
RA	Router Advertisements
RADIUS	Remote Authentication Dial-In User Service
RDP	Remote Desktop Protocol
RF	Radio Frequency
RFC	Request for Comment
RG	Radio Guide

RIP	Routing Internet Protocol
RJ	Registered Jack
RPO	Recovery Point Objective
RSSI	Received Signal Strength Indication
RTO	Recovery Time Objective
RTP	Real-Time Protocol
SaaS	Software as a Service
SAN	Storage Area Network
SC	Standard Connector/Subscriber Connector
SCADA	Supervisory Control and Data Acquisition
SDN	Software-Defined Network
SDWAN	Software-Defined WAN
SFP	Small Form-factor Pluggable
SFTP	Secure File Transfer Protocol
SIEM	Security Information and Event Management
SIP	Session Initiation Protocol
SLA	Service Level Agreement
SLAAC	Stateless Address Auto Configuration
SMB	Server Message Block
SMTP	Simple Mail Transfer Protocol
SNMP	Simple Network Management Protocol
SOA	Start of Authority
SQL	Structure Query Language
SRV	Service Record
SSH	Secure Shell
SSID	Service Set Identifier
SSL	Secure Sockets Layer
SSO	Single Sign-On
ST	Straight Tip or Snap Twist

SYSLOG	System Log
TACACS+	Terminal Access Control Access Control System+
TCP	Transmission Control Protocol
TFTP	Trivial File Transfer Protocol
TIA/EIA	Telecommunications Industry Association/Electronic Industries Alliance
TKIP	Temporal Key Integrity Protocol
TLS	Transport Layer Security
TTL	Time to Live
TX/RX	Transmit and Receive
UDP	User Datagram Protocol
UPC	Ultra Polished Connector
UPS	Uninterruptible Power Supply
VIP	Virtual IP
VLAN	Virtual Local Area Network
VNC	Virtual Network Connection
vNIC	Virtual Network Interface Card
VoIP	Voice over IP
VPN	Virtual Private Network
VRRP	Virtual Router Redundancy Protocol
WAN	Wide Area Network
WDM	Wavelength Division Multiplexing
WLAN	Wireless Local Area Network
WMS	Warehouse Management System
WPA	Wi-Fi Protected Access

Network+ Proposed Hardware and Software

Here you will find a list of hardware and software that can help assist you in preparing for the Network+ exam. The hardware and software in the list are not required, but having access to the hardware and software will better prepare you for taking the exam. We've repeated them here exactly as listed by CompTIA.

Equipment

- Optical and copper patch panels
- Punchdown blocks
- Layer 2 switch
- Layer 3 switch
- PoE switch
- Router
- Firewall
- VPN headend
- Wireless access point
- Basic laptops that support virtualization
- Tablet/cell phone
- Media converters
- VoIP system (including a phone)

Spare hardware

- NICs
- Power supplies
- GBICs
- SFPs
- Managed switch
- Wireless access point
- UPS
- PoE injector

Spare parts

- Patch cables
- RJ11 connectors
- RJ45 connectors, modular jacks

- Unshielded twisted pair cable spool
- Coaxial cable spool
- F connectors
- Fiber connectors
- Antennas
- Bluetooth/wireless adapters
- Console cables (RS-232 to USB serial adapter)

Tools

- Telco/network crimper
- Cable tester
- Punchdown tool
- Cable stripper
- Coaxial crimper
- Wire cutter
- Tone generator
- Fiber termination kit
- Optical power meter

Software

- Protocol analyzer/packet capture
- Terminal emulation software
- Linux OS/Windows OS
- Software firewall
- Software IDS/IPS
- Network mapper
- Hypervisor software
- Virtual network environment
- WiFi analyzer
- Spectrum analyzer
- Network monitoring tools
- DHCP service
- DNS service
- NetFlow analyzer
- TFTP server
- Firmware backups for upgrades

Other

- Sample network documentation
- Sample logs
- Defective cables
- Cloud network diagrams

Chapter

1

Domain 1.0: Networking Fundamentals

THE FOLLOWING COMPTIA NETWORK+ OBJECTIVES ARE COVERED IN THIS CHAPTER:

✓ **1.1 Compare and contrast the Open Systems Interconnection (OSI) model layers and encapsulation concepts.**

- OSI model
    - Layer 1 - Physical
    - Layer 2 - Data link
    - Layer 3 - Network
    - Layer 4 - Transport
    - Layer 5 - Session
    - Layer 6 - Presentation
    - Layer 7 - Application
- Data encapsulation and decapsulation within the OSI model context
    - Ethernet header
    - Internet Protocol (IP) header
    - Transmission Control Protocol (TCP)/User Datagram Protocol (UDP) headers
    - TCP flags
    - Payload
    - Maximum transmission unit (MTU)

✓ **1.2 Explain the characteristics of network topologies and network types.**

- Mesh
- Star/hub-and-spoke
- Bus
- Ring
- Hybrid
- Network types and characteristics
    - Peer-to-peer
    - Client-server
    - Local area network (LAN)
    - Metropolitan area network (MAN)
    - Wide area network (WAN)
    - Wireless local area network (WLAN)
    - Personal area network (PAN)
    - Campus area network (CAN)
    - Storage area network (SAN)
    - Software-defined wide area network (SDWAN)
    - Multiprotocol label switching (MPLS)
    - Multipoint generic routing encapsulation (mGRE)
- Service-related entry point
    - Demarcation point
    - Smartjack
- Virtual network concepts
    - vSwitch
    - Virtual network interface card (vNIC)
    - Network function virtualization (NFV)
    - Hypervisor

- Provider links
  - Satellite
  - Digital subscriber line (DSL)
  - Cable
  - Leased line
  - Metro-optical

✓ **1.3 Summarize the types of cables and connectors and explain which is the appropriate type for a solution.**

- Copper
  - Twisted pair
    - Cat 5
    - Cat 5e
    - Cat 6
    - Cat 6a
    - Cat 7
    - Cat 8
  - Coaxial/RG-6
  - Twinaxial
  - Termination standards
    - TIA/EIA-568A
    - TIA/EIA-568B
- Fiber
  - Single-mode
  - Multimode
- Connector types
  - Local connector (LC), straight tip (ST), subscriber connector (SC), mechanical transfer (MT), registered jack (RJ)
    - Angled physical contact (APC)
    - Ultra-physical contact (UPC)

- RJ11
- RJ45
- F-type connector
- Transceivers/media converters
- Transceiver type
  - Small form-factor pluggable (SFP)
  - Enhanced form-factor pluggable (SFP+)
  - Quad small form-factor pluggable (QSFP)
  - Enhanced quad small form-factor pluggable (QSFP+)
- Cable management
  - Patch panel/patch bay
  - Fiber distribution panel
  - Punchdown block
    - 66
    - 110
    - Krone
    - Bix
- Ethernet standards
  - Copper
    - 10BASE-T
    - 100BASE-TX
    - 1000BASE-T
    - 10GBASE-T
    - 40GBASE-T
  - Fiber
    - 100BASE-FX
    - 100BASE-SX
    - 1000BASE-SX
    - 1000BASE-LX

- 10GBASE-SR
- 10GBASE-LR
- Coarse wavelength division multiplexing (CWDM)
- Dense wavelength division multiplexing (DWDM)
- Bidirectional wavelength division multiplexing (WDM)

✓ **1.4 Given a scenario, configure a subnet and use appropriate IP addressing schemes.**

- Public vs. private
  - RFC1918
  - Network address translation (NAT)
  - Port address translation (PAT)
- IPv4 vs. IPv6
  - Automatic Private IP Addressing (APIPA)
  - Extended unique identifier (EUI-64)
  - Multicast
  - Unicast
  - Anycast
  - Broadcast
  - Link local
  - Loopback
  - Default gateway
- IPv4 subnetting
  - Classless (variable-length subnet mask)
  - Classful
    - A
    - B
    - C
    - D
    - E
  - Classless Inter-Domain Routing (CIDR) notation

- IPv6 concepts
    - Tunneling
    - Dual stack
    - Shorthand notation
    - Router advertisement
    - Stateless address autoconfiguration (SLAAC)
- Virtual IP (VIP)
- Subinterfaces

✓ **1.5 Explain common ports and protocols, their application, and encrypted alternatives.**

- File Transfer Protocol (FTP) 20/21
- Secure Shell (SSH) 22
- Secure File Transfer Protocol (SFTP) 22
- Telnet 23
- Simple Mail Transfer Protocol (SMTP) 25
- Domain Name System (DNS) 53
- Dynamic Host Configuration Protocol (DHCP) 67/68
- Trivial File Transfer Protocol (TFTP) 69
- Hypertext Transfer Protocol (HTTP) 80
- Post Office Protocol v3 (POP3) 110
- Network Time Protocol (NTP) 123
- Internet Message Access Protocol (IMAP) 143
- Simple Network Management Protocol (SNMP) 161/162
- Lightweight Directory Access Protocol (LDAP) 389
- Hypertext Transfer Protocol Secure (HTTPS) [Secure Sockets Layer (SSL)] 443
- HTTPS [Transport Layer Security (TLS)] 443
- Server Message Block (SMB) 445
- Syslog 514
- SMTP TLS 587

- Lightweight Directory Access Protocol (over SSL) (LDAPS) 636

- IMAP over SSL 993

- POP3 over SSL 995

- Structured Query Language (SQL) Server 1433

- SQLnet 1521

- MySQL 3306

- Remote Desktop Protocol (RDP) 3389

- Session Initiation Protocol (SIP) 5060/5061

- IP protocol types

  - Internet Control Message Protocol (ICMP)

  - TCP

  - UDP

  - Generic Routing Encapsulation (GRE)

  - Internet Protocol Security (IPSec)

    - Authentication Header (AH)/Encapsulating Security Payload (ESP)

- Connectionless vs. connection-oriented

✓ **1.6 Explain the use and purpose of network services.**

- DHCP

  - Scope

  - Exclusion ranges

  - Reservation

  - Dynamic assignment

  - Static assignment

  - Lease time

  - Scope options

  - Available leases

  - DHCP relay

  - IP helper/UDP forwarding

- DNS
  - Record types
    - Address (A)
    - Canonical name (CNAME)
    - Mail exchange (MX)
    - Authentication, authorization, accounting, auditing (AAAA)
    - Start of authority (SOA)
    - Pointer (PTR)
    - Text (TXT)
    - Service (SRV)
    - Name server (NS)
  - Global hierarchy
    - Root DNS servers
    - Internal vs. external
    - Zone transfers
    - Authoritative name servers
    - Time to live (TTL)
    - DNS caching
    - Reverse DNS/reverse lookup/forward lookup
    - Recursive lookup/iterative lookup
- NTP
  - Stratum
  - Clients
  - Servers

✓ **1.7 Explain basic corporate and datacenter network architecture.**

- Three-tiered
  - Core
  - Distribution/aggregation layer
  - Access/edge

- Software-defined networking
  - Application layer
  - Control layer
  - Infrastructure layer
  - Management plane
- Spine and leaf
  - Software-defined network
  - Top-of-rack switching
  - Backbone
- Traffic flows
  - North-South
  - East-West
- Branch office vs. on-premises datacenter vs. colocation
- Storage area networks
  - Connection types
    - Fibre Channel over Ethernet (FCoE)
    - Fibre Channel
    - Internet Small Computer Systems Interface (iSCSI)

✓ **1.8 Summarize cloud concepts and connectivity options.**

- Deployment models
  - Public
  - Private
  - Hybrid
  - Community
- Service models
  - Software as a service (SaaS)
  - Infrastructure as a service (IaaS)
  - Platform as a service (PaaS)
  - Desktop as a service (DaaS)

- Infrastructure as code
  - Automation/orchestration
- Connectivity options
  - Virtual private network (VPN)
  - Private-direct connection to cloud provider
- Multitenancy
- Elasticity
- Scalability
- Security implications

When I first started on my career path as a network professional 25 years ago, I began by learning the basic concepts of networking by reading a book similar to this one. The original networking concepts have not really changed all that much. Some concepts have been replaced by new ones, and some have just become obsolete. This is because networks have evolved and networking needs have changed over the years. Over the course of your career, you too will see similar changes. However, most of the concepts you learn for the objectives in this domain will become your basis for understanding current and future networks.

When learning network concepts, you might feel you need to know everything before you can learn one thing. This can be an overwhelming feeling for anyone. However, I recommend that you review the sections again once you've read the entire chapter. Not only does this help with review and memorization, but the pieces will make more sense once you see the entire picture.

 For more detailed information on Domain 1's topics, please see *CompTIA Network+ Study Guide,* 5th ed. (978-1-119-81163-3) or *CompTIA Network+ Certification Kit,* 5th ed. (978-1-119-43228-9), published by Sybex.

1.1 Compare and contrast the Open Systems Interconnection (OSI) model layers and encapsulation concepts.

The movement of data from one network node to another is a very complex task, especially when you try to perceive everything happening all at once. The communications between various hardware vendors is also mind boggling. Thankfully, the OSI model was created to simplify and standardize the interconnection of hardware vendors. In this section you will learn all about the OSI model as it pertains to network communications.

OSI Model

The Open Systems Interconnection (OSI) reference model was created by the International Organization for Standardization (ISO) to standardize network connectivity between applications, devices, and protocols. Before the OSI was created, every system was proprietary. Of course, this was back in the days of mainframes and early microcomputers! Today, the OSI layers are used to build standards that allow for interoperability between different vendors.

Besides interoperability, the OSI layers have many other advantages. The following is a list of the common networking advantages the OSI layers provide:

- The reference model helps facilitate communications between various types of hardware and software.

- The reference model prevents a change in one layer from affecting the other layers.

- The reference model allows for multi-vendor development of hardware and software based on network standards.

- The reference model encourages industry standardization because it defines functions of each layer of the OSI model.

- The reference model divides a complex communications process into smaller pieces to assist with design, development, and troubleshooting.

- Network protocols and connectivity options can be changed without affecting applications.

The last advantage is what I consider the most important for any network administrator. The network communications process is a complicated process. However, when we break the process down into smaller pieces, we can understand each piece as it relates to the entire process.

When you understand what happens at each layer of the OSI model, you will have a better grasp of how to troubleshoot network applications and network problems. When I first learned the OSI layers over 25 years ago, I never thought I would use this knowledge—but I could not be as successful as I am without understanding this layered approach. When we review the upper layers of the OSI (Application, Presentation, and Session), you will not have as deep an understanding as you do of the lower layers. The upper layers are generally where developers create applications, whereas the lower layers are where network administrators support the applications.

In Figure 1.1 you can see the seven layers of the OSI model. The top three layers are where applications operate. The Transport and Network layers are where TCP/IP operates. The Data Link and Physical layers are where connectivity technology, such as wireless or Ethernet, operates. These groupings are considered macro layers and will help you understand the OSI layers better as we progress through each individual layer.

FIGURE 1.1   The layers of the OSI

Application Layer

The Application layer (layer 7) is the highest layer of the communication process. It is the layer that provides the user interface to the user and often the beginning of the communication process. Applications like Edge or Internet Explorer have an interface for the user, and they are considered network applications. Applications such as Microsoft Word do not communicate with the network and are therefore considered end-user applications or stand-alone applications. Although you can store your Word document on the network, the purpose is not to facilitate network communications such as Edge or Internet Explorer do. There is a running joke in networking that some problems are layer 8 problems; that would be the user.

The Application layer defines the role of the application, since all network applications are generally either client or server. A request for information is started at the Application layer through one of three methods: a *graphical user interface (GUI)*, a console application, or an *application programming interface (API)*. These terms are synonymous with the Application layer. A request for information can begin with a click of a mouse, a command in an application, or via an API call.

The Application layer also defines the purpose of the application. A file transfer application will differ significantly in design from an instant messaging application. When a programmer starts to design a network application, this is the layer the programmer begins with because it will interface with the user. As firewalls have advanced throughout the years, it is now common to find firewalls operating at layer 7. Chapter 2, "Domain 2.0: Network Implementations," covers next-generation firewall (NGFW) layer 7 firewalls that operate at these higher layers.

Many events begin at the Application layer. The following are some common application layer events, but in no way is this a complete list. The list of application protocols—and the events that begin at this layer—grows by the minute.

- Sending email
- Remote access
- Web surfing
- File transfer

- Instant messenger
- VoIP calls

Presentation Layer

The Presentation layer (layer 6) is the layer that presents data to the Application layer. This layer is responsible for encryption/decryption, translation, and compression/decompression. When a stream of data comes from the lower layers, this layer is responsible for formatting the data and converting it back to the original intended application data.

An example is a web request to a web server for an encrypted web page via Transport Layer Security (TLS), which was formerly the Secure Sockets Layer (SSL) protocol. The web page is encrypted at the web server and sent to the client. When the client receives the page, it is decrypted and sent to the Application layer as data. This process is bidirectional, and it is important to note that the presentation layer on both the client and server make a connection to each other. This is called peer-layer communications, and it happens at all layers of the OSI model in different ways.

An example of translation services that are performed at this layer is converting Extended Binary Coded Decimal Interchange Code (EBCDIC) data to American Standard Code for Information Interchange (ASCII) or converting ASCII to Unicode.

Examples of compression and decompression, often referred to as codecs, are MP3 to network streaming protocols and H.264 video to streaming protocols. In addition, JPEG, GIF, PICT, and TIFF operate at the Presentation layer by compressing and decompressing image formats when used in conjunction with a network application like your web browser.

Session Layer

The Session layer (layer 5) is responsible for the setup, management, and teardown of a session between two computers. This layer is also responsible for dialogue control. Application developers must decide how their application will function with the network at this layer in respect to the network conversation. There are three basic forms of communications a network application can use at the Session layer:

- *Half-duplex* is a two-way communication between two hosts where only one side can communicate at a time. This is similar to a walkie-talkie and is how many protocols operate. A web browser will request a page from the web server and the web server will return the page. Then the web browser asks for the other elements contained in the Hypertext Markup Language (HTML) web page. In recent years, web developers have made half-duplex seem like a full-duplex conversation with Ajax (Asynchronous JavaScript and eXtensible Markup Language, or XML) requests by sending each keystroke and querying a response. However, it is still a half-duplex conversation.

- *Full-duplex* is two-way communication between two hosts where both sides can communicate simultaneously. Not only is this type of communication similar to a telephone call, but it is used by VoIP to make telephone calls over a network. This type of dialogue control is extremely tough for programmers since they must program for real-time events.

- *Simplex* is a one-way communication between two hosts. This type of communication is similar to tuning to a radio station—you do not have any control of the content or communications received.

Transport Layer

The Transport layer (layer 4) is the first layer that we network administrators are responsible for maintaining. A good grasp of the upper three layers is important so that we can properly troubleshoot these lower layers.

The Transport layer for TCP/IP contains two protocols that you will learn more about in objective 1.5, "Explain common ports and protocols, their application, and encrypted alternatives." The Transmission Control Protocol (TCP) and User Datagram Protocol (UDP) protocols operate at the Transport layer, and the programmer of the network application must decide which to program against. At this layer, the operating system presents the application with a socket to communicate with on the network. In the Windows operating system, it is called a *Winsock*; in other operating systems like Linux, it is called a *socket*. When we discuss the socket in the context of networking, it is called a *port*. All of these terms are basically interchangeable. I will refer to it as a port for the remainder of this section.

When a network server application starts up, it will bind to the port, as shown in Figure 1.2. The server application will then listen for requests on this port. The programmer will choose which port and protocol to use for their server application. Because UDP/TCP and the port number define the application, it is common to find firewalls operating at this layer to allow or block application access.

FIGURE 1.2   Transport server port binding

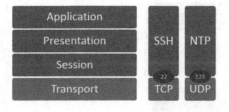

So far I have discussed how the server application listens for requests. Now I will explain how client applications use ports for requests. When a client needs to request information from a server, the client application will bind to a port dynamically available above 1023 as the source port. This dynamic allocation and short lifespan of the port number to facilitate network communications is also referred to as an *ephemeral* port numbers. On the other hand, port number 1023 and below are defined in RFC 3232 (or just see www.iana.org). These lower port numbers are called *well-known* port numbers, and they're reserved for servers. In the example in Figure 1.3, a web browser is creating a request for three elements on a web page to the server. The client will bind to port numbers 1024, 1025, and 1026 to the web browsers and send the request to the destination port number of 80 on the web server. When the three requests return from the web server, they will be returning from the source port number of 80 on the web server to the destination port numbers of 1024, 1025, and 1026 on the client. The client can then pass the proper element to the web page via the incoming data on the respective port number. Once the client receives the information, both the client and server will close the session for the port and the port can be recycled. UDP port numbers will be automatically recycled after a specific period of time, because the client and server do not communicate the state of the connection (UDP is connectionless). TCP port numbers are also automatically recycled after a specific period of time, but only after the conversation is finished using the port number. TCP communicates the state of the connection during the conversation (TCP is connection-based).

FIGURE 1.3   Transport client requests

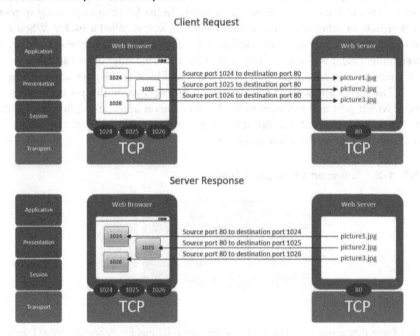

It is important to note a few concepts that are resonated throughout this discussion of the OSI layers. The first concept is each layer of the OSI communicates with the same layer on the other host—this is called *peer-layer communications*. The second concept is that every layer communicates with the layer above and the layer below. The Transport layer performs this communication to the layer above with the use of a port number. The Transport layer communicates with the layer below by moving information down to the network layer from either the TCP or UDP protocol. In the next section, you will learn how this information is conveyed and used by the Network layer.

Network Layer

The Network layer (layer 3) is responsible for the logical numbering of hosts and networks. The Network layer is also responsible for transporting data between networks through the process of *routing*. Routers operate at the network layer to facilitate the movement of packets between networks; therefore, routers are considered layer 3 devices. Figure 1.4 details three networks that are logically numbered with IP addresses, each belonging to a unique network. We will explore network routing in Chapter 2, "Domain 2.0: Network Implementations," in the section "Compare and contrast routing technologies and bandwidth management concepts" (objective 2.2).

FIGURE 1.4   Logical network addressing

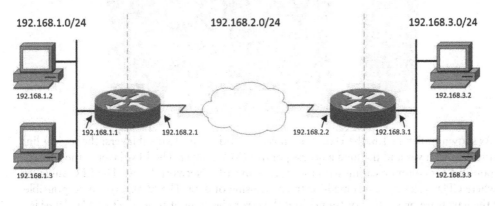

The IP protocol is not the only protocol that functions at this layer; ICMP also functions at the Network layer. There are many other Network layer protocols, but for the remainder of this discussion of objective 1.1 we will focus on the IP protocol.

The IP protocol at the Network layer communicates with the layer above by using a protocol number. The protocol number at the Network layer helps the IP protocol move the data to the next protocol. As you can see in Figure 1.5, when the protocol number is 6, the data is decapsulated and delivered to the TCP protocol at the Transport layer. When the protocol number is 17, the data is delivered to the UDP protocol at the Transport layer. Data does not always have to flow up to the Transport layer. If the protocol number is 1, the data is moved laterally to the ICMP protocol.

Data Link Layer

The Data Link layer (layer 2) is responsible for the framing of data for transmission on the Physical layer or media. The Data Link layer is also responsible for the static addressing of hosts. At the Data Link layer, unique MAC addresses are preprogrammed into the network cards (computers) and network interfaces (network devices). This preprogramming of the unique MAC address is sometimes referred to as being burnt-in, but modern network interface cards (NICs) allow you to override their preprogrammed MAC address. The Data Link layer is only concerned with the local delivery of frames in the same immediate network. At the Data Link layer, there are many different frame types. Since we are focused on TCP/IP, the only frame types we will discuss are Ethernet II frame types. Switching of frames occurs at the Data Link layer; therefore, this layer is where switches operate.

FIGURE 1.5 Network layer protocol numbers

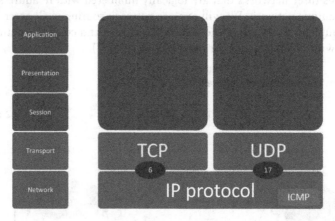

As shown in Figure 1.6, the Data Link layer is divided into two sublayers: the logical link control (LLC) layer and the media access control (MAC) layer. The LLC layer is the sublayer responsible for communicating with the layer above (the Network layer). The LLC sublayer is where CPU cycles are consumed for the processing of data. The MAC layer is responsible for the hardware processing of frames and the error checking of frames. The MAC layer is where frames are checked for errors, and only relevant frames are passed to the LLC layer. The MAC layer saves CPU cycles by processing these checks independently from the CPU and the operating system. The MAC layer is the layer responsible for the transmission of data on a physical level.

FIGURE 1.6 The Data Link layer and the sublayers within

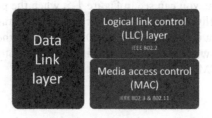

The LLC layer communicates with the Network layer by coding a type of protocol field in the frame itself, called the Ethernet type. It carries the protocol number for which traffic is destined, as shown in Figure 1.7. You may ask whether IP is the only protocol used with

TCP/IP, and the answer is no. Although TCP/IP uses the IP protocol, a helper protocol called the Address Resolution Protocol (ARP) is used to convert IP addresses into MAC addresses. Other protocols that can be found in this field are FCoE, 802.1Q, and PPPoE, just to name a few.

FIGURE 1.7   The LLC sublayer and the Network layer

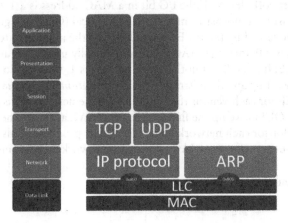

The MAC address layer is responsible for the synchronization, addressing, and error detection of the framing. In Figure 1.8 you can see the complete Ethernet II frame with the LLC layer (type field). The frame begins with the preamble, which is 7 bytes of alternating 1s and 0s at a synchronization frequency according to the speed of the connectivity method. The start frame delimiter (SFD) is a 1-byte field and technically it's part of the preamble. The SFD contains an extra trailing bit at the end of the byte to signal the start of the destination MAC address (10101011). The preamble and SFD help the receiving side form a time reference for the rest of the frame signaling; the preamble synchronizes the physical timing for both sides of the transmission. Hence, it is the way the Data Link layer communicates with the layer below (the Physical layer). The destination MAC address is a 6-byte field and represents the physical destination of the data. The source MAC address is a 6-byte field and represents the physical source of the data. The type field is a 2-byte field, as described earlier, and is part of the LLC sublayer. The data field can vary between 46 bytes and a maximum of 1500 bytes. The frame check sequence (FCS) is a *cyclic redundancy check (CRC)*, which is a calculation of the entire frames for error detection. If the CRC does not match the frame received, it is automatically discarded at the MAC address sublayer as invalid data.

FIGURE 1.8   An Ethernet II frame

A MAC address is a 48-bit (6-byte) physical address burned into the network controller of every network card and network device. The address is normally written as a hexadecimal expression such as 0D-54-0D-C0-10-52. The MAC address format is governed by, and partially administered by, the IEEE. In Figure 1.9, a MAC address is shown in bit form. The Individual Group (I/G) bit controls how the switch handles broadcast traffic or individual traffic for the MAC address. If the I/G bit in a MAC address is 0, then it is destined for an individual unicast network device. If the I/G bit in a MAC address is a 1, then the switch treats it as a broadcast or multicast frame. The Global/Local (G/L) bit signifies if the MAC address is globally governed by the IEEE or locally set by the administrator. If the G/L bit in the MAC address is a 0, then the MAC address is globally unique because it has been governed by the IEEE. If the G/L bit in the MAC address is 1, then it is locally governed— that is, it is statically set by an administrator. The *organizationally unique identifier (OUI)* is governed by the IEEE for each vendor that applies to make networking equipment. The I/G bit, G/L bit, and the OUI make up the first 24 bits of a MAC address. The last 24 bits are assigned by the vendor for each network controller that is produced. This is how the IEEE achieves global uniqueness of every MAC address for networking equipment.

FIGURE 1.9   MAC address format

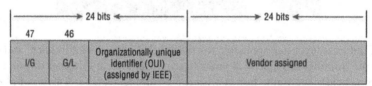

Example: 0000.0c12.3456

The IEEE publishes the list of OUIs that have been registered for network controller production. With this list, you can determine the manufacturer of the device from the first six hexadecimal digits of a MAC address. Many protocol analyzers use this same list to translate the source and destination fields in a frame to a friendly manufacturer ID. The complete list changes daily and can be found at https://regauth.standards .ieee.org/standards-ra-web/pub/view.html#registries. The site www.wireshark.org/tools/oui-lookup.html has a friendly search function for parsing this list and returning the vendor.

Physical Layer

The Physical layer is responsible for transmitting the data of 1s and 0s that is passed down from the Data Link layer. The data consisting of 1s and 0s is modulated or encoded for transmission via radio waves, light, electricity, or any other physical method of transmitting data.

The Physical layer is an integral component of many different types of transmission methods such as wireless (802.11), fiber optics, and Ethernet, just to name a few. In all cases, the Physical layer is tied directly to the Data Link layer, so together the Physical layer and the Data Link layer are considered a macro layer. This macro layer allows an application to transmit in the same way over an Ethernet connection as it does a wireless connection, such as when you disconnect and go wireless. Hubs and repeaters operate at the Physical layer because they are not tied to the Data Link layer—they just repeat the electrical signals.

The Physical layer also defines the connection types used with the various networking technologies. The physical layer is the most common place to find problems, such as a loose connection or bad connection. A list of the different connection types and transmission media can be found in the section "Summarize the types of cables and connectors and explain which is the appropriate type for a solution" (objective 1.3).

Protocol Data Units

The term *protocol data units (PDUs)* is how we describe the type of data transferred at each layer of the OSI model. Using the proper PDUs when describing data can avoid misconceptions of problems when speaking with other network professionals. Throughout this book I will use PDUs to describe data; see if you take notice when I do refer to a PDU and try to match it with the layer it operates on.

The layers of the OSI model and their corresponding PDUs can be seen in Figure 1.10. The first three layers of the OSI model (Application, Presentation, and Session) reference the components of an application. The PDU for these upper layers is considered user datagrams, or just datagrams. The datagrams are created by the application and passed to the Transport layer. The Transport layer is where segments are created from the datagrams, and then the segments are passed to the Network layer. At the network layer, packets are created from the segments and passed to the Data Link layer. The Data Link layer creates frames for transmitting the data in bits at the Physical layer.

FIGURE 1.10   OSI layers and PDUs

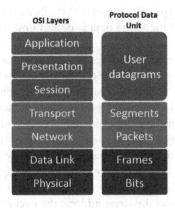

Data Encapsulation and Decapsulation

Throughout this review of the OSI model, you may have noticed a running theme. Every layer has identifying information such as a port number, the TCP or UDP protocol, IP address, and a frame. Each layer communicates with the layer above and the layer below using this information. Let's review the data encapsulation process as shown in Figure 1.11.

FIGURE 1.11   Encapsulation and decapsulation

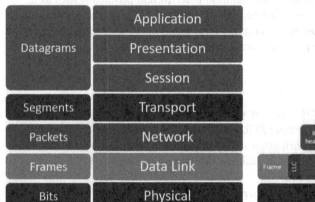
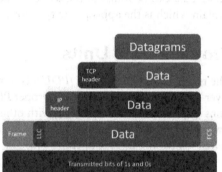

As data is transmitted, data encapsulation is the process of passing a PDU down to the next layer in the protocol stack. When it reaches this layer, information is written into the PDU header or type field (frame). This information explains to the current layer which upper layer the payload (data) came from; this will be important for the decapsulation process. The prior PDU is now considered nothing more than payload of data at this layer in the transmit process.

As data is received, data decapsulation is the process of passing the payload (data) up to the next layer in the protocol stack. When the payload is decapsulated, the information is read from the PDU header or type field (frame). This allows the current layer to know which upper layer to pass the payload to. As the data is passed upward in the stack, it becomes a PDU again.

In simple terms, if there were two buildings and a worker on the 7th floor of one building wanted to send a message to a worker in the other building on the 7th floor, the worker in the first building would write a note (datagram). This note would then be placed into an envelope and information would be written on the envelope detailing whom it came from. In addition, this envelope (segment) would have department information, such as which department it came from and which department it is going to (port numbers). The first worker would also choose the delivery company, either speedy delivery with no guarantees of delivery (UDP) or slow and steady delivery with acknowledgment of delivery (TCP). This envelope would then be placed into another envelope (packet) and on this envelope they would fill out information such as the street address the packet was coming from and going to. They would also make a note as to which delivery service was handling the message. This envelope would then go into another envelope (frame) detailing which door it came from and which door it was going to.

Encapsulation is basically envelopes inside of envelopes; each envelope performs its own function at each layer in the protocol stack. When the data arrives at the destination, each envelope is opened up and the envelope inside is handed off to the next destination it is intended for. Now let's take a closer look at these headers that will hold the information describing where data came from and how to hand it off on the other side of the conversation.

UDP

The User Datagram Protocol (UDP) is a transport protocol for TCP/IP. UDP is one of two protocols at the Transport layer that connect network applications to the network. When application developers choose to use UDP as the protocol their application will work with, they must take several considerations into account.

UDP is connectionless, which means that data is simply passed from one IP address over the network to the other IP address. The sending computer won't know if the destination computer is even listening. The receipt of the data is not acknowledged by the destination computer. In addition, the data blocks sent are not sequenced in any way for the receiving computer to put them back together. In Figure 1.12 you can see a UDP segment; the header has only a source port, destination port, length of data, and checksum field.

FIGURE 1.12   UDP segment

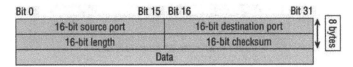

You may be wondering at this point why you would ever use UDP. We use UDP because it is faster than TCP. The application developer must make the application responsible for the connection, acknowledgment, and sequencing of data if needed. As an example, a Network Time Protocol (NTP) client uses UDP to send short questions to the NTP server, such as, What is the time? We don't need a large amount of overhead at the Transport layer to ask a simple question like that. Other protocols, such as the Real-time Transport Protocol (RTP) VoIP protocol, don't care to acknowledge segments or retransmit segments. If a segment of data doesn't make it to the destination, RTP will just keep moving along with the voice data in real time.

TCP

Transmission Control Protocol (TCP) is another transport protocol for TCP/IP. Just like UDP, TCP is a protocol at the Transport layer that connects network applications to the network. When application developers choose to use TCP as the protocol their applications will work with, the protocol is responsible for all data delivery.

TCP has all the bells and whistles for a developer. TCP is a connection-oriented protocol. During the transmission of information, both ends create a virtual circuit over the network. All data segments transmitted are then sequenced, acknowledged, and retransmitted if lost in transit. TCP is extremely reliable, but it is slower than UDP.

When the sending computer transmits data to a receiving computer, a virtual connection is created using a three-way handshake, as shown in Figure 1.13. During the three-way handshake, the window buffer size on each side is negotiated with the SYN and ACK flags in the TCP header. When both the sender and receiver acknowledge the window's size, the connection is considered established and data can be transferred. When the data transfer is completed, the sender can issue a FIN flag in the TCP header to tear down the virtual connection.

FIGURE 1.13   TCP three-way handshake

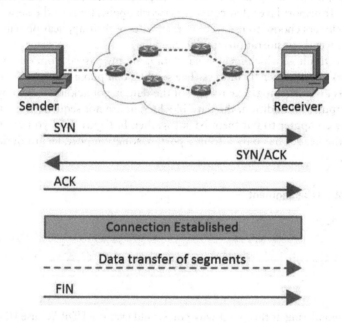

The buffer size negotiated in the three-way handshake determines the sliding TCP window for acknowledgment of segments during the transfer. As shown in Figure 1.14, the negotiated TCP sliding window size is 3. After three sequenced packets are delivered and put back in order on the receiving computer, the receiving computer sends an acknowledgment for the next segment it expects. If a segment is lost and the window cannot fill to the negotiated three-segment window size to send the acknowledgment, the acknowledge timer will be triggered on the receiver, and the receiver will acknowledge the segments it currently has received. The sender's retransmit timer will also expire, and the lost segment will be retransmitted to the receiving computer. This is how the sequencing and acknowledgment of segments operate with the use of TCP sliding windows. In Figure 1.15, the TCP header is shown with all the fields just described.

FIGURE 1.14   TCP sliding window example

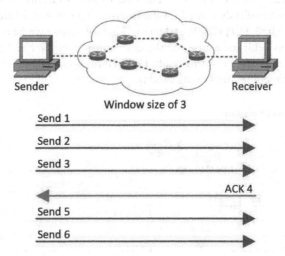

FIGURE 1.15   TCP segment

16-bit source port		16-bit destination port	
32-bit sequence number			
32-bit acknowledgment number			
4-bit header length	Reserved	Flags	16-bit window size
16-bit TCP checksum		16-bit urgent pointer	
Options			
Data			

IP

The Internet Protocol (IP) is a Network layer protocol that allows for the logical addressing of networks and hosts. The addressing of networks is the mechanism that allows routing to be used. The addressing of the hosts within the networks is the mechanism that allows end-to-end connectivity to be achieved over the network.

UDP and TCP function on top of the IP protocol. UDP and TCP are protocols that handle the data for the applications. The IP protocol is responsible for encapsulating these protocols and delivering it to the appropriate addresses. At this point, you are probably imagining a letter that is folded and put into an envelope that is addressed from the sender to the destination. You would be correct—the IP protocol handles the delivery of data segments from applications in IP packets.

Figure 1.16 shows the fields that are contained in an IP packet header. I will cover the most important fields as they pertain to this exam. The first 4 bits contain the version of IP;

this is how IPv4 and IPv6 packets are differentiated. The priority and type of service (ToS) fields are used for *quality of service (QoS)* The time to live (TTL) field is used for routing so that packets are not endlessly routed on the Internet. The protocol field defines where to send the data next—UDP, TCP, ICMP, and so on. Then of course we have the source and destination IP address fields for routing to the destination computer and responding of the destination computer. Throughout this book, I will be covering TCP/IP in depth because it is the predominant protocol in all networks today.

FIGURE 1.16   An IP packet

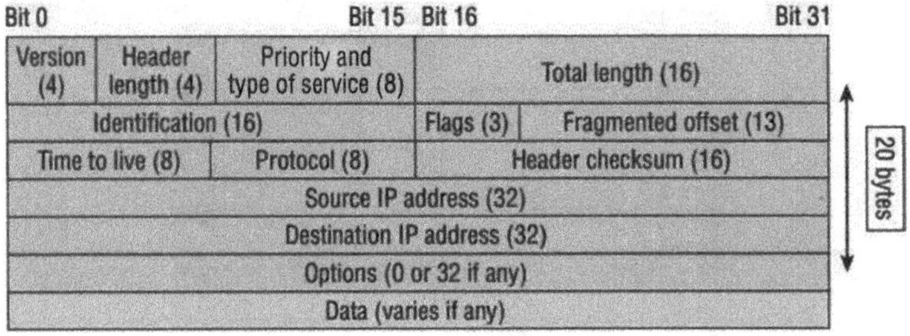

Bit 0			Bit 15 Bit 16		Bit 31	
Version (4)	Header length (4)	Priority and type of service (8)	Total length (16)			
Identification (16)			Flags (3)	Fragmented offset (13)		
Time to live (8)		Protocol (8)	Header checksum (16)			
Source IP address (32)						
Destination IP address (32)						
Options (0 or 32 if any)						
Data (varies if any)						

20 bytes

MTU

The *maximum transmission unit (MTU)* is the largest size of the data that can be transferred at the Data Link layer. The data being transferred is also known as the payload of the frame. The MTU for Ethernet is 1500 bytes. Adding 12 bytes for the destination and source MAC address, a 2-byte type field, and 4 bytes for the frame check sequence (FCS) brings the MTU to 1518 bytes. The smallest MTU is 46 bytes, or 64 bytes if including the frame fields.

The MTU is often referred to as a layer 3 data size. When data is passed down to the Data Link layer, the packet is sized to the MTU of the Data Link layer. Therefore, we can consider the MTU a constraint on the Network layer. However, it is usually adjustable only at the Data Link layer, such as when you're configuring a switch port on a switch.

The Ethernet specification allows for either an MTU of 1500 bytes or an MTU of 9000. When the MTU is increased to 9000 bytes, the frame is considered a jumbo frame. I will discuss jumbo frames in greater detail in Chapter 2, "Domain 2.0: Network Implementations."

Exam Essentials

Understand the various layers of the OSI and how they facilitate communications on each layer. The Application layer is the beginning of the communication process with the user and is where applications are defined as client or server. The Presentation layer converts data formats, encrypts and decrypts, and provides compression and decompression of data. The Session layer is responsible for setup, maintenance, and teardown of the communications for an application as well as dialogue control.

The Transport layer is responsible for flow control of network segments from the upper layers. The Network layer is responsible for the logical assignment and routing of network and host addresses. The Data Link layer is the layer responsible for the framing of data for transmission via a physical media. The Physical layer is the layer at which data is transmitted via air, light, or electricity.

Know the various protocol data units. Protocol data units (PDUs) are used to describe payloads of data at each layer of the OSI model. Using the proper PDU to describe data, network professionals can avoid miscommunication while dealing with network problems. PDUs not only describe the data, they also directly describe the layer being discussed.

Understand the encapsulation and decapsulation process. Encapsulation is the process in which data is passed down the protocol stack and each upper layer becomes a data payload at the next layer down along with identifying information for the decapsulation process. The decapsulation process is the reverse of the encapsulation process, taking the payload and decapsulating it back to the next layer, while passing it to the proper protocol above in the protocol stack.

Know the common TCP flags used for communication. The three-way handshake uses the SYN and ACK flags to establish a virtual communication circuit between two network nodes. When an established virtual circuit is complete, an RST or FIN flag is sent that tears down the established virtual communication circuit.

Understand the difference between headers for various layers of the OSI. UDP has an 8-byte header because it is a connectionless protocol and requires very few fields. The TCP header has quite a few more fields than UDP because TCP is a connection-based protocol and must sequence and acknowledge segments transmitted. Both TCP and UDP contain the element of a port number to direct information to the destination service and back to the requesting application. The IP header is used to route packets and therefore has destination and source IP address fields and other fields related to routing. In addition, it contains a protocol field that explains the payload of data and assists in handing the payload to upper layer protocols. Ethernet frames contain destination and source fields as well as a protocol field called the type field. This type field describes the payload of the frame and also assists the Data Link layer in handing the payload to upper layer protocols.

1.2 Explain the characteristics of network topologies and network types.

The topology of a network defines the shape in which the network is connected. Many of the topologies I will cover are no longer relevant for networking. However, you should understand how information moves within the topology, because you will see other technologies use these topologies.

The topology is a schematic of the overall network. Besides the topology of our network, sections of our network are defined by functional type such as local area network (LAN) and wide area network (WAN). In this and the following sections, you will learn about various functional types of networks.

A new emerging technology called the *Internet of Things (IoT)* is becoming the responsibility of the network administrator. There are several networking technologies that you must understand to support IoT devices. We will explore several common networking technologies used with IoT in the following sections.

Wired Topologies

I'll discuss several wired topologies that are no longer used for Ethernet networking. However, that doesn't mean they are deprecated and no longer used. You will see many of these topologies in other areas of technology, such as storage area networks (SANs), industrial control systems, and WANs.

Logical vs. Physical

There are two main types of topologies: physical and logical. If you ever sit down to document a network and end up with a mess of lines and details, you are trying to display both the physical and logical in one drawing. The logical topology of a network should be a high-level view of the information flow through semi-generic components in your network. This shows how the network operates and should be your first drawing. The physical topology defines why it works, such as which port on the router is connected to which port on a switch, and so on.

Star

The star topology is currently used in networks today, and it's the main topology used to connect edge devices (end users). All network devices are wired back to a hub or switch. The computers can be next to each other or spread out across an office space, but all communication goes back to a central location. This topology has been widely adopted because it concentrates the failure and diagnostic points in a central location. Another added benefit is that we can swap out the edge switches all from the same location. A disadvantage is that if a switch fails, every device connected to the switch is affected. Many buildings will have multiple star topologies; as an example, the edge switch is wired back to a larger switch, sometimes called a core switch. In Figure 1.17, you see a typical example of a star topology.

FIGURE 1.17   A typical star topology

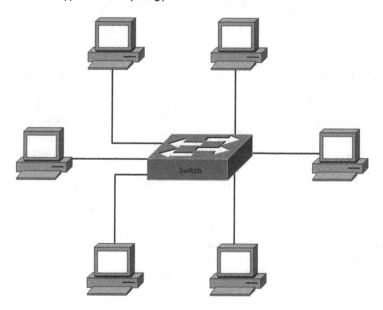

Ring

Ring topology was used over 25 years ago, and it was called token ring IEEE 802.5. IBM produced a lot of the hardware used in token ring networks, operating at a maximum speed of 4 Mbps and 16 Mbps. The networked devices would pass a token around the ring; any device that could seize the token could transmit a message around the ring. In Figure 1.18, you can see a logical ring topology. Physically the computers had one wire connected, similar to networks today. The wire consisted of a ring in pair and a ring out pair.

Token ring is now a deprecated technology for LAN connectivity with the IEEE 802.5 specification. However, token ring topologies are still used in industrial control system (ICS) applications. Token ring is also still used for WAN connectivity; it is used with *SONET rings* and *Fiber Distributed Data Interface (FDDI)* rings. I will cover LANs and WANs in this chapter. Token ring is still popular in WAN design because it can be designed to be resilient in the case of a failure.

FIGURE 1.18   A logical ring topology

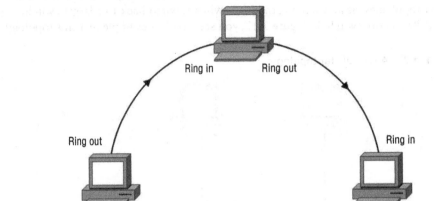

Mesh

The full mesh is a topology often used in data centers because it allows for redundant connection in the event of a component failure. Cloud computing uses a lot of mesh type connectivity because a failure should not hinder the customer(s). You will not see this used at the edge of a network where end-user computers connect to the network, mainly because it is too costly. If you wanted to calculate how many connections between four switches you would need to achieve a full mesh, you would use the following formula:

$$[n(n-1)]/2 = \text{total number of connections}$$
$$[4(4-1)]/2 =$$
$$[4(3)]/2 =$$
$$12/2 = 6 \text{ cable connections}$$

In this example, you would need six cable connections between the switches using the formula. More importantly, you would need to have three switch ports available on each switch because each cable has two ends (6 ÷ 2 = 3). In Figure 1.19, you can see a full mesh between four network switches. If you have a failure on any cable or switch, the network will continue to function. If a switch were to go down, the failure would be isolated to the failed switch.

FIGURE 1.19   A physical topology of a full mesh

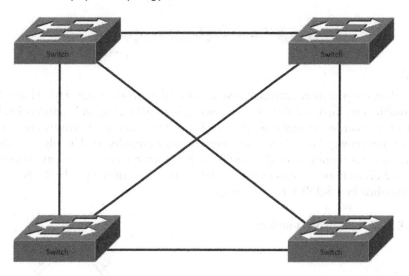

The Internet is not really a full mesh; it is a partial mesh. This is due to the costs of running cables to every provider on the Internet. So providers have partial meshes connecting them to upstream providers. When there is a failure on the Internet, it is usually localized to the path to the provider. Many providers have their own redundancy internally in their networks and use full meshes internally.

Bus

The bus concept is the most important networking concept to understand. It established the baseline for nearly all networking concepts and improvements that followed. The bus topology was common in networks 25 years ago; it is now considered legacy in its design. It used coaxial cables joining computers with BNC connectors. The reason it is deprecated is that a failure on the bus would affect all the computers on the bus. These networks also required external terminators on the ends of the bus segment. They are basically resistors; terminators stopped the reflection of electrical signals reflecting back in the direction it came from. So why are we talking about bus networks? Bus networks are how SCSI, RS-422 (industrial serial), and many other types of technologies work. It is important to understand how they work so that you can diagnose problems in these other technologies. When a computer wants to communicate on a bus network, it sends the signal out and all other computers see the message. Only the computer it is destined for by its destination MAC address processes the message and responds. SCSI disk networks use a device ID similar to how the MAC address is used on computer bus type networks. You can see this comparison in Figure 1.20.

FIGURE 1.20 A comparison of bus networks to SCSI disk networks

Hybrid

The hybrid topology is more representative of internal networks today. Hybrid topology design combines multiple topologies for resiliency, load balancing, and connectivity. In Figure 1.21, you can see several different topologies being used to effectively create redundancy and connectivity. You can also see several types of topologies. The edge switches are connected in a star topology, the distribution switches are connected in a partial mesh, and the core and distribution are connected in a full mesh. Also notice that the WAN connectivity is being supplied by a SONET ring topology.

FIGURE 1.21 A hybrid topology

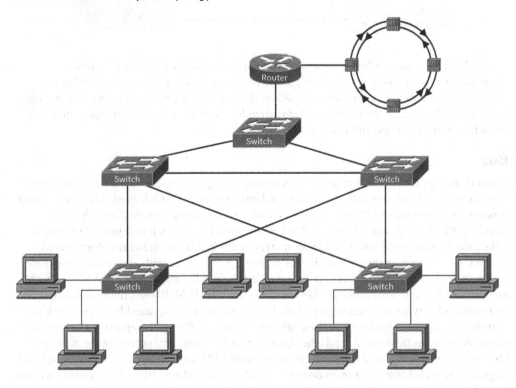

Types

When we refer to parts of our network, we classify the section of network with a type. This designation of type helps us generalize its use and function. Consider your property; you have inside doors, outside doors, and storm doors. The inside doors serve the function of privacy. The outside doors function the same but add security. The storm doors are used for security and safety. Our network has different areas that we label with these types so that we can quickly identify the areas' purpose. The type of network also helps us plan for infrastructure that the network will serve.

Client-Server

When I think back to when I first started 25 years ago in networking, I remember the dominant network operating system was Novell Netware. Although it has been discontinued for almost a decade, it still serves a purpose as an example of a strict client-server network operating system. Servers were only servers and could only serve up printers or files and clients could only be clients and could not serve files or printers. Clients used the resources from the servers, such as printers or files, and servers only existed to serve the clients.

Today, we have a more traditional peer networking model where clients can be both clients and servers, same as servers can be both. However, this model can still be applied to applications where clients access the resources for information. An example of this is a typical mail client that accesses the mail server. There is a strict client-server relationship with this example, where the client cannot serve mail because it was designed with one purpose, to act as a client. Same as such with the mail server; it was designed with one purpose, to act as server.

These client-server models should always be identified with network applications because it will help you understand the flow of information. If a client retrieves information from a server, then the server must have ports exposed to the client; so information can be accessed. If a firewall is involved, then you may have to open ports on the firewall for client connectivity. If there is a client-based firewall, then ports may need to be opened on the client side to egress the network.

Peer-to-Peer

You have probably heard of peer-to-peer networking, but it has probably been in a dark manner of piracy. True enough, the first time many of us heard of peer-to-peer networking was in the light of illegal activities. However, peer-to-peer networking existed way before these activities made headlines. A peer is nothing more than a network node that can act as both a client and server at the same time. This model breaks the strict client-server model because it allows a network host to access files and printers as well as serve them simultaneously.

The aspect of peer-to-peer information sharing is also applicable to network operating system functions. Many operating system functions have been adopted from the idea of peer-to-peer information sharing because it allows for decentralized functions. An example of this is a protocol called Link-Local Multicast Name Resolution (LLMNR), which is used as a peer-to-peer name resolution protocol. There is no one source of information since it is a distributed name resolution protocol where everyone is a peer to the information.

LAN

A local area network (LAN) defines the company's internal network. As its name infers, it is the "local area" of your network that is locally managed. As it pertains to infrastructure implementation, there should be little or no consideration for the placement of resources within the LAN. LAN speeds "should" always be the fastest within your network design and can be internally upgraded as needed. Figure 1.22 represents a typical LAN; where there is a resource local to the clients, it is considered an intranet.

FIGURE 1.22   Typical LAN

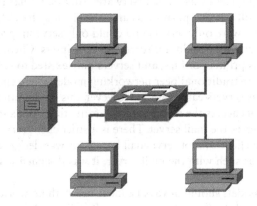

WLAN

A wireless local area network (WLAN) is a company's internal wireless network. As LAN infers, it is the "local area" that is locally managed. The WLAN is a wireless extension of our wired local area network. As it pertains to infrastructure, we should always design the wireless network for the wireless client density it could serve. Although wireless networks are upgradable, because of the physical location of wireless access points (WAPs), such upgrades are usually costly. When designing WLANs, we should always start with a site survey to estimate the best placement of WAPs. Figure 1.23 represents a typical WLAN. The WAP extends the wired network to wireless clients.

WAN

A wide area network (WAN) is a network that interconnects your network location together via a provider, and as the acronym infers, it is over a "wide area." These locations could be within the region or different regions of the world. An example of this is two locations that are connected with a point-to-point leased line within a state. As is pertains to your infrastructure implementation, a consideration is the placement of your resource within your various networks that are interconnected. This is mainly due to the fact that WAN connections usually operate at lower speeds than your internal networks. So resources should be placed closest to the users. They also could use different protocols than your internal networks do, so certain broadcast-based technologies might not work. Keep in mind that the term *WAN* is a generic description, and it does not pertain to any one solution. You could have leased lines, broadband, private fiber, public fiber, or any solution that connects your offices together over a wide area. Figure 1.24 represents a typical leased-line WAN; you can see that the branch office is connected to the central office via a leased-line.

FIGURE 1.23   Typical WLAN

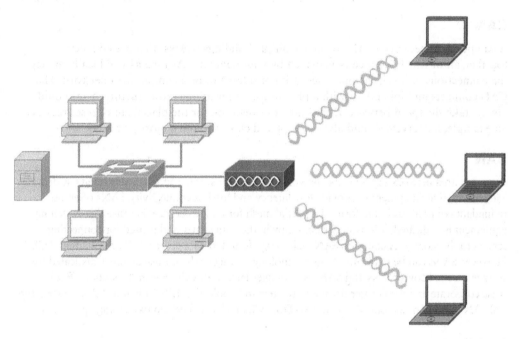

FIGURE 1.24   Typical WAN

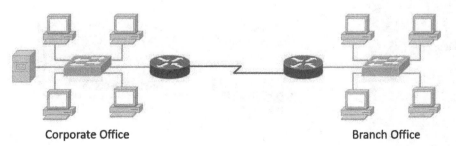

Corporate Office   Branch Office

MAN

A metropolitan area network (MAN) is a type of WAN. It is connected over a defined geographical area and has a higher connection speed between network locations via a provider. The area could be a city or a few-block radius or region of a state. The infrastructure implementation is similar to a WAN; the difference is the speed of the connection, because a MAN is built out by the provider as the backbone for your network locations. As it pertains to your infrastructure implementation, the placement of resources is less of a concern because of the higher speeds between the locations. An example of this is a company that has a branch office in the next town. You may have no administrators at that location, so centralizing the server at the primary location is the design goal. This requires a higher speed and reliable backbone between the locations.

CAN

A campus area network (CAN) defines multiple buildings (LANs) that are connected together, all of which are locally managed by your company. As long as you locally manage the connections between the buildings, it is considered to be a campus area network. The CAN connects multiple LANs with a private communications infrastructure. You should always take the speed between LANs into consideration for the placement of resources. As an example, file servers should always be placed closest to the majority of users.

SAN

A storage area network (SAN) is the network reserved for storage access. SANs often use dedicated switching equipment to provide low latency and lossless connectivity. SANs often use redundant connections in the form of a partial mesh for fault tolerance. Because this switching equipment is dedicated, it is usually found only in the data center and is used for connecting servers to the storage. A common SAN technology found in data centers is Fibre Channel (FC). However, SANs can be made up of any technology as long as the infrastructure is dedicated for storage access. I cover SANs and SAN technologies later in this chapter in the section "Explain basic corporate and data center network architecture" (objective 1.7). In Figure 1.25, we see a typical SAN that connects four servers to two Fibre Channel switches and two storage processors.

FIGURE 1.25 Typical SAN

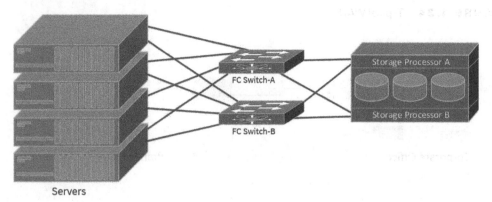

Servers

PAN

A personal area network (PAN) defines an ultra-small network for personal use. If you have a smartphone that is paired to your vehicle, you probably have a PAN. Many people walk around using a PAN every day: smart watches, smartphones, and personal fitness devices transmit data back and forth. A protocol often used with PANs is Bluetooth. However, PANs can use any protocol and any media. They can be wired or wireless, as long as they enable communications for devices near the person and are used for personal access.

MPLS

Multiprotocol Label Switching (MPLS) is an emerging WAN technology that uses packet-switching technology. It operates by adding MPLS labels to each packet generated from the customer and switching them in the provider's network. This MPLS label allows the MPLS provider to packet-switch the data based on the label and not the layer 3 network addressing. This is why MPLS is considered to work at layer 2.5; it is not a true layer 2 protocol because it is augmented with an MPLS label. It is also not a true layer 3 protocol since the destination IP address is not used for routing decisions. This makes it an extremely efficient protocol for moving data. It is considered a packet-switched technology and can be used across many different types of connectivity technologies, such as SONET, Ethernet, and ATM, just to name a few. The key takeaway is that an underlying leased line is required for MPLS to operate. MPLS is a great connectivity method for branch offices to a centralized corporate office. Cost is increased with the addition of each branch office, so at some point these lease lines become uneconomical.

SDWAN

Software-defined wide area network (SDWAN) is another emerging WAN technology. The centralized approach of bringing all network communications from branch offices back to the centralized corporate office was fine when all the resources were in a centralized location. For example, a typical branch office user would store their document on a server back at the corporate office where all the servers were located. This model just made sense for the past 25+ years. However, with the adoption of cloud-based services such as Microsoft 365, Salesforce, and Amazon Web Services, our office workers only need access to the Internet for connectivity and their documents are stored in the cloud. This can present new challenges, such as how do we police certain applications and assure bandwidth for other applications? This is where SDWAN solves a lot of problems.

All network communications use the layers of the OSI model, but depending on the purpose of the communications is what defines the plane of communications. The three basic planes are the data plane, where data is moved; the control plane, where data flow is controlled; and the management plane, where the administrator manages the control plane. SDWAN decouples the control plane from branch routers and centralizes the control plane at the SDWAN controller. Now in lieu of Border Gateway Protocol (BGP) and Open Shortest Path First (OSPF) routing protocols deciding how to route a packet, the SDWAN control now decides based upon congestion or application response. This is something that traditional protocols just can't do, because the control protocols are based upon path and getting packets routed fasted and not which server in the cloud responds quicker.

This control allows an administrator to centrally control policies for branch office routers to prioritize and route traffic over an existing Internet connection or leased line. The administrator can prioritize Voice over IP (VoIP) traffic over basic web surfing and differentiate web surfing from web-based line-of-business applications. Because SDWAN is application aware, it can differentiate between application traffic and intelligently control the flow of information over an Internet connection. SDWAN can also be combined with traditional technologies such as virtual private networks (VPNs) to maintain access to centralized resources back at a corporate office.

Generic Routing Encapsulation (GRE) is a protocol used to create a virtual tunnel over the Internet or an internetwork. The GRE protocol only creates a tunnel between two routed points; it does not provide encryption. GRE is used in conjunction with encryption protocols to provide security over the tunnel. In practice, it is used all the time to create point-to-point virtual tunnels on the Internet. The Internet Protocol Security (IPSec) protocol is then employed to encrypt the transmission over the tunnel.

The problem with GRE tunnels is that a tunnel must be built for each endpoint and between endpoints. This isn't much of a problem if you have a few locations, but once you get more than a few routers it becomes extremely difficult to manage. In Figure 1.26 we see a corporate office with multiple branch offices distributed across the Internet. Multipoint Generic Routing Encapsulation (mGRE) solves problems with scale and complication of configuration. The mGRE protocol allows an administrator to configure multiple GRE paths throughout the enterprise; it also allows branch offices to create logical tunnels between each office. Keep in mind that you still have to encrypt the traffic over these tunnels for privacy, but that is the easy part once the tunnels are configured.

FIGURE 1.26   Example of multiple GRE tunnels

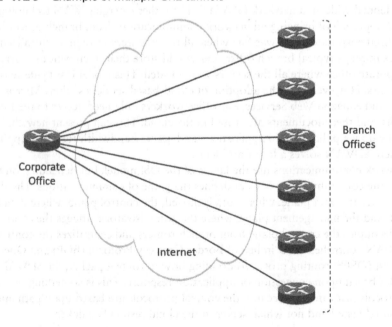

Service-Related Entry Point

The service-related entry point is yet another characteristic of service. It defines the point in a network that a provider terminates their responsibility for their service and it becomes the customer's responsibility. It also defines how the service is handed off to the customer, sometimes referred to as the *handoff*.

Many different WAN technologies can hand off the Internet connection in several different methods to the customer. The most common is Ethernet, but if distance is a factor, then fiber optic maybe specified in the buildout of services. Wireless can also be an option, when wiring is too costly or impossible due to terrain. All of these handoffs are outlined in the buildout of the services from the provider to the customer; it is generally a component of the initial setup costs. However, the buildout costs can sometimes be absorbed into the monthly reoccurring costs of service over the length of the contract for services.

No matter what method is chosen, the other side of the connection containing the customer premises equipment (CPE) is your responsibility. This is the sole function of the termination—it terminates the provider's responsibility for equipment and signaling.

Demarcation point

Demarcation point, often referred to as the demarc, is terminology used with lease lines and telephone equipment. Copper phone lines are considered legacy connections today because of cheaper alternatives from cable providers and fiber to the premise providers. However, back when the phone company ran a copper phone line to your dwelling, you were responsible for all internal wiring. The telephone company would install a box on the outside of your house that would segment your internal wiring from the telephone company's local loop wiring. This box was called the network interface connection (NIC), and it was the demarcation point for the phone company. The phone technician would pull a jumper on the NIC and test the phone connectivity. If it worked fine, then the problem was inside your dwelling and was your responsibility. Of course, they would be happy to fix it for a cost!

Today, with many other connectivity options such as broadband cable and fiber to the premises, the demarc has become the equipment that hands off service to the customer. The technician will disconnect the rest of your network and test basic Internet connectivity. Most problems can even be diagnosed from the home office of the provider, since all of the equipment has built-in diagnostics to reduce the number of technicians dispatched.

Leased lines like T1s and Integrated Services Digital Network (ISDN) lines have a mechanical jack called an RJ-48X (registered jack) at the patch panel. When the RJ-48 is removed, a shorting block bridges the connection to create a loopback. These mechanical jacks have largely been replaced with a device called a smart jack, which I will cover after the following section on CSUs/DSUs.

CSU/DSU

Channel service units/digital service units (CSUs/DSUs) are devices that convert serialized data such as T1 and ISDN to a serial protocol compatible with routers. The CSU/DSU sits between the router and the leased line circuit. In the past, it was a separate piece of equipment, but many newer routers have CSUs/DSUs built in.

The CSU/DSU will handle the receipt of clocking data from the data communication equipment (DCE) on the provider's network. The clocking data helps the CSU/DSU convert the channelized data into digital data so that data terminal equipment (DTE) such as a router can understand the data. The CSU/DSU also helps convert data back into serialized data when the router (DTE) sends information on the provider's network (DCE).

The CSU/DSU uses the RJ-48C universal service order code (USOC) to connect to the provider's demarcation point. The CSU/DSU is considered part of the customer premises equipment (CPE), so it is the customer's responsibility. The router side of the CSU/DSU generally has connections for RS-232 or V.35, and in most cases the CSU/DSU is built into the router.

Smart Jack

Smart jacks are normally used with leased line circuits such as T1 and ISDN. The smart jack is a diagnostic point for the provider and is generally the demarcation point. It has largely replaced the RJ-48C electromechanical jacks. Smart jacks allow the provider to convert protocols and framing types from the provider's network. The router still requires a CSU/DSU, but the smart jack can change the framing type the CSU/DSU expects.

The smart jack also offers advanced diagnostic capabilities to the provider. Smart jacks allow the provider to put the circuit into a loopback mode. This loopback mode enables the provider to diagnose signal quality and error rates. The smart jack also offers alarm indication signaling so the provider can determine whether the problem is on their premises equipment or the customer's. This alarm indication signaling enables the provider to dispatch technicians when the problem is discovered.

Virtualization

Before virtualization became a mainstream standard, applications had a one-to-one relationship with servers. When a new application was required, we purchased server hardware and installed an operating system along with the application. Many of these applications never used the full resources of the servers they were installed on.

Virtualization solves the problem of acquisition of server hardware and applications not fully utilizing server hardware. Virtualization allows for the partitioning of server hardware with the use of a hypervisor by enabling each virtual machine (VM) to use a slice of the central processing unit (CPU) time and share random access memory (RAM). We now have a many-to-one relationship with applications to servers. We can fit many applications (operating systems) onto one physical server called physical host hardware. Each operating system believes that it is the only process running on the host hardware, thanks to the hypervisor.

Virtual Networking Components

So far we have covered components that support physical infrastructure. A virtualized infrastructure uses networking components similar to the physical components you have learned about already. You should have a good working knowledge of virtualized networking components, since virtualization is here to stay and is growing rapidly.

Virtual Switch

A *virtual switch* (vSwitch) is similar to a physical switch, but it is a built-in component in your hypervisor. It differs in a few respects; the first is the number of ports. On a physical switch, you have a defined number of ports. If you need more ports, you must upgrade the switch or replace it entirely. A virtual switch is scalable compared to its physical counterpart; you can just simply add more ports.

The virtual switch also performs the same functions as a physical switch, with the exception of how the MAC address table is handled. The virtual switch only cares about the MAC addresses of the VMs logically attached. It doesn't care about everything else, since all other MACs can be sorted out after forwarding the frame to a physical switch. When a physical switch doesn't know the port a MAC address is associated with, it floods the frame to all the active ports. If the MAC address is unknown, the virtual switch will forward it to a physical switch via the uplink port and allow the physical switch to forward the frame. This is how we can achieve low latency switching on a hypervisor virtual switch.

Virtual NIC

The *virtual network interface card (vNIC)* is just like any other virtualized hardware in the VM. The vNIC is a piece of software that pretends to be physical hardware. It communicates directly between the VM and the virtual switch.

The virtual NIC is usually generic hardware that is installed in the VM. Examples are the DEC 21140 NIC and the Intel E1000 NIC. Some hypervisors also have more advanced cards that support unique features such as VMware's VMXNET3 NIC card. The VMXNET3 NIC can support IPv6 TCP segment offloading (TSO), direct paths into the hypervisor's I/O bus for performance, and 10 Gbps data rates. These virtual NICs require the VMware drivers since they are not generic hardware presented to the VMs. Hyper-V has a virtual NIC called a synthetic NIC; the NICs allow for similar functionality with features such as IPv6 TSO, single-root I/O virtualization (SR-IOV), direct ties into the Hyper-V VMBus, and 10 Gbps data rates. It too requires the VM to install the guest services software.

Network Function Virtualization (NFV)

Network functions such as firewalls and routing can all be virtualized inside the hypervisor. They operate just like their physical versions, but we don't have to worry about power supplies failing, CPUs going bad, or anything else that can cause a physical network device to fail. We do have to worry about the host that runs the virtual network functions; however, redundancy is built into many hypervisors. Personally, I prefer to virtualize as many functions as I can possibly virtualize.

Virtual Firewall

A *virtual firewall* is similar to a physical firewall. It can be a firewall appliance installed as a virtual machine or a kernel mode process in the hypervisor. When installed as a firewall appliance, it performs the same functions as a traditional firewall. In fact, many of the traditional firewalls today are offered as virtual appliances. When virtualizing a firewall, you gain the fault tolerance of the entire virtualization cluster for the firewall—compared to a physical firewall, where your only option for fault tolerance may be to purchase another unit and cluster it together. As an added benefit, when a firewall is installed as a virtual machine, it can be backed up like any other VM and treated like any other VM.

A virtual firewall can also be used as a hypervisor virtual kernel module. These modules have become popular from the expansion software-defined networking (SDN). Firewall rules can be configured for layer 2 MAC addresses or protocol along with tradition layer 3 and layer 4 rules. Virtual firewall kernel modules use policies to apply to all hosts in the cluster. The important difference between virtual firewall appliances and virtual firewall kernel modules is that the traffic never leaves the host when a kernel module is used. Compared to using a virtual firewall appliance, the traffic might need to leave the current host to go to the host that is actively running the virtual firewall appliance.

Virtual Router

The virtual router is identical to a physical router in just about every respect. It is commonly loaded as a VM appliance to facilitate layer 3 routing. Many companies that sell network hardware have come up with unique features that run on their virtual routing appliances; these features include VPN services, BGP routing, and bandwidth management, among others. The Cisco Cloud Services Router (CSR) 1000v is a virtual router that is sold and supported by cloud providers such as Amazon and Microsoft Azure. Juniper also offers a virtual router called the vMX router, and Juniper advertises it as a carrier-grade virtual router.

Hypervisor

The virtual networking components would not be virtualized if it weren't for the *hypervisor*. The hypervisor sits between the hardware or operating system and the VM to allow for resource sharing, time sharing of VMs to the physical hardware, and virtualization of the guest operating systems (VMs). The hardware that the hypervisor is installed on is called the host, and the virtual machines are called guests. There are three different types of hypervisors, as shown in Figure 1.27.

FIGURE 1.27 Hypervisor types

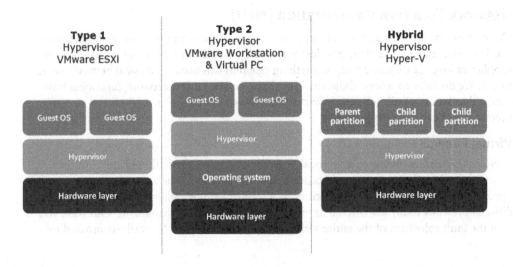

| Type 1 Hypervisor VMware ESXi | Type 2 Hypervisor VMware Workstation & Virtual PC | Hybrid Hypervisor Hyper-V |

A *Type 1 hypervisor* is software that runs directly on the hardware; its only purpose is to share the hardware among VMs running as the guest operating system. This concept is not as new as you might think. IBM offered mainframes that perform this partitioning of hardware as early as 1967! Examples of Type 1 hypervisors are Xen/Citrix XenServer, VMware ESXi, and Hyper-V. Although Hyper-V fits into the third category of hypervisors, it is still considered a Type 1 hypervisor.

A *Type 2 hypervisor* is software that runs on the host operating system. It runs as a process in the host operating system. Despite what you may think, Type 2 hypervisors do talk directly to the CPU via Intel VT or AMD-V extensions, depending on which vendor you are using. Memory utilization is similar to CPU utilization, but the host operating system parlays the requests via Direct Memory Access (DMA) calls. All other hardware is proxied through the host operating system. Examples of Type 2 hypervisors are VMware Workstation, VirtualBox, Parallels for macOS, and the open-source QEMU.

Hybrid hypervisors are a bit different than Type 1 or Type 2 hypervisors. They function outside of the norm of cloud computing hypervisor models. They require a host operating system but function as a Type 1 hypervisor. As an example, Hyper-V requires the Microsoft operating system to be installed, but the host operating system is a guest called the parent partition. It is treated the same as guest or child partitions, but it is required for management of the hypervisor. Examples of hybrid hypervisors are Linux Kernel–based Virtual Machine (KVM), FreeBSD bhyve (pronounced beehive), and Microsoft Hyper-V.

Service Type

The service type defines the service from the provider, also known as the provider link. For example, broadband cable is a cable company service type, and DSL is a phone company service type. There are many different service types well beyond those covered in the following sections. However, these are the most common service types that you will see for WAN connectivity service offerings.

Leased-Line

Leased-lines where the most popular service type 25 years ago. You might wonder why they would be covered in the Network+ exam if they are so old? It's because they serve a purpose and newer leased-line technologies like MPLS can be overlaid on top of these service types.

ISDN

Integrated Services Digital Network (ISDN) is a useful service for voice calls, but it's not that useful for data. You will probably never use it for data services, and if you run into it, you will probably be migrating away from it. It is a popular connectivity technology for phone systems, like private branch exchanges (PBXs). You may have to interface with a PBX for integrated voice services someday. ISDN is still used today by phone service providers. It is deployed in two different modes: Basic Rate Interface (BRI) and Primary Rate Interface (PRI). PRI, which I will cover later, is the most common implementation.

T1/T3

A *T1*, or tier 1, of service is sometimes referred to as a DS-1, or Digital Service tier 1. You specify the tier of service that you require when ordering service as a T1. The T1 provides 1.544 Mbps of bandwidth.

A T1 is a group of 24 channels of serial data. Think of the T1 as a conveyor belt consistently moving from one location to another. On the conveyor belt there are 24 buckets, and each bucket is a channel of data (DS0). We use a special device called a channel service unit/data service unit (CSU/DSU) to convert the channels back into a stream of data. If each channel is 64 Kbps and we have 24 channels, in total we have 1.544 Mbps of bandwidth. Channels can be used for voice or data. We can even divide T1 so that some of the channels are for the PSTN and some are for data. We can even purchase only a few channels of data; this is called a fractional T1.

A *T3*, or tier 3, of service is sometimes referred to as a DS-3. It is the next step up from a T1 when you need more bandwidth. You may be wondering what happened to the T2. It existed at one point, but T1 and T3 became the popular ordering standard. A T3 is 28 T1 connections, or 672 DS0 channels, combined together to deliver 44.736 Mbps of bandwidth.

E1/E3

An *E1* is only common in Europe and interconnections to Europe. It too works by channelizing data in 64 Kbps buckets, the same as a T1. However, it has 32 channels. This gives us 32 channels of 64 Kbps, for a total of 2.048 Mbps. An *E3* is the European standard and consists of 16 E1 connections, or 512 DS0s, combined together to deliver 34.368 Mbps of bandwidth.

PRI

Primary Rate Interface (PRI) is an ISDN circuit, and it can be used for voice and data. When you purchase an ISDN circuit, you basically purchase a T1 lease line with ISDN signaling. A T1 has 24 channels of 64 Kbps. The ISDN functions by using one of the channels as a control channel called the D (delta) channel. The other 23 data channels are called the B (bearer) channels; this is sometimes noted in shorthand as 23B + D.

The D channel will control call setup, and the B channels will carry data or voice calls. Twenty-three channels at 64 Kbps is 1472 Kbps (1.472 Mbps) of bandwidth. This is how ISDN excels when it is used for voice communications, since the D channel communicates call information for the other 23 channels to both ends (provider and PBX). In doing this call setup, it avoids something called call collisions. Call collisions happen when a call is coming in and going out on the same channel. It is a popular technology for voice but not for data.

OC3-OC1920

The *OC* stands for optical carrier, since these services are delivered over fiber-optic cables. They still have channelized data and require a CSU/DSU—it just happens to be delivered over a fiber cable via a SONET ring. An OC1 has a speed of 51.84 Mbps. Unfortunately, there is some overhead in an OC1, which takes usable bandwidth to approximately

50 Mbps. We use the 51.84 Mbps when calculating OC speeds. An OC3 is three OC1s combined together to supply approximately 150 Mbps of bandwidth. An OC12 is 12 OC1s combined together to supply approximately 600 Mbps of bandwidth. You can see how the OCs are calculated. An OC-1920 is 1920 OC1s combined together to supply 100 Gbps, which is currently the top speed of optical carriers.

DSL

Digital Subscriber Line (DSL) uses copper phone lines to transmit data and voice. These lines are already running to your house or business, which is why telephone providers (POTS) became ISPs. The provider will have a piece of equipment called a DSL Access Multiplexer (DSLAM) at the local central office (CO) where your phone line is wired for dial tone. The DSLAM is between the POTS in the CO and your house or business (premise). The DSLAM communicates with the modem at your premise by using the frequencies above 3400 hertz. The POTS system filters anything above 3400 hertz, which is why music sounds terrible over a phone call. Filters are placed on the existing phones at your premise, so your calls do not interrupt data communications and your voice calls are not disturbed with the modem's screeching of data. Figure 1.28 shows a typical DSL connection and its various components.

FIGURE 1.28   A DSL network

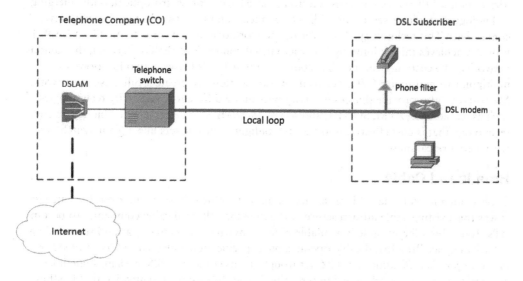

ADSL

Asymmetrical Digital Subscriber Line (ADSL) is the most common DSL offering to home and small business. The download speed is asymmetrical to the upload speed. ADSL has a typical download rate of 10 Mbps and an upload speed of 0.5 Mbps (512 Kbps). The upload speed is usually 1/20th of the download speed. Although this connectivity method has a decent download speed, you will be limited by the upload speed. ADSL is good for users who require Internet access for web surfing, but it is not the ideal technology for hosting services and servers.

SDSL

Symmetrical Digital Subscriber Line (SDSL) is a common DSL offering for small business. The download speed is similar to the upload speed: 1.5 Mbps. SDSL is comparable with T1 leased lines, which is relatively slow for most businesses today. SDSL is cheaper in comparison to leased lines, so for many businesses that do not require high speed, it is a good option.

VDSL

Very-high-bitrate Digital Subscriber Line (VDSL) is today's replacement for ADSL and SDSL, and it lacks speed. VDSL can supply asymmetrical speeds of 300 Mbps download and 100 Mbps upload, or symmetrical speeds of 100 Mbps download and 100 Mbps upload. Just like ADSL and SDSL, it can handle these data speeds across the same phone lines you use to make phone calls.

Metropolitan Ethernet

Metropolitan Ethernet, sometimes referred to as Metro-E or Metro-optical, is an emerging technology that allows service providers to connect campus networks together with layer 2 connectivity. This technology allows for the network over a large area to act like a LAN. The provider achieves this by building Ethernet virtual connections (EVCs) between the campus networks. The customer can purchase point-to-point EVCs between two locations, or multipoint-to-multipoint EVCs between several locations, to create a full meshed network. Metro-E can also provide this connectivity over many different connectivity technologies, such as leased lines, ATM, SONET, and so on. Metro-E is an extremely flexible connectivity technology that is cost effective and easy to configure, since it acts like a giant switch between network campuses.

Broadband Cable

Cable companies introduced Internet access on their cable infrastructure over 20 years ago. It was this existing cable infrastructure at the time that allowed cable companies to become ISPs. Today broadband cable is available almost anywhere in metro areas and surrounding suburban areas. Broadband cable operates on a specification called *Data Over Cable Service Interface Specification (DOCSIS)*, through the use of a DOCSIS modem, sometimes referred to as a cable modem. It can typically deliver 300 Mbps download and 100 Mbps upload speeds.

A cable modem communicates over coax lines that are run to your house or business and lead back to a fiber-optic node (see Figure 1.29). The fiber-optic node is a device in your area that converts coax communications to a fiber-optic line that ultimately leads back to the head end. The head end is the cable company's router and distribution of its Internet connection. One disadvantage is the shared coax line that leads back to the fiber node. Congestion and interference on this shared coax line can degrade services and speed for everyone in your service area.

FIGURE 1.29   The broadband cable network

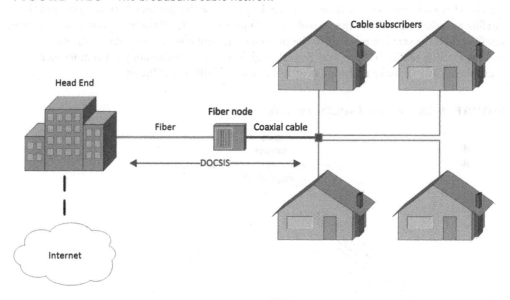

Dial-up

Dial-up uses modems on the public switched telephone network (PSTN) using a plain old telephone service (POTS) line. It has a maximum theoretical speed of 56 Kbps with the V.92 specification, although North American phone systems limited speeds to 53 Kbps. Dial-up is too slow to browse the web, but it is extremely useful for out-of-band management of routers, switches, and other text-based network devices. All you need is a phone line and you can dial in to the device. You may ask why you need it, if you have an IP address configured on the device. It is often used if the device loses connectivity from the Internet or network and is too far away to drive to. You can just dial in to troubleshoot it. Dial-up is a backup control for network outages since it uses the PSTN network for connectivity.

Satellite

Satellite communications allows unidirectional and bidirectional communications anywhere there is a line of site to the earth's equator. There is a group of satellites about 22,000 miles above the equator in a geosynchronous orbit used for communications. If you have a satellite dish, you are pointed to one of these satellites. In a unidirectional setup, you can receive video, voice, music, and data, but you cannot send information back. Your satellite dish operates in this mode of communication. It is also popular for command and control situations where first responders need to only view camera feeds and data such as weather. In a bidirectional setup, you can also send data back through the use of a *very small aperture terminal (VSAT)*, which is a dish that can transmit and receive data. Although this technology sounds amazing, there are some issues such as the transmission distance and the speed of light at about 186,000 miles per second, which is how fast your transmission travels. There are four transmissions that need to traverse the distance between you and the satellite and the satellite and the provider (see Figure 1.30). You first send your request to the satellite; then the satellite relays it to the provider, the provider replies back to the satellite, and the satellite replies back to you. So although it is a great technology for remote locations, the delay can make real-time protocols such as VoIP very difficult.

FIGURE 1.30   A typical satellite network

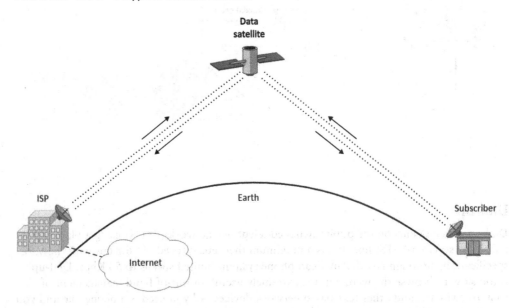

 In recent news, SpaceX started launching satellites for a service called Starlink. Although it is currently in beta in the United States, it is scheduled to be released globally in the future. The service boasts a low-latency connection to the Internet for the consumer and really fast speeds. It achieves this by maintaining a very low earth orbit and lots of satellites because of the curvature of the earth and line of sight.

Service Delivery

Regardless of which type of Internet provider you select, the provider will hand off service to you with one of three methods; copper, fiber optic, or wireless. You should be familiar with these methods, their uses, and their limitations. In the discussion of objective 1.3, I will cover connectivity methods and standards much more thoroughly.

Copper

Copper cable is a popular handoff from the provider when the network equipment is within 100 meters or less from the provider's termination point. The various services that copper is used with include leased lines, broadband cable, DSL, and dial-up. Metropolitan Ethernet services can be ordered as either a copper or fiber handoff from the provider. Copper has limited distance and speed, so fiber handoffs from the provider are more common.

Fiber

Fiber-optic cable (fiber) is used to provide extremely fast connectivity for long distances. Typical speeds of 10, 40, and 100 Gbps are transmitted on fiber, but higher speeds can be achieved. Distances will vary with the speed and type of cable being used; the typical range can be 150 meters to 120 kilometers (75 miles).

Fiber comes in two variations from the service provider: lit fiber and dark fiber. Lit fiber, also called managed fiber, is similar to Verizon's FiOS service. The provider is responsible for installing the fiber cable and for the equipment and maintenance on each end. Dark fiber is just a piece of fiber from one location to another, and the customer is responsible for lighting it and maintaining it. Dark fiber is used inside the network campus, and it can also be used for WAN connectivity. Dark fiber is the cheaper option after the upfront cost for equipment. Fiber is used to deliver several of the services covered in this chapter.

Wireless

Wireless transmission mediums are normally used when cabling cannot be accomplished or is too expensive. An example of this is Internet connectivity for ships and planes; other examples are remote locations in mountainous terrains.

Some services are exclusively delivered via wireless. *Worldwide Interoperability for Microwave Access (WiMAX)* is a connectivity technology similar to Wi-Fi in respect to delivering Internet over wireless. It is defined by the IEEE as 802.16 and operates on 2 GHz to 11 GHz and 10 GHz to 66 GHz. It can be used line of sight or non–line of sight when there are obstructions such as trees. The service provider will mount a WiMAX radio on a tower, similar in concept to cellular communications. The WiMAX tower can cover areas as large as 3,000 square miles (a 30-mile radius). This allows rural areas, where running dedicated lines is impossible, to have Internet connectivity. Subscribers need either a WiMAX card in their computer or a WiMAX router to connect to the tower. When WiMAX originally launched, it was capable of delivering speeds of 40 Mbps; it can now deliver speeds up to 1 Gbps. It is commonly used by many cellular providers to backhaul cellular traffic from remote cell towers.

Exam Essentials

Know the various wired topologies.   Logical topologies provide a high-level overview of the network and how it operates. The physical topology is a more detailed view of the network and why it can operate. Star topologies are used for Ethernet networks. Ring topologies are used for WAN connectivity. Mesh topologies are commonly found in the core of the network. Bus topologies are no longer used for Ethernet, but bus topologies can be found in many other technologies.

Know the various types of networks.   A local area network (LAN) is the locally managed network. The wireless local area network (WLAN) extends the LAN for wireless capabilities. The wide area network (WAN) allows a site to get access to another site or Internet access. The metropolitan area network (MAN) is a type of WAN that is constrained to a metropolitan area. The campus area network (CAN) is a relatively small area that is locally managed. The storage area network (SAN) is exclusively used for connecting to storage. The personal area network (PAN) is a network that is for personal use.

Know the function and understand the fundamentals of virtual networking components.   A virtual switch functions similarly to a physical switch, except for the difference of how the MAC addresses are handled. You can install virtual firewalls as a virtual appliance, and some virtualization software offers a kernel mode firewall in the hypervisor. The virtual NIC is a software emulated generic network card in the guest operating system. Virtual routers are similar to hardware routers. Hypervisors allow the hardware resources to be shared among virtual machines.

Know the various service types of WAN technologies.   ISDN PRI operates on a T1 leased line and reserves one of the 24 channels for call setup. T1 lines are point-to-point serial connections with a speed of 1.544 Mbps. E1 lines are similar in function to a T1 and are used mainly in Europe. T3 lines consist of 28 T1 connections. E3 lines consist of 16 E1 connections. Optic carriers (OCs) are based off an OC1 at around 50 Mbps. Metropolitan Ethernet is a WAN technology. Broadband cable uses a coaxial network to communicate back to a fiber node that is wired to the head end at the cable company. Dial-up is a legacy technology. SDWAN is a routing technology that is application aware. MPLS is a packet forwarding technology that is used for WAN connectivity. mGRE is a protocol that allows multiple GRE tunnels to be set up for scalability.

Know the various termination points of provider services.   The demarcation point is the end of the provider's responsibility. The CSU/DSU converts channelized serial data from the provider's network to digital serial data for the customer premises equipment. The customer premises equipment is usually the customer's router. The smart jack enables the provider to remotely diagnose a leased line connection.

1.3 Summarize the types of cables and connectors and explain which is the appropriate type for a solution.

In the discussion of this objective, I will cover the common cabling, connectors, termination points, and wiring specifications involved in connecting a network together. Over your career as a network professional, you will need to deploy the proper cabling for a given network connectivity scenario. At the end of this discussion, you should be able to describe the practical application of the cabling, connectors, termination points, and specifications for a network design.

Media Types

When wiring a network, you will have two main media types: copper cabling and fiber-optic cabling. The decision between the two is based on a number of factors that I will detail in the following sections. After the selection of the appropriate cable type for the network design, there are several different specifications of these cables that we will cover later.

Copper

As a network professional, you will be responsible for identifying cabling, diagnosing cabling problems, and ordering the proper cabling for the installation required. Coaxial cable is not used for networking anymore, but you should be able to identify and understand its practical application.

UTP

Unshielded twisted-pair (UTP) is the most common cabling for Ethernet networks today, and it is the least expensive option for cabling a network. It is unshielded from electromagnetic interference (EMI), so the placement of cables in a network should avoid EMI sources. UTP should always be cabled away from electrical lines and non-network cabling. Because of the lack of shielding, electrical lines can induce erroneous electrical signals if the cables are run in parallel with electrical lines. UTP cable has a PVC or Teflon cable jacket, as shown in Figure 1.31; inside are four pairs of wires (eight conductors). Each of the four pairs has a specific number of twists per inch. I will cover the category specification that defines speed in relation to the twists and how the pairs are separated in a later section, "Copper Cabling Standards."

STP

Shielded twisted-pair (STP) is commonly used in industrial settings, where *electromagnetic interference (EMI)* can induce erroneous data into the cable. STP cables should be used when running network cables around or near large motors, welding equipment, HVAC equipment, high-voltage lighting, and so on. There are several different types of STP cable depending on the severity of EMI. The most common STP cable consists of a PVC or Teflon jacket as well as a metal weaved shielding that protects the four pairs of twisted wires, as shown in Figure 1.32. Depending on the application, the individual pairs may have foil shielding as well. The cabling is significantly more expensive in price than UTP and more difficult to install because of the Ethernet jack shielding and RJ-45 shielding required.

FIGURE 1.31   A common UTP cable

FIGURE 1.32   A common STP cable

 When installing cable in an industrial setting such as a factory where cabling is exposed to vibrations, chemicals, temperature, and EMI, the MICE (Mechanical, Ingress, Climatic, Chemical, and Electromagnetic) classification should be followed. The standard is defined in an ISO/IEC (International Organization for Standardization/International Electrotechnical Commission) publication. It is best to engage an engineer to define the type of cabling to use when in doubt for an industrial setting because safety can be compromised.

Coaxial

Coaxial cable is no longer used in networks today for Ethernet communications on the local area network (LAN). Coaxial cable is still used for security cameras and broadband cable networks. A coaxial cable contains a solid core wire that carries the signal. The core is surrounded by a dielectric foam that keeps it perfectly centered in the cable, while not conducting any electricity. The dielectric foam is then surrounded by a shielding that is a conductive common ground. The entire cable is then protected with a jacket made from either PVC or Teflon, as shown in Figure 1.33. In the data center, you can use a connectivity method between servers and switching equipment called Twinax. A Twinax cable is a fixed-size coaxial cable with transceivers on each end. It usually comes in lengths of 1 meter, 5 meters, and 10 meters.

FIGURE 1.33   Coax cable elements

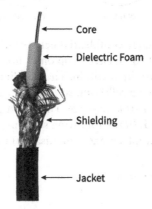

Core

Dielectric Foam

Shielding

Jacket

Stranded vs. Solid Core

Stranded network cabling is used for patch cables such as wiring from the network jack to the computer or wiring from the patch panel to the network switch. Stranded cabling is flexible and used for wiring that requires being moved around often. Stranded cabling should never be used for installs that require wire to be run in a riser since stranded cabling lacks a strength member. The proper RJ-45 end should be used with stranded network cabling, and the teeth that crimp into the wire should be perfectly straight. Stranded wire also cannot be punched down to a punch panel.

Solid core network cabling is used for permanent installation such as wall wiring from the patch panel to the network jack. It is not flexible like stranded network cabling. The solid core allows for the wire to be punched down to a patch panel or network jack. Solid core wire also can be identified by its strength member inside the jack. The strength member allows for cabling to be run in a riser. The strength member prevents the copper from weighing down the cable when run vertically and stretching the copper conductions. The proper RJ-45 end should be used with solid core, and the teeth that crimp into the wire should be offset on an angle opposing each other. This is done to clench the wire between the angle of the offset inside the RJ-45 end. Both solid and stranded core cables are shown for comparison in Figure 1.34.

Fiber

Fiber-optic cable (fiber) is often used to transmit high data rates over longer distances than conventional copper cable. It is also used in applications where the EMI is too high for copper cable, such as running cable in the proximity of an electric blast furnace. Fiber-optic

FIGURE 1.34   Cross section of solid core vs. stranded core cables

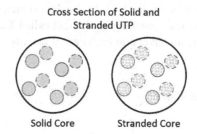

Cross Section of Solid and
Stranded UTP

Solid Core   Stranded Core

cable can also be used for extremely confidential networks because unless you are spliced in directly, it emits no emissions of RF to eavesdrop on. A fiber-optic cable contains a core of glass that the light signal is transmitted within. The cladding is used to contain the light in the core, as well as aid in creating a reflection so the light can bounce down the core. The buffer protects the cladding layer from damage. The jacket protects the entire cable from damage, as shown in Figure 1.35. In the following sections, I will discuss the different modes and sizes of fiber, as well as their advantages and disadvantages.

FIGURE 1.35   A typical fiber-optic cable

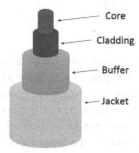

Core

Cladding

Buffer

Jacket

Single-Mode

Single-mode fiber-optic cable (SMF) is used for high-speed and long-distance communications. SMF offers less dispersion of light traveling down the glass fiber, so it is considered a single mode of light when it reaches the destination. It achieves this by using an extremely small core of 8 to 10 microns and precision lasers called transceivers. Normally, SMF is advertised as 9-micron fiber. It should be used in any application that requires 10 Gbps or higher data rates and can span up to 120 kilometers (approximately 75 miles) before it needs to be repeated. It is commonly used in long-distance communications and internal building wiring. It should be used in any new installations to future-proof bandwidth requirements. The standard color of SMF patch cables is yellow, but it is always best to check the cable's numbering. Arguably, it is easier to terminate than other types of fiber cable—since the diameter is so small, a smaller area needs to be polished.

Multimode

Multimode fiber-optic cable (MMF) is used for short to medium distances. MMF disperses light into numerous paths inside the core, which is why it is called multimode. MMF has a maximum speed of 10 Gbps at very short distances and a maximum distance of 3000 feet. It is mainly used for internal building connectivity. MMF is available in both glass core and plastic core, but speed is limited with plastic core. The core size of MMF is 50 microns, it is usually used for Fibre Channel and network connectivity, and the patch cable color is often aqua. MMF is also available in a 62.5-micron core size, and the patch cable color is often orange. See Table 1.1 for details.

TABLE 1.1 Fiber-optic cable specifications

Core size	Fiber type	Max distance	Max speed	Patch cable color
9 microns	SMF	75 miles	Over 400 Gbps	Yellow
50 microns	MMF	3000 feet	10 Gbps	Aqua
62.5 microns	MMF	2000 feet	10 Gbps (under 26 meters)	Orange

Connector Types

After the cabling is installed in the network, you will have the task of adding connectors to the cable ends. This is commonly called terminating the ends of the cable. There are two main connector types: copper and fiber-optic. In the following sections, I will discuss the advantages of each different connector for the respective connector types.

Copper Connectors

Copper connectors are not made out of copper as their name suggests. They are usually made of a harder metal and copperplated. Copper is soft and can wear over time from connecting and disconnecting the connectors. These connectors allow us to easily connect wires between two devices. Without connectors, we would be using a screwdriver and screwing down wires to screw terminals, like back in the mainframe days. Connectors serve a second useful purpose: providing an easy diagnostic point for when connectivity is the suspected problem.

RJ-45

The RJ-45 is a connector used for connecting network equipment, such as network switches, routers, and network interface cards (NICs). Today it is a worldwide standard for wired Ethernet connectivity. If you have a wired connection to your computer from a network, it is most likely an RJ-45 connector. The RJ-45 connector has four pairs (eight wires) attached to eight pins, as shown in Figure 1.36. I will cover the TIA/EIA wiring standard for these connectors later in this chapter.

FIGURE 1.36   An RJ-45 connector

RJ-11

The RJ-11 is a connector used for telephone connections. It is commonly used in the United States and most other countries. If you have a land line telephone, then it is connected to the phone jack with an RJ-11 patch cord. The RJ stands for *registered jack* and is designated a *universal service order code (USOC)* of 11. This standard was adopted by Bell Systems from the FCC for customer compliance in connecting phone equipment. The RJ-11 connector has two pairs (four wires) attached to the four pins, as shown in Figure 1.37. There is a primary pair that is green and red, and a secondary pair that is yellow and black. This allows you up to two phone lines on one cable. You will encounter this wiring in networks only if you are making a connection to a fax machine, modem, or DSL modem.

FIGURE 1.37   An RJ-11 connector

BNC Connector

The BNC in *BNC connector* stands for Bayonet Neill-Concelman or British Naval Connector, depending on whom you ask. BNC connectors, shown in Figure 1.38, were used in networking for 10Base2 LAN coaxial networks. These connectors are now considered legacy in terms of LAN networking. They are still used for T3 (DS-3) *wide area network (WAN)* connections, radio equipment, and security camera systems that use coax cameras. The connector operates with a slight spring tension when inserted; then you twist it slightly to lock it into place.

FIGURE 1.38   A BNC connector

F-Connector

The F-connector, shown in Figure 1.39, is a coaxial connector used with RG-6 or RG-59 cabling. You will commonly see this connector used for cable TV and cable modem connections. Coaxial cabling with F-connectors are also used for *Media over Coax Alliance (MoCA)* networking. This type of networking is typically used by providers to allow networking between set-top boxes (STBs) inside your house or business. It can even be used to transmit data of up to 2.5 Gbps. When using an F-connector, you insert the exposed coaxial core into a female F-connector and then thread it on until it is tight.

FIGURE 1.39   An F-connector

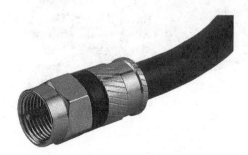

Fiber Connectors

There are several different fiber connectors to use in a fiber-optic installation. I will cover the most common fiber connectors used in networks today. Each fiber connector has a benefit or purpose in a fiber-optic installation. It is important to know the visual differences between the fiber connectors and their respective names.

LC

The local connector (LC) resembles an RJ-style connector; it has a spring-loaded detent similar to the RJ connector that allows it to be held in place. The LC connector has become a popular cable connector because of its size; this allows greater density of ports on a switch. The connector is commonly found on MMF and SMF optic cables. The cable cannot be disassembled like the SC connector (see Figure 1.40), so transmit and receive fiber lines cannot be swapped side to side.

FIGURE 1.40   An LC connector

ST

The straight tip (ST) connector, shown in Figure 1.41, was originally designed by AT&T for fiber-optic cables. It is commonly used with single-mode fiber, discussed earlier. The connector is one of the most popular connectors to date with fiber optics for WAN connectivity on SMF. The cable connector can be found in both SMF and MMF cable installations. The cable operates similar to a BNC connector; it is a bayonet-style mechanism that you twist and lock into position. The benefit to this cable is that it will not come loose over time because of the positive locking mechanism.

FIGURE 1.41   An ST connector

SC

The standard connector (SC) is a square connector with a floating ferrule that contains the fiber-optic cable, as shown in Figure 1.42. The cable comes with a plastic clip that holds the transmit and receive cables secure for insertion. These clips generally allow you to disassemble the cable ends so transmit and receive can be swapped. The SC connector is often referred to by installers as "Square Charlie," and it's the way I've remembered the shape throughout the years. It can be found in SMF and MMF installations, but it is most popular with MMF installations. The SC connector is larger than most modern connectors, so it is starting to be replaced in new installations. The cable operates with a push-on/pull-off mating mechanism.

FIGURE 1.42   An SC connector

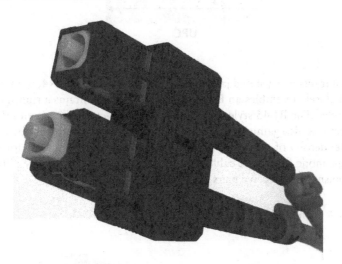

APC vs. UPC

The terms *angled physical contact (APC)* and *ultra-physical contact (UPC)* describe the polished finish on SC connectors. Fiber-optic cable is susceptible to insertion loss—the loss of signal due to the gap between the adjoining optics. Fiber is also susceptible to reflection loss—the loss of signal due to reflection back at the source. Both APC and UPC try to minimize insertion loss with a tight physical contact (PC). UPC cable ends have a polished dome to focus light into the center of the core. APC cable ends have an 8-degree angle to combat reflection loss, since any light reflected back from the cable will be at an 8-degree angle, as shown in Figure 1.43. UPC cable ends are blue, and APC cable ends are green. If APC or UPC is used in your network in lieu of the standard PC fiber-optic polished finish, the proper cable ends must be used or additional loss can occur. Most network patch cables will have a UPC finish on them, depicted by the blue cable ends. If the cable end is white, it should be assumed to have a standard PC finish.

FIGURE 1.43 APC vs. UPC

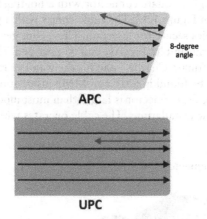

MTRJ

The mechanical transfer registered jack (MTRJ), shown in Figure 1.44, is another RJ-style connector that closely resembles an RJ-45 connector. It too contains a transmit-and-receive pair of fiber cables. The RJ-45 style detent locks it into place, similar to an Ethernet connector. The connector is also gaining popularity with networking equipment because of its size; it allows greater density of ports on a switch. The connector is commonly found on multimode and single-mode fiber-optic cables. The cable cannot be disassembled like other cables to swap the transmit-and-receive pairs.

FIGURE 1.44 An MTRJ connector

Transceivers

The job of the *fiber-optic transceiver* is to convert between the internal electrical signaling of the network equipment and light. The job of a copper transceiver is to convert between the Ethernet and the internal electrical signaling of the network equipment. Most network cards have a built-in transceiver, but modular network cards and modular networking equipment allow for transceivers to be inserted. The equipment usually has a top speed that cannot be exceeded, but slower transceivers can be inserted to lower monetary costs and design requirements. Transceivers can be used for a wide range of applications such as Fibre Channel, Ethernet, and SONET. Another important factor is distance versus speed versus compatibility of the transceiver. All transceivers require a specific media type for a specific distance.

SFP

The small form-factor pluggable (SFP) transceiver is a hot-swappable module used for both fiber-optic and copper media (see Figure 1.45). Its small design allows for a high density of ports on networking equipment such as network switching. SFPs can be found in both MMF and SMF installations, and they can support up to 1 Gbps of network connectivity. Depending on the SFP chosen for the installation, the speed and distance will vary according to the vendor's specifications for each model.

FIGURE 1.45   A typical SFP transceiver

SFP+

The small form-factor pluggable+ (SFP+) transceiver is also a hot-swappable module used for both fiber-optic and copper media. It looks identical to the SFP and is differentiated only by its part number. However, the SFP+ can support speeds of 10 Gbps or higher (up to 400 Gbps). The SFP+ also has the added benefit of providing controller data to the equipment, such as signal loss and TX/RX power. The SFP+ is slowly replacing the SFP because of speed and functionality. Distances will also vary, just as with the SFP specification.

QSFP

The quad small form-factor pluggable (QSFP), shown in Figure 1.46, is another popular transceiver. It also allows for hot-swappable operations and is used for high port density on switching equipment because of its size and quad transceiver. The QSFP contains a quad transceiver that allows for 4×1 Gbps (4 Gbps) operation. The QSFP modules can also be purchased as a fanout cable; this cable separates each transceiver to a separate connection. This is useful when connecting other switches contained in the same rack space. One QSFP transceiver can connect up to four switches at 1 Gbps.

FIGURE 1.46   A QSFP transceiver

QSFP+

The quad small form-factor pluggable+ (QSFP+) is slowly becoming a current standard in switching products. Just like its prior form-factor of QSFP, it allows for hot-swappable operations and is used for high port density on switching equipment. The QSFP+ also contains a quad transceiver that allows for 4×10 Gbps, and 4×25 Gbps (40 Gbps and 100 Gbps) operation. And like the QSFP module, it can be purchased as a fanout cable. Just think about this, you can connect up to four switches in the same rack at 25 Gbps each with one transceiver.

Media Converters

Copper Ethernet has a defined limitation of 100 meters (330 feet), which limits what copper Ethernet can be used for. A common problem is remote locations where you need Ethernet connectivity, such as for a VoIP phone or a security camera, but the distance is over 100 meters. This is where we can benefit from media converters, because they allow us to convert from copper Ethernet to fiber-optic cable back to copper Ethernet again, as shown in Figure 1.47. Media converters and the fiber optics that accompany extending copper Ethernet raise the costs of a project and introduce failure points, so they should be used sparingly.

In addition to converting from fiber-optic cable to copper Ethernet, there are converters that convert one type of fiber such as multimode fiber to single-mode fiber and vice versa. These are not common because you can run the proper fiber-optic line (SMF or MMF) and just use the proper transceivers, eliminating extra potential faults. However, this is a perfect-world scenario and sometime we must deal with existing cabling and don't have the option to re-pull fiber-optic cabling. This is extremely common when you have buried cable and the cost to re-pull it outweighs the total cost of ownership of dealing with potential problems.

FIGURE 1.47   A media converter

Characteristics of Fiber Transceivers

When choosing a transceiver, you should look up the compatibility matrix of the equipment it is being used in. This compatibility matrix will describe the speeds supported, distances supported, cabling to be used, and the model number of the transceiver to be used. Depending on the application of the fiber transceiver, you can buy bidirectional or duplex transceivers. Typically you will find bidirectional transceivers in WAN connectivity scenarios.

Unidirectional

Most of the internal fiber-optic cabling you will use inside your network will be a *duplex connection*. The duplex fiber-optic transceiver reserves one fiber-optic strand for transmit and the other for receive per each side of the fiber-optic connection. The fiber-optic strands on the other side of the connection are mapped to the receive and transmit strands, respectively. Each side of the transceiver is unidirectional, because it only transmits in one direction. Most of the transceivers you will work with internally in your network will be transmit and receive on a single wavelength of light, such as 850 nm, 1310 nm, or 1550 nm, just to name a few. When you work with external fiber-optic connections used in WAN applications, you want to use every bit of bandwidth a strand of glass can deliver. These applications are usually called dark fiber, since you are responsible for lighting and maintaining both sides of the glass (sort of speak).

There are two common methods that multiplex several different wavelengths of light onto the same glass media at a time; they are called coarse wavelength division multiplexing (CWDM) and dense wavelength division multiplexing (DWDM). Regardless of the method used, the principle is the same: on the transmit end several different wavelengths are multiplexed (mux) onto the glass media. On the receive end the various wavelengths are demultiplex (demux) back to their respective receivers.

Coarse Wavelength Division Multiplexing (CWDM)   Allows for up to 18 separate channels to be multiplexed together. It uses large chunks of light wave space to achieve a nominal 10 Gbps per channel for Ethernet and 16 Gbps per channel for Fibre Channel. Of course speeds depend on the vendor and their implementation of CWDM.

Dense Wavelength Division Multiplexing (DWDM)   Allows for up to 80 separate channels to be multiplexed together. It uses narrower chunks of light wave space to pack as much data into the bandwidth of the glass. You will find DWDM in high-capacity applications, such as long-distance connections for Internet providers. DWDM can deliver 100 Gbps per channel depending on the vendor and their implementation of DWDM.

Bidirectional

Fiber-optic cable can be expensive to install. It is even more expensive to lease since it is a reoccurring cost based on scarcity and distance of the connection. Bidirectional transceivers allow the use of a single fiber-optic cable to both transmit and receive data. It is common in WAN scenarios to purchase two fiber strands and use bidirectional transceivers on both. The bidirectional transceivers are usually more expensive than duplex transceivers. This allows for fault-tolerant connection in case a transceiver goes bad on one end.

A bidirectional transceiver operates on two different light wave frequencies, which is called bidirectional wavelength division multiplexing (WDM). For example, Device A is transmitting on 1310 nanometers, and Device B is transmitting on 1490 nanometers. Because of these two different wavelengths, the bidirectional transceivers are purchased as a pair. One transceiver is considered the upstream transceiver, and the other is considered the downstream transceiver. In each of the transceivers, a semi-reflective mirror diverts the incoming transmitted light wave to an optical receiver. The transceivers are using different light wavelengths in opposite directions to communicate on the same strand of fiber-optic cable. In Figure 1.48 you can see how a typical bidirectional transceiver functions internally.

FIGURE 1.48   How bidirectional transceivers work

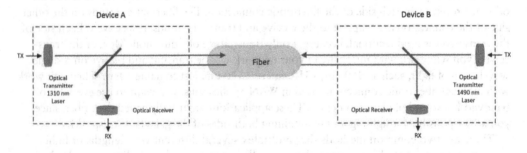

 Bidirectional transceivers are widely used with Internet providers and bandwidth-intensive applications like television. In certain large-scale installations, bidirectional transceivers are used with DWDM technology to deliver extremely high throughput.

Termination Points

Termination points are useful as a diagnostic point or termination of responsibility. When you are dealing with a telco provider, it is usually the 66 block where the service comes into the building. When dealing with a fiber provider, it is the fiber distribution panel. The provider is responsible for a clean, clear signal to that point. It is also useful as a diagnostic point when used internally within your organization.

Punchdown Block

Punchdown blocks are almost always used with analog or digital time division multiplexing (TDM) phone installations. The exception is Voice over IP (VoIP), which uses a Power over Ethernet (PoE) network connection. It is true the network's cables are punched down at some point, but they are punched down to an network patch panel, which I will discuss later. In the following sections, you will find many of the common analog and TDM punchdown blocks used with telephony hardware.

66 Block

The 66 block, shown in Figure 1.49, is commonly used for analog wiring of telephone equipment. Its main purpose is to supply a *plain old telephone service (POTS)* line access to a business or apartment building. Voice providers use the 66 block as a diagnostic point or demarcation point when supplying a dial tone. There are four prongs: the two on the left are connected to each other, and the two on the right are connected to each other. The center prongs have a clip that connects the two sides. Wires are punched down to each of the outer prongs: one to the telephone equipment and one to the dial-tone source. When you are diagnosing a telephone issue, you remove the clips in the middle to isolate the dial-tone source from the telephone equipment. The prongs are also long enough so that a lineworker's handset can clip on for testing a dial tone.

110 Block

The 110 block, shown in Figure 1.50, is commonly used for analog wiring of telephone equipment. These 110 blocks can often be found side by side with wire pairs punched down between them. Often one side will lead back to the *private branch exchange (PBX)* and the other side to the phone equipment; this is called a cross-connect. It is a common setup on in-house wiring or on-premises wiring. The fixed wiring to the phone or PBX is punched down with a tool on the back side of an insert. The wire pairs are then punched down to the front side, which allows for the wire pairs to be removed and re-punched down in a different spot for reconfiguration.

Krone

A Krone block panel is often mistaken for a 110 block panel. In Figure 1.51 you see a typical Krone block panel. It is often found in the northeastern region of the United States and it is predominantly used in the United Kingdom. It differs from the 110 block because the punchdown spades where the wire is punched down are larger and it requires a special Krone punchdown tool. You should never use a 110 block punchdown tool on a Krone block panel.

FIGURE 1.49   A 66 block panel

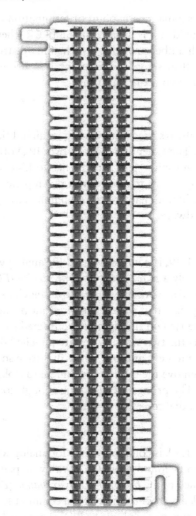

FIGURE 1.50   A 110 block panel

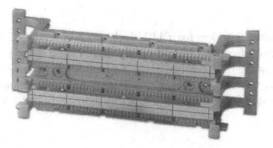

FIGURE 1.51   A Krone block panel

BIX

The Building Industry Cross-connect (BIX) is a type of punch block panel created by Nortel in the 1970s. The BIX punch block panel is almost always found in Nortel phone switch installations. The BIX punch block panel has a double-sided punch and requires a special BIX punchdown tool. The wires from the Nortel switch are punched on the back of the BIX punch block panel. The front is used for cross-connecting a 110 or 66 block that leads to the phone extension.

Patch Panel

Patch panels, like the one shown in Figure 1.52, are commonly used in wiring closets as a diagnostic point for Ethernet network connections. The back side of the patch panel is punched down to the network cabling that is installed to the computer terminal RJ-45 jack. The front side of the patch panel is connected with a patch cable to the network switching equipment, which is how the patch panel gets its name. This termination point of a patch cable allows for a field technician to check the wiring end-to-end first; then they can remove the patch cable on each end and test with a known good cable. This can be done on each end until the problem is isolated.

FIGURE 1.52   A typical patch panel

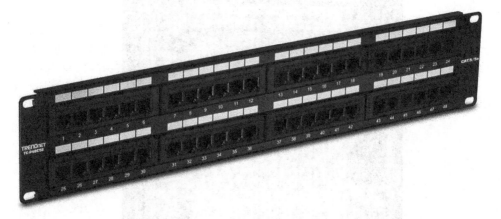

Fiber Distribution Panel

When fiber-optic cabling is installed in your network, it is generally one cable with multiple pairs of fiber. Fiber-optic cable can normally be purchased with 4, 6, 12, and 24 strands in a single cable binding. Fiber distribution panels like the one in Figure 1.53 are used to terminate the individual fragile strands to a common fiber-optic connector. Fiber distribution panels serve two purposes: distributing the individual strands and serving as a diagnostic point for troubleshooting.

FIGURE 1.53   A typical fiber distribution panel

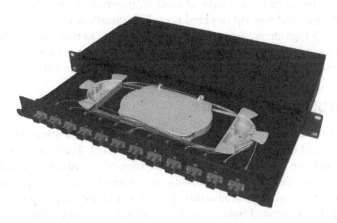

Cable Management

Regardless of the cable type being installed, copper voice, copper network, or fiber-optic cable, you should have some type of cable management in your installation. Cable management serves two distinct purposes: it makes everything look organized, and it takes the weight of the cable off of the cable ends, as shown in Figure 1.54. Making the final product look organized is a symbol of pride that network technicians take in their work. There are many examples on the Internet that will simply amaze you. The overall weight of a patch cable should also be taken into consideration because it will hang on the two cable ends and strain the cable. Network patch cables do not contain a strength member like solid-core cable used for premises wiring.

FIGURE 1.54   Cable management example

Cable management is a must-have in your network, but sometimes it is overdone and can be a detriment to the next technician. If cable management is overdone to the point where each cable is perfect and zip ties hold the whole installation together, when a change is needed it can be a nightmare. You must always keep in mind that patch panels are there so you can patch a switch to the premises wiring, and sometimes that changes. So you should always use a sensible amount of cable management and try to plan ahead.

Copper Cabling Standards

Network cabling has been categorized jointly by the Telecommunications Industry Association (TIA) and the Electronic Industries Alliance (EIA). These standards allow for the proper cabling to be installed as per the specification of a network. The differences between the various categories of network cabling are the number of twists per inch to reduce crosstalk, how the pairs are separated inside the jacket, and the thickness of the conductors. When the pairs are twisted tighter, an electrical balance is created between the wires to reduce noise from other pairs; this noise is called crosstalk. The better they are separated, the less crosstalk you encounter if wires become tangled inside the jacket. A thicker conductor allows for higher frequencies and larger data rates. Table 1.2 shows the maximum speeds for each category of cabling.

TABLE 1.2   Cable categories and speeds

Category	Maximum speed	Maximum distance	Cable type	Certified frequency
Cat 3	10 Mbps	100 meters	UTP	16 MHz
Cat 5	100 Mbps	100 meters	UTP	100 MHz
Cat 5e	1 Gbps	100 meters	UTP	100 MHz
Cat 6	1 Gbps	100 meters	UTP	250 MHz
Cat 6	10 Gbps	55 meters	UTP	250 MHz
Cat 6a	10 Gbps	100 meters	UTP	500 MHz
Cat 7	10 Gbps	100 meters	STP	600 MHz
Cat 7a	10 Gbps	100 meters	STP	1000 MHz
Cat 8	40 Gbps	30 meters	STP	2000 MHz

Category 7, 7a, and 8 cabling is a shielded twisted-pair (STP) type cable and requires special RJ-45 ends. It is much harder to work with than normal Category 6a and therefore more expensive for installations. It is usually chosen when a vendor requires the specification for an installation, or a bandwidth higher than 10 Gbps is required.

Cat 3

Category 3 cable is classified as a cabling for 10 Mbps networks; it is sometimes referred to as voice-grade cable. It was commonly used for PBX wiring and network wiring. Category 3 cabling is legacy cabling because there is no difference in price between Cat 3 cabling and Cat 5e cabling. All installations should have at least Cat 5e cabling or higher to future-proof the installation. This includes wiring to be run for PBX voice installations (non-VoIP).

Cat 5

Category 5 cable is classified as a cabling for 100 Mbps networks. It has been superseded by Category 5e cable. Cat 5e cable is classified as a cabling for 1 Gbps networks. There is a nominal price difference between Cat 3, Cat 5, and Cat 5e cable, so all installations should be using Cat 5e or higher.

Cat 6

Category 6 cable is classified as a cabling for 1 Gbps and 10 Gbps networks. This cabling has a maximum distance of 33 to 55 meters for 10 Gbps and a maximum distance of 100 meters for 1 Gbps networks. It should be used in data centers where the distance is 55 meters (approximately 180 feet) or less when 10 Gbps speeds are required. This cabling has a plastic separator that keeps the four pairs spaced and separated. Most often different RJ-45 ends must be used to accommodate the larger diameter of cable.

Cat 6a

Category 6a cable is also classified as a cabling for 10 Gbps networks. This cabling has a maximum distance of 100 meters. The Category 6a specification will soon become the standard for cabling of 10 Gbps and replace the Category 6 standard. It should be used as cabling for networks to future-proof installations for 10 Gbps. This cabling has a plastic separator that keeps the four pairs spaced and separated. Most often, different RJ-45 ends must be used to accommodate the larger diameter of cable.

Cat 7

Category 7 cable is not recognized by TIA/EIA as a defined standard and is considered an unofficial standard. It allows for 10 Gbps network speeds at distances up to 100 meters. The unofficial standard requires GG-45 connectors, which look similar to RJ-45 connectors with the addition of four top connectors on each side of the cable detent. The GG-45 female jack is backward compatible with standard RJ-45 connectors. Category 7 cable is a shielded twisted-pair (STP) cable type; the shielding is normally a foil type wrapped around each color pair with a mesh metal shielding around all of the pairs. It is extremely difficult to work with and very costly for installations and therefore Category 6a is normally used. TIA/ EIA decided to ratify the standard of Category 8 cable and skip over Category 7/7a.

Cat 7a

Although Category 7 and 7a were ratified by the International Organization for Standardization (ISO)/International Electrotechnical Commission (IEC), they were not recognized by TIA/EIA as standards. Category 7a is identical to Category 7, except that it tests at a higher frequency of 1000 MHz. Category 7a isn't certified for any higher speeds than 10 Gbps Ethernet, just a higher testing frequency. Category 7a is, however, used by many AV vendors to transmit video because of its high frequency and ability to transmit high data rates. Although these installations look like a network jack, the signal is proprietary to the equipment on both ends.

Cat 8

Category 8 is the next generation of cable specification ratified by TIA/EIA as a standard. Just like Category 7 and Category 7a, Category 8 cable is an STP cable type and is made up of foil shielded pairs surrounded by a wire mesh shielding. However, unlike Category 7 and Category 7a, Category 8 cable can use normal shielded RJ-45 connectors. Category 8 can transmit at 25 Gbps or 40 Gbps, but it has a maximum distance of 30 meters or 98.4 feet. It can also operate at 10 Gbps and 1 Gbps for backward compatibility.

The Category 8 specification is often found inside data centers, often run between switches from rack to rack or from a top-of-rack (TOR) switch to each individual server. Data center switches normally operate at 25 Gbps or 40 Gbps, which allows you to migrate or future-proof an installation using the same cable; today 25 Gbps, and tomorrow you want to upgrade to 40 Gbps.

The NIC in a data center host can normally operate at 25 Gbps or 40 Gbps, depending on the switch they are attached to using autonegotiation. You won't find Category 8 wiring in client-side networking due to the cost of installation and the short distances. It's also rare to find workstations that need 25 Gbps or 40 Gbps bandwidth speeds.

When purchasing cabling, you will notice an MHz rating on the cable as well as the category. This MHz rating is for certification after installation; specialized equipment called cable certifiers are used to test and certify the cable. The MHz rating is the highest frequency that can be transmitted on the cable before data crosstalk occurs. It is not directly related to the speed at which the network operates. When a cable is certified, it means that it can pass the recommendations of the TIA/EIA or the manufacturer's specifications. Beware of inflated numbers that the manufacturer advertises; cable certifications should always be benchmarked against TIA/EIA specifications. This should be part of the scope of work when contracting a cable installer.

RG-59 and RG-6

RG-59 and RG-6 are both 75-ohm coaxial cable specifications, typically used for security camera and broadband cable installations. RG-59 is thinner in diameter than RG-6 and should not be used for infrastructure wiring. RG-6 has a larger inner core, larger insulator, and better shielding than RG-59. Many suppliers have stopped selling RG-59 or have limited supplies of RG-59 because RG-6 has become a standard in new installations of coaxial cable. The price difference is nominal between the two cables, so bigger is better!

Coaxial cables are constructed of an inner core of copper, an insulator (dielectric foam), a foil shielding, a metal weaved shielding, and a protective jacket. RG-59 and RG-6 are usually terminated (crimped) with either BNC connectors or F-connectors.

Twinaxial

Twinaxial cable, also known as Twinax, is a popular standard in data center installations. The cable comprises a fixed length coaxial cable in 1-, 5-, or 10-meter lengths. On each end of the cable an SFP+ or QSFP+ transceiver is affixed, which in turn connects the data center switch and the NIC in the data center host. You can find Twinax in speeds of 1, 10, 25, 40, and 100 Gbps. Twinax is purchased as passive or active cabling. Passive cabling is used for short distances such as 1 and 5 meters. Active cabling is used for longer distances, such as 10 meters and above. Your equipment must explicitly support active cabling because the transceiver requires higher-power levels to boost the signal over the longer-distance coaxial cable.

When comparing Twinax and traditional fiber-optic cabling, the following should be considered. With fiber-optic cabling, you need two matching fiber-optic transceivers and the fiber-optic cable itself. It's fragile because the core is glass. Also it's overkill because most of the time you are patching a host into the network over a rather short distance. So there are a lot of disadvantages to traditional fiber-optic cable in the data center. The advantage of Twinax is it saves you money versus the traditional fiber-optic cabling because the transceivers are part of the cable and the cable is made up of a pretty tough coaxial cable (at least tougher than glass). The disadvantage is that the cable is a fixed length, so you can't cut to fit a cable.

 Twinaxial cable is being replaced slowly by Category 8. This is mainly because of the price, Category 8 cable is cheaper than Twinax because it does not need transceivers affixed on a cable of predetermined length. The disadvantage is Category 8 has a maximum speed of 40 Gbps.

Copper Termination Standards

When terminating the RJ-45 connectors on the ends of a patch cable, use the defined standard of wiring for the RJ-45 connector set forth by the TIA/EIA. The TIA/EIA specification of 568 has published two standards for this wiring that I will cover in the following section. When you are punching down the wires on a patch panel, the manufacturer will often have its own standard coloring code. The proper wiring standard should be used when terminating patch cables or punching down onto a patch panel. If these standards are not used, the network cabling could fail certification or may not work at the speeds expected.

TIA/EIA 568A/B

The TIA/EIA 568A specification was originally created back when 10 Mbps networks were standard. Today all patch cables use the TIA/EIA 568B specification on both ends. However, that doesn't mean that the TIA/EIA 568A specification is obsolete. It is cabled on one end when you need a crossover cable, as I will explain shortly. Figure 1.55 shows the wiring specification for TIA/EIA 568A and TIA/EIA 568B along with the position of pin 1 through pin 8 on an RJ-45 connector.

FIGURE 1.55   TIA/EIA 568A and 568B wiring standard

EIA/TIA 568A

Position	Color
1	White-Green
2	Green
3	White-Orange
4	Blue
5	White-Blue
6	Orange
7	White-Brown
8	Brown

EIA/TIA 568B

Position	Color
1	White-Orange
2	Orange
3	White-Green
4	Blue
5	White-Blue
6	Green
7	White-Brown
8	Brown

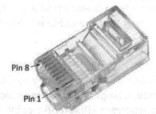

Pin 8

Pin 1

Straight-Through Cables

A network cable that has the TIA/EIA 568B specification terminated on both ends is considered a straight-through network cable. A network cable can have the TIA/EIA 568A specification terminated on both ends and also be considered a straight-through cable. However, the TIA/EIA 568A is deprecated for straight-through cables; it was originally used with Category 3 cable.

As seen in Figure 1.56, the computer expects to transmit data on pins 1 and 2 and receive data on pins 3 and 6. Conversely, the switch expects to transmit data on pins 3 and 6 and receive data on pins 1 and 2. The straight-through cable aligns pins 1 and 2 for transmitting (computer side) to pins 1 and 2 on the adjoining equipment (switch side) for receiving. Pins 3 and 6 are receiving (computer side) from pins 3 and 6 on the adjoining equipment (switch side) for transmitting.

Straight-through cables should be used for the following scenarios:

- Connecting computers to switches
- Connecting routers to switches
- Connecting computer to hubs

FIGURE 1.56   Straight-through cable wiring

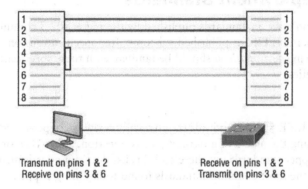

Transmit on pins 1 & 2
Receive on pins 3 & 6

Receive on pins 1 & 2
Transmit on pins 3 & 6

Crossover Cables

A network cable terminated with the TIA/EIA 568A and TIA/EIA 568B specification is considered a crossover cable. This aligns pins 1 and 2 for receiving with pins 3 and 6 on the other end for transmitting (see Figure 1.57). This is because both switches and/or computers expect a straight-through cable to be attached.

FIGURE 1.57   Crossover cable wiring

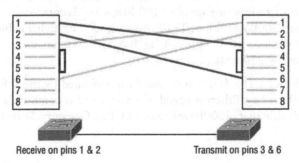

Receive on pins 1 & 2

Transmit on pins 3 & 6

On newer switches, a feature called *auto MDI-X (Medium Dependent Interface Crossover)* allows for automatic detection of the transmit and receive pair. The auto MDI-X will auto-crossover the connection when a straight-through cable is present connecting a switch to another switch.

Crossover cable cables should be used in the following scenarios:

- Connecting switches to switches
- Connecting routers to routers (via Ethernet)
- Connecting computers to computers
- Connecting hubs to hubs
- Connecting hubs to switches

Ethernet Deployment Standards

Ethernet is based on a set of standards published by the *IEEE 802.3* committee. Over the past three decades, the IEEE has published subcommittee specifications on 802.3 that I will cover in the following sections. You should be familiar with these specifications and their respective capabilities.

Copper

The first group of IEEE 802.3 standards that we will review is copper-based. You would find these standards using the media of a twisted-pair connection, either UTP or STP. There are plenty of other copper standards out there and this list does not constitute all of them. The following are just the most common standards found today using copper.

10BaseT   The 10BaseT standard is defined by the IEEE as 802.3i. It is capable of an Ethernet speed of 10 Mbps and is just referred to as Ethernet. The standard originally made use of TIA/EIA Category 3 or higher cabling and only used two of the four pairs in the cabling. It has a maximum distance limitation of 100 meters (330 feet). You can usually spot patch cables made for 10BaseT applications as both ends will be terminated with the TIA/EIA 568A color code. All standards after the 10BaseT standard used the TIA/EIA 568B color code.

100BaseTX   The 100BaseTX standard is defined by the IEEE as 802.3u. It is capable of an Ethernet speed of 100 Mbps and is commonly referred to as Fast Ethernet. 100BaseTX uses TIA/EIA Category 5 or higher cabling and uses only two of the four pairs in the cabling. It has a maximum distance limitation of 100 meters (330 feet).

1000BaseT   The 1000BaseT standard is defined by the IEEE as 802.3ab. It is capable of an Ethernet speed of 1 Gbps and is commonly referred to as Gigabit Ethernet. 1000BaseT uses TIA/EIA Category 5e or higher cabling and uses all four pairs in the cabling. It has a maximum distance limitation of 100 meters (330 feet).

10GBaseT   The 10GBase-T standard is defined by the IEEE as 802.3an. It is capable of an Ethernet speed of 10 Gbps and is commonly referred to as 10 Gigabit Ethernet. 10GBaseT uses TIA/EIA Category 6 or higher cabling. Category 6 cable has a maximum distance of 55 meters, and Category 6a cable has a maximum distance limitation of 100 meters (330 feet).

40GBaseT   The 40GBaseT standard is defined by the IEEE as 802.3bq. It is capable of an Ethernet speed of 40 Gbps and is commonly referred to as 40 Gigabit Ethernet. The standard is also backward compliant with 25GBaseT since both standards are defined in the IEEE 802.3bq working group. Both standards also require Category 8 STP cable with the appropriate shield RJ-45 ends. The specification has the distance limitation of 30 meters, which coincides with the Category 8 cable specification. The 40GBaseT standard is almost exclusively found in data centers.

Although NBase-T and MGBase-T are not part of the CompTIA Network+ objectives, it is important to be aware that these new standards exist. With the higher speeds that 802.11ac and 802.11ax deliver, a 1 Gbps connection is just not fast enough. The IEEE created the working group 802.3bz to address this issue, and the 2.5Base-T and 5Base-T standards were created. The 2.5Base-T allows for 2.5 Gbps over Cat 5e, while the 5Base-T allows for 5 Gbps over Cat 6. Many newer switches support 100 Mbps, 1 Gbps, 2.5 Gbps, 5 Gbps, and 10 Gbps all on the same interface.

Fiber Optic

The second group of IEEE 802.3 standards that we will review is fiber-optic-based. These standards use multimode fiber (MMF) or single-mode fiber-optic (SMF) cable. The purpose of fiber-optic standards is that data is transferred over light with all of these standards. These standards are also used in applications where copper cabling cannot be used because of electromagnetic interference (EMI), security, or distance since light in a glass media is not susceptible to these problems.

100BaseFX   The 100BaseFX standard is defined by the IEEE as 802.3u. It is capable of Fast Ethernet speeds of 100 Mbps using a 1300 nm laser over 50-micron fiber-optic cable. 100BaseFX has a maximum distance of 2 kilometers (1.2 miles) using multimode fiber. The 100BaseFX is a dated standard, just like the copper standard of 100BaseT. It is quickly being replaced with 1000Base and 10GBase standards.

100BaseSX The 100BaseSX standard is based upon the IEEE 802.3u specification. It is capable of Fast Ethernet speeds of 100 Mbps, just like the 100BaseFX. However, it is a cheaper alternative since it uses an LED-based source versus the 100BaseFX that uses a laser-based source. Because of this it has a much shorter distance than the 100BaseFX standard, and therefore it is commonly called "short haul." It uses an 850 nm signal over 50-micron or 62.5-micro fiber-optic cable for a maximum distance of 550 meters (1804 feet). It too is quickly being replaced with 1000Base and 10GBase standards.

1000BaseSX The 1000BaseSX standard is defined by the IEEE as 802.3z. It is capable of an Ethernet speed of 1 Gbps over multimode fiber. It is commonly called "short haul" because it is used for short distances. It uses an 850 nm laser with either 62.5-micron or 50-micron fiber-optic cabling. You can use 62.5-micron fiber to achieve a maximum distance of 220 meters. You can use 50-micron fiber to achieve a maximum distance of 550 meters.

1000BaseLX The 1000BaseLX standard is defined by the IEEE as 802.3z. It is capable of an Ethernet speed of 1 Gbps over 9-micron single-mode fiber with a 1300 nm laser. It is commonly called "long haul" because of the distances it can achieve of up to 10 kilometers (6.2 miles).

10GBaseSR The 10GBaseSR standard is defined by the IEEE as 802.3ae. It is capable of delivering a speed of 10 Gbps over multimode fiber-optic cable with an 850 nm laser. It is commonly called "short range" because it has a maximum distance of 400 meters (1312 feet). The standard is perfect for connectivity inside a building where 10 Gbps is needed over existing fiber-optic cable and your install is budget conscious.

10GBaseLR The 10GBaseLR standard is defined by the IEEE as 802.3ae, just like the 10GBaseSR standard. It is also capable of delivering a speed of 10 Gbps, but it uses single-mode fiber with a 1310 nm laser. It is commonly called "long range" because it has a maximum distance of 10 kilometers (6.2 miles). This standard works well in areas where distance is required. Keep in mind cost goes up, as the max distance goes up.

Exam Essentials

Know the types of copper cables. The most common cables used in networks today are UTP, STP, and coaxial cable. UTP cabling is the most common cable used in networks today. STP cabling is used in networks that have high amounts of EMI from machinery. STP cabling is usually used in industrial Ethernet circumstances and is more expensive than UTP. Coax cable is commonly used for security cameras and broadband cable installations. RG-6 is the most common cable used for coax cabling; it is slightly bigger than RG-59 and provides less signal loss.

Know the types of fiber-optic cable. There are two main types of fiber-optic cable: single-mode fiber, which is normally 9 microns (yellow patch cables), and multimode fiber, which includes 50 microns (aqua patch cables) and 62.5 microns (orange patch cables). Single-mode fiber can span distances of 75 miles, and multimode fiber can span distances of 3000 feet.

Be familiar with various copper connectors. Although there are several different types of connectors, RJ-45 connectors are the most common in networks today. Know the physical characteristics of each connector and their application.

Be familiar with the various fiber-optic connectors. There are many different fiber-optic connectors that provide unique advantages; you should be familiar with these and understand their purpose. Know the physical characteristics of each connector and their design.

Be familiar with the various transceivers. Most all transceivers are hot swappable. The SFP transceiver has a maximum speed of 1 Gbps. The SFP+ transceiver is slowly replacing the SFP transceiver. The SFP+ can operate at over 10 Gbps up to 400 Gbps. The GBIC transceiver has a maximum speed of 1 Gbps and is an older standard. The QSFP+ transceiver has a quad transceiver in one module; it can support speeds of 1 Gbps to 100 Gbps. The QSFP+ transceiver can also be purchased as a fanout cable that can supply four 10 Gbps links' switches in the same rack. Bidirectional transceivers can use a single strand of fiber for bidirectional communications. Duplex transceivers use two strands of fiber for communications; one strand is a transmit strand and the other is a receive strand.

Know the various termination points. A 66 block is generally used by telco providers to create a termination point for POTS lines. A 110 block is generally used with PBX systems and in-house wiring for connecting telephones. A Krone block looks similar to a 110 block but has wider lugs. A BIX block looks like a 110 block and was used with Nortel equipment. A patch panel is used to create a diagnostic point for troubleshooting purposes. Fiber distribution panels are used to separate the strands in a fiber-optic cable; they allow for distribution on signal and serve as a diagnostic point.

Know the categories of UTP cables and their purpose. Category 5e cable supports a maximum speed of 1 Gbps at 100 meters. Category 6 cable supports a maximum speed of 10 Gbps at 55 meters. Category 6a cable supports a maximum speed of 10 Gbps at 100 meters. Category 7 cable is an unofficial standard that supports a maximum speed of 10 Gbps at 100 meters. Category 8 cable is an official standard that can deliver speeds of 25 and 40 Gbps for the data center.

Know the copper termination standards. The EIA/TIA 568A specification is an older specification for 10 Mbps networks, and EIA/TIA 568B is the current specification for cable termination. When you terminate a cable with 568A and 568B, it creates a crossover cable. Normal patch cables have the 568B specification terminated on both ends.

Know the various Ethernet deployment standards. You will need to memorize the various standards and their capabilities.

1.4 Given a scenario, configure a subnet and use appropriate IP addressing schemes.

When building networks, we must plan the logical IP address space for both the internal and external networks. We must also plan the default gateway and subnet mask and alter the subnet mask to accommodate subnetting.

In the discussion of this domain, we will explore several concepts, such as classful versus classless IP addresses as well as how to use CIDR notation. These concepts will allow you to build logical networks for the flow of information. In addition, you must understand how IP addresses are assigned statically and dynamically. Several methods of dynamic IP address assignment are available, such as DHCP, APIPA, and EUI64 for IPv6.

Private vs. Public

When assigning addresses on an internal network, you should be familiar with RFC 1918. It defines the private IPv4 address spaces that are reserved for internal networks. These addresses are non-Internet routable—as a matter of fact, Internet routers abide by RFC 1918 and have no routes in their table for these addresses. RFC 1918 defines three categories of IP addresses for private assignment:

- **Large networks**—10.0.0.0/8 with a range of 10.0.0.0 to 10.255.255.255
- **Medium networks**—172.16.0.0/12 with a range of 172.16.0.0 to 172.31.255.255
- **Small networks**—192.168.0.0/16 with a range of 192.168.0.0 to 192.168.255.255

It should be noted that small networks have a range of 192.168.0.0 to 192.168.255.255 using the /16 (255.255.0.0) mask. The network IDs in this range are normally subnetted with a mask of /24 (255.255.255.0) to provide a smaller range of 254 usable addresses. We will discuss subnetting in a later section.

Public IP addresses are Internet routable and used on the exterior of networks for Internet connectivity. Public IP addresses are coordinated by the Internet Assigned Numbers Authority (IANA). IANA assigns public blocks of IP addresses to private companies, government entities, and the regional Internet registry (RIR). Because of the shortage of IPv4 addresses, IANA no longer assigns IPv4 addresses to private companies and government entities. The RIR is the Internet registry in your region of the world:

- **AFRINIC:** Africa Region
- **APNIC:** Asia/Pacific Region
- **ARIN:** Canada, the United States, and some Caribbean Islands
- **LACNIC:** Latin America and some Caribbean Islands
- **RIPE NCC:** Europe, the Middle East, and Central Asia

The RIR for your region is responsible for the assignment of IPv4 address blocks to private companies. These blocks are much smaller than the legacy assignments of IANA, and often they are assigned to Internet service providers (ISPs). The ISPs are then responsible for the management and assignment of IP addresses to their customers.

IANA publishes the entire IPv4 address space at www.iana.org/ assignments/ipv4-address-space/ipv4-address-space.xhtml. Many of the IP addresses will still resolve to the address prefixes registered. For example, as of this writing, icloud.com will resolve to 17.253.144.10 and identity.apple.com will resolve to 17.32.194.99, which are registered to Apple Computer Inc. These are just two examples, since Apple owns every IP address that starts with 17. These private registrations are quickly being returned to the respective RIR, and companies are using caching services like Akamai for content delivery.

NAT/PAT

Network address translation (NAT) is used for translating one network address to another. This process is required when using a private IP address scheme and you want to request resources on the Internet. We call the device in our house a router, but in actuality it is a NAT device. There are other instances when we need NAT, such as when we have an overlapping IP address scheme. This normally happens when a company merges and you can't pick the IP address scheme because it's already in use at the other company. There are several types of NAT, and I will cover them next.

Static NAT

Static network address translation (SNAT) is used for one-to-one mappings between local (private or inside) and global (Internet) addresses. This requires an IP address on the outside of the NAT process for each IP address inside your network.

In Figure 1.58 you see a group of internal computers on the left; these IP addresses are considered the inside local addresses. When a message is sent to the router from the host (packet A), the source IP address is 192.168.1.10, and the destination IP address is 208.215.179.146. When the packet arrives at the router, a table lookup is performed in the NAT table, and the source IP address is replaced with 24.20.1.2 from the table (packet B). This IP address is called the inside global IP address because it is controlled inside your network, but it is globally routed on the Internet. The packet is then sent on the Internet to the destination, called the outside global IP address (packet C) because it is outside of your network and control and it is globally routed on the Internet. The server then sends the packet back to a destination IP address of 24.20.1.2 (packet D). When it returns at the router performing NAT, it is looked up in the table, and the destination address is replaced with the inside local IP address (packet E). The router then sends it to the original requesting host (packet F). The host never knew that the packet's source and destination address were altered during the process.

FIGURE 1.58   The static NAT process

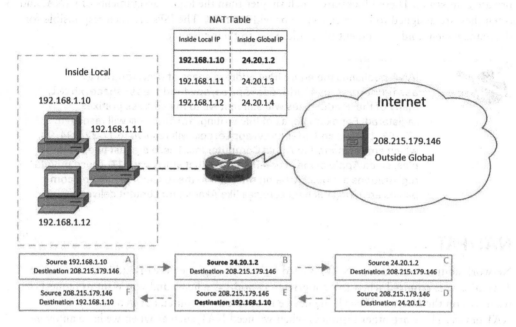

Dynamic NAT

Dynamic network address translation (DNAT) functions similarly to static NAT, as shown in Figure 1.59. DNAT is a one-to-one mapping of IP addresses, with the difference that a pool of IP addresses is attached to the NAT process. When an internal host (inside local) is destined for the Internet through the NAT router, an IP address (inside global) is mapped dynamically from the pool to the inside local IP address and the entry is added to the table. This dynamic mapping is allocated for a set period of time; after the time period is up, the IP address can then be recycled. This process still requires as many IP addresses on the inside global side as you have inside local IP addresses. The benefit is that each IP address does not require a static mapping.

PAT

Port address translation (PAT) is a many-to-one mapping of IP addresses. It is basically what your home NAT router does. It uses a single public (inside global) IP address to translate all of the private (inside local) IP addresses in your house or business. It performs this by adding the inside local (private) IP address and port number to the table. PAT then maps the inside global (public) IP address and port number. The important concept here is that the inside local port number does not need to be the same as the inside global port number since it will be translated in the table. In Figure 1.60, I've purposely used a different port number to illustrate the NAT table lookup and this concept. You can see the translation of IP address and port number in packets B and E. Although I didn't include the outside global address in the table for simplicity, it's in there. PAT will include the outside global address in the table since many requests from host(s) to the same server could exist and this will allow for proper translation.

FIGURE 1.59   Dynamic NAT process

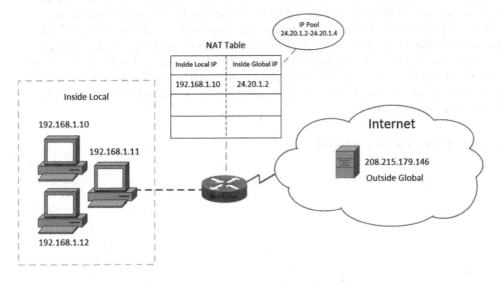

FIGURE 1.60   Port address translation process

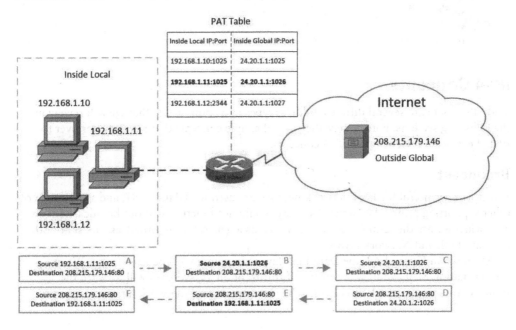

Port Forwarding

Port forwarding is a PAT concept, but for the remainder of this section I will refer to it as NAT. Port forwarding allows outside global (public Internet) hosts to contact services on an inside local (private) host in your network behind a NAT. It performs this function with a manual static entry mapping of the inside local IP address and port to an IP address on the public interface of the router. When a packet destined for the IP address and the port is remapped to the internal host IP address and port number, think of it as a reverse NAT entry. It allows the administrator to publish services on servers internally on the internal network. In Figure 1.61 you see a port forwarding entry for an internal web server with an IP address of 192.168.1.15. The entry is mapped to the outside IP address on the router of 209.160.245.2 and port 80. When a connection is made to the outside IP address, it is forwarded to the internal server.

FIGURE 1.61   Port forwarding example

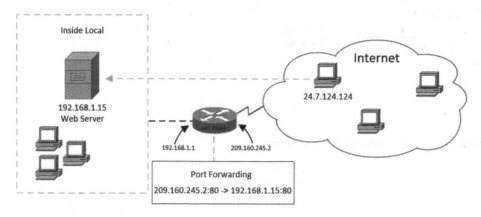

IPv4 Concepts

With IPv4 there are several different address types and components that we will review in the following sections. Fortunately, they are all simple concepts that also transfer over to IPv6. Let's begin reviewing the IPv4 concepts.

Broadcast

Broadcasts are useful for IPv4 networking, they are used for DHCP, ARP, and a multitude of other supporting protocols. Networks today would not function without broadcasts! However, when we use the term *broadcast*, it is used as a general term. Broadcasts exist at both the Data Link and Network layers.

As shown in Figure 1.62, the Data Link layer can contain a broadcast frame. When the destination MAC address is ff:ff:ff:ff:ff:ff:ff:ff: or all 1s, switches will forward the frame to all active network interfaces. When a network card (network interface) receives a broadcast frame, it will process the data to the Network layer. The Network layer protocol does not have to be the IP protocol shown in Figure 1.62; it can be ARP or DHCP. However, in Figure 1.62 we see an IP packet at the Network layer with a destination address of 255.255.255.255. When the destination IP address is all 1s (or in this case, 255.255.255.255), the broadcast is considered a Network layer broadcast. The operating system at this point processes the data within the packet when a Network layer broadcast is received.

FIGURE 1.62   A broadcast frame and IP packet

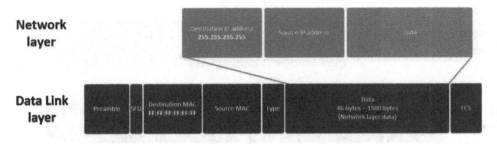

 Not all Data Link layer broadcasts are forwarded to the Network layer. Where a broadcast gets forwarded to next depends on the protocol type in the frame. It is safe to say that all network broadcasts are also Data Link layer broadcasts.

Multicast

Multicasts are similar to broadcasts in that communications is a one-to-many flow of information. This is sometimes referred to as point-to-multipoint communications. However, that is where the similarities end. Multicast is a smart type of broadcast controlled by the switch. Multicast traffic is delivered only to the devices participating in the multicast session. This multicast process helps reduce bandwidth usage for computers not participating in the multicast communications.

A special range of IP addresses is set aside for multicast addressing. The address range for multicast is 224.0.0.0 to 239.255.255.255. When a multicast session is created, the first host begins by registering a multicast IP address, and the port on the switch becomes part of the multicast group. When other hosts join the session, they register with the same IP address, and their ports are added to the multicast group; this process is called the *Internet Group Management Protocol (IGMP)* join.

When any host participating in the multicast group sends data to the switch with a specially crafted MAC address, the data will be forwarded to only the members of the multicast group. All multicast MAC addresses start with 01:00:5e; the rest of the MAC address is a bitwise calculation of the multicast IP address.

Unicast

Unicast communications is a one-to-one conversation between two network devices. Unicast communications should make up 95 to 98 percent of the bandwidth in a typical network.

As you can see in Figure 1.63, the destination MAC address at the Data Link layer is a specific MAC address on the network. A switch will forward this frame only to the port associated with this MAC address. In Chapter 2, "Domain 2.0: Network Implementations," I will cover switching functions in more depth.

FIGURE 1.63 A unicast frame and packet

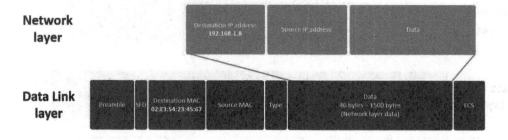

Once the frame is delivered to the host with the destination MAC address, the data is passed to the Network layer. If the destination IP address matches the host, then the data is further processed.

Anycast

An anycast IP address is a one-to-closest-one relationship. Multiple hosts will share the same IP address so they can serve the closest client. Although anycast is a type of IP address, it's not the address itself that makes it an anycast; it's what is done with the specific IP address. An anycast IP address will have multiple route statements to different hosts across a wide geographic area. So, it's more about the trickery in the routing protocol than the IP address itself. A great example of this is the root servers for Domain Name System (DNS). There are only 13 root servers in the root server list, but these 13 IP addresses actually map to hundreds of servers across the globe.

The complete DNS root server list can be found at www.iana.org/domains/root/servers. If you want to see the individual servers, https://root-servers.org contains an interactive map with all of the servers and their locations in the world.

Loopback and Reserved

In addition to the address types covered in the previous sections, there are several reserved IPv4 addresses that are used for special purposes. You should be familiar with RFC 5735, which defines these special-use IP addresses. The loopback is one of these special IP addresses used as a "loopback" to the internal IPv4 address stack. The most important special use IP addresses are defined here:

- 0.0.0.0/8 addresses in this block refer to the source host on the immediate network. It can also be used to define all addresses by using 0.0.0.0/0 and is used in default routing statements.
- 10.0.0.0/8 addresses are defined as private IP addresses in RFC1918.
- 127.0.0.0/8 addresses are reserved for use as loopback addresses.
- 169.254.0.0/16 addresses are reserved for link-local addresses (APIPA).
- 172.16.0.0/12 addresses are defined as private IP addresses in RFC 1918.
- 192.88.99.0/24 addresses are reserved for 6to4 relay anycast addresses.
- 192.168.0.0/16 addresses are defined as private IP addresses in RFC 1918.
- 224.0.0.0/4 addresses are reserved for multicast IP address assignment.
- 240.0.0.0/4 addresses are reserved for future use and not assigned or used.
- The address of 255.255.255.255/32 is used for limited broadcasting for layer 3 broadcasts.

In the following sections, I will cover the special-use IP addresses listed here in further detail. You should commit this list to memory since these are the most common ones. IP addresses not mentioned here are used for documentation purposes and can be found in RFC 5735.

IP Address Elements

For every IP address assigned to a network host or device there are certain elements that need to be configured along with the IP address. Every IP address must at least have an IP address itself and a subnet mask to be valid. The default gateway and options are not required for valid function, but having them adds functionality for the network host or device.

Default Gateway   The default gateway is the IP address that provides routing out of the immediate network. The default gateway is an option for configuration of an IP address on a host since leaving the network is optional. It is sometimes called the gateway of last resort when referring to the routing table. When there is no specific route in the routing table for the destination network, the packet will take the gateway of last resort to another router that can hopefully provide a route to the destination network. Hosts also contain a routing table; however, they usually have only the immediate network configured in the table along with the default gateway.

Subnet Mask   When a source host begins to send information to a destination host, it calculates the immediate network it belongs to. This is done by ANDing the subnet mask and its IP address; the result is the network that the source host belongs to. Next the source will calculate its subnet mask against the destination IP address; the result is the network that the source believes the destination host is a part of.

If both of these addresses match, then the traffic is deemed to be local on the immediate network. The source host will send an Address Resolution Protocol (ARP) request for the destination IP address to obtain the MAC address of the destination host. If the results are not equal, then the destination is deemed remote. The source host will send an ARP request for the default gateway IP address to obtain the MAC address of the default gateway.

When the source host calculates the immediate network and the destination network, the subnet mask is responsible for both of these calculations. It is the perception of the host's immediate network to the destination network that is the deciding factor of sending the traffic to the local host or the default gateway.

Options   IP address options are just that, they are optional parameters that extend functionality usually configured via Dynamic Host Configuration Protocol (DHCP). A great example of this is DNS; you don't need a DNS server configured for network communications. However, DNS servers make it a lot easier for hosts to communicate on the network. Time servers can be specified for keeping time and even the default gateway can be configured via DHCP options. There are hundreds of other options that can be configured and even custom options can be configured.

IPv6 Concepts

IPv6 was developed by the IETF and was published in 1998. It is now 20 years later and it is still slowly being adopted! The motivation for IPv6 was the exhaustion of the IPv4 address space; in the year 2000, half of the IPv4 addresses were allocated. Through the years since the IPv4 exhaustion was first forecasted, many technologies were developed to lessen the impact. One such technology was network address translation (NAT), covered earlier in this chapter. IPv6 has many unique features that you will learn.

Addressing

Before you learn about IPv6, let's compare it to IPv4. The IPv4 address consists of a 32-bit network and host address. A 32-bit address is capable of supplying 4.3 million IP addresses. However, with the classification of IP addresses, we really have only 3.7 million usable addresses. In comparison, there are 7.5 billion people on the planet. So I think you can see the problem? The IPv6 address consists of a 128-bit address and can supply 3.4×10^{38} usable addresses.

There is a learning curve to the IPv6 address, but it is actually easier than IPv4. No complicated binary math is involved with subnetting; the IETF built it into the IPv6 address. However, it is a really large number to notate compared to IPv4, and we must use hexadecimal in the addressing. This is probably the biggest intimidation factor for IPv6, but trust me, it is simple.

Figure 1.64 shows an IPv6 address. The first half (64 bits) is the network ID, and the second half (64 bits) is the interface ID—resulting in a 128-bit address. It is written in hexadecimal, so each digit represents 4 bits. There are 32 digits in an IPv6 address, each containing 4 bits of information, and 32 × 4 = 128 bits. The first 48 bits are called the global prefix and are assigned by the RIR, just like an IPv4 network address. The next 16 bits are the subnet bits, and although they comprise the network ID, they can be assigned by the organization assigned to the global prefix. The last 64 bits make up the interface ID that we will discuss later.

FIGURE 1.64   IPv6 address example

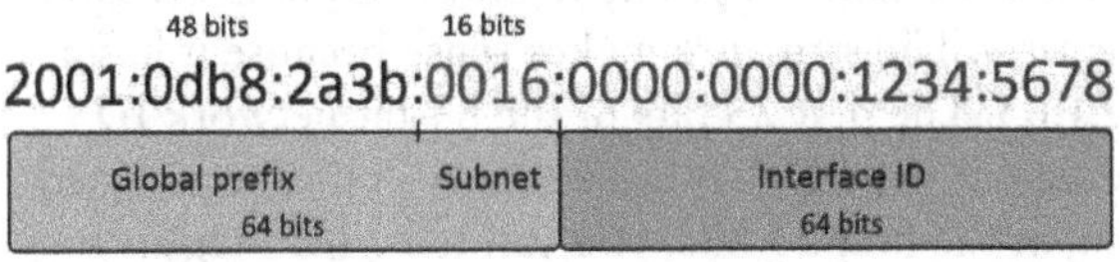

IPv6 Shorthand

Because an IPv6 address is long, there are a few ways to shorten it. When you're shortening an IP address, you need to follow a few rules. Here is an example of an IPv6 address in its uncondensed form:

```
2001:0db8:0045:0000:0000:0056:0000:0012
```

We can condense it by first removing all of the leading zeros between the colons. The leading zeros need to be there for a complete IPv6 address, but the IETF has given us a shortcut. Consider this: We don't have $0010; we have $10. This is an easy way to remember the leading zero concept. When we are done, the IPv6 address will look like this:

```
2001:db8:45:0:0:56:0:12
```

We can condense it further by removing the zeros between the colons, but you can only do this once. So either IPv6 address here is correct:

```
2001:db8:45:0:0:56::12
2001:db8:45::56:0:12
```

In the second IPv6 address, we removed a colon completely. When the host puts the address back together for processing, it will first add the leading zeros back to the address (using the second example):

```
2001:0db8:0045::0056:0000:0012
```

The host will then add the zeros between the double colons to create a 128-bit address again. Here's another example:

```
2001:0db8:0000:0000:0000:0000:0001:0012
2001:db8::1:12
```

Address Types

There are many different IPv6 address types, and again they are not all that different than their IPv4 counterparts. *Internet Assigned Numbers Authority (IANA)* is responsible for mandating addressing of IPv6 prefixes. In the following definitions, I will compare with the IPv4 counterpart:

Unicast packets in IPv6 are the same as unicast packets IPv4. They are direct communications between two hosts. Just as in IPv4, there are public IP addresses and private IP addresses. The only things that change are the terminology and the address prefix.

Global unicast addresses (2000::/3) are the same as public IP addresses in IPv4. They are assigned by a regional Internet registry. The structure makes sense because it has a logical hierarchy, as shown in Figure 1.65. The first 23 bits of the 64-bit network ID define the RIR. The next 9 bits are assigned to an ISP, and the next 16 bits are assigned to a company. In other words, looking at the first 23 bits, you can tell which registry assigned the network ID. Looking at the first 32 bits, you could tell which registry and ISP assigned the network ID. Finally, looking at the first 48 bits, you could tell the registry, ISP, and company the network ID was assigned to. The largest block an ISP can assign is a /48 block because the final 16 bits are used by the company to subnet the address further.

FIGURE 1.65   Breakdown of an IPv6 global unicast address

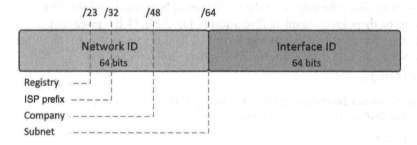

Link-local addresses (fe80::/10) are the same as link-local addresses in IPv4. In IPv4 Microsoft calls a link-local address an *Automatic Private IP Addressing (APIPA)* address. These addresses are used for local access on a network and are unrouteable. As shown in Figure 1.66, the first 10 bits will always start with 1111 1110 10, or written in hexadecimal, fe80. This might confuse you at first, because fe80 is actually 16 bits and I'm stating that the first 10 bits are mandated by IANA. It is true—the last 6 bits can be anything as long as the first 10 bits are fe8. IANA notates all prefixes as 16-bit hexadecimal addresses.

FIGURE 1.66   A link-local prefix

64 bits	64 bits
fe80	Interface ID

1111 1110 10

Unique local addresses (fc00::/7) are similar to private IP addresses in IPv4. The addresses are used for internal routing and not intended for Internet routing. The first 7 bits are mandated by IANA, and the other 57 bits can be assigned by the organization. Whenever you see fc00 as the prefix, it is a link-local address. Again, IANA only mandates the first 7 bits to be fc, but IANA notates all addresses in a 16-bit hexadecimal address.

Multicast addresses (ff00::/8) are similar to multicast addresses in IPv4. A multicast is a one-to-many address used in lieu of broadcasts in IPv6. In IPv6 broadcast addresses no longer exist. In lieu of broadcasts, IPv6 uses multicasting. IANA mandates that the first 8 bits are all 1s or ff. So whenever you see an address starting with ff, know that it is an IPv6 multicast address.

Anycast addresses are also similar to their IPv4 counterparts. Anycast addresses are used for a one-to-nearest connectivity. The address is a standard global unicast address, but it is populated in multiple routing tables. The root DNS servers function with this special address type. You should make note that although anycast addresses are global unicast addresses, the IETF has reserved the first 128 addresses for each /64 for use with anycast addressing.

Tunneling

Tunneling is used as a transition technology for IPv6 networking over an IPv4 network. There are several different technologies for achieving coexistence between an IPv6 network and an IPv4 network. These technologies are commonly used because an application must function with IPv6 or a particular service requires IPv6.

6to4 encapsulates IPv6 packets inside an IPv4 packet using network protocol 41. 6to4 can be used in two ways; the first is site-to-site over an IPv4 network such as the Internet. The 6to4 router will encapsulate an IPv6 packet over the IPv4 Internet to the destination 6to4 router, where it is decapsulated and routed on the IPv6 network. The second way 6to4 can be used is to allow an IPv6 network to communicate over the IPv4 Internet to the IPv6 Internet, as shown in Figure 1.67. When it is used in this scenario, your 6to4 router must be pointed to a 6to4 router connected to the IPv6 Internet. These 6to4 endpoint routers use an anycast address of 192.88.99.1 as the IPv4 destination network address.

FIGURE 1.67   6to4 tunneling

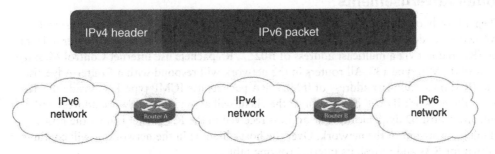

Toredo tunneling is another IPv6 transitional technology. It is used when an IPv6 host is behind a network address translation (NAT). The IPv6 packets are sent as UDP/3544 IPv4 packets to a Toredo server that is connected to the IPv6 network. Many ISPs have Toredo servers for public use to the IPv6 Internet. A Toredo relay is a router that interacts with a Toredo server to facilitate IPv4 clients to IPv6 hosts.

Intra-Site Automatic Tunnel Addressing Protocol (ISATAP) allows dual-stack hosts to communicate on an IPv4 network to an IPv6 router. When a dual-stack host is configured for ISATAP, it will resolve the DNS ISATAP well-known entry. This request will resolve to an IPv4 ISATAP router that will allow the host to communicate to the IPv6 network. The client will then obtain an IPv6 network address and communicate with the IPv6 router by using IPv6-in-IPv4 encapsulation.

Dual Stack

When the IPv4 OSI layers work together, it is known as a network stack. The IPv6 OSI layers are similar to IPv4, with the exception of IPv6 at the Network layer; IPv6 is also considered a network stack. A dual-stack router or host is considered to have both the IPv4 and IPv6 network stacks running simultaneously, as shown in Figure 1.68. This allows the router or host to communicate on both versions of the IP protocol.

FIGURE 1.68   Dual stack example

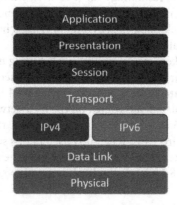

Router Advertisements

When a host boots up in an IPv6 network, the host will configure itself with a link-local IPv6 network address starting with fe80. This IPv6 address is used to send a Router Solicitation (RS) request via a multicast address of ff02::2. RS packets use Internet Control Message Protocol (ICMP) type 133. All routers in the network will respond with a Router Advertisement (RA) on a multicast address of ff02::1. RA packets use ICMP type 134. Inside this RA packet the network ID will be contained; the client will assume this network address and configure a host ID dynamically. The address received in the RA packet is now the host's default gateway out of the network. Over the host's lifetime in the network, it will continue to listen for RAs and refresh its internal routing table.

Neighbor Discovery

When an IPv4 host needs to communicate with another IPv4 IP address on the link-local network, it requires the MAC address. The process requires an ARP request and ARP reply, which is broadcast-based. IPv6 has eliminated broadcasts, and ARP with the ICMPv6 protocol calls the Neighbor Discovery Protocol (NDP).

When an IPv6 host needs to communicate with another IPv6 host on the link-local network, it will multicast a Neighbor Solicitation (NS) called a solicited node multicast to a multicast address of ff02::1. The NS packets use ICMPv6 type 135. The neighbor will then reply with a Neighbor Advertisement (NA) with its MAC address. The NA packets use ICMPv6 type 136. The requestor will then cache this address in the neighbor cache, which is similar to the ARP cache in IPv4. This entire process is similar to IPv4 ARP requests and replies, but it uses multicast to facilitate the traffic and eliminate broadcasts.

Address Assignments

We can assign IP addresses in one of three ways: auto-assignment, dynamic assignment, and static assignment. IPv6 operates with auto-assignment of IPv6 addressing, although we can use DHCPv6 for dynamic assignments. Dynamic assignment allows for centralized management of IP addresses. IPv4 supports both auto-assignment and dynamic assignment, but auto-assignment of IP addresses is nonroutable, as you will see later. We also always have the choice of statically assigning IP addresses for both IPv4 and IPv6.

DHCP

Dynamic Host Configuration Protocol (DHCP) is responsible for automatic configuration of IPv4 IP addresses and subnet masks for hosts from a pool of IPv4 addresses. It is also responsible for configuration of such options as default gateways, DNS server addresses, and many other IP-based servers. It performs configuration of the host in a series of network broadcasts and unicasts.

The process of DHCP for a client is called DORA—Discover, Offer, Request, Acknowledgment. In Figure 1.69, you see a DHCP client and a DHCP server. The client begins by sending a DHCP Discover broadcast packet to the network. The server hears the broadcast and processes the request based on the client's MAC address and IP address availability in the pool. The server sends a unicast frame back to the client with a DHCP Offer of an IP address, subnet mask, and any options. The client still doesn't have an IP address, so it broadcasts a DHCP Request for the IP address, subnet mask, and options. The request for the configuration is then acknowledged by the DHCP server with a DHCP Acknowledge unicast to the client. At this point, the client assumes the IP address, subnet mask, and options, and a lease timer starts. I will cover the DHCP lease period later in this chapter.

FIGURE 1.69   The DHCP DORA process

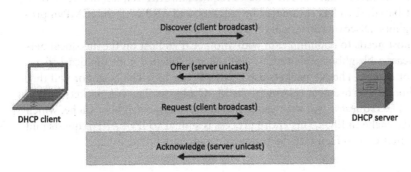

FIGURE 1.69   The DHCP DORA process

Stateless Address Autoconfiguration (SLAAC)

Stateless Address Autoconfiguration, also known as SLAAC, is defined in RFC 4862 and is the default IPv6 address assignment method for IPv6. When an IPv6 host becomes active in the network, it is automatically configured with an IPv6 link-local address starting with a prefix of fe80::. The link-local address is non-routable and only used in the process of obtaining a routable IPv6 address.

The host then sends a Router Solicitation (RS) to the multicast address of all routers ff02::2 from the link-local address automatically configured and checked. This RS message is an Internet Control Message Protocol (ICMP) packet type 133, as shown in Figure 1.70. All the routers in the multicast network will receive the RS packet and send back a Router Advertisement (RA) ICMP packet containing the network address for the immediate

FIGURE 1.70   The SLAAC process

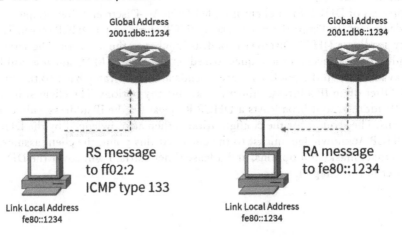

network. The host will then auto-assign the interface ID portion of the IPv6 address randomly with a 64-bit value, which is the default method on Microsoft Windows, or with the EUI-64 method reviewed in the next section.

 Periodically all routers will send an RA message ICMP type 134 to the multicast address of ff02:1 (all IPv6 devices); the RA message contains the network prefix and default gateway. When a host becomes active, it sometimes cannot wait for this message and preempts with a RS message to ff02:2 (all IPv6 routers) as discussed in the prior section.

EUI-64

Extended Unique Identifier 64 (EUI-64) is used with IPv6 addressing. EUI-64 provides a mechanism for logical assignment of the host's MAC address in the interface ID of the host's IPv6 address. By default with many operating systems, a random interface ID is created and checked for possible duplication. This is the default auto-assignment process for IPv6.

If EUI-64 is enabled, the MAC address of 48 bits will be padded and inserted into the 64-bit interface ID. The EUI-64 process is a two-step process. First, the MAC address is split into two 24-bit pieces and padded with fffe, as shown in Figure 1.71. Anytime you see the fffe in the middle of the interface ID, you can assume that the interface ID is an EUI-64 address.

FIGURE 1.71   Padding process of EUI-64 addresses

Next, we must flip the universal/local bit, which is the seventh bit from the left of the interface ID. This bit identifies whether this interface identifier is universally or locally administered. If the bit is 0, the address is locally administered; if the bit is 1, the address is globally unique. Although most of the time this bit will be a 1, you should know that RFC 4291 recommends the bit be flipped. Flipped means that it will be the opposite of what it is—a 1 will become a 0 and a 0 will become a 1. So the next step is to flip the bit on our IPv6 address, as shown in Figure 1.72.

Our interface ID is now complete as the address of 0212:34ff:ffaa:bbcc. The full address might look like 2001:0db8:0045:0000:0212:34ff:feaa:bbcc, with the first 64 bits being the network ID.

FIGURE 1.72   Bit flipping for EUI-64 addresses

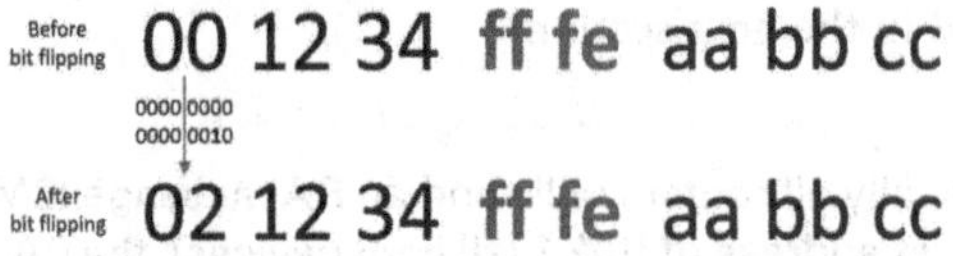

^{Before}
Before bit flipping   00 12 34 ff fe aa bb cc

0000|0000
0000|0010
↓

After bit flipping   02 12 34 ff fe aa bb cc

DHCPv6

Dynamic Host Configuration Protocol v6 (DHCPv6) is the IPv6 version of DHCP for IPv4. DHCP in IPv6 can be deployed in stateless mode and stateful mode. It is often deployed in stateless mode because IPv6 automatic address assignment is built into IPv6.

In stateless mode as described earlier, DHCPv6 is only used for the assignment of DHCP options. In this mode, DHCPv6 does not fully function like its IPv4 counterpart. DHCPv6 doesn't assign IPv6 addresses in this mode; SLAAC is used to assign an IP address. However, throughout this process the DHCP options are never transmitted by the router. This is where stateless DHCPv6 service comes in—it provides the DHCP options for critical services such as DNS. These options are transmitted via an RA message that has the O flag set to 1 for "other stateful configuration." This might be confusing because DHCPv6 in stateless mode has the "other stateful configuration" flag set! Keep in mind that we are forcing the client to take these options, so we are forcing the state—hence the name.

In stateful mode, DHCPv6 is responsible for the assignment of IPv6 network addresses and interface IDs, similar to its IPv4 counterpart. In fact, it operates exactly like an IPv4 DHCP server; it will assign the IP address and keep the state of the IP address it has assigned the client, just as its mode states (no pun intended). The stateful DHCPv6 service operates similarly to an IPv6 router, listening and responding to RS packets with RA packets. However, the RA packet contains an M flag set to 1 for "managed address configuration." This tells the client to accept both the network address and interface ID from the RA packet. The M and O flags can be set to provide both the IPv6 address and the options.

Static

Dynamic IP addressing is the standard in small-to-large networks when configuring client computers. Static IP addressing should only be used under certain circumstances for client computers since it is not very scalable and a nightmare to keep track of manually. DHCP allows for a central management of the IP address space versus static assignment of individual hosts (which is decentralized). Static IP addressing should only be used on network resources such as routers, network printers, and servers. Figure 1.73 shows the IPv4 configuration page of a network adapter on Windows Server 2019, although the dialog box has not changed at all since Windows 95.

FIGURE 1.73   The Windows DHCP/static IP address dialog box

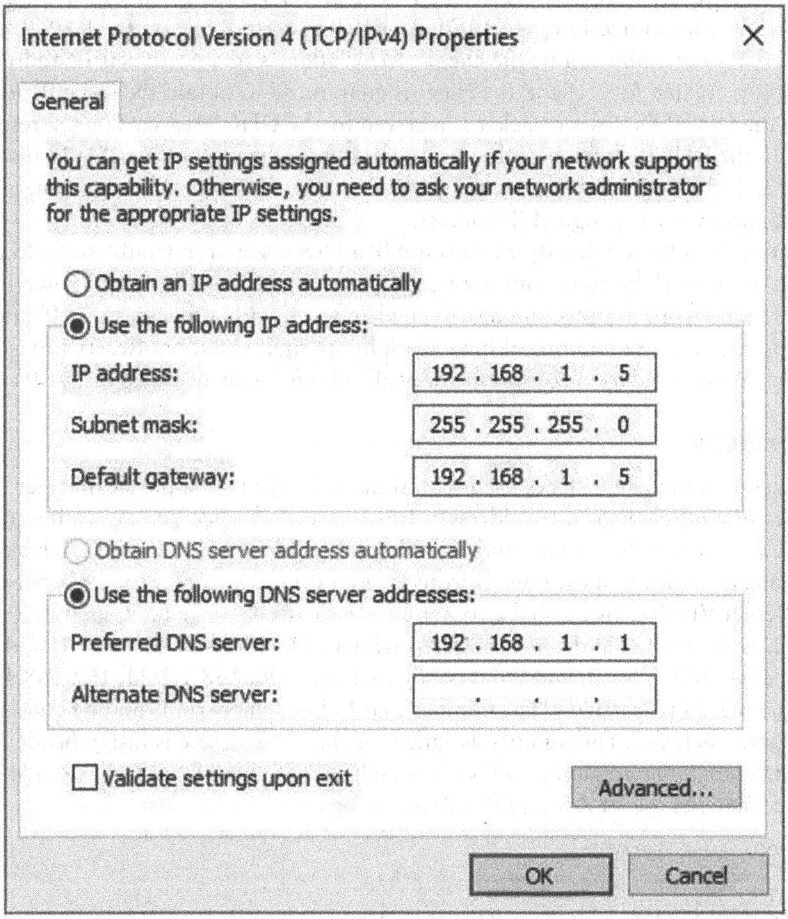

Internet Protocol Version 4 (TCP/IPv4) Properties	✕

General

You can get IP settings assigned automatically if your network supports this capability. Otherwise, you need to ask your network administrator for the appropriate IP settings.

○ Obtain an IP address automatically

⦿ Use the following IP address:

IP address:	192 . 168 . 1 . 5
Subnet mask:	255 . 255 . 255 . 0
Default gateway:	192 . 168 . 1 . 5

○ Obtain DNS server address automatically

⦿ Use the following DNS server addresses:

Preferred DNS server:	192 . 168 . 1 . 1
Alternate DNS server:	. . .

☐ Validate settings upon exit   Advanced...

OK   Cancel

APIPA

Automatic Private IP Addressing (APIPA) is a Microsoft term for link-local addressing defined in RFC 3927. This auto-assignment of IP address allows for multiple hosts to automatically obtain an IP address. Although the IP address is auto-assigned, the default gateway is not used. So APIPA allows for local network connectivity but not internetwork connectivity.

APIPA addressing always starts with 169.254.x.x, so it's easy to recognize. APIPA only auto-assigns the IP address if the DHCP server is unavailable. If you see an APIPA address on an interface adapter, it probably means that DHCP has failed or is unavailable. On Windows operating systems, the DHCP client will continue in the background to obtain an IP address if DHCP becomes available.

Reservations

When a client requests an IP address from a DHCP server via the DORA process, the client's MAC address is transmitted in the CHADDR DHCP packet. A rule on the DHCP server called a *DHCP reservation* can tie the client's MAC address to a particular IP address. When a reservation is created for a client, the client is guaranteed to obtain the same IP address every time the DHCP Discovery packet is received by the DHCP server. When a reservation is created on the DHCP server, no other hosts can obtain the reservation IP address unless they have the MAC address that matches the reservation. This type of assignment is considered a dynamically static-assigned IP address.

Reservations can be very handy when static IP addresses are too troublesome to configure, such as network printers with poor configuration options. I've been known to set a reservation on network printers and move on when faced with a finicky static IP address process. You too can save an hour of busy work in the right situation. Reservations can also be useful when you need to make specific firewall rules for a client based on its IP address.

Subinterfaces

Subinterfaces are unique interfaces used with routers. They allow a physical router interface to contain multiple logical IP addresses. It is very useful when you are configuring a router or a WAN technology that requires multiple IP addresses configured, such as MPLS. The following configuration example is from a Cisco router used as a router between several different VLANs, also called a router on a stick (RoaS). The main interface is the interface FastEthernet 0/0 and it is configured with an IP address of 192.168.1.1/24. The subinterfaces are 0/0.2, 0/0.3, and 0/0.4 configured with 192.168.1.2/24, 192.168.1.3/24, and 192.168.4.1/24 respectively. The number that follows the period can be between 1 and 4,294,967,296, inclusive. The number assigned for the subinterface is insignificant, but it should match what you are doing so it's not a nightmare to read later. For example, each subinterface matches the VLAN and IP subnet configured.

```
RouterA#configure terminal
RouterA(config)#interface FastEthernet 0/0
RouterA(config-if)#ip address 192.168.1.1 255.255.255.0
RouterA(config-if)#no shutdown
RouterA(config-subif)#interface FastEthernet 0/0.2
RouterA(config-subif)#encapsulation dot1q 2
RouterA(config-subif)#ip address 192.168.2.1 255.255.255.0
RouterA(config-subif)#interface FastEthernet 0/0.3
RouterA(config-subif)#encapsulation dot1q 3
RouterA(config-subif)#ip address 192.168.4.1 255.255.255.0
RouterA(config-subif)#interface FastEthernet 0/0.4
RouterA(config-subif)#encapsulation dot1q 4
RouterA(config-subif)#ip address 192.168.4.1 255.255.255.0
RouterA(config-subif)#
```

Subnetting

Subnetting is the process of changing the subnet mask to break a logical network into smaller logical networks. Subnetting is often used for addressing of physical locations, such as point-to-point WAN connections. Subnetting is also used for network segmentation—for example, to facilitate routing between VLANs. In all cases, subnetting changes the host's immediate network in which it is assigned.

Because of the ANDing process on the host, when the host calculates its immediate network and the destination network, the subnet mask is directly responsible for the results. If we change the subnet mask, we can change the results.

The term *ANDing* explains a logic calculation and not an arithmetic calculation. With the AND process, 0 AND 0 equates to a 0; 0 AND 1 or 1 AND 0 equates to 0' 1 AND 1 equates to 1. As you can see, the only time 1 is a result is when 1 is ANDed against itself, as shown in Table 1.3.

TABLE 1.3   AND Truth Table

Bit 1	Bit 2	Result
0	0	0
0	1	0
1	0	0
1	1	1

As shown in Figure 1.74, host A performs the ANDing process against its subnet mask to produce the network it belongs to. Then host A performs the ANDing process against the destination address and host A's subnet mask to produce the second result. This second result is the perceived distance of the destination host from host A's perspective, because host A must decide if the frame will go directly to the destination or be sent to a router.

FIGURE 1.74   The ANDing process

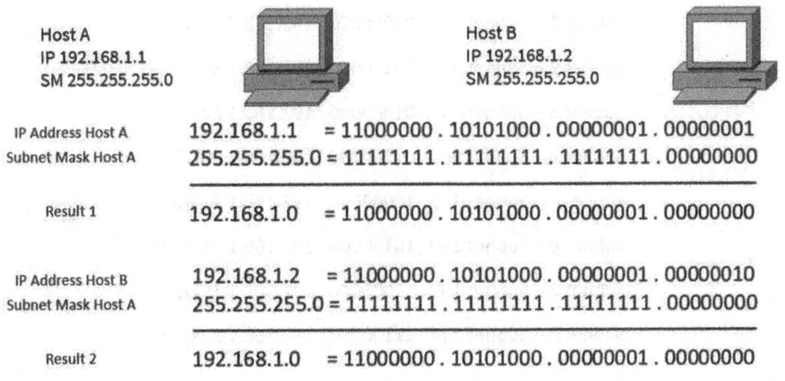

Host A IP 192.168.1.1 SM 255.255.255.0		Host B IP 192.168.1.2 SM 255.255.255.0

IP Address Host A	192.168.1.1	= 11000000 . 10101000 . 00000001 . 00000001
Subnet Mask Host A	255.255.255.0	= 11111111 . 11111111 . 11111111 . 00000000
Result 1	192.168.1.0	= 11000000 . 10101000 . 00000001 . 00000000
IP Address Host B	192.168.1.2	= 11000000 . 10101000 . 00000001 . 00000010
Subnet Mask Host A	255.255.255.0	= 11111111 . 11111111 . 11111111 . 00000000
Result 2	192.168.1.0	= 11000000 . 10101000 . 00000001 . 00000000

An analogy of this is if you had to decide if you were going to deliver a letter personally or just send it to the post office. You would first look at your address and identify your city and state, then you would look at the destination and identify the city and state. If it matched, you could probably save a stamp and deliver it yourself (local network). If it didn't match, then it's probably worth the stamp and dropping it off to the post office (router). The IP address and subnet ANDing process is identical. You first identify your network ID, then you use your same subnet mask and apply it to the destination address to see if you get the same result. By changing the subnet mask you will get different results because you're changing the network you belong to. We will look closer at the ANDing process in Chapter 2, "Domain 2.0: Network Implementations."

In Figure 1.75, an IP address is detailed in quad dotted-decimal notation and its underlying binary equivalent. The IP address of 192.168.1.1 has a default subnet mask of 255.255.255.0. Therefore, the first three octets define the network ID, and the last octet of 8 bits defines the host ID. If we subnet this network ID further, we must borrow bits from the host section for the subnet ID. This borrowing of bits becomes part of the subnet mask, as seen in the figure. The new subnet mask would now be 255.255.255.224 because 11100000 is 224 in decimal.

FIGURE 1.75   Subnetting of an IP address

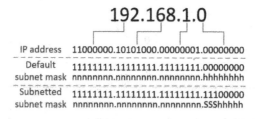

Figure 1.76 shows the eight different subnets that are created when we subnet the IP network from the previous example. As you can see, the last octet is written out, detailing the 3 bits we borrowed from the host section. As we count up in binary, the subnets identify themselves.

FIGURE 1.76   Subnet IDs

Subnet 1 – Subnet 0   **000**00000   192.168.1.0/27

Subnet 2 – Subnet 32   **001**00000   192.168.1.32/27

Subnet 3 – Subnet 64   **010**00000   192.168.1.64/27

Subnet 4 – Subnet 96   **011**00000   192.168.1.96/27

Subnet 5 – Subnet 128   **100**00000   192.168.1.128/27

Subnet 6 – Subnet 160   **101**00000   192.168.1.160/27

Subnet 7 – Subnet 192   **110**00000   192.168.1.192/27

Subnet 8 – Subnet 224   **111**00000   192.168.1.224/27

When calculating the host IDs, you must follow a few rules. The first rule is that all zeros in the host ID identify the network address and cannot be used as a host ID. The second rule is that all 1s in the host ID are the broadcast IP address for the immediate network. This address cannot be used to assign to a host. As shown in Figure 1.77, the last octet has been written out in binary format to show the mechanics of subnetting and calculating the valid host IDs.

Understanding the binary mechanics that are underlying in subnetting is useful. However, when we are subnetting, it is inefficient and confusing—mainly because our brains have a hard time switching between binary and decimal and applying artificial rules of subnetting to the mathematics. In Figure 1.78, I've detailed how to create a subnet calculator. This calculator is the fastest method for making subnetting calculations. Let's look at the two bottom lines; if we borrow 3 bits from the host ID, then we count from left to right and use the column with 224 and 32. The bottommost line is the subnet mask 255.255.255.224. The middle line is the subnet IDs; as in the previous example, we would count from 0 by 32. It's really that simple!

FIGURE 1.77   Host ID calculations

Subnet 1 – Subnet 0	00000000 = 192.168.1.0	Network ID
	00000001 = 192.168.1.1	First Valid ID
	00011110 = 192.168.1.30	Last Valid ID
	00011111 = 192.168.1.31	Broadcast ID
Subnet 2 – Subnet 32	00100001 = 192.168.1.33	First Valid ID
	00111110 = 192.168.1.62	Last Valid ID
Subnet 3 – Subnet 64	01000001 = 192.168.1.65	First Valid ID
	01011110 = 192.168.1.94	Last Valid ID
Subnet 4 – Subnet 96	01100001 = 192.168.1.97	First Valid ID
	01111110 = 192.168.1.126	Last Valid ID
Subnet 5 – Subnet 128	10000001 = 192.168.1.129	First Valid ID
	10011110 = 192.168.1.158	Last Valid ID
Subnet 6 – Subnet 160	10100001 = 192.168.1.161	First Valid ID
	10111110 = 192.168.1.190	Last Valid ID
Subnet 7 – Subnet 192	11000001 = 192.168.1.193	First Valid ID
	11011110 = 192.168.1.222	Last Valid ID
Subnet 8 – Subnet 224	11100001 = 192.168.1.225	First Valid ID
	11111110 = 192.168.1.254	Last Valid ID
	11111111 = 192.168.1.255	Broadcast ID

Let use the calculator and try to solve a subnetting problem. If we wanted to segment a network into four logical networks, we would use the formula of $2^x = $ or > 4, where x should be equal to or greater than 4. We can use the top line to calculate this formula. As seen in Figure 1.79, if we plug 2 into the formula, then we get 4 ($2^2 = 4$). The 2 represents the number of bits we are borrowing from the host ID for the network ID, just as in the previous example. So we count from left to right on the two bottom lines and circle them. We now have our subnet mask of 255.255.255.192 and the subnet IDs of 0, 64, 128, and 192.

FIGURE 1.78   Creating a subnet calculator

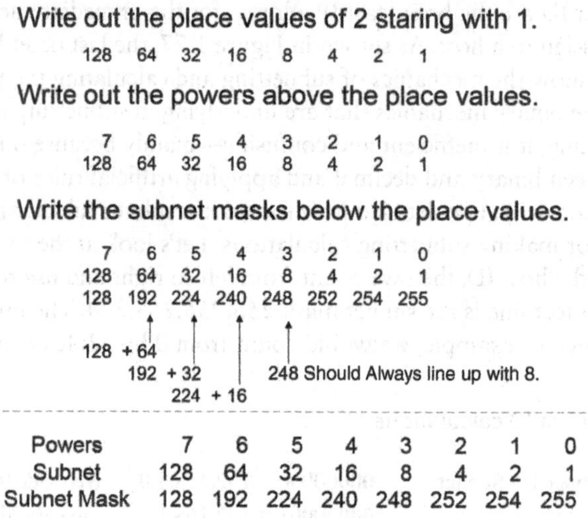

Write out the place values of 2 staring with 1.

128   64   32   16   8   4   2   1

Write out the powers above the place values.

7	6	5	4	3	2	1	0
128	64	32	16	8	4	2	1

Write the subnet masks below the place values.

7	6	5	4	3	2	1	0
128	64	32	16	8	4	2	1
128	192	224	240	248	252	254	255

128 + 64
192 + 32   248 Should Always line up with 8.
224 + 16

Powers	7	6	5	4	3	2	1	0
Subnet	128	64	32	16	8	4	2	1
Subnet Mask	128	192	224	240	248	252	254	255

To calculate the host ID, we follow the +1 from the network ID and –2 from the next ID, so for the first IP address range it would be 192.168.1.1 to 192.168.1.62. The next range is 192.168.1.65 to 192.168.1.126, and so on. As you can see, we have 62 valid IP addresses in each of the four network IDs. We use the calculation of $2^x - 2$ to equal the valid network IP addresses ($2^6 - 2 = 62$). So where did the 6 come from? We had 8 bits in the host ID and we used 2 for the network ID (subnet), leaving us with 6 bits for the host ID.

FIGURE 1.79   The subnet calculator

Powers	7	6	5	4	3	2	1	0
Subnet	128	64	32	16	8	4	2	1
Subnet Mask	128	192	224	240	248	252	254	255

We can switch the formulas to calculate a subnet that will accommodate x number of clients. However, you must pay close attention to the subnet ID. In Figure 1.80, if we need 6 clients per subnetwork, we can use the formula of $2^x - 2 =$ or > 6. When we use the calculation $2^3 - 2 = 6$, the 3 bits are now used for the host ID, and we must figure out the network bits (8 bits – 3 for the host = 5 for the network). We then use this 5 to count from left to right on the bottom two rows. Our subnet mask is 255.255.255.248, and our subnet IDs are 0, 8, 16, 24, 32, and so on.

FIGURE 1.80   Subnetting for hosts

Powers	7	6	5	4	3	2	1	0
Subnet	128	64	32	16	8	4	2	1
Subnet Mask	128	192	224	240	248	252	254	255

So far we have been subnetting the last 8 bits of an IP address. Larger addresses like 170.26.0.0 have a default subnet mask of 255.255.0.0. So we have 16 bits to subnet with in the last two octets. The same rules apply with larger numbers. For instance, if we needed 8 subnets, our network IDs would be 170.26.0.0, 170.26.32.0, and 170.26.64.0 to 170.26.224.0 for the last network ID. The subnet mask would be 255.255.224.0; this is derived by counting from the left for the number of subnet bits on the calculator. Just remember we are subnetting across 16 bits, so the 224 belongs to the third octet. This gives us a number of 32, which we use to calculate the subnets. The total number of networks would be $2^3 = 8$ subnetworks, each containing $2^{13} - 2 = 8,190$ hosts each ($3 + 13 = 16$ bits). The host IDs are a bit different to calculate because we have two octets to deal with, as shown in Figure 1.81.

FIGURE 1.81   Valid host IDs for a 13-bit host ID

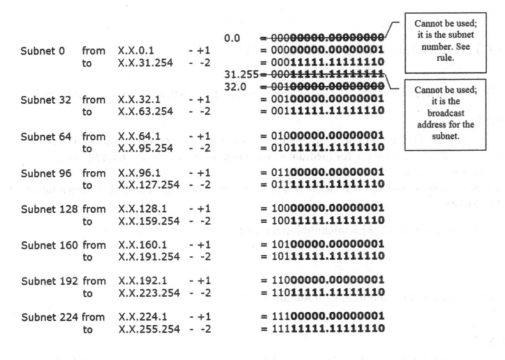

Classful

When we discuss the default subnet mask a network ID has, we are talking about its IP class. Classful IP network addresses are addresses that follow this strict classification. We often use the term *classful* when describing routing protocols. A classful routing protocol is a routing protocol that does not abide by subnetting. As an example, if a network had the default subnet mask of 255.255.0.0 and we subnetted the network as 255.255.224.0, the routing protocol would treat all the network IDs the same under the classful assignment of 255.255.0.0. Fortunately, RIPv1 is the only routing protocol that does this; RIPv2 abides by the subnetted IDs.

The different IP classes were originally proposed and drafted by the Internet Engineering Task Force (IETF). They define large, medium, and small networks, along with specialized IP assignments. The class of an IP address is defined by the first octet of the IP address, as you'll see in the following sections.

Class A

Class A network IDs have a defined range of 1 to 126 for the first octet and a default mask of 255.0.0.0. They are for really large networks with $2^{24} - 2 = 16,777,214$ hosts, although we would subnet this down further.

The leading bit in the 32-bit IP address is always a zero, so that defines a range of 0 to 127:

00000000.hhhhhhhh.hhhhhhhh.hhhhhhhh = 0

to

01111111.hhhhhhhh.hhhhhhhh.hhhhhhhh = 127

All zeros are reserved by RFC 5735 for special use, and 127.0.0.0 is reserved for loopbacks.

Class B

Class B network IDs have a defined range of 128 to 191 for the first octet and a default mask of 255.255.0.0. They are for medium-sized networks with $2^{16} - 2 = 65,534$ hosts, although we would subnet this down further.

The leading bit in the 32-bit IP address is always a one and a zero, so that defines a range of 128 to 191:

10000000.nnnnnnnn.hhhhhhhh.hhhhhhhh = 128

to

10111111.nnnnnnnn.hhhhhhhh.hhhhhhhh = 191

Class C

Class C network IDs have a defined range of 192 to 223 for the first octet and a default mask of 255.255.255.0. They are for small networks with $2^8 - 2 = 254$ hosts.

The leading bit in the 32-bit IP address is always a one, a one, and a zero, so that defines a range of 192 to 223:

11000000.nnnnnnnn.nnnnnnnn.hhhhhhhh = 192

to

11011111.nnnnnnnn.nnnnnnnn.hhhhhhhh = 223

Class D

Class D network IDs are not used for individual networks. They are specialized IP addresses for multicasting purposes, as defined originally by the IETF and RFC5735. Just like Classes A, B, and C, they follow the same premise of leading bits. Class D IP addresses start with 1110 for a usable range of 224 to 239. Multicast IP addresses (Class D) do not have a default subnet mask because of their specialized purpose.

Class E

Class E network IDs are not used at all—they are considered for experimental use only and were never used. A while back, the IETF investigated and allowed this range of unused IP addresses to be used again. However, it was found that all networking devices would have to be reprogrammed, mainly because they all follow classifications of IP addressing. The idea was scrapped, and the range from 240 to 254 is not used to this day. Class E defines the leading bits of the IP address starting with 1111.

Theoretically, there would have been a Class F and further classifications. Following the binary mechanics of classifications, we could have 248 to 254. However, all of these addresses are grouped into the Class E assignment.

Classless

The classless IP address category specifies that we do not adhere to the classful assignment of the IETF. With the scarcity of IPv4 addresses, we need to subnet! It also means that we can *supernet*, which is the opposite of subnetting. The RFC1918 address of 172.16.0.0/12 (255.240.0.0 mask) is supernetted. The 172 address falls between the Class B assignment range, but the mask is going the other way. We are mandated by Class B addressing to have a mask of /16 (255.255.0.0 mask), but we elect to group multiple /16 networks into a /12 network. This is supernetting, and it wouldn't be possible without classless IP addresses.

VLSM

In all our subnet examples, we've assumed that all the networks use the same subnet mask. However, this is extremely inefficient, because not all subnetworks require that same number of hosts. Luckily, every host makes the determination of where to forward the frame based on the destination network address. As long as we do not overlap addressing, we can vary the subnet mask. Figure 1.82 shows a small network requiring a different number of hosts. The router on the left in the figure has a routing table with a single entry pointing to the router on the right. The router on the right contains the routing table that will forward the packet to the appropriate subnet.

The smallest assignment of a network is a block of four addresses. Two of the four addresses will be used for the network ID and broadcast ID, which leaves us with two usable valid IP addresses. To calculate variable-length subnet mask (VLSM) networks, we simply create a spreadsheet or table using a block size of 4. Inside the table we can allocate block sizes of 4, 8, 16, 32, 64, and 128, but the block must start on a multiple of those numbers. As shown in Figure 1.83, we calculated the four subnets used in the previous example without overlapping addresses.

FIGURE 1.82 A variable-length subnet mask (VLSM) network

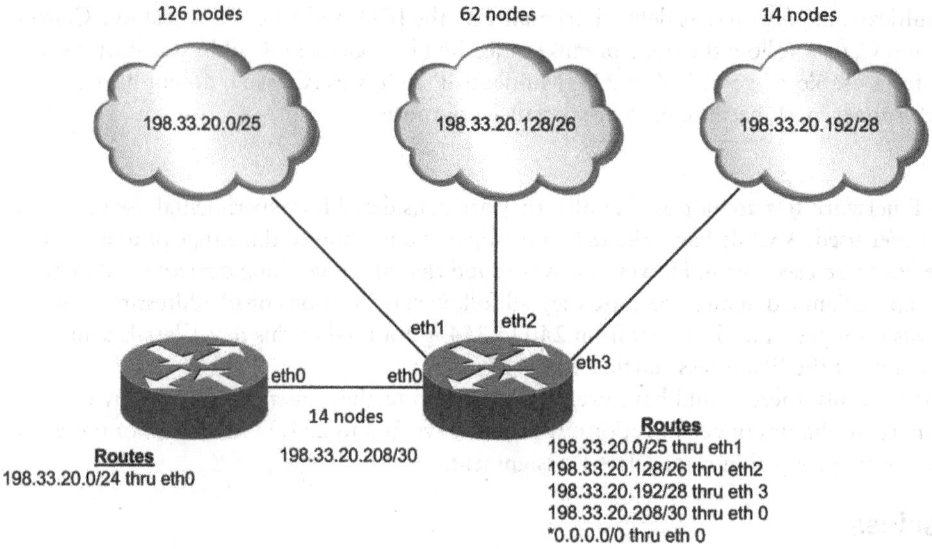

FIGURE 1.83 VLSM worksheet

0		64		128		192	
4		68		132		196	
8		72		136		200	
12		76		140		204	
16		80		144		208	
20		84		148		212	
24		88		152		216	
28		92		156		220	
32		96		160		224	
36		100		164		228	
40		104		168		232	
44		108		172		236	
48		112		176		240	
52		116		180		244	
56		120		184		248	
60		124		188		252	

Subnet 1 - 198.33.20.0/25 usable range of 198.33.20.1 to 198.33.20.126
Subnet 2 - 198.33.20.128/26 usable range of 198.33.20.129 to 198.33.20.190
Subnet 3 - 198.33.20.192/28 usable range of 198.33.20.193 to 198.33.20.206
Subnet 4 - 198.33.20.208/30 usable range of 198.33.20.209 to 198.33.20.210

CIDR Notation (IPv4 vs. IPv6)

Classless Inter-Domain Routing (CIDR) notation is a network engineer's shorthand. It is just another way of writing out the network mask. We count the number of bits and represent it using a / and the number. So a subnet mask of 255.255.255.248 is 11111111.11111111.111 11111.11111000 in binary, and in CIDR notation it is $8 + 8 + 8 + 5 = 29$, or /29.

In Figure 1.84 you can see a simple CIDR calculator. I have something similar hanging by my desk for when I need to double-check a subnet mask or block size.

FIGURE 1.84   A CIDR calculator

Subnet	128	64	32	16	8	4	2	1
Subnet Mask	128	192	224	240	248	252	254	255
CIDR 4th octet	/25	/26	/27	/28	/29	/30	/31	/32
CIDR 3rd octet	/17	/18	/19	/20	/21	/22	/23	/24
CIDR 2nd octet	/9	/10	/11	/12	/13	/14	/15	/16
CIDR 1st octet	/1	/2	/3	/4	/5	/6	/7	/8

With IPv6, CIDR notation is the only way to notate the network ID. It really is, because the number is so large and it is in hexadecimal. So we always see CIDR notation with the 128-bit IPv6 addresses. As an example, 2001:db8:45:0/64 would represent our network ID in IPv6.

Virtual IP (VIP)

The default gateway is the only way out of our network. However, if a router fails or needs to be serviced, the default gateway will become unavailable. This might not be a problem for average web surfing. However, if VoIP depends on the default gateway, we now have a bigger problem.

Since the default gateway is just an IP address configured on every host that responds to ARP requests, we can virtualize it using a *first-hop redundancy protocol (FHRP)*. We can create a highly available default gateway by letting more than one router respond to an ARP request. As you can see in Figure 1.85, all we need to do is use a virtual IP address and virtual MAC address. No one router owns the virtual IP address or the virtual MAC address. However, they all respond to ARP requests with the configured virtual MAC address. Two protocols are used for creating highly available default gateways: *Virtual Router Redundancy Protocol (VRRP)* and *Hot Standby Router Protocol (HSRP)*.

VRRP is an open standard FHRP for creating highly available routers. VRRP functions in an active/passive configuration; only the active router will answer requests for ARP requests for the virtual IP address with the associated virtual MAC address. If the active router fails, the passive router will become the new active router and start serving ARP requests for the virtual IP address and the associated virtual MAC address.

HSRP is a Cisco proprietary FHRP for creating highly available routers. HSRP also functions as an active/passive configuration. The operation of HSRP is identical to VRRP, except that all devices must be Cisco devices.

FIGURE 1.85   Typical FHRP setup

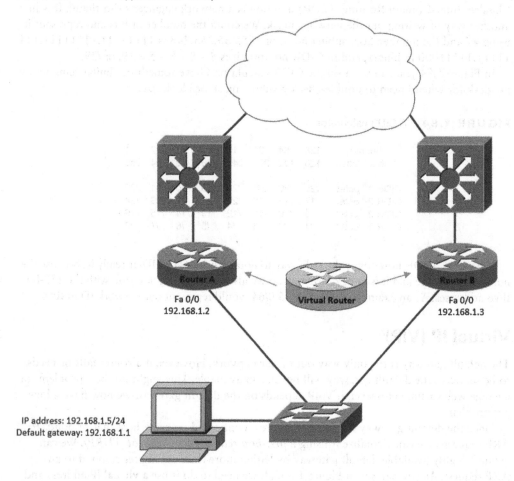

IP address: 192.168.1.5/24
Default gateway: 192.168.1.1

Exam Essentials

Know the various private and public IP address schemes. RFC 1918 defines the three private IP address schemes for Class A, Class B, and Class C networks of 10.0.0.0/8, 172.16.0.0/12, and 192.168.0.0/16. Public IP addresses are assigned by IANA and the RIR for your region.

Know the various special IP addresses that are considered reserved. Several special IP addresses are reserved, as per RFC 5735. The short list of special IP addresses discussed in the section "Loopback and Reserved" should be committed to memory; they are the most common reserved IP addresses.

Understand how the default gateway is used in networks for routing. The default gateway is configured to the IP address of the router in the network. The router allows for hosts on the immediate network to be routed to the remote networks. It serves as a gateway out of the immediate network.

Understand the concepts of NAT and PAT.   Network address translation (NAT) allows IP addresses to masquerade as different IP addresses on a network or the Internet. The translation between the two IP addresses allows for network address overlap and private IP addresses to be routed on the public Internet. Port address translation (PAT) allows for multiple IP addresses to use a single IP address. PAT creates a translation that includes the source and destination port of the packet.

Understand the concepts of port forwarding.   Port forwarding is used when a host is behind a NAT process. It allows for a specific destination port from the outside IP address to be translated to the inside IP address and destination port.

Understand how virtual IP addresses are used to create redundancy.   A virtual IP address and virtual MAC address are associated with a first-hop redundancy protocol (FHRP). FHRPs used for redundancy are Virtual Router Redundancy Protocol (VRRP) and Hot Standby Router Protocol (HSRP).

Understand the relevance of the subnet mask and how it is used.   The subnet mask defines the network the host belongs to. Through the process of ANDing, the host calculates its immediate network. Then the host calculates the network of the destination address. These two calculations help the host decide if the traffic is local or remote.

Be able to articulate key concepts of IPv6.   IPv6 was created by the IETF to combat the problem of IPv4 address exhaustion. IPv6 is a 128-bit address written as a hexadecimal. There are various ways to shorten the IPv6 address, such as by removing the leading zeros and multiple zeros between the colons in the address. Global unicast addresses (2000::/3) are the same as public IP addresses in IPv4. Link-local addresses (fe80::/10) are the same as link-local addresses in IPv4 and always start with fe80. Unique local addresses (fc00::/7) are similar to private IP addresses in IPv4 and always start with fc00. Multicast (ff00::/8) is similar to multicast addresses in IPv4 and always starts with ff00. Router Advertisement and Router Solicitation packets are ICMPv6 packets used to support IPv6 network assignment, gateway discovery, and neighbor discovery.

Understand how subnetting is performed and how it is used.   Subnetting is the process of creating smaller logical networks from a larger logical network. This is performed for routing between VLANs and geographic use of IP networks for WAN connections, among other reasons. We subnet a logical network by using the bits from the host section of the IP address and changing its subnet mask. CIDR notation is the total number of bits used for the network address and is expressed with a slash after the network address, followed by the number of bits used.

Know the various methods of assigning IP addressing for hosts via auto-assignment, dynamic assignment, and static assignment.   Static assignment should be reserved only for servers and networking equipment that must always have the same IP address. DHCP is the most common method for assigning IP addressing to hosts because it is centrally administered. Auto-assignment is the method used with IPv6 because DHCPv6 can be used to assign options or addresses for IPv6. When auto-assignment is used with IPv4, it is nonroutable and often called APIPA addressing.

1.5 Explain common ports and protocols, their application, and encrypted alternatives.

As a network professional, you will be expected to be fluent in acronyms. You'll run across lots and lots of acronyms, and knowing their definitions is going to be the easy part. Understanding the practical application of these protocols will be what defines your knowledge of networking concepts.

Protocols and Ports

In the following sections, I will introduce numerous protocols that are used to support network communications and administer networking components as well as configure and troubleshoot networking components. The following are associated with each of these protocols:

- A Transport layer protocol in which it operates
- A port number where it listens for requests

SSH (22)

Secure Shell (SSH) is a cryptographic protocol that is used to remotely administer Linux servers and network equipment through a text console. The SSH protocol uses public-key cryptology to authenticate and encrypt network access from the remote computer. This allows the user to securely log in without risk of the password being transmitted in clear text. Once the user is authenticated, all network transmissions are uniquely encrypted. The SSH protocol listens for incoming requests on TCP port 22. It is common practice for cloud providers to use SSH for authentication of administrators. The cloud provider will supply the private key of the keypair to the administrator. The private key is downloaded only one time by the administrator because it is not stored on the cloud provider's server. The private key is also protected by a passphrase (password) that unlocks the key and allows authentication of the administrator's credentials.

DNS (53)

Domain Name System (DNS) is a distributed directory of domain resource records. The resource records are primarily used in translating *fully qualified domain names (FQDNs)* to IP addresses, such as www.sybex.com to an IP address of 208.215.179.132. DNS can also be used for other lookups, such as IP addresses to FQDNs (called reverse DNS lookups) and for locating services such as Lightweight Directory Access Protocol (LDAP) servers. I will cover DNS in more depth in objective 1.6, "Explain the use and purpose of network services." DNS resolvers operate on UDP port 53 for simple lookups. DNS servers also use TCP port 53 (called the zone transfer) for data replication.

SMTP (25)

Simple Mail Transport Protocol (SMTP) is a protocol used by *mail transfer agents (MTAs)* to deliver emails to a destination email server. The protocol is used only in the process of delivering the email to the email server. Other protocols (such as Internet Message Access Protocol [IMAP] and Post Office Protocol [POP]) on the email server are responsible for client access. I will cover both of these protocols later. SMTP operates on TCP port 25, where the server awaits an incoming delivery of email from the MTA.

SMTP TLS (587)

The Simple Mail Transport Protocol (SMTP) can operate over Transport Layer Security (TLS). When SMTP is encrypted over TLS, it uses TCP port 587. All mail will be encrypted in transit when SMTP TLS encryption is used. SMTP TLS also requires authentication depending on the service you use it with, such as Office 365.

SFTP (22)

Secure File Transfer Protocol (SFTP) is a file transfer protocol that uses the SSH inner workings. When SSH is installed on a system such as Linux, SFTP is automatically enabled to transfer files. The command used on many of these systems is scp, which stands for Secure Copy Protocol. Since SFTP is used with the SSH protocol, the server awaits an incoming connection on TCP port 22.

FTP (20, 21)

File Transfer Protocol (FTP) is a legacy file-sharing protocol that is still commonly used on the Internet. FTP is slowly being replaced with SFTP because SFTP offers encryption and doesn't have the firewall issues FTP has. FTP is an odd protocol; it consists of a control channel and a data channel. FTP also operates in two modes: active and passive. In both modes, the command channel, also known as the control channel, listens for requests on TCP port 21 on the FTP server. This is generally why we associate FTP with port 21. The control channel is responsible for receiving commands from the FTP client and processing those commands.

The data channel works differently in active mode than it does in passive mode, as shown in Figure 1.86. In active mode, when a server needs to transfer a file or information (such as a directory listing) to the client, the information comes from TCP port 20 on the server and is sent to a destination port above TCP 1023 directed to the client; this port is communicated through the control channel. This behavior creates a problem on firewalled networks and networks that use network address translation (NAT) because the client awaits the incoming request from the server on a different port than it initially communicated on. Passive mode was created to address this problem; in passive mode, the client initiates the data channel from a port above TCP 1023 and sends it to a waiting port on the server above TCP 1023. The behavior of the client initiating the transmission to the server for the data channel is what firewalled and NAT networks expect as a dataflow.

TFTP (69)

Trivial File Transfer Protocol (TFTP) is a handy protocol because it provides no security and is simplistic in its operation. TFTP is used to boot computers over the network with the Preboot Execution Environment (PXE). It is also used to transfer software images for network devices such as routers and switches during software upgrades. Network devices also use TFTP to back up and restore configurations. The TFTP server listens for requests on UDP port 69. It is often used during upgrades and configuration backup/restores, and the network administrator starts the TFTP server on their workstation. The network administrator can then copy the file(s) to or from the TFTP server to complete the task.

FIGURE 1.86   FTP active and passive modes

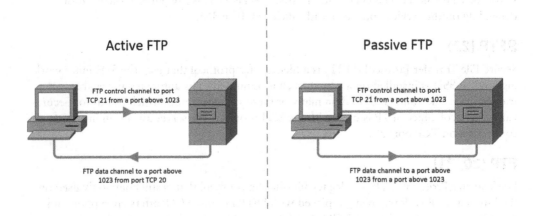

Telnet (23)

Telnet is another legacy protocol slowly being replaced by the SSH protocol. The Telnet protocol allows remote administration of network devices through a text-based console. One major disadvantage of Telnet is its lack of encryption compared to SSH. A Telnet server or device will await connection on TCP port 23.

DHCP (67, 68)

Dynamic Host Configuration Protocol (DHCP) is a protocol that provides automatic configuration of IP addresses, subnet masks, and options such as Domain Name System (DNS) servers and the remote gateway to network devices. DHCP operates in a connectionless state because during the process the client does not yet have an established IP address. During the configuration process, the DHCP server waits for a request from clients on UDP port 67. Clients will send the initial request from UDP port 68, as shown in Figure 1.87. When the server responds to the client, it responds to UDP port 68 from UDP port 67. You will find DHCP in use in everything from small home networks to large enterprise networks.

FIGURE 1.87   An overview of the DHCP process

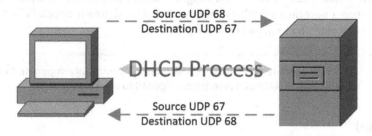

HTTP (80)

Hypertext Transfer Protocol (HTTP) is an application protocol for web data communications. When a web page is requested from a web server, an HTTP request is made for the Hypertext Markup Language (HTML) page. When the page is returned to the web browser, subsequent requests are made for the elements in the HTML page (such as images and JavaScript); all of this is done via HTTP. Web browsers are only one type of user agent (UA) that can request objects via HTTP. Many other UAs exist, including web crawlers and mobile apps. The server listens for incoming requests on TCP port 80.

HTTPS [Transport Layer Security (TLS)] (443)

Hypertext Transfer Protocol over Secure Sockets Layer (SSL), also known as HTTPS, is also a method for web data communications. It provides the same functionality as HTTP but also allows for the encryption of these transfers via Secure Sockets Layer (SSL). SSL is a cryptographic suite of protocols that uses Public Key Infrastructure (PKI). The web server listens for requests on TCP port 443. A private key must be imported into the web server from a mutually trusted source to allow SSL to properly work. The name HTTPS should carry a disclaimer since SSL has been deprecated from the SSL suite of protocols as per the Internet Engineering Task Force (IETF) because of security issues. SSL is referred to as both a protocol and a suite of protocols, that contains SSL and TLS. As of the writing of this book, TLS 1.3 is the current standard used for encryption with HTTPS SSL cryptography suite.

SNMP (161/162)

Simple Network Management Protocol (SNMP) is a protocol used for the management of servers and network devices. SNMP can be used to collect data from servers and network devices such as memory, CPU, and bandwidth. When used in this way, the data is read from a centralized network management station (NMS). The NMS is then responsible for arranging the data into an acceptable display such as a graph; this allows an administrator to create a baseline of performance.

SNMP can also be used in a trap configuration. If a certain variable such as CPU usage crosses a threshold the administrator has set, the SNMP agent can send a trap message to the NMS. Traps are sent to UDP port 162. The NMS will then notify an administrator that something is wrong using a text message or email.

SNMP can also be used in a writable mode. This is often done with network equipment because SNMP requests can be sent to reconfigure the equipment. An example of reconfiguration is changing a port on a switch to another virtual local area network (VLAN). SNMP agents and servers listen for requests on UDP port 161.

 SNMP operates on UDP by default and is commonly supported via UDP. However, SNMP can also be configured to operate on TCP.

RDP (3389)

Remote Desktop Protocol (RDP) is a Microsoft protocol used for connecting to another Microsoft computer or server for remote administration. RDP has been built into the Microsoft operating systems since Windows 2003. Prior to Windows 2003, it was called Terminal Services. The RDP client built into the Microsoft operating system is `mstsc.exe` (the Microsoft Terminal Services Client). The operating system listens for requests on TCP port 3389.

NTP (123)

Network Time Protocol (NTP) is a network protocol that is optimized for synchronizing clocks between computers over the Internet. Because there is a round-trip delay in requesting time over the Internet, NTP uses an algorithm for calculating the precise time accounting for this delay. NTP listens for requests on UDP port 123. The requesting host will send requests from UDP port 123 as well. NTP is a rare protocol that uses a symmetrical port for both the request and reply of the NTP packet.

SIP (5060, 5061)

Session Initiation Protocol (SIP) is a communication protocol for the setup and signaling of Voice over IP (VoIP) calls. SIP does not transport the media stream—it only assists in setting up the media stream for the communication session. SIP is a text-based protocol developed by the *Internet Engineering Task Force (IETF)*. It is extremely extensible, so new functionality can be added. You will find that many VoIP private branch exchange (PBX) manufacturers add functionality to SIP. These proprietary functions add functionality to the vendors' SIP phones while providing basic backward compatibility with other SIP phones. The SIP protocol operates on UDP port 5060, although it can operate on TCP as well. SIP can also use encryption via *Transport Layer Security (TLS)* on UDP port 5061 and can be changed to TCP if needed.

A VoIP PBX will communicate with VoIP phones and the SIP provider via SIP. When a VoIP phone joins the VoIP PBX, a SIP registration is exchanged and authentication occurs. Once the VoIP phone is registered to the VoIP PBX, SIP notifications occur that act as a keepalive and register the state of the VoIP phone. Information transmitted in the notify packets can include line events, message-waiting indicator status, and do not disturb status. During a call setup, the VoIP phone will communicate with the VoIP PBX to negotiate codecs for the call and the IP address and port number that the Real-time Transport Protocol (RTP) will use to transport the voice data.

In addition to VoIP phones, SIP is used for the SIP trunk. The SIP trunk connects the VoIP PBX to the public switched telephone network (PSTN).

SMB (445)

The Server Message Block (SMB) protocol is a common network file and printer sharing protocol that is used with Microsoft products. It is also referred to as the Common Internet File System (CIFS). However, when referring to SMB as CIFS, it is implied that SMB 1.*x* is in use. Many network attached storage (NAS) units support the SMB protocol as the filer protocol. I cover storage technologies in Chapter 2, "Domain 2.0: Network Implementations." Linux also has an SMB filer called Samba that is compatible with the SMB file protocol for file and printer sharing. The SMB protocol is enabled on every server and client in a Microsoft network. The SMB protocol waits for a connection on TCP port 445.

Over the years Microsoft has updated the SMB protocol to overcome security issues, speed, negotiation, and failover. The current specification of SMB is 3.1.1. SMB 3.1.1 is used for database and virtual machine storage over the network. It now supports many features of block-level storage protocols, such as remote direct memory access (RDMA), failover, and *Advanced Encryption Standard (AES) encryption.*

 The term *filer* is used to describe the function of file sharing with high-level protocols, such as Server Message Blocks (SMBs) and Network File System (NFS). You find the term used throughout this book.

POP (110)

The Post Office Protocol (POP), also known as POP3, is a legacy protocol, but it's still used on the Internet today. POP is slowly being replaced with IMAP.

POP allows email clients, also called *mail user agents (MUAs)*, to log in and retrieve email. Common email clients are Microsoft Outlook and Mozilla Thunderbird. POP listens for requests to the server on TCP port 110. When an email client initially connects to the POP server, it will download the mail from the server. This creates a problem when multiple email clients are used because only the last email client to access the POP server will have the latest mail.

POP3 over SSL (995)

Although POP3 is a legacy protocol, it is still used for legacy applications and transmits information in clear text. Therefore, POP3 over SSL can be employed to encrypt any data in transit. The caveat is that the mail client must support POP3 over SSL, which operates on TCP port 995.

IMAP (143)

Internet Message Access Protocol (IMAP) is used to allow email clients to retrieve and read email on the email server. IMAP allows for multiple email clients to access the same email box simultaneously. This multi-email client access is one of the reasons IMAP is so popular and POP is becoming outdated. IMAP also uses flags on the messages so that email clients can keep track of which emails are read and unread. IMAP listens for incoming connections on the email server from email clients on TCP port 143.

IMAP over SSL (993)

IMAP can also operate over SSL, because by default it is a clear-text protocol. So, any data in transit can be intercepted on TCP port 143. When encryption is used, all data transmitted is encrypted on TCP port 993.

LDAP (389)

Lightweight Directory Access Protocol (LDAP) is an application protocol that can search a directory service for objects. Microsoft Active Directory (AD) is an example of a directory service that uses LDAP to locate objects. AD uses directory services to locate objects such as domain controllers (DCs) and user objects for Group Policy (GP) application. An LDAP client communicates to LDAP servers on TCP port 389; it can also use UDP port 389.

LDAPS (636)

Lightweight Directory Access Protocol over SSL (LDAPS) is the application protocol of LDAP when SSL is configured. By default, on Microsoft networks LDAP traffic is unencrypted. However, by installing an SSL certificate into AD, you enable the LDAPS protocol. Any open-source versions of LDAP also allow for LDAPS to be enabled with the same process of installing an SSL certificate. LDAPS operates on TCP port 636 and can also use UDP port 636.

H.323 (1720)

H.323 is a recommendation by the ITU Telecommunication Standardization Sector (ITU-T) for communications over the Internet. The H.323 protocol is similar to the SIP protocol but different in the respect that it encompasses all of the communications technologies used by VoIP and videoconferencing. The H.323 protocol performs call setup on TCP port 1720.

The H.323 protocol has four main functionality areas:

- Terminal control, which provides endpoint signaling such as the VoIP phone itself

- Gateway services that provide transcoding functionality as well as communications with circuit-switched and packet-switched networks

- Gatekeeper services that provide admission control (authentication and authorization), bandwidth control, and management of endpoints (also known as zone management)

- The multipoint control unit (MCU), which provides conference call capabilities and call control of data, voice, and video for future in-call conferencing

Syslog (514)

A syslog server sits and waits for a syslog message: it sounds simple and it really is. However, the main purpose of syslog is to allow for postmortem of problems and security-related events. For example, if you had a fan failure on a router and it just rebooted, all logs would be gone because they are stored in RAM. However, if a syslog server was configured, you would have a good chance of understanding why the router died. A message would be sent to the syslog server showing that the fan died; at least that is what should happen. If it's a security-related event, then the logs may help put together what actually happened. Syslog awaits messages on UDP port 514.

SQL (1433)

Structured Query Language (SQL) is a generic term for the language a SQL server talks, and it does not specify a particular implementation. However, the term *SQL server* is synonymous with Microsoft SQL Server. The key take-away is that when you see TCP port 1433, you associate it with Microsoft SQL Server traffic.

MySQL (3306)

MySQL is an open-source relational database system, similar to Microsoft SQL Server. The language of MySQL is extremely similar to the Microsoft implementation, and if you wanted to use a query, very minor changes would need to be made. The key take-away is that when you see TCP port 3306, you associate it with MySQL.

SQLnet (1521)

SQLnet is a proprietary networking software developed by Oracle. It enables communication between Oracle databases, so information can be exchanged for queries. The protocol enables client-to-server or server-to-server operations. The SQLnet protocol operates on TCP port 1521.

IP Protocol Types

We just finished a review of different protocols at the upper layers of TCP/IP. During the review of these protocols, I made several references to TCP and UDP. Both of these protocols are part of the TCP/IP protocol stack and provide support for the application and application protocols you just learned. In the following sections, we will take a closer look at the protocols that make up the TCP/IP stack.

ICMP

Internet Control Message Protocol (ICMP) is a support protocol for TCP/IP that operates alongside of the IP protocol on the Network layer. It is used by networking devices such as routers to identify operation problems, such as a gateway that is no longer responsive. A router will create an ICMP packet back to the originating host of network traffic if the destination network is unreachable.

The `ping.exe` and `traceroute.exe` commands also use ICMP to help technicians perform troubleshooting of the network. ICMP operates at layer 3 of the OSI.

In IPv6, the ICMP protocol has a much larger role than it does in IPv4. ICMP in IPv6 is responsible for the Neighbor Discovery Protocol (NDP), which is the equivalent of the Address Resolution Protocol (ARP) in IPv4. ICMP in IPv6 is also responsible for the discovery of the network gateway(s) with ICMP *Router Solicitation (RS)* and *Router Advertisement (RA)* packets so that hosts can find a way out of the network. In addition, ICMP in IPv6 performs duplicate address detection (DAD) so that hosts do not duplicate IPv6 addressing.

UDP

The User Datagram Protocol (UDP) is a transport protocol for TCP/IP. UDP is one of two protocols at the Transport layer that connect network applications to the network. UDP is a connectionless, non-sequenced, and non-acknowledged protocol. Many of the applications that use UDP don't need the overhead of TCP. These applications include request/response and real-time protocols. As an example, the DNS protocol used UDP port 53 to request the IP address for a particular fully qualified domain name (FQDN). The request is usually one segment of data and the response is one segment of data back. No need to sequence the segments and acknowledge them. If the client doesn't get an answer, then the client will just ask again. Same with NTP; if a client doesn't get a response back, the client will ask again.

Real-time protocols use UDP because the segments are time-sensitive. If data is lost and one side were to wait for the data or be delayed because of TCP acknowledging the data, a snowball effect would happen, introducing delay. RTPs just elect to forget the data ever got transmitted. Think back to the last VoIP call you had. When people start to sound like robots because of network congestion, it's because packets are getting dropped or the RTP application is just moving along to keep up so the conversation is in real time.

TCP

Transmission Control Protocol (TCP) is another transport protocol for TCP/IP. Just like the UDP protocol, TCP is a protocol at the Transport layer that connects network applications to the network. TCP is a connection-oriented, sequenced, and acknowledged protocol. Applications that use TCP are applications that are moving data. The developer chose to use TCP because they wanted to ensure that the data is populated by the requesting client. If the user has to wait, then so be it; as long as the data is eventually received, it doesn't matter. An example of this is when you request a web page and there is congestion on the network, the page will painfully render. HTTP and HTTPS are protocols that use TCP for its ensured delivery. You also find that some protocols like DNS use UDP and TCP. DNS uses UDP port 53 for simple queries, but when a zone transfer needs to take place, TCP port 53 is used. The general rule of thumb is any application that needs to move non-time-sensitive data will use TCP.

Generic Routing Encapsulation (GRE)

Generic Router Encapsulation (GRE) is a layer 3 protocol that allows you to create tunnels over an Internetwork, such as the Internet. The concept of overlay and underlay networks is a component to understanding GRE. The GRE tunnel itself is considered an overlay network because it travels over an underlay network like the Internet. When it comes to understanding overlay and underlay networks, this is probably the easiest way to understand the concept. You will see this concept throughout this exam, usually in relation to software-defined networks, but it is also applicable for GRE. In Figure 1.88, we see the overlay network for GRE, and we also see the Internet that GRE overlays on top. Office A and Office B believe they are directly connected by Router A and Router B, even though there are several Internet routers between them.

FIGURE 1.88   GRE tunnel example

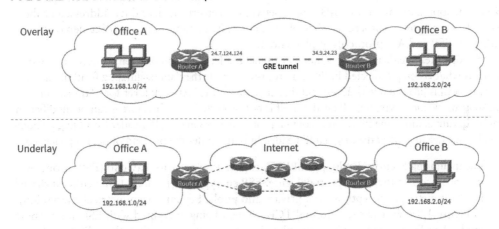

So, you may wonder how this benefits us and what application it serves? Without GRE, using a routing protocol such as Open Shortest Path First (OSPF) between two offices separated by the Internet would be impossible. However, because the overlay network believes Router A and Router B are directly connected using GRE, OSPF will work perfectly fine. GRE performs this by encapsulating the original packet with a GRE header, then sending the GRE packet to the destination router in a regular IP packet, as shown in Figure 1.89. GRE is a Network layer protocol and inside the IP packet the protocol number is 47.

FIGURE 1.89   A GRE Packet

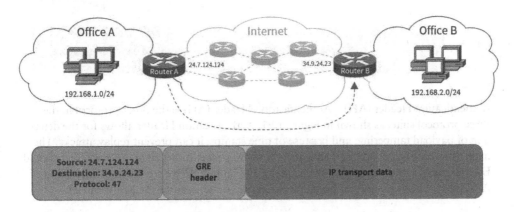

GRE sounds like a great protocol for tunneling data from end to end. However, be warned: GRE is a clear-text protocol. Although we can tunnel packets through an Internetwork, we have no assurance of privacy.

Internet Protocol Security (IPSec)

Internet Protocol Security (IPSec) is a combination of two protocols that encrypt data (Encapsulating Security Payload [ESP]) and assure that data has not been altered in transit (Authentication Header [AH]). IPSec allows private tunnels to be created that are impervious to eavesdropping or tampering. IPSec is a Network layer protocol, and it's addressed at the network layer with a protocol number of 50 and 51. It is common to see IPSec deployed with both ESP and AH protocols implemented.

IPSec operates in either transport mode or tunnel mode. The main different between the two modes is what is being protected in IPSec. In transport mode the data originating from the transport protocol is protected with IPSec and then it is sent to the Network layer for IP transit. In transport mode the originating IP header itself is not protected, and therefore it can be modified in transit. In tunnel mode the IPSec protocol will protect the originating IP header by adding an additional IP header to protect the original IP header. In both modes the payload of data is protected.

Encapsulating Security Payload (ESP)   Encapsulating Security Payload (ESP) is one of two protocols in the IPSec protocol suite. ESP encrypts the payload using either a shared key (symmetrical encryption) or a private and public keypair (asymmetrical encryption). In Figure 1.90, we can see a normal TCP segment being encrypted with ESP in transport mode. The Transport layer is encapsulated as data and encrypted with an ESP header and ESP tail. The ESP authentication data is then used to authenticate the ESP header data and ESP tail. The payload data and ESP tail are encrypted.

FIGURE 1.90   ESP Packet

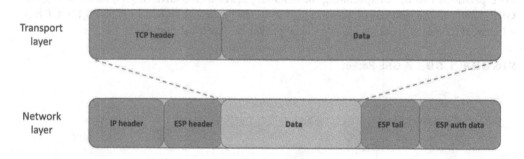

Authentication Header (AH)   Authentication Header (AH) is the other protocol in the IPSec protocol suite, as shown in Figure 1.91. Authentication Header allows for the detection of payload tampering, and because of time stamps, it can prevent replay attacks. The main difference is that AH authenticates the entire packet rather than just the ESP data and ESP tail, such as the case with just ESP alone. In Figure 1.92 we see the implementation of AH and ESP. It's important to note that the entire packet is authenticated with AH.

FIGURE 1.91   AH packet

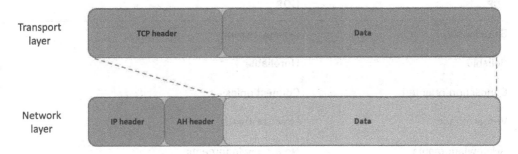

FIGURE 1.92   AH and ESP

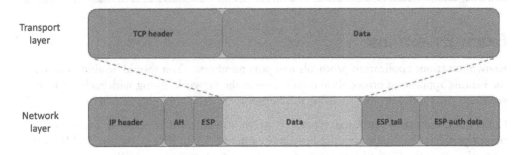

Connection-Oriented vs. Connectionless

A connection-oriented protocol is the TCP protocol. During the conversation with the destination computer, both the source and destination share information about each other and the progress of the data transfer. TCP establishes a connection with the other computer using a three-way handshake. During the three-way handshake, information about both sides of the connection is shared, and the connection is established.

A connectionless protocol is the UDP protocol. During the transfer with the destination computer, neither the source nor the destination knows the progress of the data transfer. That statement does not imply that the data transfer is unknown—it is only unknown at the Transport layer. Upper-layer protocols that use UDP might keep track of the data transfer depending on the application. If the application is TFTP and you are transferring a file, the TFTP application is going to be responsible for retransmission of missing segments of data.

Because UDP and TCP are both used at the Transport layer for the TCP/IP protocol, it is important to understand the differences between the two protocols. Both protocols are used to connect network applications to the network, and both UDP and TCP are used differently by the developer of the application.

It is important to note that if an application solely uses either TCP or UDP, unless it is rewritten, you as the administrator cannot change the protocol. Table 1.4 shows a list of features for both UDP and TCP.

TABLE 1.4   Key features of UDP and TCP

TCP	UDP
Sequenced	Unsequenced
Reliable	Unreliable
Connection-oriented	Connectionless
Virtual circuit	Low overhead
Acknowledgments	No acknowledgments
Windowing flow control	No windowing or flow control of any type

Exam Essentials

Know the various application protocols and port numbers.   You should be able to define the various application protocols and their uses in the network. Along with each application protocol, you should be able to define the transport protocol and port number.

Understand the various protocol types.   ICMP is a protocol that helps with the notification of problems to the originating host in IPv4 networks. In IPv6 networks, ICMP is an integral part of the IPv6 addressing and communications processes. UDP is a connectionless Transport layer protocol; it is fast and normally used for question-and-answer type dialogues. TCP is a connection-oriented Transport layer protocol; it is slower than UDP and more reliable.

Know the various tunneling protocols.   The GRE protocol is a tunneling protocol that allows a tunnel to be created over an internetwork. The GRE protocol is a layer 3 clear-text protocol. IPSec is a layer 3 tunneling protocol used for privacy over a network. IPSec contains two subprotocols, ESP and AH; ESP is used for encryption, and AH is used for packet integrity.

Know the differences between connection-oriented and connectionless protocols.   Connection-oriented protocols, such as TCP, create a virtual connection between the two endpoints for data transfer. Connectionless protocols such as UDP do not create connections at the Transport layer. The applications are expected to create a connection between the endpoints if reliability of data is required. You should know the differences between UDP and TCP.

1.6 Explain the use and purpose of network services.

When we are building networks, there are essential services that all networks require to operate: name resolution, dynamic assignment of IP addresses, synchronization of time, and management of IP address resources. As networks scale out, these essential services help manage and maintain the network and are usually centrally managed.

DNS

The hosts file is a static file that was originally used for translation of hosts to IP addresses. It was centrally managed and used in the early days of the ARPAnet, when there was a limited number of hosts. However, as the ARPAnet expanded into the Internet back in 1983, DNS was proposed and created to decentralize the name resolution process. The hosts file still exists today locally on operating systems as an override to DNS.

Domain Name System (DNS) is a decentralized hierarchical database used for resolving fully qualified domain names (FQDNs) to IP addresses. An FQDN is a name that has been registered with a name authority and resolves to an IP address. An example of an FQDN is www.wiley.com, which resolves to 208.215.179.146. Computers need the numeric IP address to retrieve our data, but as humans we have a hard time remembering phone numbers let alone IP addresses. We also use DNS to resolve for other name resolution record types, as I will discuss in the following section.

Record Types

DNS is decentralized technology using zone files to partition the domain namespace. This partitioning allows for the namespace to be delegated. The zone file contains resource records, such as FQDN–to–IP address records. These resource records allow DNS to perform more than just IP address lookups. In the following examples, I will use the *Berkeley Internet Name Domain (BIND)* file convention. These example are the most common records you will encounter on a DNS server.

A (Address Record)

A records allow a host to resolve an FQDN to an IPv4 address, also called a forward DNS query. We use these records every time we visit an address like www.wiley.com or www.sybex.com; they resolve to an IP address.

```
; host   class  record   IP address
  ns1     IN     A        192.168.1.1
  ns2     IN     A        192.168.1.2
  www     IN     A        192.168.1.3
```

AAAA (Quad A Record)

AAAA records are the IPv6 equivalent of an A record. It allows a host to resolve an FDQN to an IPv6 IP address.

```
; host       class  record   IP address
  mail       IN     AAAA     2001:db8::1
  www        IN     AAAA     2001:db8::2
  terminal   IN     AAAA     2001:db8::3
```

TXT (SPF, DKIM)

TXT records allow for text to be queried from DNS. TXT records are often used for proof of ownership of a domain name, such as management of search engine crawling. Mail servers use TXT records for identifying the authorized IP addresses of originating mail servers. The Sender Policy Framework (SPF) record is used to define these IP addresses so that other mail servers can combat spam. Domain Keys Identified Mail (DKIM) records allow for organizations to authenticate messages sent through a cryptographic key stored in the TXT record.

```
; SPF Record
@        IN TXT "v=spf1 mx a ptr ip4:208.215.179.0/24"


; DKIM Record
1500514958.wiley._domainkey.www.wiley.com. IN TXT (
"v=DKIM1;t=s;p=MIGfMA0GCSqGSIb3DQEBAQUAA4GNADCBiQKBgQC3pAs2gR+4d0Bjl9nE7n20LJyY"
         "XcabqzpAgsjquwf73TOoNJKto/adyB3zHGAriQWAWja8hBdrlFX28Q8vG/11F0nu"
         "/xda3KcdNWIHC71oKkY3WNAEOTj3ofXJ7w4R/lucZGh5+fr1PCU2Ym0x6w5ZOO+0"
         "e6LKFS64pVRRM3OLpQIDAQAB")
```

SRV (Service Locator Records)

SRV records are used for locating services such as LDAP, which is used by Active Directory and Linux for login services. The SRV record is formatted with the service name and protocol followed by the time to live (TTL), class (Internet), SRV, priority, weight, port number, and target FQDN. The lowest priority gets used first and the weight helps the client decide if multiple entries for the same service exist.

```
;_service._proto.name.TTL    class record priority weight port target
_ldap._tcp.wiley.com. 86400 IN    SRV    10       50     389  ldap.example.com.
_sip._tcp.wiley.com.  86400 IN    SRV    10       50     5060 sip.example.com.
```

MX (Mail Exchanger)

MX records assist a mail server in identifying the mail server for your domain. You must publish an MX record for your mail server if you want to receive mail from other mail servers. The @ symbol refers to the domain the zone file belongs to, and the priority is how the sending server picks the host to send mail to; the lowest priority is chosen first.

```
;      class record  priority  target
@      IN    MX       10        mail1.example.com.
@      IN    MX       20        mail2.example.com.
@      IN    MX       30        mail3.example.com.
```

CNAME (Canonical Name)

CNAME records allow an FQDN to resolve to an A record. This is quite handy when you have one host that has multiple names. Although multiple A records could be created if you ever change the IP address, all of them would need to be updated. With a CNAME record that points to a single A record, only the A record's IP address would need to be changed.

```
; host   class  record  target
  sftp   IN     CNAME   www.example.com.
  ftp    IN     CNAME   www.example.com.
  www    IN     A       192.168.1.3
```

NS (Name Server)

NS records contain all the servers responsible for a particular zone file. If a DNS server does not have an NS record, it is not allowed to perform a zone transfer (copying the zone).

```
;      class  record  target
@      IN     NS      192.168.1.1
@      IN     NS      192.168.1.2
```

SOA (Start of Authority)

SOA records define a zone file and allow secondary DNS servers to know when the zone file has changed via the serial number, using a reverse date code; how often to check the primary zone file for changes via the refresh interval; how often to keep checking if it becomes unavailable via the retry interval; and what the default TTL (time to live) is for caching via the TTL. The NS records and their corresponding A records always follow the SOA record.

```
@ 1D  IN  SOA ns1.example.com. hostmaster.example.com. (
                  2017071901 ; serial yyyymmddss
                  1H ; refresh
                  15 ; retry
                  1w ; expire
                  1h ; ttl
                )
;      class  record  target
@      IN     NS      192.168.1.1
@      IN     NS      192.168.1.2
```

```
; host   class  record   IP address
  ns1    IN     A        192.168.1.1
  ns1    IN     A        192.168.1.2
```

PTR (Pointer Record)

PTR records allow a client to resolve an IP address to an FQDN. PTR record queries are called reverse lookups. This is useful for learning the name of a host. PTR records are mainly used by administrators.

```
; 1.168.192.IN-ADDR.ARPA. zone file
; host  class  record   FQDN
  1     IN     PTR      ns1.example.com.
  2     IN     PTR      ns2.example.com.
  3     IN     PTR      www.example.com.
```

Dynamic DNS

Dynamic DNS allows hosts to add and update their own A records. These records are normally only edited manually. However, when we use dynamic updates, we allow the hosts to maintain these records for us. Dynamic updates can also add and update PTR records by the host or with the assistance of a DHCP server. This allows reverse lookup PTR records to be automatically maintained as well. Dynamic updates help automate the entries into DNS and maintain the entries thereafter; they provide consistency for the administrator and services dependent on DNS.

Windows Server and Active Directory add an extra layer of protection with Active Directory integrated zones. The protection is provided to the entries by adding security information to the record when the host adds the record, and therefore only the host can modify or delete it. You can even prevent non-domain members from adding entries into DNS with the use of Secure Updates.

Internal vs. External DNS

Name authorities can be public, such as the root servers and registrar server, or they can be an internal DNS zone file (database), in which all the clients are pointed to a particular DNS server for name resolution.

It is common to have DNS servers dedicated to resolution of hosts on the Internet and DNS servers dedicated to resolution of hosts on the interior of our network. The two servers must be managed separately; this is called a *split-brain DNS* model. We need to do this because the DNS we provide for internal clients will resolve to private IP addresses, such as www.wiley.com to 192.168.1.1. Public DNS will resolve to a public IP address, such as www.wiley.com to 208.215.179.146.

It is best practice to separate out the internal DNS servers from external DNS servers. We can always use a different namespace outside versus inside, such as wiley.com and wiley.local. However, if the same server is used for both internal and external DNS, a malicious user can try to query internal names from the DNS and gain internal information.

Third-Party/Cloud-Hosted DNS

It is common practice as described in the preceding section to use separate DNS servers for internal and external queries. We do a good job as administrators of securing and operating internal DNS, but sometimes it is easier to outsource the external DNS.

When a public domain name (FQDN) is registered, it is common that the registrar will provide DNS for you. This solves the dilemma for the administrator of setting up an external DNS server. The registrar will often provide a simple web page to configure the DNS records for the FQDN.

If the number of records and maintenance of the external DNS is large, then we can always use IaaS. Many cloud providers, such as Amazon Web Servers (AWS), will provide cloud-based DNS. AWS offers a service called Route 53 that allows administrators to host DNS in the cloud. This service offers many features; one such feature allows a DNS record to be queried differently from a different region of the world via a route policy. Another unique feature allows for a DNS client to receive the lowest latency IP for servers hosted in the AWS cloud. Each provider will have unique features that average administrators would be hard-pressed to support themselves.

Hierarchy

DNS is a distributed hierarchy; think of it as a directory of directories where you will eventually resolve the FQDN to a resource record (IP address). In Figure 1.93, we see this distributed hierarchy.

When FQDNs are resolved, they are resolved from right to left with a dot at the end; this signifies the root of all DNS resolution. The root DNS servers point to the registrars of com, net, and gov, and the registrars point to the owner's DNS server, which keeps a database of resource records. In Figure 1.93 you see an example of two resource records for www and ftp for wiley.com.

FIGURE 1.93   DNS hierarchy

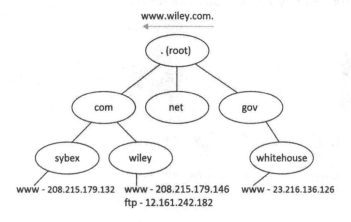

In the prior example, I explained the hierarchy of the DNS as it pertains to the Internet. Internal DNS environments also have a hierarchy. However, the internal domain is the starting zone record in lieu of the root domain. An example of this is `wiley.local.`, which would be hosted as a zone on the DNS server that all clients are pointed to for resolution.

In the following sections I will cover the most common types of DNS server configurations. A DNS server's job is either to resolve DNS on behalf of the client or to host a DNS zone, which can be considered a database of records. A DNS server can do both jobs, resolving clients and hosting zone files, or they can be specifically purposed.

Primary DNS Server

A primary DNS server's job is to host a domain's zone file. When the primary zone is hosted on the DNS server, the DNS server is considered the primary DNS server when referring to that particular zone. A zone must have at least one primary DNS server, which hosts the primary zone. This special primary zone is the only writable copy of the DNS zone file. The primary name server is called the authoritative name server since it is the only server that can write new records.

Secondary DNS Server

A secondary DNS server is not required, but it's a good idea to have one, since it is the backup copy of the zone file. The secondary zone file is updated through a zone transfer from the primary zone file. The server hosting the secondary zone is considered the secondary DNS server for that zone. A DNS server can both be a primary and secondary server, depending on which domain DNS zone file you are speaking about.

In Figure 1.94 we have two DNS servers hosting two different DNS zones. Server A is the primary DNS server for sybex.com and the secondary DNS server for wiley.com. Server B is the primary DNS server for wiley.com and the secondary DNS server for sybex.com. Server A and server B are both a primary and secondary DNS server, when speaking in the context of the zone file.

FIGURE 1.94   Primary and secondary DNS servers

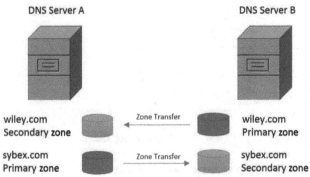

Zones and Zone Transfer

A zone is a database of resource records for a particular DNS path; for example, `wiley.com` would contain the records for `www`, `ftp`, `mail`, just to name a few. The writable copy of the zone is located on the primary DNS server and the secondary DNS server contains a copy as we learn the roles of the primary and secondary servers.

The Start of Authority (SOA) record is primarily responsible for keeping records up-to-date on the secondary servers. When a zone is created, the SOA record gets created and a serial number and refresh parameter are written. The refresh interval tells the secondary DNS servers how often to request a refresh of the SOA records. If the SOA serial number has gone up, then a zone transfer is performed.

There are two different types of zone transfers that can be performed by the primary DNS server: full and incremental. A full zone transfer is pretty obvious; it performs a full zone transfer of the zone file to the secondary server. An incremental zone transfer just sends the changes since the SOA serial number had incremented. In either case, zone transfers are normally performed over TCP port 53.

Time To Live (TTL)

Resource records can become stale, meaning that a resource might change its IP address. So, there is a time to live (TTL) that every record will abide by in a client or caching DNS server cache. The TTL can be set on a per-resource-record basis, or it can be defaulted in the SOA record.

Forwarding/Caching DNS Server

A forwarding DNS server is a server that forwards requests for DNS to another server such as an Internet service provider (ISP) DNS server. The server saves bandwidth by caching the answers, so the server does not need to make another request to the ISP's DNS server for the same thing. A forwarding/caching DNS server can also maintain a primary or secondary zone file.

Recursive Lookups/Iterative Lookups

In Figure 1.95, you see a typical DNS query path from client to the server hosting the resource record. The client is at the far left and it has a DNS resolver and cache. On the Windows operating systems this component is the DNS Client service. When the operating system needs to resolve an FQDN, it requests it from either your ISP's DNS server or an internal DNS server, such as in Figure 1.95. This is normal practice and it probably happens in your home with your router, where your router acts as a forward caching DNS server. The type of query sent is considered an iterative lookup since it is a directed query to the internal DNS server. The internal DNS server will cache the result and it can simultaneously host a zone. The internal server then performs an iterative query to your ISP's DNS server if it doesn't have the answer. The ISP's DNS server will most likely not have an answer to the query, so it will need to query the root server for the top-level domain (TLD) name server. Then the ISP's server will query the TLD server for the domain name. The ISP's server will then query the DNS server hosting the domain name for the resource record. This volley back and forth with the ISP's server and various servers, starting with root server to the resource record server, is called a recursive lookup.

FIGURE 1.95   DNS queries

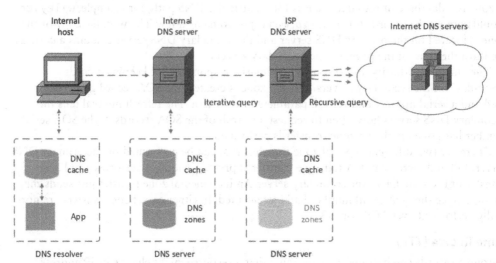

 Nothing stops you from performing recursive queries from your internal corporate DNS server. However, one consideration is security, because you will need to allow your internal DNS server to egress your network on UDP port 53 for any IP address. If you just allowed your ISP to do the recursive lookups, you only need one firewall entry to the ISP's DNS server for UDP port 53.

Forward vs. Reverse Zone

In the preceding sections, I covered the various DNS server types. You learned that primary DNS servers host the editable copy of the DNS zone file and the secondary DNS server is a read-only copy. When we host a zone file on the DNS server, there are two different types of zone files: forward and reverse zones.

Understanding the differences between forward and reverse zone types is easier once you know what a reverse zone is used for. Reverse zone types are used for reverse IP address resolution. This is handy when we are troubleshooting and we want to know the hostname an IP address belongs to. We can use reverse DNS with a reverse zone type and PTR records to reverse the IP to an FQDN.

Reverse zone files are named in reverse of the IP address. Let's use an IP address of 192.168.1.3 as an example. When we look at the IP address, the least specific portion starts with 192 and the most specific is the end of, 3. However, when we look at a DNS FQDN of www.example.com., the least specific is the root at the far right of the FQDN. The most specific portion is the www portion of the FQDN at the far left. Therefore, when hosting a reverse zone, we must reverse the IP address. In the example of 192.168.1.3, it would be

reversed as shown here. The 3 is the PTR record that is mapped to the FQDN of www
.example.com. The complete zone file with the SOA record is detailed here so that you can
see a working reverse zone file. It should be noted that the semicolon is nothing more than a
comment line. It allows you to create sections in a zone file for readability purposes.

```
; 1.168.192.IN-ADDR.ARPA. zone file example
@  1D    IN   SOA ns1.example.com. hostmaster.example.com. (
                        2017071901 ; serial yyyymmddss
                        1H ; refresh
                        15 ; retry
                        1w ; expire
                        1h ; ttl
                        )
; PTR records
1        IN   PTR    ns1.example.com.
2        IN   PTR    ns2.example.com.
3        IN   PTR    www.example.com.
4        IN   PTR    sip.example.com.
```

Forward zone files are used for lookups by DNS clients for destination and informational purposes. So, basically all other queries other than reverse queries are forward queries.
I've shared a complete zone file example from the individual examples covered earlier in
this section.

```
; example.com. zone file example
@  1D    IN   SOA ns1.example.com. hostmaster.example.com. (
                        2017071901 ; serial yyyymmddss
                        1H ; refresh
                        15 ; retry
                        1w ; expire
                        1h ; ttl
                        )
; name servers
@        IN   NS     192.168.1.1
@        IN   NS     192.168.1.2
; SPF Record
@        IN   TXT "v=spf1 mx a ptr ip4:208.215.179.0/24"
; mail servers
@        IN   MX  10   mail1.example.com.
@        IN   MX  20   mail2.example.com.
@        IN   MX  30   mail3.example.com.
; host records
sftp     IN   CNAME    www.example.com.
```

```
ftp       IN    CNAME    www.example.com.
ns1       IN    A        192.168.1.1
ns2       IN    A        192.168.1.2
www       IN    A        192.168.1.3
sip       IN    A        192.168.1.4
mail      IN    AAAA     2001:db8::1
www       IN    AAAA     2001:db8::2
terminal  IN    AAAA     2001:db8::3
; SRV records
_sip._tcp 86400 IN SRV 10 50 5060  sip.example.com.
```

DHCP Service

The purpose of the DHCP service is to assign an IPv4 address to clients dynamically as they join the network. Figure 1.96 shows the Windows Server 2019 DHCP server management console. This dialog box has not changed much since Windows NT 4.0, although new features have been added throughout the years, such as fault tolerance and load balancing. Microsoft server operating systems have supported DHCP since the NT product line was launched.

FIGURE 1.96   The Windows DHCP management console

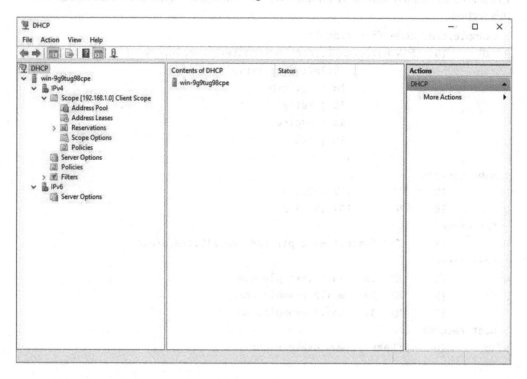

This is only one example of DHCP services. Linux and Unix operating systems also support DHCP services. They are just as common in networks as Microsoft DHCP servers. Router operating systems also support DHCP services. Most routers have a built-in process, and many default to serving out DHCP IP addresses. You more than likely have one in your home today.

Regardless of which DHCP server you run on your corporate network or even your home network, it will have common components that you will learn in the following sections. In Figure 1.97 you will see the various components of DHCP that we will review.

FIGURE 1.97   DHCP Components

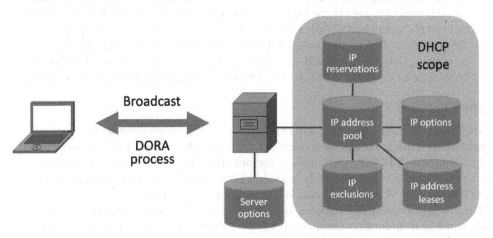

MAC Reservations

Dynamic assignment is preferable in networks via DHCP because we have centralized management of the IP addresses and associated options. We can change options such as DNS servers, and the DHCP clients will receive the changes next time they boot or renew their lease. However, sometimes we need a DHCP client to receive a specific IP address or the same address all the time. If we statically changed the IP address, we would be burdened with manually changing the DNS server if it ever changed.

Nearly all DHCP services allow for MAC address reservations. We can enter the MAC address of the DHCP client into the DHCP service and specify the desired IP address in the DHCP pool. In Microsoft DHCP services, we can right-click a current lease and convert it to a MAC reservation as well. When we add a reservation, the client will behave as if it is a DHCP client, but it will receive the same IP address every time.

Scope

DHCP pools are a logical grouping of consecutive IP addresses a DHCP server can serve out to clients. DHCP pools are called DHCP scopes in Microsoft terminology; both terms mean the same thing. You can have several DHCP scopes on the DHCP server. It is best practice to organize DHCP scopes for each subnet that is configured on the DHCP server. If possible, the DHCP scopes should be labeled with a description so that the purpose is clear to other administrators. Microsoft DHCP and most servers allow for a description.

IP Exclusions

As you learned in the previous section, IP pools, also called scopes, are consecutive IP addresses. An example of a consecutive range is 192.168.1.1 to 192.168.1.254. However, we need some reserved IP addresses for the gateway and possible servers in the range.

IP exclusions allow us to exclude a range of these IP addresses for service use. When we add an exclusion range, the DHCP server will exclude this range from the IP addresses served out. It is typical to reserve the lower portion of an address space for IP services. An exclusion example would be 192.168.1.1 to 192.168.1.10, using the earlier scope example.

It is also important to note that most DHCP servers will allow you to simply exclude ranges by entering only the range of IP addresses you want to serve to clients. An example would be to enter a range of 192.168.1.11 to 192.168.1.254, using the previous examples.

Scope Options

A DHCP server at a bare minimum will only serve out an IP address and subnet mask to clients. Although this is enough for a client to function on the local network, we need extra configurations called DHCP options. These options allow the client to leave the network, obtain name resolution, and obtain the complete DNS name for the host. You can even extend functionality of options via custom user-specific parameters.

The most important DHCP option is the router option. The router option configures a default gateway IP address on the client computer. This default gateway is how the client can leave the network through a router, so you can communicate with other subnets or the Internet. Another vital DHCP option is the DNS server IP address. Without DNS, we would need to memorize IP addresses; going to www.sybex.com would look like http://208.215.179.132. So a DNS server IP address configured on the client is also a bare necessity. We can configure another DHCP option for DNS called the DNS suffix or DNS domain name. This option allows the DNS resolver in your computer to append the DNS suffix to a request. As an example, when you enter http://www in a web browsers and the client is configured with a DNS suffix of sybex.com, the DNS resolver will try to resolve the FQDN of www.sybex.com. We can configure many other DHCP options for the client, but the router, DNS server, and DNS suffix options are the most important.

The Internet Assigned Numbers Authority (IANA) provides a complete list of DHCP options for reference at www.iana.org/assignments/bootp-dhcp-parameters/bootp-dhcp-parameters.xhtml. The client must understand how to use the various options.

Lease Time/TTL

A DHCP lease specifies a period of time the IP address given out by the DHCP server is good for. Both the server and the client keep track of the lease time. The server does not keep track if the IP address is in use; it only knows that the lease has been granted for a time period.

When the time period has expired or the lease is manually deleted, the IP address can be served to another computer. A DHCP lease should never be manually deleted from the server, unless you know it is no longer in use by the client.

After the initial DHCP DORA process, the server does not communicate with the client in reference to the DHCP lease period. It is the responsibility of the client to renew its lease. I will use the default lease cycle for a Windows DHCP server of 8 days for the following explanation of the DHCP lease life cycle in Figure 1.98. When the lease is granted to the client, the lease timer is started. At 50 percent of the lease (the fourth day), the client is responsible for renewing its lease with the DHCP server via a DHCP Request packet. If successful, the lease time is restarted for 8 days. If the DHCP server does not acknowledge the lease, the client will wait until 87.5 percent of the lease cycle (the seventh day), where it will send a DHCP Request to any server in hopes of "rebinding" the lease to another server. If a DHCP server does not acknowledge the rebind request, at 100 percent (the eighth day) of the lease, the client must release the IP address. The client will continue with the DHCP DORA process to obtain another IP address from any responding server.

FIGURE 1.98   The DHCP client lease life cycle

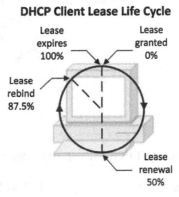

DHCP Client Lease Life Cycle

DHCP Relay/IP Helper

As I discussed earlier, the DHCP DORA process is dependent on broadcasts for a client to obtain a DHCP assigned address. Routers stop broadcasts and this presents a problem when we want to centrally manage DHCP from one point for all routed subnets. Luckily there is a fix for this problem: we can use an IP helper statement on a router or a DHCP relay agent.

We configure an IP helper/UDP forwarder on a router interface to intercept broadcasts for DHCP and forward them directly to the configured DHCP server IP address. In Figure 1.99, we see a network that is segmented with a router. The router will listen for DHCP Discover packets and forward them directly through unicast to the DHCP server. The DHCP server will send a unicast DHCP Offer packet back to the router, where the router will forward it back to the client. This process continues until the DORA process is complete.

A DHCP relay agent is a configured service on a server that intercepts broadcasts for DHCP and forwards them directly to the configured DHCP server IP address. The network in Figure 1.99 is configured like the one in Figure 1.100. The DHCP relay agent operates identically to an IP helper on a router. The difference is that it is a service on a server. If this was a branch office and the router didn't support IP helper configuration, a local file or print server could be configured as a DHCP relay agent.

FIGURE 1.99 An example of a network router configured with an IP helper

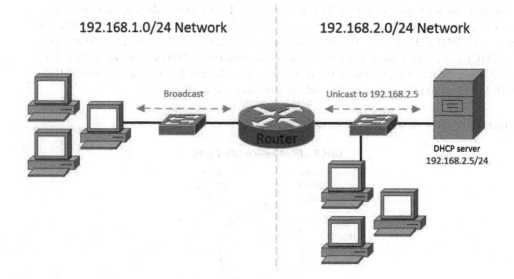

FIGURE 1.100 An example of a DHCP relay agent configured on a server

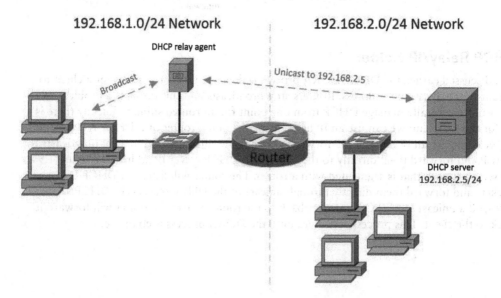

You may be wondering how the DHCP server knows which scope to serve the remote subnet when an IP helper or DHCP relay agent is used. The answer is the GIADDR (Gateway Interface Address) field of the DHCP packet is used when an IP helper or DHCP relay agent is present. The GIADDR field is filled with the IP address of either the IP helper interface or the DHCP relay agent IP address on which the broadcast was heard. It is the router or DHCP relay agent's responsibility to complete the GIADDR field. When the DHCP server receives the unicast packet from the DHCP relay agent, the scope to be served from is matched against the GIADDR IP address and the proper subnet scope is served.

NTP

Network Time Protocol (NTP) is a network protocol that is optimized for synchronizing clocks between hosts over the Internet. NTP uses a hierarchy of precision clocks called stratums.

A stratum 0 is the highest precision clock; it is generally an atomic cesium or rubidium clock. A stratum 1 is a host system that derives its clock from a stratum 0. A stratum 2 is a host system that derives its clock from a stratum 1, and so on. The highest stratum (lowest precision) is a stratum 15; a stratum 16 means that the host system's clock is not synchronized. NTP is also a client-server application and network devices can be both a client and server at the same time, Because it is hierarchal, each client will be a higher stratum from its source clock.

Because there is a round-trip delay in requesting time over the Internet, NTP uses an algorithm for calculating the precise time accounting for this delay. With the expansive growth of cloud computing, NTP is becoming an extremely important protocol for synchronization of time among computer systems. When virtual machines (VMs) run on a hypervisor, the clocks in the VMs are emulated and drift quickly over time. NTP prevents these emulated clocks from large time skews that could affect client access.

Exam Essentials

Understand what the various DNS resource records are and how they are used.   The A record or host record is used for FQDN-to–IP address resolution. The AAAA record (quad A) is used for FQDN-to–IPv6 address resolution. TXT records are used for various purposes where text should be returned when a record is queried. SRV records, called service locator records, are used for host lookup of a service on the network, such as LDAP or SIP servers. MX records, called mail exchanger records, are used for lookup of a destination mail server. CNAME records, or canonical name records, allow for an FQDN to be mapped to another FQDN that has an A record for resolution. NS records, or name server records, are used by the DNS servers to define who can have a copy of the DNS zone file. SOA records, or start of authority records, are used to define the parameters of a zone file, such as the primary DNS server, refresh intervals, and TTL. PTR records, or pointer records, are used solely for reverse DNS queries.

Understand the differences and considerations between external DNS and internal DNS.   External DNS is used for resolution of public IP addresses for services published externally on the Internet. Internal DNS is used for resolution of private IP addresses for services published internally on the network.

Understand the hierarchy of DNS systems.   DNS is a decentralized distributed database of databases, where all resolution starts at the root or far right of an FQDN. Primary DNS servers own the editable copy of the DNS zone file. Secondary DNS servers contain the copy of a particular DNS zone file, but the copy is read-only. Forwarding DNS servers may not contain any zone files, but they allow DNS requests to be forwarded to another DNS server such as an ISP's server; these servers often cache the queries as well.

Understand the difference between forward and reverse zone lookups.   Reverse zone lookups allow for IP address–to–FQDN resolution using PTR records. Forward zone lookups allow for all other name resolution, such as FQDN–to–IP address lookups, TXT lookups, and so on. You should review the structure of a zone file for both forward and reverse zones.

Understand the various components of DHCP.   DHCP MAC reservations allow for a host to be treated like a DHCP client yet always retain the same IP address. The DHCP pool is the range of servable IP addresses that can be allocated via DHCP. IP address exclusions allow us to exclude a range from the DHCP pool for statically assigned hosts such as servers. Scope options are additional parameters that can be supplied along with the IP address and subnet mask from DHCP pools.

Understand the DHCP lease process.   The lease time of the IP address is always the client's responsibility to renew. DHCP clients renew the lease at 50 percent of the lease cycle. If the original server does not respond, then at 7/8ths of the lease cycle the client will send DHCP discover packets to all listening servers in hopes of a new lease. If this does not occur, then at the end of the lease cycle the client must release the IP address.

Understand how an IP helper and DHCP relays work.   An IP helper is a process on a router interface. The IP helper intercepts DHCP broadcast messages and sends them via unicast to a defined remote DHCP server. A DHCP relay performs the same service as an IP helper and is often a server on the immediate network that is configured to intercept DHCP broadcasts and send them as unicast to the remote DHCP server.

Understand how NTP is used and how it operates.   Network Time Protocol (NTP) is used to synchronize time between hosts on the Internet. NTP uses a series of stratum levels; lower is more precise and higher is less precise.

1.7 Explain basic corporate and datacenter network architecture.

If this was a lesson in corporate data centers 10 years ago, it would have looked very different than corporate data centers today. Everything has become faster and more scalable with software-defined networking, not just in the data center, but also in the corporate network. In the following sections, I will discuss basic design of corporate networks and data center networks.

Three-Tiered Model

The three-tiered networking model was introduced over 20 years ago by Cisco and it's been the gold-standard for network design. Even though it was introduced over 20 years ago, it is still very much valid today for any hardware vendor. However, in today's small to mid-sized network designs, the collapsed-core model has been adopted to save the expense of additional network switching, as shown in Figure 1.101. The elements of both models are similar in function.

FIGURE 1.101   Three-tier vs. collapsed core model

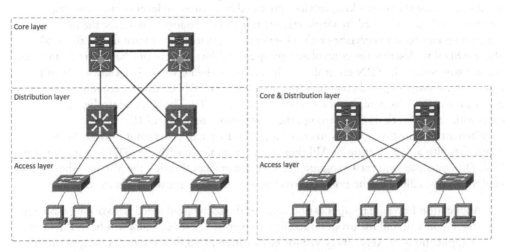

Core Layer   The core layer is also considered the backbone of the network. It is where you will find connectivity between geographic areas with WAN lines. It should be designed for high availability and only provides routing and switching of the entire network. Nothing should be done at the core layer to slow it down!

Distribution Layer   The distribution layer is often referred to as the workgroup layer or the aggregation layer because it allows for connectivity to multiple access layer switches. The distribution layer is where the control plane is located and is where packet filtering, security policies, routing between VLANs, and defining of broadcast domains are performed. You can think of it as the distribution of switching from the core to the access layer.

Access Layer   The access layer is often referred to as the edge switching layer, and it connects the end user hosts. The access layer provides local switching and the creation of collision domains. It is simply designed for access to the network and it is where support begins for QoS, Power over Ethernet, and security (802.1x, web-auth, DHCP snooping).

The collapsed-core model was adopted to save cost and complexity in networks. With the powerful switching of today, we can support both the core layer and distribution layer on the same piece of network switching equipment. It still performs the same functions as the core and distribution layer, it is just collapsed into one piece of switching equipment.

Software-Defined Networking

Software-defined networking (SDN) is a broad term used by *virtualization* vendors, cloud providers, and network hardware vendors. Virtualization vendors and cloud providers often use it to describe the networking services provided at a software level of the *hypervisor*. The term *SDN* is often used by virtualization and cloud vendors to describe the internal network service their hypervisor or cloud service can perform. Network hardware vendors also use SDN to describe the control and programmability of network hardware from a centralized controller. The SDN controller is the brains of the network that allows centralized control to all switching and routing in the network. The SDN controller communicates to applications and APIs with the *northbound interface (NBI)*. The SDN controller communicates with the network devices through the *southbound interface (SBI)*.

When an administrator wants to create a policy, they can program it into the SDN controller with an application or API that will communicate with the SDN controller via the NBI. The controller will then program the network devices through the SBI, and the network equipment will adhere to the policy across the enterprise, as shown in Figure 1.102.

Application Layer   The application layer of the software-defined networking model is where you will find the programmability elements. These elements will be in the form of applications or APIs. Every vendor has a different application or set of applications that are designed for the SDN controller. These applications can be in the form of monitoring, management, troubleshooting, network policies, security policies, network automation, and network configuration, just to name a few.

Northbound Interface(NBI)   The northbound interface (NBI) is the interface between the application layer and the control layer. It specifically allows applications and APIs access to the SDN controller's logic to monitor and manage network devices that are south of the controller.

FIGURE 1.102   Software-defined networking

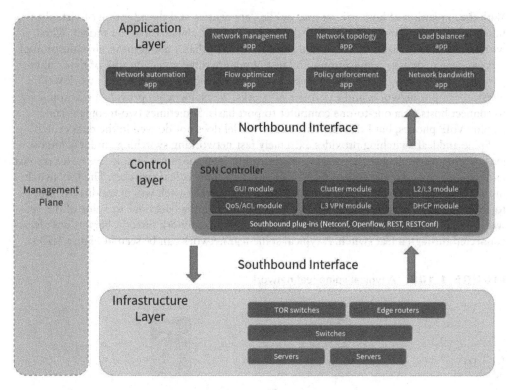

Control Layer   The control layer in the software-defined network model is essentially the SDN controller since the SDN controller is controlling the hardware. The use of the term *control plane* is similar to how it is used with traditional networking concepts, and the function is identical. The control layer will control everything, such as networking hardware, protocols, and the flow of data.

Southbound Interface (SBI)   The southbound interface (SBI) is used by the SDN controller to communicate with the network hardware. SDN controller vendors will support a wide variety of various network hardware vendors. The main goal is the overall flexibility and compatibility with their SDN controller and your network.

Infrastructure Layer   The infrastructure layer is where the network hardware is located. The hardware can be routers, switches, VPNs, or any other type of device. The device can be hardware-based or a software appliance, since many of the hardware devices today are being sold as virtualized alliances. The key takeaway is that this layer is where the data plane lives and is responsible for data management.

Management Plane   The management plane is how devices are managed for the control and flow of data. The management plane really stretches across all of the layers of the SDN model. However, the management of devices should always be performed through the application layer.

Spine and Leaf

With the expansion of both private and public data centers and the adoption of virtualization, a switching technology was needed that didn't fit the classic three-tier model. When we talk about virtualization, we should be open-minded that it could mean virtualization of servers, clients, storage, applications, and just about anything you can think of that can be partitioned over many hosts. The classic three-tier and collapsed-core models work well in physical campus networks and enterprise networks; access switches provide a star topology to connect hosts on a one-to-one computer to port basis. Sometimes two-to-one, if you employ VoIP phones, but I digress. This classic model does not do well in the data center.

Spine and leaf switching provides extremely fast networking switching, and it is almost exclusively used in data center network architecture. The concept is simple: create a very fast and redundant backbone (spline) that is only used to connect leaf switches. The leaf switches in turn connect the hosts (servers) in the data center. A leaf switch will never directly talk to another leaf switch; it will always need to talk through the backbone or spine of the network. Servers will never be connected to the spine of the network directly. Servers are always connected through a leaf switch. A typical spine-leaf network can be seen in Figure 1.103.

FIGURE 1.103   A typical spine-leaf network

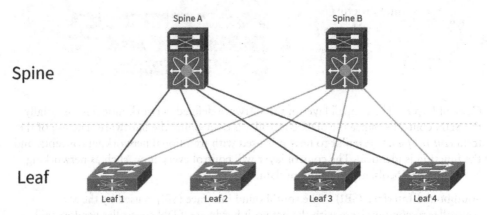

As you see in Figure 1.103, the Spine A switch is connected to every leaf switch and the Spine B switch is connected to every leaf switch as well. This allows extremely fast switching between Leaf 1 and Leaf 4 as well as any other leaf switch. Switching between two leaf switches is always two hops away no matter where they are in the network. It will traverse to the spine switch, then to the destination leaf switch. The concept of spine-leaf switching is often referred to as a CLOS network, named after Charles Clos, who formalized the concept in 1938 of multistage circuit-switching. Spine-leaf switching creates a two-tier circuit-switched network.

The control plane of spine-leaf switching is provided by software-defined networking. An underlay is built using an IP address–based network that uses either External Border

Gateway Protocol (eBGP) or Open Shortest Path First (OSPF) for layer 3 connectivity between the spine and leaf switches. The routing protocol ensures that data always flows through the fastest path via one of the spines. The overlay network will typically be a virtual extensible local area network (VXLAN). Using a VXLAN enables us to move data in the data center for a VLAN over the fastest path using layer 3. The VXLAN accomplishes this by encapsulating the frame within an IP packet, which allows the frame to traverse data centers and retain VLAN information. It also allows for the integration of virtual infrastructure without compromise of the virtual network traffic.

All things considered with spine-leaf architecture, it helps support building massively scalable data centers (MSDCs). So far, I've explained the logical connectivity for spine-leaf network design. The physical network design is much more straightforward and simple. In any given data center you will find a row of network racks; each row or section of the data center will typically contain a spine switch. Each rack is a standard 46- or 48-unit space that can accommodate 46 or 48 one-unit servers. So, each rack is dedicated a top-of-rack (ToR) switch that is considered a leaf. Sometimes the leaf switches are larger and will service more than one rack, but the concept remains the same. Each of these TOR switches are leaf switches in our spine-leaf network design. You may hear the terminology end-of-row (EoR) and even middle-of-row (MoR). These terms just dictate where the aggregation switch is located. To save space in a rack, you may locate the switch at the end of the row and wire everything back to the EoR switch. The MoR switch works the same way and requires shorter cables since it's in the middle of the row.

Traffic Flows

The traffic in a data center is critical since it can carry many different latency sensitive protocols, like iSCSI and virtualized storage traffic, just to name a couple. When we talk about traffic patterns in a data center, we talk about North to South and East to West directions.

Any traffic that stays on its respective VLAN is considered to be East to West traffic, as shown in Figure 1.104. We always want to keep time-sensitive traffic on the same VLAN as it reduces latency. The latency between Server 1 and Server 2 (both on VLAN 2) is most likely sub-millisecond. However, if traffic must traverse a router such as Server 1 (VLAN 2) communicating with Server 3 (VLAN 3), then it must do so and additional latency is introduced. We can expect a nominal latency of 10 milliseconds when traversing through a router. When traffic travels up to a router and then back down to its destination, the traffic is considered to be North to South.

North to South traffic patterns should be avoided at all costs if possible, unless the destination traffic is intended to traverse the router. An example of this is client access to servers; they are expected to be on different VLANs since they are different workgroups. The lines blur when we introduce virtualization into the picture because the host server may be in multiple VLANs at the same time. The virtual machines will also be members of virtual networks that operate on various VLANs. When a virtual machine is live-migrated from one host to another, the storage traffic, memory movement, and CPU load will all need to be migrated East to West. Also, during the live migration, client access is simultaneously happening, most likely North to South.

FIGURE 1.104   Data center traffic

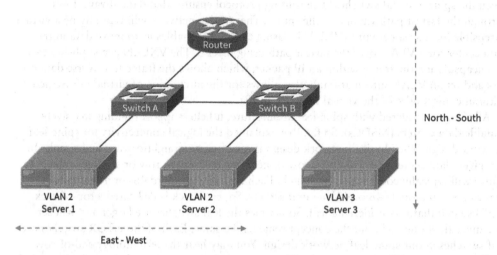

Traffic flow is really a design concept. If we look at each aspect of a live migration we can see the various traffic patterns. Storage traffic is designated for a specific VLAN. The memory movement and CPU state are designated to another VLAN and the client access is another VLAN. Although the client access might seem like a time-sensitive task, storage and memory/CPU movement have to be extremely fast. Now ask yourself, what if everything was traversing the router? Latency is the answer, and although one live migration might not seem too intensive. What if there were multiple moves, such as when a host is placed into maintenance mode?

Host Locations

As administrators we have lots of options as to where to host our servers. We can host our servers in the public cloud, in our own data center, at a branch office, or even at a coloca-tion. Each location has an advantage and disadvantage as you may have guessed.

Public Cloud   Hosting in the public cloud is a great option if you do not have a data center established already. For a monthly fee, you can rent the infrastructure you need. You will learn more about the public cloud later in this chapter in the discussion of objective 1.8, "Summarize cloud concepts and connectivity options." Keep in mind that this option doesn't always require Amazon Web Services or Azure; many Internet service providers (ISPs) also have a public cloud offering. The biggest disadvantage to public cloud hosting is the monthly reoccurring fee. You can't capitalize an expenditure for the public cloud because you are renting time on someone else's equipment. So it becomes an operational expense.

Company-Owned Data Center   Company-owned data centers, also known as on-premises hosting, allow us to exercise the greatest control when we host applications and servers. Well, at least we have as much control as the budget allows. You will find out that you need data center grade switching, servers, UPS backup systems, generators, and cooling. Building a data center can be very costly. It is, however, a capital expense that can be deprecated over several years. The other disadvantage is the location in a building, which I've always found was an afterthought in the building process. I've been to several privately owned data centers and most all of them suffer from the same potential problem of water and fire damage. In one case the water main was running through the data center, right above the servers! With great control comes great responsibility too. You will need to maintain service contracts for all of the equipment.

Branch Office Branch offices, otherwise known as remote offices/branch offices (ROBOs), are universally disliked by administrators for a number of reasons. Placement of the corporate servers at the main location means that ROBO users must use WAN technologies to access files and resources. Sometimes these connections are slow and problematic. Also, most branch offices do not have a full-time administrator, so it can be challenging; especially when technology runs your business. As administrators we should embrace ROBO and use it to our advantage, such as placing resources at the ROBO for disaster recovery. Keep in mind that if you do not have a full-time admin and you want to house a lot of technology at the ROBO, you will need to be good at troubleshooting remotely.

Colocation A colocation is a space or location where you are permitted to place servers and network resources but you do not own the space or location. The cost of colocations can be via simple landlord agreements or they can be in the form of a monthly reoccurring charge. A very common colocation scenario is hosting your equipment at an ISP's data center. ISPs usually have what they call ping and power space, which means they have UPSs, generators, cooling, and connectivity to the Internet. Colocations are great places to place off-site backup units and disaster recovery servers since they are physically separated from your main data center. However, they do require a monthly operational expense, and this can sometimes be considered an insurance policy in the event of a disaster.

Network Storage Types

Virtualization hypervisors allow resources to be shared among virtual machines. The three main resources shared are compute, network, and storage. Hypervisors share the resources of RAM and CPU, which fall under compute resources. However, hypervisors need storage, and this is where network storage enters the cloud computing model. Two main storage types exist for hypervisors: *network attached storage (NAS)* and *storage area networks (SANs)*. Each type has its own unique benefit to the hypervisor or cluster.

It is important to note that over the past few years a third type of storage called hyperconverged storage has become popular. It is a cross between a SAN and *direct attached storage (DAS)*, and the hypervisor is responsible for the storage. With hyper-converged storage, the hypervisor is responsible for maintaining the DAS while communicating with the other hosts in the cluster. You should expect to see this type of storage become popular in the coming years because it removes the requirement of external storage.

Although I introduced this section on network storage focused on hypervisors, network-based storage is not exclusively used for hypervisors. It just seems to be the current trend of the market since virtualization is mainstream. Network-based storage is also used as storage for Microsoft Exchange, SQL databases, file servers, and many other nonvirtualized applications.

NAS

Network attached storage (NAS) is technically nothing more than a file server. Although I've oversimplified NAS as a file server, the important fact is that NAS serves file-based storage via a filer process. Examples of these filers are *Server Message Blocks (SMBs)* and *Network File System (NFS)*. When the hosts read, write, and delete files, the commands sent are to a higher-level process such as SMB. SMB is then responsible for performing the commands against a file structure such as NTFS. An important aspect of NAS is that the security for the data is facilitated by the filer process and the filesystem. In other words, the NAS unit is responsible for filing and processing the requests for storage over the existing network.

NAS is commonly used as storage of files in an appliance-based solution. These appliances come in all shapes and sizes, but all have similar major components, such as hard drives, CPU, network connectivity and software that makes all the components work together. You can find NAS appliances serving files to clients where a server-based file server is administratively too costly, as in a remote office/branch office (ROBO). NAS appliances allow for features like backup and replication that normally require a high level of administration. Because NAS appliances are purpose built, these functions are easy to set up and maintain for the administrator.

NAS can also be used for hypervisor support, but certain protocols, such as SMB 2.0 or lower, will not handle the requirements of the hypervisor. With the introduction of Hyper-V 2012, SMB 3.1 is now supported and can handle many of the requirements of a hypervisor in respect to storage. NFS is commonly used for Linux NAS storage as a filer protocol.

SAN

A storage area network (SAN) is separated either logically or physically from the local area network (LAN). When we talk about a SAN, we generally refer to the unit itself, but a SAN refers to the entire network for storage. The most dominant SAN technology on the market today is Fibre Channel (FC). Fibre Channel equipment is expensive to purchase and difficult to maintain. It is common to find one admin dedicated to Fibre Channel storage networks in large companies. However, many networks already have data center switching in place, so Internet Small Computer System Interface (iSCSI) is becoming popular as a replacement for Fibre Channel. I will cover both Fibre Channel and iSCSI later in this chapter.

SANs perform an important function: they provide block-level storage. Block-level storage is different from file-level storage in that the host connecting to the storage is responsible for storage of information directly to the volume on the SAN. This is coordinated by the use of a special adapter card called the *host bus adapter (HBA)* card when using *Fibre Channel* or the Ethernet card when using *iSCSI*. The hypervisor sends data to the HBA or the iSCSI initiator, which then formats the data to be written or read directly to the *logical unit number (LUN)* in a block format. This gives the host better performance and lower latency to the storage since read and write commands are at a very low level.

SANs performs security of the volume at a hardware layer. In Fibre Channel, zoning is used to partition devices to a LUN. This creates a logical layer of security that prevents one host from accessing a LUN dedicated to another host. In iSCSI, security is performed in the initiator and target as part of the iSCSI protocol. Since block-level storage gives the host hardware-level access, it is important to logically separate out the LUNs on a SAN or data loss could occur.

 Storage is a complex part of a hypervisor structure and networks today. The CompTIA Network+ exam covers basic concepts on the subject of storage. If you want to learn more about storage, I recommend *Information Storage and Management: Storing, Managing, and Protecting Digital Information in Classic, Virtualized, and Cloud Environments,* Second Edition, G. Somasundaram and Alok Shrivastava (Wiley, 2012).

Connection Type

When you're connecting SANs to your hosts, you can choose from several different connectivity methods. I've covered two of the types of network storage: NAS and SAN. Next I will discuss the four common connection types for SANs: Fibre Channel, iSCSI, FCoE, and InfiniBand. Several others exist, but these are the most common found in storage area networks today.

Fibre Channel

SANs have different requirements than an Ethernet network, such as a lossless connection. Let's first explore potential problems of using a LAN for the storage network. Normal network switching performs a best-effort delivery of data, with the expectation that upper-level protocols will retransmit lost data. This retransmitting of data creates latency for the storage connection. At this point you may expect that data is not lost in transit in this day and age, and you are correct. However, normal switching equipment performs a function called blocking when too much data enters the switching equipment's interface buffer. There are expensive ways to fix this problem, such as nonblocking Ethernet data center switching equipment. This is one of the reasons Fibre Channel SANs are a choice for hypervisor clusters—they are designed for storage at wire speeds and lossless in their connections since they handle congestion differently.

The Fibre-Channel protocol operates by encapsulating SCSI commands. It uses buffer credits to avoid congestion. The buffer credit system allows for the source and destination to agree upon a buffer size. The source and destination use a hardware address called a worldwide name (WWN), similar to a MAC address. WWNs are generally 128 bits or 64 bits, depending on the age of the equipment. Common Fiber Channel speeds are 1, 2, 4, 8, and 16 Gbps.

Fibre Channel SANs also addresses redundancy and fault tolerance. Just as your Ethernet network has redundancy considerations, the Fibre Channel SAN is even more important because if a failure occurs, it will result in loss of data. The host's HBA has two connections, and each is connected to a separate storage switch for redundancy. Each of the storage processors on the Fibre Channel SAN storage unit are then connected to each Fibre Channel switch; this creates a storage fabric. As seen in Figure 1.105, if there is a fault on any storage processor, switch, or connecting lines, the SAN will remain operational.

FIGURE 1.105   A typical storage area network

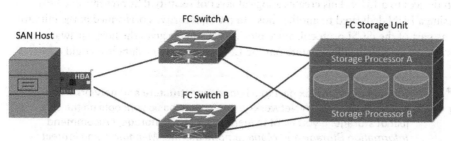

It is important to note that although FC SANs require FC switches and an FC fabric, Fibre Channel can be connected without an FC switch in an arbitrated loop. The arbitrated loop is often used for direct connection of storage equipment that is not shared to other hosts. The Fibre Channel arbitrated loop is often referred to as FC-AL.

FCoE

Fibre Channel over Ethernet (FCoE) is becoming a popular connectivity method for hosts. This technology was developed for data centers to reduce the complexity of cabling. When you add a new host to your data center and you run Fibre Channel, you need two power cables (A side and B side), two Ethernet cables for host communications, and two Fibre Channel connections. FCoE reduces all of the cables (except for power) to two Ethernet cables. We can perform this magic with the help of a special card called a converged network adapter (CNA) and a data center switch that is FCoE compliant.

The CNA acts as a Fibre Channel HBA and an Ethernet card. The host addresses both of these functionalities separately, as if you had two separate cards installed. In most cases, the CNA requires two separate drivers as well, one for the FC HBA and one for Ethernet. When Fibre Channel commands are sent to the CNA, it encapsulates the FC data into an Ethernet frame and sends it to the data center switch. The data center switch then reads the frame and forwards it to the FC switching plane and eventually to the FC storage unit. In Figure 1.106 you see a network with a separate FC network and one with a converged FC network.

iSCSI

When you implement an iSCSI SAN, you are using Ethernet to transmit data over the existing switching equipment. SCSI commands are encapsulated with TCP/IP headers, typically TCP port 860 and TCP port 3260. These SCSI commands can then be sent over a normal TCP/IP network. The expectation is that you have similar redundancy and the proper data center switching equipment in place, such as nonblocking Ethernet.

iSCSI is a cheaper alternative to Fibre Channel—that is, if you have the proper equipment in place already. It can deliver faster speeds than Fibre Channel implementations on the market today and uses the open standard of the iSCSI protocol. Typical speeds of iSCSI can range from 1 Gbps to 40 Gbps.

When sharing out a LUN to a host, you will associate the LUN with a target. The iSCSI target listens for requests from iSCSI initiators on the SAN storage device. This iSCSI target is where you implement security via MAC addresses, IP addresses, and a shared key called the Challenge Handshake Authentication Protocol (CHAP).

The initiator is a piece of software on the host operating system that connects to the iSCSI target. The initiator's job is to authenticate to the target, create SCSI commands, and encapsulate them in an IP packet. Most all operating systems today support iSCSI.

FIGURE 1.106 A comparison between separate SAN and network switching vs. a converged FCoE network

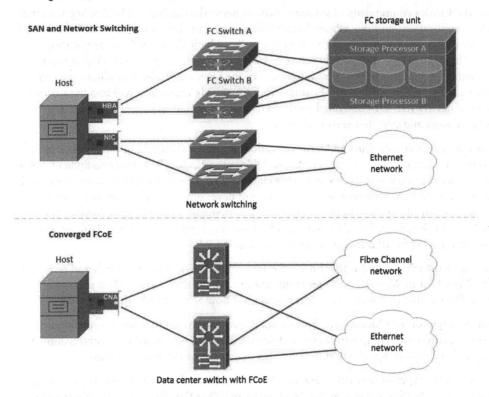

InfiniBand

InfiniBand (IB) is a standard high-performance computing network protocol that is used as a SAN connectivity type. It is different from Ethernet because it was designed to be an extremely low-latency, high-throughput, and lossless connection. It requires an InfiniBand switched fabric dedicated to the SAN similar to Fibre Channel. The major difference is that very few companies produce this high-end switching equipment.

The host units connecting to storage require a host channel adapter (HCA), and the storage unit contains a target channel adapter (TCA). There are several different InfiniBand types that are out of the scope of the Network+ exam. The current specification of Infini-Band, called FDR, can deliver speeds of 56 Gbps to the storage target.

Exam Essentials

Understand the classic three-tier and collapsed-core model.   The core layer should be the fastest bandwidth and nothing should be done to slow traffic down; only routing and switching should occur at the core layer. The distribution layer is where packet filtering, routing of VLANs, and the control plane are located. The access layer is for client connectivity and where you find PoE, QoS, and other client protocols. The collapsed-core model combines the core and distribution layers.

Know the various components of software-defined networks (SDNs).   The Application layer is where applications and the API are located that control the infrastructure. The northbound interface (NBI) is a component of the SDN controller, which allows API and application access. The control layer is basically the SDN controller; everything is controlled at this layer. The southbound interface (SBI) is a component of the SDN controller that allows it to communicate with the infrastructure. The infrastructure layer is where you will find the various hardware devices that are controlled by the SDN controller. The management plane is used to manage devices and stretches across all layers.

Know the various components and basic operation of spine-leaf switching.   Spine-leaf switching is found in data centers to provide fast, scalable networks for data center equipment. Spine servers connect to each leaf switch and never connect hosts or other network equipment. Leaf switches only communicate with spine switches and never directly with other leaf switches. Leaf switches are always within two hops from their destination via the spine switch. The underlay is an IP address–based network, and the overlay is normally a VXLAN to encapsulate the original packet for IP transit across the underlay.

Understand the principal of traffic flow.   Routed traffic flows South to North and switched traffic flows East to West. Data center traffic should always flow East to West to minimize latency. Only traffic to the clients or Internet should flow South to North.

Know the types of host locations.   You should know the advantages and disadvantages of hosting data center equipment in the public cloud, company-owned data center, branch office, and colocation. Know the differences between each of the host locations.

Understand the types of network storage.   Network attached storage (NAS) is a file-level storage system. NAS requires a higher-level protocol called the filer to process file requests. Storage area networks (SANs) are block-level storage systems. The two main types of SAN are Fibre Channel and iSCSI. SAN storage allows the host to access a LUN directly and read and write at the data block level.

Know the different storage connection types.   Fibre Channel normally required dedicated FC switches and was designed for wire speeds and lossless connections for storage. With Fibre Channel over Ethernet, a single Ethernet cable carries both the Ethernet traffic and the Fibre Channel traffic. iSCSI is becoming a popular replacement for Fibre Channel because existing Ethernet data center switching can be used for connectivity. InfiniBand requires a similar fabric as Fibre Channel and was created for high-performance computing.

1.8 Summarize cloud concepts and connectivity options.

The traditional compute model was based on a one-to-one relation of application to server. However, most applications only use a fraction of the compute resources during idle periods, and all applications collectively seldom use all of the compute resources at the same time.

Virtualization allows us to partition compute resources for each guest operating system (OS) supporting an application running on the host hardware. The hypervisor allows the partitioning of compute resources. The partitioning of virtualization allows each OS to operate as if it had exclusive control of the host hardware. Compute resources consist of the central processing unit (CPU), memory, and devices related to a physical server.

Cloud services allow us to pool the resources together collectively for each host server providing virtualization. When the resources of computer, network, and storage are pooled together, the cloud gains fault tolerance and scale. This allows us to lose a host and still maintain the ability to compute the workload of the guest operating systems supporting our applications. It also allows us to add resources of compute, network, and storage to scale the cloud out for additional workloads. The scale of workloads is referred to as elasticity.

The cloud model is based on a many-to-many model where the exact location of the resources doesn't matter to the end user. We can create an application by allocating available resources to a guest OS from a pool of resources. The guest OS will then gain the fault tolerance of the cloud along with the added benefit of elasticity of the cloud.

Characteristics of a Cloud

The National Institute of Standards and Technology (NIST) defines cloud computing with five distinct characteristics: on-demand self-service, broad network access, resource pooling, rapid elasticity, and measured service. Any service that contains these characteristic can be considered a cloud-based service or application.

On-Demand Self-Service A customer can provision computer capabilities and resources, such as CPU, memory, storage, the network, instance of a virtual machine, or any other component of the service, including the service itself, without any human interaction.

Broad Network Access The capabilities are accessible over a network and are not a contrived system like the old mainframe systems, where you needed a proprietary connection. Broad access includes the device as well, such as mobile devices, laptops, desktop computers, just to name a few.

Resource Pooling The intent of cloud computing is to time-share a pool of resources over many several virtual instances. If it is a public cloud, the resource pools can be allotted by customer or organization. If it is a private cloud, then chances are the resource pool will be allotted to virtual instances in the same organization.

Rapid Elasticity   Computer capabilities can be elastically provisioned based on the customer's requirements at the time, such as load. The same capabilities can be released when the customer's requirement requires less resources. An example of rapid elasticity is a web-based company that requires additional capacity during a peak busy time. The resources can be allocated during the peak and deallocated when the traffic reaches a nominal level.

Measured Service   Any cloud service should have the capability to meter the resources of CPU, network, storage, and accounts, just to name a few. In addition, most cloud services charge based on any or all of these resources. Resources usage should be monitored, reported, and ultimately controlled without the consumer ever realizing that any of these are being applied.

The five characteristics of cloud computing can be found in the National Institute of Standards and Technology (NIST) publication SP 800-145. This document is titled "The NIST Definition of Cloud Computing" and it sets the guidelines for cloud computing. The document can be accessed with the URL https://csrc.nist.gov/publications/detail/sp/800-145/final.

Cloud Delivery Models

When we discuss the cloud, names like Amazon AWS and Microsoft Azure come to mind. However, anyone can own their own cloud as long as the resources meet the criteria of the NIST standard for cloud computing. We can classify the ownership of these models within the four main categories of public, private, hybrid, and community.

I often find that companies will begin entering into the cloud via a public cloud provider. Using these public clouds is like renting compute power. The costs are charged to an operational expense budget because there is no equity in the service, much like renting a house. Once companies realize the savings of virtualization, they often purchase the equipment to transform into a private cloud. The purchase of the equipment is a capital investment because we have equity in the equipment, much like owning a house.

Private

The private cloud model is defined as cloud infrastructure that is provisioned for exclusive use by a single organization, as shown in Figure 1.107. It can be owned, managed, and operated by the organization, a third party, or a combination of both. The infrastructure can also be located on- or off-premises. This makes the cloud resources exclusive to the owner.

There are several reasons to move to a private cloud deployment, such as regulations, privacy, monetary and budgetary impact, and overall control. Private clouds give the owner ultimate control of the cloud and its design. Sometimes the public cloud may not offer certain features or hardware that a private cloud can be built to support. The creation of the private cloud might not be for purposes of new technology; it could be designed to support legacy systems that may not be compatible with public cloud offerings.

FIGURE 1.107   A private cloud

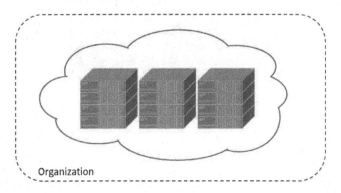

The private cloud model has the advantage of ultimate control, with a price that is not immediately evident. When equipment is purchased such as compute, network, and storage, the company must forecast growth over a nominal five- to seven-year period. In a public cloud, resources can be purchased on demand and relinquished when not needed, but in the private cloud model, we must acquire these additional resources and are burdened with the ownership.

Obsolescence of the equipment must also be considered, because the average expected life of compute, network, and storage resources is usually five to seven years. Private clouds often need hardware refreshes every five to seven years because of newer features or end-of-life warranties.

Public

The public cloud model is defined as infrastructure that is provisioned for open use by the general public. It can be owned, managed, and operated by a business entity, government organization, or a combination thereof. However, the infrastructure exists on the premises of the cloud provider, as shown in Figure 1.108.

The public cloud is often a public marketplace for compute, network, and storage in which you can rent or lease compute time. This compute time, of course, is segregated from other customers, so there is a level of isolation between customers on the same infrastructure. Examples of public cloud providers are Amazon Web Services (AWS), Microsoft Azure, and Google Cloud; these are just a few providers, and the list grows every day.

A benefit of the public cloud is the pay-as-you-go utility model. You can purchase the compute power you need for a period of time. You are charged only for the compute time that you use or purchase, and there is no initial capital investment on the part of the customer.

FIGURE 1.108   A public cloud

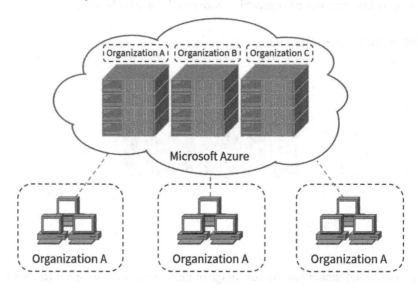

Another benefit to the public cloud is the elasticity of compute, network, and storage resources. If a customer is an online retailer and needs extra compute power for the holiday season, the customer can purchase more scale-out, and when the busy period is over, they can relinquish the resources.

A disadvantage to the public cloud is the lack of control and hardware configuration. If custom hardware is required, then the public cloud is not an option. Heavily regulated industries might not be able to use the public cloud because of restrictions on where data can be stored and who can access it.

Hybrid

The hybrid cloud model is a combination of both the private and public cloud models. It is the most popular model because many businesses leverage public cloud providers while maintaining their own infrastructure, as shown in Figure 1.109.

Many cloud providers now offer integration for private cloud software, such as Microsoft Hyper-V and VMware vSphere. This integration allows private clouds to gain the on-demand elasticity of the public cloud. When a private cloud uses the public cloud for elasticity of resources or additional capacity, it is called cloud bursting.

Community

The community cloud model is a rare model for the average organization to adopt. The community cloud is a group of organizations that share a particular tenant or shared infrastructure, as shown in Figure 1.110. In order to adopt the community cloud, the organization must have specific requirements, such as security or special access to another member's cloud. Community clouds are commonly used by the healthcare and financial sector, but they are not limited to those sectors. Education and government are also big adopters of the community cloud.

FIGURE 1.109   A hybrid cloud

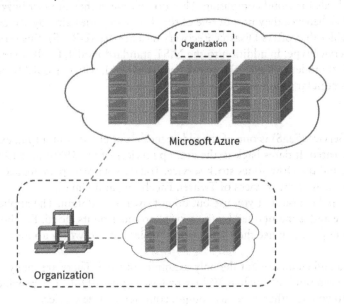

FIGURE 1.110   A community cloud

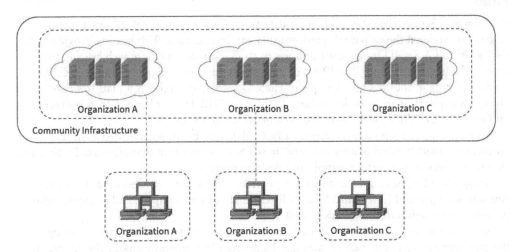

Types of Services

The term *cloud* has become a ubiquitous buzzword in IT, applied to anything involving hosted services. However, the *National Institute of Standards and Technology (NIST)* has defined three service types for cloud computing: Software as a Service (SaaS), Platform as a Service (PaaS), and Infrastructure as a Service (IaaS).

There are many more service types than the three mentioned, but they are not defined by the NIST standards for cloud computing. That doesn't mean they are just buzzwords; it just means that NIST believes they fit into one of the three categories already. An example of this is a cloud provider that offers Disaster Recovery as a Service (DRaaS); this service would fit into the IaaS service type. In addition to the NIST standard model, I will cover an immerging aaS (as a Service) model called Desktop as a Service (DaaS), which is quickly becoming an offering that is popular among providers.

SaaS

Software as a Service (SaaS) is one of the oldest models of cloud computing, existing before the term was created. It dates back to the dial-up services of the 1980s and 1990s like CompuServe, AOL, and the Dow Jones stock service. Today, SaaS providers are accessed through a web browser, such as the services of Twitter, Facebook, and Gmail.

SaaS is any application that you use but do not own or maintain. The application is the provided service and is maintained by the service provider on its cloud. Facebook and Gmail are popular examples; you use their services and never have to worry about the underlying infrastructure.

Social media and email are not the only examples of SaaS. There are many others that you might not even think of, such as WebEx by Cisco and GitHub. The provider extends these services to you as either a pay-as-you-go, contract, or free service.

PaaS

Platform as a Service (PaaS) is another model of cloud computing. PaaS allows a customer to generate code on the provider's platform that can be executed. Web hosting providers like GoDaddy and A Small Orange are examples of PaaS. You can purchase web hosting from these providers and set up a WordPress or custom web application using PHP or ASP.Net.

Web hosting is not the only example of PaaS. Google App Engine is a platform that allows an application to be coded in Java, Python, or PHP. The application then is executed on Google's PaaS cloud; Web hosts can even provide storage like SQL.

SaaS applications can be produced on a PaaS platform. Evernote is hosted as of this writing on Google's cloud platform. Evernote is a SaaS application that allows collecting and sharing of ideas across various mobile and desktop devices.

Google App Engine is not the only PaaS provider—there are countless other providers. Amazon Web Services (AWS) and Microsoft Azure are other examples, and countless other providers have begun to offer PaaS as well.

Applications are isolated between customers. The processes are allotted resources by the customer and can scale out for demand. PaaS providers generally charge the customer according to CPU cycles used.

IaaS

Infrastructure as a Service (IaaS) is the established model of computing that we generally associate with cloud computing. Amazon Web Services (AWS), Microsoft Azure, and Rackspace are just a few providers. Customer are allowed to use the provider's infrastructure of compute, network, and storage.

When the customer needs IaaS, it is as simple as purchasing an instance of compute resources and then choosing an operating system and region of the world for the instance and connecting to it. The customer will not know the exact host server, network equipment, or storage the guest VM is running upon. All of the worries of the infrastructure are left up to the provider.

Computing resources are not the only services that you can purchase from a cloud provider. For example, Amazon Web Services and Microsoft Azure offer backup services. You can purchase space on the provider's cloud and back up straight to it.

Any infrastructure that you would normally purchase as a capital expense (lease or own) can be converted into an operational expense (rent) via services from the provider. Whenever I am looking to purchase physical infrastructure, I incorporate IaaS into my cost analysis. However, you must also weigh the nonmonetary saving such as infrastructure maintenance and overall administration of the infrastructure. You must ask yourself, is it better to own this infrastructure or rent this infrastructure long term?

DaaS

Desktop as a Service (DaaS) is the latest offering by cloud providers, such as Microsoft and VMware, just to name a couple. In a normal compute model, the end-user computer, also known as the edge device, processes the data. This also means that the edge device can retain a copy of the data and that data can be copied off onto a USB drive. The edge device can be stolen and depending on the data, it might mean that your company has to report it as a data loss. Another emerging threat is for the end-user computer to get infected and ransom the data. These scenarios can cost a company a lot of money to remediate.

DaaS doesn't solve all the problems, but it does give the administrator a lot more control by pushing the processing of data to the cloud. Because the edge device is no longer responsible for processing the data, it can be a repurposed computer, tablet, Chromebook, or any other device. These devices are called thin clients because the only software they need to support is the client for DaaS. In many cases all that a person needs is a web browser to access the desktop in the cloud. This allows for mobility and flexibility in provisioning desktops for workers. You can even scale up or down depending on usage. Coupled with a bring your own device (BYOD) policy, a company could save some real money.

Administrators gain the greatest amount of control when an organization decides to switch to DaaS. Data can be tightly controlled by turning off clipboard sharing between the thin client and the virtual desktop. USB access can be controlled, printing can be controlled, and these are just a few examples. Security patches can be centrally controlled and quickly installed as they are released. Antivirus and antimalware can be managed and monitored to thwart ransomware attempts. The best part is that, with the right mix of policies, the data remains in the cloud and never makes it to the edge device. So there is no chance of data loss, and costly proceedings can be avoided.

Infrastructure as Code

Infrastructure as Code (IaC) gives developers the ability to provision infrastructure and operate as an extension of IT. The ability to develop and operate as IT personnel is actually how we get the term *DevOps*. There are some development best practices that go with that title, but in short it's the ability to develop and provision resources as needed.

Before we get into why we need IaC, let's look at a typical development cycle. A developer will create code, that code needs to be tested, and then if the test succeeds, the code will be put into production. So, at bare minimum a developer will require a test and production environment that are identical. This model assumes we have one developer working on the code, and in reality, you could have several developers all working on different code simultaneously. The standard before was when a developer needed a production environment created, they would submit a ticket to the network operations people. The server would get created and the developer had a place to run their code. The same held true for the test environment: a ticket was submitted and the test environment was diligently created by someone outside of development to mimic the production environment. This is called a silo approach to development and network operations and it works, but it's not fast and it's not pretty.

Today, developers can stand up infrastructure on a cloud provider by writing a simple automation script. The best part is that developers usually know what they want; it's the network operation people that usually slow things down. As an example, maybe a developer needs a web server running PHP and a simple database instance. Normally the developer would need to wait for someone to manually create the server. What if you needed one for each of your 50 developers? That is where orchestration software comes to the rescue. There are two approaches to orchestrate the tasks of installing an application: imperative and declarative. Both come with advantages and disadvantages.

Imperative   An imperative approach is probably the route most of us would take. It's a classic approach of listing all of the steps to get to the desired state. For example, an imperative approach might look like the following pseudocode. You might think that the pitfall is configuring specifics like hostname or IP, but those can be turned into variables. The pitfall is actually the fact that the install of PHP is dependent on the Apache web server getting installed properly. If this were more complex and step 234 errored, we would need to debug the other 233 lines to see what changed.

```
Install Ubuntu 20.04
Configure hostname:ServerA
Configure IP:192.168.1.10
Install Apache 2.4.24
Set home directory
Install PHP 7.4.13
Enable PHP module
Install MySQL 5.7.23
Set MySQL password:Password20!
Configure firewall:open TCP 80
```

Declarative   A declarative approach is a desired state that you want to reach in the end. Basically, we know that when we are done we want to have an Ubuntu 20.04 server with Apache, PHP, and MySQL installed. How we get there is really irrelevant to the script or the developer. The same defaults need to be set, such as the hostname, IP address, MySQL password, and so on. The following pseudocode represents a declarative approach. The orchestration software would contain the specifics on how to install the appropriate pieces.

```
Ubuntu::install { '20.04':
  hostname => 'ServerA',
  ip       => '192.168.1.10',

}
apache:package install { 'dev.wiley.com':
  port    => '80',
  docroot => '/var/www/',
  module  => 'php'
  open_fw => 'true'
}
mysql:package install { 'db_app':
  password => 'Password20!'
}
```

Orchestration Software

Orchestration software can enable developers to spin up and spin down servers on demand. A developer can create a VM when they start their day and discard it at the end of the day since we normally pay for computer time by the second. With these tools, your development staff has become scalable; a developer just needs the script and they will have a test server that is identical to the production server(s).

There are several different orchestration software packages available for a DevOps automation. Every cloud provider will prefer a specific software package. However, nothing stops you from running your preference of orchestration software on your private cloud. You don't even need to be a developer to reap the benefits. You can use orchestration software for installing specific services for a reference server you use often. In any case, in the following list are the most popular orchestration software packages. There are many other packages that can be adopted. A whole book could be dedicated to how each operates and there are fundamental differences.

Chef   Chef is a client-server architecture and its configuration is performed with a Ruby domain-specific language (DSL). Ruby DSL differs from normal Ruby because it is limited to a specific domain, such as particular tasks like installing services and applications. It removes a lot of the extraneous code so that the focus can be placed on the task at hand. Chef uses a pull method of installation from a master server with the SSH protocol. The agent periodically polls the master server for infrastructure changes. Chef is also an imperative approach to orchestration, so the learning curve can be incredibly steep.

Puppet   Puppet is a client-server architecture as well, and its configuration is also performed with Ruby DSL and Embedded Ruby (ERB) templates. This blend of configuration languages makes the Puppet language so unique that it is called the Puppet DSL. Agents are installed on the endpoints and periodically poll the master server with the XML-RPC protocol over HTTPS. Puppet is a declarative orchestration tool, but because of the Puppet DSL language, it has a steep learning curve.

Ansible   Ansible is probably the best orchestration tool, mainly because it was created as a replacement for Chef and Puppet. Its design goal was to simplify complex orchestration and to scale. Ansible is a declarative approach to orchestration, but it also allows for commands to be implanted, similar to imperative tools, so it is really considered a hybrid orchestration tool. The configuration files are YAML Ain't Markup Language (YAML)-based. The best feature about Ansible is that it can push commands sequentially to destination servers and services and therefore does not require an agent to perform it orchestration tasks. These pushes are done with the SSH protocol.

Connectivity Methods

Before public clouds, the applications, authentication, and users were all within a local area network (LAN) or the organization's network. Public clouds allow us to host our application in data centers located in the public cloud. However, users still need to access these applications, and the applications still need to access authentication systems in our data center. Some of these applications also need access to legacy systems that can only be hosted in our private data centers. The client access is not much of a concern because cloud providers offer broad network access. The Internet is usually the way we access these applications located in the public cloud.

As for the applications that need access to our private data center, there are two main methods that we can use to provide access and remain secure.

VPN   Cloud providers often sell virtual private network (VPN) virtual appliances that can create a VPN tunnel back to our data center. You don't necessarily need the provider's virtual appliance; you can always install your own in the public cloud if there is a particular VPN package you elect to use. These VPN virtual appliances allow for data to be transmitted over the Internet in an encrypted tunnel.

The VPN method is the simplest, mainly because within an hour you can have a VPN tunnel created back to your company. The downside is you have no level of quality of service end to end, so applications that are prone to latency might run poorly. A couple of examples of latency-sensitive applications are real-time communications and VoIP.

Private-Direct Connection   The other method of connectivity is to build out a private WAN to the public cloud, with the help of a WAN provider or Internet service provider (ISP). This method requires planning and often ties you to a particular data center location because dedicated fiber-optic lines run directly from your location to the cloud provider.

The private-direct method of connectivity is probably the costliest, but it does provide a high level of security and very low latency. Since you are the only one on the fiber-optic connection direct to the cloud provider, you have the entire fiber-optic line for your company's traffic.

There are many other connectivity methods available, depending on your ISP and location in the world. As an example, Multiprotocol Label Switching (MPLS) is a popular method of connectivity that resembles a private-direct connection but uses a shared packet switching technology.

Multitenancy

The term *tenant* is used to describe a group of users or devices that share a common pool of resources or common access with specific privileges. A popular example of a tenant is the Microsoft 365 platform. When you sign up your organization and associate it with Microsoft 365, each user or device you add is grouped to your tenant. You can then manage the privileges for your users across your entire organization. Another classic example of a tenant is when you create a private virtualization cloud in your organization with Hyper-V or VMware vSphere. You have a single tenant that can share the pool of resources and you can define policies for all of the VMs across your organization.

Now that we have a broad definition of a tenant, let's get into what a multitenant is. Simply put, it's a platform that supports multiple tenants at the same time. Microsoft 365 is a great example of this, when your organization is created it is scaled over many different servers. These servers also have other organizations (tenants) processing on them, so they are considered multitenant.

Another example of a multitenant is a virtualization cloud. It is possible to have two organizations defined on the same set of hardware. Using resource pool policies, the multiple tenants could be configured so they would not affect each other. This is common practice with ISPs that offer a hosted virtualization service. There is often middleware that allows the users to create and modify VMs without directly accessing the hypervisor platform.

Elasticity

Elasticity is one of the five essential characteristics of cloud computing and it is defined below, as per the NIST publication SP 800-145:

> A consumer can unilaterally provision computing capabilities, such as server time and network storage, as needed automatically without requiring human interaction with each service provider.

Cloud providers offer configuration of virtual CPU, virtual RAM, network bandwidth down and up, storage, and many other resources for a virtual machine or virtual service. When that service needs more resources, elasticity allows the consumer to add or remove the resources without any human interaction from the hosting provider. The customer of course has to pay for these resources, but in traditional circumstances of real hardware, your only option would be to purchase new hardware or add upgrades to existing hardware. Elastic upgrades can normally be performed through a GUI, a command line, or an API for automation and orchestration. They can sometimes even be added without a reboot or disruption of service.

Scalability

Scalability follows along the same lines of elasticity. Both elasticity and scalability technically increase resources for an application or service. Elasticity is considered to be tactical in its approach, and scalability is considered to be strategic in its approach. As an example, if you see a rise in CPU for a virtual machine, you can simply increase the virtual CPU count and decrease its virtual CPU when the load has subsided.

What if your company has a website in a US data center where 80 percent of your business is and your company wanted to expand to an overseas location? Strategically, you should place the web server across both data centers. This is where a scale-out cluster comes in handy. With the use of a load balancer, you could scale your website over several data centers all over the world.

The previous example is a classic geographic scale-out scenario. There are many other examples like this, but the concept remains pretty much the same: they are all strategic in nature. Keep in mind that the application needs to support scalability, and some applications are written as to be optimized for scalability. Your organization needs to take a strategic approach from the design of the application to deployment of the application to make it scalable.

Security Implications/Considerations

When using cloud providers, keep in mind several security implications. When applications are moved to the provider's cloud, we give up the control of the hardware and data running on it. We trust that the provider takes proper precautions to protect our data, but we cannot rely on it. Another consideration is connectivity to the applications and data. Most of the time it is across the Internet, where *man-in-the-middle (MitM)* attacks and eavesdropping can occur.

When data is transmitted or accessed to or from the public cloud, the data should be encrypted in transit. The protocol used to encrypt the data during transit should allow for authentication of the data and strong encryption to prevent replay attacks, MitM attacks, and interception of the data. Application authentication should also be encrypted to prevent theft of the identity of services running the application and users accessing the application.

When data is at rest in the storage medium of the public cloud, the data should also be encrypted. This restful encryption will ensure that our data residing on the hardware at the provider is safe in the event of theft, misplacement, or any other circumstance out of our control.

In addition to security, identity management must be considered. When applications are moved to the public cloud, we should ensure that we maintain *single sign-on (SSO)*. It is common practice to create a VPN tunnel to the cloud resources we have purchased so that we can allow for native authentication back to our identity systems.

SSO can also be in the form of a federated identity solution such as Microsoft Federated Services or the Shibboleth federated service. Federated services allow for the authentication of users and computers on our immediate network. We then provide the application with a response-token guarantee that we have authenticated the user or computer.

Relationship Between Local and Cloud Resources

It is common for most enterprise networks to be built on a hybrid cloud model. There are many applications that should be hosted locally in the company's private cloud, such as file services. Then there are applications that should be hosted remotely in the public cloud, such as external websites.

When looking at the resources we can host locally and remotely, we must consider how to leverage the public cloud to our advantage. When we back up our local server farm, we want to do it locally because the resources we are backing up are local. However, if we leverage cloud storage and transmit the month-end backups to the public cloud, we can guarantee that if we have a local disaster the data will still be available.

Compute power is another resource I touched on briefly when discussing the hybrid cloud. We can burst our local cloud and bring on resources from the public cloud to scale out our service. One use of cloud bursting might be to scale out our intranet web servers or a particular application that was in high demand but didn't warrant the purchase of more equipment. Cloud bursting is also used when the equipment will take too long to acquire.

There are countless other examples of augmenting the local private cloud with public cloud resources. When the local private cloud is secured and augmented with public cloud resources, it is commonly known as a virtual private cloud (VPC). However, when making these decisions, we should consider where our user base is located, consider how long the resources will be needed, perform a cost analysis between purchasing the equipment and using the public cloud, and of course, calculate what the potential savings will be to our company.

Exam Essentials

Know and understand the various type of cloud services.   Software as a Service (SaaS) allows us to use an application provided and maintained by the service provider. Platform as a Service (PaaS) is a platform for designing applications that are compiled and executed in the cloud. Infrastructure as a Service (IaaS) allows the customer to rent the infrastructure of compute, network, and storage from the cloud provider. Desktop as a Service (DaaS) is a service that provides the end user with a virtual desktop that lives in the cloud.

Know and understand the various cloud delivery models.   In a private cloud, resources are owned by the organization and exclusively used by the organization. In a public cloud, defined resources at the provider are provisioned and used by the general public. The public cloud allows a pay-as-you-go strategy that is similar to renting the equipment rather than owning it. A hybrid model is a blend of both the public cloud and private cloud within an organization. A community model is a grouping of organizations for a cloud resource that share a common access requirement.

Understand common connectivity methods to the public cloud.   When we host resources in the public cloud, we need local resources such as authentication. Virtual private networks (VPNs) are used to allow an encrypted tunnel to be built across the public Internet. VPNs allow for the agility of change, such as switching data centers. Public wide area networks (WANs) can be built out from the customer to the public cloud provider; these connections are exclusive for the customer.

Understand the basic operations of Infrastructure as Code (IaC).   Infrastructure as Code empowers DevOps to provision servers with code-based automation and orchestration tools. The two common approaches of deploying IaC are imperative and declarative. An imperative approach requires a step-by-step script to be created for the end goal. A declarative approach only defines the end state and it is left to the orchestration tool to get to the end goal. Three common tools for IaC are Chef, Puppet, and Ansible.

Know the various characteristics of the cloud.   The characteristic of multitenancy means that more than one organization shares a piece of hardware or service. Elasticity defines that resources can be added to a service or application during peak utilization and removed when the utilization is nominal. Scalability is a strategic scaling out of a service or application based upon demand.

Understand security implications and considerations for public cloud applications.   Data should be transmitted with encryptions to prevent eavesdropping of the data. When data lands on the public cloud, it should be encrypted at rest on the disk. In addition to encryption of data, we should consider identity management and maintaining a single sign-on (SSO) environment for our users.

Understand the relationship between local and cloud resources.   There are several different ways to augment the local resources of compute and storage with the public cloud. An example of using the public cloud for local compute resources is cloud bursting, when purchasing the equipment is too expensive or it will take too long to acquire. Storage resources can be used for month-end backups of our local server farm; this moves the backups away from our physical location in the event of disaster.

Review Questions

1. On which layer of the OSI model does encryption and decryption occur?
   A. Application
   B. Presentation
   C. Session
   D. Transport

2. Which layer in the OSI model provides framing of data?
   A. Application
   B. Physical
   C. LLC
   D. Data Link

3. What is the proper protocol data unit for data at the Application layer?
   A. Bits
   B. Segments
   C. User datagrams
   D. Frames

4. Which connectivity method is locally owned, managed by an organization and used to connect the organization's LAN together?
   A. MAN
   B. CAN
   C. WAN
   D. WLAN

5. Which network topology design has a centralized switch connecting all of the devices?
   A. Star topology
   B. Full mesh topology
   C. Partial mesh topology
   D. Hybrid topology

6. Which is a direct benefit of a full mesh topology?
   A. Increased bandwidth
   B. Increased redundancy
   C. Decreased switch count
   D. Increased complexity

7. Which core diameter is commonly associated with single-mode fiber-optic cabling?

   A. 50 microns

   B. 125 microns

   C. 62.5 microns

   D. 9 microns

8. Which transceiver type allows for the connection of up to four different devices from one transceiver?

   A. SPF

   B. SPF+

   C. QSPF+

   D. GBIC

9. What is the functional purpose of an APC fiber-optic connection end?

   A. Vendor interoperability

   B. Increased speed of the connection

   C. Extremely polished surface

   D. Minimized reflection loss

10. Which cabling standard was the first to support 10 Gbps data speeds?

   A. Category 5

   B. Category 5e

   C. Category 6

   D. Category 7

11. Which method will allow you to use RFC 1918 addresses for Internet requests?

   A. CIDR

   B. Classful addressing

   C. NAT

   D. VPN

12. Why is IPv6 needed in the world today?

   A. It does not require NAT to operate.

   B. The IPv4 address space is exhausted.

   C. IPv4 is considered legacy, and IPv6 is the replacement.

   D. IPv6 does not require subnetting.

13. Which is true of the IP address 135.20.255.255?

   A. It is a Class A address.

   B. It is a broadcast address.

   C. It is the default gateway address.

   D. It has a default mask of 255.0.0.0.

14. You have been given an IP address network of 203.23.23.0. You are asked to subnet it for two hosts per network. What is the subnet mask you will need to use to maximize networks?

    A. 255.255.255.252

    B. 255.255.255.248

    C. 255.255.255.240

    D. 255.255.255.224

15. Which IPv6 address is not a valid address?

    A. 2001:db8:f::0000:1e2:2c0:2

    B. 2001:0db8:0:0:0:8d8:242:1

    C. 2001:0db8::10e:0:12

    D. 2001:0db8:45::102::12

16. You need to provide text console–based access to a server for administration. Which protocol will provide encrypted text console–based access for the server?

    A. Telnet

    B. RDP

    C. SSH

    D. SFTP

17. Which protocol is built into Microsoft servers for remote access purposes?

    A. SNMP

    B. LDAP

    C. Telnet

    D. RDP

18. Which Transport layer protocol provides assured delivery and retransmission of segments lost in transmission?

    A. ICMP

    B. UDP

    C. IP

    D. TCP

19. You need to make sure that a printer is configured with the same IP address every time it is turned on. However, the printer is too troublesome to configure a static IP address. What can be done to achieve the goal?

    A. Configure an A record for the printer in DNS.

    B. Configure a DHCP exclusion for the printer.

    C. Configure a DHCP reservation for the printer.

    D. Configure a PTR record for the printer in DNS.

20. Which record type is used for an IPv4 address mapping to FQDN for DNS queries?

    A. The A record

    B. The CName record

    C. The PTR record

    D. The AAAA record

21. Which should only be performed at the core layer?

    A. Routing

    B. Supporting clients

    C. Configuring ACLs

    D. Switching

22. Where is the hybrid topology most commonly seen in the three-tier design model?

    A. Core layer

    B. Distribution layer

    C. Access layer

    D. Routing layer

23. Where is the full mesh topology commonly seen in the three-tier design model?

    A. Core layer

    B. Distribution layer

    C. Access layer

    D. Routing layer

24. Hosting a disaster recovery (DR) site on Microsoft Azure is an example of which National Institute of Standards and Technology (NIST) type of cloud service?

    A. IaaS

    B. DRaaS

    C. PaaS

    D. SaaS

25. A hosted medical records service is an example of which cloud model?

    A. PaaS

    B. IaaS

    C. SaaS

    D. BaaS

Chapter

2

Domain 2.0: Network Implementations

THE FOLLOWING COMPTIA NETWORK+ OBJECTIVES ARE COVERED IN THIS CHAPTER:

✓ **2.1 Compare and contrast various devices, their features, and their appropriate placement on the network.**

- Networking devices
    - Layer 2 switch
    - Layer 3 capable switch
    - Router
    - Hub
    - Access point
    - Bridge
    - Wireless LAN controller
    - Load balancer
    - Proxy server
    - Cable modem
    - DSL modem
    - Repeater
    - Voice gateway
    - Media converter
    - Intrusion prevention system (IPS)/intrusion detection system (IDS) device
    - Firewall
    - VPN headend

- Networked devices
    - Voice over Internet Protocol (VoIP) phone
    - Printer
    - Physical access control devices
    - Cameras
    - Heating, ventilation, and air conditioning (HVAC) sensors
    - Internet of Things (IoT)
        - Refrigerator
        - Smart speakers
        - Smart thermostats
        - Smart doorbells
- Industrial control systems/supervisory control and data acquisition (SCADA)

✓ **2.2 Compare and contrast routing technologies and bandwidth management concepts.**

- Routing
    - Dynamic routing
        - Protocols [Routing Internet Protocol (RIP), Open Shortest Path First (OSPF), Enhanced Interior Gateway Routing Protocol (EIGRP), Border Gateway Protocol (BGP)]
            - Link state vs. distance vector vs. hybrid
    - Static routing
    - Default route
    - Administrative distance
    - Exterior vs. interior
    - Time to live
- Bandwidth management
    - Traffic shaping
    - Quality of service (QoS)

✓ **2.3 Given a scenario, configure and deploy common Ethernet switching features.**

- Data virtual local area network (VLAN)
- Voice VLAN
- Port configurations
    - Port tagging/802.1Q
    - Port aggregation
        - Link Aggregation Control Protocol (LACP)
    - Duplex
    - Speed
    - Flow control
    - Port mirroring
    - Port security
    - Jumbo frames
    - Auto-medium-dependent interface cross-over (MDI-X)
- Media access control (MAC) address tables
- Power over Ethernet (PoE)/Power over Ethernet plus (PoE+)
- Spanning Tree Protocol
- Carrier-sense multiple access with collision detection (CSMA/CD)
- Address Resolution Protocol (ARP)
- Neighbor Discovery Protocol

✓ **2.4 Given a scenario, install and configure the appropriate wireless standards and technologies.**

- 802.11 standards
    - a
    - b
    - g
    - n (WiFi 4)
    - ac (WiFi 5)
    - ax (WiFi 6)

- Frequencies and range
  - 2.4GHz
  - 5GHz
- Channels
  - Regulatory impacts
- Channel bonding
- Service set identifier (SSID)
  - Basic service set
  - Extended service set
  - Independent basic service set (Ad-hoc)
  - Roaming
- Antenna types
  - Omni
  - Directional
- Encryption standards
  - Wi-Fi Protected Access (WPA)/WPA2 Personal [Advanced Encryption Standard (AES)/Temporal Key Integrity Protocol (TKIP)]
  - WPA/WPA2 Enterprise (AES/TKIP)
- Cellular technologies
  - Code-division multiple access (CDMA)
  - Global System for Mobile Communications (GSM)
  - Long-Term Evolution (LTE)
  - 3G, 4G, 5G
- Multiple input, multiple output (MIMO) and multi-user MIMO (MU-MIMO)

In the prior chapter, "Domain 1.0: Networking Fundamentals," I covered the networking fundamentals such as how protocols operate, and we took a detailed look of various layers of the OSI model that form the networking stack. In this chapter we will apply that knowledge to the implementation for the various devices you will find in networks today. This might sound relatively simple, but the considerations when implementing a device always adds a level of complexity. In this chapter you will learn about the various components, their implementation, and some of the considerations when implementing them, and the chapter will also provide a detailed look at routers, switches, and wireless.

2.1 Compare and contrast various devices, their features, and their appropriate placement on the network.

The various building blocks inside a network perform the vital functions of moving, distributing, protecting, and controlling data. Each of these devices performs specific functions. It is important for you to understand the function of each device so that you can make an educated decision when implementing them in your network infrastructure. In the following sections, I will cover the functionality of each device you will commonly find inside a network.

Network Devices

There are lots of different network devices to choose from when building a network. Each performs the important functions of segmentation of collision domains, segmentation of broadcast domains, security of protocols, security of applications, and extending the wireless infrastructure as well as many other functions. The key difference between network devices and networked devices is that network devices are used to connect networked devices. For example, a switch (network device) is used to connect a VoIP phone (networked device). It's a minor detail, and the key take-away is that you understand how all the pieces come together to create a network. Let's start by reviewing some common network devices and their functions at the various layers of the OSI model.

Hubs

Hubs are considered legacy devices and are not currently used in LANs However, it is important to understand network hub functionality so that you do not use hubs in lieu of a switch. Hubs function at layer 1 (Physical layer) of the OSI model because they are nothing more than multiport repeaters. If you used a four-port hub similar to the one in Figure 2.1 and a device on any of the ports transmitted on an Ethernet frame, the frame would be repeated on all the other connected ports. This behavior forces devices that are not directly participating in the exchange of data to listen to the conversation. It may not seem to be a problem, since devices not participating in the exchange of data will just disregard, or more specifically drop, the frames. However, this robs useful bandwidth from those devices not participating in the exchange of data. Although full-duplex hubs can be purchased, they are always referenced as being half-duplex devices. Hubs typically operate at speeds of 10 Mbps or 100 Mbps. Hubs can be useful when you want to capture a conversation between two computers with a packet analyzer since the frame is repeated to all connected ports. Advanced managed switches now have these capabilities built-in. In Figure 2.2, you see a visual representation of a hub or repeater as it is applied to the OSI model, along with the logical symbol for a hub.

FIGURE 2.1 Four-port active hub

FIGURE 2.2 Hubs, repeaters, and the OSI model

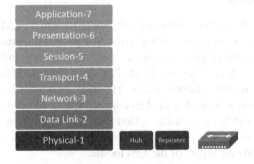

Repeaters

Repeaters do nothing more than repeat an incoming signal back out the exiting end. They were used originally in networking when attenuation of a signal was an issue. It would repeat the original signal so the new signal would have a chance of reaching its destination. However, today everything is digital and functions typically within 100 meters of each device.

Repeaters are not entirely useless; they have plenty of useful applications. You can find repeaters in WAN applications like fiber-optic communications. They are used to boost the fiber-optic signal every 200 Kms, when fiber-optic lines are run across a long distance. Later I will also explain how repeaters are used in wireless communications. However, they are not commonly used in local area networks (LANs) today as a network connectivity device.

Media Converters

Technically, media converters can be considered a type of physical repeater. A media converter repeats a digital signal on a different media, thus converting and repeating the digital signal on the new media.

Copper Ethernet has a defined limitation of 100 meters (330 feet), which limits what copper Ethernet can be used for. A common problem is needing Ethernet connectivity, such as for a VoIP phone or a security camera, in remote locations but the distance is over 100 meters. This is where we can benefit from media converters, because they allow us to convert from copper Ethernet to fiber-optic cable back to copper Ethernet again. Media converters and the fiber optics that accompany extending copper Ethernet raise the costs of the project and introduce failure points, so they should be used sparingly.

Switches

Switches are the main connectivity device within networks today. They function at layer 2 (Data Link layer) of the OSI model, which makes them extremely efficient. Switches that only perform layer 2 functionality are often referred to as layer 2 switches. They do not have the same problems associated with hubs, since they perform two important functions at layer 2: MAC address learning and forward filter decisions based on the MAC addresses learned. These functions are performed by application-specific integrated circuits (ASICs). Figure 2.3 shows some managed switches you will typically find in wiring closets and data centers; they vary in configuration options and port density. The arrangement and sophistication of ASICs dictates the switching speed and price. Managed switches can also perform a third vital function: loop avoidance through STP (Spanning Tree Protocol), which I will cover in this chapter in the discussion of objective 2.3, "Given a scenario, configure and deploy common Ethernet switching features." Managed switches offer several features, most notably VLANs. VLANs allow you to make virtual switches inside the physical switch to segment the network further for security and control of broadcasts. I will also cover a number of these features in the discussion of objective 2.3. In Figure 2.4, you see a visual representation of a switch as it is applied to the OSI model, along with the logical symbol for a switch.

FIGURE 2.3 Typical managed switches

FIGURE 2.4 Switches and the OSI model

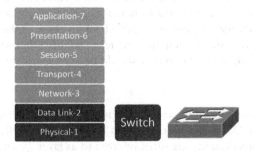

Bridges

Bridges perform functionality identical to that of switches. They perform address learning and forward filtering decisions based on the MAC address table. They can even use STP. However, bridges have a limited number of ports and are usually software-based switches. They do not have the extremely fast ASICs switches do. They were the very first implementation of switching and still have useful purposes today; most current operating systems support bridging. You can use Microsoft Windows to extend the wireless network to the Ethernet network attached to the Windows computer via bridging. Linux also supports bridging between Ethernet adapters and can even perform STP. Even applications like VMware Workstation can bridge traffic between a virtual machine (VM) and the host's network interface card (NIC).

The word *bridge* today is used as a function of bridging traffic via the operating system rather than to describe a particular network device in the network.

Routers

Routers are the heart of our networks and the Internet. I like to think of them as intelligent pumps, which sort and move data packets to their intended network destination. They perform these routing decisions on the destination IP address of the packet, so they are considered layer 3 (Network layer) devices. Figure 2.5 shows a typical router found at the edge of our internal networks today. In Figure 2.6, you see a visual representation of a router as it is applied to the OSI model, along with the logical symbol for a router.

FIGURE 2.5 Typical edge router

FIGURE 2.6 Routers and the OSI model

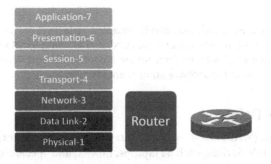

Another vital function routers perform is the segmentation of broadcast domains. A broadcast domain defines the boundary of the network where a broadcast message can be heard. This is why you get an IP address from your home router and not your neighbor's router. Outside of the DHCP protocol, there are many other useful broadcast-based protocols that require a certain amount of network bandwidth. Even basic network communications require broadcasting, such as the case with the Address Resolution Protocol (ARP). If we didn't have routers, the Internet would be a very slow and loud shouting match of devices!

Layer 3 Switches

You are probably wondering, can switches perform both switching functionality and routing functionality? The answer is yes, they are called layer 3 switches and they are commonly found in networks today. They perform all of the functionality that a layer 2 switch would commonly perform, but they also have a special ASIC that allows for routing functionality. This give you the functionality of routing between VLANs on the same switching equipment, which gives you the benefit of low latency. In many instances, switchports can be converted to routed ports, so the layer 3 switch can act as a router to other network devices.

Depending on the type or model of switch purchased, they can even participate in dynamic routing protocols. Dynamic routing protocols will be covered in the discussion of objective 2.2, "Compare and contrast routing technologies and bandwidth management concepts." In Figure 2.7, you see a visual representation of a layer 3 switch as it is applied to the OSI model, along with the logical symbol for a layer 3 switch.

FIGURE 2.7   Layer 3 switches and the OSI model

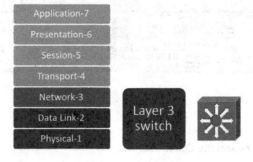

Many layer 2 switches can be enabled as layer 3 switches by purchasing additional licensing from the vendor. Switching vendors sell these license-enabled switches, so the customer can grow into the product and not have to repurchase equipment later on.

Wireless Access Point

A wireless access point (WAP) is a device that extends the wired network to a wireless network. This allows mobile devices, such as laptops, tablets, and specialized wireless-enabled equipment, to access your network infrastructure. The functional role of a WAP is similar to a layer 2 switch. A WAP's main function is to switch traffic between wireless clients as well as wired components. Each WAP can be directly wired to your network infrastructure, or WAPs can join other WAPs already wired, creating a wireless mesh. This is useful in designs where cabling back to a switch would cost too much or the distance is too great. Many municipalities use these wireless mesh technologies to add IP cameras to busy intersections. In Figure 2.8 you can see two common configurations of WAPs with internal and external antennas. Stand-alone WAPs are sometimes called autonomous WAPs when they are used without a wireless controller, because they function autonomously of each other. In Figure 2.9, you see a visual representation of an access point as it is applied to the OSI model along with the logical symbol for an access point.

FIGURE 2.8   WAPs with internal and external antennas

FIGURE 2.9   Access points and the OSI model

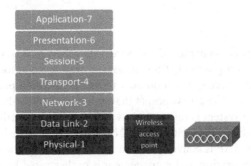

Wireless LAN Controller

One of the problems with using multiple autonomous WAPs in a wireless network is channel assignment when the roaming between the WAPs is not coordinated for the client. This can be solved with a wireless LAN controller (WLC or WLAN controller). The WLAN controller can provide coordination services for the client as well as deployment services for the access points.

When we look at the traffic a wireless LAN controller facilitates, there are three main types of data: the data in the control, data, and management planes. These terms are universal with all networking equipment, not just wireless equipment. The control plane is the data that WAPs use to control internal functions, like SSID and channel assignment. The data plane is the data that WAPs move between the wireless clients and the network. The management plane is the management data for configuration and diagnostics. In Figure 2.10, you see an autonomous access point deployment versus a WLAN controller deployment, along with the three planes of data.

FIGURE 2.10   Wireless LAN controller functionality

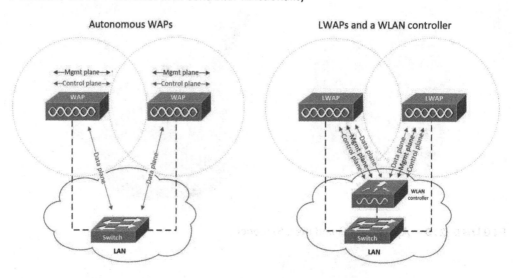

When a WLAN controller is deployed to coordinate access points, the access points don't need their full operating system. They no longer need to be autonomous, as they will have a WLAN controller directing them on how to handle the data plane. A trimmed-down operating system is used for the access points that will join the WLAN controller. This trimmed-down operating system is referred to as a lightweight operating system. The access points deployed in a configuration with a WLAN controller are called lightweight access points (LWAPs). When a WAP is converted to an LWAP, their autonomous capabilities are surrendered and all configuration and management is orchestrated by the WLAN controller. Not all WAPs can become an LWAP, and many vendors sell their wireless equipment as autonomous or lightweight and offer conversion between the two modes.

The Control And Provisioning of Wireless Access Points (CAPWAP) protocol is often used between the LWAPs and the WLAN controller. CAPWAP is an open standard used for facilitating all the various data planes. The management plane is facilitated when the LWAP boots up, joins the controller, and is provisioned with a name identifier and IP address. This is considered the underlay network because it will facilitate the movement of data for each LWAP to the WLAN controller. After the LWAP is booted and provisioned, the control and data planes are tunneled back to the controller using UDP port 5246 for the control plane and UDP port 5247 for the data plane. This is considered the overlay network because it will use the underlay network established during bootup and provisioning to move data. You may wonder, why tunnel data and control traffic to the controller? By centralizing the control plane and data plane, the WLAN controller can effectively manage all wireless clients.

Split MAC is another common deployment mode of wireless communications; often vendors will have their own variation of split MAC. For example, Cisco calls this mode Flexconnect mode. The principle behind it is splitting the MAC layer of the OSI between the WLAN controller and the LWAP. This allows the LWAPs to focus on real-time data, like encryption/decryption, channel monitoring, and rogue detection, just to name a few. The controller can then focus on the control of the access points, and in many cases this can decentralize the switching of the data plane. This mode allows for local switching on the LWAP for traffic that is local to the access point. Every vendor has a variation of split MAC, and their implantation is usually the "special sauce" that makes their product unique.

With either mode deployed, the controller assists the LWAPs in broadcasting the same SSID but on different channels in each of the wireless cells the LWAP creates. The controller also uses 802.11 extensions to communicate with the client, so the client can switch to the new channel based on signal strength. However, one of the most frustrating issues with WLAN controllers is the wireless clients attached to the LWAPs, since it's ultimately up to them to switch between WAPs and channels.

 The operation of a WLAN controller is often really complex, especially for the average consumer. However, the average consumer sometimes needs the functionality that comes with a WLAN controller, such as a single SSID across multiple access points in their house that is centrally controlled by a WLAN controller. Luckily the consumer market has created products like Google Nest WiFi and Amazon eero, just to name a couple. These products create a simple and easy deployment of Wi-Fi for the average consumer with the functionality of complex WLAN controllers and LWAPs.

Wireless Range Extender

A wireless ranger extender is often referred to as a wireless repeater. It operates by associating to a wireless network and rebroadcasting the SSID. It can be useful in wireless networks that have a dead zone, but a major drawback is that the bandwidth is reduced by 50 percent. This is because all network communications now must travel two wireless signals to reach the wired network. Wireless range extenders are usually only found in *small office, home office (SOHO)* networks.

There is an argument that with the inexpensive mesh type systems on the market today, wireless range extenders should not be used. However, they are a cheaper alternative to purchasing a complete wireless system for the average consumer.

Load Balancer

Load balancers allow administrators to distribute the load of requests from users to multiple resources or even multiple locations. Load balancers typically function at layer 4 (Transport layer) and layer 3 (Network layer), inspecting the Transport layer ports and destination IP addresses. The load balancer then makes a decision, based on the load of ongoing requests from other users, to forward the new request to the next available server. Load balancers also function at layer 7 (Application layer) for redirection of users to the server with the least amount of load or to the closest server. It is common to find load balancers distributing load to web servers since websites have static content and they are the perfect candidates for this technology. It is also common to employ geographic load balancers, because applications are now global and directing a user to the closest server provides the fastest response to the end user. With the expansion of cloud services, geographic load balancing is a popular technology.

Websites are not the only candidate for load balancers. Microsoft Server 2019 has a built-in load balancing mechanism that can be configured for load-balancing DHCP. Load balancers are also used for Terminal Services and virtual desktop servers. They can be found in just about any service that has a stateless request for resources. They can be configured to provide affinity for a server until the user is done with the request. Load balancers can be hardware or software solutions—they are commonly deployed today as software solutions since virtualization and cloud services have become mainstream for corporate hosting of services.

Proxy Servers

Proxy servers are used to proxy a connection from a user to a web application. When we proxy something, we are sending the request to the intermediary (proxy), which fetches the request on behalf of our request and returns the data. Proxies provide an administrator with a single point of egress (*forward proxy* or just proxy) or ingress (*reverse proxy*). This provides not only a layer of protection, but also a way to centrally log access to the data. We can also filter access since the proxy is the single exit point or entry point. When we filter access on a proxy, it becomes the control point—this is how content filters work. The most useful property of a proxy is the caching ability; when we enable caching, this type of proxy is referred to as a caching proxy. When we enable caching, we significantly reduce bandwidth consumption and load on web servers we maintain.

In Figure 2.11 you can see a typical internal network on the left and the Internet on the right. When implementing a proxy server, administrators will block clients from directly connecting to web servers on the Internet at the router. The clients will be forced to use the proxy server to connect to the web servers on the Internet. When a request is made for a web page, the request will be directed to the proxy server, which will request the page on behalf of the client. When the reply comes back from the Internet web server, it is returned to the proxy server and the proxy server returns the web reply back to the client. To the left of the proxy server is a caching and filtering (content filter) engine. Proxy servers do not have to use caching engines. However, if they do, we benefit from reduced bandwidth. All of the consecutive requests to the same web page will never generate a request to the Internet until the cache timer expires on the content. We can also employ content filtering that can restrict the user from inappropriate web pages.

FIGURE 2.11   Overview of a proxy server implementation

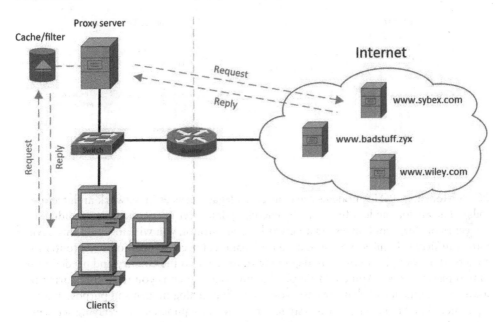

Reverse proxy servers serve clients as well, but in the reverse order of requests. In Figure 2.12 you see the Internet on the left and a private network or cloud service provider on the right. You'll notice the router and switch are only there for connectivity. In this example, a client on the Internet requests a web page from www.wiley.com. However, in lieu of requesting the web page directly from the server, the client sends the request to a reverse proxy. The client doesn't know that the request is being proxied on the backend. This reverse proxy then requests the web page from the actual server(s), and the server responds to the reverse proxy. The reverse proxy then responds back to the client. The benefit of a reverse proxy is caching, for the simple reason of saving CPU cycles to render the page on the actual server. It also reduces the server's load by handling encryption, security certificates, and authentication to enable a single sign-on to access multiple services. Reverse proxies are useful for load balancing when more than one actual server is used. They are also very handy to mitigate denial of service (DoS) attacks that create an enormous amount of web page requests, resulting in CPU cycles wasted and denying legitimate users access to the web pages. Reverse proxies are often referred to as server publishing.

Modems

The term *modem* is actually two opposite terms combined: *modulation* and *demodulation*. Modulation is the act of encoding a digital signal into an analog signal. Demodulation is the act of reversing the encoding back into a digital signal again. These modulated analog signals are used with plain old telephone service (POTS) modems, Digital Subscriber Line (DSL) modems, and cable modems.

FIGURE 2.12   Overview of a reverse proxy server implementation

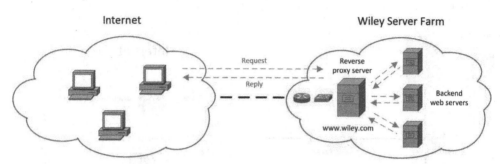

POTS Modems   POTS modems are considered legacy devices in network architecture today. The analog modem functions by encoding data over telephone lines as audible screeches of chirps and hisses. As a network administrator, you will not build this device into your network unless you need an out-of-band connectivity method for a router or switch—for example, if you were deploying routers across the country and needed to be in two places at once. You could simply dial into one router as you were configuring the local router. Outside of that use case, you might find analog modems in purpose-built equipment like fire panels, alarm systems, and elevator equipment for relaying service-related information. So it is useful to know what you are dealing with.

Cable Modems   Cable modems are used in broadband Internet connectivity from your local cable provider. Using the existing cable lines that already carry TV programming to your home or business, data can be modulated/demodulated onto a channel to carry your data. The cable modem directly communicates with the fiber node in your local area. The fiber node's job is to modulate/demodulate the signal to your cable modem and carry the traffic back to the provider's head end over fiber-optic cable.

DSL Modems   A DSL modem acts similarly to a POTS modem by modulating and demodulating chirps and hisses onto a POTS line to the phone company's central office (CO). The difference is it uses a frequency higher than 3,400 Hz, way into the inaudible range of even 4 MHz. DSL technology shares your existing phone line back to the central office, and it is necessary to install filters on every phone in the house. These filters block any tones above 3,400 Hz from disrupting the DSL modem's data stream.

VoIP PBX

Voice over IP (VoIP) private branch exchange (PBX) is a private phone system that communicates with VoIP. PBXs have been around for several decades. They provide phone communications using specialized phones often called *time-division multiplexing (TDM)* phones. PBX systems allow for call forwarding from the individual phones, call pickup groups, conference calling, and many other enterprise-type call features. With the expansive adoption of VoIP, the VoIP PBX has become a popular upgrade path that moves away from the vendor lock-in of TDM phone equipment. You will find that VoIP phones and VoIP PBXs offer features that are vendor-specific as well. However, with VoIP phone systems, we no longer need to maintain a separate wired infrastructure; it is all treated like data. This is a tremendous selling point when you're deciding to convert to a VoIP PBX, since the sunk cost of switching equipment has probably already been made. An added benefit that the VoIP PBX enables is the ability for remote offices to use the same VoIP PBX as the main office for all end-user communications' needs. VoIP PBXs can be software or hardware appliances, depending on the number of users and features required.

VoIP PBXs offer all of the features a traditional TDM PBX phone system does. Many other advanced features can be purchased along with the VoIP PBX, such as Unified Communications (UC). UC is a collaboration of applications and VoIP services. In business today, information is not bound to a phone call or a voicemail. UC combines VoIP, instant messaging, voicemail, interactive voice response (IVR), and web conferencing, just to name a few. An example of UC is when you dial into your bank and are presented with an IVR requesting your account number and purpose of the call. Your call is routed to an agent, and that agent now has your information on their screen, ready to assist. Microsoft recently purchased Skype as a building platform for UC to replace a prior product called Microsoft Lync. Microsoft is not the only company—Cisco and other phone system providers offer their own version of UC.

VoIP Gateway

A VoIP gateway allows a VoIP PBX to interface with an existing PBX or the *public switched telephone network (PSTN)*. The VoIP gateway is often referred to as a PSTN gateway when describing its functionality. VoIP gateways do not need to be used exclusively with a VoIP PBX. UC platforms such as existing Microsoft Lync or Skype often use a VoIP gateway to interface with the existing TDM PBX (see Figure 2.13). Most TDM PBXs use either ISDN PRI interfaces or T1 interfaces to connect to the PSTN. VoIP gateways can interface with the TDM PBXs as if they were the PSTN. This enables the reuse of a phone system with UC platforms.

FIGURE 2.13   UC platform and VoIP gateway

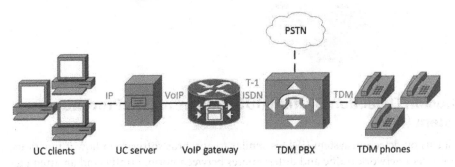

VoIP gateways are also used when you want to convert your TDM PBX to use a VoIP provider to send and receive phone calls (see Figure 2.14). If the PBX is too old, it might not support VoIP directly. A VoIP gateway will act as the PSTN and hand off a T1 of ISDN PRI to the PBX as if it were the PSTN, thus lowering calling costs via VoIP.

FIGURE 2.14   VoIP gateway acting as the PSTN

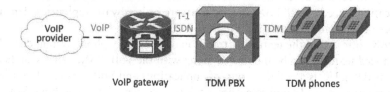

Another common use of the VoIP gateway is to provide a plain old telephone service (POTS) dial tone for fax machines, alarm systems, and so forth. The VoIP gateway can then be used to imitate the PSTN for dial-tone services (see Figure 2.15). The POTS equipment will send and receive phone calls over a VoIP network without ever knowing it is doing so. This strategy helps bridge the gap of technology when transitioning to VoIP.

FIGURE 2.15   VoIP gateway serving POTS

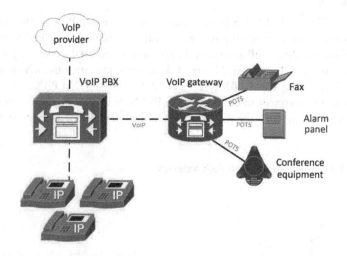

Intrusion Detection System (IDS) and Intrusion Prevention System (IPS)

An intrusion detection system (IDS) is similar to antivirus software in how it functions. The IDS watches network traffic and differentiates between normal traffic and an attempted intrusion. It performs this function in two ways: signature-based or anomaly-based.

Signature-based detection matches signatures from well-known attacks. These signatures are generally a subscription from the IDS provider, similar to antivirus signatures. The anomaly-based detection method detects abnormal traffic patterns or packets. Each IDS anomaly algorithm is the IDS provider's "special sauce." The most notable function of an IDS is that when it detects an intrusion, it gathers, identifies, and logs the traffic and then alerts administrators responsible for security. This functionality is useful when you have dedicated security response personnel or need to perform postmortem network analysis to prevent future intrusions.

An intrusion prevention system (IPS) is similar to an IDS in that they both use signature-based and anomaly-based detection. They are often referred to as intrusion detection and prevention systems. They gather, identify, and log traffic and then alert administrators. However, the IPS will try to prevent the intrusion by dropping the packets of the malicious transmission, or it will actively block the offending IP address. Most firewalls today have this functionality built-in to avert attacks and intrusions based on signature subscriptions from the provider. This is often part of a maintenance agreement with the provider.

Although the CompTIA objective is based on the generic term *IDS* and *IPS*, you may see other variations of IDS and IPS depending on how they are deployed. A network-based intrusion prevention system (NIPS) is usually in the form of a network appliance or virtual machine that sits on the network and prevents intrusion. If the IPS is host-based, then it will be referenced as a host-based intrusion prevention system (HIPS). This implementation involves a piece of software the runs on the operating system and prevents intrusion. Just as there are variations of the IPS for network-based versus host-based, there are also IDS systems that are implemented the same way.

Firewall

Firewalls control and protect data inside the internal network as well as protect against access from outside the internal network. Firewalls can be either a hardware appliance (see Figure 2.16) or a software solution. Since the release of Windows XP SP2, Microsoft has included a built-in firewall with the operating system. *Linux* has a built-in firewall called IPTables, and macOS has a built-in firewall called the Application Firewall. These OSs or application firewalls can control how applications are allowed to communicate inside your network. However, OS firewalls are not the only software firewalls out there; pfSense, McAfee, Cisco, Barracuda, and many other companies offer software-based firewalls that perform like hardware firewalls. With the ever-growing expansion of virtualization and cloud computing, the list of firewall solutions grows daily.

FIGURE 2.16   A typical hardware firewall appliance

The protection functionality of a firewall is synonymous with the term *firewall*. The definition of firewall is a wall or partition to inhibit or prevent the spread of fire. A firewall partitions your network with rules or groups of rules called policies that the administrator configures to prevent unauthorized access to data by filtering access at various levels of the OSI model. The rules in a firewall are configured as conditions and actions. Conditions can be configured on layer 3 protocols and IP addressing, layer 4 ports and states, and even specific application requests. Actions are triggered when conditions are met. The most common actions are permit traffic, block traffic, and log traffic. More advanced firewalls can slow traffic down when a condition is met. Firewalls can also control packets based on malicious activity such as port scanning or threat detection. In Figure 2.17, you see a visual representation of a firewall as it is applied to the OSI model, along with the logical symbol for a firewall.

FIGURE 2.17   Firewalls and the OSI model

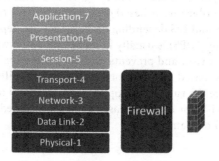

NGFW/Layer 7 firewall

Next-generation firewalls (NGFWs) are layer 7 firewalls that help protect applications by inspecting the layer 7 traffic. Most traditional firewalls inspect traffic at layer 3 (Network layer) and layer 4 (Transport layer). These inspections of traffic at layers 3 and 4 do not mitigate malicious intent to applications that are allowed past these traditional firewall rules. An example of this is your public mail server; you may have Outlook Web Access (OWA) configured for your users to access mail when they are away from the office. A traditional firewall rule will stop SYN floods and other DoS attacks, but it will not prevent a malicious user from trying to access the Exchange control panel from outside your corporate network. This level of firewalling must be done at layers higher than 3 and 4. This is where an NGFW helps mitigate security problems. We can create a policy that restricts any user who is not on the internal network from accessing the Exchange control panel via the Uniform Resource Locator (URL) for the control panel.

NGFWs do much more than just restrict access based on URLs. Most NGFWs perform something called deep packet inspection (DPI) and use an IPS to mitigate known threats. This can often be tricky when using Secure Sockets Layer (SSL) encryption because everything is encrypted. Most NGFWs allow for the termination of this encryption at the firewall itself so that DPI can be performed. In addition to DPI, NGFWs help with quality of service and bandwidth management at the application level. In Figure 2.18, you see a visual representation of an NGFW as it is applied to the OSI model, along with the logical symbol for an NGFW.

FIGURE 2.18   NGFW and the OSI model

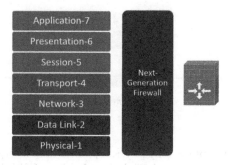

VPN Headend

A virtual private network (VPN) is an encrypted tunnel across the public Internet or an unsecured network. A VPN headend, also called a concentrator, protects data at ingress or egress points in your network. VPN concentrators are normally used for remote access users as a concentrated point into the network through a VPN tunnel. The VPN concentrator is responsible for terminating the encrypted tunnel back to the original unencrypted packets. VPN concentrators function at layer 3 (Network layer) by encrypting the original data and encapsulating it inside of various VPN protocols. Common VPN protocols are *Point-to-Point Tunneling Protocol (PPTP)*, *Layer 2 Tunneling Protocol (L2TP)*, and *IPSec*. VPN concentrators can also create a VPN tunnel between two locations, such as a branch office and the main office. VPN concentrators can be hardware or software. However, for large numbers of users, hardware VPN concentrators are the best option because they usually have specific hardware for cryptography of data during the encryption and decryption process.

VoIP Phones

A voice over IP (VoIP) phone is a networked device that allows phone calls to and from the user. There are three main types of phones you will find used in organizations today:

Physical Phones   A physical phone is the most common phone found in many organizations today, mainly because organizations are used to having a physical phone on workers' desks. Just as the name implies, a physical phone is just that, a physical phone. The VoIP phone is wired from the network with a network cable that supplies Power over Ethernet (PoE) to power the phone. The VoIP phone will contain a network port to connect it to the network. It will also have another network connection to connect the phone to the computer. This is so you can use one wire to supply the network connection to both the VoIP phone and the desktop computer. The VoIP phone achieves this by containing a small switch inside itself, as seen in Figure 2.19.

FIGURE 2.19   Typical wired VoIP phone

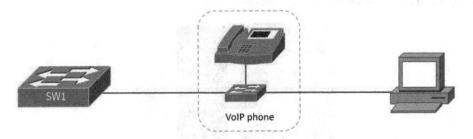

Wired VoIP phones are not the only physical phones used in organizations today. Wireless VoIP phones are also used. With the adoption of 802.11 wireless, many organizations have also adopted wireless VoIP phones. This frees the worker from being pinned to the desk during a conversation, and it also allows a degree of privacy. A worker can now simply walk to a private location without calling the other party back. This sounds like a great option when adopting VoIP, but be warned: your wireless network must support the level of service needed to make crystal clear calls. When supporting VoIP on 802.11 wireless, you'll find you may need twice as many wireless access points to accommodate the real-time communications a phone call requires.

Soft Phones   A soft phone is a piece of software that looks like a physical phone but only exists as a piece of software. Soft phones were created for maximum flexibility of both the organization and their workers. Today's workforce is ever changing, and more and more people are working from home or on the road. Organizations normally supply their workers with a laptop or mobile device when the organization needs this level of flexibility for their workers. Workers that work from home will use their existing network connection at their home to connect the device. For workers that are on the road, such as salespeople, the device is usually outfitted with wireless wide area network (WWAN) connectivity, such as a cellular card. Outside of the device, the user will only need a headset and the soft phone becomes a fully functional phone.

Virtual Phones   A virtual phone really describes a hybrid of the physical phone and soft phone that mixes both VoIP and plain old telephone service (POTS). These virtual phones are sometimes called find-me-anywhere solutions, or they are part of an overall unified communications (UC) solution. These solutions are often deployed as a cloud-based services. You configure all of your physical phone and soft phone numbers into the service. Then when the virtual phone rings, it rings on all of the configured devices. You see the caller ID on your cell phone, home phone, work phone, or any other phone you've configured to ring. The benefit to the worker is availability without surrendering their privacy. The caller never sees the worker's direct personal number, just the virtual number they dialed. This can also be tied to a 4 to 6 digit extension vs. a specific 10 digit number. This solution is very popular with technical services where, the technician will never want the user to call them directly. There are endless possibilities and this is just one of them.

There are many different VoIP phones on the market today, but generally you will need to stick to the vendor that supports your VoIP private branch exchange (PBX). Many of the vendor-specific features will only be supported when you use the vendor's VoIP phones. Features that might not be supported on the third-party phone could be transfer of phone calls, merging calls, and forwarding, just to name a few. VoIP PBX vendors will generally support basic VoIP features on any VoIP phone that you currently own. This allows a gradual migration to their product over a period of time, without breaking your business continuity.

Printers

Printing to a printer sounds simple, but it is a very complicated process when a network is involved. When the printer doesn't print, it could be a network issue, it could be a printer issue, or the printer could just be out of paper. It is probably the most hated process in the network by administrators. There is a lot going on when you hit the print button, and understanding the process is key to understanding how these devices are networked.

When you hit the print button on your client, the application renders the document using the graphic display interface (GDI) against the first portion of the print driver for the particular printer. This first step converts the print to a language called an Enhanced Meta File (EMF). The EMF file is required so we can transmit the document across the network, as seen in Figure 2.20. When it arrives at the destination, the EMF file is then processed by the driver and rendered with the other portion of the print driver that converts the EMF to the printer language. The printer language can be Postscript, Printer Control Language (PCL), or something proprietary; it is basically the printer instructions to print the document. The printer language is then transmitted to the printer, either across the network or to a directly connected device. It really is a complicated process, and those steps don't even include the point-and-print functionality of distributing the driver. The Windows operating system performs point-and-print functionality in the background to distribute the printer driver to the client upon adding the printer or double-clicking on it.

FIGURE 2.20   Network print process

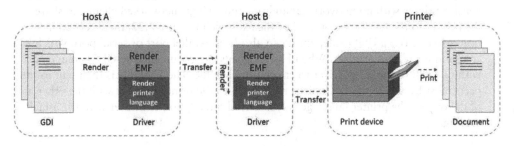

The second portion of the rendering from the EMF to the printer language can happen at one of three locations. This location dictates one of three printing scenarios with printing:

Decentralized Printing   Decentralized printing is probably the easiest to understand. It means that the printer's print language is rendered locally for the document being printed. The printer language is then transmitted to the printer directly, as shown in Figure 2.21. Keep in mind that this scenario can happen on multiple computers at one time, each computer managing its own print job from render to transmit over the network.

FIGURE 2.21   Decentralized print process

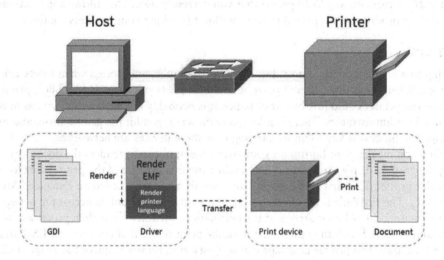

Peer-to-Peer Printing   Every Windows client can also be a Windows server; this is the definition of a peer. In small office/home office (SOHO) networks and small business networks, peer-to-peer printing works well. The Windows client operating system, such as Windows 10, has a limitation of 20 concurrent connections, so peer-to-peer printing only works in small networks.

The principle behind peer-to-peering printing is that you can purchase a relatively inexpensive printer with no network capabilities and a single networked client can share the printer to the rest of the office. For the example in Figure 2.22, the direct connection for Host B is a USB cable, but it can also be a parallel port or serial port, which is common for receipt printers. When Host A prints the document, the GDI is rendered with one half of the print driver to create the EMF file. The EMF file is then sent to the peer (Host B), where the EMF file is rendered into the print language with the other half of the driver. The printer language is transferred directly to the printer with the attached cabling.

FIGURE 2.22   Peer-to-peer print process

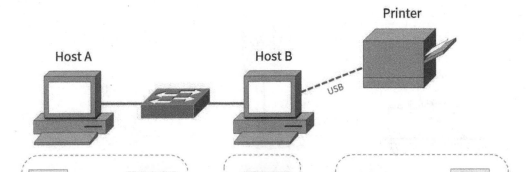

Keep in mind that if the printer has network capabilities, then peer-to-peer printing should not be used. You should set up decentralized printing in that case because peer-to-peer printing requires the host sharing the printer to be on when someone prints a document.

Centralized Printing   Centralized printing is the most common printing scenario in mid-size to large networks. It gives the administrator a great amount of control and audit capabilities because every print job will go through the centralized print server before being transmitted to the printer. The print process is almost identical to the peer-to-peer print process with the exception of how the printer is attached. It is directly attached to the network, as shown in Figure 2.23.

To properly administer a centralized printer, you have to force everyone to print to the server versus printing directly to the networked printer. You can achieve this with access control lists (ACLs), as we will discuss later in this book. Because the hosts are printing to the print server, we can then use Windows security, such as group-based ACLs to control printer access. You can even audit and control how much someone can print with third-party applications.

Physical Access Control Devices

Network security is based upon the management of users and groups and their access to resources. If a user has a particular permission to a resource, then that user can access the resource. If the user lacks the permission to the resource, then the user is denied access to the resource. As administrators we always like to manage groups of people and not individuals. So, the marketing group might have access to the latest development files, but the salespeople might not be granted access to those same files.

FIGURE 2.23   Centralized print process

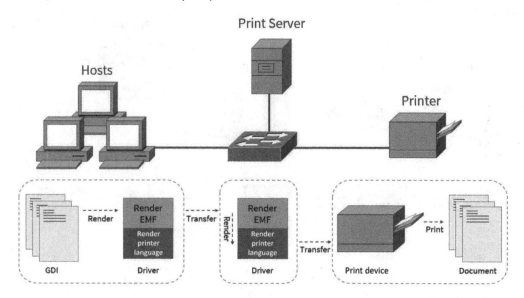

When we start to look at physical security, the system of permissions and access breaks down with traditional physical lock and key systems. A key can be given to another person that should never have access, or the key can be lost. There is no way to track a key's use, and auditing is another issue. When a master key is lost, basically you need to rekey all of your locks. These are just some of the issues with physical lock and key systems. Fortunately, as administrators of the network we can employ a new technology like access control. Access control makes physical lock and key systems obsolete!

Access control systems have two distinct parts: the Ethernet network and the low-voltage network, as shown in Figure 2.24. The Ethernet network is just how it sounds: it is the network that connects devices and computers with switches. It is also used to connect the access control panel to the network. The low-voltage network has wiring between the access control panel and various devices at the control point. The control point will normally contain a reader and a door lock. The wiring to the control point is usually a proprietary standard.

Although every access control system has its own proprietary components, each component can be described by one the following terms:

Security Console   The security console exists on the Ethernet network and communicates with the access control servers (ACSs) for user enrollment into the access control system. Although the term *security console* tends to describe a physical console, it is usually just an application on your security officer's desktop computer. The security console should be in a protected area where the average person cannot physically access it in an attempt to alter their own access permissions. The security console is also where audit reports are created, so you can audit when people gained access or tried to gain access to various control points.

FIGURE 2.24   Access control schematic

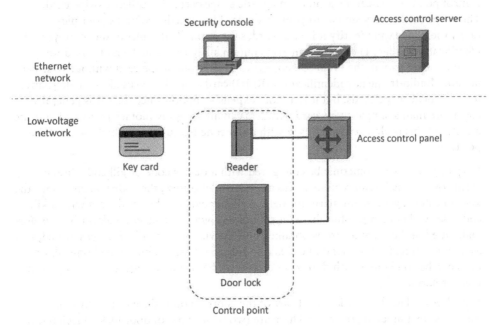

Access Control Server   When a user is enrolled in the access control system, an entry will be created in the access control server describing the user's access for various control points. The access control server will then either respond to access control panel requests or will download the database to all the access control panels. In today's networks, the access control server is usually just a virtual machine or a physical server.

Access Control Panel   The access control panel and access control server are usually made by the same vendor and almost always proprietary. The access control panel is the bridge between the Ethernet network and the low-voltage network. The access control panel is where the control point is logically configured (reader to door) and physically connected (reader and door). The connections at minimum are a reader and door lock, but these configurations can be much more elaborate, including multiple door locks and door position sensors for creating a man trap to prevent tailgating by unauthorized people. One attribute of an access control panel is its ability to function in the event of a network outage, which is called survivability. Some access control panels make access requests as they are required and some panels download the database from the access control server and make local requests. The cost of the access control panel is going to be directly proportional to the number of control point devices that can be connected. The more devices that the panel can control and read, the higher the price. You will also have multiple access control panels in an installation.

Reader   *Reader* is a generic term, and it can describe a number of technologies. The control point reader can be a simple magnetic stripe card, also called a swipe card. The swipe card is very similar to your credit card but usually contains your picture so someone can identify it is your card, so it normally doubles as an employee identification badge. The reader can also contain a key pad, which can be used for two-factor security in the event someone tries to use your swipe card without your permission. Radio-frequency identification (RFID) cards can also be used as an alternative to traditional swipe cards, but it is a more expensive option since the cards generally cost more than a simple swipe card. Readers can also employ biometrics to authenticate a user, but this is almost always used with a pin code because of the high rate of false positives.

Keypad readers can sometime be configured with a duress code or kill code. In the event someone is forcing you to access a space under duress, the code you enter into the keypad can trigger a silent alarm for help. A reader can also be configured with a kill code that will effectively shut that control point down and trigger an alarm. This is normally used in the event a card is obtained and the victim cannot be further harmed, such as in a mugging. It may sound like cloak-and-dagger features, but many home alarm systems can be configured with duress codes as well. It's a simple feature that can prevent theft or harm.

Door Lock   The door lock is the heart of the control point, since it literally controls the access by unlocking the door. There are two main types of door locks: mechanical door locks and magnetic locks. A mechanical door lock controls the latch or the door strike to allow access for a person. A mechanical door lock is usually a solenoid that retracts the latch or retracts a pin in the strike to allow the door to open. A magnetic lock is nothing more than a giant magnet that keeps the door locked when energized. These types of locks require a request to exit (REX) bar on the secured side of the door to allow people to leave. The problem with magnetic locks is that they fail to open in a power outage. They are normally used internally in a building or as part of a man trap.

Tailgating is a common tactic used to gain access into a secure area. A tailgater will "tail," or follow, behind someone that has swiped or authenticated their entry device. It can be as simple as grabbing the door before it closes or walking in behind someone like you own the place. A man trap is a tailgating prevention method that employs a series of two controlled doors and a corridor between them. You must successively authenticate the first door and then the second door. The prerequisite for authenticating the second door is the first door being in a closed position. The corridor makes it impossible for someone to sneak in, since there is line of sight to the first door. It also makes it very uncomfortable being in a small room with a stranger.

Cameras

Cameras are the backbone of physical security. It is the only detection method that allows an investigator to identify what happened, when it happened, and, most important, who made it happen. Two types of cameras can be deployed: fixed and *pan-tilt-zoom (PTZ)*. Fixed cameras are the best choice when recording for surveillance activities. Pan-tilt-zoom (PTZ) cameras allow for 360-degree operations and zooming in on an area. PTZs are most commonly used for intervention, such as covering an area outside during an accident or medical emergency. PTZ cameras are usually deployed for the wrong reasons, mainly because they are cool! PTZs are often put into patrol mode to cover a larger area than a fixed camera can. However, when an incident occurs, they are never pointed in the area you need them! It is always best to use a fixed camera or multiple fixed cameras, unless you need a PTZ for a really good reason. They are usually more expensive and require more maintenance than fixed cameras.

Cameras can be deployed with two common media types: coaxial cable and Ethernet. Coaxial cable is used typically in areas where preexisting coaxial lines are in place or distances are too far for typical Ethernet. These systems are called *closed-circuit television (CCTV)*. Coaxial camera systems generally use appliance-like devices for recording of video. These CCTV recorders generally have a finite number of ports for cameras and a finite amount of storage in the form of direct attached storage (DAS).

Ethernet (otherwise known as IP) surveillance is becoming the standard for new installations. Anywhere an Ethernet connection can be installed, a camera can be mounted. Power over Ethernet (PoE) allows power to be supplied to the camera, so additional power supplies typically used with coaxial cameras are not needed. Ethernet also provides the flexibility of virtual local area networks (VLANs) for added security so that the camera network is isolated from operational traffic. IP surveillance uses *network video recorder (NVR)* software to record cameras. Because NVRs are server applications, we can use traditional storage such as network area storage (NAS) or storage area network (SAN) storage. This allows us to treat the video recordings like traditional data.

Coaxial camera networks can be converted to IP surveillance networks with the use of a device called a media converter. These devices look similar to a CCTV recorder. They have a limited number of ports for the coaxial cameras and are generally smaller than the CCTV recorder. This is because they do not have any storage. The sole purpose of the media converter is to convert the coaxial camera to an Ethernet feed to the NVR.

The use of IP video surveillance allows for a number of higher-end features such as camera-based motion detection, *license plate recognition (LPR),* and motion fencing. Advanced NVR software allows cameras to send video only when motion is detected at the camera; this saves on storage for periods of nonactivity. LPR is a method of detecting and capturing license plates in which the software converts the plate to a searchable attribute for the event. With motion fencing, an electronic fence can be drawn on the image so that any activity within this region will trigger an alert. Among the many other features are facial recognition and object recognition.

Heating, Ventilation, and Air Conditioning (HVAC)

In our homes today, we are realizing the benefits of smart thermostats. The thermostat turns down the heat when we are not there and turns it back up before we are expected to arrive. They can also adjust the temperature according to outdoor conditions. Ultimately this will save you some money on your monthly bill. Corporations that have extremely large-scale HVAC installations can save even more money by electronically controlling the HVAC equipment. Also, something must orchestrate the entire system and this is where HVAC controllers enter the picture. An example of an HVAC system is show in Figure 2.25.

FIGURE 2.25 HVAC schematic

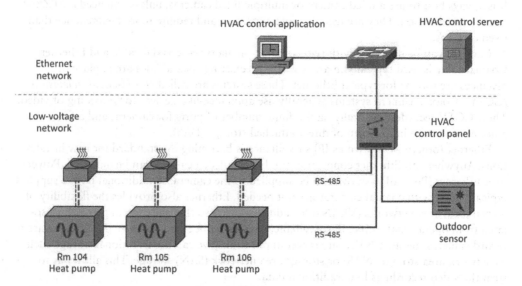

Just like an access control system, an HVAC control system will have two distinct parts: the Ethernet network and the low-voltage network. The Ethernet network is how the HVAC application communicates to the HVAC control server and how the HVAC control server communicates with the HVAC control panels. The low-voltage network is usually a serial communication network that can be daisy-chained from one unit to another. A common protocol used in these low-voltage networks is RS-485, but it can also be RS-422 or RS-232, and in some cases it can be proprietary. There are several components to an HVAC system:

HVAC Control Application The HVAC technician will need to set work schedules and adjust temperatures as well as monitor and troubleshoot the HVAC system. The HVAC control application is where the technician performs these tasks. The application is usually highly customized by the installer because each building will have a different floor plan and HVAC components. However, once the application is customized, it can usually be accessed from either a mobile device or computer. The HVAC control application will normally communicate directly with the HVAC server.

HVAC Control Server   A typical HVAC installation will usually have more than one HVAC control panel. So an HVAC control server is set up to manage all of the various HVAC control panels. Although the server acts as an intermediate layer, it is also used to log data. This logging allows a technician to troubleshoot, for example, why it's 90 degrees in the conference room. Maybe it's because of a failure or maybe one of the components has failed. The control server can usually be set up with notification so the technician can be notified and intervene before that conference room becomes a hot box. Every HVAC control system will have different features and the feature set is usually related to the price.

HVAC Control Panel   The HVAC control panel is where all the magic happens. The HVAC control server will push programming instructions to the HVAC control panel. The control panel will then run those instructions and usually function autonomously from the server. The HVAC control panel will periodically send reading back to the server for logging purposes. It is very similar to a programmable logic controller (PLC). As a matter of fact, many of the vendors that create PLCs for industrial control systems also make HVAC control panels. When an HVAC control system is purchased, it is normally very proprietary in nature. If you purchase a panel from a specific vendor, the server software and other panels will need to be from this vendor so the system can act as one system.

HVAC Components   The HVAC components can consist of a multitude of devices such as, for example, heat pumps, condensers, return air handlers, and cooling towers. The list can go on since HVAC is a profession on its own. Components are usually broken down into two categories: control points and sensors. Control points are any devices in the HVAC system that need be turned on or off or controlled in some fashion. The control point will be connected to the HVAC control panel with a daisy-chained line running a serial protocol, as discuss previously. Each control point will have a unique ID number that corresponds to the unit. As a command is sent down the serial line, only the device with the matching ID will act upon the command. Sensors, on the other hand, will send information back to the HVAC control panel. These devices can be wired directly to the HVAC control panel, and some of them can be wired on the serial line the control points use.

At some point in your career as a network professional, you will need to work with HVAC control systems. I urge you to learn as much as you can about these systems; they are truly fascinating and complex. Most HVAC installations require several engineers to create a final design, from the size of the unit to cool an area to the size of the duct work, to allow necessary air flow. Everything is taken into consideration in the design.

Internet of Things (IoT)

Over the past 20 years, IP-based technology has become cheaper and the availability of technology has improved. The Internet of Things (IoT) is a direct result of this expanse in

IP-based technology. Wireless technology further propelled IoT to become a standard in our homes today. The following are some common IoT devices you will find in home networks today.

Refrigerator   The refrigerator has been the hub for every family. The refrigerator door displays our bills, our photos, our messages, and the shopping list for the week, among other things. The smart refrigerator operates pretty much the same way a traditional refrigerator does. The only difference is a smart refrigerator has a touchscreen on the door that resembles a giant smart phone and everything you displayed on the refrigerator is now an app. A smart refrigerator usually runs the Android operating system and allows many different types of apps to be downloaded. The apps can display pictures you took with your phone, weather conditions, messages from another member of the household, and shopping lists, and this is just a few of the most common apps.

Smart Speakers   The smart speaker is more than just a speaker, it is an audible way to use the Internet, control other smart devices in your home, and have a digital assistant at your beck and call. By saying "Hey Google," "Alexa," or "Hey Siri," you can prompt the smart speaker to listen. You can then follow up with a task, such as asking what time it is, setting a reminder, checking the weather, controlling the lights, or even playing some music. The most common smart speakers on the market today are the Google Nest, Amazon Echo, and Apple HomePod. There is one major advantage with smart speakers, and that is synchronized playback of an audio source. You can listen to music, the news, an audiobook, or a podcast and have all the smart speakers play the same audio source.

Smart Thermostats   The old round mechanical thermostat was a foolproof mechanism that has heated and cooled houses for decades. However, with the modern technology of electronics and the Internet, the smart thermostat has forever changed the way our home is made comfortable. Smart thermostats don't just cycle heating when it's cold and cooling when it's hot, they perform in an economical way. Since everyone has a cellphone and no one leaves the house without it, the thermostat can track when you are home and when you aren't. The thermostat will turn the cooling or heating cycle off when you are not home, and it can even turn them back on when you are expected to be home. The smart thermostat learns your habits and adjusts the heating and cooling cycles. In addition, it can do all of this in conjunction with the current weather in the area. Most all smart thermostats also have an app for your cellphone that allows you to remotely control the thermostat over the Internet. If it is used in conjunction with a smart speaker, you can even control it with your voice!

Smart Doorbells   With the rise of eBay, Amazon, and many other online retailers, it is ever so common to have packages dropped off at your door. It has also become common to have these packages stolen. The thieves even have the nickname "porch pirates." Now you can secure your home and packages with a simple smart doorbell. The smart doorbell communicates with the Internet and an app on your cellphone. When someone walks up to the door, it will sense motion and instantly send an alert to your cellphone with video and the ability to talk back to the person. Outside of theft, it's a great way to ignore salespeople and other annoyances. It's also a great way to give the presence of someone being home, to thwart burglary. Because these devices record video upon motion, it has now become common practice for law enforcement to use the video. Now when there is a crime that has happened outside of your house that requires a police investigation, your doorbell can unwittingly help solve the crime!

Although, this section is focused on IoT home devices, IoT is much bigger than home gadgets. The smart devices we use in our homes are the by-product of big data and machine learning. These applications of big data and machine learning can also be applied to industry, such as agriculture, manufacturing, and research, just to name a few. IoT devices are pretty cheap and expendable units, so a couple dozen might be deployed in a crop field to monitor soil dampness. IoT devices might also be used to monitor heat in factory devices to signal a foreseeable failure. The solutions are limitless; if you can monitor it and forecast the outcome, you can use IoT to achieve better results.

Industrial Control Systems/Supervisory Control and Data Acquisition (SCADA)

Industrial control systems are the systems that are used in manufacturing processes. Products come into the process on an assembly or production line and exit as a final product. Supervisory control and data acquisition (SCADA) is an automated system used to control and monitor products such as energy production, water, electric distribution, and oil and gas, just to name a few. An example of what an industrial control system/SCADA system looks like is in Figure 2.26. Although industrial control systems are typically used in manufacturing and SCADA systems are used to create and distribute resources, they both share common components and the two are sometimes indistinguishable.

FIGURE 2.26   SCADA systems

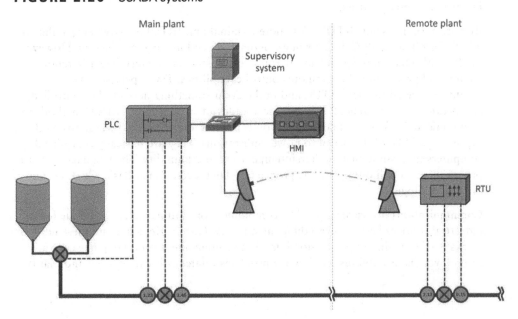

Supervisory System   All plant operations require a supervisory system to measure, monitor, and control plant production. They are often redundant systems because if a server fails, it could mean the entire production line stops. Supervisory systems also have a database where production metrics are stored for quality control and customer usage in the case of utilities. The supervisory system is usually located in the server farm at the main plant and not in the cloud because it needs to be as low latency as possible.

Programmable Logic Controller (PLC)   A programmable logic controller (PLC) is nothing more than a bunch of logic circuits performing a task. On PLCs there is often inputs and outputs. The inputs might be wired to buttons, switches, or position sensors, just to name a few. The outputs may be wired to solenoids, motors, or even robotic, and again, these are just a few things a PLC may control. It is up to the manufacturing engineer to design and program the PLC to perform a task. The programming language a PLC uses is actually not a language. The programming resembles a type of logic circuit. It is called ladder logic and it is quite popular. A specialized program is usually required for programming of PLCs; it is used to develop and program the ladder logic into the controller. Once the ladder logic is programmed into the PLC, the controller will run the program until it is powered off or programmed to stop.

Human Machine Interface (HMI)   The human machine interface (HMI) is used by plant operators so an overview of the production line can be observed. The HMI might have an oversimplified drawing of the production line with metrics displayed so a plant operator can adjust processes. In the event of a failure on the production line, it is used to identify where the fault exists. Just like PLCs, the HMI is programmed with specialized software. Once programmed, they will continue to operate until turned off and the programming software is no longer required, unless a major change is needed. The HMI can interface with the PLC and the supervisory system, depending on the requirements by the plant and operators.

Remote Terminal Unit (RTU)   A remote terminal unit (RTU) is extremely similar to a PLC. Just like the PLC, it can run autonomously and manage production. However, the RTU also has an independent microprocessor, so it can be installed at a remote facility and programmed for remote control capabilities. The supervisory system would oversee all the field RTUs, and in the event something needs to be controlled, an operator can intervene. RTUs can use a multitude of communications' methods to communicate back to the main plant. You can find these units everywhere from oil rigs in the middle of the ocean to power substations. They are basically ruggedized computers that can withstand harsh temperature and humidity. The language they are programmed in will differ, such as proprietary languages, Visual Basic, C#, C++, and even ladder logic.

Communications Infrastructure   The communications infrastructure is unique for industrial controls because everything must be low latency. Keep in mind these networks need to maintain production lines. If a canning line is processing five cans a second, you have a 200 ms window for problems if latency is experienced and that is cutting it close! There are a number of protocols and wiring you will find in industrial control systems, such as Modbus, Profibus, Hart, EtherNet/IP (Rockwell), and RS-485, and these are just a few of them. Every PLC and RTU will use a set of standardized protocols that will work with the various components like the HMI, sensors, and actuators. Some of these protocols are compatible with Ethernet and some are completely proprietary to industrial controls. The PLCs and RTUs will normally support Ethernet and IP-based connectivity back to the supervisor systems. However, the production network is often logically or physically separated from the operational network, so the two do not interfere with each other. Lessons have been learned from the 2010 Stuxnet infection that targeted PLCs and used the production network as an entry point. It is important to isolate a problem on the operations network, so production is not affected.

Exam Essentials

Know the functions and applications of various network devices.   Hubs operate at layer 1 and are nothing more than multiport repeaters. Switches perform three important functions: forwarding of filter decisions, MAC address learning, and loop avoidance. Switches function at layer 2, forwarding and filtering frames via the destination MAC addresses. Bridges perform functionality identical to that of switches, but they are usually software implementations of switches and have a limited number of ports. Routers function at layer 3, performing routing decisions based on destination IP addresses. Firewalls protect data with condition- and action-based rules and groups of rules called policies. Modems are legacy devices but are still useful for out-of-band management of network equipment. Wireless access points are used to extend a wired infrastructure to a wireless infrastructure for mobile device access. Media converters allow us to extend copper Ethernet past 100 meters by converting it to fiber-optic media. Wireless range extenders are useful for SOHO networks where you need a wireless dead spot covered.

Know the functions and applications of various networked devices.   A VoIP phone is any device that is the final destination of a voice call over VoIP. Printers can be deployed as decentralized, centralized, and peer-to-peer devices. Physical access control is a method of providing access to a person or group of people via a swipe card, biometrics, or PIN code. Cameras can be connected to a network to provide both PoE power and centralized recording with a NVR. HVAC systems are connected with a controller that can be programmed for automation of the HVAC system. The Internet of Things allows for big data and machine learning to augment household and commercial applications. Industrial control systems and SCADA have five major components: supervisory system, PLCs, HMI, RTUs, and communications infrastructure.

2.2 Compare and contrast routing technologies and bandwidth management concepts.

Without routing, networks would be captive to only the service they provide themselves. The size of a network would also be a critical factor since you need a logical routed segmentation between groups of clients to reduce broadcast traffic. In the following sections, I will cover routing and bandwidth management with switches and routers.

Routing

All network hosts are configured with a logical IP address. This IP address has two parts: a logical network and a logical host section. Routing is the process of moving data to the destination logical network that contains the logical host contained within it. Routers do not care about the host—routers base all routing decisions on the destination network.

The process is similar to the post office with the use of zip codes. The mail is sent to your local town, and then the post office within your town is responsible for delivering the mail to your specific address.

Routers perform this critical decision-making based on routing tables, which are statically entered or dynamically entered via routing protocols. Let's examine how routers make these decisions based off a static routing table for a simple network. In Figure 2.27 you see two networks separated by a router. Computer A sends a packet to the destination IP address of 192.168.2.2 (step 1). The router receives the packet, looks at the destination IP address, and calculates the network it belongs to. The router then looks at its internal routing table (step 2) and makes a decision on which interface to send the packet out for the destination IP address. The router also decrements the time to live (TTL) in the IP header by 1 before routing out the exit interface. Computer B then receives the packet (step 3), and the process starts again in the opposite direction when Computer B responds. The source address in the packet is never relevant in this process—with the exception of Computer B so that it can respond to the originating source. The TTL prevents packets from routing around the Internet forever; when the TTL reaches 0, the packet is considered unrouteable and it's dropped.

Routing Types

There are three basic types of routing that all routing processes and protocols fall into. Figure 2.27 shows a simple network with two networks containing one router. This example is extremely simple because only one router is used. Depending on the number of routers and where the routers are located, you will need to decide which routing type to use for the given scenario.

FIGURE 2.27   The basic routing process

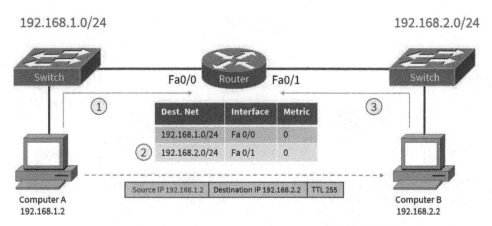

Static Routing

Static routing is the simplest of all the types of routing we can perform. It is generally used in small networks without much change because it is time-consuming for the network administrator. However, the benefit of static routing is that it doesn't change!

In Figure 2.28 we have three networks with two routers. Below each of the routers we have a routing table. The routing table consists of the destination network, exit interface, and a metric. On router A, networks 192.168.1.0/24 and 192.168.2.0/24 are directly connected because an IP address belonging to those networks is configured on the respective interfaces. When an IP address is configured on a router's interface, an entry is automatically placed into the routing table for the network it belongs to. This is a form of static routing because the IP address is statically configured; therefore, the routing entry is considered to be statically configured.

In Figure 2.28, we use the exit interface as the gateway because it is a serial line and any packets that enter the serial line are transmitted to the other side. However, the exit interface can also be an IP address. For router A, we can substitute S0/0 for the gateway of 192.168.2.2, and for router B we can substitute S0/0 for 192.168.2.1. In Ethernet networks, you must specify the gateway by IP address because the packets can take any path, unlike serial links in the figure.

On router A, we can see that a third entry is configured for the 192.168.3.0/24 network. This entry was configured by an administrator because router A doesn't know about the third network of 192.168.3.0/24. We can also see the opposite exists for router B. If a third network was introduced, we would need to manually update both router A and router B with the new entry. If something changed in the network, we would need to manually update all the routers. So static routing is reserved for small networks with very little change.

FIGURE 2.28   Two-router network

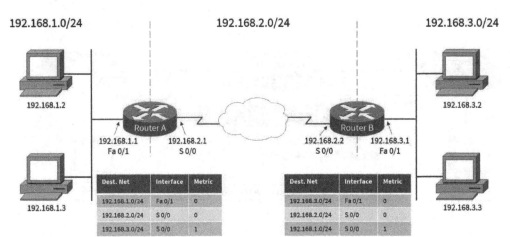

Dynamic Routing

Dynamic routing reduces the amount of administrator intervention by automating the trading of routing tables or entries with the use of routing protocols. This allows routers to learn new routes to networks from other routers participating in the dynamic routing process.

Routing decisions are optimized with the use of routing protocols in the dynamic routing process. Multiple routes to the same destination network can exist; the routing protocol will select the best route based on the metric.

There are three types of dynamic routing protocols: distance-vector, link-state, and hybrid. I will cover dynamic routing protocols in a bit.

Default Routing

Default routing is useful in stub networks where all destination networks are reachable through a particular gateway or interface. An example of this is the Internet.

In Figure 2.29 we have two routers connecting two networks and the Internet. Router A is the stub of the network; therefore, we do not need an entry for 192.168.2.0/24. The default route of everything, 0.0.0.0/0, will push packets out of the S0/0 interface, and router B will route the packets to the appropriate destination. This special route is also known as the gateway of last resort. Router B is also a stub of the network in respect to the Internet; therefore, anything that is not matched in the routing table will be routed to the Internet router via the S0/1 interface.

Routing Protocols (IPv4 and IPv6)

Routing protocols have two responsibilities: dynamic routing updates, as discussed earlier, and optimized routing decisions. There are several different methods that routing protocols use to populate and update routes among the participating routers.

FIGURE 2.29 Default routing example

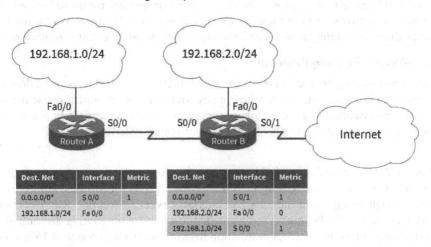

Dest. Net	Interface	Metric
0.0.0.0/0*	S 0/0	1
192.168.1.0/24	Fa 0/0	0

Dest. Net	Interface	Metric
0.0.0.0/0*	S 0/1	1
192.168.2.0/24	Fa 0/0	0
192.168.1.0/24	S 0/0	1

Each routing protocol also uses a different algorithm to calculate routing decisions from a set of metrics. Every router will trust one routing protocol over another routing protocol. Cisco calls these trust levels the administrative distance (AD). Table 2.1 is a list of the various ADs.

TABLE 2.1 Cisco administrative distances

Routing protocol	Administrative distance
Directly connected interface	0
Static route	1
EBGP	20
Internal EIGRP	90
OSPF	110
RIP	120
Internal BGP	200
Unknown	255

There are many different dynamic routing protocols to choose from, and each has its own characteristics as I will cover in the following sections. One of the characteristics of routing protocols is that it will be used internally in the network or externally. If it is used internally, it is considered an interior routing protocol, and if it is used externally, it is considered an external routing protocol. With the exception of Border Gateway Protocol (BGP), all of them are considered interior routing protocols. This means that they are meant to be used on the interior of your network and not the exterior of your network (Internet). BGP is used on the Internet as the main routing protocol and therefore considered an exterior routing protocol.

Distance-Vector Routing Protocols

Distance-vector routing protocols use the metric of distance to calculate routing decisions. The metric used is hop count, which is how many routers a packet must traverse to get to the destination network. Distance-vector routing protocols are susceptible to routing loops because they only look at the number of hops and no other criteria.

RIP

The *Routing Information Protocol (RIP)* is a true distance-vector routing protocol. It is an older protocol used for dynamic routing in small networks. RIP sends the complete routing table to the neighboring router out all active interfaces every 30 seconds. RIP uses the hop count as a metric and the Bellman–Ford algorithm to calculate the routing decision. RIP has a maximum hop count of 15. A destination network with a hop count of 16 is deemed unreachable. There are several versions of RIP:

RIP version 1 uses broadcasts to send routing updates and the initial routing table. RIP version 1 can only use classful routing because the subnet mask is not transmitted in the routing updates. This means that all networks need to use the associated subnet mask and cannot be broken down into subnets.

RIP version 2 uses the multicast address of 224.0.0.9 to send routing updates and the initial table to participating routers. The use of multicast helps with bandwidth concerns of broadcasts, but the protocol still has the limitations of 15 hops. RIP version 2 also addresses the problem of using subnets in the network. RIP version 2 transmits the table with the subnet mask included; this is called classless routing.

RIPng (RIP next generation) is an IPv6 implementation of the RIP routing protocol. Like the IPv4 versions, RIPng uses hop count and the Bellman–Ford algorithm to calculate routing decisions and has a maximum hop count of 15. RIPng uses an IPv6 multicast address of ff02::9 to transmit route updates and the initial table every 30 seconds out of all active interfaces.

All versions of RIP have a slow convergence time because routers must pass the complete table around the network. A router four hops away might need to wait up to 90 seconds to obtain the full table. Because of the slow convergence time with RIP, it is susceptible to routing loops. A few techniques exist to prevent routing loops:

Split horizons prevent routing updates from being received on the same interface that a route update was sent from, in which the update states that the destination network is down. This creates an artificial horizon where a router cannot be told a path to its own network is available via another router.

Poison reverse exploits the maximum hop count of 15 to stop routers from receiving an update to an alternate path to the same network. When a router detects a network that it manages is down, it will adjust the hop count to 16 and continue to populate the route entry. This will poison all the tables in the network for the affected network. When it comes back up, the route entry will be adjusted back.

Hold-downs are used to slow down routing updates for an affected network. It allows all the tables in the network to converge by holding down any updates for the affected network. The normal hold-down time is six times the update period of 30 seconds, for a total of 180 seconds.

Link-State Routing Protocols

Link-state routing protocols do exactly what their name says; they not only keep track of neighbors, they also track the state of their neighbor's links. This is the main difference between distance-vector routing protocols and link-state routing protocols. Link-state routing protocols make independent decisions based on the links versus distance-vector protocols that can only make decisions based on what other routers preprocess.

OSPF

Open Shortest Path First (OSPF) is a true link-state protocol. It is an open standard, which means that it can be configured on any manufacturer's router—that is, if it is included in the feature set. OSPF is extremely scalable and is used for very large networks. OSPF uses the Dijkstra algorithm to construct the initial shortest path tree and calculates routes based on the bandwidth metric. The hop count of OSPF is unlimited, unlike EIGRP and RIP.

OSPF uses the concept of areas to create a hierarchal routing structure. All OSPF configuration must start with an area of 0, sometimes referred to as the backbone area of 0.0.0.0. The use of areas allows the OSPF protocol to be scalable, because routing updates can be constrained to routers participating within the area to control bandwidth. Areas communicate with other areas to send summary route advertisements through routers called area border routers (ABRs). In addition, OSPF areas can connect other autonomous systems such as EIGRP, BGP, and so on. The routers that connect OSPF to other autonomous systems are called autonomous system boundary routers (ASBRs).

When the OSPF process starts on a router, it selects the highest IP address on the router and uses this IP address as the router ID (RID). The RID is how the routers are tracked by OSPF. The Hello protocol is used for neighbors to form on the multicast address of 224.0.0.5 and is also used for link-state advertisements (LSAs). However, in order for routers to become neighbors, the same area IDs must match, the authentication password must match (if used), and Hello/Dead intervals must match.

OSPF will form an adjacency with neighboring routers; adjacent routers permit the direct exchange of route updates for OSPF route calculation. However, adjacencies are not formed with all neighbors—only with routers that share a direct link, such as a point-to-point connection. Adjacencies are also formed with designated routers (DRs). A router becomes the DR by having the highest RID in an election. The designated router is used in broadcast networks such as Ethernet and is allowed to form adjacencies with other routers in the same broadcast network. In broadcast networks, a multicast address of 224.0.0.6 is used for LSAs.

OSPF contains tables (databases) similar to EIGRP protocol tables. It maintains a neighborship database, a topological database, and of course, the routing table. The neighborship database is populated by the process described earlier. The topological database is built by the OSPF process and feeds the routing table with respective routes to destination networks.

OSPFv3 is the IPv6 version of OSPF version 2 (IPv4). In OSPF version 2, the RID is calculated on the router as the highest IP address. In OSPFv3, the RID is an IPv4 address configured on the router because IPv6 addresses are too long and sometimes autoconfigured. OSPFv3 works similar to how its IPv4 counterpart works—it still requires the first area to be area 0.0.0.0. The multicast addresses used are FF02::5 for point-to-point routers and ff02::6 for broadcast routers.

Hybrid

Hybrid routing protocols are protocols that have characteristics of both a link-state routing protocol and a distance-vector routing protocol. EIGRP is the only hybrid routing protocol covered on the CompTIA Network+ exam objectives, but it is the clearest example of a hybrid routing protocol.

EIGRP

The *Enhanced Interior Gateway Routing Protocol (EIGRP)* is a Cisco proprietary protocol and is only available on Cisco products. EIGRP is not a true distance-vector routing protocol. It has the characteristics of both distance-vector and link-state protocols.

EIGRP is a more modern protocol than RIP and therefore has many more features. It allows for scalability with the use of autonomous system (AS) numbers. This allows routers within an AS to participate in routing updates. EIGRP also has a default hop count of 100 and a maximum of 255; both of these features support scalability of the protocol so it can be used in large networks. EIGRP supports classless routing (subnets), variable-length subnet masking (VLSM), discontiguous networks, and summarization of networks.

EIGRP doesn't use hop count solely for routing decisions; it can use a combination of bandwidth, delay, load, reliability, and maximum transmission units (MTUs). By default, to compute routing decisions EIGRP uses a combination of bandwidth and delay called a composite metric. The algorithm EIGRP uses is the Diffusing Update Algorithm (DUAL). The algorithm makes use of protocol-dependent modules (PDMs), which allows IPv4, IPv6, or any other protocol to be used with DUAL.

EIGRP uses three main tables: the neighbor table, the topology table, and the routing table (see Figure 2.30). EIGRP starts by associating with neighboring routers through a process called neighbor discovery. Router A will send a multicast Hello packet to 224.0.0.10; router B and router C will respond with a Hello/ACK packet. In the Hello packet, the AS number and metrics (K values) will be sent. In order for an EIGRP neighboring router to be considered a neighbor, three pieces of information must be exchanged: Hello and ACK packets, matching AS numbers, and identical metrics. When this occurs, the neighboring router will be added to the neighbor table.

The topology table is populated by the DUAL algorithm. DUAL will inspect the neighbor table and calculate the metrics to the destination networks. In this case, two paths exist to the destination network of 10.0.0.0/8: one through the S0/0 (router B) and another through the S0/1 (router C). DUAL will choose a successor route and a feasible successor router to 10.0.0.0/8. The successor route will be sent to the routing table, and the feasible successor will remain in the topology table. If the successor route fails, then the feasible successor route will become the successor route and move to the routing table.

FIGURE 2.30 EIGRP tables

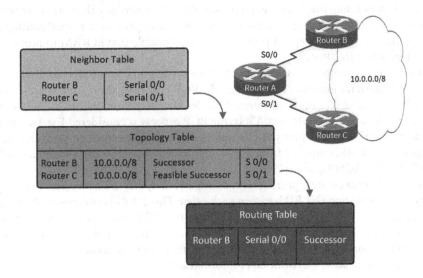

EIGRP maintains the neighbor table with the Reliable Transport Protocol (RTP). RTP will multicast Hello packets every 60 seconds to the multicast address of 224.0.0.10. RTP will maintain a list of neighbors who have responded and those who have not. If a neighbor does not respond to a multicast, RTP will unicast Hello packets to the neighbor. After 16 unicast attempts, the neighbor will be dropped out of the neighbor table and DUAL will recalculate. This is one of the reasons EIGRP is not considered a true distance-vector protocol!

EIGRPv6 is the IPv6 version of EIGRP and functions the same as EIRGP for IPv4. Since DUAL supports PDMs, IPv6 is treated the same as IPv4. There are a few minor differences, such as how it is configured. The IPv6 multicast address is FF02::A, which is easy to remember because A equals 10 in hex, and the IPv4 multicast address is 224.0.0.10.

Path-Vector Routing Protocol

A path-vector routing protocol is similar to a distance-vector routing protocol because it uses the distance to the destination. It performs this based upon path and not next hop. One aspect of a path-vector protocol is that it requires the entire content of all possible routes.

BGP

Border Gateway Protocol (BGP) is a path-vector routing protocol. The protocol is most commonly used for Internet routing of IPv4 and IPv6. Although you could use it internally in your network, there are better protocols that are made for internal routing, such as OSPF. Path-vector routing protocols are classified as distance-vector routing protocols because they listen to peer routers for their information. BGP uses a process called the BGP Best Path Selection algorithm for choosing the best route to the destination network.

BGP is often used by enterprises to either load-balance connections over two Internet providers or provide failover between two Internet service providers (ISPs). When it is used with a single connection to each ISP, it is considered a single multihomed connection. When an enterprise needs to populate the Internet with routes and a single ISP, it is considered a single-homed connection. There are other variations of the connection, but these two are the most common.

BGP is resource intensive on a router when used in a multihomed connection because your router is processing the routes learned from the ISPs. Currently there are over 600,000 IPv4 routes for the Internet that your router must learn and process. The BGP routing tables are almost one gigabyte in size, and routers often need double that in RAM to process and function; this is just for IPv4.

The BGP routing protocols uses an autonomous system number (ASN) to allow routers inside an ASN to share internal routes. When the BGP peer (neighbor) routers are inside an ASN, the BGP process is considered Internal Border Gateway Protocol (iBGP). When the BGP peers are between two different ASNs, the BGP process is considered External Border Gateway Protocol (eBGP). Before you can use BGP to populate routes on the Internet, you must register for an ASN number from a *regional Internet registry (RIR)*—such as ARIN, RIPE, AFRINIC, LACNIC, and APNIC.

When BGP routers create a peering with another router, they transmit Network Layer Reachability Information (NLRI) between each other. This NLRI is composed of length and prefix. The length is the *Classless Inter-Domain Routing (CIDR)* notation of the network mask, and the prefix is the network address. BGP peers send a keepalive every 60 seconds via a unicast message on TCP/179. BGP is a unique routing protocol because it uses the Transport layer to communicate Network layer information.

Bandwidth Management

Networks are used to transmit all sorts of data, from iSCSI to web surfing. Depending on which IP services you use in your network, some services should take priority over others. For example, VoIP should take a higher precedence in the network than simple web browsing or even file-based access because it is a time-sensitive service. You will learn several techniques in the following sections to make VoIP or iSCSI take precedence over other non-time-sensitive network traffic.

Traffic Shaping

Traffic shaping is implemented on routers to shape traffic to the speed of the connection. If you had a 1 Gbps interface but pay for overage costs for over 800 Mbps of traffic, you need to slow down the outgoing traffic. This is where traffic shaping comes in handy.

With traffic shaping, we allow the output queue to send data for a specific bit rate, and then we wait for the remainder of the cycle. In Figure 2.31 you see a time reference of 1 second on the bottom of the legend. If we were to transmit the full rate of the interface (which is 1 Gbps), then it would take an entire second. However, with traffic shaping we will transmit only 800 million bits in 800 milliseconds, and then we will wait the remainder of the cycle, or 200 milliseconds. We have effectively slowed the bit rate down to 800 Mbps!

FIGURE 2.31   A traffic shaping example

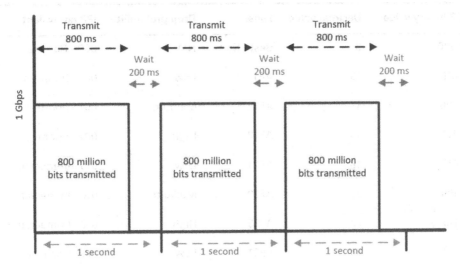

This example is exaggerated for explanation purposes. An interval of 200 ms is an eternity for data to wait for the next transmit cycle of data. Therefore, in a practical application we would divide 1000 ms by 100 and use a cycle of 10 ms. We would transmit for 8 ms and wait 2 ms. The effect is the same because we have, over a 1-second interval, shaped the data to 800 Mbps.

QoS

Quality of service (QoS) is the concept of the prioritization of protocols. You always want time-sensitive protocols like VoIP or iSCSI to have priority in networks over web surfing traffic or file access. QoS can be achieved at layer 3 and layer 2 of the OSI model. It is important to note that, although your internal routers and switches can be programmed to abide by the layer 3 and layer 2 QoS markings, Internet routers usually don't care.

Diffserv

Differentiated Services Code Point (DSCP), or DiffServ, is a 6-bit value contained in the 8-bit Type of Services (ToS) field of an IP header at layer 3. Before DiffServ was created, the first 3 bits in the 8-bit ToS field were used for IP Precedence (IPP) QoS markings. IPP is deprecated and no longer used (the DSCP markings are now used), but the IPP markings are still present for backward compatibility. So when you see the DSCP priorities in Table 2.2, the Class Selector (CS) values are there for backward compatibility with IPP.

The DSCP Assured Forwarding (AF) values are a combination of a two-digit value. The first digit identifies the queue, where 1 is worst and 4 is best. The second digit is the drop probability, where 1 is low and 3 is high. Traffic classified with a DSCP value of AF12 has a higher probability of being dropped and queued later than traffic classified with a DSCP marking of AF31.

TABLE 2.2 DSCP markings

DSCP binary value	Decimal value	Label	Drop probability	IPP equivalent
000 000	0	Best Effort	N/A	000 - Routine
001 010	10	AF11	Low	001 - Priority
001 100	12	AF12	Medium	001 - Priority
001 110	14	AF13	High	001 - Priority
010 010	18	AF21	Low	010 - Immediate
010 100	20	AF22	Medium	010 - Immediate
010 110	22	AF23	High	010 - Immediate
011 010	26	AF31	Low	011 - Flash
011 100	28	AF32	Medium	011 - Flash
011 110	30	AF33	High	011 - Flash
100 010	34	AF41	Low	100 - Flash Override
100 100	36	AF42	Medium	100 - Flash Override
100 110	38	AF43	High	100 - Flash Override
001 000	8	CS1		1
010 000	16	CS2		2
011 000	24	CS3		3
100 000	32	CS4		4
101 000	40	CS5		5
110 000	48	CS6		6
111 000	56	CS7		7
101 110	46	EF		Critical

CoS

Class of Service (CoS) is a 3-bit field in the layer 2 802.1Q frame. CoS is used for the prioritization of traffic between switches on 802.1Q trunk links. In Figure 2.32 you can see the 802.1Q frame and the 3-bit value for priority. The 3-bit value maps to a priority of eight possible queues (0 through 7), where 0 is best effort (worst) and 7 is the highest priority (best). VoIP traffic normally uses a priority value of 5, and web traffic normally uses a priority value of 0.

FIGURE 2.32   An 802.1Q frame

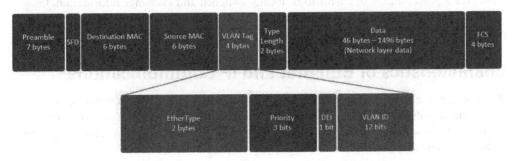

Exam Essentials

Understand the various concepts of routing.   Routing allows for information to be passed between logical IP networks with the use of routing tables. Static routing requires administrator intervention to program the routes into the routing table. Dynamic routing allows for the routing tables to be exchanged automatically between routers. Default routing is used on stub networks, where all routes exist through a particular gateway. Distance-vector routing protocols exchange information about their routes and report the distance they calculated. BGP is a path-vector protocol and is used on the Internet for routing. Link-state routing protocols calculate their own costs from routes learned. Hybrid routing protocols contain characteristics of both distance-vector and link-state routing protocols.

Know the various routing protocols.   Router Internet Protocol (RIP) is a distance-vector routing protocol that is used for small-scale internal routing in our networks. Enhanced Interior Gateway Routing Protocol (EIGRP) is a hybrid routing protocol that is proprietary to Cisco and used for medium to large company networks. Open Shortest Path First (OSPF) is a link-state routing protocol that is extremely scalable and used for extremely large networks. Border Gateway Protocol (BGP) is a path-vector routing protocol that is used for routing the Internet.

Know the various bandwidth management features used in a network.   Traffic shaping allows for the queuing and timing of packets to slow down traffic exiting an interface. The timing allows for a defined amount of bits to leave and interface for a specific amount of time before a waiting period during a time interval. Quality of service (QoS) is a concept in which protocols are prioritized so that time-sensitive protocols have higher priority. Differentiated Services Code Point (DSCP), or DiffServ, is a layer 3 QoS mechanism for layer 3 devices such as routers. Class of Service (CoS) is a layer 2 QoS mechanism used with 802.1Q frames for prioritization of frames.

2.3 Given a scenario, configure and deploy common Ethernet switching features.

Switching is equally as important as routing, if not more important. Switching services allows for a great number of clients to be locally switched and exchange information. In the following sections, I will cover switching services, the characteristics of Ethernet, and a number of switching features commonly found on network switches.

Characteristics of Ethernet and IP Communications

We no longer use hubs and repeaters because they cause collisions that slow traffic. It is important to understand what a collision domain is and how it can affect network communications. Broadcasts, on the other hand, are part of IP communications and we need to understand how they affect the network as well.

Collision Domains

A collision will occur when two nodes send a frame simultaneously on the same physical network or media. The key concept is that frame collisions happen at the Physical layer. Collisions are common on networks that use hubs because hubs communicate using half-duplex Ethernet. The same pair of wires used to transmit data is the same pair of wires used to receive data. Therefore, data could possibly be transmitted on the same pair simultaneously by two nodes, thus causing a collision.

When a collision occurs, all the nodes on the physical network must stop and wait for a random period of time via the CSMA/CD contention method. No data can be transmitted during this wait time. (I will explain CSMA/CD later in this discussion of objective 2.3.) This wait time means that bandwidth is reduced as more collisions occur. A typical 10 Mbps connection with only two or three computers may be able to sustain a top speed of only 6 or 7 Mbps due to collisions.

The best way to solve collisions is to replace all hubs with switches and verify full-duplex Ethernet connectivity. As shown in Figure 2.33, a switch will place each node in its own collision domain regardless of half-duplex or full-duplex operation. Full-duplex communications can only be achieved with switches. Switches reserve a pair of wires for transmit and a pair of wires for receive; this guarantees that collisions will not occur.

Broadcast Domains

The broadcast domain is defined as a group of devices on a network segment that hear all broadcasts transmitted on the network segment. These broadcasts are generally layer 2 broadcasts. I will discuss different types of broadcasts later.

FIGURE 2.33 Hubs, switches, and collision domains

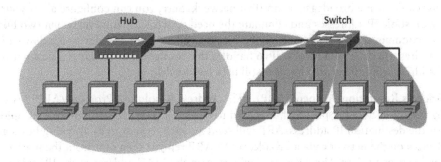

Excessive broadcast traffic in a network can create congestion for unicast network traffic. Some broadcast traffic in a network is considered a healthy portion of traffic. We can't totally get rid of broadcast traffic because many supporting protocols rely on it. For example, you could try getting rid of DHCP by putting a static IP address on each computer. However, ARP is still required for resolving IPs to their associated MAC addresses. ARP is required for normal communications, and it is a broadcast-based protocol, just like DHCP. Broadcast traffic will always have a destination MAC address of ff:ff:ff:ff:ff:ff:ff:ff. When a switch see the broadcast MAC address, it forwards the frame to all of the active switchports.

As your network grows, the broadcast traffic required to support it also increases. To combat congestion that can be caused by broadcasts, we can simply create more broadcast domains and limit the number of devices affected. As we increase the number of broadcast domains, we reduce the number of computers affected by the broadcasts in each domain. This is commonly done by creating additional network segments and connecting the segments together with a router, because routers stop broadcasts. In Figure 2.34 you see two network segments with four computers in each broadcast domain. The broadcast traffic generated by the computers in the first segment will not affect computers in the second segment. However, the computers in the first segment can still communicate with the computers in the second segment via the router connecting the two segments.

FIGURE 2.34 Two broadcast domains connected with a router

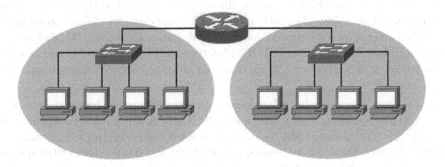

Helper Protocols

You just can't escape broadcasts in an IPv4 network. Sure, you can configure all of your hosts with static IP addresses and eliminate the need for DHCP. However, when two hosts begin to communicate, a broadcast will be necessitated by layer 2 to derive the destination MAC address on an IPv4 network. IPv6 handles this resolution of the layer 2 destination MAC address a bit differently, but it is still uses bandwidth.

Address Resolution Protocol (ARP)   The Address Resolution Protocol (ARP) is used by layer 2 as a helper protocol. It is used to derive the layer 2 destination MAC address for the destination IP address. ARP will send an ARP request to all listening hosts and devices on the network via a broadcast. An ARP reply is then sent from the matching hosts or devices. The ARP reply will contain the MAC address of the IP address requested; the requesting host will then store the IP address and MAC address mapping in the ARP table and continue processing the frame at the Data Link layer. All consecutive requests for the MAC address will be resolved from the ARP table in memory until the entry is expired from the ARP table.

The ARP table is a temporary table in memory to reduce ARP requests for IP address–to–MAC address mappings. When a packet is created at the Network layer, it is passed down to the Data Link layer for framing. The source MAC address is known because it is the host the data was initiated on. However, the destination MAC address is unknown, so the ARP protocol is used to find the MAC address for the destination IP address.

ARP is a broadcast-based protocol and an IPv4 network cannot work without ARP. ARP is one of the reasons we need to segment the network. As networks grow in size, so does the residual bandwidth from ARP. The ARP traffic only exists to support IP-based conversations.

Neighbor Discovery Protocol (NDP)   ARP is exclusively used by IPv4 and it's broadcast-based. So, if a host is not participating in the conversation, hosts must still process the broadcast message. IPv6 was designed to eliminate all broadcast traffic. It performs this by using multicast traffic. It's not a perfect solution since multicast members must still process the message, but it does cut down on residual traffic.

IPv6 uses Neighbor Discovery Protocol (NDP) as a replacement for ARP. It performs the same function as ARP by resolving the destination layer 2 MAC address for a given destination IPv6 address. The NDP protocol performs this critical function by using ICMPv6 and the message types of Neighbor Solicitation (NS) using IMCPv6 type 135 and Neighbor Advertisement (NA) ICMPv6 type 136. The initial NS is sent as a multicast packet to all participating in the multicast group, but the NA is sent back as a unicast message.

The neighbor solicitation and advertisement process might sound familiar to you. It's similar to Stateless Address Auto Configuration (SLAAC), in which Router Solicitation (RS) and Router Advertisement (RA) messages are used. Another similar protocol that is used with ICMPv6 is Duplicate Address Detection (DAD), and it is similar to NDP in how it performs. It uses NS and NA messages to identify a duplicate address in the network.

Common Switchport Characteristics

Although a switchport can be configured in a number of different ways depending on the features the switch is purchased with, there are three defining characteristics that every switchport has on all switches.

Speed   The speed of the port is measured in bits per second, such as 10 Mb/s, 100 Mb/s, 1 Gb/s, 10 Gb/s, 25 Gb/s, and so on. A port is usually backward compatible with slower speeds, but this is not a rule. It is common to find a switch that will support 25Gb/s and 10 Gb/s. It is, however, uncommon to find that the 25 GB/s port will backwardly support 100 Mb/s. So, it is always best to check with the vendor of the equipment.

Duplex   The duplex of the port is either half-duplex or full-duplex. A port operating at half-duplex means that the same wires are used to transmit and receive. When a port operates in half-duplex mode it creates a single collision domain for both devices connected. Therefore, the protocol of carrier-sense multiple access with collision detection (CSMA/CD) is used to arbitrate collisions. When a port operates in full-duplex mode, a set of wires is dedicated for transmitting and a set is dedicated for receiving data. The port can now send and receive without the risk of a transmission causing a collision.

The duplex of the port is also tied to speed. If a switchport is operating at full-duplex, the switch can now send and receive the full speed of the wire bidirectionally. If a switch supports 1 Gb/s and it can switch at wire speed, the switchport can potentially switch 2 Gb/s simultaneously: 1 Gb/s for transmitting and 1 Gb/s for receiving data. If a switch port operates a half-duplex, then collision will slow traffic down by up to 50 or 60 percent of the speed of the connection.

Flow Control   Ethernet has a mechanism called flow control, 802.3x pause frames, or blocking ports. The names all mean the same thing, and the mechanism exists for access layer switching where the port needs to communicate back to the sender to slow down and temporarily stop sending data. This happens if the switchport buffers are full and need to process. An 802.3x pause frame will be sent to the sender. Although flow control is fine at the edge of our network, the core of our network should never pause Ethernet. Real-time protocols such as iSCSI will develop performance problems and in extreme cases disconnect! The flow control of a port is often overlooked when selecting a switch for an application that requires high uninterrupted speeds. When selecting a data center or core switch, you should always make sure the ports are non-blocking.

CSMA/CD

Carrier Sense Multiple Access with Collision Detection (CSMA/CD) is a wired Ethernet contention method. CSMA allows the network controller to sense a carrier to transmit data. CSMA also provides a path for multiple computers to talk or have access to the same network. I often use the example of a group of people meeting. All the people in the group have equal access to speak. Each person can also sense when they can speak by listening for silence in the group. Network nodes work the same way; when a node wants to talk, it will first check for the presence of a signal on the wire. If the wire is clear, the node can begin transmitting the data.

The CD, or collision detection, method is used to detect a collision of two nodes talking at the same time within the same collision domain. When a collision occurs, both nodes begin transmitting a temporary jam signal; this prevents any other nodes from creating additional collisions. All nodes that hear the jam signal use a back-off algorithm to determine a random amount of time before they can attempt to transmit again. The CD method is similar to two people in the group talking at the same time. They both stop and give courtesy to the other person, and then one of them starts the conversation again after a random amount of time. One difference is that after the back-off algorithm is triggered, all nodes have equal access to transmit.

Basic Switch Functions

A switch will perform three basic functions of MAC address: leaning, forward filtering, and loop avoidance. Although loop avoidance is a feature found in more expensive switches, every switch will perform MAC address learning and forward filtering at the very least. More advanced switches will offer VLAN and routing capabilities, as you will learn.

MAC Address Learning/Filtering

The MAC address table is responsible for associating a MAC address or multiple MAC addresses with a physical port on the switch. The MAC address table is sometimes referred to as content-addressable memory (CAM).

When a switch is first started, a table is created in memory, appropriately called the MAC address table. When Computer A sends a message to Computer D in Figure 2.35, a frame is created with the source MAC address of Computer A (step 1). When the switch receives the frame, it inspects the source MAC address of the frame (step 2) and records it in the MAC address table on the port it was received on. This is the MAC address learning function of a switch; more specifically, it is called source address learning. The switch then needs to forward the frame to the destination MAC address/port, but the table is empty other than Computer A's entry. So it floods the MAC address to all of the ports (step 3). The process of deciding the destination port based on the MAC address table is the forward filtering function of the switch. However, since the switch was just started and the table is empty, it must flood the frame to all ports. When Computer D responds to Computer A (step 4), a frame is received by the switch, and the source MAC address is entered in the MAC address table (step 5). A forward filter decision can now be made based on the destination MAC address (step 6). The frame is now delivered directly to Port 1 (step 7). All communication between Computer A and Computer D will now be isolated to their respective ports based on the MAC address table.

FIGURE 2.35   The MAC address learning process

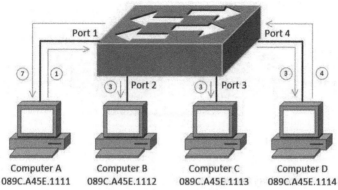

MAC Address Table	
Port	MAC Addresses
1	089C.A45E.1111 ② ⑥
2	
3	
4	089C.A45E.1114 ⑤

Switching Loops/Spanning Tree

Multiple paths between switching equipment in a network should exist for redundancy. However, multiple paths can also create switching loops, and these instantly kill bandwidth on a network. In Figure 2.36 you see an example of two switches with a redundant link between them. The unicast frames sent from host A will enter into the first switch, only to be forwarded out each link of the switch to the adjacent switch. The far side switch will then receive two frames, which it will forward to host B; this cuts the bandwidth in half. Although that is a problem, you could probably still function—that is, until a broadcast frame is introduced into the network. In Figure 2.37, you see host A send a broadcast frame to the first switch; this switch then forwards it to all ports. The adjacent switch does the same, and this begins what is called a broadcast storm. All hosts are instantly crushed with bandwidth, and the MAC address table is thrashed from multiple MAC address entries. The host's network cards accept the data and pass it to the layer above, so the hosts also see a spike in CPU utilization as the operating system processes the broadcast.

We can create redundant connections in our network and avoid switching loops if we use the Spanning Tree Protocol (STP). STP will monitor redundant links and block data from being switched on a redundant link to avoid the problems just mentioned. STP manages the redundant link and allows data to pass if the primary link goes down.

FIGURE 2.36 Duplicate unicast packets

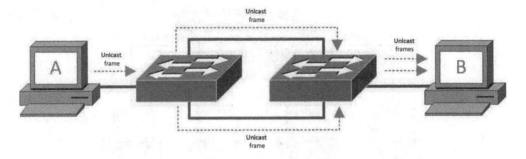

FIGURE 2.37 A broadcast storm

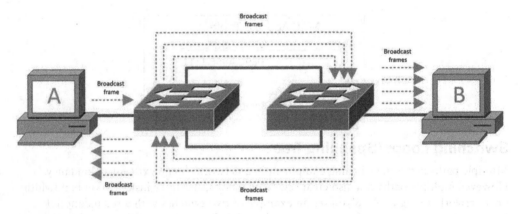

STP (802.1D)

The original Spanning Tree Protocol was developed by Digital Equipment Corporation (DEC) back in 1993. The IEEE later created its own version of STP called 802.1D (STP). STP uses the Spanning Tree Algorithm (STA) to block redundant links from causing a switching loop. The STP (802.1D) protocol is still used today because it manages redundant links very well, but it has its shortcomings, as you will see.

Before you begin learning how STP operates, here are a few terms you must learn:

Root Bridge   The root bridge is the switch with the lowest bridge ID. The switches participating in STP will elect a root bridge. The root bridge becomes the root of the network, and all redundancy is managed with the root as the focus of the network. All of the other switches must make a path to the root bridge. The root bridge is often where the servers are located.

Non-Root Bridges   These are switches that are not the root bridge. Non-root bridges participate in STP by exchanging Bridge Protocol Data Units (BPDUs).

Bridge ID   The bridge ID is a calculation of the lowest MAC address on the switch and the priority. The default bridge priority is 32,768 for most switches. The bridge priority can be adjusted in multiples of 4096 to force a switch to become the root bridge.

Port Cost   The port cost helps determine the fastest connection to the root bridge. When there is a redundant connection to an adjacent switch, the port cost determines which port is turned to a blocking mode. In Table 2.3, you can see the IEEE port cost for each link speed.

TABLE 2.3   IEEE STP link costs

Link speed	IEEE cost
10 Mbps	100
100 Mbps	19
1,000 Mbps	4
10,000 Mbps	2

Root Port   The root port is the port leading to the root bridge on the adjacent switch. If there is more than one port from the same switch leading to the root bridge, the port with the lowest cost becomes the root port.

Forwarding Port   A forwarding port is a port that is allowed to forward frames. A forwarding port is marked as a designated port that assists in forwarding frames to a root bridge and has the lowest cost.

Blocking Port   A blocking port is a port that is not allowed to forward frames. It is the redundant link that has a higher cost to the root bridge. Although blocking ports will not forward data, they will forward BPDUs.

STP Operations

Now that you've learned some of the terminology, let's see how STP operates by blocking redundant links and avoids switching loops. Figure 2.38 shows three switches redundantly connected. All of the switches have the same default priority, so the lowest MAC address will win the election of the root bridge. All of the links between the switches also have the same cost.

Once the root bridge is selected, as in Figure 2.39, we can label the forwarding ports on switch A. All ports on the root bridge will be in a forwarding mode. The root ports (RPs) can then be labeled on switches B and C, since they are the ports on the adjacent switches that lead back to the root bridge. Now the link between switch B and switch C is the remaining link that is redundant. The switch with the lower cost (switch B) will have its port put into a forwarding mode. The switch with the higher cost (switch C) will have its port put into a blocking mode. If anything in this network changes, STP will recalculate.

FIGURE 2.38   Three switches with redundant links

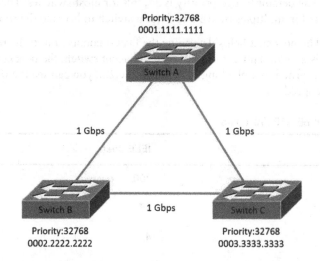

FIGURE 2.39   Three switches with STP calculated

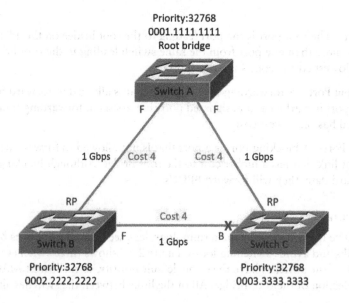

STP Port States

When a port becomes active on a switch, the port transitions between several states before allowing frames to be forwarded. These port transitions are necessary to avoid switching loops in the network, but during this time we cannot forward traffic. The possible port states are as follows:

Disabled   This port state is not really an STP port state; it is just a state of any port that has been disabled by an administrator.

Blocking   This is the first state of any active port; it ensures that a loop will not occur. During the blocking mode, BPDUs are still transmitted so that the STA can calculate redundant paths.

Listening   This port state allows the port to listen for BPDUs.

Learning   This port state works in conjunction with a listening port; it allows the switch to listen to BPDUs of other switches so that it can calculate its own STP database.

Forwarding   If the port does not have a redundant path or is the lowest cost port, it then transitions into the forwarding mode. In this mode, frames are allowed to be forwarded.

STP Convergence

STP convergence is the process of placing all ports on the switch into either a forwarding or blocking mode as they become active. The STP convergence time is 50 seconds; during this time no data is passed. If at any time an STP port needs to recalculate, it will block frames for a total of 50 seconds. This convergence time can cause a significant impact to a network. Simply unplugging a connection and plugging it back in can cause a 50-second wait for frames to be forwarded during this convergence period.

An active port will transition to blocking while listening and learning; it will then either remain blocking if it is the higher cost redundant link or transition to forwarding if it is the lower cost redundant link. This transition process can be modified for servers and clients when you can guarantee there are no redundant links in the network. Spanning Tree Port-Fast allows for forwarding, listening, and learning based on the convergence to either remain forwarding or blocking.

RSTP (802.1w)

The *Rapid Spanning Tree Protocol (RSTP)* is a newer IEEE standard of STP that fixes many of the issues with STP (802.1D). The first feature that RSTP has is fast convergence time; because RSTP is more proactive with calculations, it does not need the 50-second convergence time. RSTP is also backward compatible with STP and can be configured on a port-by-port basis on most switches. Some terminology has changed slightly with RSTP. For example, see the port states shown in Table 2.4. RSTP will transition from discarding, to learning, to forwarding or remain discarding if it is a higher cost redundant link.

Another main difference with RSTP compared to STP is that path cost is taken into account when calculating forwarding ports. The entire path is calculated versus the individual port cost. RSTP introduces two other port modes of backup and alternate ports. In Figure 2.40 you see switch B connected to another segment of C; one port is placed into a designated port role, and the other redundant port is placed into a backup port role. On switch C there is an alternate path to the root bridge from segment C if the designated port were to fail. The original STP specification would have just placed these ports into a blocking mode and treated convergence time the same.

TABLE 2.4 802.1D vs. 802.1w port states

802.1D state	802.1w state
Disabled	Discarding
Blocking	Discarding
Listening	Discarding
Learning	Learning
Forwarding	Forwarding

FIGURE 2.40 Backup and alternate ports

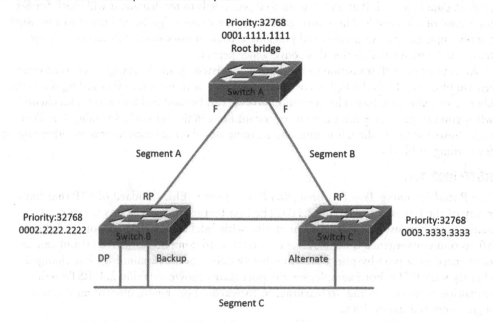

Segmentation and Interface Properties

Segmentation of a network is necessary to control broadcast domains and manage collision domains. In the following sections, I will cover the mechanisms for segmenting a network such as VLANs, trunks, and tagging of frames. In addition, there are several properties of switched interfaces that will be covered, such as the duplex, port mirroring, and the Spanning Tree Protocol (STP).

VLANs

Virtual local area networks (VLANs) are the primary mechanism to segment networks. However, before we can understand the need for VLANs, let's examine a network without VLANs. In Figure 2.41 you see one network segment connected with a switch; this is considered a flat network because there is no segmentation, and all clients share the same broadcast domain. We can add additional switches, but that will only extend the broadcast domain further. Regardless of the job function, the hosts share the same switch; in the figure you can see Sales and HR on the same physical switch. It is important to note that VLANs are usually described with numbers from 1 to 4,096, but for the remainder of this section we will use friendly names.

FIGURE 2.41   A flat switched network

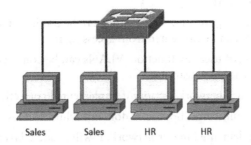

| Sales | Sales | HR | HR |

As shown in Figure 2.42, when we implement VLANs in a network, we can logically segment a network inside a physical switch. We can even connect switches together and extend the VLANs to additional switches (I will explain how later). The key point is that we have created two separate broadcast domains in the same physical switch, thus reducing the number of broadcasts that can be heard by each client.

VLANs help control broadcasts by creating logical segmentation (logical switches) inside a switching infrastructure; these are virtual switches. When we create multiple logical segments inside the switch infrastructure, it allows the network to become scalable to thousands of hosts without repercussions for bandwidth from broadcasts. VLANs also help provide flexibility to the daily maintenance of adding and moving clients within a job function. If a salesperson were to move from one floor to another floor, we can simply reconfigure the switches with the appropriate VLANs and the salesperson is within the same VLAN.

FIGURE 2.42   A network using VLANs

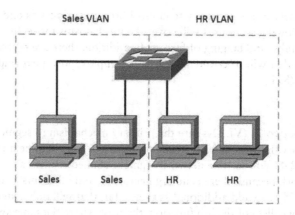

VLANs are more commonly used today in conjunction with security. Because we can group users together inside a switch, we can apply access control lists (ACLs) to the VLANs and restrict traffic between them.

Here is a short list of benefits to implementing VLANs:

- Network adds, moves, and changes are achieved with ease by just configuring a port into the appropriate VLAN.

- A group of users that require a level of security can be put into a VLAN so that users outside of the VLAN can be prevented from accessing it.

- As a logical grouping of users by function, VLANs can be considered independent from their physical or geographic locations.

- VLANs greatly enhance network security if implemented correctly.

- VLANs increase the number of broadcast domains while decreasing their size.

When VLANs are implemented in our network, it will create a layer 2 segmentation. However, we still need to get unicast traffic to communicate between the two segments. This requires a router so that unicast traffic can be routed between the two segments. Additionally, we must provide a layer 3 logical address scheme for each of the VLANs. As shown in Figure 2.43, the Sales VLAN is assigned an IP address scheme of 192.168.1.0/24, and the HR VLAN is assigned an IP address scheme of 192.168.2.0/24. If the Sales VLAN needs to communicate with the HR VLAN, it must send the traffic to its default gateway (router), and the traffic will be routed to the appropriate VLAN and host. Routing between VLANs is required, even if the VLANs are all in the same physical switch.

Trunking (802.1Q)

Up to this point I have covered VLANs within the same switch. When we need to extend a VLAN infrastructure past a single switch, we use trunking. Trunking allows the VLAN information to be prepended to the switched frame as it traverses the switches. When the adjacent switch receives this frame, the trunking information is stripped off and the frame is forwarded to the appropriate port(s).

FIGURE 2.43   Routed VLANs

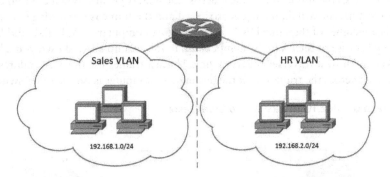

There are two main trunking protocols that are used today in switching. One is *Inter-Switch Link (ISL)*, which is proprietary to Cisco equipment. The other trunking protocol is *802.1Q*, which is an IEEE standard that is compliant with all switching equipment, including Cisco. The 802.1Q trunking protocol is nothing more than a prepended field on an Ethernet frame. As you can see in Figure 2.44, the top frame looks identical to a standard Ethernet II frame, with the exception of the 4 bytes for VLAN tagging. The EtherType field, or type field, contains the first 2 bytes that a VLAN tag comprises; the position of these first 2 bytes is what the LLC sublayer would expect for the position of a normal (non-802.1Q) frame. Since the type field is set to 0x8100 (802.1Q), this tells the device that the frame has tagging information inside. The original type field is still there—it is right before the data—and it will reflect the upper protocol the data is destined for after it is put on the proper VLAN. Inside the VLAN tag, a priority is embedded for a length of 3 bits; this is a QoS value that we will discuss later in this section. A discard eligibility indicator appears after the priority bits; it is normally not used for Ethernet. Then at the end we have the VLAN ID, for a total of 12 bits. Since we are using 4 bytes for this VLAN tag, we must subtract it from the data payload, so rather than being able to transmit 1500 bytes, we can transmit only 1496 bytes.

FIGURE 2.44   An 802.1Q frame

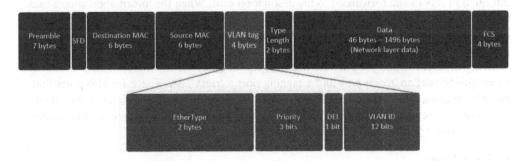

When we connect a switch to another switch and configure an 802.1Q trunk between them, we allow multiple VLANs to traverse the trunk link. The example in Figure 2.45 shows computer C in the HR VLAN sending a broadcast message. When the switch receives the broadcast, it forwards the broadcast to all other computers on the switch in the same VLAN. The switch also tags the frame and sends it across the 802.1Q trunk. When the frame is received at the adjacent switch, the tag is processed and the frame is forwarded to computer H because it is a member of the same HR VLAN. All other computers—A, B, E, F, and G—never see the frame because of their VLAN membership. In this example I've shown you a broadcast frame/packet and how it traverses the trunk link. Unicast frames use the MAC address table and are directed across the trunk link if the destination computer is on the other switch.

FIGURE 2.45   802.1Q trunk link and broadcasts

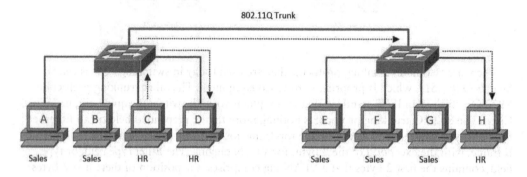

Tagging and Untagging Ports

As you know, 802.1Q trunks tag packets with VLAN tagging information; these ports are considered to be tagging ports. Normal network clients don't need to see the 802.1Q tagging information. For the most part, they never really know what VLAN they are in—it's the switches' job to put them in the respective VLAN.

In Figure 2.46, you can see a client and switch connected to another switch with an 802.1Q trunk link. When the frame leaves the PC, it is untagged as a normal Ethernet II frame. If the destination computer is on the far side switch, then it must traverse the 802.1Q trunk link. When it leaves this port, it receives the VLAN tagging information; therefore, the 802.1Q trunk port is considered a tagging port. When it is received on the adjacent switch, the tagging information is read and forwarded to the destination host. When the information comes back from the far side switch, it is again tagged as it leaves the far-side trunk port. It is then read by the adjacent switch and forwarded onto the respective VLAN/port. When it leaves the host port, the tagging information is removed; hence, this port is called an untagging port.

Many different switch vendors use different terminology for this functionality. Cisco calls an untagging port an *access port* and a tagging port a *trunk port*. There are also ports that listen for tagging information so that VoIP data can be switched properly; these are called *voice ports*. Many generic switch vendors will refer to these ports as tagging and untagging ports. The concept is identical between all vendors.

Voice VLAN

When a switchport must support both a VoIP phone and a computer, we can employ a voice VLAN. The voice VLAN is a combination of a tagged port for the VoIP traffic and an untagged port for the computer's data traffic. This all works because every phone has a small switch

FIGURE 2.46 Untagging and tagging ports

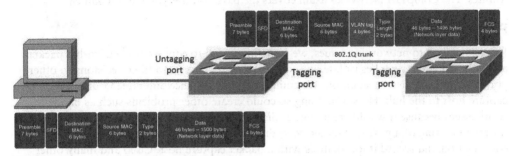

inside that can divert traffic tagged with the voice VLAN to the phone and untagged traffic to the computer, as seen in Figure 2.47. In the figure you can see how the switch received the traffic. When a frame is tagged for the voice VLAN, it will have a VLAN tag in lieu of the type field. Ordinary data traffic will look like a standard frame to the switch and therefore it will be switched appropriately to the computer. Basically, a voice VLAN port will act as both a tagged and untagged port at the same time, but only one VLAN (voice) can be tagged on the port.

FIGURE 2.47 Voice VLAN ports

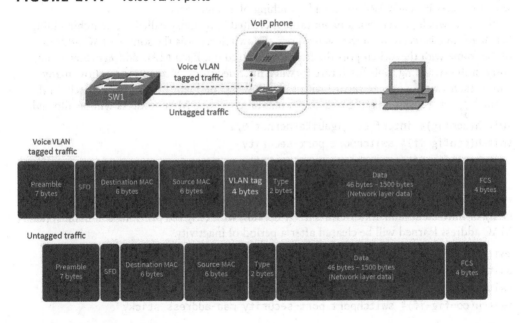

Switching Features

There are several different features that can be enabled on a managed switch. Some of these features can help you diagnose problems, such as port mirroring. Some can help you secure your network, such as port security, and these are just a few that I will cover in the following sections.

You will find the more expensive switches that are managed come with a number of switching features. The CompTIA Network+ exam covers the basic features you will encounter.

Port Mirroring

When we run into networking issues, we sometimes need to capture packets with a packet analyzer. However, switches isolate our conversation with forward filter decisions so other ports do not hear the conversation. We could put a hub in place and attach our packet capture host to the hub. However, doing so could create other problems such as bandwidth issues because it would create one collision domain. Most managed switches allow for the mirroring of a port to another port; this functionality allows us to eavesdrop on a conversation and record it for analysis with a packet capture host. Cisco and many other vendors refer to port mirroring as the *Switched Port Analyzer (SPAN)* feature.

Port Security

Port security is a method of restricting specific MAC addresses or a specific number of MAC addresses on a physical access mode switch port. Port security is supported on many different vendor switches, but I will focus on the Cisco switching platform for this section; all switches support similar port security function. Port security is commonly implemented by the network administrator to mitigate the threat of end users plugging in hub, switches, or wireless access ports (WAPs) to extend switching of a single port.

When a switch powers on, a blank table is created in memory called the switching table. When a frame is received on the switch port, the switch records the source MAC address of the frame with the switch port the frame is received on. Each MAC address receives an entry in the switching table for future forward filter decisions. We can restrict how many entries each switch port can record with the following commands on a Cisco switch. In the example, port security is configured, and a maximum of one MAC address will be allowed.

```
switch(config)# interface gigabitethernet 0/1
switch(config-if)# switchport port-security
switch(config-if)# switchport port-security maximum 1
```

By using `switchport port-security mac-address sticky`, we can configure the switch to record the first MAC address and limit the port to only that MAC address indefinitely or until an administrator clears it. By default, with only the previous commands, the MAC address learned will be cleared after a period of inactivity.

```
switch(config)# interface gigabitethernet 0/1
switch(config-if)# switchport port-security
switch(config-if)# switchport port-security maximum 1
switch(config-if)# switchport port-security mac-address sticky
```

We can also constrain the switch port to a specific MAC address statically. In lieu of the `switchport port-security mac-address sticky` command, we can specify the specific MAC address to limit the switch port to. When we configure the following command, the MAC address will be locked to 0678.e2b3.0a02 for the switch port:

```
switch(config)# interface gigabitethernet 0/1
switch(config-if)# switchport port-security
```

```
switch(config-if)# switchport port-security maximum 1
switch(config-if)# switchport port-security mac-address 0678.e2b3.0a02
```

Port Aggregation

Port aggregation is a mechanism for aggregating ports together for increasing bandwidth between switches—say, if you had two switches and needed to provide more bandwidth between the connected switches than the current 1 Gbps link. You could add another 1 Gbps link and aggregate both ports together to provide 2 Gbps of bandwidth, as shown in Figure 2.48. Most switches will allow two to eight links to be aggregated together.

FIGURE 2.48 LACP port aggregation between two switches

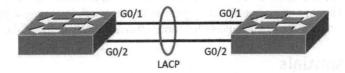

A common protocol used for port aggregation is IEEE 802.3ad, *Link Aggregation Control Protocol (LACP)*. LACP is an open standard that will allow aggregation of ports between two different vendors. Another port aggregation protocol is the Cisco proprietary protocol called *Port Aggregation Protocol (PAgP)*. PAgP can only be configured on Cisco switches and routers.

Auto-Medium-Dependent Interface Crossover (MDI-X)

On newer switches, a feature called *auto MDI-X (Medium Dependent Interface Crossover)* allows for automatic detection of the transmit and receive pair. The auto MDI-X will auto-crossover the connection when a straight-through cable is present, connecting a switch to another switch.

Jumbo Frames

Jumbo frames are just that, bigger frames! The maximum size of an Ethernet frame is 1500 bytes, and a jumbo frame is 9000 bytes. iSCSI storage benefits from these jumbo frames. If jumbo frames are used, data is less likely to be fragmented into smaller 1500-byte frames. When packet fragmentation occurs, the higher-level protocol of IP at layer 3 must reassemble the fragments. The reassembly of these fragmented packets causes latency and higher CPU utilization. Latency is the enemy of SANs.

A caveat to jumbo frames is that all the network equipment in the switching path must support this larger framing of data, also called the maximum transmission unit (MTU). If one of the switches doesn't support the jumbo frames MTU and you turn on jumbo frames at each end (initiator and target), you could end up with a performance decrease of up to 30 percent or higher!

PoE and PoE+ (802.3af, 802.3at)

Power over Ethernet (PoE) allows for the both power and data to be transmitted on a standard Ethernet connection. This technology is what allows VoIP phones to be powered from the switching equipment without the need for power adapters. It is also used for devices, such as video surveillance cameras and wireless access points (WAPs), in remote locations that could not be powered otherwise.

Two standards for PoE exist: PoE (802.3af) and PoE+ (802.3at). The PoE (802.3af) standard is used to supply up to 15.4 watts of power and is commonly used with phone and video surveillance cameras. The PoE+ (802.3at) standard is used to supply up to 25.5 watts of power. PoE+ (802.3at) is sometimes required for the latest wireless standards on WAPs that require more power than PoE (802.3af).

It is important to note that identification protocols such as *Link Layer Discovery Protocol (LLDP)* and the *Cisco Discovery Protocol (CDP)* communicate power requirements to the switch. These power requirements conveyed to the switch lower the supply wattage of PoE and PoE+ at the switch. This allows for more efficient power usage of the end devices.

Exam Essentials

Understand the various characteristics of Ethernet and IP-based traffic.   A collision domain is a segment of the network where two or more nodes can send a frame simultaneously on the same physical network or media, which causes a collision. CSMA/CD is a contention method used with Ethernet. A broadcast domain is a segment of the network where all the hosts can see a broadcast. Helper protocols such as ARP and NDP use broadcasting and multicasting to resolve MAC addresses from IP addresses.

Understand the basic functionality of a switch.   Switches perform three basic functions: MAC address learning, forward filter decisions, and loop avoidance. MAC address learning is always based on the source MAC address seen on a certain port. Forward filter decisions are made once the MAC address table is established. Loop avoidance is performed by STP, in which one of the higher-cost ports is placed into a blocking mode.

Understand and be able to describe the segmentation of networks and interface properties.   Virtual local area networks (VLANs) allow for the logical segmentation of a physical network. VLANs support segmentation of networks by creating broadcast domains. Trunking allows multiple VLANs to be transmitted between switches using a process of 802.1Q tagging. Tagging ports will tag VLAN information on frames so that the frames can be transmitted across a trunk port. Untagging ports removes the VLAN information from frames before the traffic leaves the port.

Know the various switching features found on many switches.   Port mirroring such as SPAN allows for a copy of the frames on one interface to be mirrored on another interface for packet capture. Port security works by restricting a specific MAC address or a total number of MAC addresses with a switchport. Port aggregation is the process of combining 2 or more switchports to act as a single interface, increasing the bandwidth to the other device. Jumbo frames allow for larger frames to be sent containing 9000 bytes of data compared to 1500 bytes in a normal Ethernet frame. The PoE (802.3af) standard is used to supply up to 15.4 watts of power. The PoE+ (802.3at) standard is used to supply up to 25.5 watts of power.

2.4 Given a scenario, install and configure the appropriate wireless standards and technologies.

Wireless technologies are useful for mobility and ease of access. In the past 20 years, mobile computing has become expected in society and networks. The expansive growth of mobile computing has required more bandwidth and better wireless coverage, which has led to steady advancements in wireless hardware and protocols. Ease of access is another reason wireless has become a required technology. When network access is too expensive or logistically impossible to wire, wireless technologies come to the rescue.

The following sections cover both the mobility and ease of access for wireless technologies. We will first explore the various 802.11 standards, and then we will cover cellular technologies, along with the supporting technologies from almost two decades of enhancements.

802.11 Standards

Wireless standards are developed by the Institute of Electrical and Electronics Engineers (IEEE) 802.11 working group. The original 802.11 wireless standard was ratified in 1997. The original specification had a maximum bandwidth of 1 and 2 Mbps.

Over the past 20 years, new standards have been ratified by various 802.11 working subgroups. When we discuss 802.11a, the "a" stands for the working subgroup of the IEEE, and it also represents the ratified standard.

Wireless equipment vendors will adhere to these standards when producing new wireless hardware. However, when new standards are to be ratified soon, vendors will often prerelease standards hardware. This allows the vendor to get a jump on the market, and when the specification is formally ratified, the vendors will release firmware for the ratified standard.

802.11b

The 802.11b standard was ratified in 1999. It was the first wireless protocol to become popular with wireless networks and was responsible for the expansive growth of wireless in the following years.

The 802.11b standard operates on the 2.4 GHz frequencies in the industrial, scientific, and medical (ISM) radio band. It can use 11 frequency channels in North America and only 3 of the 11 channels are non-overlapping. The standard uses *direct-sequence spread spectrum (DSSS)* modulation. It is capable of a maximum speed of 11 Mbps and a maximum distance of 350 feet. As the signal gets weaker, the speed drops at these intervals: 11, 5.5, 2, and 1 Mbps.

The 802.11b standard is considered legacy because it requires the channel it's operating on to shift from newer modulation techniques to DSSS. When an 802.11b client enters the network, all other devices on the network must shift back to 802.11b for backward compatibility since the WAP is now operating with this older modulation. Most administrators completely turn off 802.11b functionality for this reason.

802.11a

The 802.11a standard was ratified in 1999 alongside of 802.11b. The 802.11a standard was mainly used in corporate networks for bridging between buildings via wireless. In the early 2000s, 802.11a was not as popular as 802.11b, and the equipment was more expensive.

The 802.11a standard operates on the 5 GHz frequencies in the *Unlicensed National Information Infrastructure (U-NII)* radio band. The standard can use 12 frequencies of non-overlapping channels. It uses *orthogonal frequency-division multiplexing (OFDM)* modulation, which has become the standard for all subsequent wireless standards. 802.11a is capable of a maximum speed of 54 Mbps and a maximum distance of 190 feet. As the signal gets weaker, the speed drops at these intervals: 54, 48, 36, 24, 18, 12, 9, and 6 Mbps.

The 802.11a standard is also considered legacy because the 802.11n standard can access 23 non-overlapping frequency channels. The *Federal Communications Commission (FCC)* released an additional 11 channels in 2004 and 2008.

802.11g

The 802.11g standard was ratified in 2003 and served as an updated standard for 802.11b. This new standard became very popular because the cost was about the same and the standard introduced newer features.

The 802.11g standard operates on the 2.4 GHz frequencies in the ISM radio band. It can use 11 frequency channels in North America and only 3 of the 11 channels are non-overlapping. The 802.11g standard is capable of a maximum speed of 54 Mbps and a maximum distance of 310 feet. Just like other standards, as the signal gets weaker, the speed drops at these intervals: 54, 48, 36, 24, 18, 12, 9, and 6 Mbps.

The updated standard switched to the OFDM modulation and was backward compatible with the DSSS modulation (802.11b). This backward compatibility comes with a cost to all other clients on the WAP: everyone will be switched back to a maximum of 11 Mbps!

802.11n

The 802.11n standard was ratified in 2009 and introduced faster speeds, more channels, and longer distances. The 802.11n standard is also marketed as WiFi 4 by the Wi-Fi Alliance. I would consider the 802.11n standard to be the best advancement in wireless since wireless was first introduced. The standard introduced many features that newer standards have built upon.

The 802.11n standard operates on the 2.4 GHz frequencies in the ISM radio band and the 5 GHz frequencies in the U-NII radio band. The standard can use 23 frequencies of non-overlapping channels in the 5 GHz radio band and can use all 11 of the channels in the 2.4 GHz radio band in North America. It allows for bonding of up to two 20 MHz channels to provide a single 40 MHz channel for higher speeds. However, bonding of channels should be avoided on 2.4 GHz because of the limited number of non-overlapping channels. I will cover channel bonding later.

The 802.11n standard is backward compatible with 802.11g and 802.11a by working in a mixed mode and reading the preamble of the wireless frame. It is also backward compatible with 802.11b at the cost of everyone's speed, because 802.11b uses a different modulation.

The 802.11n standard uses OFDM modulation along with multiple input, multiple output (MIMO), called MIMO-OFDM. The standard will allow up to four spatial streams of MIMO. I will cover MIMO later. The 802.11n standard is capable of a maximum speed of 600 Mbps, with 4×4 MIMO and a 40 MHz channel. However, it is not common to find a WAP that supports 4×4 MIMO, and the nominal maximum bandwidth is found to be 450 Mbps with 3×3 MIMO. The maximum distance for 802.11n is 230 feet.

802.11ac

The 802.11ac standard was ratified in 2013 and is the current gold standard for wireless. It is marketed as WiFi 5 by the Wi-Fi Alliance. The 802.11ac standard built upon many of the new technologies that 802.11n introduced to produce fast speeds.

The 802.11ac standard operates on the 5 GHz frequencies of the U-NII radio band and ISM. The standard can use 25 frequencies of non-overlapping channels. It allows for bonding of up to eight 20 MHz channels to provide a single 160 MHz channel for higher speeds. The 802.11ac standard is backward compatible with all previous 5 GHz wireless standards.

The 802.11ac standard uses MIMO-OFDM modulation and will support up to eight spatial streams of MIMO for the downlink. A theoretical maximum speed of 6.93 Gbps is possible with *802.11ac Wave 2*. The 802.11ac standard allows for 160 MHz channel bonding. However, there are only 23 non-overlapping channels, and bonding of 8 channels diminishes usable channels to two 160 MHz channels, so it is not commonly done in enterprise networks. It is common to bond channels into 80 MHz channels and use 3×3 MIMO to provide 1.3 Gbps.

The 802.11ac standard supports 1.3 Gbps at a maximum distance of 90 feet. However, 802.11ac allows for a greater distance at slower than 1.3 Gbps speeds, so distance is a trade-off for top speed.

802.11ax

The 802.11ax standard is to be ratified early 2021 by the IEEE. It is also expected to replace 802.11ac as the gold standard for wireless. 802.11ax is marketed as WiFi 6 by the Wi-Fi Alliance.

The 802.11ax standard operates on the 5 GHz frequencies of the U-NII radio band and can also operate on the 2.4 GHz radio band, unlike 802.11ac. In the future, the 802.11ax standard will operate on 6 GHz radio frequencies, and it has been dubbed WiFi 6E (E for extended). Currently there are only 25 non-overlapping channels in the 5 GHz radio band and they can be bonded for up to two 160 MHz per channels.

Just like the 802.11ac standard, 802.11ax will use MIMO-OFDM modulation and will support up to eight spatial streams of MIMO. However, the 802.11ax standard will support both downlink and uplink for MIMO-OFDM modulation. The spatial frequencies can now be colored by adding an identifier. So now the spatial frequency can be differentiated from neighboring wireless equipment. All of this means that the 802.11ax standard can achieve greater density of clients.

A new feature added to the 802.11ax standard is Target Wake Time (TWT), and it can extend battery performance for mobile and IoT wireless devices. The wake interval is negotiated between a client and an access point. This allows the device to enter into a sleep cycle and wake up at a specific time to receive information or transmit to the access point.

The 802.11ax standard can deliver a theoretical speed of 14 Gbps at a relatively short distance away from the access point. However, a realistic speed is around 3.5 Gbps and that is twice as fast as 802.11ac.

Frequencies

The frequencies used with wireless local area networks (WLANs) vary by standard. The two main frequencies used are 2.4 GHz and 5 GHz. The 2.4 GHz frequencies are governed by the industrial, scientific, and medical (ISM) radio bands. The 5 GHz frequencies are governed by the Unlicensed National Information Infrastructure (U-NII) radio band. It is important to note that in the future, 6 GHz frequencies will be used with the second release of 802.11ax called WiFi 6E.

2.4 GHz

The 2.4 GHz spectrum is governed by the ISM radio band. The 802.11b/g/n standards operate on 2.4 GHz frequencies. The band consists of 14 channels 22 MHz wide. In North America only the first 11 of the channels can be used for wireless. In Japan all 14 channels can be used, and almost everywhere else in the world the first 13 channels can be used.

Only 3 of the 14 channels are considered non-overlapping, as seen in Figure 2.49. The channels of 1, 6, and 11 are considered prime channels for WLAN because they do not overlap with the other channels in the channel plan. Therefore, three WAPs can function in an extended service set (ESS) without experiencing interference from each other.

FIGURE 2.49 The 2.4 GHz channel plan

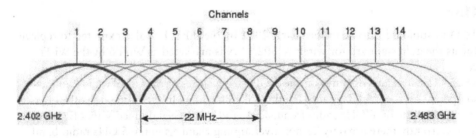

Channels

1 2 3 4 5 6 7 8 9 10 11 12 13 14

2.402 GHz |←——— 22 MHz ———→| 2.483 GHz

The 2.4 GHz ISM radio band is nearing the end of its life because of the limited number of channels and non-overlapping channels. The latest standard of 802.11ac does not support 2.4 GHz. WAPs that support 802.11ac and allow 2.4 GHz connection have dual radios built in and use 802.11 b/g/n for the 2.4 GHz radio. However, the 2.4 GHz band is still useful, because it goes further with less power. So, the 802.11ax standard has revived the 2.4 GHz band and supports both 5 GHz and 2.4 GHz.

5 GHz

The 5 GHz frequencies are governed by the Unlicensed National Information Infrastructure (U-NII) radio band. The 802.11 a/n/ac/ax standards operate on the 5 GHz frequency spectrum.

As seen in Figure 2.50, the band consists of 25 non-overlapping channels. In North America the 802.11a standard can function on 12 channels consisting of 36, 40, 44, 48, 52, 56, 60, 64, 149, 153, 157, and 161. Each regulatory domain restricts the number of channels and specific channels for the region.

In North America, the 802.11ac standard can use 25 of the non-overlapping channels as seen in Figure 2.50. In Europe and Japan the channels are limited to the U-NII 1, U-NII 2, and U-NII 2E list of channels. The 802.11n standard only allowed the first 24 channels in North America, because channel 165 is in the ISM band.

FIGURE 2.50   The 5 GHz channel plan

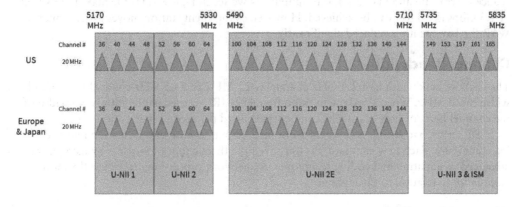

Wireless Considerations

When installing a wireless system, there are a number of considerations. Some of these considerations might mean adding additional access points dependent on distance. In addition, antenna type can allow for various installations. The goal of the following sections is to familiarize you with technologies and theory that fill the gaps of wireless communications.

Speed and Distance Requirements

The distance of wireless outdoors will always be better than wireless indoors. Wireless outdoors has the advantages of an open space environment, which reduces the backscatter and absorptions of wireless signals.

Wireless signals bounce off any surface and create this backscatter of RF that attributes to *wireless multipath* interference, thus reducing the overall signal quality. We can see this effect in a room that has an audible echo. The echo can sometimes be so extreme it drowns out a conversation. Wireless signals experience this same effect when backscatter is severe.

Wireless signals also suffer from absorption into materials. In a house or commercial building, we generally have sheetrock and wood. These materials tend to absorb the signal, which lowers the strength of the signal on the other side. Although backscatter and absorption are only two of the many problems we can have with wireless signals, they are the two most common.

Speeds will always be higher on 5 GHz wireless, such as the 802.11 a/n/ac standards. The 802.11ac standard can use a maximum of 25 non-overlapping channels. However, the 802.11 b/g/n standards are restricted to the 2.4 GHz wireless band with three non-overlapping channels. To future-proof new installations of wireless, focus on 5 GHz coverage and hardware. The 802.11ac standard exclusively covers 5 GHz.

Regardless of the standard used, there is a relationship between distance and speed. As the client station moves further away from the WAP, the speed is automatically reduced for a reduced error rate and maximum throughput. As we see in Figure 2.51, the maximum speed of 1.3 Gbps at 90 feet can be achieved. However, as the client station moves away from the WAP, the bandwidth is reduced significantly.

Channel Bandwidth

The channel bandwidth of a 2.4 GHz channel is 22 MHz and a 5 GHz channel has a bandwidth of 20 MHz. When speaking in radio frequency (RF) terms, bandwidth is the width of the channel hertz or how many bits can be transmitted per second (per cycles).

In RF terms, bandwidth is different from throughput because of modulation and coding techniques. Each new standard has improved the throughput of wireless by using more advanced modulation and coding techniques. As network professionals, we use the term *bandwidth* in relation to throughput.

Channel Bonding

With the introduction of the 802.11n wireless standard, bonding adjacent channels together became possible. When channels are bonded together, we gain increased throughput for the combined channels. With the introduction of 802.11ac, we can now bond eight 20 MHz channels together for 160 MHz of bandwidth. With modern modulation and coding techniques, we can obtain the throughput of 14 Gbps over these bonded channels!

Bonding can create bonded channels of 20, 40, 80, and 160 MHz, as detailed in Figure 2.52. One of the problems with channel bonding is the reduction of channels that are non-overlapping. With 25 non-overlapping channels, we can have twelve 40 MHz channels, six 80 MHz channels, or two 160 MHz channels. This limits the number of non-overlapping channels and the complexity of your design for maximum throughput.

It is also possible to bond channels with the 2.4 GHz radio band. However, because there are only three non-overlapping channels, it is not practical.

FIGURE 2.51 802.11ac data rates vs. distance

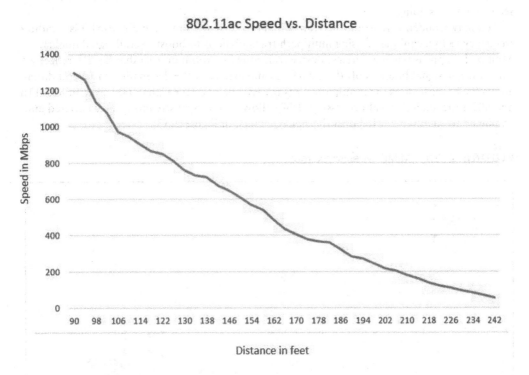

FIGURE 2.52 Channel bonding in the 5 GHz radio band

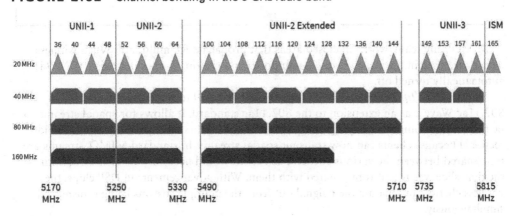

MIMO/MU-MIMO

Multiple input, multiple output (MIMO) technology allows for wireless devices to transmit and receive the same signal across multiple antennas. These signals are called spatial streams and are often referred to as 2×2, 3×3, 4×4, and 8×8. The 2×2 designation means that two antennas on the WAP are used and two antennas on the client are used; 3×3 means that three antennas on the WAP are used and three antennas on the client are used. I think you see where this is going.

You may wonder, why would we transmit and receive the same signal? MIMO is a radio frequency (RF) technique of using multipath transmissions to boost overall signal quality. Multipath happens when a wireless device transmits in a room or area that has RF reflective surfaces. The signal bounces off these surfaces and arrives at the destination in several different paths. In most cases the multipath transmissions degrade the signal. However, in 802.11n and 802.11ac, digital signal processing (DSP) allows for several streams to be compared and combined to simultaneously boost the signal, as seen in Figure 2.53.

FIGURE 2.53   MIMO wireless example

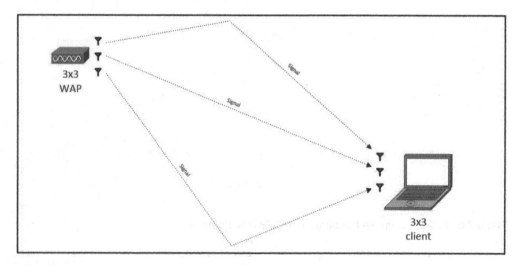

MIMO only really works in closed areas that propagate RF multipath. When wireless devices are used in open spaces such as outdoors and multipath does not exist, MIMO is automatically turned off.

Multiuser multiple-input, multiple-output (MU-MIMO) technology was released in 802.11ac Wave 2 as an extension to the 802.11ac standard. It allows for spatial streams to be transmitted simultaneously to multiple users. In 802.11ax, the spatial streams are bidirectional because clients can now transmit spatial streams. In standard MIMO, streams are time-shared between the various clients. Each client would need to wait their turn, until the time slice was round-robin shared with them. With advancements in DSP chips, the wireless clients can separate their signal out from the multiple streams being transmitted simultaneously.

Unidirectional/Omnidirectional

Wireless antennas can be purchased in many different functional designs. Each design of antenna produces gain with a certain pattern. The patterns along with the gain information are often found on the wireless vendor's website in the section typically referred to as the ordering guide.

In Figure 2.54, you see a unidirectional antenna called a *Yagi antenna*. It has a decibel gain of 13.5 dBi and operates on the 2.4 GHz radio frequency band. As you can see in the figure, there is an *azimuth plane* radiation pattern and an *elevation plane* radiation pattern. The azimuth plane is the radiation pattern left to right. The elevation plane is the radiation pattern from top to bottom. With these two patterns, we can effectively cover an area, depending on the application. In the case of the Yagi antenna design (unidirectional) in Figure 2.54, the shape would look like a blunt cone emanating from the antenna.

FIGURE 2.54   A Yagi antenna radiation pattern example

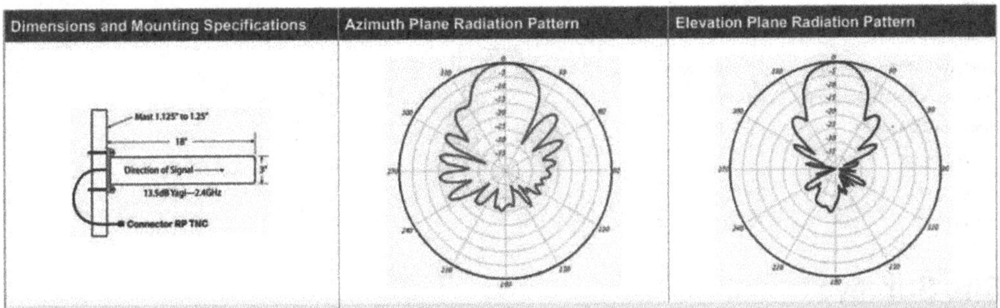

Frequency Range	2.4-2.83 GHz
VSWR	Less than 2:1, 1.5:1 Nominal
Gain	13.5 dBi
Front to Back Ratio	Greater than 25 dB
Polarization	Vertical
Azimuth 3dB Beamwidth	30 degrees
Elevations 3dB Beamwidth	25 degrees
Antenna Connector	RP-TNC
Cable Length	3 ft. (91 cm)
Dimensions	18 in. x 3 in. (45.72 cm x 7.62 cm)
Wind Rating	110 MPH
Mounting	Mast/Wall Mount

The most common antenna is the omnidirectional antenna because it produces a uniform radiation pattern. The radiation pattern of the azimuth plane (left to right) is uniform in all directions. The elevation will vary from antenna to antenna, but it will be somewhat uniform. If we were to image the 360-degree view, it would look like a giant doughnut around the antenna. An example of an omnidirectional antenna can be seen in Figure 2.55.

FIGURE 2.55   An omnidirectional antenna radiation pattern example

Dimensions and Mounting Specifications	Azimuth Plane Radiation Pattern	Elevation Plane Radiation Pattern
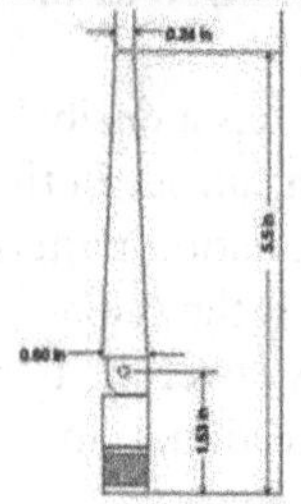	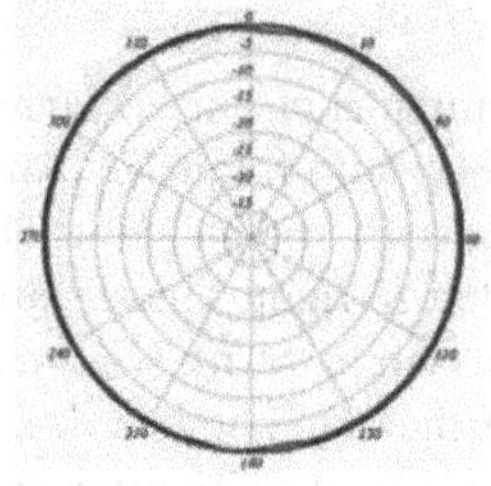	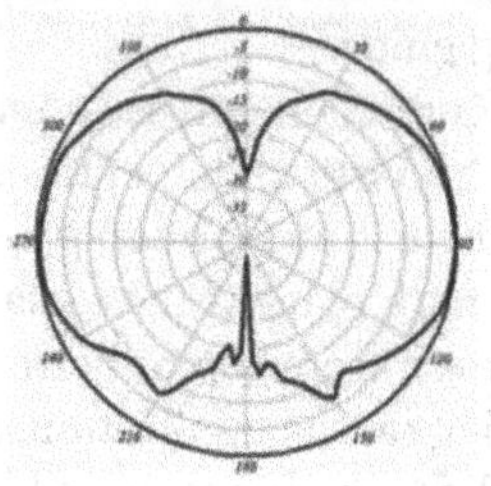

Frequency Range	2.4-2.484 GHz
VSWR	Less than 2:1
Power	5 watts
Gain	2.2 dBi
Polarization	Linear
Azimuth 3dB Beamwidth	Omnidirectional
Elevations 3dB Beamwidth	65 degrees
Antenna Connector	RP-TNC
Cable Length	None
Dimensions	5.5 in.
Mounting	To RP-TNC Connector

Site Surveys

Carpenters have a saying, "Measure twice, cut once." When we are designing a wireless network. the placement of the WAPs is critical, for both cost and coverage. Often we need to mount these WAPs on a high ceiling and run the wiring in conduit for fire code reasons. So the carpenter's saying holds very true in these situations. Before ordering WAPs we should have a good understanding of where they are going to be mounted and what the coverage is going to look like.

Fortunately, site surveys can help us future-proof the wireless design. During a site survey, the equipment is temporarily positioned in the estimated location. This positioning can be done with a special tripod with extensions that allow for high elevation, or it can just be zip-tied to the spot. The key is that it is temporary so that we can take measurements. The equipment should be the exact model, firmware, and antenna so that our readings are as close to the future design as possible.

Once the equipment is temporally mounted, we can take our readings around the expected coverage area. Software like Netscout AirMagnet allows for a drawing of the coverage area to be imported; then we can simply click the spot we are standing in and the software will register: signal strength, *signal-to-noise ratio (SNR)*, and various other metrics from the laptop's wireless card. After several points are registered, the software can create a heat map of the coverage area.

Because of the cost and acquisition of the wireless equipment and software for a site survey, it is general practice to purchase these services from the reseller. The reseller can then be the single point of contact when the coverage is not as expected or needs to be expanded upon. If you contract these services, be careful to scrutinize the *scope of work (SOW)*.

Wireless Modes of Operation

The concept of wireless topologies is very similar to that of wired topologies. The various modes define how the infrastructure is logically connected. With wireless, we are creating logical connections between wireless infrastructure and wireless clients via radio frequency (RF). Or we are creating logical connections directly between clients with RF.

Service Set Identifier (SSID)

The various modes of operation are directly tied to the equipment being used and how the service set identifier (SSID) is managed. The SSID is the friendly network name that the user will see in their wireless connections when they join a network or check the status of an already joined network. However, to the wireless devices it identifies a set of wireless services between two clients or between a client and an access point. The service can even span multiple access points and allow the user to roam between the access points.

Ad Hoc

Most wireless devices that we use daily function in infrastructure mode. Even when connecting to another wireless device, we use a wireless access point (WAP) to connect. However, when we need to connect two wireless devices and don't have any wireless infrastructure, ad hoc networks, also called independent basic service sets, can be created. Ad hoc wireless networks are impromptu networks that do not require any infrastructure at all, as shown in Figure 2.56. They are peer-to-peer network connections between two or more devices over 802.11 wireless (although other wireless technologies have ad hoc modes as well).

FIGURE 2.56   Ad hoc wireless network example

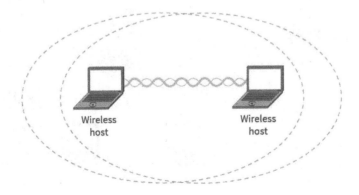

Wireless host   Wireless host

A disadvantage to ad hoc mode is that we can normally connect only two devices together. WAPs arbitrate wireless communications between devices with request-to-send and clear-to-send (RTS/CTS) signaling. When we use ad hoc mode, both clients must arbitrate the RTS/CTS signaling, which limits the connection to usually two devices—although it is possible to have as many wireless clients connected in ad hoc mode as wireless bandwidth or the operating system will allow.

Another disadvantage is the distance at which two devices can communicate. Normally we would have a WAP between two clients, allowing an average range of 100 feet. This would enable two clients to have a maximum distance between them of 200 feet, assuming the WAP is in the middle. When we use ad hoc mode, the distance is usually less than 100 feet. This is because of the transmitting power of the client wireless adapters, which is normally lower than that of WAPs on average. Also the client's antenna is smaller in size than WAP antennas.

Infrastructure

Infrastructure mode extends the wired network to a wireless network with the use of a wireless access point (WAP). Wireless devices communicate directly to the WAP, even if the devices are communicating with each other and right next to each other. The WAP arbitrates connections with request-to-send and clear-to-send (RTS/CTS) signaling, which is a carrier-sense multiple access with collision avoidance (CSMA/CA) contention method.

Basic service set (BSS) is the simplest building block for designing 802.11 wireless networks. A BSS consists of a single WAP wired to a network that provides access to a group of devices, as shown in Figure 2.57. If this sounds familiar, it should be, since it is probably how you have your wireless set up at home.

FIGURE 2.57   Basic service set example

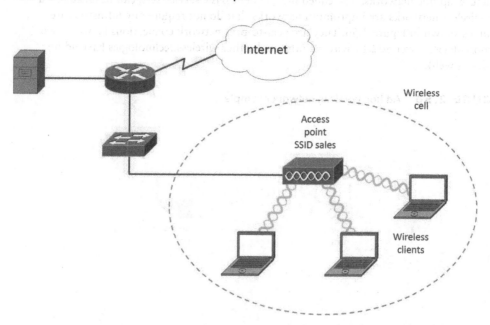

Extended service set (ESS) is a grouping of basic service sets to serve a common group of wireless devices. An ESS allows us to cover greater distances and enables a wireless device to roam between WAPs. Figure 2.58 shows an example of a typical ESS. Because wireless clients can roam between WAPs, we should implement a *wireless LAN controller (WLC)* to coordinate channels between WAPs, authentication of the client, security credentials, and overall roaming. However, a WLC is not required to create an ESS. The ESS consists of multiple BSSs with the same SSID and security settings.

FIGURE 2.58 Extended service set example

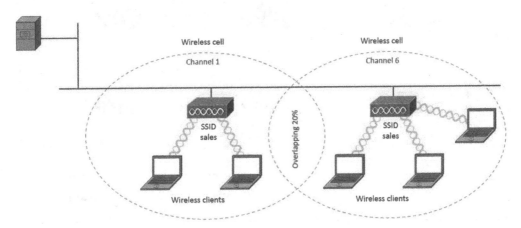

I often find that people purchase two WAPs and place them at far ends of their house for extended coverage only to find that their devices suffer disconnects and poor performance. This is because there is no coordination of channels between the WAPs. Both WAPs could use the same channel, which will limit bandwidth. Also, clients would connect to the first WAP and never be told to roam to the other WAP. When WAPs are used without a WLC, they are considered autonomous WAPs. An ESS can be created without the use of a WLC; however, each BSS cell will operate autonomously and could be problematic.

Mesh

In a wired mesh network, each switch is connected to the other switches in a mesh-type fabric of redundant connections. In a wireless mesh, each WAP can wirelessly connect to the other WAPs over RF.

The running joke is, wireless is not wireless—meaning that we still need to wire the WAPs back to the wired network. We have to wire WAPs back to the physical network for power and data. However, in many cases we cannot wire the WAPs back to the network because of cabling costs or the installation location. This is where mesh wireless networks come in.

Let's examine the use case of a 100,000-square-foot warehouse that requires wireless coverage throughout. WAPs are mounted on ceilings, and the cable runs in the middle would be too long to use Ethernet cabling. As shown in Figure 2.59, if we use mesh WAPs, we can wire in the WAPs closest to the switching equipment and allow the other WAPs to mesh together. All we need to do is supply power!

FIGURE 2.59   Mesh WAP example

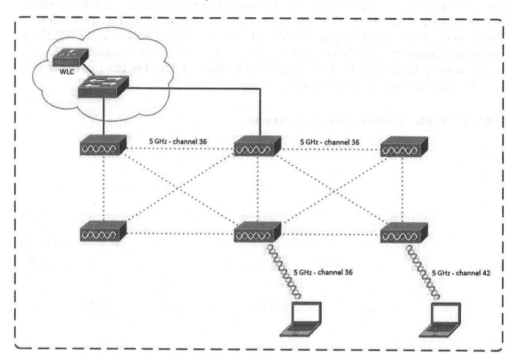

Mesh requires a wireless LAN controller for the coordination of channel assignment and forwarding traffic between WAPs. Mesh WAPs will use one channel for backhaul data (between WAPs) and other channels for serving the wireless clients.

Recently, many consumer networking equipment vendors started selling mesh WAP systems under $500 that can cover an average house of 2000 square feet. In residential houses, we have only one centralized spot where our Internet comes in and the first WAP is located. However, it is rarely in the middle of the house! These consumer-grade WAPs have a built-in WLC that allows meshing of the other WAPs to cover the entire house, and all you need is power for the other locations.

Wireless Security

802.11 wireless extends an organization's internal LAN to the outside world via radio frequency (RF). Much care is taken to secure the internal network and the external network via the firewall, but wireless should be equally protected.

Two aspects of wireless should be focused on for security purposes: encryption and authentication/authorization. Encryption of data is important because wireless can be eavesdropped on and data can be stolen as it is being transmitted. Authentication and authorization are important to keep unauthorized users away from protected portions of your network, which also protects you from theft of services and data.

Wireless Standards

There are several different encryption standards to choose from when securing a network. However, most wireless networks secured today will use the latest measure of security of WPA2. The rule of thumb is that if the equipment can handle the latest and greatest security, then it should be used. If the equipment does not support the latest and greatest, then there is probably a firmware to upgrade it. Encryption standards are usually upgradable with firmware, depending on the device.

WPA

Wi-Fi Protected Access (WPA) was standardized by the Wi-Fi Alliance in 2003 in response to the vulnerabilities in *Wired Equivalent Privacy (WEP)*. WPA uses 256-bit keys versus the 64-bit and 128-bit keys WEP used previously. WPA operates in two modes of preshared key (PSK, also called personal mode) and enterprise mode. PSK is the most common because it can easily be implemented. Enterprise mode requires a certificate server infrastructure and is also called WPA-802.1x. Enterprise mode uses the 802.1x protocol, RADIUS, and EAP; it is often used in corporate environments.

WPA introduced many improved security features over WEP, such as *message integrity checks (MICs)* that detect packets altered in transit. WPA also introduced *Temporal Key Integrity Protocol (TKIP)*, which uses the RC4 algorithm that provides per-packet keying to prevent eavesdropping on wireless conversations. However, despite the improvements in security, WPA is considered exploitable and is no longer used for wireless security. A common exploit used against WPA is an attack on the helper protocol of Wi-Fi Protected Setup (WPS). WPS is used for consumer ease of setup and should be turned off for security purposes.

WPA2

Wi-Fi Protected Access 2 (WPA2), also known as 802.11i, is the successor to WPA. WPA was deprecated in 2006, when WPA2 became a wireless security standard. Just like WPA, WPA2 operates in both personal mode (PSK) and enterprise mode.

WPA2 uses the Advanced Encryption Standard (AES) algorithm to protect data. AES is more secure than the RC4 algorithm used with TKIP. WPA2 replaced TKIP with Counter Cipher Mode (CCM) with Block Chaining Message Authentication Code Protocol (CCMP). However, TKIP can be configured as a fallback for WPA backward compatibility. Just like WPA, WPA2 is exploitable if the WPS service is enabled. WPS should be turned off for security purposes, since it is just as exploitable as the WPA version.

TKIP-RC4

Temporal Key Integrity Protocol (TKIP) uses the RC4 encryption algorithm protocol as its cipher. TKIP seeds the RC4 algorithm with a key that is derived from the MAC address and initialization vector. TKIP also works in conjunction with message integrity checks (MICs) to check the integrity of messages received by the access point. The MIC protocol is also called Michael, a 32-bit cyclic redundancy check (CRC). If two CRC MICs fail within 60 seconds, the access point requires TKIP to rekey the RC4 seed value.

CCMP-AES

Counter Mode with Cipher Block Chaining Message Authentication Code Protocol
(CCMP) – Advanced Encryption Standard (AES) uses a 128-bit key to seed the AES encryption and a 128-bit cipher block. The prior ciphered text is used to encrypt the next block of
text; this type of cipher is called code block chaining (CBC). CCMP-AES also uses a MIC
to check the integrity of wireless data received. If the MIC fails, the CCMP-AES rekeys
the session.

Authentication and Authorization

The ciphering of data and integrity checks of data are important for the confidentiality
of the data being transmitted. WPA2 is only exploitable if the attacker is already authorized
on the wireless network. It is just as important to secure the network from unauthorized
connections as it is to protect the confidentiality of the data being transmitted. The following sections focus on the method of securing wireless using authentication and authorization
of devices.

EAP

Extensible Authentication Protocol (EAP) is an IETF standard that allows supplicants
and authenticators to use various methods of encryption for authentication purposes over
802.1x, as shown in Figure 2.60. These authentication methods are defined by modules that
both the supplicant and the authenticator must have in common. These shared modules can
be replaced with other modules that expand authentication method functionality, which is
why we consider EAP to be extensible. There are many different EAP methods that can be
used. I will discuss only the three common EAP methods as per the objectives for this exam.

FIGURE 2.60   Wireless authentication for 802.1x/EAP

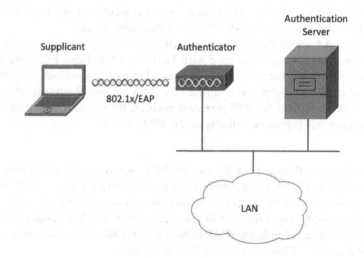

PEAP

Protected Extensible Authentication Protocol (PEAP) was jointly developed by Cisco, Microsoft, and RSA Security. PEAP is used in conjunction with 802.1x authentication systems and provides Transport Layer Security (TLS). TLS protects EAP messages by providing an encrypted tunnel as well as authentication between the host and the authenticating server before credentials are passed. The authenticator will provide the supplicant with a certificate from the authentication server signed by a certificate authority. It is important to note that the supplicant must trust the issuing certificate authority so that the authentication server's certificate is valid.

EAP-FAST

Extensible Authentication Protocol – Flexible Authentication via Secure Tunneling (EAP-FAST) is a Cisco proposed standard to replace the older Cisco proprietary protocol of Lightweight Extensible Authentication Protocol (LEAP). EAP-FAST operates in three phases; the first phase, called Phase 0, is when in-band provision occurs to create a shared secret that will be used for Phase 1 to establish a secure tunnel. Once the second phase called Phase 1 establishes the secure tunnel, then the third phase called Phase 2 allows authentication to occur between the supplicant and authentication server. Because of its use of shared keys, it is faster than PKI for tunnel creation.

EAP-TLS

Extensible Authentication Protocol – Transport Layer Security (EAP-TLS) is an open standard defined by the IETF. Because it is an open standard, many vendor and operating systems support EAP-TLS. EAP-TLS can be deployed with a preshared key (PSK), but it is more common for EAP-TLS to be deployed in conjunction with a certificate authority. When EAP-TLS is deployed in conjunction with a certificate authority, the deployment is more secure because each user or computer is issued an individual certificate. EAP-TLS is the underlying protocol used for WPA enterprise mode and WPA2 enterprise mode. When this protocol is used, EAP transmits the credentials over TLS.

Shared or Open

Shared passphrases are used with Wired Equivalent Privacy (WEP). When WEP is used, it provides 64- or 128-bit encryption via the shared passphrase. The passphrase can easily be cracked with tools like *Aircrack-NG* and is no longer used to secure wireless.

Open security is just that—it is open with no passphrase or authentication protocol. Open security was originally how all wireless access points (WAPs) were shipped to the customer. Open security still has its uses when used in conjunction with guest wireless.

Preshared Key

A preshared key (PSK) is widely used with the wireless protocols WPA and WPA2 personal mode for home wireless applications. A preshared key is a symmetrical encryption, where the key that encrypts the data also decrypts the data. PSK can also be used with other authentication protocols, such as EAP-TLS, but PSK is rarely used for EAP-TLS deployments outside of testing.

MAC Filtering

MAC address filtering is used to secure wireless by providing only whitelisted MAC addresses access to the wireless system. It is extremely effective because an attacker will not have knowledge of which MAC addresses are whitelisted. However, there is an administrative burden in entering the MAC addresses to be whitelisted. MAC address filtering is commonly used in wireless deployments that have few clients or static clients that do not change frequently.

Geofencing

Geofencing is a method of controlling mobile devices by their location. Geofencing creates a virtual perimeter around an area with the use of mapping software. The device requires an agent to be installed that reports back the Global Positioning System (GPS) coordinates. When a device is outside of the perimeter, it is considered in violation of compliance and can be applicable to a device wipe to prevent data loss.

Cellular

Cellular connectivity methods are typically not used for connecting our businesses to the Internet since most data usage is metered by the provider on a monthly basis. Where this technology excels is for the mobility of workers with a laptop and cell card. This connectivity is also used in remote equipment locations that don't need a constant stream of data, such as digital signage, equipment monitoring, and even payphones in remote locations.

TDMA

Time-division multiple access (TDMA) is a legacy cellular network protocol that is no longer used by carriers. TDMA provided 2G network services and has been incorporated into GSM cellular network protocols. The bandwidth of TDMA was 14.4 Kbps to 64 Kbps.

CDMA

Code division multiple access (CDMA) was originally designed by Qualcomm in the United States as a competitor to GSM networks. Several cellular providers still use CDMA as their 3G cellular network protocol. Sprint, Verizon Wireless, and Virgin Mobile are just a few that used CDMA.

CDMA cellular phones and equipment are not compatible with GSM networks. Although CDMA cell equipment contains a subscriber identification module (SIM) card, the cell equipment retrieves the subscriber information from the provider's servers.

CDMA-2000 is a 3G protocol used by many of the providers that support CDMA. The protocols can deliver a maximum of 3 Mbps for data. Evolution-Data Optimized (EV-DO) CDMA will not allow simultaneous voice and data, but Simultaneous Voice and EV-DO data (SV-DO) does. The more common CDMA protocol is EV-DO because North American carriers have not adopted SV-DO.

GSM

Global System for Mobile Communications (GSM) is a standard developed by the *European Telecommunications Standards Institute (ETSI)*. GSM is a global standard used around the world. It is not compatible with CDMA equipment. AT&T and T-Mobile are among the providers that use GSM networks. Several carrier technologies are built upon GSM:

Enhanced Data Rates for GSM Evolution (Edge) is used as a connectivity method for cellular data on 2G networks. It has a maximum data speed of 1 Mbps but is normally limited to 500 Kbps. It can provide backward compatibility with GSM networks, which operate at 43.2 Kbps. Many providers have moved away from Edge to the current standards of LTE.

Third-Generation (3G) operates on GSM networks worldwide and CDMA networks in the United States and limited areas. When 3G was first introduced, it had a maximum speed of 200 Kbps, but with a number of variations on 3G from providers, it can deliver up to 4 Mbps. The speed depends on whether the receiving object is stationary or moving.

High-Speed Packet Access Plus (HSPA+) is a variation of third-generation cellular that uses GSM networks. It has a theoretical speed of 168 Mbps download and 23 Mbps upload, but it is often limited by the carrier since it requires enormous RF bandwidth to achieve those speeds. Typical speeds are around 42 Mbps download and 11 Mbps upload. It is still supported with 3G phones and devices for certain carriers.

LTE/4G

Long-Term Evolution (LTE) fourth generation (4G) was the current standard of cellular data up until the year 2020, as it is slowly being replaced with 5G technology. LTE/4G is based on GSM/EDGE and HSPA technologies. LTE/4G is not a CDMA technology; it uses orthogonal frequency-division multiple access (OFDMA).

The current maximum data throughput for LTE/4G is 299 Mbps download and 75.4 Mbps upload, although typical consumer bandwidth is much lower at 12 Mbps download with a peak of 50 Mbps and 5 Mbps upload. LTE Advanced is proposed to support 1 Gbps download and 500 Mbps upload speed.

5G

Fifth generation (5G) is the new standard of cellular data that was released at the beginning of 2020. 5G was created by the 3rd Generation Partnership Project (3GPP), which is a partnership of seven organizations from Asia, Europe, and North America. Therefore 5G is not owned or maintained by any one communication company, making it a true next generation cellular standard.

The technology offers lower latency of less than 10 milliseconds versus latency of LTE/4G that was 20 to 30 milliseconds. This lower latency means that the user experience on 5G is crisp and responsive. In addition to lower latency, the technology offers higher capacity of devices within a wireless cell. The improvement of higher capacity addressed problems with dense areas like schools, hospitals, and other areas with a high density of users. The technology can support 100x more devices than LTE/4G.

The theoretical maximum data throughput for 5G is 20 Gbps, although most marketing material for 5G boasts the maximum is 10 Gbps. In either case, for many of us, this maximum speed means that we would hit our data cap in under 1 minute. Most providers will throttle the speed down to 50 to 400 Mbps for downloads and 50 to 250 Mbps for uploads.

Exam Essentials

Know the various 802.11 standards and features for each standard. 802.11b operates on 2.4 GHz and can supply a maximum bandwidth of 11 Mbps. 802.11a operates on 5.0 GHz and can supply a maximum bandwidth of 54 Mbps. 802.11a can use a maximum of 12 non-overlapping frequency channels. 802.11g operates on 2.4 GHz and can supply a maximum bandwidth of 54 Mbps. 802.11n operates on 2.4 and 5.0 GHz and can possibly of supply a maximum bandwidth of 600 Mbps. 802.11n introduced multiple-input, multiple-output (MIMO) technology and channel bonding. The 802.11ac operates solely on 5.0 GHz to supply 1.3 Gbps. 802.11ax is the latest standard and can supply a theoretical speed of 14 Gbps.

Know the two standard wireless frequencies used with 802.11. 2.4 GHz consists of 14 channels 22 MHz wide. Only channels 1, 6, and 11 of the 14 channels are non-overlapping. 5.0 GHz consists of 25 non-overlapping channels 20 MHz wide. The 5.0 GHz wireless frequencies are governed by the Unlicensed National Information Infrastructure (U-NII) radio band.

Understand the concepts of speed and distance with 802.11 wireless. Wireless speed on 5.0 GHz wireless will usually be higher than 2.4 GHz wireless because of the number of non-overlapping channels available. Wireless in outdoor settings has better distance capabilities because there is less reflection and absorption of the wireless signal.

Understand the concept of channel bandwidth vs. throughput. A 2.4 GHz wireless radio channel has a bandwidth of 22 MHz, and a 5.0 GHz wireless radio channel has a bandwidth of 20 MHz. The channel bandwidth is the capability of signals per second (cycle). The throughput can be higher because of modulation and encoding techniques.

Understand the concept of channel bonding for wireless. Channel bonding is the ability to join two adjacent non-overlapping channels to function as one operational channel. Bonding can create bonded channels of 20, 40, 80, and 160 MHz.

Understand the concept and functionality of MIMO and MU-MIMO. Multiple-input, multiple-output (MIMO) technology allows wireless devices to transmit and receive on multiple antennas. MIMO helps produce more usable bandwidth by using the multipath bounce of a wireless signal to increase the usable throughput.

Understand the concepts of unidirectional and omnidirectional antennas. Unidirectional antennas focus the signal in one general direction both up and down (elevation) and left to right (azimuth). Omnidirectional antennas focus the signal in all directions for elevation and azimuth.

Know the various modes of operation for wireless. The ad hoc wireless mode is normally point-to-point connections between two wireless devices, without the use of a wireless access point. Infrastructure wireless mode can consist of basic service sets (BSSs) or extended service sets (ESSs). A BSS is a wireless access point (WAP) connected to a wireless network providing service to a common group of computers. An ESS is several WAPs working together to extend wireless coverage for a wired network.

Know the various methods to protect information transmitted over wireless networks. Wi-Fi Protected Access (WPA) encrypts data using a 256-bit key utilizing the RC4 cipher and can be deployed in personal mode or enterprise mode. TKIP-RC4 is the method of encryption for the WPA wireless security protocol. Message integrity checks (MICs) are used in conjunction with TKIP-RC4 to provide rekeying if a cyclic redundancy check (CRC) fails. Wi-Fi Protected Access 2 (WPA2), also known as 802.11i, is a successor to WPA and operates in personal mode or enterprise mode, similar to WPA. Counter Mode with Cipher Block Chaining Message Authentication Code Protocol (CCMP-AES) also works in conjunction with MIC to provide encryption with Advanced Encryption Standard (AES) and rekeying if CRC checks fail.

Know the various cellular standards and their accompanying features. TDMA is a legacy cellular standard that provided 2G cellular; it has a bandwidth of 14.4 Kbps to 64 Kbps. CDMA is a 3G cellular technology that Sprint, Verizon Wireless, and Virgin Mobile use. CDMA-2000 can supply a maximum of 3 Mbps of bandwidth per subscriber. Evolution-Data Optimized (EV-DO) CDMA will not allow simultaneous voice and data, but Simultaneous Voice and EV-DO data (SV-DO) will allow simultaneous voice and data. GSM is a European standard globally adopted and is used by 2G and 3G cellular standards. High-Speed Packet Access Plus (HSPA+) is a variation of 3G cellular. LTE/4G is the latest 4G cellular standard capable of a maximum data throughput of 299 Mbps download and 75.4 upload.

Review Questions

1. Which devices provide the lowest latency and highest bandwidth for connectivity?
   A. Hubs
   B. Switches
   C. Bridges
   D. Routers

2. Which networking component allows you to detect and prevent malicious network activity?
   A. Firewall
   B. IDS/IPS
   C. Proxy server
   D. Content filter

3. Which device will act as a multiport repeater in the network?
   A. Hub
   B. Switch
   C. Bridge
   D. WAP

4. Which is a function of a layer 2 switch?
   A. Forwarding the data based upon logical addressing
   B. Repeating the electrical signal to all ports
   C. Learning the MAC address by examining the destination MAC addresses
   D. Determining the forwarding interfaces based upon the destination MAC address and tables

5. You need to deploy a surveillance camera in an area that requires you to record the equipment from the time it has entered your data center to the time it is installed. Which type of surveillance camera should you deploy?
   A. CCTV
   B. PTZ
   C. Coaxial
   D. PoE

6. You need to protect against threats for specific URLs on your web server. Which device should you implement?
   A. IDS
   B. Proxy server
   C. NGFW
   D. Router

7. Which component is commonly found inside of a SCADA system?

   A. HMI

   B. Access control panel

   C. Security console

   D. Smart speaker

8. Which routing type is best implemented in stub networks?

   A. Default routing

   B. RIP routing

   C. Static routing

   D. Dynamic routing

9. You are obtaining another Internet provider for your company's connectivity to the Internet. You want to make sure that if there is a failure, the routing protocol will advertise your company's IP addresses and fail over. Which routing protocol should you use?

   A. RIPv2

   B. EIGRP

   C. OSPF

   D. BGP

10. Which quality of service (QoS) method is used at layer 2 of the OSI?

    A. 802.1Q

    B. ToS

    C. Diffserv

    D. CoS

11. Which routing protocol uses path-vector metrics?

    A. BGP

    B. RIP

    C. OSPF

    D. EIGRP

12. You have two different routing protocols with routes to the same destination. How will the best route be chosen?

    A. Round robin

    B. Hop count

    C. Congestion

    D. Administrative distance

13. What must you always configure first when implementing OSPF?

   A. Area 1

   B. Backbone 0.0.0.0

   C. ABR

   D. LSA

14. Which protocol uses a 6-bit value for QoS?

   A. DSCP

   B. ToS

   C. CoS

   D. QoS

15. Several of your users are complaining that the network slows down several times a day. You recently added a large number of clients to the immediate network. What should be done to reduce the impact of the additional hosts?

   A. Create a single broadcast domain.

   B. Create a single collision domain.

   C. Create several broadcast domains.

   D. Assign static IP addresses to all computers.

16. What is the normal maximum transmission unit (MTU) size for an Ethernet network?

   A. 1500 bytes

   B. 1548 bytes

   C. 9000 bytes

   D. 1648 bytes

17. You captured network traffic with a network capture utility. Several of the MAC addresses are ff:ff:ff:ff:ff:ff:ff:ff. What could these packets be?

   A. ICMP traffic

   B. Broadcast traffic

   C. Multicast traffic

   D. IGMP traffic

18. You need to trunk two switches from two different vendors together. Which trunking protocol should you use?

   A. ISL

   B. 802.1D

   C. 802.1Q

   D. 802.1w

19. When calculating Spanning Tree Protocol (STP), which switch will always become the root bridge?

    A. The switch with the highest priority

    B. The switch with the highest MAC address

    C. The switch with the lowest MAC address

    D. The switch with the lowest priority

20. You need to restrict a switch port to a maximum of two devices. What should you implement to guarantee only two devices can communicate on the switch port?

    A. Jumbo frames

    B. 802.1x

    C. ACLs

    D. Port security

21. You have recently deployed several POE security cameras on a switch. You had chosen the switch because it met the power requirements of the cameras. However, several ports will not power up and you have now discovered that you are drawing too much power. Which option will quickly rectify the problem?

    A. Purchase cameras with a lower power requirement.

    B. Purchase a new switch that can provide more power.

    C. Turn on POE+ support on the switch.

    D. Turn on LLDP on the switch.

22. Which wireless standard first introduced channel bonding?

    A. 802.11n

    B. 802.11ac

    C. 802.11g

    D. 802.11a

23. Which cellular standard was developed by the European Telecommunications Standards Institute (ETSI)?

    A. TDMA

    B. CDMA

    C. GSM

    D. LTE/4G

24. Which three wireless channels on 2.4 GHz wireless are non-overlapping?

    A. 1, 3, and 9

    B. 1, 9, and 11

    C. 1, 6, and 11

    D. 1, 6, and 12

25. Which Cisco proprietary protocol is used to transmit credentials for 802.1x authentication systems?

A. LEAP

B. EAP

C. PEAP

D. NAC

Chapter

3

Domain 3.0: Network Operations

THE FOLLOWING COMPTIA NETWORK+ OBJECTIVES ARE COVERED IN THIS CHAPTER:

✓ **3.1 Given a scenario, use the appropriate statistics and sensors to ensure network availability.**

- Performance metrics/sensors
- Device/chassis
    - Temperature
    - Central processing unit (CPU) usage
    - Memory
- Network metrics
    - Bandwidth
    - Latency
    - Jitter
- SNMP
    - Traps
    - Object identifiers (OIDs)
    - Management information bases (MIBs)
- Network device logs
    - Log reviews
        - Traffic logs
        - Audit logs
        - Syslog
    - Logging levels/severity levels

- Interface statistics/status
    - Link state (up/down)
    - Speed/duplex
    - Send/receive traffic
    - Cyclic redundancy checks (CRCs)
    - Protocol packet and byte counts
- Interface errors or alerts
    - CRC errors
    - Giants
    - Runts
    - Encapsulation errors
- Environmental factors and sensors
    - Temperature
    - Humidity
    - Electrical
    - Flooding
- Baselines
- NetFlow data
- Uptime/downtime

✓ **3.2 Explain the purpose of organizational documents and policies.**

- Plans and procedures
    - Change management
    - Incident response plan
    - Disaster recovery plan
    - Business continuity plan
    - System life cycle
    - Standard operating procedures

- Hardening and security policies
    - Password policy
    - Acceptable use policy
    - Bring your own device (BYOD) policy
    - Remote access policy
    - Onboarding and offboarding policy
    - Security policy
    - Data loss prevention
- Common documentation
    - Physical network diagram
        - Floor plan
        - Rack diagram
        - Intermediate distribution frame (IDF)/main distribution frame (MDF) documentation
    - Logical network diagram
    - Wiring diagram
    - Site survey report
    - Audit and assessment report
    - Baseline configurations
- Common agreements
    - Non-disclosure agreement (NDA)
    - Service-level agreement (SLA)
    - Memorandum of understanding (MOU)

✓ **3.3 Explain high availability and disaster recovery concepts and summarize which is the best solution.**

- Load balancing
- Multipathing
- Network interface card (NIC) teaming

- Redundant hardware/clusters
    - Switches
    - Routers
    - Firewalls
- Facilities and infrastructure support
    - Uninterruptible power supply (UPS)
    - Power distribution units (PDUs)
    - Generator
    - HVAC
    - Fire suppression
- Redundancy and high availability (HA) concepts
    - Cold site
    - Warm site
    - Hot site
    - Cloud site
    - Active-active vs. active-passive
        - Multiple Internet service providers (ISPs)/ diverse paths
        - Virtual Router Redundancy Protocol (VRRP)/ First Hop Redundancy Protocol (FHRP)
    - Mean time to repair (MTTR)
    - Mean time between failure (MTBF)
    - Recovery time objective (RTO)
    - Recovery point objective (RPO)
- Network device backup/restore
    - State
    - Configuration

In previous chapters, I discussed the networking concepts that help you understand how a network functions as well as the infrastructure that allows us to build networks from these networking concepts. In this chapter you'll learn how to maintain the infrastructure through the management and planning of daily operations. Regardless if you just built the network or you already have a preestablished network, you need to maintain its operations.

The concepts discussed in this chapter help you maintain network operations through documentation, business continuity, disaster recovery, performance, patch management, remote access, policies, and best practices. You must master all of these topics to maintain the operations of a network.

3.1 Given a scenario, use the appropriate statistics and sensors to ensure network availability.

Understanding network concepts to be able to build a network is only the beginning. Keeping the network up and running is an ongoing task. In the following sections, I will cover the important metrics, collection of those metrics, analysis of logs, common errors and alerts, and environmental factors. Understanding these concepts will build your knowledge as a network analyst, which is just one of the many roles you will perform in your job as a network professional.

Performance Metrics

If I asked how well your car ran on 87 versus 89 octane gasoline, what would your answer be? The answer might be very subjective, such as fine or better. However, those answers would not gauge the true performance of the better octane level. What if all of a sudden your car started losing power or feeling like it was losing power? Would you know, for sure, if there is actually a problem? How would you describe the problem? And when would you know if it is truly fixed?

In order to gauge performance and diagnose problems, we need an objective approach. Performance and troubleshooting can only be managed or gauged on their effectiveness if metrics are defined and compared. If a metric can be defined, then you have a measure of success. This concept can be applied to anything, not just networks. Fortunately, there are some very well-defined metrics for both networked devices and the networking that connect these devices.

Device Metrics

Every device on our network can succumb to overheating, overutilization, or just plain running out of resources. These devices can include everything from a network switch to the database server, just to give a range of examples. Most devices will have some form of a sensor, which allows the end user to gauge the performance or condition of the device.

Temperature   Temperature can be a problem because of two different factors: the external environment and the internal temperature of the component(s). The external temperature and the internal temperature are related to each other. For example, if a component is not properly cooled (high external temperature), the fans will just blow hot air through it and eventually it will overheat.

Let's assume that the external cooling in the environment is optimal and consistent. The metric of temperature can also be related to the utilization of an internal resource of the component. High temperature usually means that the central processing unit (CPU), random access memory (RAM), logic circuits, or any other component is being highly utilized.

Temperature is usually related to CPU utilization, but in some cases it can be tied to another external factor, such as dust. If dust builds up inside a component, it won't properly cool regardless of the external cooling factors. So this metric is a great metric to collect because it can be used to identify issues with equipment.

CPU Utilization   The central processing unit (CPU) for any device is a key metric to describe the utilization of the device. There are a few exceptions to this, such as embedded logic circuits like the application-specific integrated circuit (ASIC) chips found in many switches today. The ASIC chips will do the bulk of the work forwarding frames and the CPU is only responsible for the control of traffic and management of the switch. However, these fringe cases are the exception to the rule.

It basically comes down to devices with a high CPU utilization are doing more work than devices with low CPU utilization. The gauge of what is high CPU utilization and what is low CPU utilization is best left to understanding baselines, which I will discuss later in this chapter.

Capturing the metric of CPU utilization will give you a clear picture of how much work a device is doing. To correct the problem, it may require adding processing capacity, changing the application of the device, or upgrading it entirely. However, without capturing and analyzing the metric of CPU utilization, you will not have a clear picture of usage for the device.

Memory   The memory for a device is typically used as temporary storage of information and instructions for the CPU; it is called random access memory (RAM). However, memory can also be used for storing the configuration and operating system for a device; that is called non-volatile RAM or flash memory. Router and switches will load their operating system from flash into RAM and then load their configuration from non-volatile RAM.

The metric of RAM is probably the most important metric to capture compared to other types of memory. This is mainly because configuration changes will happen infrequently to necessitate capturing non-volatile RAM as a metric. Also, the flash memory will only change during an upgrade of the router or switch's operating system, so capturing flash memory as a metric won't identify a performance problem. RAM is the most dynamic of the various types of memory. High RAM utilization might mean that there are too many processes or applications being loaded into RAM. It can also mean that the operating system is processing too much data.

Generally, if you are monitoring the metric of RAM on an operating system and there is high memory utilization, you will also see high CPU utilization and disk utilization. This is because most operating systems use the concept of swapping memory from RAM to disk, in an effort to free up RAM. When a trend of high utilization is tracked over time, it usually means that the RAM needs to be upgraded or the device needs to be upgraded, depending on the RAM upgrade options.

Storage   Although storage is not in the objectives for the exam, it can be considered a type of memory for devices, depending on the type of device. I'm including it for completeness on the topic of device metrics. The storage capacity needed for long-term data storage, applications, and the operating system depends on the type of device. For the purpose of this discussion, I will refer to disk storage as it relates to an operating system like Windows or Linux, mainly because there are too many devices that can use storage in too many ways and they are the most common.

We normally want to capture the capacity of storage to identify a problem before we completely run out of space on the device. We can also capture other metrics if the storage is not directly connected, such as throughput and latency, and I will discuss those metrics in the next section, "Network Metrics." You can run out of space on the operating system for a number of reasons. The most common is lack of planning, which is why most software vendors have gigantic storage requirements for their products. Software vendors know their product can be utilized in so many ways, so they also state the highest storage recommendation in an effort to force you to plan.

Although lack of planning is the most common reason to run out of storage, there could be other reasons, such as a large update that utilizes the disk storage or an event that is rarely seen. In any case, the metric of storage is valuable in preventing problems. When an operating system runs out of space, the failure is often subtle and could cause long-term corruption.

Network Metrics

The network is the first thing to get blamed when performance problems are encountered with networked applications. Sometimes the problem is the network, and sometimes the problem is the device that the application is processing on. Luckily there are established metrics that can be used to diagnosis most network performance problems.

Bandwidth   Bandwidth can be measured in two different ways; the first is available bandwidth and the second is bandwidth utilization or throughput. When we talk about bandwidth utilization or throughput, we simply refer to it as utilization.

The bandwidth of a connection is often referred to as a connection's speed, and it is measured in bits per second (bps). The throughput can never exceed the bandwidth for a given connection, as shown in Figure 3.1. Throughput measurement is often performed on a connection such as the Internet. We will collect the metric by measuring the path to a given host on the Internet. It's not a perfect measurement because a host can sometimes be down or overwhelmed with other traffic. However, most of the time the destination host has a much bigger connection than the Internet connection you are connected with.

FIGURE 3.1   Bandwidth vs. utilization

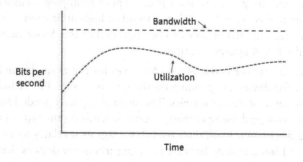

Another way of collecting this metric is to use a point-to-point measurement with a tool such as iPerf. This method requires a dedicated computer on both ends of the connection, one acting as a server and the other acting as a client. If you are continually collecting throughput, a dedicated server will be required. One consideration is that you will be flawing the result by consuming bandwidth for the test while other traffic is flowing, thus giving you a false reading. Another consideration is the direction of throughput; for an accurate test you should see the utilization for both directions.

The collection for the utilization metric is much more defined and accurate. The utilization metric is typically a percentage of the total link speed (potential bandwidth), or the metric can also be in bits per second (bps). Most switches and routers have a defined counter that can be collected using the Simple Network Management Protocol (SNMP). However, this metric is not limited to routers and switches, it can also be collected from other operating systems. Measuring the utilization of a connection can help you see how busy the interface or host is at a given point in time.

Latency   Latency is the time it takes a packet or frame to travel from source to destination, and it is measured in milliseconds (ms), as shown in Figure 3.2. You will always have some form of latency in a network; switching creates latency, routing creates more latency. If you are communicating on the Internet, processes like network address translation (NAT) will create even more and we didn't even discuss the possible congestion along the path. So, latency is a very important metric to collect, especially during trouble periods.

FIGURE 3.2   Latency vs. time

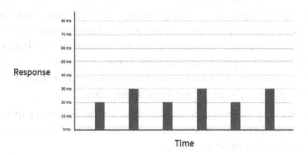

When dealing with real-time protocols such as Voice over IP (VoIP), latency of 125 ms or more could create an echo. Just to put things in perspective, the average latency across the Internet is 10 ms to 20 ms and100 ms is 1/100 of a second. Fortunately, there are algorithms built into the codec used with VoIP to help with echo cancellation. Other real-time protocols such as Internet Small Computer Systems Interface (iSCSI) can also be affected, although these protocols usually don't travel across the Internet. A latency of 300 ms, or 3/100 of a second, could wreak havoc on a datastore on an iSCSI storage area network (SAN).

Collecting this metric is often done by using the round-trip time of a packet. The round-trip time is the time it takes for a packet to reach the destination and make it back to the sender. This is really latency × 2, assuming the path back is the same as the original path. So, acceptable latency is always calculated for this round-trip time. This is fine, because if you create a request, you'll be expecting an answer back, even if you are just sending data, as in the case of iSCSI. The Internet Control Message Protocol (ICMP) can measure the round-trip time, and since it operates at layer 3 of the OSI model, it's pretty accurate.

Jitter   Jitter is the variation of latency from packet to packet and is also measured in milliseconds (ms). For example, if there are three packets sent and they are received with 10, 40, and 70 ms of latency, then the jitter is 30 ms. If packets are sent and they are received with 10, 20, and 10 ms of latency, the jitter is 10 ms, as shown in Figure 3.3.

FIGURE 3.3   Jitter vs. time

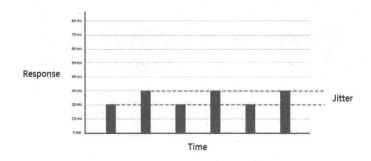

Network protocols and applications are very tolerant of latency, but not jitter. This is similar to a car driving down a smooth road versus driving down a bumpy road; in both instances the car can maintain a comfortable speed if the road conditions are consistent. However, if you consistently go from a smooth to a bumpy road and then back again, you will slow down even more because of the adjustment period between conditions. Network protocols and applications have the same affect. We always want low jitter measurements for our networked applications. An acceptable amount of jitter should be below 15 to 25 ms for the average network application.

Collecting the jitter metric only requires calculating the difference of latency between packets. ICMP is used for this process of collecting the initial latency, again because it operates at layer 3 and is most accurate.

Although this section is about the collection of network-based metrics with the Simple Network Management Protocol (SNMP), one-off tests can be done with third-party websites. For example, http://meter.net/ping-test/ is a great way to check your latency and jitter. The website also gives you a graphical format of the results. This is not the only service. There are several other sites like this one. With this simple test you can obtain your nominal metrics and then you can identify whether or not you actually have a performance problem.

SNMP

The Simple Network Management Protocol (SNMP) is protocol that allows the collection of metrics, also known as counters. SNMP can also be used for the reporting events from a device back to a centralized *network management station (NMS)*. Although the expansion of the acronym SNMP includes the word *simple* it is not a simple protocol because there are many components, as shown in Figure 3.4. But don't worry, I will discuss each component in detail in the following sections. As always, you might feel like you need to know everything about this subject before you can understand a specific topic about this subject. For that reason, I recommend reading the following sections twice.

FIGURE 3.4   SNMP components

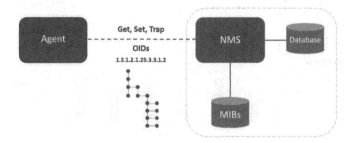

Agent

The agent is a small piece of software that resides on the device or operating system to be monitored. The agent is responsible for answer requests from a network management station (NMS), or the agent will send messages to the NMS. The agent is configured with a specific set of counters (metrics) called object identifiers (OIDs) for which it is responsible. It will be responsible for collecting the values for these counters and presenting them upon a request. The agent can also be set up to transmit to an NMS if a counter crosses a threshold value.

NMS

OpenNMS, and PRTG Network Monitor are two examples of network management systems. An NMS is responsible for collecting statistics such as bandwidth, memory, and CPU from devices and operating systems. An NMS can also be configured to store these counters in a database, so you have the ability to review past performance. When a service goes down or stops responding to NMS queries, an NMS can send an alert or notification for network administrator intervention. We can also set thresholds for specific counters, and when a counter crosses the threshold, alerts and notifications are sent to the administrator from the NMS. For instance, if we are collecting the metric of temperature and the value crosses a threshold we set in the NMS, an email can be sent to the administrator with a warning.

Network management systems are generally used for the ongoing collection of statistics from network devices and operating systems. This constant recording of statistics creates baselines for comparison over time. It also helps us identify trends and problematic periods of time. As seen in Figure 3.5, around 17:00 hours of bandwidth spiked up to 9.2 Mbps. Looking at the weekly graph, these spikes seem normal for brief periods of time.

Commands

Network management stations (NMSs), can operate with two basic command methods: SNMP get command and SNMP trap command, as seen in Figure 3.6. An SNMP get command is a solicited request to the OS or network device for an *object ID (OID)* value; SNMP get commands are considered polling requests since they happen at a set interval. An SNMP trap command is unsolicited information from the OS or network device. An SNMP trap command is sent when the threshold on the device has been exceeded, such as a bandwidth setting, disk space, or in the event an interface goes down. These SNMP trap commands can be configured on the SNMP monitor to create alerts and notifications for the administrator.

There is a third command method called the SNMP set command and it is not normally used by the NMS. It allows a variable to be set on the device or operating system. It functions similarly to an SNMP get command, with the exception you are setting a value. The SNMP set command is normally initiated by a technician or script when setting a value, such as a password on a group of network devices.

FIGURE 3.5   SNMP monitor graph

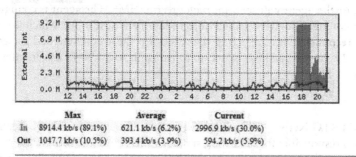

Daily Graph (5-minute average)

	Max	Average	Current
In	8914.4 kb/s (89.1%)	621.1 kb/s (6.2%)	2996.9 kb/s (30.0%)
Out	1047.7 kb/s (10.5%)	393.4 kb/s (3.9%)	594.2 kb/s (5.9%)

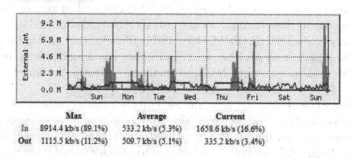

Weekly Graph (30-minute average)

	Max	Average	Current
In	8914.4 kb/s (89.1%)	533.2 kb/s (5.3%)	1658.6 kb/s (16.6%)
Out	1115.5 kb/s (11.2%)	509.7 kb/s (5.1%)	335.2 kb/s (3.4%)

FIGURE 3.6   SNMP get and trap methods

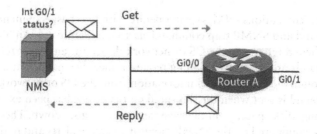

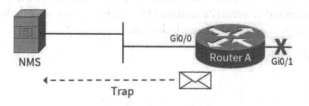

SNMP operates on two different ports, 161 and 162, depending on if you are sending an SNMP get command to retrieve a value for a counter or a device is reporting an event. All SNMP get and set commands (polling type commands) are sent via UDP port 161. SNMP trap commands are sent from the agent to the NMS on UDP port 162. By default, SNMP uses UDP since the messages sent are simple commands that require simple responses. However, TCP can be configured for moving data in an environment where data delivery is not always assured, such as across the Internet.

Community Name

The community name is a shared passphrase authentication for SNMP versions 1 and 2c. SNMPv3 uses community names, but it is not the main authentication method. The SNMP community name allows an NMS or technician to send SNMP commands to an SNMP instance running on a device or operating system. The default community name for read-only (get commands) is public. The default community name for read-write (set commands) is private. So, we often refer to the community name as public and private regardless of the actual community name. Obviously if someone obtains the community name, they can read sensitive information such as configuration information and possibly write new configurations if they obtain a read-write community name.

Versions

SNMP version 1, known as SNMPv1, is obviously the first version of SNMP and it is the oldest. SNMPv1 was defined in RFC 1155 and 1157 back in 1990. It is old (30 years) and should no longer be used; it is covered for historical purposes only. SNMPv2 expanded on SNMPv1 by adding support for 64-bit counters for handling large counter numbers. SNMPv2c added support for proxy agents. Both version 1 and version 2c lack any kind of encryption or authentication outside of the community name string. They should both be avoided when setting up SNMP, but many vendors still promote setting up SNMPv2c.

SNMPv3 was released in 2002 and added the much-needed encryption and authentication that prior versions lacked. User accounts can be set up along with a type of access control called an SNMP view. The SNMP view is a way of scoping access down to a specific OID or group of OIDs. SNMPv3 is a lot more difficult to set up, but it is a lot more secure than prior versions. My personal recommendation is to use it over SNMPv1 and v2c, but every situation has its considerations.

OIDs and the MIB

Object identifiers (OIDs) are uniquely managed objects on a device or operating system that can be queried or configured. The OIDs are organized into a hierarchal tree and are noted in dotted decimal notation, such as .1.3.6.1.2.1.2.2. Each number represents a portion of the hierarchy, from least significant on the left to most significant on the right. For example, the OID.1.3.6.1.2.1.2.2 is broken down to iso(1) identified-organization(3) dod(6) internet(1) mgmt(2) mib-2(1) interface(2) ifTable(2). So, if this

OID is queried, a value will be returned for each interface on the system. From there, you can choose which interface you want to query and the specific attribute. To query interface 3, the OID would look like this .1.3.6.1.2.1.2.2.3, adding a 3 on the rightmost OID string. The attributes would then follow, such as .1.3.6.1.2.1.2.2.3.5 for ifSpeed. This might look like dark magic, but it is all very well documented in the MIB.

The guide of attributes is always contained in the *management information base (MIB)*. The MIB is a database of OIDs published by the vendor of the OS or network device. The MIB defines the OID counters along with the type of data the OID offers for collection. Otherwise the value you get back is just an arbitrary value. The MIB gives definition to the value, such as an interface error rate, bandwidth, or many other attributes of an interface. The NMS will require a specific MIB for the device or OS in order to collect statistics for the counter. Without a proper MIB installed, the SNMP process on the NMS cannot be configured to retrieve the values.

As I stated before, SNMP is not a simple protocol as its name states, mainly because it has many different components. For the exam you should know the various components and not their intricacies, as an entire book could be devoted to those topics. That being said, if you would like to learn more about the MIB file referenced in this section, visit www.net-snmp.org/docs/mibs/IF-MIB.txt and browse the file. Net-SNMP is the de facto standard used by many devices and operating systems. The website at www.net-snmp.org is a great source for documentation on the subject.

Network Device Logs

Logging events is important for a number of reasons, such as post-mortem analysis and auditing as well as identifying what happened and who or what caused it in the event of a security breach. Most network devices and operating systems will log locally to a file, but this will cause a problem in the event of device failure because the log files will be inaccessible. The optimal strategy for logging is to point all of the network devices and operating systems to one centralized logging server. This centralized logging server will create a central repository of logs for the entire network. However, do not underestimate the massive amounts of logs that are collected daily. Depending on what exactly is being collected, these servers might require really big and very fast disks.

When reviewing logs, we must first isolate and drill down to the device we need to focus on. Most log management tools like Splunk and Kibana, just to name a couple, provide drill-down of log data for the system. After you isolate the device in the log, you then need to isolate the normal log data from the abnormal log data. This will allow you to find the root cause of a problem or identify a performance problem depending on the situation, as shown in Figure 3.7. In this particular example, a filter was created to remove anything that wasn't a normal log entry. This is called removing the noise in the logs. This is an art in itself because of the complexity of the data as well as the problem you are trying to solve.

FIGURE 3.7   Example of an Elasticsearch with Kibana

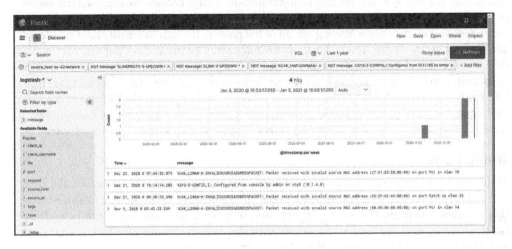

All log viewing tools have a facility to filter log data—even the built-in *Event Viewer* in the Microsoft operating system has this functionality. In Figure 3.8, you can see I filtered out everything in the application log, except for Critical and Error levels. Every tool will have some method of removing the noise from the logs. I've only presented two tools here, but there are hundreds of tools on the market.

FIGURE 3.8   Event Viewer filtering

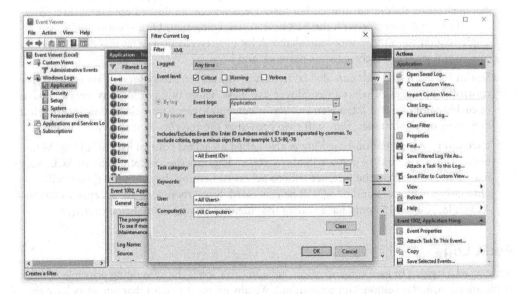

Something else that should be considered when viewing network logs is correlation. Correlation of data is a reason to use centralized log collection. This is because we can correlate events between devices for a given time period. For example, maybe we have a device that is rebooting for no reason. You may begin filtering out all of the noise in the logs to identify only shutdowns and startups for the device. You end up only finding startup events and nothing else for the device, which would mean the device doesn't know it is going to reboot. If you widen the scope of the search to include the networked UPS the device is plugged into, you might find that the UPS has issues that could lead to the mysterious reboots. If the times of the UPS errors correlate to the device rebooting, you've solved the mystery. Of course, this correlation of data can be done in a decentralized fashion, but it often takes longer and data is sometimes overlooked.

Traffic Logs

Traffic logs can be attained in a number of ways, depending on your requirements. I'm sure you will want to collect everything traffic-wise, but these logs can be gigantic in size because they represent the traffic flows for your network; therefore, their size should not be underestimated. In the following list I will cover some of the most common traffic logs you may collect. There are countless scenarios; these are just the common ones.

Overview   Overview-based traffic logs are simply based upon the source and destination traffic communicating out of your network. Often the top-talkers can be identified, and it's the best way to understand traffic patterns to your network. Overview-based traffic logs are great at showing you a 10,000-mile view of the network while also allowing you to scope down to the specific sender and receiver.

Session   Session-based traffic logs are the start and end of a particular session or transmission on the network. There is no one way to capture these types of logs and a session can mean several different things. For instance, a session might be based on a three-way-handshake and conclude with the FIN or RST flag being sent. Or a session might be a single request for a three-way-handshake. A lot of firewalls now offer this as an option, so you can see what accessed your network and how.

Session-based traffic logs can also be from a proxy server. Proxy servers are effective for controlling policies of what an employee can view. These types of logs are very effective in curbing non-work-related web surfing. When employees know that you capture what they view on the Internet, they will stop browsing the Internet as if they were home.

Exception   An exception-based log is also called an access control list (ACL) log. Many firewalls, routers, and switches will allow you to log only the exceptions to an ACL. So, if a particular host on the Internet tries to access something they shouldn't, they will obviously get blocked and a log will be generated. Since these logs are exceptions to the ACL rule, you tend to only have entries that identify attacks or malicious activity.

Audit Logs

Auditing and logging of user authentication and authorization is the accounting principle of AAA (authentication, authorization, and accounting). We always want to trust that our users have the best intentions. This leads us to the mantra of auditing and logging, which is to trust and audit.

Logging of user authentication activity helps us audit who among our users are accessing the organization's systems and when. It holds the users accessing the network systems accountable for their actions. We always believe our users have good intentions, but what happens if a user's account is compromised? Reviewing of the log files helps identify failed attempts or successful logins by a bad actor.

Logging of authorization is similar to logging of authentication, with the exception of the amount of data generated. When a user accesses a piece of information that is being audited to create a log event, it generates a log entry. If we are auditing for successful authorization requests, everything a user does could potentially create a log entry. This helps us identify what a user is doing, but it creates a massive amount of data. If we audit only for failures of authorization, it will lower the amount of data collected, but we see only failures and not what the user is accessing. A delicate balance of success auditing and failure auditing must be established. One tactic is to choose carefully what to audit, such as only sensitive information for successful authorization and failed attempts.

Syslog

Throughout these sections on network device auditing, I've discussed the best practices of logging and described servers that store these logfiles. However, I have not covered how you get the logs to the server and exactly what kind of server accepts these messages. This is where the Syslog protocol comes into this discussion.

Syslog is a client-server protocol that allows just about any device on the network to send logs as they happen. The protocol operates on UDP port 514 and it's considered a "fire-and-forget" type protocol. This means that the device sending the message never receives an acknowledgment that the message was received. So you really need to make sure that the logs are being collected at the syslog server.

It is also important to note that by default network devices and Linux/Unix operating systems will write a file called syslog because it contains local events for the device. This comes in handy when troubleshooting, but it also causes challenges if the device completely fails. Therefore, it's always best to ship the logs off the network device or operating system with the Syslog protocol pointed to a syslog server.

The syslog message format is standardized, as shown in Figure 3.9. The message will start with a timestamp so you know when it was created. On some network devices, sequence numbers can be used in lieu of timestamps. Sequence numbers are useful because some events can happen simultaneously and the sequence number helps sort out which happened first. The next field, called the Device-id, is optional. By default, for most network devices, the Device-id is not sent. However, it's useful to send it if you are sending these messages to a centralized syslog server. The Device-id can be a hostname, an IP address, or any string that identifies the device. The next field actually comprises three different parts: the facility, severity, and mnemonic. The facility is the internal system inside the device that has generated the log message. The severity is standardized based upon a 0–7 severity level that I will discuss in the next section. The mnemonic is nothing more than the action the facility took, and the value is a simple string. The last section of a syslog message is the message text itself. This is what exactly happened to generate the syslog message.

FIGURE 3.9   Anatomy of a syslog message

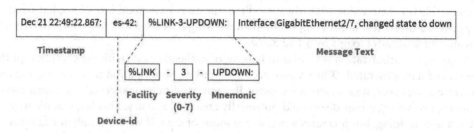

Logging Levels/Severity Levels

Most services like DNS and DHCP have some sort of debug feature to help you diagnose problems. The debug feature will produce some form of logs, either on the screen or to a file. Keep in mind that when logs are produced, you will end up with a certain level of noise from normal events. So, some services allow you to specify a logging level in an effort to reduce the noise or dive deeper into the problem. This of course all depends on what you specify, your mode of diagnostic, and your tolerance for the noise in the log file.

The Syslog protocol/service is used solely for logging events on network devices and operating systems. Therefore, it has a built-in logging level called a severity level. These severity levels range from the most critical level of 0 (emergency) to the least critical of 7 (debug). This gives you a total of eight levels to choose from, as shown in Table 3.1.

TABLE 3.1   Severity levels

Level	Severity	Description
0	Emergency	System is unusable.
1	Alert	Action must be taken immediately.
2	Critical	Critical conditions.
3	Error	Error conditions.
4	Warning	Warning conditions.
5	Notice	Normal, but significant conditions.
6	Informational	Informational messages.
7	Debug	Debug-level messages.

A level can be throttled back and forth depending on what you are trying to capture. The severity level is also inclusive of lower levels. This means that if you choose a level of 3, it will include the logging that would be produced at level 2 and level 1. For example, if you configure the severity level to the lowest value of 0, you will only receive the emergency messages. However, if you configure the severity level to 4, you will receive all of the warning (4), error (3), critical (2), alert (1), and emergency (0) messages.

Interface Statistics/Status

The interface statistics and status for a connection is probably the most important information to have when you're trying to diagnose a connection problem. The information can be collected a number of ways from the various operating systems. For example, on the Windows operating system, the PowerShell command `Get-NetAdapterStatistics` can be used to get detailed statistics. In the following example, counters for various Ethernet and IP statistics are displayed when the command is executed.

```
PS C:\Users\Jon> Get-NetAdapterStatistics | Format-List
Caption                  : MSFT_NetAdapterStatisticsSettingData 'Realtek GbE'
Description              : Realtek Gaming GbE Family Controller
ElementName              : Realtek Gaming GbE Family Controller
InstanceID               : {1893BDFE-A5EF-473C-B0D8-84F0D5C92F96}
InterfaceDescription     : Realtek Gaming GbE Family Controller
Name                     : Ethernet
Source                   : 2
SystemName               : Centaur
OutboundDiscardedPackets : 0
OutboundPacketErrors     : 0
RdmaStatistics           :
ReceivedBroadcastBytes   : 1834282
ReceivedBroadcastPackets : 416
ReceivedBytes            : 5150835981566
ReceivedDiscardedPackets : 1182
ReceivedMulticastBytes   : 21010513
ReceivedMulticastPackets : 3261
ReceivedPacketErrors     : 0
ReceivedUnicastBytes     : 5150813136771
ReceivedUnicastPackets   : 122000286
RscStatistics            :
SentBroadcastBytes       : 13885725
SentBroadcastPackets     : 303561
SentBytes                : 100858698741
SentMulticastBytes       : 14335203
```

```
SentMulticastPackets     : 85009
SentUnicastBytes         : 100830477813
SentUnicastPackets       : 1678156163
SupportedStatistics      : 4163583
PSComputerName           :
ifAlias                  : Ethernet
InterfaceAlias           : Ethernet
ifDesc                   : Realtek Gaming GbE Family Controller


PS C:\Users\Jon>
```

Using another PowerShell command, Get-NetAdapter | Format-List *, detailed information about the interface, such as speed, duplex, link state, and so much more, can be viewed. However, most of the time you're going to be diagnosing the problem from the network switch. This is done mainly because it's a fast way to see if there is a problem as well as what the problem might be. In the following example, by using the command show interface on a Cisco switch and specifying the interface name and number, we can view detailed information about the interface.

```
es-29#show interface gigabitEthernet 4/27
GigabitEthernet4/27 is up, line protocol is up (connected)
  Hardware is Gigabit Eth Port, address is 843d.c6bc.b922 (bia 843d.c6bc.b922)
  Description: FX-70 EMS Controller #1
  MTU 1500 bytes, BW 100000 Kbit/sec, DLY 100 usec,
     reliability 255/255, txload 1/255, rxload 1/255
  Encapsulation ARPA, loopback not set
  Keepalive set (10 sec)
  Full-duplex, 100Mb/s, link type is auto, media type is 10/100/1000-TX
  input flow-control is off, output flow-control is off
  Auto-MDIX on (operational: on)
  ARP type: ARPA, ARP Timeout 04:00:00
  Last input never, output never, output hang never
  Last clearing of "show interface" counters never
  Input queue: 0/2000/0/0 (size/max/drops/flushes); Total output drops: 0
  Queueing strategy: fifo
  Output queue: 0/40 (size/max)
  5 minute input rate 0 bits/sec, 0 packets/sec
  5 minute output rate 0 bits/sec, 0 packets/sec
     110016673 packets input, 33461502152 bytes, 0 no buffer
     Received 72917 broadcasts (99 multicasts)
     232 runts, 0 giants, 0 throttles
     112085 input errors, 111853 CRC, 0 frame, 0 overrun, 0 ignored
     0 input packets with dribble condition detected
```

```
        161829497 packets output, 20291962434 bytes, 0 underruns
        0 output errors, 0 collisions, 3 interface resets
        0 unknown protocol drops
        0 babbles, 0 late collision, 0 deferred
        0 lost carrier, 0 no carrier
        0 output buffer failures, 0 output buffers swapped out
es-29#
```

In the following sections, I will cover the most important parts of this output.

Link State (Up/Down)

Normally on a network interface, if you want to see the link state you'll just look at the lights. If the green connectivity light is lit up solid and the yellow activity light is blinking, then it's probably working. However, when you are working on the other side of a campus or on the other side of the world, you might not have the opportunity to view a connection status by just looking at it. In that case, the easiest way is to remote to the switch hosting the connection and view the link state.

When analyzing the output of the show interface command, note that the first line is the status of the connection. In the following example, the interface is up and the line protocol is up, so it is considered connected. The first status of GigabitEthernet4/27 is up is the Physical layer connectivity, which is the wiring of the Ethernet connection. The second status of line protocol up is the Data Link connectivity for the connection.

```
es-29#show interface gigabitEthernet 4/27
GigabitEthernet4/27 is up, line protocol is up (connected)
   Hardware is Gigabit Eth Port, address is 843d.c6bc.b922 (bia 843d.c6bc.b922)
   Description: FX-70 EMS Controller #1
   MTU 1500 bytes, BW 100000 Kbit/sec, DLY 100 usec,
      reliability 255/255, txload 1/255, rxload 1/255
   Encapsulation ARPA, loopback not set
[ Output Cut ]
```

It is rare to see the line protocol in a down state for Ethernet. Therefore, if the interface is in an up state, then the line protocol will be in an up state. It is common to see an interface in an administratively down state, as in the following example. This means that the interface has been put into a down state because of an error or an administrator.

```
es-29#show interface gigabitEthernet 1/8
GigabitEthernet1/8 is administratively down, line protocol is down (disabled)
   Hardware is Gigabit Eth Port, address is 84b8.02d6.d723 (bia 84b8.02d6.d23)
   Description: DISABLED - R024-1
   MTU 1500 bytes, BW 100000 Kbit/sec, DLY 100 usec,
      reliability 255/255, txload 1/255, rxload 1/255
   Encapsulation ARPA, loopback not set
[ Output Cut ]
```

Speed/Duplex

The speed and duplex of a connection can be viewed with the show interface command. In the following example, the interface is set to Full-duplex and the speed is set to 100Mb/s. The actual interface of the switchport has the capabilities of running at 10, 100, or 1,000 Mb/s.

```
es-29#show interface gigabitEthernet 4/27
GigabitEthernet4/27 is up, line protocol is up (connected)
  Hardware is Gigabit Eth Port, address is 843d.c6bc.b922 (bia 843d.c6bc.b922)
  Description: FX-70 EMS Controller #1
  MTU 1500 bytes, BW 100000 Kbit/sec, DLY 100 usec,
    reliability 255/255, txload 1/255, rxload 1/255
  Encapsulation ARPA, loopback not set
  Keepalive set (10 sec)
  Full-duplex, 100Mb/s, link type is auto, media type is 10/100/1000-TX
  input flow-control is off, output flow-control is off
  Auto-MDIX on (operational: on)
  ARP type: ARPA, ARP Timeout 04:00:00
[ Output Cut ]
```

The default for switchports on a switch is auto for speed and auto for duplex. However, it is best practice to statically set the speed and duplex on important connections, such as your Internet router. The command speed 100 and duplex full can configure the port statically for 100 Mb/s and full-duplex operations, as seen in the following running configuration.

```
es-29#show running-config interface gigabitEthernet 1/4
Building configuration...

Current configuration : 209 bytes
!
interface GigabitEthernet1/4
 description M-FL2-TMarketing Printer - R015-30
 switchport access vlan 9
 switchport mode access
 power inline never
 speed 100
 duplex full
 spanning-tree portfast
end

[ Output Cut ]
```

By setting the speed and duplex statically, you can stop the port from renegotiating automatically at less desirable settings. You should verify that the other side is set to auto for both speed and duplex or set statically to match the switchport. This is done to avoid having a speed or duplex mismatch.

Send/Receive Traffic

Examining the send and receive traffic can help determine the average traffic from a layer 2 (Data Link) perspective. The send and receive traffic can be examined in a few different spots within the output from the show interface command, as seen in the following example. The line that displays the txload and rxload is a point-in-time reading for the interface load. These values are proportions to the speed of the connection. As an example, a value of 25 for the txload means that 1/10 of the connection speed is being used to transmit data. The second spot that traffic can be examined is the 5 minute input rate and 5 minute output rate, which will give you an estimate of what the interface has received and sent in bits per second for the past 5 minutes.

```
es-29#show interface gigabitEthernet 4/27
GigabitEthernet4/27 is up, line protocol is up (connected)
  Hardware is Gigabit Eth Port, address is 843d.c6bc.b922 (bia 843d.c6bc.b922)
  Description: FX-70 EMS Controller #1
  MTU 1500 bytes, BW 100000 Kbit/sec, DLY 100 usec,
     reliability 255/255, txload 1/255, rxload 1/255
  Encapsulation ARPA, loopback not set
  Keepalive set (10 sec)
  Full-duplex, 100Mb/s, link type is auto, media type is 10/100/1000-TX
  input flow-control is off, output flow-control is off
  Auto-MDIX on (operational: on)
  ARP type: ARPA, ARP Timeout 04:00:00
  Last input never, output never, output hang never
  Last clearing of "show interface" counters never
  Input queue: 0/2000/0/0 (size/max/drops/flushes); Total output drops: 0
  Queueing strategy: fifo
  Output queue: 0/40 (size/max)
  5 minute input rate 0 bits/sec, 0 packets/sec
  5 minute output rate 0 bits/sec, 0 packets/sec
     110016673 packets input, 33461502152 bytes, 0 no buffer
     Received 72917 broadcasts (99 multicasts)
[ Output Cut ]
```

The send and receive traffic for a particular interface allows us to determine if there is a problem with the switchport or if the host is just busy with traffic. The load of the line can tell you a lot about the traffic patterns, and most NMS servers collect the load counter and graph it over time. The load of the interface is the best determining factor for upgrading a connection to a higher speed.

The reliability counter in the show interface output can determine an interface's reliability to transmit data without error. The counter is a proportional value, just like the `txload` and `rxload` counters. The value should always be 255 over 255, meaning the connection is 100 percent reliable. The reliability is calculated with the formula *reliability = number of packets / number of total frames*. The formula calculates that each packet will be sent by a frame. If the frame does not make it to the destination, then there is a problem with the line and that decreases the reliability.

Protocol Packet and Byte Counts

Protocol packets and byte counts help us to inspect an interface from a layer 3 (Network) perspective. These counters should be closely examined if it's determined there is a high load of incoming or outgoing traffic. The counters can help identify abnormal layer 3 traffic from a 10,000-mile perspective. A protocol analyzer can be used to see individual packets, but these counters allow for a quick assessment if that is a necessary next step.

In the following output from the show interface command, a few details can be attained quickly, such as the 5 minute input rate and 5 minute output rate for the number of packets per second. These counters will allow you to see the layer 3 load for input and output of packets for an interface.

```
es-29#show interface gigabitEthernet 4/27
GigabitEthernet4/27 is up, line protocol is up (connected)

[ Output Cut]
  Last input never, output never, output hang never
  Last clearing of "show interface" counters never
  Input queue: 0/2000/0/0 (size/max/drops/flushes); Total output drops: 0
  Queueing strategy: fifo
  Output queue: 0/40 (size/max)
  5 minute input rate 0 bits/sec, 0 packets/sec
  5 minute output rate 0 bits/sec, 0 packets/sec
     110016673 packets input, 33461502152 bytes, 0 no buffer
     Received 72917 broadcasts (99 multicasts)
     232 runts, 0 giants, 0 throttles
     112085 input errors, 111853 CRC, 0 frame, 0 overrun, 0 ignored
     0 input packets with dribble condition detected
     161829497 packets output, 20291962434 bytes, 0 underruns
     0 output errors, 0 collisions, 3 interface resets

[ Output Cut ]
```

The total number of received packets can be attained from the `packets input`, as well as the total number of bytes received. The counters also detail the number of `packets output` as well as the accompanying byte totals that follow after the packet output. When these totals are compared to the number of received broadcasts and multicasts packets, a conclusion can be made about traffic. Keep in mind this is a high-level view. In the preceding example, the interface seen has a total number of 110,016,672 packets input, 72,917 broadcasts, and 99 multicast packets. If broadcasts are compared in proportion to the number of input packets using the formula of *broadcast percentage = broadcasts × 100 / packets input*, it can be concluded that broadcast traffic is about 7 percent of the traffic. A percentage can be calculated for the multicast packets using the formula *multicast percentage = multicasts × 100 / packets input*.

These counters are accumulative, so if something has been changed and the counters need to be reevaluated, they can be cleared. By issuing the command `clear counters gigabitEthernet 4/27`, you can clear the counters back to zero for reevaluation for the gi4/27 interface.

Cyclic Redundancy Checks (CRCs)

The cyclic redundancy check (CRC) counter in the output of the `show interface` command displays layer 2 errors, as shown in the following example. If any CRC errors are present on the interface, it means that there is or was a problem on the interface. The CRC counter increments when the switchport receives a frame and it fails the check against the last 4 bytes of the frame, which is the frame check sequence (FCS).

```
es-29#show interface gigabitEthernet 4/27
GigabitEthernet4/27 is up, line protocol is up (connected)

[ Output Cut]
  5 minute input rate 0 bits/sec, 0 packets/sec
  5 minute output rate 0 bits/sec, 0 packets/sec
    110016673 packets input, 33461502152 bytes, 0 no buffer
    Received 72917 broadcasts (99 multicasts)
    232 runts, 0 giants, 0 throttles
    112085 input errors, 111853 CRC, 0 frame, 0 overrun, 0 ignored
    0 input packets with dribble condition detected
    161829497 packets output, 20291962434 bytes, 0 underruns
    0 output errors, 0 collisions, 3 interface resets

[ Output Cut ]
```

Interface Errors or Alerts

Now that you have the basics of reading statistics and identifying the status of a connection, let's shift our focus to interface errors or alerts. Nothing is perfect, and you will unfortunately end up with interface errors. It could be that a simple wire is loose or not crimped properly, there is electrical interference, or the interface is just configured wrong. All of the interface errors I will cover in the following sections are related to layer 2 (Data Link) or layer 1 (Physical) issues. The goal is to identify the various counters that will help us troubleshoot problems.

In the examples in the following sections, I will be using the output of the show interface command on a Cisco switch. Every vendor has its own way to see the interface counters, and as long as you understand the theory, the knowledge can be applied to other vendors' hardware.

CRC Errors

Cyclic redundancy check (CRC) errors happen when the last 4 bytes of the frame (FCS) fail to verify the incoming frame. As we see in the following example, this interface has both input errors and CRC errors. Input errors are any error encountered on the interface, whereas CRC errors are exclusively failed FCS checks. Both of these counters are accumulative and need to be manually cleared with the clear counters command, specifying the interface name and number, such as gigabitEthernet 4/27.

```
es-29#show interface gigabitEthernet 4/27
GigabitEthernet4/27 is up, line protocol is up (connected)

[ Output Cut]
     Received 72917 broadcasts (99 multicasts)
     232 runts, 0 giants, 0 throttles
     112085 input errors, 111853 CRC, 0 frame, 0 overrun, 0 ignored
     0 input packets with dribble condition detected
     161829497 packets output, 20291962434 bytes, 0 underruns
     0 output errors, 0 collisions, 3 interface resets

[ Output Cut ]
```

It important to understand that you can only view incoming CRC errors. Outgoing frames are the responsibility of the other side of the connection, to be checked against the FCS. Common causes of CRC errors usually involve wiring, but having the wrong duplex manually configured on both sides can also cause CRC errors.

Giants

Giant frames are just what their name suggests; they are large frames. When the interface receives an incoming frame larger than the configured maximum transmission unit (MTU) for an interface or VLAN, the giant frame counter will increment. The giants' counters can be found in the output of the show interface command, as shown in the following example. The default MTU for Ethernet is 1500 bytes. It is very common to see this counter increment if the connected host is sending jumbo frames with an MTU of 9000 bytes.

```
es-29#show interface gigabitEthernet 4/27
GigabitEthernet4/27 is up, line protocol is up (connected)

[ Output Cut]
    Received 72917 broadcasts (99 multicasts)
    232 runts, 0 giants, 0 throttles
    112085 input errors, 111853 CRC, 0 frame, 0 overrun, 0 ignored
    0 input packets with dribble condition detected
    161829497 packets output, 20291962434 bytes, 0 underruns
    0 output errors, 0 collisions, 3 interface resets

[ Output Cut ]
```

Runts

If giant frames are large frames, then logically, runts are small frames. When an interface receives an incoming frame smaller than 64 bytes, the frame is considered a runt. This commonly happens when there are collisions, but it can also happen if you have a faulty connection. In the following example, the interface has received a number of runt frames, but no collisions were detected. However, the interface has received a number of CRC errors, so this is probably a bad physical connection.

```
es-29#show interface gigabitEthernet 4/27
GigabitEthernet4/27 is up, line protocol is up (connected)

[ Output Cut]
    Received 72917 broadcasts (99 multicasts)
    232 runts, 0 giants, 0 throttles
    112085 input errors, 111853 CRC, 0 frame, 0 overrun, 0 ignored
    0 input packets with dribble condition detected
    161829497 packets output, 20291962434 bytes, 0 underruns
    0 output errors, 0 collisions, 3 interface resets

[ Output Cut ]
```

Encapsulation Errors

When we encounter encapsulation errors and interfaces, it means that the Data Link encapsulation protocol is misconfigured on the interface or the host. This commonly happens because an interface can be configured as an access link or a trunk. To further complicate things, a trunk can be configured with 802.1Q or the Cisco proprietary protocol Inter-Switch Link (ISL). I am of course assuming we are just configuring Ethernet. If we are configuring a wide area network (WAN), there are several protocols, such as Point-to-Point Protocol (PPP), High-Level Data Link Control (HDLC), and Frame Relay, just to mentions a few. So, there is a huge margin for error when configuring encapsulation.

There are many different scenarios in which you can have an encapsulation error, but the most common is a misconfiguration of Ethernet encapsulation. It normally happens when the switch interface is statically configured as a trunk (802.1Q) and you connect a host. There is no warning message that you will see; the host just won't be able to communicate properly on the network. This happens because the host is not encapsulating traffic with an 802.1Q encapsulation. The interface can quickly be checked by either reviewing the running configuration or using the show interfaces trunk command, as shown in the following example.

```
es-42#show interfaces trunk
Port        Mode        Encapsulation    Status      Native vlan
Gig0/1      on          802.1q           trunking    1
Gig0/2      on          802.1q           trunking    1

[ Output Cut ]
```

If you are connecting a switch to another switch, where one switch is configured as a trunk switchport and the other is configured as an access switchport, you will get the following alert at the console on the switch configured as an access switchport. No data will pass because the interface will be placed into a blocking mode by the Spanning Tree Protocol (STP).

```
es-29#
%LINK-5-CHANGED: Interface GigabitEthernet0/1, changed state to up

%LINEPROTO-5-UPDOWN: Line protocol on Interface GigabitEthernet0/1,
changed state to up
%SPANTREE-2-RECV_PVID_ERR: Received 802.1Q BPDU on non trunk
GigabitEthernet0/1 VLAN1.

%SPANTREE-2-BLOCK_PVID_LOCAL: Blocking GigabitEthernet0/1 on VLAN0001.
Inconsistent port type.
es-29#
```

By checking the running configuration on both switches, you can avoid these problems. By default, Cisco switches are set to auto-negotiate trunks. So this problem only happens when the mode of the switchports is statically configured.

Environmental Factors and Sensors

The environment in which network equipment is maintained is directly related to its potential for failure. Fortunately, the environment in which our network equipment is maintained can be monitored with environmental sensors. The sensors allow for monitoring temperature, humidity, electricity, and flooding. The sensors can be purchased as stand-alone devices that audibly alert you, but it is now common to find these sensors on the network. Networked environmental sensors work with SNMP and a centralized NMS. When these devices are purchased, they come with the MIBs that are loaded into the NMS. The thresholds can be modified and alerts can be configured so that an administrator can be alerted if something happens outside of the normal parameters. In the following sections I will cover how environmental conditions affect network equipment and how to effectively protect the equipment.

Temperature

Temperature is the most common factor that leads to component failure. Most components inside of our network devices, such as the CPUs and ASICs, will fail when the temperature of the component is over 125 degrees Celsius (257 degrees Fahrenheit). That temperature seems really hot, but in reality, most devices operate at a pretty hot temperature already, especially when under a load. It's not uncommon for a chip to run at a constant 90 or 100 degrees Celsius. The manufacturer obviously anticipated this heat, and components will have either a heat sink that is cooled by the flow of air through the network device or a heat sink that is cooled by a fan. In either case, the ambient air is used to cool the component.

It is best practice to maintain a constant temperature between 68 to 71 degrees Fahrenheit (20 to 22 degrees Celsius) in a server room or where network devices are installed. If the ambient air gets hotter, we could be on our way to component failure. This is one of the reasons that temperature monitoring is so important. If an air-conditioning (AC) unit fails, the ambient air could heat up in a matter of 20 to 30 minutes.

Although dust is not normally monitored, excessive dust leads to components running warmer over time. When dust builds up on the circuit boards inside of the network equipment, the dust creates an insulating barrier that prevents proper cooling. In extreme cases, dust can clog up the heatsinks and prevent the components from getting sufficient air flow. Most commercial AC units will contain a dust filter. The filters will help, but a preventative maintenance schedule should be followed to blow network equipment out with a low-pressure air source and change AC filters.

Humidity

Humidity is an important factor for network equipment as well. Problems can arise if the air is too dry or too wet. Little or no humidity and high humidity are usually linked to the weather and the season. Generally, in the wintertime humidity can drop below 20 percent and in the summertime humidity can rise to over 80 percent.

If the humidity is below 20 percent, the potential for electrostatic discharge (ESD) becomes a risk. Electrostatic discharge is a silent killer that can make components fail without warning. Unfortunately, a byproduct of most air-conditioning is lower and dryer humidity levels. This is why the condenser side of the air-conditioner drips water; it evaporates the water out of the air. Special heating, ventilation, and air-conditioning (HVAC) units can replace the water evaporated out of the air because they remove the humidity during the cooling process.

If the humidity is over 80 percent, the potential for short circuits becomes a risk. Water by itself will not conduct electricity. The water needs particles to carry the charge inside the water. However, when water condenses out of the air on a dusty component, it can cause these short circuits because the dust acts as the conductor. To mitigate this risk, a specific amount of water should be removed out of the air with the HVAC unit.

The optimal humidity for a server room is between 40 to 60 percent humidity. Special HVAC units can monitor and adjust the humidity level. As I stated before, air-conditioning dries the air as it is cooling the air. However, when the HVAC reaches the set point, the evaporative cooling methods stop, and humidity can spike back up. In some HVAC units, the air-conditioner will continue to run to bring the humidity level down, and an auxiliary heater will warm the air back up to maintain the set point temperature. These HVAC units humidify the air by heating a body of water and allowing the water to reenter the air. The process is similar to boiling water on a stove, just using much lower temperatures.

Electrical

The condition of the electrical power is another important factor in maintaining uptime for the network equipment. Obviously, if we lose power, the equipment stops working. However, there are many other electrical problems we can encounter that will affect our network equipment and interrupt operations.

Sags An electrical sag is created when the line voltage dips below the nominal operating voltage. Normally the voltage should stay consistent at 90 percent of the voltage specification. An electrical sag is considered an event if the voltage drops within a 1/2 second to 3 seconds of a power cycle.

Spike Power spikes are created when the line voltage increases over the nominal operating voltage. A voltage spike can be tens of thousands of volts, but the event only lasts 1 to 2 nanoseconds.

Surges Power surges are also created when the line voltage spikes over the nominal operating voltage. However, the difference between a spike and a surge is that a surge can last over 3 nanoseconds.

All of these electrical conditions, including power failure, can be avoided with the use of an uninterruptible power supply (UPS). UPS systems can avoid power spikes and surges by absorbing the excess voltage. They can avoid power sags and failures by supplying the appropriate voltage during trouble periods. They can also avoid short-term power outages by supplying power from the batteries they contain.

Most UPS systems have the option of network connectivity so that these events can also be monitored by your NMS and can provide administrator notification. I will cover the various UPS systems when I discuss facilities and infrastructure support later in this chapter.

 A power sag is a drop in line voltage, but this term should not be confused with brownouts. A brownout is a condition of the power grid where the line voltage drops over a much longer period of time, sometimes hours or even days. Brownouts usually happen because of upstream demand, such as a really hot day when everyone is using their air-conditioning units.

Flooding

Water and electrical components don't mix, and from both an equipment safety and personal safety aspect, flooding is another risk. You may think that you only have to worry about flooding if your server room is located in the basement. However, that is very far from the truth because flooding can occur anywhere there is the potential for water. You cannot totally prevent flooding, but you can mitigate the risk. The most obvious prevention is to avoid placing networking equipment in basements or low levels of a building that could flood. However, the location of water pipes, drainage pipes, and HVAC cooling lines should also be considered. Some HVAC systems use water and ethylene glycol (antifreeze) as coolant; these systems can contain hundreds of gallons of this mix. If a pipe were to spring a leak, your equipment will get damaged by this mix.

Most flooding happens slowly, so by deploying monitoring in strategic locations, we can be alerted before it gets too bad. Most of these monitors can also be connected to a network and pointed to the NMS.

Not all flooding happens by accident. Flooding can occur in response to another emergency, such as fire. Many fire suppression systems are designed to dump water in the event of an emergency. This is usually a concern if the network equipment is installed in an existing location. However, new building design will generally account for a different fire suppression technology to be used in areas where your network equipment is located. Substitutes such as chemical or carbon dioxide fire extinguishers are used in place of water.

Performance Baselines

It's important to document the network and its configuration so that you can easily troubleshoot problems when they arise. These documents also serve as a point of diagnostics for others in your group, which relieves the burden of day-to-day operations. Unfortunately, not every problem is as evident or black-and-white as a network outage. Performance problems are the toughest and often take a great deal of time to resolve. I will discuss troubleshooting further in Chapter 5, "Domain 5.0: Network Troubleshooting," but for now we will focus on how documentation can help solve problems quicker. When you experience a performance problem, the first question to come to mind is "How was it performing before?" This is where a performance baseline comes in handy.

The performance baseline should be captured over a period of time that involves normal activity. An example of normal activity is Monday through Sunday during hours of business and normal times of inactivity. The best scenario is to constantly monitor and record the performance of selected network services. There are several tools you can use to monitor performance and compile baselines of the performance of the network. Microsoft includes a tool called Performance Monitor that is built into the operating system. Other performance monitoring tools are Multi Router Traffic Grapher (MRTG) and Paessler AG's PRTG, which use Simple Network Management Protocol (SNMP). There are also many different applications that you can purchase that can monitor performance—too many to mention.

The performance baseline serves two purposes. First, it describes what normal activity looks like and answers the question "How was it performing before?" The second purpose it serves is to validate that you have solved the performance problem because the baseline is a basis of comparison.

Sometimes problems are compounded, such as a web server performing poorly and at the same time the SQL database for the web server is performing poorly. These problems can be next to impossible to solve because if you try to implement a solution to the web server, the SQL database is still performing poorly. However, if you had a performance baseline for both the web server and the SQL database, you could visually see if the solution implemented fixed a portion of the system.

NetFlow Data

NetFlow is a Cisco proprietary protocol that allows for the collection of traffic details as the traffic flows through a router. NetFlow version 1 was originally created back in 1996, and the current version is version 9. It has become so popular that an open standard was created called IPFIX, and it is based on version 9 of NetFlow. NetFlow can be used to gain insight into the traffic patterns on our router. It can be used to identify high bandwidth utilization culprits and provide security monitoring of IP packets. It is an extremely useful protocol that is used to plan, analyze, account for traffic, and secure traffic on the network.

The NetFlow protocol is responsible for creating and updating the NetFlow cache inside of the router as packets traverse, as show in Figure 3.10. When a packet enters an interface and is deemed routable, an entry will either be created in the flow cache or updated to reflect the entry's new byte count totals. Several key pieces of information are written down in the cache, such as source and destination IP, source and destination port, source interface, protocol, and of course the number of bytes. The flow cache can contain hundreds of thousands of entries or even millions, so memory on the routers is a key consideration when deploying NetFlow.

FIGURE 3.10   Anatomy of NetFlow

Flow Cache

Source IP	Destination IP	Source port	Destination port	Source interface	Protocol	Bytes
23.24.34.56	24.7.124.124	2345	80	0	TCP	1423
34.45.64.67	24.7.124.124	4567	80	0	TCP	956
24.7.124.124	23.24.34.56	80	2345	1	TCP	1534
24.7.124.124	34.45.65.67	80	4567	1	TCP	1043

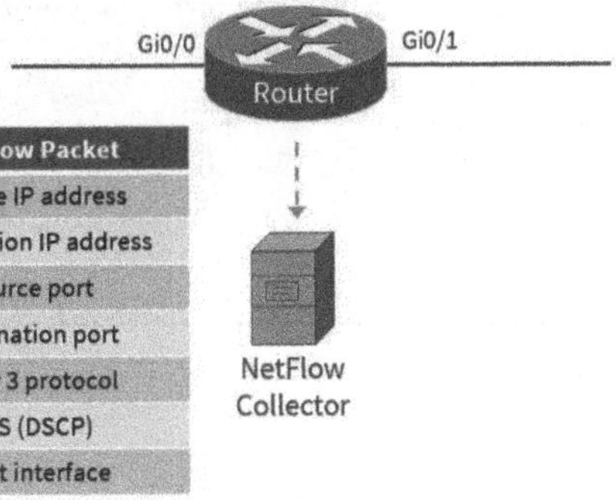

As flows expire, they will be exported to a centralized server called the NetFlow collector. The NetFlow collector is responsible for collating the information into a timeline so traffic pattern can be reported upon. The NetFlow collector can provide visual representation for the data, so it can be reviewed from a high level with the option to drill down to a lower level of details. Some of the visualizations might be top talkers in the network, a network topology from traffic patterns, or threats detected, and these are just a few.

Uptime/Downtime

A function of an NMS is to calculate uptime and downtime for the network; uptime/downtime is also called the availability. The network as a whole is made up of many different services on the various servers. The uptime calculated by the NMS is the total time all network services are up and responding to requests. The downtime is how long the network services were down and not responding to requests. The NMS will check each service and keep a running tally of down services, as shown in Figure 3.11. It will then calculate the outages and display the total uptime of the network.

FIGURE 3.11   Network management station availability

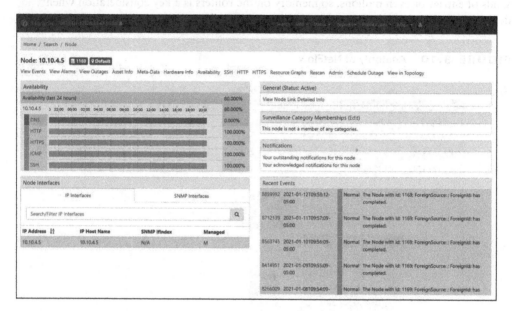

Exam Essentials

Understand the various metrics used to monitor devices.   Hosts and network devices are monitored for temperature, CPU usage, and memory usage. Temperature is monitored so the network device does not overheat and it is related to the load on internal components. CPU and memory utilization is monitored so that nominal performance can be maintained.

Understand the various metrics used to monitor the network.   The network metrics monitored are bandwidth, latency, and jitter. Bandwidth utilization is the overall bandwidth consumed on the link. Latency is a delay as packets are routed throughout a network or the Internet, and it is measured in milliseconds. Jitter is the difference between variation of latency and is measured in milliseconds as well.

Know the various components of SNMP.   SNMP is a protocol used to collect metrics from network devices. The network management station (NMS) is loaded with the management information base (MIB) that details all of the various counters on a network device. The NMS uses SNMP get messages to poll the object ID (OID) counters. SNMP devices can also use trap messages to send notifications to an NMS.

Know the various logs found on network devices. As a best practice, network devices and hosts should be configured to send all logs to a centralized server so they are searchable and you can provide correlation between devices. Traffic logs provide an overview of traffic, details of various sessions, and security monitoring. Audit logs provide a record of authentication of users and authorization of resources. Syslog is a client-server protocol that operates on UDP port 514 and transmits log entries.

Understand how logging levels are used and the severity levels used with Syslog. Severity levels are used to either view more detail in logs or less detail in logs, depending on where you are at in the diagnostic process. Severity levels are used with Syslog and provide a way to configure eight different levels of logging from 0 to 7. The severity levels are as follows: emergency (0), alert (1), critical (2), error (3), warning (4), notice (5), informational (6), and debug (7).

Know the various statistics and status of interfaces. You should be familiar with the output of the show interface command. A link status is usually the layer 1 status and layer 2 status, reported as either up/up or down/down, and in some cases layer 2 can be down. Speed and duplex can be statically set to avoid renegotiation. Send and receive traffic, as well as packets and byte counts, are detailed in the output, along with cyclic redundancy checks (CRCs).

Understand the various interface errors and alerts. A CRC error represents a frame that fails the frame check sequence when received by a switchport. A giant is a frame that exceeds the maximum transmission unit set on the switchport. A runt is a frame that is received and is under 64 bytes. Most encapsulation errors are due to a mismatch of configuration on the switchports.

Know how the various environmental factor affect network devices. Components will fail when temperatures are over 125 degrees Celsius (257 degrees Fahrenheit). Dust can cause an insulating effect on components inside of network devices and prevent cooling. Dust can also clog heatsinks and prevent cooling. Humidity can cause a short in the network equipment. Electrical problems can be complete outages, sags in voltage, spikes in voltage, or surges in voltage. Flooding can be mitigated with planning of the network device placement in a building.

Understand the how NetFlow is used and the data it provides. NetFlow is a Cisco proprietary protocol used to collect traffic statistics. It performs the collection of traffic details by building and maintains a flow cache. When cache expires, it is exported to a Flow Collector, where it can be reported on.

3.2 Explain the purpose of organizational documents and policies.

It's important to document the network and its configuration so that you can easily troubleshoot problems when they arise. Examples of these configurations are the installation procedure for software, network wiring diagrams, and so forth. However, it is not just the elements of a network that require documentation. Soft elements such as policies and procedure should also be documented and enforced. When policies and procedures are documented, the organization has an enforceable structure. Many of the policies, procedures, and documents I will discuss in this chapter are common to any organization.

Plans and Procedures

When organizations create policies, they will outline specific processes to adhere to the policies. Throughout this discussion you may see the words *policy* and *plan*. Policies are also considered plans for the organization; once a plan is ratified, it becomes a policy. Put another way, a policy is a matured and enforced plan of action. Each process derived from the plan or policy will have a list of procedures that are called *standard operating procedures (SOPs)*, as shown in Figure 3.12. All of these components are part of the documentation process for a *quality management system (QMS)*. QMSs are created to meet certain International Organization for Standardization (ISO) requirements. A common ISO certification is ISO 9001. When a company is ISO certified, it means that they adhere to strict quality standards for consistent outcomes and have a detailed operation plan. There are many information technology ISO standards that your organization can be certified with. You have probably seen these certifications in a sales manual at some point.

FIGURE 3.12   Policies, processes, and procedures

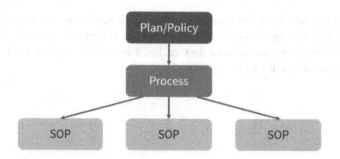

A process in a QMS is just that—a process. A process is defined as taking an input and creating an output. Here's an example: A specific server requires to be decommissioned, which is the input to the process of decommissioning a server and the output of the process is that the server is wiped clean of corporate information. The process in this example is the decommissioning of a server. (I am oversimplifying the process in this example.) Most processes have an input specification and an output specification.

The SOP in this example outlines how to perform the process of decommissioning of the server. The SOP should clearly explain who and what is responsible and the standard they must achieve for the process. In the example of a decommissioned hard drive, the SOP would define the following:

- Who is responsible for removal of the server from the rack
- Who is responsible for wiping the drives in the server
- What standard should be used to wipe the drives
- Who is responsible for removing DNS entries
- Who is responsible for removing firewall rules
- Who is responsible for clearing the BIOS
- In which order the tasks are performed

Several tasks are created from the SOP document. Each task is defined as part of your procedure to achieve the decommissioning of the server. The work instructions serve two primary purposes. The first is to detail how each task should be performed. The exact steps are detailed in the work instructions and for the previous example may include the following:

- How to remove the server from the rack
- How to wipe the drives in the server
- How the drive should be wiped
- How to remove the DNS entries
- How to remove the firewall rules
- How to clear the BIOS

The second purpose of the work instructions is to provide a training process for new employees. The work instructions are a more detailed portion of the procedure, so it becomes a training item for new employees on how to perform their job.

Change Management Documentation

Change management is a process often found in large corporations, publicly held corporations, and industries such as financial services that have regulatory requirements. The purpose of change management is to standardize the methods and procedures used to handle changes in the company. These changes can be *soft* changes of personnel or processes or *hard* changes of network services.

A change advisory board often meets once a week to discuss changes detailed in the change management documentation. The change advisory board can then evaluate the changes to reduce their impact on day-to-day operations.

The key to the change management documentation is knowing your audience. The *change advisory board* is often composed of people from the entire organization, not just from information technology. Some change advisory boards are strictly IT stakeholders, so you must understand who will review the proposed changes.

The change control form details several pieces of key information:

Item to Be Changed   The item that is being requested for a change. Examples of items are software, hardware, firmware, configuration, or documentation, just to name a few.

Reason   The reason the item is being submitted for a change. Examples are legal, marketing, performance, software bug, or process problem.

Priority   The urgency, or priority, of the change will be documented in this section of the form, although this should also be conveyed in the reason for the change. The priority is often a separate field on the change control form. Examples are emergency, urgent, routine, or a specific date.

Change Description/Plan   The description or plan for the change is documented in this section. For changes in configuration, you would detail the changes to the configuration and why each part of the configuration is being changed. Firmware changes would list the version being upgraded from and the version being upgraded to.

Change Rollback Plan   The rollback plan describes the steps to roll back from a failed primary plan. If it was determined that the primary plan could not be completed, you would implement either an alternate plan or a rollback plan depending on the changes proposed.

Technical Evaluation   In this section of the form, you will document why the primary plan will succeed. The changes should be tested in a lab environment closest to the production environment and documented in this section. When you're creating the technical evaluation, specific objective goals should be outlined along with the metrics with which they can be measured.

Duration of Changes   Here, you will document the estimated duration of the change process. Any service outages will be documented in this section.

Each organization is different, and each change management document will be slightly different. However, the sections described here are the most common found on these documents. The change management document must be approved by the majority of change advisory board members or by specific board members.

Incident Response Plan

The incident response plan defines how a computer incident is handled, such as a security-related incident or outage. The incident response plan is also called the incident response policy because it is enforceable for an organization. The policy should focus on the prioritization, communication, and lessons learned so that the *computer incident response team (CIRT)* is prepared for future incidents.

The policy should include the priority of the incident based on the impact to the organization. For example, if a server was down, the impact on the organization would be moderate. In comparison, if a workstation was down, there would be very little impact on the organization, and the severity would reflect the impact. This prioritization helps the CIRT handle the most severe incidents in a timely manner.

Having a good response plan in place that prioritizes incidents is important. Communications should also be defined in the policy so that the CIRT can effectively relay information to technicians and upper management. During a time of crisis, communication is important to a fast recovery of failed or compromised systems.

The last piece of an incident response policy is the follow-up to the incident with documentation. The CIRT should focus on the lessons learned during the incident. Reflecting back on lessons learned helps the CIRT make better decisions in the future and avoid bad ones from past incidents.

 The National Institute of Standards and Technology (NIST) has published a guide named "Computer Security Incident Handling Guide - SP 800-61 Rev. 2." It is necessary reading for anyone who is creating a CIRT or handling an organization's incident policy. The document can be viewed at https:// csrc.nist.gov/publications/detail/sp/800-61/rev-2/final.

Incident Documentation

An *incident* is any event that is unusual or outside of the normal processes. You may encounter many different types of incidents as a technician: network security incidents, network outage incidents, and even customer service incidents. Regardless of which type of incident transpires, an incident document should be completed so that there is a record of the event. A record of the incident allows for further review after the incident has subsided so that it is not repeated.

The incident document should be completed as soon as possible so that key details are not forgotten. This document is often used as an executive brief for key *stakeholders* in the company, such as C-level people—for example, the *chief information officer (CIO)*. The incident document can also be public-facing and used to inform customers of the incident. When used in this fashion, the incident document allows the organization to communicate with transparency for a major incident they may or may have not experienced. Following are some common elements of a network incident document:

Date and Time   The date and time of the incident is probably the most important because several incidents could happen on the same day. The date and time allows you to distinguish between various incidents. The date and time should be referenced using the *Universal Time Code (UTC)* so that someone anywhere in the world does not need to calculate the time offset.

Summary   The *incident summary* is another important piece of information that should be documented. It will often be the first thing that is looked at because it describes the summary of what happened during the incident.

Root Cause The *root cause* is the ultimate reason the incident occurred. Every incident needs to have a root cause defined; otherwise, the incident could happen over and over again. The network team's first responsibility is to identify the root cause.

Actions Taken The actions taken are the actions that transpired during the incident to rectify the situation. Most of the time, they are temporary actions so that business can resume.

Remediation The *remediation* is the ultimate fix that will repair the root cause of the incident. This could be as simple as installing a patch, or it could be as complex as redesigning a network component.

Services Impacted The services impacted section details all the network systems and business units that were impacted during the incident. This section defines the severity of the incident.

Recommendations The recommendations section details the next steps to take to remediate the issue. It also details how to avoid similar incidents in the future.

Although these are the most common elements to an incident document, the incident document is not limited to these elements. Each organization will have different needs for the process of reviewing network incidents. A template should be created so that there is consistency in the reporting of incidents.

Business Continuity Plan/ Disaster Recovery Plan

All companies rely on network services in some way for their day-to-day operations. These companies use network services for the storage of internal financial data, communications, client records, and so forth. Many companies such as online retailers and service providers can lose money by the second when there is an outage.

It is important for an organization to have both a business continuity plan and a disaster recovery plan. The two go hand in hand with each other. The business continuity plan will outline how an organization will continue to function during a disastrous event. The business continuity plan cannot account for every disaster, but each critical sub-organization in the organization should have a contingency plan if their function is affected by disaster. As an example, if a company derived their business from online sales and the risk is the servers failing, the company should have an alternate method of completing sales detailed in the business continuity plan.

The disaster recovery plan is how the company transitions from a disaster back to normal operations. If the disaster was the sales database getting completely wiped out, the business continuity plan would detail how to continue business during the outage. The disaster recovery plan would detail how to restore systems so that business functions normally.

Disasters can be critical files deleted by accident, files destroyed or lost because of a virus or ransomware, or unexpected events like fire and flooding.

The network administrator is responsible for the recovery of IT systems during a disaster. Therefore, a disaster recovery plan should be prepared for high risk disasters.

If your server room is on the bottom floor of a building, then the server room flooding is a high risk. The business continuity plan for each of the departments would detail how they would function while the servers were down. However, your responsibility is to get them back up and running and this is the purpose of a disaster recovery plan. Although there are many different types of disasters, the disaster recovery plan should outline the following:

Responsibilities of Personnel   A detailed list of who is responsible for each system involved in the disaster recovery effort. This should also include scheduling, since a disaster can span longer than an eight-hour work shift and you will probably need a second team for the next shift or two.

Processes and Procedures   The processes used to recover from the disaster should be detailed in the document as well as the procedures to perform the tasks to recover the organization.

Systems Involved in Recovery   Documentation should outline each of the systems that are involved in the recovery effort. This list should coincide with the list of responsible personnel for each system.

Recover Point Objective (RPO)   The RPO is the point in time to which you can recover the organization. It is commonly used to describe the restoration of files from a backup restore. If the recovery effort requires the restoration of data from the prior backup, then the expectation for RPO should be the point in time when the backup initially ran. Having the RPO documented allows for everyone involved to have an adequate expectation.

Recovery Time Objective (RTO)   The RTO is the time it will take to recover from the disaster. This is really subjective because it depends on the scope of the recovery effort. The term is also commonly used with backup and restoration of files. However, if it is a simple recovery of files, an approximate time can be documented. If the recovery is getting a new server because the old one is under water, then the time it takes to purchase, install, and configure a new server is the RTO. The documentation of the RTO allows everyone involved to have an expectation of when the organization can recover from a disaster.

I have been in many network outages where the information about the network was on the network and only on the network. This creates a chicken-and-egg scenario that you don't want to find yourself in during a panic situation. It is a best practice to create hard copies of key information about your network and compile it into a binder. Articles to be included are network diagrams, IP addresses of vital equipment, support numbers, and account information. Back in the mainframe days, we called this collection of documents "crash books." If and when the system crashed, it was the first book you would grab.

Real World Scenario

The 2020 COVID-19 pandemic was unexpected and unprecedented in many organizations. Many organizations shut down for several months, and in some cases, organizations continued to operate. It was all dependent on their product or service. Regardless of the product or service, some organizations supplied back-office functions needed to continue, such as accounts payable, payroll, bookkeeping, just to name a few.

Many organizations quickly reacted to the disaster of the pandemic and formed a business continuity plan. A lot of these plans directly involved technology and the IT departments. The disaster recovery effort IT faced was bringing these back-office functions online virtually with a work-from-home strategy. The COVID-19 pandemic was unforeseen, but was your organization ready to launch a work-from-home strategy? Was there a plan in place for an event such as the pandemic?

System Life Cycle

The life cycle for IT systems is cyclical and differs slightly depending on the assets. The typical life cycle for IT systems consists of purchasing, deploying, managing, and retiring. When an asset is purchased, it becomes an asset to the organization and is depreciated over its useful life in the organization. Once the asset is purchased, it is deployed. The deployment phase could involve plugging the equipment into the network and turning it on. Or the deployment phase could involve imaging, configuring, or installing software on the IT system. The management of the system is usually performed directly by the IT department once the system is deployed. However, the management of the system can also involve the end users—for example, in the case of an accounting software package. Eventually all IT systems near the end of their useful life and are retired.

The retirement of IT systems can be done several different ways depending on the type of equipment. End-user computing equipment might be sold for scrap costs, or they could be appropriated elsewhere in the organization. In the case of server and SAN equipment, these systems are usually moved to less critical workloads, such as development or development testing. An organization will commonly have generations of equipment, retiring the prior generation of equipment to another part of the organization. It is also important to note that the retirement process dovetails with the planning and repurchasing process that begins the life cycle again.

The last phase of the equipment life cycle is asset disposal. There are two responsibilities of the IT department and the organization pertaining to asset disposal. The first responsibility is to prevent data loss when equipment is disposed of. A procedure should be in place to wipe organization data from systems that are disposed of. The second responsibility is an ethical and legal responsibility to properly dispose of equipment. There are several environmental issues that can arise from trashing electronic equipment. Often electronics end up in landfills, and depending on the equipment and the local laws, the organization can be liable for fines. When selling equipment for scrap value, the buyer should be able to provide documentation to shield the company from legal ramifications if equipment is dumped.

Hardening and Security Policies

When we think of hardening of our network, we immediately think of the default configuration many products come with out of the box. These initial configurations/installs are often lax in security or contain exploits. The lax security is easily remedied by changing the default password and installing the latest updates. I will cover these basic hardening techniques in Chapter 4, "Domain 4.0: Network Security."

Changing passwords, installing updates, and limiting access are all examples of hard control an administrator can employ. The following sections will focus on the soft controls we can use with the use of written policy to force users to be secure. Remember that policies drive processes, which in turn guide procedures. It is the enforcement of these policies that keeps our networks secure. Administrators are burdened with the knowledge of keeping the network safe and secure, but end users do not have this same mindset. Therefore, these policies force the end user to apply a level of discretion and security to their daily activities in the workplace.

Password Policy

As network administrators, we are generally familiar with the hard controls of a password policy. We can require users to change passwords every 90 days and require password complexity, and we can even ensure that prior passwords are not reused. However, as we make the password policy more difficult for the users, the users often resort to lax security practices, such as writing down passwords.

The soft controls of a password policy should be drafted between the HR department and the IT department. It should detail the conduct expected of employees regarding their passwords. The document should outline various expectations such as the following:

- Passwords should never be shared between employees.
- Passwords should never be disclosed to others, including IT employees.
- Passwords should never be written down.
- Passwords should not be guessable, such as using the date it was changed (for example, *password*-04017).

When developing a password policy for your organization, the sensitivity of the information the users handle should be taken into consideration. The frequency of password changes, password length, and password complexity should be dictated by the sensitivity of information. A user who handles accounts payables should adhere to a stricter password policy than a laborer.

Acceptable Use Policy (AUP)

There can be many different resources employees use that the organization supplies to conduct its business. An *acceptable use policy (AUP)* helps protect the organization from employee abuse of these resources. Email is an example of one such resource. It is generally not acceptable for an employee to use an organization's email for religious, political, or personal causes; illegal activities; or commercial use outside of the organization's interest.

The AUP should be developed by the organization's legal counsel, HR department, and IT department. The systems that should be included in the AUP are telephone, Internet, email, and subscription services. The AUP might not be exclusive to electronic resources; the organization might also include postage and other nonelectronic resources that could be abused.

Bring Your Own Device (BYOD)

The traditional workforce is slowly becoming a mobile workforce, with employees working from home, on the go, and in the office. Mobile devices such as laptops, tablets, and smartphones are used by employees to connect to the organization's cloud resources. *Bring your own device (BYOD)* has been embraced as a strategy by organizations to alleviate the capital expense of equipment by allowing employees to use devices they already own.

Because employees are supplying their own devices, a formal document called the BYOD policy should be drafted. The BYOD policy defines a set of minimum requirements for the devices, such as size and type, operating system, connectivity, antivirus solutions, patches, and many other requirements the organization will deem necessary.

Many organizations use *mobile device management (MDM)* software that dictates the requirements for the BYOD policy. MDM software helps organizations protect their data on devices that are personally owned by the employees. When employees are terminated or a device is lost, the MDM software allows a secure remote wipe of the company's data on the device. The MDM software can also set policies requiring passwords on the device. All of these requirements should be defined in the organization's BYOD policy.

Remote Access Policies

Remote access policies, just like many other policies for organizations, have a soft control and hard control. The soft control for an organization's remote access policy starts with defining who has access and why they have access as it pertains to their job function. The remote access policy can serve as an AUP for accessing the company's data remotely.

Hard controls can be configured in Microsoft Windows Server for remote VPN access. VPN access is controlled via a *Network Policy Server (NPS)*. The NPS can be configured to require security group membership, time of day criteria, and connection type, just to name a few. It is important to note that a freshly installed NPS will not allow connection by default until configured to do so. On Linux and Unix systems, *Remote Authentication Dial-In User Service (RADIUS)* can control remote access. It is also important to note that the Microsoft NPS functions as a RADIUS server.

As network administrators, we can implement hard controls to make sure users adhere to a specific number of characters in their password or deny users access to certain areas of the network. We must help administer soft controls (policies) as well. These soft controls should be made in conjunction with your company's legal counsel and human resources (HR) department. Policies are rules and procedures that employees are expected to follow. Best practices are a suggested set of rules that should be followed every time to ensure a positive outcome, such as destruction of a hard drive before sending it to the trash.

Onboarding/Off-Boarding procedures

As employees are hired in your organization, a certain amount of initial interaction with IT is required. This interaction is called the onboarding procedure and is often coordinated with the HR department in your organization. During the onboarding procedure, the IT representative will help the user log in for the first time and change their password. The password policy is often the first policy discussed with the user. Other policies such as bring your own device (BYOD), acceptable use policy (AUP), and information assurance should also be discussed during the onboarding procedure. Email, file storage, and policies should also be covered with the user during the onboarding process. Each organization will have a different set of criteria that make up the onboarding procedures.

Eventually, employees will leave your organization. The off-boarding procedure ensures that information access is terminated when the employment of the user is terminated. The off-boarding procedure will be initiated by the HR department and should be immediately performed by the IT department. This process can be automated via the employee management system used by the organization. The procedure can also be manually performed if the employee management system is not automated. However, the procedure must be performed promptly since access to the company's information systems is the responsibility of the IT department. During the off-boarding procedure, email access or BYOD is removed via the mobile device management (MDM) software, the user account is disabled, and IT should make sure the user is not connected to the IT systems remotely. The off-boarding procedure may also specify that a supervisor assume ownership of the terminated employee's voicemail, email, and files.

Security Policy

The security policy for an organization is the document that brings everything together under one enforceable policy. It is typically part of the employee handbook or it is referenced in the handbook to an independent document. The security policy is tailored for the particular organization it is written for. For example, the security policy for a law firm will be very different than one for a retail chain. In the case of a law firm, confidential information is much more important than physical theft, which would be relevant to a retail chain. However, both types of organizations can suffer from a faulty policy. Here are some of the policies you can find in the security policy:

- Acceptable use policy (AUP)
- Backup policy
- Bring your own device (BYOD) policy
- Confidential data policy
- Data classification policy
- Email policy
- Encryption policy
- Guest access policy

- Incident response policy
- Mobile device policy
- Network access policy
- Network security policy
- Outsourcing policy
- Password policy
- Physical security policy
- Remote access policy
- Retention policy
- Security incident report
- Social media policy
- Third-party policy
- Wireless policy
- Destruction of sensitive trash policy

> The preceding list includes just a few common polices; there are hundreds more. The creation of these policies can be a full-time job and often are for the chief security officer (CSO). However, small organizations can still have a strong security policy, and it can be developed over time to encompass all of the organization's security. A good place to start is by using a template and customizing it for your organization. The SANS institute has a number of these templates via www.sans.org/information-security-policy.

Data Loss Prevention

When an organization suffers data loss, the information is not lost—it is just out of the control of the organization. Data loss prevention (DLP) is a system used to ensure that end users do not send sensitive and/or critical information outside the organization. An example of sensitive information is a Social Security number or the secret sauce recipe for a hamburger chain. The user may not even know they are doing anything wrong in many instances.

DLP systems ensure that data loss will not occur because the damaging effects can be long term. A common DLP system is an outbound email filter. The email transport filters can sanitize or restrict information such as credit card numbers, Social Security numbers, or any type of data they are programmed to detect. Microsoft Exchange Server allows administrators to create custom DLP policies or use prebuilt DLP policies that ship with Microsoft Exchange. Other systems can classify data based on their sensitivity and restrict users from emailing the information to users outside the company or uploading the information to public cloud services.

DLP systems are efficient at identifying potential data loss and they provide a hard control for administrators, but it is best practice to implement soft controls as well by working with the organization's HR department to develop policies and effective training for end users.

Common Documentation

Documentation is extremely important to an information technology department, not to mention the entire organization. It serves many different purposes, such as educating new IT workers, recording work performed, highlighting problems, and describing normal functionality, and these are just a few. However, documentation is usually the one of the functions that suffer the most when projects are hurried and there is a push to start the next project.

In the following sections, I will cover the most common documents that help support the information technology department and day-to-day operations. Some of these documents are prepared by collecting information in a specific manner and then detailing the results, like site surveys and baseline configurations. However, many of these documents just detail how the network is connected and how it functions. The documentation process of the existing network components is usually the best way to learn the network.

Logical vs. Physical Diagrams

Before you begin documenting and diagramming the network, you must decide what type of drawing you are creating. A *logical diagram* details how a network system operates by showing the flow of information. A *physical diagram* details why a network system operates by showing how the devices are physically connected. An example of a logical diagram appears in Figure 3.13.

FIGURE 3.13   A logical diagram

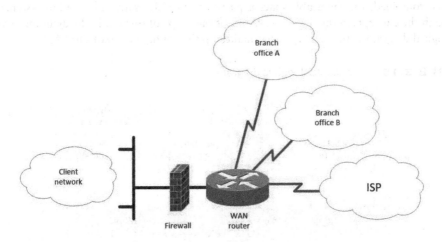

The diagram does not need to be exclusively logical or physical, but the diagram's main purpose should be one type of diagram or the other. Let's suppose you are diagramming your main site in a physical drawing and have several branch sites. The focus of the drawing is the main site; all connections for the main site's network should be detailed. However, the branch sites should only represent a logical connection and should be detailed in a future diagram, as seen in Figure 3.14.

FIGURE 3.14 A physical diagram

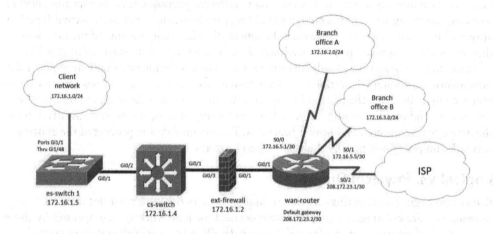

Diagrams do not need to be confined to network topologies. They can also represent the ideas and concepts of a system. For example, we can use a logical diagram to detail each abstract layer so that we can easily understand the system as a whole. Figure 3.15 shows a complex SAN and how the disks are allocated to two RAID groups. The RAID groups are then combined, and the usable space is partitioned to LUNs and allocated to systems. Although the concepts in the drawing are out of the scope of this book, the diagram serves as a logical diagram with each layer that makes up the configuration of our SAN.

FIGURE 3.15 A conceptual logical diagram

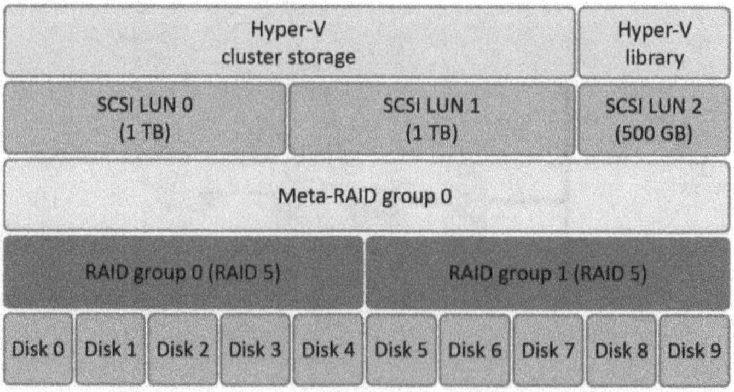

Hyper-V cluster storage		Hyper-V library
SCSI LUN 0 (1 TB)	SCSI LUN 1 (1 TB)	SCSI LUN 2 (500 GB)
Meta-RAID group 0		
RAID group 0 (RAID 5)	RAID group 1 (RAID 5)	
Disk 0 Disk 1 Disk 2 Disk 3 Disk 4 Disk 5 Disk 6 Disk 7 Disk 8 Disk 9		

Floor Plan

The floor plan is a physical drawing that is often overlooked and underestimated in its potential. In large environments, it helps the IT worker locate network assets. This drawing might depict the location of a computer in an office building or a piece of networking equipment on a factory floor, for example. The floor plan also allows new employees to get acclimated with an organization's network equipment.

The floor plan in a data center is really important for two reasons: planning and locating equipment. The planning aspect is critical in a data center because of environmental factors such as temperature, humidity, electricity, and network connections. Locating equipment is equally important, since one rack of equipment can look like the next in the data center.

The *American National Standards Institute (ANSI)* and *Telecommunications Industry Association (TIA)* have standardized a generic naming convention for the location of network equipment in the ANSI/TIA-606-B standard. As seen in Figure 3.16, the floor space is divided into quadrants. These quadrants are then identified on one axis with letters and on the other axis with numbers. So, grid coordinate K9 defines a specific floor space in an office or server room. It is a common practice to label server racks with this naming scheme on the server room floor. The rack location should coincide with the rack diagrams, so you know exactly what equipment is in rack K9 or any other rack in the grid.

FIGURE 3.16 A floor plan drawing

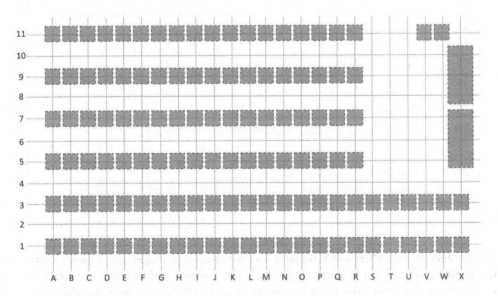

Rack Diagrams

Rack diagrams help us to document the configuration of our server racks for three purposes. The first purpose is obvious: being able to locate the servers in the rack. The second purpose is the planning of new server locations. The third purpose is creating a physical diagram to detail how the racks are wired.

A typical server rack is 42 rack units high, and each rack unit is approximately 1.75 inches, or 44.45 millimeters, for an overall height of about 73.5 inches. The typical rack numbering starts at the bottom of the rack with number 1 and the top of the rack with 42. In data centers, it's all about density. Therefore, it's also common to see rack units that are 48 units high for a total height of 84 inches.

When I create this type of documentation, I simply use a Microsoft Excel document and detail each rack unit in the server racks with the server equipment that occupies the rack unit(s), as shown in Figure 3.17. This allows for quick changes when equipment is decommissioned or added and ensures that all administrators can update the documentation. This documentation also helps with planning when a new piece of equipment is ordered and you need to move servers and equipment around.

FIGURE 3.17 A rack diagram

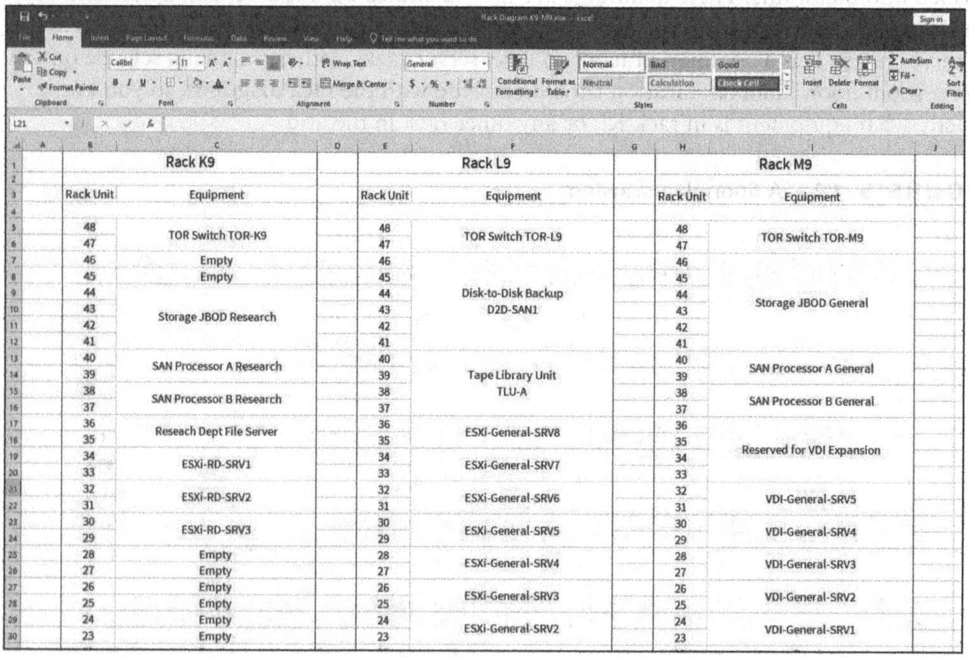

Rack K9 Unit	K9 Equipment	Rack L9 Unit	L9 Equipment	Rack M9 Unit	M9 Equipment
48	TOR Switch TOR-K9	48	TOR Switch TOR-L9	48	TOR Switch TOR-M9
47		47		47	
46	Empty	46		46	
45	Empty	45		45	
44	Storage JBOD Research	44	Disk-to-Disk Backup D2D-SAN1	44	Storage JBOD General
43		43		43	
42		42		42	
41		41		41	
40	SAN Processor A Research	40	Tape Library Unit TLU-A	40	SAN Processor A General
39		39		39	
38	SAN Processor B Research	38		38	SAN Processor B General
37		37		37	
36	Reseach Dept File Server	36	ESXi-General-SRV8	36	Reserved for VDI Expansion
35		35		35	
34	ESXi-RD-SRV1	34	ESXi-General-SRV7	34	
33		33		33	
32	ESXi-RD-SRV2	32	ESXi-General-SRV6	32	VDI-General-SRV5
31		31		31	
30	ESXi-RD-SRV3	30	ESXi-General-SRV5	30	VDI-General-SRV4
29		29		29	
28	Empty	28	ESXi-General-SRV4	28	VDI-General-SRV3
27	Empty	27		27	
26	Empty	26	ESXi-General-SRV3	26	VDI-General-SRV2
25	Empty	25		25	
24	Empty	24	ESXi-General-SRV2	24	VDI-General-SRV1
23	Empty	23		23	

Many vendors offer Microsoft Visio templates for ongoing management of server racks. These templates allow for a finished diagram of network-server racks in the Visio application. I often use these templates when I am working as a contractor because it provides a finished look to the work being performed or pitched to the customer.

IDF/MDF Documentation

Intermediate distribution frame (IDF) and *main distribution frame (MDF)* were terms originally used by telephone providers to describe the distribution of communications. Today, they are used to describe the wiring distribution points of our internal networks.

The IDF is the switching closets where cabling is distributed to end-client computers. Patch panels are often labeled with the naming scheme adopted by the builder. Often, these numbers do not match the actual room numbers because rooms get renumbered and reconfigured over the years. A document detailing the translation of these room and patch numbers should be kept up-to-date and available at the IDF locations for network technicians.

The MDF is the central location from which each IDF is supplied network connectivity. The MDF is usually wired to the IDF closets with fiber-optic cabling. Over time the MDF will have several fiber-optic connections, each leading to a different IDF closet. These fiber-optic cables should be documented extensively because the other end of the fiber-optic cable can be a great deal of distance away.

Wiring Diagrams and Labeling

A tremendous amount of time can be wasted if wiring and port locations are not properly documented. The consequences can be seen each time your network team wastes time chasing down the other end of the cable.

When a building is being constructed, the low-voltage contractor is responsible for the installation and naming scheme of network cabling in the building. The contractor will often use the architect's room numbers as the naming scheme. However, the architect's room numbers will not always match the final room numbers decided by your organization after the building is finished. This is a common problem, and most of the time it cannot be avoided, but it can be documented.

Cabling that is installed after a building is finished is the responsibility of your organization. Some organizations have an internal maintenance department that installs required cabling, and some organizations contract this work. Regardless of who provides the labor, a naming scheme should be standardized for your organization and provided before the installation of the cabling is performed. Do not leave it up to the person(s) providing the labor of cable installation—you may find that nothing is documented!

Wiring diagrams are essential when troubleshooting equipment of any type that the IT department is responsible for maintaining. The diagram can help the technician quickly locate the connection so that a test can be performed, or the connection can simply be plugged back in. In Figure 3.18, you will see a wiring diagram for audiovisual equipment. The diagram details the type of cabling and the label on the cabling so a technician can quickly diagnose a problem. These diagrams are sometimes called as-built diagrams because the drawings represent wiring that was revised as the system was built.

FIGURE 3.18   Typical wiring diagram

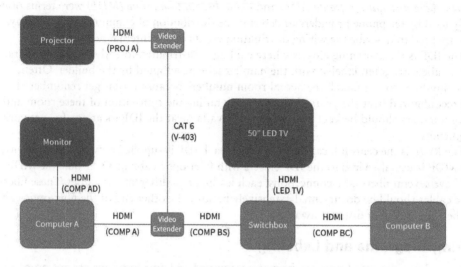

When planning a naming scheme for wiring, you must make it scalable for the entire building. A common naming scheme used internally in buildings looks like this:

Building: E9

Room: 405

Grid coordinates: A05

Patch panel: PP05

Outlet: 01

Using this naming convention, *E9-405-A05-PP05-01* defines a specific location the cable serves as well as the patch panel on which it is terminated. This naming scheme then becomes the labeling scheme used for the cabling so that your network team never needs to hunt down a cable again.

Labeling for network cabling is produced with printed wraps, as seen in Figure 3.19. These wraps are often printed on plastic-coated protective labels so that they resist damage and do not wear off. Labels can be generated with standard inkjet and laser printers on a sheet when labeling several cables at a time, or they can be generated individually on hand-held labelers.

When labeling permanent cabling, use the naming scheme previously explained. The label should be clearly marked with the source and destination on both sides. The naming convention used for labeling should be consistent so that the field technician can decipher it.

Network equipment should also be labeled so that field technicians know which server to reboot or which piece of equipment has a fault. The labeling should contain the network name of the device as well as any key IP address information. I'm sure you would hate to be the technician who took the website down by mistake!

FIGURE 3.19   Network cable label wrap

Site Survey Report

The site survey report is a special document that pertains to wireless coverage, and it is often called a heat map. A site survey is typically performed before wireless equipment is purchased so that proper coverage can be attained and a build of materials (BOM) can be compiled. A site survey should also be performed after the wireless equipment is installed. The site survey report will then guide any adjustments to the wireless parameters, as well as document the as-built wireless network. An example of a site survey report can be seen in Figure 3.20.

Audit and Assessment Report

An audit and assessment report is simply a report that details how well a system is secured. The systems audited and assessed can be your entire network or just a system within the network. The assessment and audit processes along with the document creation are typically performed by a third party so that the final report has integrity.

The security assessment portion of the report is performed with a member of the IT staff in a nonconfrontational way to assess overall security. Policies and procedure are reviewed along with the measures taken to secure the system. The National Institute of Standards and Technology (NIST) published the Cybersecurity Framework that is applied to the system being assessed, shown in Figure 3.21. The Cybersecurity Risk Assessment details what the system does, how it is protected, how security issues are detected, the response to security issues, and the recovery from security issues.

In addition to the Cybersecurity Risk Assessment, a regulatory assessment might be performed to assure compliance. A control assessment might also be performed, in which controls of information and processes are assessed. There are a number of publications that can guide your organization in preparation for these assessments. They are based upon your organization's function, such as healthcare, financial, education, and utility, just to name a few.

FIGURE 3.20   Typical site survey report

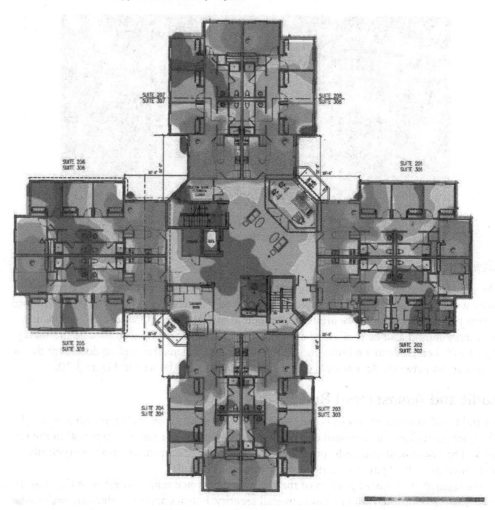

FIGURE 3.21   NIST Cybersecurity Framework

The audit portion of the report is usually performed without forewarning of IT staff and it is carried out in a confrontational manner to identify weak security. Audits can also be called penetration tests, when the entire network is being audited. The goal of a penetrations test is to penetrate the network externally or internally. The testing doesn't always need to be network-based. Often the easiest way to gain information is to just ask someone who is helpful by employing social engineering.

Baseline Configurations

A baseline configuration is a group of agreed-upon settings for a network device or system. These settings are often related to security of the device or system. For example, network switches will often have admin username and password, SSH service, SNMP service, management IP address, and certificates as part of its initial configuration, and specific services might be turned off. By creating a baseline for these common settings, you ensure that every switch setup will be identically secured. Not all settings are security-related; some settings can be organizational preference. However, all of these configuration settings are incorporated into the baseline configuration so there is uniformity in configuration across devices and systems.

Common Agreements

There are several agreements that you will need to be familiar with for the Network+ exam. This short list does not constitute all of the agreements you might have to abide by as a network professional. These are just the most common that you might need to follow or create.

NDA

When an organization hires a new employee, the employee may be privileged to certain proprietary information. This information could be a company's secret sauce, passwords to administrative systems, or customer information. A nondisclosure agreement (NDA) legally protects an organization from an employee disclosing this information to a person outside the organization. The NDA is a document that defines the consequences of disclosure by termination and legal recourse. The NDA should be developed by the organization's legal counsel, HR department, and stakeholders of proprietary information in the organization.

SLA Requirements

The *service-level agreement (SLA)* is an expected level of service that the service provider will adhere to for uptime. The SLA is detailed in the service contract as a percentage of uptime per year; it is often called "the nines." When a service provider exceeds the percentage of uptime defined in the SLA, the provider is in breach of the contract. The contract will often identify what is considered in the SLA requirement as well as the terms if they breach the SLA requirement.

You should be careful with SLAs because being up 99 percent of the time means the service provider can be down 3 days and 15 hours over the course of a year before breaching the contract. A service provider with 5 nines (99.999 percent) can be down 5 minutes and 15 seconds over the course of a year before breaching the contract. Table 3.2 details the different nines of an SLA for uptime.

TABLE 3.2   Uptime for nines of an SLA

SLA %	Downtime per year	Downtime per month	Downtime per day
99% (two nines)	3.65 days	7.2 hours	14.4 minutes
99.9% (three nines)	8.76 hours	43.8 minutes	1.44 minutes
99.99% (four nines)	52.56 minutes	4.38 minutes	8.64 seconds
99.999% (five nines)	5.26 minutes	25.9 seconds	864.3 milliseconds
99.9999% (six nines)	31.5 seconds	2.59 seconds	86.4 milliseconds

Memorandum of Understanding (MOU)

The memorandum of understanding (MOU) is a mutual agreement between two or more parties. The MOU is not a legal contract, but the terms, conditions, and deliverables stated in the MOU can be legally binding. It is drafted when the parties do not want to interfere with an established agreement or slow the process down by creating a new formal legal agreement. The MOU is often used in situations where a union and the organization are currently contracted. The MOU then serves as an amendment to an already established agreement. Therefore, the MOU is commonly agreed upon before it is drafted in a formal contract.

Exam Essentials

Understand and identify common plans and procedures.   Standard operating procedures are derived from the processes that are defined by an organization's policy or plan. Change management is used to minimize the impact of a change to the organization's various processes and ultimately its product. The incident response plan details how incidents are handled by the organization and who is responsible for each piece of the process. Incident response policies help the computer incident response team (CIRT) react to current incidents and plan for future incidents. The business continuity plan and disaster recovery plan details how the organization can continue doing business and its plan to recover from a disaster. The system life cycle details how equipment is received, used, and disposed of in a responsible fashion by the organization.

Know what the basic elements of a change management document are and why the document is used.   Change management documentation is used to minimize the impact of changes on day-to-day operations. A change advisory board reviews the changes and signs off on them. A change management request will contain the item to be changed, reason for the change, priority, description/plan, rollback plan, technical evaluation, and duration of the change.

Know the various hardening and security policies.   A password policy enforces complex passwords of a minimum length. The acceptable use policy (AUP) helps protect an organization from abuse of organization-owned resources. A bring your own device (BYOD) policy defines requirements for employees supplying their own equipment for organizational use. Remote access policies define who has remote access to the organization. Onboarding procedures are created for new employees so that a level of IT training and expectations is established. Off-boarding procedures are used to ensure that access for terminated employees is ended at the time they leave the organization. The security policy encompasses all of the organization's policy, and it is usually found in the employee handbook for an organization. Data loss prevention (DLP) systems minimize the risk of data loss by restricting sensitive information from being moved, viewed, or emailed.

Understand the differences between logical and physical diagrams.   Logical diagrams detail how information flows in the network or system. The exact detail of connections between the symbols is less important than why they are connected. Physical diagrams detail how the network or system is actually wired together and operates. Physical diagrams emphasize details of the network.

Understand why we create rack diagrams.   Rack diagrams help us locate the servers in the rack and plan locations of new servers and detail how the racks are wired. A standard rack is 42 rack units high and each rack unit is 1.75 inches high for a total height of 73.5 inches.

Understand the importance of wiring and port location documentation.   Wiring and port location documentation assists field technicians in locating cabling so that it can be tested or repaired in a timely fashion. Naming schemes for wiring help to standardize the description of wiring locations so that a field technician can trace the wire back to the patch panel.

Understand the importance of IDF and MDF documentation.   The intermediate distribution frame (IDF) is the distribution point of cabling for end clients. The IDF patch panels should be documented with a naming scheme to assist field technicians in locating wiring. The main distribution frame (MDF) is the central distribution point for cabling to the IDFs. The cabling that runs between the MDF and IDF is generally fiber-optic cable. It should be well-documented to assist in troubleshooting since fiber-optic cable can travel large distances.

Understand the importance of documenting network configuration and performance baselines.   Network configuration should be documented to help with troubleshooting of network-related problems. The network configuration should be placed in a shared location. Some network configurations should be printed in the event the network is unreachable during a problem. Performance baselines assist in troubleshooting performance problems. The performance baseline establishes a level of normal operations of the network. It is used to validate a problem and assist in validating a solution.

Know the common agreements that are found in organizations.   The nondisclosure agreement (NDA) is an agreement between the organization and the employee when sensitive information proprietary to the company is shared. The service-level agreement (SLA) is an expectation of service uptime and is often incorporated into a contract with a provider. The memorandum of understanding (MOU) is a mutual agreement between two or more parties, which usually precedes a formal contract. It is often drafted as an amendment to an existing contract.

3.3 Explain high availability and disaster recovery concepts and summarize which is the best solution.

High availability concepts support business continuity and are a preventive measure before failure happens. If you build the network services with resiliency to a failure, you have supported the continuity of your business during minor or major component failures. Each availability concept requires a different degree of cost; therefore, they are often viewed as an insurance policy for your business.

But high availability concepts shouldn't just be viewed as an insurance policy. Some availability concepts support the continuity of network services when there are severe loads on the network services. This type of availability allows you to scale out your servers to accommodate the load. However, if this type of high availability is not planned, under a severe load you could suffer a failure of the network services.

Of course, it is impossible to foresee every disaster. Some disasters you just can't avoid, like a user deleting important files by accident. Therefore, we should build disaster recovery concepts into our normal everyday process. In the following sections, I will cover common high availability and disaster recovery concepts.

Load Balancing

Load balancing allows requests to an incoming service to be balanced across several servers. Load balancing helps support business continuity by preventing a loss of service from being overwhelmed with requests. A use case for load balancing is a web server with high CPU utilization due to requests. We can add another web server and place a load balancer in front of both web servers. The load balancer will then distribute the load across both web servers. We can even add more web servers as demand increases. When we add servers to satisfy demand, it is called *scaling out*, as seen in Figure 3.22.

Load balancers can be purchased as hardware appliances, or they can be configured as software services. *Network Load Balancing (NLB)* is a service included in the Microsoft operating system for load balancing of services. HAProxy is a Linux open-source solution for load balancing of TCP services.

Multipathing

Multipathing is used to provide redundant paths between servers and the storage unit over the storage area network (SAN). Multipathing is a high availability concept because the components that connect the servers to the storage unit can fail or become congested. Multipathing is also known as multipath IO (MPIO) and many vendors license features to avoid congestion. A typical multipath iSCSI setup is shown in Figure 3.23. This setup is not exclusive to iSCSI; it is common for any storage area network, such as Fibre Channel (FC) and Infiniband, for example.

FIGURE 3.22   Scaling out a web server

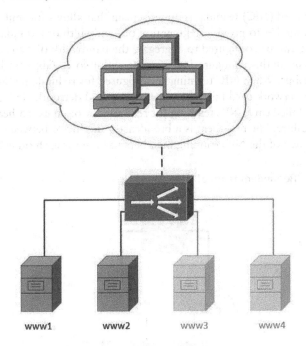

FIGURE 3.23   Typical multipath iSCSI setup

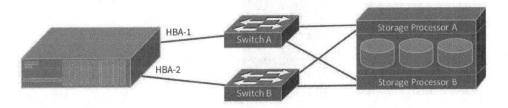

The server will contain a network controller card called a host bus adapter (HBA), which will have two network connections. Separate HBA cards in the server are the best for high availability, but servers are often tight on space, so it is common to use a dual port HBA card. Each port of the HBA card will plug into a separate network switch. This allows a complete switch to fail and the system can retain availability. The storage unit itself will have two separate storage processors that support high availability in the case of a failure. Each storage processor will also have two connections, each of which will connect to each of the switches.

Network Interface Card (NIC) Teaming

Network interface card (NIC) teaming is a mechanism that allows for multiple network cards to function together to provide aggregation of bandwidth or redundancy of connections. *NIC teaming* can be configured to aggregate the bandwidth of two connections to the switching equipment. In this configuration, a server with two 10 Gbps cards could aggregate bandwidth to 20 Gbps. When NIC teaming is configured for redundancy, as shown in Figure 3.24, if one network card fails, the other card would detect the failure and resume operations for the failed card. NIC teaming for redundancy often uses a heartbeat between cards to detect a failure. The heartbeat is a broadcast or multicast between the two or more NICs that allows each of the NIC teaming members to monitor each other's connectivity.

FIGURE 3.24   Redundant team of NICs

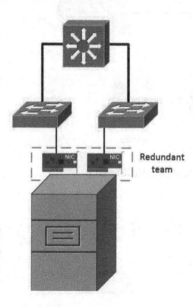

NIC teaming was always a function of the software driver of the network card driver. However, with the introduction of Microsoft Windows Server 2012, Microsoft allows the operating system to team network cards together, even if the software driver never supported the functionality. However, the cards must be of the same speed.

Redundant Hardware/Clusters

Fault tolerance is the ability of a system to remain running after a component failure. Redundancy is the key to fault tolerance. When systems are built with redundancy, a component can suffer a failure and an identical component will resume its functionality. Systems should be designed with fault tolerance from the ground up.

If a power supply in a piece of network equipment malfunctions, the equipment is dead. With the best support contracts, you could wait up to 4 hours before a new power supply arrives and you are back up and running again. Therefore, dual-power supplies are a requirement if high availability is desired. Fortunately, most networking equipment can be purchased with an optional second power supply. Dual-power supplies operate in a few different ways:

- *Active/passive* dual-power supplies allow only one power supply to supply power at a time. When a power fault occurs, the entire load of the device is shifted to the passive power supply, and then it becomes the active power supply. One problem with active-passive dual-power supplies is that only one power supply operates at a time. If the passive power supply is worn with age and the load is transferred, it has a higher chance of not functioning properly.

- *Load balancing* dual-power supplies allow both power supplies to operate in an active-active configuration. Both power supplies will supply a portion of the power to balance out the load. Load balancing dual-power supplies have a similar problem as active-passive dual-power supplies, because one will eventually have to carry the entire load.

- *Load-shifting* dual-power supplies are found in servers and data center equipment. As power is supplied by one power supply, the load, or a portion of the load, is slowly transferred to the other power supply and then back again. This method allows for testing of both power supplies, so problems are identified before an actual power outage.

When installing the operating system on a hard drive or *Secure Digital (SD) card*, you should mirror the operating system onto an identical device, as seen in Figure 3.25. Redundant Array of Independent Disks *(RAID-1)* is also called mirroring , which supports the fault tolerance of the operating system in the event of a drive or card failure.

FIGURE 3.25   RAID-1 (mirroring)

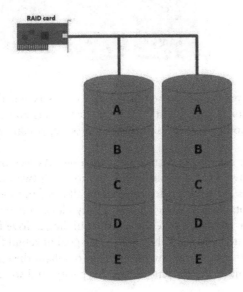

The data drives should be placed on a RAID level as well, but mirroring is too expensive since it requires each drive to be mirrored to an equal size drive. Striping with parity, also called *RAID-5*, is often used for data drives. RAID-5 requires three or more drives and operates by slicing the data being written into blocks, as seen in Figure 3.26. The first two drives receive the first two sequential blocks of data, but the third is a parity calculation of the first two blocks of data. The parity information and data blocks will alternate on the drives so that each drive has an equal amount of parity blocks. In the event of failure, a parity block and data block can create the missing block of data. Read performance is enhanced because several blocks (drives) are read at once. However, write performance is decreased because the parity information must be calculated. The calculated overhead of RAID-5 is 1/N: if three drives are used, one-third of the capacity is used for parity; if four drives are used, one-fourth of the capacity is used for parity; and so on.

FIGURE 3.26 RAID-5 (striping with parity)

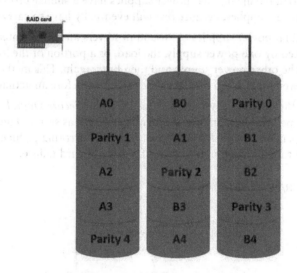

RAID-5 has its disadvantages. Because of the larger data sets, when a drive fails, the other drives must work longer to rebuild the missing drive. This puts the other drives under a severe stress level. If another drive fails during this process, you are at risk of losing your data completely.

Luckily, *RAID-6* helps ease the burden of large data sets. As seen in Figure 3.27, RAID-6 achieves this by striping two blocks of parity information with two independent parity schemes, but this requires at least four drives. RAID-6 allows you to lose a maximum of two drives and not suffer a total loss of data. The first parity block and another block can rebuild the missing block of data. If under a severe load of rebuilding a drive fails, a separate copy of parity has been calculated and can achieve the same goal of rebuilding. The overhead of RAID-6 is 2/N: if four drives are used, two-fourths, or one-half, the capacity is for parity; if five drives are used, two-fifths the capacity is used for parity; and so on.

FIGURE 3.27   RAID-6 (striping with two parity schemes)

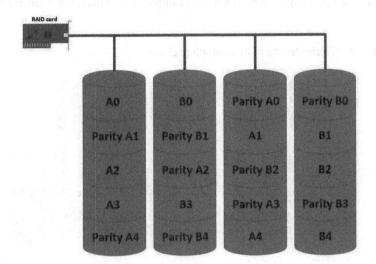

Disks are prone to failure because they have spinning magnetic platters. However, disks are not the only component that can fail in a system. Power supplies can also fail. Systems should always be built with dual power supplies. In the event one power supply fails, the second power supply will pick up the load and the system will continue to function. Newer server hardware can even manage faults related to a CPU and the motherboard will switch processing to the second CPU. Memory faults can be predicted and managed so that information is not lost in the event of memory failure. All of these redundant systems can operate, and the only noticeable event will be an amber warning light on the server to notify the administrator the system requires attention.

Today's servers can be purchased with full redundancy so they maintain functionality in the event of any component failure. However, component redundancy does not address periods in which you need to take the system down for maintenance, nor does it address the load of processes that require several servers processing together.

Clusters are redundant groupings of servers that can balance the load of processes and allow maintenance or complete failure on a node without consequence to overall operation. The Microsoft Server 2019 product contains a feature called Failover Clustering that allows applications to run in a high availability mode. If one server fails or is put into maintenance mode, then the application will fail over to another server. The application must be written for failover clustering, and although it was popular 5 to 10 years ago, today it has been upstaged by virtualization clusters.

Microsoft Hyper-V, VMware vSphere, and Citrix Hypervisor (XenServer) are a few examples of popular virtualization cluster software found in data centers today. These platforms can cluster operating systems for both servers and workstation access. Workstation access is commonly known as virtual desktop infrastructure (VDI). Applications can also be placed into containers on these platforms with the use of Kubernetes or Docker. This allows the application to be treated the same as a virtual machine without the higher cost of ownership associated with an operating system. A logical example of a virtualization cluster is shown in Figure 3.28.

FIGURE 3.28 Example of a high availability cluster

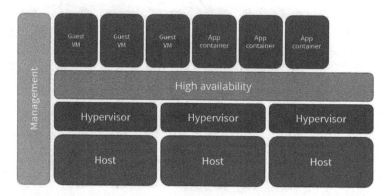

Typically, the host will be similar to the rest of the hosts in the cluster, which is also sometimes call the stack. Each host will have a hypervisor installed that will allow the sharing of resources such as computer, network, and storage. Most vendors will allow you to download their hypervisor and use it free of charge in this capacity, since it will function autonomously from the other hypervisor hosts. However, when the hypervisor hosts work together, they form a cluster and the service that ties them together is high availability. The feature of high availability is something the vendor of the hypervisor software will usually reserve as a premium feature that requires a cost to the organization. Along with the high availability feature is an overall management of the stack. Vendors will differ slightly in their costs and features that complement their basic hypervisor.

Switches

I've discussed ways to create high availability for compute and storage. We can also create high availability for networks that connect the hosts (computer) and SANs (storage) because the links between network switches can fail as well. As discussed in Chapter 2, "Domain 2.0: Network Implementations," we want redundancy of network connections in the event of failure. Spanning Tree Protocol (STP) blocks frames on redundant links so that we don't have broadcast storms and duplicate frames. However, if a link fails, STP recalculates and allows frames to be forwarded across the redundant link. We can even bypass entire switches by building redundancy into the network, as seen in Figure 3.29. The distribution layer or core layer can suffer a loss and continue to forward the information. Purchasing redundant switches is costly, but depending on your day-to-day operations and cost, if a failure occurs, the insurance of redundancy might be worth the price.

FIGURE 3.29   Redundancy in a network

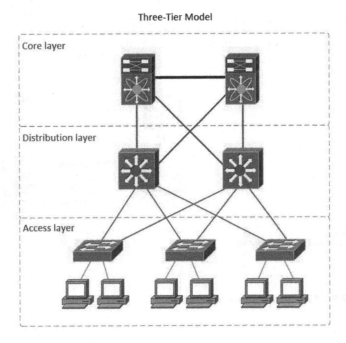

Three-Tier Model

Core layer

Distribution layer

Access layer

Routers

Routers as well as the provider can also be made redundant with the use of *first-hop redundancy protocols (FHRPs)*, such as *Hot Standby Router Protocol (HSRP)* and *Virtual Router Redundancy Protocol (VRRP)*. Both of these protocols allow you to configure a highly available default gateway by providing a coordinated virtual router, as shown in Figure 3.30. If a router goes down for maintenance or failure, the other router will respond to requests and route packets in behalf of the virtual router's IP address. I will cover FHRPs in greater detail in the section "Virtual Router Redundancy Protocol (VRRP)/First Hop Redundancy Protocol (FHRP)" later in this chapter.

Firewalls

Firewalls can also be implemented for high availability using the same standard FHRPs that routers commonly use, as shown in Figure 3.31. One consideration is that the provider supports FHRPs for a redundant firewall connecting to the Internet. Although we can use FHRP for redundancy of outbound traffic, the provider would need to support FHRP for redundancy of inbound traffic. If your organization is using two different providers, then the problem becomes much more complex. Another consideration is that both firewalls have the same configuration or you risk a potential security problem.

FIGURE 3.30   First-hop redundancy protocols (FHRPs)

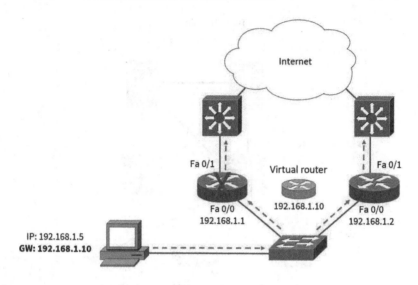

FIGURE 3.31   FHRP and Firewalls,

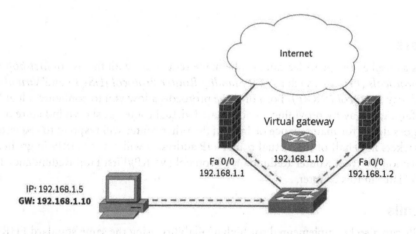

Facilities and Infrastructure Support

The facilities where our network equipment is housed and maintained must have the proper infrastructure support. This is commonly known as "ping and power," but it is far from being simply network and power management. The term "ping and power" encompasses everything from cooling, heating, and humidity (also known as HVAC) to fire suppression.

Of course, power outages are going to be the most eminent threat to our equipment, but proper HVAC maintenance and preventing fires is just as important. In the following sections, I will cover all of the infrastructure that is critical to maintaining network equipment in a facility.

Uninterruptible Power Supply (UPS)

An *uninterruptable power supply (UPS)* is a battery backup system that allows for power conditioning during power sags, power surges, and power outages. A UPS should only be used until a power generator can start supplying a steady source of power. For workstations and server installations where backup generators are not available, the UPS allows enough time for systems to gracefully shut down. UPSs are most often used incorrectly as a source of power generation during a power outage. The problem with this scenario is that there is a finite amount of power in the battery system. It may allow you some time to stay running, but if the power is out for too long, the UPS will shut down when the batteries are depleted.

UPS systems should be used to supply power while a power generator is starting up. This protects the equipment during the power sag that a generator creates during its startup after a power outage has triggered it.

There are several types of UPS systems that you may encounter. The main types are as follows:

- A *standby UPS* is the most common UPS, the kind you find under a desk protecting a personal computer. It operates by transferring the load from the AC line to the battery-supplied inverter, and capacitors in the unit help to keep the power sag to a minimum. These units work well, but they are not generally found in server rooms.

- A *line interactive UPS* is commonly used for small server rooms and racks of networking equipment. It operates by supplying power from the AC line to the inverter. When a power failure occurs, the line signals the inverter to draw power from the batteries. This might seem similar to a standby UPS, but the difference is that the load is not shifted. In a standby UPS, the load must shift from AC to a completely different circuit (the inverter), whereas on a line interactive UPS, the inverter is always wired to the load but only during the power outage is the inverter running on batteries. This shift in power allows for a much smoother transition of power.

- An *online UPS* is the standard for data centers. It operates by supplying AC power to a rectifier/charging circuit that maintains a charge for the batteries. The batteries then supply the inverter with a constant DC power source. The inverter converts the DC power source back into an AC power circuit that supplies the load. The benefit of an online UPS is that the power is constantly supplied from the batteries. When there is a power loss, the unit maintains a constant supply of power to the load. The other benefit is that the online UPS always supplies a perfect AC signal.

Power Distribution Units (PDUs)

In data centers, each rack is supplied an A and B electric circuit. Each rack will have two power strips, called *power distribution units (PDUs)*. The A PDU supplies the first power supply in a dual-power supply configuration; the B PDU will supply the second power supply. In the event of a problem with one electrical circuit, the second circuit will continue supplying the load. It is also common for each A and B circuit to have separate dedicated UPSs and generators with independent fuel supplies.

Power Generators

Power generators supply power during a power outage. They consist of three major components: fuel, an engine, and a generator. The engine burns the fuel to turn the generator and create power. The three common sources of fuel are natural gas, gasoline, and diesel. Diesel-fueled generators are the most common type of generator supplying data centers around the world.

As mentioned earlier, generators require a startup period before they can supply a constant source of electricity. In addition to the startup period, there is also a switchover lag. When a power outage occurs, the transfer switch moves the load from the street power to the generator circuit. UPSs help bridge both the lag and sag in electricity supply during the switchover and startup periods.

HVAC

The heating, ventilation, and air conditioning (HVAC) system supports the environmental conditions of network equipment and servers. If it is too cold, you run the risk of condensing water on components and shorting electronics. If it is too warm, you run the risk of overheating components. The HVAC system also regulates the humidity; if the humidity is too high, dust will soak up the water in the air and short-circuit components. If the humidity is too low, there could be static discharge and static buildup on components. The HVAC will regulate the temperature and humidity and is critical for longevity of equipment. In addition to conditioning the air, HVAC systems serve another purpose, which is keeping dust down. Many HVAC systems have specialized air filters to filter out particulates from the air.

Data centers often employ hot and cold aisles designed to maximize cooling of equipment, as shown in Figure 3.32. The design concept is simple: the rack fronts are pointed toward each other and this makes up the cold aisle. In the cold aisle, cool air is pumped up from the floor vents. The equipment pulls the air in and the air then turns warm. The backs of each equipment rack are pointed toward each other to make the hot aisle. Since hot air rises, the air intakes are mounted above the back of the racks. The intake vents often have a funnel-style shroud to collect as much hot air it can. One consideration to this design is that empty spaces in the racks require blank spacers to keep a division of hot and cold aisles. If you even need to work in a data center aisle for a long period of time, always opt to work in front of the servers in the cold aisle.

FIGURE 3.32   Hot and cold aisles in a data center

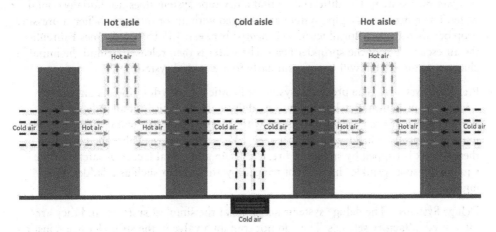

Large-scale data centers require an immense amount of cooling and air conditioning. Some of these data centers require 8 megawatts per building, which is the equivalent to a small town's power requirements. So there is a tremendous environmental impact to a data center. Thankfully, the cloud compute community has developed a metric called power usage effectiveness (PUE) to help providers be efficient with their power requirements. A measurement of 2 PUE means that for every watt of compute power additional watts are used to cool, condition, and distribute power for the compute equipment. A measurement of 1 PUE means that 1 watt is used exclusively for compute, which is the desired goal. Most data centers operate around 1.1 to 1.2 PUE. More information about PUE can be found at www.thegreengrid.org/en/resources/library-and-tools/20-PUE:-A-Comprehensive-Examination-of-the-Metric.

Fire Suppression

Fire suppression in your facility is critical. Even more critical is the type of fire suppression you deploy. If a fire breaks out and the fire suppression system contains it but the wrong type of fire suppression was deployed, you could still end up with a catastrophe. There are five basic types of fire suppression you may find in a facility.

Wet Pipe System   This is the most common fire suppression system found in facilities such as office complexes and even residential buildings. The wet pipe system is constantly charged with water from a holding tank or the city water supply. The sprinkler head contains a small glass capsule that contains a glycerin-based liquid that holds the valve shut. When the glass capsule is heated between 135 to 165 degrees Fahrenheit, the liquid expands, breaking the glass and opening the value. Gallons of water will dump in that area until either the fire is extinguished or another head opens from excessive heat.

Dry Pipe System   Although the name is deceiving, a dry pipe system uses water, similar to a wet pipe system. The difference is that a dry pipe system does not initially contain water. The pipes in a dry pipe system are charged with air or nitrogen. When a pressure drop occurs because a sprinkler head is heated between 135 to 165 degrees Fahrenheit, the air escapes out of the sprinkler head. The water is then released behind the initial air charge and the system will operate similarly to a wet pipe system.

Preaction Systems   The preaction system is identical to the dry pipe system in operations. The preaction system employs an additional mechanism of an independent thermal link that pre-charges the system with water. The system will not dump water unless the sprinkler head is heated between 135 to 165 degrees Fahrenheit and the thermal link is tripped by smoke or fire. This is an additional factor of safety for the equipment, so a sprinkler head is not tripped by an accident such as a ladder banging into it.

Deluge Systems   The deluge systems are some of the simplest systems, and they are often used in factory settings. They do not contain a valve in the sprinkler head, just a deflector for the water. When a fire breaks out, the entire system dumps water from all of the sprinkler heads.

Clean Agent   There are many different clean agents available on the market today. These systems are deployed in data centers worldwide because they do not damage equipment in the event of a fire. The principle of operation is simple: the system displaces oxygen in the air below 15 percent to contain the fire. The clean agent is always a gas, and these systems are often mislabeled as halon systems. Halon 1301 was a popular displacement gas, but it was found to be harmful to the environment so it has largely been replaced by halocarbon-based and inert gases. A halocarbon gas is a man-made gas and is often used as a replacement gas for halon. Inert gases are used in new clean agent installations and are made up of nitrogen, argon, and CO^2 or a mixture of those gases. Inert gas clean agent systems are cheaper to maintain and have small environmental impact.

Redundancy and High Availability (HA) Concepts

We can create redundancy within the host, the rack, and even the facility. However, what happens if an entire facility suffers a catastrophe? These were lessons learned in 2001, when the Twin Towers fell in New York City. Entire data centers were solely contained inside the Twin Towers. Although other branch offices were still intact, many organizations just couldn't continue doing business because all of the financial records were lost. In the following sections, I will cover site redundancy and high availability (HA) concepts in respect to facilities. I will also cover many of the business continuity terms you should be familiar with when discussing facility redundancy and HA.

Cold Sites

A cold site is not a low-temperature, as its name might suggest. It is a networked space used after disaster has struck your primary site. Your network team will have to purchase network equipment since cold sites do not generally contain any equipment. Many ISPs will offer a cold site in the event you actually need one. This is the cheapest of all the disaster recovery plans because you won't invest in any equipment until after the disaster has struck. The downfall is that it will take time to acquire, set up, and configure the equipment.

Warm Sites

A warm site will contain some network equipment essential to resuming network operations. It can be a dedicated rack in an ISP or even another building that will contain the essential network equipment. The equipment is dedicated to the recovery of operations, so minimal effort will be required. However, manual intervention is required by the network team in a warm site. I've seen many companies use their prior generation of server equipment for a warm disaster recovery site.

Hot Sites

A hot site contains equipment that can resume 100 percent of the primary site's network operations. In addition, it is usually fully automated and requires no manual intervention. Some hot sites do require manual intervention, though, depending on how the automation is set up. This disaster recovery strategy is the most expensive to operate and maintain. The disaster recovery strategy is a duplication of the primary site's equipment as well as expensive automation software. However, a hot site will switch operations over with minimal downtime.

Cloud Sites

With the rapid adoption of cloud services, it's natural to look to the cloud for business continuity. An entire site can be duplicated in the cloud, and with minimal effort the organization can be back online after a disaster event. Some cloud providers even offer Business Continuity as a Service (BCaaS) as a product offering. BCaaS is a full product that is completely managed by the cloud provider. Regardless of which service you choose, BCaaS or engineering your own cloud site, the ongoing cost of maintaining a cloud site is mainly viewed as an insurance policy for the organization. The value is dependent on the potential loss in the event of an outage.

Active-Active vs. Active-Passive

When choosing a redundancy strategy, you will need to plan how the redundant site will be used in day-to-day operations. If you have implemented a warm, hot, or cloud site, you may be paying for the computer time and space regardless if it is being actively used. You may also want to geographically position your services in case of a regional disaster. In these situations, an active-active configuration allows for redundancy for the main site and backup site. A key consideration is how you will get traffic to the main site and backup site simultaneously to provide an active-active configuration. You must also consider the Internet service providers that can be affected in a regional disaster. An active-passive design can work equally well in providing redundancy by routing traffic. Dynamic routing protocols like Border Gateway Protocol can help provide failover in the event of a disaster.

Multiple Internet Service Providers (ISPs)/Diverse Paths

It's important to realize that your connection for both your external customers and your internal customers is dependent on your connection to the Internet. If your Internet link goes down, your entire business, along with productivity, can go down as well. Most of this is out of your control since it is your provider's responsibility to keep your Internet connection working.

Throughout the years, I've seen many problems with Internet communications that simply couldn't be avoided. Problems like fiber optics mistakenly being cut, cars hitting poles, fires in central offices, and those are just the physical problems. Routing loops, denial of service (DoS), flapping ports, and BGP being flooded with erroneous information are some of the technical problems that can completely take the Internet down.

The one way that you can mitigate the problem of Internet loss is to design a network with diverse paths by using multiple ISPs, as shown in Figure 3.33. Even your ISP will have diverse paths for its upstream providers. It is extremely rare for any ISP to have a single connection for its upstream provider. Some providers even have paths directly to highly used data centers such as Google, Amazon, and Microsoft. Providers also have paths directly between each other's networks; these types of links are called peering agreements and they are quite common.

FIGURE 3.33   Internet service provider connections

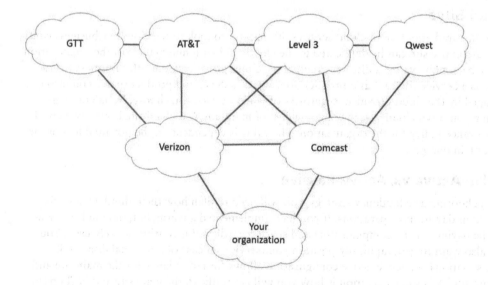

Virtual Router Redundancy Protocol (VRRP)/First-Hop Redundancy Protocol (FHRP)

Looking closer at your organization, the default gateway is the only way out of your network. If a router fails or needs to be serviced, the default gateway will become unavailable. This might not be a problem for average web surfing. However, if VoIP depends on the default gateway, you now have a bigger problem.

Since the default gateway is just an IP address configured on every host that responds to ARP requests, you can virtualize it using a *first-hop redundancy protocol (FHRP)*. You can create a highly available default gateway by letting more than one router respond to an ARP request. As you can see in Figure 3.34, all you need to do is use a virtual IP address and virtual MAC address. No one router owns the virtual IP address or the virtual MAC address. However, they all respond to ARP requests with the configured virtual MAC address. Two protocols are used for creating highly available default gateways: *Virtual Router Redundancy Protocol (VRRP)* and *Hot Standby Router Protocol (HSRP)*.

VRRP is an open standard FHRP for creating highly available routers. VRRP functions in an active/passive configuration; only the active router will answer requests for ARP requests for the virtual IP address with the associated virtual MAC address. If the active router fails, the passive router will become the new active router and start serving ARP requests for the virtual IP address and the associated virtual MAC address.

HSRP is a Cisco proprietary FHRP for creating highly available routers. HSRP also functions as an active/passive configuration, as shown in Figure 3.34. The operation of HSRP is identical to VRRP, except that all devices must be Cisco devices.

FIGURE 3.34 Typical HSRP setup

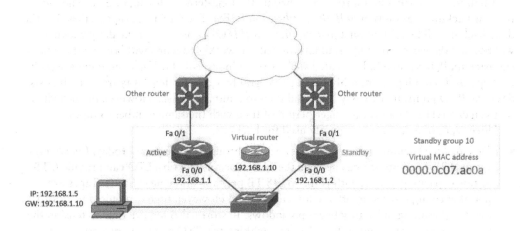

MTTR

The mean time to repair (MTTR) is the measurement of the maintainability for repairable items in a fault-tolerant system. The measurement is generally represented in hours and represents the average time required to repair the failed item.

The MTTR is often found as an article in a maintenance contract for a fault-tolerant system. The MTTR in the contract will define the average time it takes for the vendor to repair the system.

MTBF

The mean time between failures (MTBF) is the average measurement of reliability of a component. You can think of it as the expected life of the component or product. It is commonly found as an advertised specification for hard disks published in hours. A hard disk with a MTBF of 1 million hours based on a specific workload means that a failure could occur after 300,000 hours. However, 300,000 hours is roughly 34 years, and not every hard drive will last that long. That is why this is an average of reliability and not the actual reliability of the component.

Backups

Backups are not just there for disasters. For example, you may need a backup simply because of mistakes on the part of a user deleting files. However, backups are typically used for larger problems such as malicious data loss or failures of disk subsystems.

The concept of the *recovery point objective (RPO)* defines the point in time that you can restore to in the event of a disaster. The RPO is often the night before, since backup windows are often scheduled at night. The concept of *recovery time objective (RTO)* defines how fast you can restore the data. In this section I discuss backup methods, some of which can speed up the process. However, the disadvantage is that these methods will increase the recovery time, as I will explain.

Administrators will adopt a rotation schedule for long-term archiving of data. The most popular backup rotation is *grandfather, father, son (GFS)*. The GFS rotation specifies that the daily backup will be rotated on a *first-in, first-out (FIFO)* basis. One of the daily backups will become the weekly backup. And last, one of the weekly backups will become the month-end backup. Policies should be created such as retaining 6 daily backups, retaining 4 weekly backups, and retaining 12 monthly backups. As you progress further away from the first six days, the RPO jumps to a weekly basis and then to a monthly basis. However, the benefit is that you can retain data over a longer period of time with the same number of tapes.

Three types of media are commonly used for backups:

- *Disk-to-tape* backups have evolved quite a bit throughout the years. Today, *Linear Tape-Open (LTO)* technology has become the successor for backups. LTO can provide 6 TB of raw capacity per tape, with plans for 48 TB per tape in the near future. Tapes are portable enough to rotate off-site for safekeeping. However, time is required to record the data, resulting in lengthy backup windows. Restores also require time to tension the tape, locate the data, and restore the data, making the RTO a lengthy process.

- *Disk-to-disk* backups have become a standard in data centers as well because of the short RTO. They can record the data quicker, thus shortening backup windows. They also do not require tensioning and and do not require seeking for the data as tape media requires. However, the capacity of a disk is much smaller than tapes because the drives remain in the backup unit. Data deduplication can provide a nominal 10:1 compression ratio, depending on the data. This means that 10 TBs of data can be compressed on 1 TB of disk storage. So a 10 TB storage unit can potentially back up 100 TBs of data; again, this depends on the types of files you are backing up. The more similar the data is, the better the compression ratio. It is important to note that the backup utility in Windows Server only supports disk-to-disk backups. If disk-to-tape is required, third-party software must be purchased. The built-in Windows backup utility also does not support data deduplication.

- *Disk-to-cloud* is another popular and emerging backup technology. It is often used with disk-to-disk backups to provide an off-site storage location for end-of-week backups or monthly backups. The two disadvantages of disk-to-cloud is the ongoing cost and the lengthy RTO. The advantage is that expensive backup equipment does not need to be purchased along with the ongoing purchase of tapes.

Creating a complete backup every night is extremely wasteful for resources and time. All of the data doesn't change every day, and therefore there exists three methods commonly used for backups. It is common to complete a full backup one of the days of the week, like Sunday night. Then create incremental backups until the next full backup to save time. The three main methods are as follows:

Full A full backup is just that: a full backup of the entire dataset. A full backup requires the longest windows of all the methods. Therefore, full backups are generally performed on weekends. All files are backed up regardless of the archive bit state. The archive bit is an attribute of each file; when a file is created or modified, the archive bit is turned on. When a full backup is performed, all of the archive bits are reset on the files in the dataset. This type of backup is not sustainable through the week because it backs up all the files whether or not they have been modified.

Incremental An incremental backup is used to speed up backups through the week when backup windows are short. An incremental backup will copy all files with the archive bit set; after the files are backed up, the archive bit will be reset. Only the files that were created and modified from the last full or prior incremental are copied, so backups are small. However, if you need to restore from an incremental, you will need to restore the full backup as well as all of the incremental backup files up to the RPO required. This type of restore will create a longer RTO because of the multiple backups that are required.

Differential A differential backup is also used to speed up backups through the week. It will copy all the files with the archive bit set as well, but it will not reset the archive bit after it has done so. A differential will create a gradually larger backup until a full backup is completed and the archive bits are reset again. This type of backup will have a shorter RTO than incremental backups because only the full and the last differential are needed to restore to the RPO required.

Snapshots

Before snapshots, when a user called in and said, "I desperately need this file from 10 a.m.!" all we could say was, "I can restore it from last night at 10 p.m." Unfortunately, this would mean that the user would lose 2 hours or more of valuable work. So snapshots were invented just for this purpose. Starting with Microsoft Windows Server 2003, the *New Technology File System (NTFS)* included a service called the *Volume Snapshot Service (VSS)*. The VSS could snapshot an entire volume in a split second and allow the user to restore files up to the last 64 snapshots. This gives users the ability to restore their own files.

Snapshots do not copy any information; instead, they take a picture of the file and folder structure. When you change or delete a file or folder, it is archived to a protected portion of the operating system, and a pointer is placed into the snapshot. When a user performs a restore for a file or folder from the snapshot, the pointer will direct the restore to the protected storage. This allows up-to-the-minute snapshots with little performance drain on the operating system.

Snapshots are not an exclusive Microsoft technology—Microsoft's implementation is only the most common. The snapshot can also be found on SAN equipment. It is most commonly used for daily backups of data because a backup can be created from the snapshot. This allows all the files to be backed up at a precise time when the snapshot was taken.

Network Device Backup/Restore

Files are not the only thing that should be backed up on the network. Network devices should be backed up as well, since their configuration is usually completely unique. Configurations such as the various port configurations on a network switch can be a nightmare to reconfigure. Configurations can be lost because they were erased by accident or overwritten or due to just plain failure of the equipment. There are automated appliances and software that can automatically back up configuration of switches on a daily basis. Many vendors also have mechanisms so that the equipment can back itself up to a TFTP, FTP, SFTP server, or even a flash card.

In the case of a cluster host or virtualization host, configuration is not the only thing you will need to back up in the event of failure. The overall state of the device should be saved as well, in the event the device needs to be completely replaced. The software installed on the device expects MAC addresses and disk configuration to be the same when it is moved to new hardware. Otherwise, the software could need to be completely reinstalled. Thankfully many vendors allow for state to be saved. This allows a complete forklift of the operating system and data without reinstalling.

Exam Essentials

Understand the concepts of high availability for business continuity. Fault tolerance is the redundancy of components in a system to maintain the system in the event of a failure of one of its components. High availability is similar to fault tolerance because it prevents loss in the event of failure, but the redundant components work together to prevent a failure and allow maintenance in a coordinated system. Load balancing enables the load of a service to be distributed across many identical services. NIC teaming allows bandwidth to be aggregated for the host, or it can create a redundant connection in the event of a connection failure. Port aggregation enables bandwidth to be aggregated between two switches. Clustering provides failover, load balancing, and high availability for the services running on the cluster of hosts.

Understand the concepts for supplying power to network equipment.   Battery backup/ uninterruptable power supplies (UPSs) maintain voltage and the quality of the power during a power outage. A stand-by UPS is often found under a desk for an individual PC. A line interactive UPS is often used for small racks of networking equipment, and an online UPS is used for data centers. Power generators can provide a constant supply of electricity during a power outage with the use of fuel, an engine, and a generator. Dual-power supplies allow power to be fault tolerant at the network device or server level. Redundant circuits are common in data centers; each rack is supplied with an A circuit and a B circuit. Each of the circuits is plugged into one of the dual-power supplies.

Understand the concepts of recovery for business continuity.   Cold sites do not contain any equipment. Warm sites contain the equipment necessary to run the essential services but not all of the primary site's servers. Hot sites contain the same equipment as the primary site and can operate automatically if the primary site fails. Cloud sites are similar to hot sites but located in the cloud.

Understand how virtual IP addresses are used to create redundancy.   A virtual IP address and virtual MAC address are associated with a first-hop redundancy protocol (FHRP). FHRPs used for redundancy are Virtual Router Redundancy Protocol (VRRP) and Hot Standby Router Protocol (HSRP).

Understand the concepts of availability.   The mean time to repair (MTTR) is the average time required to repair a fault-tolerant system. The mean time between failures (MTBF) is the average measurement of reliability of a component. The service-level agreement (SLA) is found in service provider contracts and details an expected level of service that the provider will adhere to for uptime.

Review Questions

1. Why should performance baselines be captured over a long period of time?

    A. To define normal operations and activity

    B. To define a historical representation of activity

    C. To help validate when a problem is solved

    D. All of the above

2. You are using a network management station (NMS) to collect data for network devices. What must be loaded before you can capture data from the network devices via the Simple Network Management Protocol (SNMP)?

    A. OID

    B. MIB

    C. Traps

    D. Gets

3. Which environmental factor can cause the potential for electrostatic discharge?

    A. Temperature

    B. Electrical

    C. Humidity

    D. Flooding

4. Which interface counter will increment if a host is sending a frame size of 9000 bytes and the default MTU is configured on the interface?

    A. Runts

    B. Encapsulation

    C. CRC

    D. Giants

5. Which version of SNMP offers authentication and encryption?

    A. SNMP version 1

    B. SNMP version 2e

    C. SNMP version 2c

    D. SNMP version 3

6. Which component is responsible for visually representing data from NetFlow?

    A. NetFlow collector

    B. NetFlow cache

    C. NetFlow packet

    D. NetFlow router

7. What is the component that an SNMP agent sends information to?

   A. Syslog

   B. Network management station

   C. Object identifier

   D. Management information base

8. Which metric is the variation from another measurement between the source and destination?

   A. Latency

   B. Jitter

   C. Bandwidth

   D. Throughput

9. What type of diagram is depicted in the following exhibit?

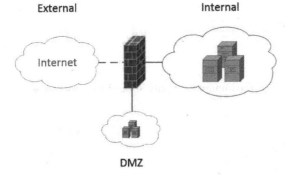

   A. Physical diagram

   B. LAN diagram

   C. Logical diagram

   D. Network schematic

10. Which document would you create to detail step-by-step instructions to decommission a server from your network?

   A. ISO document

   B. SOP document

   C. Server policy

   D. Asset destruction

11. Which group of people evaluates changes for the network to reduce the possibility of affecting day-to-day operations?

    A. Network operations

    B. Executive committee

    C. Stakeholders

    D. Change advisory board

12. When labeling cable in a switch closet, which statement is a best practice you should follow?

    A. The label should have the name of the workstation.

    B. Labels should be labeled from the least-specific to the most-specific location.

    C. Labels should be labeled from the most-specific to the least-specific location.

    D. The label should represent the purpose of the host.

13. Which type of software helps assist in tracking IT inventory?

    A. MDM software

    B. Life-cycle management software

    C. Accounting software

    D. System upgrade software

14. Which policy would you create to define the minimum specification if an employee wanted to use their own device for email?

    A. MDM

    B. AUP

    C. BYOD

    D. NDA

15. You are contracting with a new service provider and are reviewing their service level agreement (SLA). The SLA states that their commitment to uptime is 99.99 percent. What is the expected downtime per year?

    A. 3.65 days

    B. 8.76 hours

    C. 52.56 minutes

    D. 5.29 minutes

16. Configuring a group of disks with RAID level 5 is an example of which availability concept? (Choose the best answer.)

    A. Fault tolerance

    B. High availability

    C. Clustering

    D. Load balancing

17. You have a high demand of normal requests on the company's web server. Which strategy should be implemented to avoid issues if demand becomes too high? (Choose the best answer.)

 A. Clustering

 B. Port aggregation

 C. Fault tolerance

 D. Load balancing

18. Which type of recovery is the least expensive to maintain over time?

 A. Cold site recovery

 B. Warm site recovery

 C. Hot site recovery

 D. Cloud site recovery

19. A recovery from tape will take 4 hours; what is this an example of?

 A. The recovery point objective (RPO)

 B. The recovery time objective (RTO)

 C. Grandfather, father, son (GFS) rotation

 D. Backup window

20. You are the network administrator for your organization. Backup windows are starting to extend into work shifts. You have been asked to recommend a better strategy; what will speed up backups to shorten the window?

 A. Disk-to-tape backups

 B. Disk-to-disk backups

 C. Full backups

 D. GFS rotations

21. Which backup job will back up files with the archive bit set and then reset the archive bit for the next backup?

 A. Archive backup

 B. Full backup

 C. Differential backup

 D. Incremental backup

22. Which type of uninterruptable power supplies (UPS), often found in data centers, provides constant power from the battery-powered inverter circuit?

 A. Line interactive UPS

 B. Standby UPS

 C. Online UPS

 D. Failover UPS

23. Which type of backup is used for grandfather, father, son (GFS) rotations?

    A. Copy backup

    B. Full backup

    C. Differential backup

    D. Incremental backup

24. Which high availability protocol is an open standard?

    A. NLB

    B. HSRP

    C. NTFS

    D. VRRP

25. Which fire suppression system is normally found in data centers?

    A. Deluge

    B. Clean agent

    C. Preaction

    D. Dry pipe

Chapter

4

Domain 4.0: Network Security

THE FOLLOWING COMPTIA NETWORK+ OBJECTIVES ARE COVERED IN THIS CHAPTER:

✓ **4.1 Explain common security concepts.**

- Confidentiality, integrity, availability (CIA)
- Threats
  - Internal
  - External
- Vulnerabilities
  - Common vulnerabilities and exposures (CVE)
  - Zero-day
- Exploits
- Least privilege
- Role-based access
- Zero Trust
- Defense in depth
  - Network segmentation enforcement
  - Screened subnet [previously known as demilitarized zone (DMZ)]
  - Separation of duties
  - Network access control
  - Honeypot
- Authentication methods
  - Multifactor
  - Terminal Access Controller Access Control System Plus (TACACS+)

- Single sign-on (SSO)
- Remote Authentication Dialin User Service (RADIUS)
- LDAP
- Kerberos
- Local authentication
- 802.1X
- Extensible Authentication Protocol (EAP)

■ Security assessments

- Vulnerability assessment
- Penetration testing
- Risk assessment
- Posture assessment

■ Security information and event management (SIEM)

✓ 4.2 Compare and contrast common types of attacks.

■ Technology-based

- Denial-of-service (DoS)/ distributed denial-of-service (DDoS)

  ■ Botnet/command and control

- On-path attack (previously known as man-in-the-middle attack)
- DNS poisoning
- VLAN hopping
- ARP spoofing
- Rogue DHCP
- Rogue access point (AP)
- Evil twin
- Ransomware
- Password attacks

  ■ Brute-force

- Dictionary
- MAC spoofing
- IP spoofing
- Deauthentication
- Malware
- Human and environmental
    - Social engineering
        - Phishing
        - Tailgating
        - Piggybacking
        - Shoulder surfing

✓ 4.3 Given a scenario, apply network hardening techniques.

- Best practices
    - Secure SNMP
    - Router Advertisement (RA) Guard
    - Port security
    - Dynamic ARP inspection
    - Control plane policing
    - Private VLANs
    - Disable unneeded switchports
    - Disable unneeded network services
    - Change default passwords
    - Password complexity/length
    - Enable DHCP snooping
    - Change default VLAN
    - Patch and firmware management
    - Access control list
    - Role-based access

- Firewall rules
  - Explicit deny
  - Implicit deny
- Wireless security
  - MAC filtering
  - Antenna placement
  - Power levels
  - Wireless client isolation
  - Guest network isolation
  - Preshared keys (PSKs)
  - EAP
  - Geofencing
  - Captive portal
- IoT access considerations

✓ **4.4 Compare and contrast remote access methods and security implications.**

- Site-to-site VPN
- Client-to-site VPN
  - Clientless VPN
  - Split tunnel vs. full tunnel
- Remote desktop connection
- Remote desktop gateway
- SSH
- Virtual network computing (VNC)
- Virtual desktop
- Authentication and authorization considerations
- In-band vs. out-of-band management

✓ **4.5 Explain the importance of physical security.**

- Detection methods
  - Camera

- Motion detection
- Asset tags
- Tamper detection
- Prevention methods
  - Employee training
  - Access control hardware
    - Badge readers
    - Biometrics
  - Locking racks
  - Locking cabinets
  - Access control vestibule (previously known as a mantrap)
  - Smart lockers
- Asset disposal
  - Factory reset/wipe configuration
  - Sanitize devices for disposal

Network security should be the primary focus in the design and operations of your network. We build networks to internally share our organizational information and resources to authorized users. However, we must also protect the information from unauthorized individuals. Many of the unauthorized individuals will be external to the organization and have malicious intent.

In the previous chapters, you learned the fundamental theory of networking. You also learned about the various infrastructure components and how to maintain network operations. In this chapter, you will learn how to secure the network infrastructure.

4.1 Explain common security concepts.

Security can be intimidating for the average administrator, because the advanced topics can be confusing and carry a tremendous consequence if not fully understood. An administrator could have a rude awakening if their network security is insufficient; they could even end up in the unemployment line. Fortunately, just like networking concepts, there are common security concepts that build off each other. In the following sections, I will cover common security concepts that can help in understanding more advanced topics of security.

Confidentiality, Integrity, Availability (CIA)

The most elemental security concept is the CIA triad, shown in Figure 4.1. Although the Central Intelligence Agency (CIA) has the same acronym as the CIA triad, the two have nothing to do with each other. The CIA triad stands for confidentiality, integrity, and availability, and these concepts apply to information security and the storage of information.

FIGURE 4.1   The CIA triad

Confidentiality   The confidentiality of information focuses on limiting access to only the individuals allowed to access the information while denying access for those individuals who are restricted from accessing the information. Confidentiality can be achieved with physical locks (such as locked doors), file cabinets, safes, and, in extreme cases, security guards. Confidentiality can also be achieved electronically with authentication, encryption, and firewalls. Essentially, you need to decide how secure the information needs to be and that will dictate the level and method of protecting the data's confidentiality.

Integrity   The integrity of information focuses on its accuracy and how susceptible it is to being altered by an unauthorized individual. Integrity of data must be protected both at rest and in transit. The integrity of data at rest can be protected with file hashes to detect unauthorized altering of the data. Unauthorized altering of information can also be prevented with the use of access control lists (ACLs). The integrity of data in transit can be protected with the use of signatures and checksums, such as the use of the Authentication Header (AH) protocol. This ensures that the data is not altered as it is being transmitted across the network.

Availability   The availability of the information pertains to the uptime of the systems serving the information. The availability of the data can be heightened by using redundant systems or redundant components to create highly available information systems. Information can also be backed up, which also raises the availability of the information because you are creating a point-in-time snapshot of the data. The restoration of information must be considered from two perspectives: the point in time from which you can restore the data and the time it takes to restore the data to that point.

Threats

A threat is a potential danger to the network or the assets of the organization. When we think of threats, we tend to think of just cyberattack threats, where a bad actor uses the network to carry out an attack. However, threats can also be physical, such as weather or other environmental factors that have a potential to be dangerous.

As an oversimplified example, let use the trip to the grocery store to set the stage in understanding threats. If we purchase groceries and place them in the car, there are all kinds of potential dangers (threats) to our groceries. We could get into an accident on the way home, they could be stolen, or our ice cream could melt. There is a certain amount of risk for each one of these threats, known as the likelihood it will happen. If you are a good driver, then the risk of an accident is low. If you live in a relatively safe neighborhood, then the risk that the groceries will be stolen is low. However, if it's a really hot day, there is a high risk of the ice cream melting.

Unfortunately, an organization's network is a lot more complicated than a grocery store visit. In most organizations there are two types of threats: external and internal. External threats are almost always carried out by an attacker with ill intent. The risk or potential of these threats is usually our connection to the outside world, such as the Internet, email, and our Internet-facing servers. If you mitigate the risk, then the threat is less likely to occur. Internal threats, also known as a threat from within, are potentially carried out by an employee. A disgruntled employee can compromise your organization's network by intentionally leaking the organization's data or intentionally running malicious code. Internal threats can be much more dangerous than external threats because employees often know exactly how systems are configured and how to circumvent controls.

Vulnerabilities

Vulnerabilities are weaknesses in the security for an organization. These weaknesses in security can be physical- and network-based. An example of physical vulnerabilities are often doors that are not locked to sensitive areas where data is accessible. Network vulnerabilities are often found in applications, operating systems, and network products.

Vulnerabilities are the reason we need to constantly patch network systems. However, even with constant patching we can never be assured that we have eliminated all vulnerabilities. Some vulnerabilities will always exist and sometimes never be known by the owners of the system or the bad actors attempting access to these systems. Patching does, however, lower our risk or potential for an attack through known vulnerabilities.

Common Vulnerabilities and Exposures (CVE)

Common Vulnerabilities and Exposures (CVE) is a system that provides a reference-method for publicly known vulnerabilities and exposures. The CVE system was originally created in 1999 by a working group based upon a white paper published by David E. Mann and Steven M. Christey of the MITRE Corporation. The purpose of the CVE system is to create a common naming scheme for vulnerabilities while reducing any overlaps in documentation from varying agencies documenting the same vulnerability.

A typical CVE will look similar to this common nomenclature of CVE-2020-17084. This particular CVE details a buffer overflow in Microsoft Exchange Server that was discovered in 2020. By investigating this CVE on the Internet, you can see that regardless of who hosts the information, it pertains to the same vulnerability. For example, Microsoft references the same vulnerability the National Institute of Standards and Technology (NIST) references using this CVE number. All sources have the same relative information about the vulnerability, such as affected versions, a score that explains the associated risk, the impact, and references.

Keep in mind that the CVE is not a database. it is a numbering system for tracking vulnerabilities. The numbering and characterization of a CVE is up to the CVE Numbering Authority (CNA). As in the example above, Microsoft is a CNA and therefore created the initial CVE-2020-17084 document that all other CVE repositories must reference similarly. There are CNAs all around the world and most of them are software manufacturers such as IBM, Microsoft, and VMware. However, some of the CNAs are security organizations. The underlying theme is not who creates the CVE, but that once it is created, the CVE should be consistent across all references.

Zero-Day

All publicly known vulnerabilities usually have either a workaround or a patch. However, some vulnerabilities are discovered before a patch or workaround can be devised and made available. These are known as zero-day vulnerabilities, and they carry high risk because there is no way to defend from an attack. A zero-day vulnerability doesn't mean that the attack is imminent; some zero-day vulnerabilities are remediated the very next day. However, it does mean that until a patch or workaround is devised, you are vulnerable.

Exploits

A vulnerability is a weakness in security, as you have learned. An exploit is a method that acts on a weakness (vulnerability). I will use a luggage lock as an example, mainly because they are notoriously weak security solutions. A simple paperclip bent appropriately could be used to exploit the weakness and open the lock. It would be nice if all problems were as simple as getting a better lock, but networks are complicated systems that can have many complex vulnerabilities, as well as known exploits.

When we talk about exploits, we generally refer to scripts, software, or sequences of commands that exploit a known vulnerability. The CVE published against a vulnerability can be used to patch or block the exploit, depending on the vulnerability. Just like zero-day vulnerabilities, where there is a weakness that is not documented yet, there exists zero-day exploits, in which an attack is carried out without understanding the vulnerability it is carried out upon.

The term *zero-day* can be applied to both a vulnerability and an exploit. A zero-day vulnerability means that a weakness is known before the vendor has time to acknowledge a workaround or patch. A zero-day exploit is much more serious, since there is an automated method created to exploit a weakness not yet documented. You may come across the term *zero-day* used in either of these two contexts.

Least Privilege

The principle of least privilege is a common security concept that states a user should be restricted to the least amount of privileges that they need to do their job. By leveraging the principle of least privilege, you can limit internal and external threats. For example, if a front-line worker has administrative access on their computer, they have the ability to circumvent security; this is an example of an internal threat. Along the same lines, if a worker has administrative access on their computer and received a malicious email, a bad actor could now have administrative access to the computer; this is an example of an external threat. Therefore, only the required permissions to perform their tasks should be granted to users, thus providing least privilege.

Security is not the only benefit to following the principle of least privilege, although, it does reduce you surface area of attack because users have less access to sensitive data that can be leaked. When you limit workers to the least privilege they need on their computer or the network, fewer intentional or accidental misconfigurations will happen that can lead to downtime or help desk calls. Some regulatory standards require following the principle of least privilege. By following the principle of least privilege, an organization can improve upon compliance audits by regulatory bodies.

Role-Based Access

As administrators we are accustomed to file-based access controls and the granularity that accompany these access control models. However, with today's emerging cloud-based systems, we often do not need the granularity of individual permissions. Role-based access helps remove the complex granularity by creating roles for users that accumulate specific rights. The user is then given a role or multiple roles in which specific rights have been established for the resource, as shown in Figure 4.2.

FIGURE 4.2   Role-based access

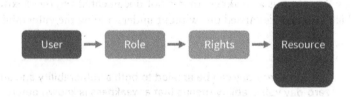

As an example, Microsoft Teams has roles for a Teams meeting. You can be an attendee, presenter, or organizer. The attendee can attend a Teams meeting and share their video and audio feed. The presenter can do that plus they can share a presentation, mute participants, and perform several other presentation key functions. The organizer can do everything the presenter can do plus they can create break-out rooms and view attendance. By changing someone's role in the meeting, from attendee to presenter, for example, we can allow them to share a document to the meeting's other attendees. If we had to find the specific permission to allow that person to perform the function, it would take a lot longer and would be prone to error.

Role-based access doesn't stop with just cloud-based applications. We can use role-based access controls in our day-to-day operations by standardizing permissions based upon specific roles in our organization. When a marketing person is hired, the standardized role of marketing can be applied. This can be performed with Active Directory groups and the permission groups we include.

Zero Trust

In a traditional trust model, everything within the perimeter of the network is trusted and everything outside is not. When an external user needs to access an internal resource, they connect to the internal network via a virtual private network (VPN). Connecting to the network with a VPN makes the device they are connecting with trusted because the user is authenticated with their credentials.

The traditional model works well when the expectation is that you drive to work and log on to a trusted computer to access sensitive information. However, with today's mixture of work from home and mobile device access, the traditional model doesn't always work. The traditional model also doesn't address cloud resource access. This is where the Zero Trust model excels. With a Zero Trust model, nothing is trusted regardless of the location and everything is authenticated. If a user logs on to a cloud resource, the device is authenticated and the user is authenticated before it can connect to the data or application. This prevents a bad actor from using a user's compromised device to access sensitive data. Every vendor has a different implementation of Zero Trust, but the concept remains the same; nothing is trusted and everything must be authenticated.

Defense in Depth

The concept of defense in depth is not the implementation of a single security measure but the combination of several different security measures. This creates a depth to our defense strategy to make is tougher for a bad actor to launch a successful attack and gain access to sensitive data. An example of a defense in depth strategy is shown in Figure 4.3 as it applies to a malicious email. The malicious email should be filtered by the spam filter, but if it makes it through the spam filter, then the antivirus and antimalware software should pick up the attempt. If none of the prior detections work at stopping the email, the end-user training should prevent the malicious link in the email from being clicked. However, if it is clicked, then the content filtering software should prevent the exploit from calling back to the server hosting the malware.

FIGURE 4.3   Example of defense in depth

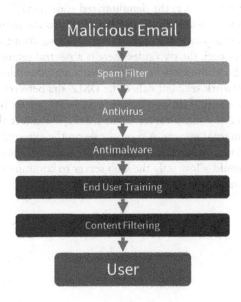

Security in this example is not left to a single mechanism. The collection of these mechanisms makes it tougher for a bad actor to succeed. The following sections cover several different security measures as per the CompTIA Network+ exam objectives, but they in no way cover all of the different security measures out there. It is always best to assess what you are trying to secure first, then identify the weaknesses. Once you understand the weaknesses, security measures can be implemented to address each weakness identified. The result will be a very diverse set of security measures and a defense in depth strategy.

Network Segmentation Enforcement

When a network is flat with no segmentation, it is impossible to secure because an intruder has potential access to all hosts and devices once the initial network is compromised. Fortunately, there are a number of methods to implement segmentation in the network. We can use physical routers, separate switches, and firewalls. However, the easiest method is to implement virtual local area networks (VLANs) in the network. When VLANs are implemented, each VLAN has a distinct network ID. The VLANs become routable networks because they create segments in the network. This concept can then be taken one step further by implementing access control lists (ACLs) between these segments to increase security.

If you are implementing a firewall to create network segmentation, the various networks are given a label and value of trust is associated with them. The labels are also commonly called zones. As an example, the Internet is often labeled as the public zone and carries the lease amount of trust. Internal networks are often labeled as private zones and carry a higher amount of trust. Rules can then be enforced that dictate that a public zone cannot communicate to a private zone, unless the private zone has initiated the connection.

Segmentation can be taken even further, by segmenting internal private networks within the organization, such as production, research, and sales, with each zone carrying a different level of trust. Enforcement rules can then be put into place to protect each segment.

Screened Subnet (Previously Known as Demilitarized Zone [DMZ])

The screened subnet is also known as the demilitarized zone (DMZ). The DMZ gets its name from the segmentation that is created between the exterior of the network and interior of the network. This is similar to where borders of two opposing countries meet with military presence on both sides. Between the two sides there is a neutral segment call the DMZ. As it pertains to a network, hosts that serve Internet clients are placed in the DMZ subnet. As shown in Figure 4.4, a network segment called the DMZ sits between an external firewall and internal firewall. The external firewall contains ACLs to restrict Internet hosts from accessing nonessential services on the server in the DMZ. The internal firewall restricts which hosts can talk to internal servers. A typical rule on the external firewall would allow HTTP access for a web server in the DMZ and would restrict all other ports. A typical rule on the internal firewall would allow only the web server to communicate with the SQL back-end database in the internal network.

FIGURE 4.4   A typical DMZ with two firewalls

Although the concept of the DMZ is still used today in network design, a screened subnet can be created between any two segments in the network. The subnets don't necessarily need to be external and internal in relation to the network. Routers containing ACLs can be implemented in lieu of firewalls to filter traffic to the screened subnet, as shown in Figure 4.5. In the figure, a network called Network A is segmented from the screened subnet by a router with ACLs filtering traffic. On the other side of the screened subnet is another network called Network B, and it too is segmented by a router with ACLs filtering traffic. Each of these two networks have equal access to the hosts in the screened subnet. These two networks, Network A and Network B, could potentially be a wireless network and the wired network, respectively.

FIGURE 4.5   A typical screened subnet with two routers

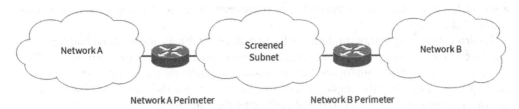

Some screened subnets are just another interface on a single firewall, as shown in Figure 4.6. In this example, the rules for both the Network A subnet and the Network B subnet would be on the same firewall. The benefit of a single firewall is centralized administration of firewall rules. Each interface is placed into a trust zone, and the firewall rules allow incoming and outgoing connections.

Separation of Duties

The separation of duties is a security concept that reduces the control or power of one individual over a process. This is done by assigning specific responsibilities for each procedure in the process and then reinforcing it with permissions.

FIGURE 4.6   A typical screened subnet with one firewall

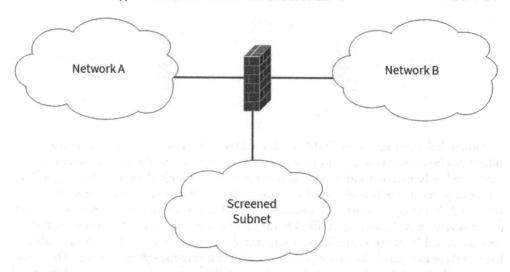

A separation of duties is commonly implemented between the firewall admin and the server admin. Each admin has their own responsibility as it pertains to the creation of firewall rules or the installation of the server. Each admin only has the given permissions to complete their own procedure in the process. This prevents the server admin from mistakenly exposing a service by misconfiguring the firewall. It also prevents the firewall admin from misconfiguration of the server.

Implementing a separation of duties helps to reduce the threat of one individual having the control or power to make a change and then cover their tracks by deleting logs. We always want to trust our employees, but we should also audit their activities and ensure the logs have integrity. If the employee has the control to delete their actions in logs, this increases the threat of illegal or immoral activity by the employee.

NAC

The 802.1X protocol is used to authenticate computers and users for access to the network. Although 802.1X can be used by itself for authentication, it is often used in conjunction with a *network access control (NAC)* system. It is often referred to as port-based network access control (PNAC).

As shown in Figure 4.7, NAC agents check the reported health and integrity of the client before allowing it on the network. The NAC agent can check the current patch level of the client, antivirus signature date, and firewall status. The NAC policy is defined by the network administrator. If the client passes the checks, the client is allowed on the network. If the client fails the checks, the client is placed into a remediation network, where the user must remediate the client. The 802.1X protocol is used to control the access of the client via the switchport. I will cover the 802.1X protocol in greater detail later in this chapter.

FIGURE 4.7 NAC and 802.1X

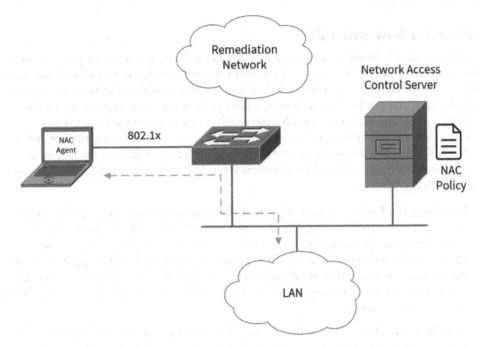

Honeypot/Honeynet

A honeypot is a physical or virtual host that is set up for the explicit purpose of allowing unauthorized access. The honeypot is a system that is tightly controlled by the administrator, but it allows an attacker to compromise the system so that you can analyze the attacker's efforts. A honeynet is a group of honeypots that work in conjunction to form a network of honeypot systems. This creates a depth of realism for the attacker.

Honeypots are useful for gathering reconnaissance on attackers. They are most notably used to detect spammers and compromised servers that send spam. Honeypot information can be used to tighten firewall rules on the production network by identifying current threats on the honeypot network.

Authentication Methods

When a user wants to access a resource, they must first provide *authentication* that they are who they say they are. A user can provide authentication credentials using several different factors. The most common authentication factors are something you know (passwords), something you have (smartcard), and something you are (biometrics). Besides the various factors of authentication, there are several protocols that can be used to transmit credentials or aid in the authentication of a user. In the following sections, I will cover in detail all of the various protocols as well as the various factors of authentication that can be used to authenticate a user or computer.

Multifactor Authentication

All authentication is based on something that you know, have, are, or do, or your location. A common factor of authentication is a password, but passwords can be guessed, stolen, or cracked. No one factor is secure by itself, because by themselves they can be compromised easily. A fingerprint can be lifted with tape, a key can be stolen, or a location can be spoofed.

Multifactor authentication helps solve the problem of a compromised single-factor authentication method by combining the authentication methods. With multifactor authentication, a single factor will no longer authenticate a user; two or more of the factors discussed in this section are required for authentication. This makes the credentials of the user more complex to compromise.

Something You Know   Computing has used the factor of something a person knows since computer security began. This is commonly in the form of a username and password. We can make passwords more complex by requiring uppercase, lowercase, numeric, and symbol combinations. We can also mandate the length of passwords and the frequency in which they are changed. However, the username/password combination is among the most common type of credentials to be stolen because they can be phished or sniffed with a keylogger.

Something You Have   Authentication based on something a person has relates to physical security. When we use a key fob, RFID tag, or magnetic card to enter a building, we are using something we have. An identification badge is something we have, although technically it is also something we are if it has a picture of us on it. Credit cards have long since been something we have to authenticate a transaction. Within the past two decades, it has also become the most thieved credentials. Recently, credit cards have implemented a new authentication method called Europay, MasterCard, and Visa (EMV). EMV will make it harder to steal and duplicate cards. However, if a card is lost, it can still be used by an unscrupulous person because it is something you physically have.

Something You Are   A decade or so ago, authenticating a user based on something they are was science fiction. We now have biometric readers built into our phones for our convenience! All we need to do is place our finger on the reader, speak into the phone, or allow the phone to recognize our face and we are instantly logged in. Computers can be outfitted with fingerprint readers to allow logon of users based on their fingerprint as well. When this technology entered the market, there were various ways to get around it, such as tape-lifting a print, playing back someone's voice, or displaying a picture of a person for the camera. These systems have gotten better since they have entered the market by storing more points of the fingerprint, listening to other aspects of a user's voice, and looking for natural motion in the camera.

Somewhere You Are   A relatively new factor of authentication is based on somewhere you are. With the proliferation of Global Positioning System (GPS) chips, your current location can authenticate you for a system. This is performed by creating authentication rules on the location. GPS sensors are not the only method of obtaining your current location. Geographic IP information queried from Geo-IP services can also be used for the authentication process. We can restrict login to a specific IP or geographic location based on the IP address provided.

Something You Do   Another relatively new factor of authentication for network systems is based on something you do. Although it has been used for hundreds of years for documents and contracts, a signature is something you do, and you don't even think about how you do it. It is unique to you and only you because there is a specific way you sign your name. Typing your name into the computer is something you do and don't think about, but there is a slight hesitation that you make without knowing it. Algorithms pick up on this and use the keystrokes as a form of authentication. Arguably, it can be considered biometrics because it is something your brain does without you consciously thinking about it.

TACACS+

Terminal Access Controller Access Control System+ (TACACS+) is a protocol developed by Cisco from the original dated protocol TACACS. Although it was developed by Cisco, it was released as an open standard. The protocol is mainly used with routers and switches for authentication, authorization, and auditing. The TACACS+ protocol is declining in popularity and has largely been replaced with RADIUS.

Single Sign-On

Single sign-on (SSO) is an aspect of authentication and not a protocol. SSO assists the user logon by allowing the user to authenticate to the first application and then reusing the credentials for other applications. This way, the user no longer has to enter the same username and password for each application they access. As shown in Figure 4.8, a user will initially log in and authenticate to the authentication server, such as Active Directory (AD). When that user then attempts to access the cloud resource, the cloud resource will call back to AD through a federation server. A claim in the form of the user's attributes will be furnished to the cloud resource, thus logging the user into the cloud resource.

Each application that participates in SSO requires an SSO agent module. The SSO agent module is responsible for retrieving the authenticating credentials for the user from an SSO policy server. The SSO policy server can be a *Lightweight Directory Access Protocol (LDAP)* directory or Active Directory Federation Services (ADFS). The protocol *Security Assertion Markup Language (SAML)* is used to exchange credentials; this is considered SAML-based SSO.

FIGURE 4.8 Single sign-on example

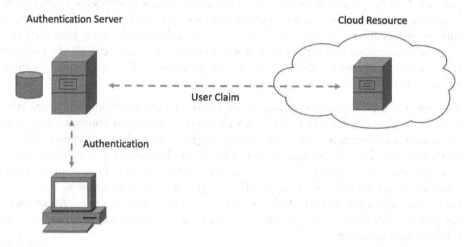

RADIUS

Remote Authentication Dial-In User Service (RADIUS) was originally proposed as an Internet Engineering Task Force (IETF) standard. It has become a widely adopted industry standard for authenticating users and computers for network systems. RADIUS creates a common authentication system, which allows for centralized authentication and accounting.

The origins of RADIUS are from the original ISP dial-up days, as its acronym describes. Today, RADIUS is commonly used for authentication of remote access systems, wireless systems, and any network system that requires a common authentication system. RADIUS operates as a client-server protocol. The RADIUS server controls authentication, authorization, and accounting (AAA). The RADIUS client can be wireless access points, a VPN, or 802.1X switches. The RADIUS client will communicate with the RADIUS server via UDP/1812 for authentication and UDP/1813 for accounting. The RADIUS server can be configured with authorization rules that use the connection's attributes. Common attributes are caller IP address, connection type, group association, and the username and password of the user.

A RADIUS server is often called an authentication, authorization, and accounting (AAA) server. The AAA model defines the basics of user administration for access to resources. The AAA system of access is easily explained as a transaction in a physical bank. In Figure 4.9, the customer (user) appears on the far left, and their money (resource) is shown on the far right. As an example, I will use the analogy of a bank transaction in which a customer will withdraw money.

A customer (user) will provide their *authentication* via their account number (something they know) and identification (something they are). The bank teller can then authenticate that they are the person they say they are.

FIGURE 4.9   AAA bank analogy

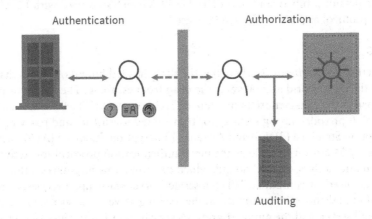

Once the teller has authenticated the customer (user), *authorization* will be checked. With the analogy of a bank, authorization might be how much money is in your bank account. However, a better example is who in the bank is allowed to enter the vault and touch the money! I'm sure even if my bank authenticates me, they won't authorize me to count and withdraw my own money. I'm pretty sure that if I tried, I would go to jail and not collect my two hundred dollars. The teller is authorized to touch the money and hand it to you. It is important to note that in this example, the teller is also authenticated when they come into work, though this authentication process is less rigorous than your authentication process.

Now that you have been authenticated and authorized to receive your money, an audit trail is created. If you had $400 and withdrew $200, your account would be debited $200. The audit trail in this example is the *accounting* process of the AAA system. Accounting allows us to trust and audit.

In a network system, when a user logs on, they will commonly authenticate with a username and password. When the user tries to access the resource, their authorization to the resource will be checked. If they are authorized to access the resource, the accounting of access will be recorded. It is important to note that accounting can record denied access to a resource as well.

LDAP

Lightweight Directory Access Protocol (LDAP) is an open standard directory service protocol originally defined by the IETF. It operates as a client-server protocol used for looking up objects in a directory service and their respective attributes. LDAP was adopted by Microsoft in 2000 for Active Directory lookups of objects on domain controllers.

An LDAP client queries requests to an LDAP server with a specifically formatted uniform resource identifier (URI). The URI will contain the object to search for and the attributes to be retrieved. In addition, filters can be supplied so that only specific objects are searched. LDAP uses a default protocol and port of TCP/389. When SSL is used with LDAP, called LDAPS, the protocol and port of TCP/636 is used.

Kerberos

In Greek mythology, *Kerberos* (Cerberus) is the three-headed hound of Hades that guards the gates of the underworld and prevents the dead from escaping. The Kerberos protocol was developed at the Massachusetts Institute of Technology (MIT) as a secure authentication protocol. It provides strong security for transmitted usernames and passwords via Triple Data Encryption Standard (3DES) and Advanced Encryption Standard (AES) encryption. It was adopted by Microsoft in 2000 as the main authentication protocol for Active Directory.

It's named after a three-headed hound, which describes how it requires a three-way trust to authenticate users or computers. When a service server starts up, it requests a service ticket (proof of authentication) from the authenticating server. A service server can be a file server or email server, and the authentication server can be a Linux/Unix Kerberos server or Microsoft Active Directory server. When the client starts up, it too requests an authentication ticket. When the client accesses the service server, the authentication tickets are exchanged and checked against the authenticating server list. Both the client and service server must trust the same authenticating server for access to be permitted. This completes the three-way trust of client to service server to authenticating server.

Local Authentication

So far we have covered centralized authentication and protocols that support the authentication process. Local authentication is useful when providing access to a small group of people because each account must be manually created on each device or server to be accessed.

Local authentication is just that—it operates by authenticating the user to a local database contained on the equipment or server. There is no need for protocols, because it's all local and nothing needs to be transmitted over the network. Local authentication is normally used for the management of network devices. It is common to configure network device management to authenticate users from RADIUS or TACACS+, with a fallback to local authentication if the network is down.

802.1X

The *802.1X* protocol is used to control access on the internal network, as shown in Figure 4.10. 802.1X commonly uses RADIUS as the authentication server. However, other AAA authentication servers can be used, such as LDAP and TACACS+. 802.1X is used for both wired and wireless network access. When you are using 802.1X with a wired connection, the physical port allows communications of 802.1X credentials. The port will not allow user traffic to be switched until the AAA process is completed and the user or computer is verified. The user's device is called the supplicant, and the port it is plugged into is called the control port, because it controls access to the organization's LAN or resources. The switch that is set up for 802.1X is called the authenticator.

FIGURE 4.10   802.1X switch control

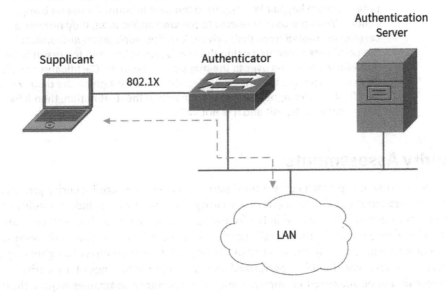

802.1X works with wireless connections, but in lieu of a physical connection an association occurs. When 802.1X is used with wireless, the control port is the port leading back to the network. All 802.1X authentication between the supplicant and the authenticator occurs over the associated connection.

Extensible Authentication Protocol (EAP)

The *Extensible Authentication Protocol (EAP)* is a framework for transmitting credentials for the user or computer accounts for authentication purposes. EAP is not a specific authentication method or authentication mechanism. Instead, the framework allows for the extensibility of authentication. For example, Cisco devices use a protocol called *Lightweight Extensible Authentication Protocol (LEAP)*, and Microsoft uses a protocol called *Protected Extensible Authentication Protocol (PEAP)*. Both are EAP-based authentication protocols as their names imply. The Cisco protocol is mainly used for wireless clients, and the Microsoft protocol is mainly used for the authentication of computers and users. EAP can be used to even extend authentication to biometrics because it is only a framework for authentication.

> Although certificates are not a formal objective of the CompTIA Network+ exam, it is important to understand how certificates are used for authentication and maintaining integrity. Certificates are a method of using a Public Key Infrastructure (PKI) to validate users and computers. When certificates are used to authenticate a user, the public key of the user's public-private keypair is mapped to the user account for the web application. When the user connects to the web application, they provide a certificate created from their private key. The application authenticates the certificate presented using the user's public key, and the result is the authentication of the user to the mapped credentials. Certificates can also be used to validate the integrity of applications by signing the data with a certificate. If the signature does not match at the destination, then it has been altered in transit and it is not valid.

Security Assessments

A security assessment is performed by a third party to assess the overall security preparedness of your organization. The methods of a security assessment can include a number of different tactics that will be covered in the following sections. Each method will generate a report and will be included in the overall security assessment. The key goal of the security assessment is to report the current security of the organization in an effort to tighten security.

A security assessment should be performed annually, and the findings of a security assessment should be addressed promptly. Some cyber insurance companies require third-party security assessments as a prerequisite to a cyber insurance policy. Security assessments can also be required by compliance regulations that apply to an organization's industry sector, such as the financial sector or healthcare sector, just to name a few.

Vulnerability Assessment

A vulnerability assessment is critical to identifying risk in your network. A vulnerability scan is normally completed on the external and internal network ranges of the organization. The first tactic is to identify the open services by using a port scanning tool such as Nmap. The next tactic performed after the port scan is complete and services are identified is a vulnerability scan. The vulnerability scan will interrogate the services in an effort to identify their weakness. There are many different tools out there to scan network vulnerabilities. The Nessus vulnerability scanner is the most popular, and it requires a subscription for large scans. The tactics of port scanning and identifying vulnerabilities are the same methods a bad actor will follow in an effort to compromise your organization.

Penetration Testing

A penetration test, also known as a pen test, will take the vulnerability assessment one step further by executing the vulnerabilities found in the vulnerability assessment. The pen tester will attempt to circumvent security and penetrate the network by using the known vulnerabilities. A penetration test is the racy part of the security assessment, because there is no script that the penetration tester follows, just wits and tradecraft.

When a pen test is being performed, there should not be a heightened security posture where the employees are expecting something to happen. You want to prevent a red team vs.

blue team circumstance, unless it is normal operating procedure. Many times, the pen tester will use any means to penetrate the network, such as physical access and phishing email with a payload that beacons back to a command and control server.

Risk Assessment

Risk is the potential for a threat to be carried out against your organization. The risk assessment is the part of the security assessment that identifies the cause and conditions, circumstances, and threats and opportunities for a bad actor. The findings from this assessment will also identify the potential of the findings being acted upon. The risk assessment will often be in the form of a report detailing the threats identified from the vulnerability assessment and penetration test, although it is not limited to these two assessments. Although the purpose of risk assessment is to identify an organization's overall risk, the outcome of the risk assessment should detail the steps to mitigate the risk. The actionable items to mitigate risk are sometimes contracted out in security firms so that the risk can be rechecked after the findings are mitigated.

Posture Assessment

A security posture assessment is the assessment of how an organization handles a breach or threat and the risk associated with it. One of the goals of the security posture assessment is to establish a benchmark. This benchmark should then be improved upon in an ongoing effort to heighten your security posture.

Fortunately, there are some objective guidelines that can be applied to network security and how network security is handled. The National Institute of Standards and Technology (NIST) Cyber Security Framework (CSF) and the International Organization for Standardization (ISO) standards 27001 specification both outline framework and standards of network security. The NIST CSF describes a cyclical process of Identify, Protect, Detect, Respond, and Recover, as shown in Figure 4.11. Each item in the NIST CSF process should be carried out when a threat is identified. The threat should then be protected, and a system should be implemented to detect further threats. A response and recover plan should then be followed or outlined, depending on the circumstance. The ISO 27001 standard is for the management of information security that an organization should follow and can be certified as practicing.

FIGURE 4.11   NIST CSF processes

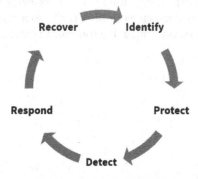

Security Information and Event Management (SIEM)

A security information and event management (SIEM) system is a piece of software or a service that combines the tasks of security information management (SIM) and security event management (SEM). The responsibilities of the SIEM system is to collect data, identify anomalies, and take appropriate actions. The collection of data is usually in the form of log collection by security systems, such as a firewall or intrusion prevention system (IPS), just to name a couple. The identification could be a simple comparison to a threat intelligence feed, or it could be a form of artificial intelligence that identifies abnormalities. The identification mechanism is usually the "special sauce" of a vendor's SIEM product. The actions that a SIEM system can execute can be a simple passive escalation to a security operation center (SOC) via email or the SIEM system can actively block a threat. The actions that a SIEM product can deliver are also what make a vendor's product unique in the market place.

Exam Essentials

Know the CIA triad and how it applies to information security.   The CIA triad consists of the three concepts of confidentiality, integrity, and availability. Confidentiality defines how data is secured. Integrity defines how data is protected from unauthorized altering. Availability defines how data in systems is kept available to users and outages are avoided.

Understand the various security concepts presented in this discussion of objective 4.1. A threat can be internal or external to your organization. A threat is the opportunity for a security event. Risk is the potential that a threat can occur. A vulnerability is an example of a threat in the form of a weakness in security. Common Vulnerabilities and Exposures (CVE) is a standardized cataloging system for vulnerabilities across all vendors. Exploits are code or techniques that can be carried out upon a vulnerability. The principle of least privilege defines that an employee is only given the access required to perform their duties. Role-based access is the technique of combining privileges together for common roles in an organization. Zero trust describes the idea that every system internal and external to the organization's network is not trusted and must be authenticated in some way.

Understand the strategy of the defense in depth concept.   A defense in depth strategy is several layers built on top of each other with the express purpose of mitigating a threat and strengthening security. No one layer is trusted to prevent the threat, but all the layers combined help to lower the risk of a threat succeeding. Network segmentation is used so that an intruder does not have the ability to roam various parts of the network. It can also be used to prevent intrusion, depending on how it is implemented. The screened subnet, also known as the DMZ, is used to screen or filter traffic to a shared resource. Separation of duties prevents any one person from having too much control. Network access control

(NAC) is a method of limiting access to the network based upon a device's security posture. A honeypot is used to distract bad actors while allowing the admins to be alerted of their tactics.

Understand the different factors that can be used for multifactor authentication. Multifactor authentication is the process of using two or more factors for authentication. An example of something you know would be a password or personal identification number (PIN). Something you have is something you physically have that can be used for authentication. An example of something you are is biometrics such as fingerprint scans and voice and facial recognition. Somewhere you are is a fairly new authentication method that uses GPS coordinates or an IP-to-geographic location database. Something you do could be considered a biometric authentication method.

Understand the various access controls that can be used within a network. 802.1X is a control protocol for wired or wireless access, commonly used in conjunction with a RADIUS server for AAA services. Network access control (NAC) works in conjunction with 802.1X by restricting access to a device until it has passed a security posture evaluation by the NAC agent on the device.

Understand common authorization, authentication, and accounting systems. Remote Authentication Dial-In User Service (RADIUS) is an industry standard that provides AAA services for users and computers on network equipment. TACACS+ is an AAA protocol developed by Cisco and released as an open standard. Kerberos is an open-standard protocol for authenticating users and computers by issuing identity and service tickets. Single sign-on (SSO) allows a user's credentials to be reused for concurrent logins for other applications. Local authentication is performed against a local database of credentials; it is not scalable. Lightweight Directory Access Protocol (LDAP) is an open standard directory service that is used by Microsoft for Active Directory. Certificates are used to authenticate users; the public portion of the public-private keypair is mapped to a user account. The principle of "trust and audit" dictates that logging and auditing should be performed on all user accounts.

Know the various components of a security assessment. A security assessment is a third-party assessment upon the security preparedness for your organization. A security assessment is the final product from a number of other assessments, such as the vulnerability assessment, penetration testing, risk assessment, and security posture assessment. The vulnerability assessment details the various vulnerabilities found externally and internally on the network. A penetration test is a test against the discovered vulnerabilities in an attempt to bypass security and gain access to the network. A risk assessment is an assessment of how likely a threat or vulnerability will be acted upon. A security posture assessment is how an organization handles security-related events and how prepared an organization is for the likelihood of a security event.

4.2 Compare and contrast common types of attacks.

Networking attacks are the most common type of intrusions for an organization. The actor or actors involved do not need to be in the same vicinity or even the same country as the network they are attacking. All network attacks focus on disrupting service, theft of services, theft of data, or direct monetary theft—all of which hurts an organization's reputation and finances. In the following sections, I will discuss several different types of network attacks.

Technology-Based

All attacks upon an organization are either technology-based or physically-based. A technology-based attack is one in which the network and operating systems are used against the organization in a negative way. Physically-based attacks use human interaction or physical access, which I will cover later. I will now cover several different types of technology-based attacks that are commonly used against networks and organizations.

DoS

A *denial-of-service (DoS)* is an attack launched to disrupt the service or services a company receives or provides via the Internet. A DoS attack is executed with an extremely large amount of false requests, resulting in the servers not being able to fulfill valid requests for clients and employees. As shown in Figure 4.12, a bad actor sends many false requests for information to a server. Then when the valid requests are sent to the server, the resources are exhausted and the server cannot fulfil the valid requests. There are several different types of DoS attacks.

FIGURE 4.12   Typical DoS attack

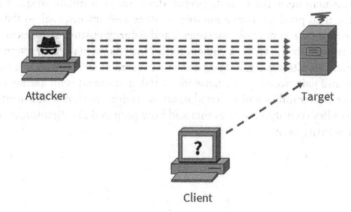

Reflective   A reflective DoS attack is not a direct attack; it requires a third party that will inadvertently execute the attack. The attacker will send a request to a third-party server and forge the source address of the packet with the victim's IP address. When the third party responds, it responds to the victim. There are two victims in this type of DoS attack; the first is the victim the attack is aimed at, and the second is the third-party server used to carry out lthe attack, as shown in Figure 4.13.

FIGURE 4.13   Typical reflective attack

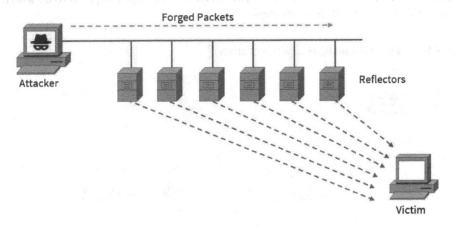

Amplified   An amplified DoS attack is a variant of a reflective DoS attack. It is carried out by making a small request to the third-party server that yields a larger response to the victim. The most common third-party servers used to carry out this type of attack are DNS and NTP. For example, an attacker will request a DNS query for a single host-name that contains 20 aliases while forging the source IP address. The victim is then barraged with the 20 answers from the query, as shown in Figure 4.14.

FIGURE 4.14   Typical amplified attack

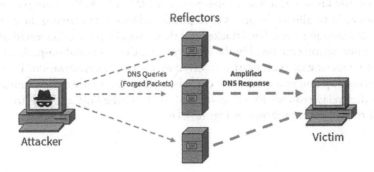

Distributed   A *distributed denial-of-service (DDoS)* is becoming the most common type of DoS, because the source of the DoS is varied. A DDoS employs many bots to create a botnet. A botnet is a series of compromised servers or hosts that are under a bad actor's control. It is common for botnets to launch DDoS attacks on organizations. When a single host is used to create a DoS, it can simply be blocked. However, when traffic is coming from millions of different hosts, it is impossible to isolate the DoS and firewall the source. A bad actor will leverage a key server called a command and control server to deliver commands to each bot in the botnet, as shown in Figure 4.15. The command and control server is often a compromised server as well; it just happens to be where the bad actor has set up shop (so to speak).

FIGURE 4.15   Components of a DDoS attack

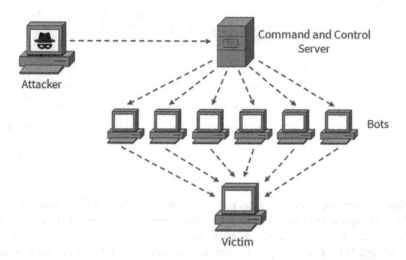

On-Path Attack (Previously Known as Man-in-the-Middle Attack)

Many of the attacks we're discussing can be used in conjunction with an on-path attack, which is previously known as a *man-in-the-middle (MitM)* attack. For example, the evil twin attack mentioned later, allows the attacker to position themselves between the compromised user and the destination server. The attacker can then eavesdrop on a conversation and possibly change information contained in the conversation. Conventional on-path attacks allow the attacker to impersonate both parties involved in a network conversation. This allows the attacker to eavesdrop and manipulate the conversation without either party knowing. The attacker can then relay requests to the server as the originating host attempts to communicate on the intended path, as shown in Figure 4.16.

FIGURE 4.16 On-path attack

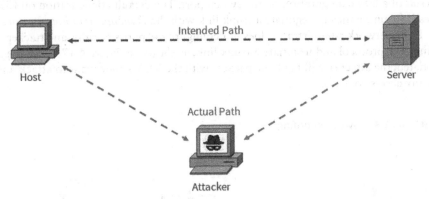

DNS Poisoning

DNS poisoning is an attack that targets an organization's DNS server. An attacker will attempt to replace valid DNS entries with a compromised server's IP address. The replacement of valid DNS entries is often performed via a DNS exploit or poisoning of a DNS cache. The attack is carried out by sending random answers to the DNS server with the bad actor's IP address. The attack hinges upon the likelihood that the DNS server asked a legitimate DNS server for the answer. When the bad actor's reply is seen, the target DNS server accepts this as its expected answer.

The attack of poisoning the DNS cache of a DNS server was a common approach by bad actors a decade ago. However, in the past decade a lot of the vulnerabilities in DNS have been patched and improvements to the DNS protocol have been made, making the protocol incredibly difficult to exploit. For example, Microsoft implemented the ability to lock the DNS cache to prevent updates from randomly being accepted. DNS socket pools were also implemented that prevented responses coming in on unexpected source ports that the server never sent out. In addition to these security improvements, Domain Name System Security Extensions (DNSSEC) was ratified by the Internet Engineering Task Force (IETF) to prevent DNS names from being spoofed. DNSSEC uses cryptographic signatures to sign DNS replies so that the answer can be validated back to an authoritative name server for the namespace.

VLAN Hopping

VLAN hopping is an attack method in which an attacker switches the VLAN that they are currently assigned to gain access to a system on another VLAN. VLAN hopping allows the attacker to bypass access controls to the protected resource. There are two primary methods of VLAN hopping that an attacker can use: one is called switch spoofing and the other is double-tagging of frames.

Switch spoofing allows for an attacker to gain a two-way conversation with the victim. It's a result of a lazy configuration on the switch port. The default configuration on Cisco switches is to automatically negotiate a trunk link with the *Dynamic Trunking Protocol (DTP)*. If the network administrator does not configure the port statically, an attacker can spoof the DTP protocol and negotiate a trunk link, as shown in Figure 4.17. Once the trunk is negotiated, the attacker will tag their packets with the VLAN they want to attack and bypass any access controls.

FIGURE 4.17   Switch spoofing

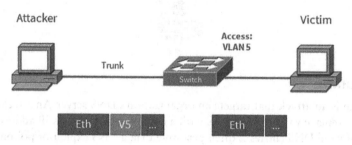

The other method of VLAN hopping is double-tagging of VLANs. This method of attack is a one-way attack since the return path will not be double-tagged. As shown in Figure 4.18, the attacker will tag the packet with the VLAN they are in as well as double-tagging the packet with the intended VLAN. When the switch receives the tagged frame on an access list, the switch removes the first VLAN tag and forwards the frame. However, when the frame is transmitted on a trunk, the adjacent switch will switch the frame on the VLAN in the second tag (now the primary tag). The result is the victim will receive the packet, but the victim computer will never make the round trip back since double-tagging is not a normal Ethernet operation. The method of double-tagging is useful when performing a DoS on the destination host.

FIGURE 4.18   Double-tagging of VLANs

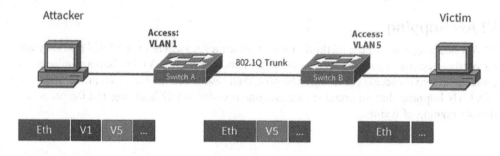

ARP Spoofing

The Address Resolution Protocol (ARP) is used by TCP/IP to resolve an IP address to a MAC address. As a packet (layer 3) becomes a frame (layer 2) and is prepared for transmission, the destination MAC address of the frame is used. However, if the destination MAC address is not known, then the sending host will send a broadcast ARP request asking who knows the MAC address for the destination IP address. The sending host is then vulnerable to this attack, since the response is not authenticated and an attacker can send a spoofed ARP reply.

This attack is normally used in conjunction with an on-path attack. The attacker will first learn the IP address of the default gateway so that they can route the packets. Then the attacker just needs to wait for the ARP request for the default gateway IP address and reply a forged Gratuitous Address Resolution Protocol (GARP) packet, as shown in Figure 4.19. GARP is used to notify hosts when a MAC address changes and the IP to MAC address mapping should be updated. When the victim receives the GARP packet, the victim will update their ARP entry for the given IP address. The attacker can then accept packets on behalf of the default gateway, sniff the contents, and pass the information on to the real default gateway.

FIGURE 4.19   Example of MAC spoofing

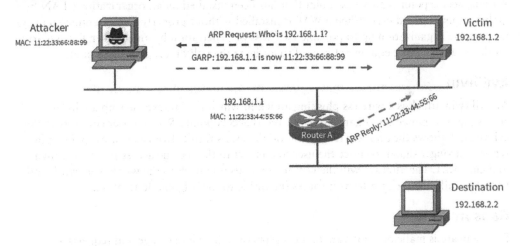

Rogue DHCP

A rogue DHCP server is an unauthorized DHCP server that an attacker will start up to hand out invalid IP addresses. A rogue DHCP server is normally used to cause a DoS by serving invalid IP addresses. However, it can also be used to redirect their traffic through an attacker's host computer by changing the default gateway being served as a DHCP option, as shown in Figure 4.20. The attacker can then passively sniff traffic and capture credentials and other key information as the information is rerouted to the original gateway via the attacker's computer.

FIGURE 4.20   Example of a rogue DHCP server

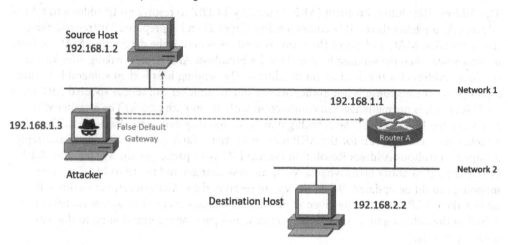

Rogue Access Point

A rogue access point is an access point that has been installed on an organization's LAN by a malicious user or end user. When a WAP is installed without properly implementing security, it opens the organization up to possible data loss or penetration by an attacker. Port security on the local switching equipment is used to mitigate the risk of a rogue access point.

Evil Twin

An evil twin attack is a wireless phishing attack in which the attacker sets up a wireless access point to mimic the organization's wireless access points. When a user connects to the evil twin, it allows the attacker to listen in on the user's traffic. Evil twin access points often report a stronger signal to entice the user to connect to the specific access point, as shown in Figure 4.21. The attacker will then create a connection back to the wireless network and passively sniff network traffic as it routes the traffic to the original destination.

Ransomware

Ransomware is malicious software that encrypts or holds files hostage and requests a ransom for decryption. Some variants will threaten disclosure of sensitive information or trade secrets in an attempt to collect the ransom. The rise of ransomware is directly tied to the anonymous currency Bitcoin. Bitcoin is used like the cliché bag of money in a ransom-themed movie because it is somewhat untraceable currency. The attackers will usually ask for an amount of money that is negligible to the organization to move on from the incident.

Ransomware is a current and emerging threat for organizations. Many phishing email campaigns target users in an effort to click and run the ransomware. Once an attacker is into the network, they will start encrypting everything and they'll even attempt to encrypt or destroy backups so an organization cannot recover to an acceptable point.

FIGURE 4.21 Evil twin attack

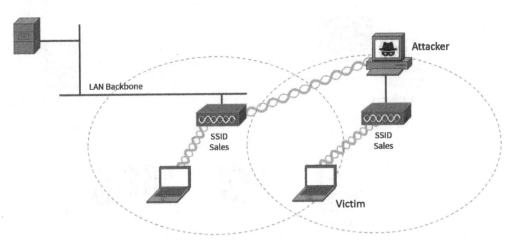

A new spin on ransomware is asking for a ransom so an organization can prevent a public disclosure of private information. Data loss of client information can be the death of any company. Some organizations have even had their intellectual property (IP) stolen. "Either pay the ransom or your 'special sauce' will be publicly disclosed," is the decision many organizations have recently had to make.

Password Attacks

When an attacker attempts to guess a password for a known username, it is considered a password attack. Usernames such as admin, administrator, and root should always be avoided since these are considered privileged accounts. You should always use passwords that are at least 10 characters or longer. Complexity should also be used when formulating a password, such as using lowercase, uppercase, symbols and numbers. An attacker will perform a password attack with two primary tactics of a dictionary attack and brute-force attack.

Dictionary Attacks A dictionary attack is just how it sounds; The attack is carried out by using a database of common words called a dictionary. These dictionary files can be kilobytes to gigabytes in size, and they contain commonly used passwords. The obvious dictionary words are *password, privilege,* and variations of *password* using numbers, such as *passw0rd*. Complexity and length will mitigate password dictionary attacks.

Brute-force Attacks Brute force is a last-ditch effort to crack a passphrase or password. A brute-force application will try every combination of a password until access is granted. These combinations will include uppercase letters, lowercase letters, symbols, and numbers. The number of combinations is exponential. with every character added to a password, so long passwords of 10 characters or more are best. There are two brute-force attack methods: the online method and offline method, as shown in Figure 4.22.

FIGURE 4.22   Brute-force password attacks

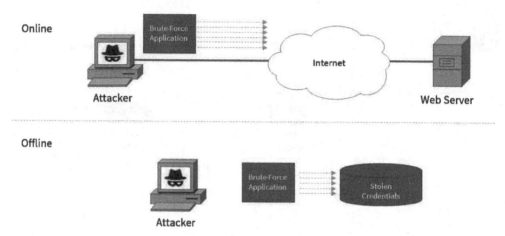

Both methods use a brute-force application to try each permutation of the password. The online method accesses the application directly and attempts to crack the password. However, the weakness to an online brute-force attack is the use of automatic lockouts after so many failed attempts and it slows the attacker down considerably. The offline method requires the theft of the credentials file and the brute-force attack is attempted directly on the offline credentials file. Passwords are never stored in clear text; they are commonly hashed. So, theft of the credential file requires hashing password combinations in an attempt to match the hash. With the use of a high-end graphics card, an attacker can try millions of password hashes a minute or even in seconds. An attacker can also employ a database of password-to-hash combinations, called rainbow tables. Rainbow tables can be terabytes in size.

MAC Spoofing

MAC spoofing is used to bypass firewalls and captive portals that employ the MAC Authentication Bypass (MAB) protocol. MAB is commonly used in networks that allow self-registration of computers, such as bring your own device (BYOD) scenarios. A valid user will register their device by MAC address. When the firewall or captive portal sees the MAC address, it will allow it to bypass any security through to the resource without further restrictions. VLAN assignment can also be used with MAB to place the host on the proper network according to the user's credentials.

The attacker carries out the attack by passively sniffing and learning the valid MAC address of a registered computer. Then when the computer is no longer connected, the attacker can spoof the source MAC address and bypass any firewalls or captive portals, as shown in Figure 4.23. Although the figure illustrates a wired network, this same technique can be used on wireless networks that employ MAB.

FIGURE 4.23   Example of MAC spoofing

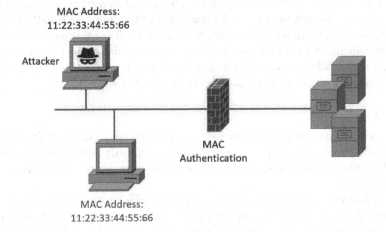

IP Spoofing

Spoofing is performed by an attacker so they can impersonate an IP address of an organization's assets. Spoofing allows the attacker to bypass access control systems and gain access to protected resources on the network. Spoofing is often used in DoS attacks to hide the attacker's IP address. As shown in Figure 4.24, the attacker forges a packet with pawn's IP address as the source IP address and proceeds to attack the victim at the destination IP address. IP spoofing can be used in more elaborate attacks involving MAC spoofing to carry on a two-way conversation.

FIGURE 4.24   Example of IP spoofing

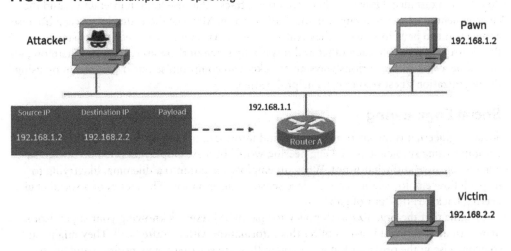

Deauthentication

The 802.11 wireless protocol contains a method for deauthentication of clients via a deauthentication frame. An attacker can send a deauthentication frame on behalf of the user, which disconnects them from the access point. Attackers will use this method in conjunction with an evil twin attack to deauthenticate the user from a valid access point so they can try to reconnect to the evil twin access point. The deauthetication attack can also be used to generate association traffic for purposes of cracking a wireless passphrase.

Malware

Malware is a broad term describing any software with malicious intent. Although we use the terms *malware* and *virus* interchangeably, there are distinct differences between them. The lines have blurred because the delivery mechanism of malware and viruses is sometimes indistinguishable.

A virus is a specific type of malware the purpose of which is to multiply, infect, and do harm. A virus distinguishes itself from other malware because it is self-replicating code that often injects its payload into documents and executables. This is done in an attempt to infect more users and systems. Viruses are so efficient in replicating that their code is often programmed to deactivate after a period of time or they are programed to only be active in a certain region of the world.

Malware can be found in a variety of other forms, such as covert crypto-mining, web search redirection, adware, spyware and even ransomware, and these are just a few. Today the largest threat of malware is ransomware because it's lucrative for criminals.

Human and Environmental

Technology-based attacks are common because the attacker can covertly attack a victim and do it from a distance. However, there are other attacks that use human interaction and the environment to carry out a physical attack on a victim. Many of these attacks succeed because people want to be helpful when they realize someone is genuinely in need of assistance. People are wired to help each other and this is why some of these attacks work. Therefore, we should be aware of the various ways an attacker can compromise our organization by using the organization's best resource, its helpful people.

Social Engineering

Social engineering is the art of extracting vital information from an organization's employees without raising suspicion. Social engineering works because employees often do not know what is sensitive and what is not. When an employee is put into a dilemma, like trying to help a fellow employee, they can disclose sensitive information. The tactics of a social engineering hacker is the "gift of gab."

Imagine that the organization's policy for password resets is knowing your supervisor's name. An attacker could easily collect this information with a crafted call. They might call someone else in the organization and explain they are starting a new position and are to meet with the target's supervisor, but they forgot the supervisor's name and are embarrassed to ask since they are new. The person on the other end of the call now has a dilemma; they can potentially save the person calling some embarrassment. If they sound reputable, would you challenge them or would you help them? This is the art of social engineering.

Phishing   Phishing is normally performed via email by an attacker in an effort to gain usernames, passwords, and other personally identifiable information (PII). An attacker will craft an email that looks like an organization's system. The email will generally contain a URL to a compromised web server where the user will be prompted for their information. Although this sounds like a technical-based attack, the potential success of phishing is dependent upon the wording and believability of the email.

Tailgating   *Tailgating* refers to being so close to someone when they enter a building that you are able to come in right behind them without needing to use a key, a card, or any other security device. Sometimes the person may even hold the door for them, thinking they are a fellow employee. Many social engineering intruders needing physical access to a site use this method of gaining entry. Educate users to beware of this and other social engineering ploys and prevent them from happening.

Piggybacking   *Piggybacking* is identical to tailgating in every way, except the person that originally swiped in never sees the attacker piggyback behind them. The attacker will watch how long the door stays open and time it so that they sneak in right behind someone. The attacker might even weight the timing in their favor with a mechanical device of some sort.

Shoulder Surfing   Another form of social engineering is known as shoulder surfing. It involves nothing more than watching someone when they enter their sensitive data. They can see you entering a password, typing in a credit card number, or entering any other pertinent information. A privacy filter can be used to block people from looking at your screen from an angle. However, privacy filters do not protect you as you are entering a password, since a shoulder surfer will watch your keystrokes. The best defense against this type of attack is simply to survey your environment before entering personal data. It is also proper etiquette to look away when someone is entering their password.

Exam Essentials

Know the common denial-of-service techniques of an attacker.   Denial-of-service (DoS) attacks target organizations in an attempt to disrupt the service or services a company receives or provides via the Internet. A distributed denial-of-service (DDoS) attack requires several different hosts to coordinate an attack on a victim. A reflective attack involves the attacker reflecting the attack off an unknowing pawn called a bot. An amplified attack is similar to a reflective attack, with the addition of amplifying the information being returned, such as querying all of the time servers that the NTP host uses.

Know the various networking attacks that are commonly used by attackers. An on-path attack, also known as a man-in-the-middle (MitM) attack, allows an attacker to impersonate both parties in an effort to eavesdrop and manipulate the conversation. VLAN hopping is an attack method where the attacker switches VLANs by double-tagging a packet or imitating a switch. A rogue DHCP server is used to launch an on-path attack by serving as a false default gateway. A rogue access point is an access point that has been installed on an organization's LAN by a malicious user or end user. An evil twin attack is a wireless phishing attack in which the attacker sets up a wireless access point to mimic the organization's wireless access points. Deauthentication is an attack that disassociates a client from an access point; it is used in conjunction with other attacks such as the evil twin attack. Malware is any software that has malicious intent for the user or system. Viruses are classified as malware, and so is spyware, ransomware, and many other types of malicious software.

Know the various spoofing techniques used by attackers. DNS poisoning is an attack against an organization's DNS server in an attempt to replace valid entries with compromised servers' IP addresses. ARP poisoning is an attack in which an attacker sends a forged ARP reply to a client to redirect traffic to the attacker's host. ARP spoofing is used in conjunction with other attacks by sending a GARP packet stating a host's MAC address has changed. MAC spoofing is the technique of assuming a valid MAC address to bypass security. IP spoofing is performed by an attacker to hide the originator of an attack or to bypass security.

Understand the various password attacks that an attacker could employ. Password attacks are attacks in which many different passwords are guessed against a known user account. The attack can be performed with a list of common passwords and combinations; this is called a dictionary attack. The attack can also employ brute-force tactics of guessing the password by trying every permutation of uppercase, lowercase, numbers, and symbols. The brute-force method can be used online or offline if the credential datastore is stolen.

Know the various non-networking attacks that are commonly used by attackers. Social engineering is an attack that is conducted by duping employees into willingly disclosing sensitive information. Insider threats are carried out by a disgruntled employee, an employee with criminal intent, or an employee participating in corporate espionage. Phishing is performed via email in an effort to gain a user's username, password, and other personally identifiable information (PII). Tailgating is performed by an attacker to gain physical access to a controlled building by tailgating behind a helpful person holding the door. Piggybacking is similar to tailgating, except that the person who swiped in never sees or acknowledges the attacker piggybacking on their credentials. Shoulder surfing is the act of an attacker watching over someone's shoulder to gain information or passwords.

4.3 Given a scenario, apply network hardening techniques.

There are many different hardening techniques we can employ to secure our networks from compromise. When evaluating the techniques to be employed in your network, you should keep a few things in mind: evaluate your risk, evaluate the overhead the hardening introduces, and prioritize your list of hardening techniques to be implemented. Many of these hardening techniques are "low-hanging-fruit" and should be employed, such as changing default passwords on network appliances and operating systems. Just make sure you have a system in place so complex passwords are not forgotten and they are kept safe. Other techniques might require much more effort, such as patch management and firmware changes. In the following sections, I will introduce you to a myriad of hardening techniques that can be used to secure your organization.

Best Practices

A best practice is a technique or methodology that has largely been adopted by the professional community. A number of security best practices are techniques that can keep the organization safe and secure. Many of the best practices will prevent some of the risk from attacks that I previously discussed. The benefits of other best practices might not be immediately apparent, but they will keep an organization safe in the long run.

Secure SNMP

The Simple Network Management Protocol (SNMP) is a network management protocol that allows an administrator to pull information or set information using the SNMP GET and SET commands. Unfortunately, SNMP can also be used by an attacker to get critical information or set information on the network device. So proper configuration of SNMP is critical to the security of an organization.

SNMP was released in three versions: version 1, 2c, and 3. Each version improved on the prior version of SNMP to expand capabilities, but only v3 addressed security. Both version 1 and 2c only used simple community names to get and set information. Both versions of SNMP allowed for configuration of read-only or read-write community names. However, if someone learned of the community name, then they could get or set information depending on the use of the community name. The common default for a read-only community name is public and the common default for a read-write community name is private. So, at bare minimum the default community names should be changed if they are configured out of the box.

SNMP version 3 was the first version to acknowledge and address security concerns. SNMP v3 allows for usernames and passwords to strengthen authentication. In addition to better authentication, encryption was added to SNMP v3, allowing for better security of information transmitted. Both of these security features can be used independently of each other.

SNMP version 3 is a little more involved than setting a community name to read or read-write. To compound the problem, there is not one universal command or instructions a vendor follows for configuring SNMP v2. However, there are four basic steps to configuration of any SNMP v3 server:

Step 1: Configure the username and accompanying password.

Step 2: Configure the view that defines the MIB tree that is visible.

Step 3: Configure the group that maps the user and view.

Step 4: Configure the access policy for request processing.

Router Advertisement (RA) Guard

The IPv6 Neighbor Discovery Protocol (NDP) uses Router Advertisement (RA) messages to advertise IPv6 prefixes (network ID), provision IPv6 addresses, and convey the default gateway for an IPv6 host. These autoconfiguration features make host configuration simple and largely replace the function of DHCP. However, because NDP operates like DHCP, these NDP features allow the IPv6 host to become susceptible to spoofing attacks and on-path attacks. An attacker can send a forged RA message and divert traffic through their own host in an attempt to capture sensitive traffic.

Every vendor has a different method configuring the RA Guard switching feature, but the concept is the same from vendor to vendor. The RA Guard switching feature will thwart attackers by restricting which port can send RA messages. When configuring RA Guard, you will specify ports containing the router and connecting other switches. These ports will then be allowed to originate RA messages. When RA Guard is applied to a host port, the host on that port will be restricted from originating RA messages.

Port Security

Port security is a method of restricting specific MAC addresses or a specific number of MAC addresses on a physical access mode switch port. Port security is supported on many different vendor switches, but I will focus on the Cisco switching platform for this section; all switches support similar port security functions. Port security is commonly implemented by the network administrator to mitigate the threat of end users plugging in hub, switches, or wireless access ports (WAPs) to extend switching of a single port.

As covered in Chapter 2, "Domain 2.0: Network Implementations," when a switch powers on, a blank table called the switching table is created in memory. When a frame is received on the switch port, the switch records the source MAC address of the frame with the switch port the frame is received on. Each MAC address receives an entry in the switching table for future forward filter decisions. We can restrict how many entries each switch port can record with the following commands on a Cisco switch. In the example, port security is configured, and a maximum of one MAC address will be allowed.

```
switch(config)# interface gigabitethernet 0/1
switch(config-if)# switchport port-security
switch(config-if)# switchport port-security maximum 1
```

By using `switchport port-security mac-address sticky`, we can configure the switch to record the first MAC address and limit the port to only that MAC address indefinitely or until an administrator clears it. By default with only the previous commands, the MAC address learned will be cleared after a period of inactivity.

```
switch(config)# interface gigabitethernet 0/1
switch(config-if)# switchport port-security
switch(config-if)# switchport port-security maximum 1
switch(config-if)# switchport port-security mac-address sticky
```

We can also constrain the switch port to a specific MAC address statically. In lieu of the `switchport port-security mac-address sticky` command, we can specify the MAC address to limit the switch port to. By configuring the following command, the MAC address will be locked to 0678.e2b3.0a02 for the switch port:

```
switch(config)# interface gigabitethernet 0/1
switch(config-if)# switchport port-security
switch(config-if)# switchport port-security maximum 1
switch(config-if)# switchport port-security mac-address 0678.e2b3.0a02
```

Dynamic ARP Inspection

Address Resolution Protocol (ARP) spoofing is an attack technique in which the attacker redirects the victim to the attacker's host. The attacker can then sniff packets for confidential information. The attack is performed by sending a crafted Gratuitous Address Resolution Protocol (GARP) packet to all of the hosts in the network. This GARP packet will explain that the MAC address has changed for a given IP address, such as the default gateway.

Dynamic ARP Inspection (DAI) is used in conjunction with the DHCP snooping switch feature. DHCP snooping records the IP address, MAC address, VLAN, and the accompanying interface in a memory resident table called the DHCP snooping binding table. The DAI process then inspects this table for each ARP request. If an ARP reply is sent back that conflicts with the DHCP snooping binding table, then the ARP reply will be dropped by the DAI process.

Control Plane Policing

Control plane policing (CoPP) is a router and switch feature that protects the route processor (RP) from denial-of-service (DoS) attacks. The feature is often found on Cisco IOS devices, but other vendors have a similar feature and it is often abbreviated as CPP.

The main purpose of a router or switch with a virtual router is to route traffic. This routing of data is considered the data plane of communications and it is optimized so the CPU is not burdened with usage. However, if you were to ping the router, the CPU will need to process the ICMP packet. The response is considered control plane traffic. CoPP helps to drop (police) large amounts of traffic directed to the control plane of the router while allowing data plane traffic to be unaffected.

Private VLANs

A virtual local area network (VLAN) is a virtual segmentation of traffic inside a switch or set of switches to create a broadcast domain, as covered in Chapter 2, "Domain 2.0: Network Implementations." A private VLAN is further micro-segmentation of the primary VLAN (standard VLAN) to create security between hosts.

The hardest part of understanding private VLANs is understanding the terminology that goes along with the topic, otherwise it really is a simple subject. The first term is *primary VLAN*, which is a standard VLAN that contains the underlying private VLANs known as the secondary VLANs. If we didn't configure a secondary VLAN, then the primary VLAN would just be an ordinary VLAN in our switched network. A secondary VLAN is the underlying VLAN that actually creates the micro-segmentation inside the primary VLAN. In Figure 4.25, there are two secondary (private) VLANs created: VLAN 10 and VLAN 11, contained in the primary VLAN of 100.

FIGURE 4.25   Private VLAN terminology

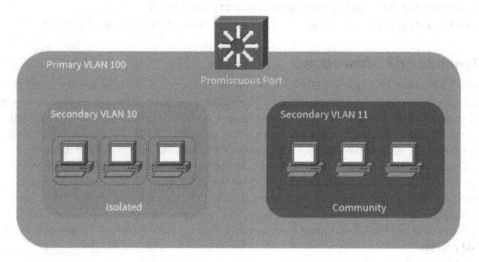

When you create a secondary VLAN, there are two types that can be created: isolated and community. When you create an isolated secondary VLAN, all of the hosts are isolated from communicating with each other. The hosts within the isolated secondary VLAN will all share a common network addressing scheme so they can communicate outside of their logical subnet. The hosts within the isolated secondary VLAN will only be able to communicate with the router port called the promiscuous port.

A community secondary VLAN allows the hosts within the community to communicate with each other and the router's promiscuous port. However, the communities are isolated from each other. You may ask, why create a secondary VLAN in the first place, since they act like a regular VLAN? The reasons will vary, but the best reason is micro-segmentation. For example, your organization might be a hosting company and the primary VLAN of 100 is the customer VLAN. This VLAN is where all customer traffic is located in your network. Then each community secondary VLAN will be allocated for each customer. This will allow the customer's hosted servers on your network to communicate with each other but no other customers. Of course, this is one example; compliance and regulatory requirements would also be reasons for using community secondary VLANs within an organization's network.

Disabling Unneeded Switchports

When we disable and/or firewall TCP/IP ports on a network operating system, we prevent remote exploits. However, physical ports are just as susceptible to exploit. If an attacker has physical access to the switching equipment, they can connect to the organization's network with only a patch cable and a laptop. The attacker can even connect a wireless access point and remotely connect to your network. Any unused switchports on network devices should be either disabled or protected with a protocol such as 802.1X.

Disabling Unnecessary Services

When services that are unneeded are enabled, it expands the surface area of attack. The surface area of attack is the range of possible exploitable services on an operating system or network device. If an operating system was a house, the entry points would be the doors, windows, and chimney. If we disable services, we remove entry points that can be exploited by attackers.

One of the major design changes to the Microsoft Server operating system was introduced with Windows Server 2008. Starting with Windows Server 2008, Microsoft disabled all services out of the box, and the firewall was turned on by default. This dramatically reduced the surface area of attack for the operating system compared to prior versions, such as Windows Server 2003 R2.

Linux and Unix have long since used this minimalistic approach to installation. When the Linux/Unix operating systems are installed, no services are installed by default. All functionality must be added via the repository tools such as apt for Ubuntu and Debian and yum for Red Hat–based systems.

Operating systems are not the only network systems that contain services; many network devices have services. Network devices are not immune to exploit; therefore, the surface area of attack should be reduced by disabling nonessential services. A typical example is a network printer; printers will often have several protocols enabled for printing, such as Server Message Block (SMB), AppleTalk, Internet Printing Protocol (IPP), and File Transfer Protocol (FTP). Unnecessary protocols and services should be disabled since each one could potentially have a vulnerability.

Changing Default Credentials

When installing a network device, the very first thing you must do is log into the device. There is often a standardized default username and password for each vendor or each vendor's product line. Most devices make you change the default password upon login to the device.

Changing the default password to a complex password is a good start to hardening the device. However, changing the username will also ensure that a brute-force attack cannot be performed against the default username. There are many different websites dedicated to listing the default credentials for network devices, so it doesn't take tremendous skill to obtain the default username and password of a device.

Avoiding Common Passwords

Avoiding common passwords is another simple measure to harden a device or operating system. There are several dictionaries that you can find on the Internet that will include common passwords. Some dictionaries are even collections of compromised passwords that have been made public.

When creating a password, it is always best practice to make the password at least 12 to 18 characters, based on the sensitivity of its use. You should always include symbols, numbers, and upper- and lowercase alpha characters. You should also resist substituting characters for symbols that looks like the character. This substitution is often called "leet speak" and it is in every downloadable dictionary on the Internet. An example of a "leet speak" passwords is *p@$$word*. Another common pitfall in creating passwords is the use of words; passwords should be random and complex. An example of a complex password is *GLtNjXu#W6*qkqGkS$*. You can find random password generators on the Internet, such as https://passwordsgenerator.net/.

DHCP Snooping

An attack called DHCP spoofing is carried out by an attacker running a rogue DHCP server on your LAN. The rogue DHCP server has particular options set such as DNS or the default gateway in an attempt to redirect valid traffic to an exploited website to further compromise the clients. A rogue DHCP server can also be introduced to create interruption of service.

DHCP snooping is a feature on Cisco switches as well as other vendor switches. It prevents a rogue DHCP server, also called a spurious DHCP server, from sending DHCP messages to clients. When DHCP snooping is configured on switches, all switchports are considered untrusted ports. Only a trusted port can forward DHCP messages; all untrusted ports are filtered for DHCP messages.

Change Native VLAN

When data is transmitted on a trunk link that is not tagged with a VLAN ID, the data will default to the native VLAN. The native VLAN is also the VLAN used for switch management. The default native VLAN is VLAN 1 on all unconfigured switches from the factory; it is also the default membership for all ports on an unconfigured switch.

This creates a potential security issue; if a new switch is plugged into the network and the default VLAN is not changed on the switch ports, a user will have direct access to the management network.

If the native VLAN is not changed from the default, an attacker can use the native VLAN to launch an attack using the Dynamic Trunking Protocol (DTP) or launch a VLAN hopping attack. A DTP attack is performed by plugging in a rogue Cisco switch to a port that is set to default trunking negotiation. An attacker can then use the untagged packets to move data on the native VLAN of the trunk. A VLAN hopping attack is when the attacker tags the frame twice. The intended VLAN is tagged, then the default VLAN of 1 is tagged. When the switch receives the frame on an access link, the first tag is stripped off and then the frame is switched onto the intended VLAN.

We can mitigate the risk of users being exposed to the management VLAN and VLAN hopping by changing the native VLAN to another VLAN number. It is common to change the native VLAN on trunks to VLAN 999 or another unused VLAN. Then do not use VLAN 1 for any device management and create another VLAN for that purpose.

Patching and Updates

When operating systems are installed, they are usually point-in-time snapshots of the current build of the operating system. From the time of the build to the time of install, several vulnerabilities can be published for the operating system. When an operating system is installed, you should patch it before placing it into service. Patches remediate the vulnerabilities found in the operating system and fixed by the vendor. Updates add new features not included with the current build. However, some vendors may include vulnerability patches in updates. Network devices also have patches and updates that should be installed prior to placing them into service.

After the initial installation of the device or operating system and the initial patches and updates are installed, you are not done! Vendors continually release patches and updates to improve security and functionality, usually every month and sometimes outside of the normal release cycle. When patches are released outside of the normal release cycle, they are called out-of-band patches and are often in response to a critical vulnerability.

Microsoft products are patched and updated through the Windows Update functionality of the operating system. However, when an administrator is required to patch and update an entire network, Windows Server Update Services (WSUS) can be implemented. A WSUS server enables the administrator to centrally manage patches and updates. The administrator can also report on which systems still need to be patched or updated.

Upgrading Firmware

When you purchase a network device, you don't know how long it's been sitting on the shelf of a warehouse. In that time, several exploits could have been created for vulnerabilities discovered. It is always recommended that a device's *firmware* be upgraded before the device is configured and put into service.

Most hardware vendors will allow downloading of current firmware. However, some vendors require the device to be covered under a maintenance contract before firmware can be downloaded. It is also best practice to read through a vendor's changelog to understand the changes that have been made from version to version of firmware.

Access Control Lists

Access control lists (ACLs) are used to control traffic and applications on a network. Every network vendor supports a type of ACL method; for the remainder of this section, I will focus on Cisco ACLs.

An ACL method consists of multiple access control entries (ACEs) that are condition actions. Each entry is used to specify the traffic to be controlled. Every vendor will have a different type of control logic. However, understanding the control logic of the ACL system allows you to apply it to any vendor and be able to effectively configure an ACL. The control logic is defined with these simple questions:

- How are the conditions of an ACL evaluated?

- What is the default action if a condition is not met?

- How is the ACL applied to traffic?

- How are conditions edited for an ACL?

Let's explore the control logic for a typical Cisco layer 3 switch or router. The conditions of the ACL are evaluated from top to bottom. If a specific condition is not met for the ACL, the default action is to deny the traffic. Only one ACL can be configured per interface, per protocol, and per direction. When you are editing a traditional standard or extended ACL, the entire ACL must be negated and reentered with the new entry. With traditional ACLs, there is no way to edit a specific ACL on the fly. When editing a named access list, each condition is given a line number that can be referenced so that the specific entry can be edited. For the remainder of this section I will use named access lists to illustrate an applied access list for controlling traffic.

In Figure 4.26 you can see a typical corporate network. There are two different types of workers: HR workers and generic workers. We want to protect the HR web server from access by generic workers.

We can protect the HR server by applying an ACL to outgoing traffic for Eth 0/0 and describing the source traffic and destination to be denied. We can also apply an ACL to the incoming interface of Eth 0/2 describing the destination traffic to be denied. For this example, we will build an access list for incoming traffic to Eth 0/2, blocking the destination of the HR server.

```
Router(config)# ip access-list extended block-hrserver
Router(config-ext-nacl)# deny ip any host 192.168.1.4
Router(config-ext-nacl)# permit ip any any
Router(config-ext-nacl)# exit
Router(config)# interface ethernet 0/2
Router(config-if)# ip access-group block-hrserver in
```

FIGURE 4.26   A typical corporate network

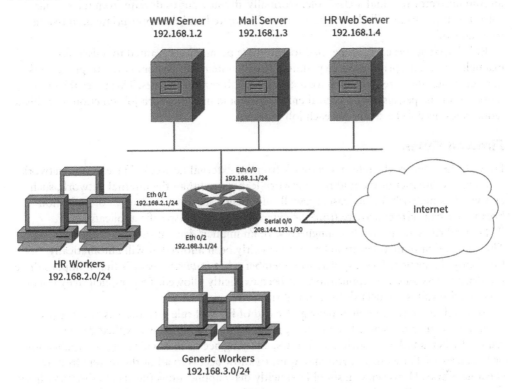

This ACL, called block-hrserver, contains two condition action statements. The first denies any source address to the specific destination address of 192.168.1.4. The second allows any source address to any destination address. We then enter the interface of Eth 0/2 and apply the ACL to the inbound direction of the router interface. The rule will protect the HR server from generic worker access while allowing the generic workers to access all other resources and the Internet.

It is important to note that the focus of this section is to understand how ACLs are used to protect resources. It is not important to understand how to build specific ACLs since commands will be different from vendor system to vendor system.

Role-Based Access

Implementing role-based access can harden security because it reduces the complexity of traditional security that requires adding layer upon layer of permission. When a user is placed into a role, such as Human Resource Worker, they will be given all of the necessary permissions to complete their job. Many different applications have adopted this model of permissions, including cloud-based applications. Most application come preconfigured with an Administrator role and a User role. Normally, if you want to deviate from the default roles, the application will allow a new role to be created and the appropriate permissions to be added.

Role-based access can also be used to automate permissions granted to a user. For example, your enterprise resource planning (ERP) system can be configured to place users in a role when they are hired or have a change of job responsibilities. This takes the guesswork out of the permissions a typical employee would have for each job function. For this to work, roles need to be set up for each job function.

Firewall Rules

Firewalls help secure the internal network from an external network. The external network could be the Internet or it could be a network less trusted than the internal network, such as a wireless network. In any case, firewall rules help harden security of an organization because we can restrict activity from the external network to specific applications.

Firewall rules are normally configured with an implicit deny at the end of the rules set. This means that if an application has not explicitly been allowed, it will automatically (implicitly) be denied. The easy way to remember what *implicit* means is that it implies there is a deny, unless a user or application has been explicitly allowed. This implicit deny operation of a firewall is the default for firewall rule sets.

Although there is an implicit deny at the end of firewall rule sets, there is also the need from time-to-time to explicitly deny an application or IP address. An explicit deny is required when another explicit rule follows, allowing access to a wide range of applications or IP addresses. For example, you may want to allow access to all of the servers from the client networks. However, you should explicitly deny applications the clients shouldn't have access to, such as Remote Desktop Protocol (RDP) or Secure Shell (SSH).

Wireless Security

The wired network is perceived to be easier to secure because we have the ability to see and control the connections. When you compare that perception to wireless connections, wireless security seems to be more elusive. That is somewhat of a true statement if we don't have fundamental knowledge of wireless security concepts. Once you understand the basic wireless security concepts, you will find that wireless security is not that mysterious. In the following sections, I will introduce wireless security concepts that will harden the wireless network and ultimately the organization's security.

MAC Filtering

MAC address filtering is used to secure wireless by providing only whitelisted MAC addresses access to the wireless system. It is extremely effective because an attacker will not have knowledge of which MAC addresses are whitelisted. There is an administrative burden in entering the MAC addresses to be whitelisted if your installation has a few clients or static clients that do not change frequently. MAC filtering is more commonly used with wireless LAN controllers (WLCs) to control specific clients by their MAC address. When it is used in conjunction with an 802.1X/NAC solution, the devices can be controlled globally from the authentication server. MAC filtering is a very effective method of security because of the difficulty an attacker has identifying the MAC addresses that are specifically allowed to be forwarded by the switch or WAP. Switches can be configured to filter specific MAC addresses as well. Port security is considered a form of MAC filtering for switching.

Antenna Placement

The placement of wireless antennas is extremely important for client coverage. However, improper placement of antennas can overextend the reach of the wireless signal outside of the network, which can allow attackers to possibly connect from other locations (the parking lot, the building next door, and so on).

There are several different factors to be taken into consideration for optimal antenna placement. The most important is client coverage, but others are antenna type, wireless band, wall density, and windows. These are just a few, since every environment will be different. The antenna type will dictate the radiation pattern of the wireless signal. The wireless band will dictate how far the signal could potentially travel. Construction material will vary and can't be judged by the human eye, although windows will generally allow signal propagation. Because of these various factors, it is always best to conduct a wireless survey to choose the best antenna placement.

Power Levels

Power levels will go hand in hand with antenna placement from a security viewpoint. Therefore, power levels should be adjusted so they don't travel past the interior of the organization's building. If they do, then someone sitting in the parking lot or an adjoining building could attempt to infiltrate the wireless network. On the chance that the signal is actually traveling too far, some access points include power level controls that allow you to reduce the amount of output provided.

The wireless protocol of 802.11h can help control power of the access point needed by each individual client. The 802.11h protocol uses Transmit Power Control (TPC) as well as Dynamic Frequency Selection (DFS) to adjust for optimal power and frequency of the client. Although this protocol should be on by default, a site survey of the wireless signal outside of your organization should be performed. These locations should include parking lots, street access, and any publicly accessible areas. Then manual adjustments to the access points' transmit power can ensure that the signal does not travel past the desired point.

Wireless Client Isolation

The wireless client isolation feature allows for better hardening of host-to-host security. Normally when you join a wireless network, such as your home, you can connect to other wireless devices joined to the same wireless network. This functionality is fine in your home, but in an organization's network it can allow an attacker to pivot their attack. If the attacker can connect to neighboring devices, they can compromise those devices or use them as a new jumping-off point.

You may think turning this feature on is a drop-dead simple decision, that it should definitely be on! However, you should consider devices like Google Chromecast, Apple iPlay, and other presentation devices. Organizations have adopted these wireless devices to allow employees to present on projectors and large TVs in conference rooms. Wireless printers may also be used in your organization. Before turning this feature on, you will need to formulate a plan for dealing with these devices.

Guest Network Isolation

Most guests in your network never need to connect to the organization's servers and internal systems. When guests connect to your wireless network, it is usually just to get connectivity to the Internet. Therefore, a guest service set identifier (SSID) should be created that isolates guest traffic from production traffic. These guest network SSIDs are usually created by default on consumer wireless devices. On enterprise wireless LAN controllers, the guest network typically needs to be created.

Some considerations for the guest network are what is open to guests, how long they have access, how much bandwidth, SSID name, and the list goes on depending on your organization. Guest networks usually don't give totally unrestricted Internet access; certain sensitive ports like TCP 25 SMTP are normally blocked. The length of time they have access is another concern. Generally a guest is just that, a guest. So, 4 hours, 8 hours, or 24 hours of access seem responsible. This needs to be thought through as too short a time will create administrative overhead and too long a window of access allows for abuse of service.

Preshared Keys (PSKs)

A preshared key (PSK) is widely used with the wireless protocols WPA- and WPA2-Personal mode for home wireless applications. A preshared key is a symmetrical encryption system where the key that encrypts the data also decrypts the data. PSKs can also be used with other authentication protocols such as EAP-TLS, but PSKs are rarely used for EAP-TLS deployments outside of testing.

EAP

Extensible Authentication Protocol (EAP) is an IETF standard that allows supplicants and authenticators to use various methods of encryption for authentication purposes over 802.1X, as shown in Figure 4.27. These authentication methods are defined by modules that both the supplicant and the authenticator must have in common. These shared modules can be replaced with other modules that expand authentication method functionality, which is why we consider EAP to be extensible. There are many different EAP methods that can be used. I will discuss only the three common EAP methods as per the objectives for this exam.

FIGURE 4.27   Wireless authentication for 802.1X/EAP

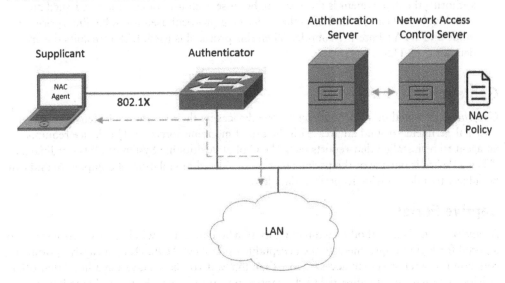

PEAP   Protected Extensible Authentication Protocol (PEAP) was jointly developed by Cisco, Microsoft, and RSA Security. PEAP is used in conjunction with 802.1X authentication systems and provides Transport Layer Security (TLS). TLS protects EAP messages by providing an encrypted tunnel as well as authentication between the host and the authenticating server before credentials are passed. The authenticator will provide the supplicant with a certificate from the authentication server signed by a certificate authority. It is important to note that the supplicant must trust the issuing certificate authority so that the authentication server's certificate is valid.

EAP-FAST   Extensible Authentication Protocol – Flexible Authentication via Secure Tunneling (EAP-FAST) is a Cisco proposed standard to replace the older Cisco proprietary protocol of Lightweight Extensible Authentication Protocol (LEAP). EAP-FAST operates in three phases; the first phase, called Phase 0, is when in-band provision occurs to create a shared secret that will be used for Phase 1 to establish a secure tunnel. Once the second phase, called Phase 1, establishes the secure tunnel, then the third phase, called Phase 2, allows authentication to occur between the supplicant and authentication server. Because of its use of shared keys, it is faster than PKI for tunnel creation.

EAP-TLS   Extensible Authentication Protocol – Transport Layer Security (EAP-TLS) is an open standard defined by the IETF. Because it is an open standard, many vendors and operating systems support EAP-TLS. EAP-TLS can be deployed with a preshared key (PSK), but it is more common for EAP-TLS to be deployed in conjunction with a certificate authority. When EAP-TLS is deployed in conjunction with a certificate authority, the deployment is more secure because each user or computer is issued an individual certificate. EAP-TLS is the underlying protocol used for WPA-Enterprise mode and WPA2-Enterprise mode. When this protocol is used, EAP transmits the credentials over TLS.

Geofencing

Geofencing is a method of controlling mobile devices by their location. Geofencing creates a virtual perimeter around an area with the use of mapping software. The device requires an agent to be installed that reports back the Global Positioning System (GPS) coordinates. When a device is outside of the perimeter, it is considered in violation of compliance and can be subject to a device wipe to prevent data loss.

Captive Portal

A *captive portal* is a method of redirecting users who connect to wireless or wired systems to a portal for login or agreement to the acceptable use policy (AUP). Using a captive portal is common for wireless system access. More than likely, if you have stayed in a hotel that offers wireless, you have been redirected to the captive portal to accept the terms. Some hotels require you to purchase the wireless service; this type of service would also redirect you to the portal for login or payment. Captive portals are not exclusively used for hotels; they are also used for corporate access to an organization's wireless system.

A captive portal redirects the user to the captive portal address on the first DNS request the web browser or application initiates. DNS name resolution for all addresses are pointed to the captive portal address, where the user is presented with the login screen. Captive portal systems commonly use a Remote Authentication Dial-In User Service (RADIUS) or Lightweight Directory Access Protocol (LDAP) server when validating credentials for a user.

When configuring the captive portal, we have several different implementations we can use. The two most common implementations are inline and out-of-band. Figure 4.28 details an inline implementation of the captive portal. In order for the client to communicate with the LAN, all traffic must pass through the captive portal. This design is common for small implementations.

FIGURE 4.28   An inline captive portal

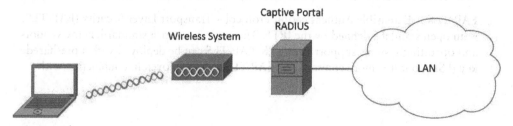

Figure 4.29 shows an out-of-band implementation. When the user first connects to the wireless system, they are placed into a registration VLAN where the captive portal is the gateway, capturing the user for login. Once the user is authenticated, the RADIUS server directs the switch to change the VLAN for the user. The captive portal is now out-of-band of the user's traffic, and the user is solely using the switching network. These implementations commonly use 802.1X for the wireless LAN controller (WLC).

FIGURE 4.29   An out-of-band captive portal

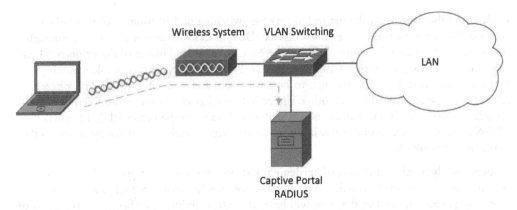

Wireless System   VLAN Switching

LAN

Captive Portal
RADIUS

IOT Considerations

The Internet of Things (IoT) is an exploding industry. You can now control everything from your lights to your thermostat with a mobile device or computer. The downside to connecting things to the Internet is that they must be patched so they are not exploitable. Hardware vendors often wire-in off-the-shelf components into the hardware, and these off-the-shelf components never get frequent updates. So, this is a major security consideration for an organization. Ease of use vs. security is the balance beam that you walk when owning IoT devices.

In recent years, attackers have harvested IoT devices for DDoS attacks. The Mirai botnet is one such popular botnet that can crush an organization's bandwidth. This can happen from the aspect of IoT devices in your network being used in a DDoS or being DDoS'ed by the botnet. To mitigate inadvertently being used in a DDoS, you can place the IoT devices on an isolated network and police their outbound bandwidth.

Unfortunately, there is not much you can do with IoT devices to prevent being attacked. If an attacker wants to DDoS your organization with IoT devices, firewalls, ISP controls, and third-party services like Cloudflare can help mitigate these attacks. This is not really an IoT consideration because any botnet can attack you and the mitigations are the same as if you are attacked by an IoT botnet.

Exam Essentials

Understand the various hardening techniques for protocols.   Default community names should be changed for SNMP, and SNMPv3 should be used if possible. Router Advertisement (RA) Guard suppresses RA messages from interfaces that contain hosts. Dynamic ARP inspection prevents ARP spoofing attacks and it is implemented with DHCP snooping. DHCP snooping stops rogue DHCP servers by filtering untrusted ports on the switch. Unneeded services should be disabled to lower the risk of attack if a service is not properly configured or vulnerable.

Understand the various hardening techniques for switching and routing.   Control plane policing (CoPP) helps prevent denial-of-service (DoS) attacks by prioritizing traffic through the router vs. traffic to the router. Private VLANs can be created inside of the primary VLAN to create a micro-segmentation within the VLAN. Private VLANs can be implemented two ways: an isolated VLAN, for host-to-host isolation, and a community VLAN, where hosts can communicate with each other. Unneeded switchports should be disabled because an attacker can just plug in and access the network. Changing the native VLAN thwarts VLAN hopping attacks and the possibility of an end user mistakenly obtaining access to the management network.

Understand the various methods of hardening network systems.   Changing default credentials for network systems will thwart brute-force attacks against default usernames. Upgrading firmware ensures that you will have any vulnerabilities patched up to the point of the firmware upgrade. Continual patching and updating of operating systems and network devices ensures that you are protected for any new vulnerabilities as well as newer features. Disabling unused services on a network system reduces the area of attack by reducing the number of services that are potentially vulnerable. Disabling unused services ensures that an attacker cannot take advantage of a vulnerability. Access control lists (ACLs) consist of conditions and actions to control traffic for applications. Role-based access can be used to remove the complication of various permissions for each user by placing users into a role that is inclusive of all the permissions necessary for the job. Internet of Things (IoT) devices should be isolated from the rest of the network. Outbound access should be policed so the IoT devices are not used in a botnet to DDoS someone else.

Understand the various access controls that can be used within a network.   Port security allows us to restrict the number of devices that can be connected to a switchport. MAC filtering is the method of restricting a specific MAC address or list of MAC addresses. Captive portals redirect an initial request to a portal where the user must log in or accept an agreement; the user is then moved into another VLAN where traffic is switched as normal. Firewall rules explicitly deny applications and users (IP address) when there is an inclusive rule that allows a larger group of applications or IP addresses. Implicit deny rules are normally found at the end of a firewall rule set if no other condition matches to allow the traffic it is implicitly denied.

Know the various methods to protect information transmitted over wireless networks.   Antenna placement is critical for wireless client coverage, but it can also allow attackers to attack the wireless network from public areas. Power levels should also be monitored and adjusted so that the wireless signal does not extend to public areas, where attackers can attack the wireless network. Wireless client isolation restricts clients from connecting to each other when joining the same SSID. Guest network isolation ensures that guests do not connect to the internal wireless network.

Know the various methods of authentication for wireless networks.   Extensible Authentication Protocol (EAP) is an extensible standard of authenticating users and computers. Protected Extensible Authentication Protocol (PEAP) was developed by Cisco, Microsoft, and RSA Security and provides Transport Layer Security (TLS) via an encrypted tunnel. Extensible Authentication Protocol – Flexible Authentication via Secure Tunneling (EAP-FAST) is a Cisco-proposed replacement to Lightweight Extensible Authentication Protocol (LEAP). Extensible Authentication Protocol – Transport Layer Security (EAP-TLS) is used with WPA2-Enterprise mode to transmit credentials securely. Geofencing is used in conjunction with mapping software to create a virtual fence to prevent data loss outside of the geofence.

4.4 Compare and contrast remote access methods and security implications.

Remote access is implemented to provide access to network systems for end users and administrative personnel at remote locations. Remote access of the network systems can be provided over the public Internet, a local area network, or a wide area network since it extends the local access of a system. You can be in another room or another country and it is considered remote access as long you are not at the local mouse and keyboard. We use remote access for a multitude of purposes, such as remote control, remote files access, remote assistance, database access, performance monitoring, and diagnostics.

VPN

A virtual private network (VPN) extends your company's internal network across the Internet or other unsecured public networks. This remote access technology allows clients and branch networks to be connected securely and privately with the company's network. There are several different ways a VPN can be used in our network architecture, and I will cover them in the following sections. A VPN achieves this private connection across a public network by creating a secure tunnel from end to end through the process of encryption and encapsulation. The encryption protocols used will vary, and I will cover them as well. Since a tunnel is created from end to end, your local host becomes part of the company's internal network along with an IP address that matches the company's internal network. We don't have to be bound to only TCP/IP across a VPN since this technology can encapsulate any protocol and carry it through the tunnel.

Site-to-Site VPN

Over the past 10 to 15 years, using high-bandwidth connections to the Internet has become cheaper than purchasing dedicated leased lines. So companies have opted to install Internet connections at branch offices for Internet usage. These lines can serve a dual purpose: connecting users to the Internet and connecting branch offices together to the main office. However, the Internet is a public network and unsecured, but site-to-site VPN connections can fix that. Companies with multiple locations have reaped the benefits of creating VPN tunnels from site to site over the Internet by ditching their leased lines, installing VPN concentrators at each location, and creating VPN tunnels. Site-to-site VPN is also much more scalable than leased lines because locations only need a connection to the Internet and a *VPN concentrator* to be tied together.

Figure 4.30 details two locations tied together with a VPN tunnel. The magic happens all in the VPN concentrator. Since VPN concentrators also have a routing function, when a tunnel is established, a route entry is created in the VPN concentrator for the remote network. When traffic is destined for the branch office with a destination network of 10.2.0.0/16, the router encrypts and encapsulates the information as data and sends it to the other side of the tunnel over the Internet. This is similar to a host-to-site VPN, the difference being the routing is performed in the VPN concentrator. When the packet is received on the other side of the tunnel, the VPN concentrator will decapsulate the data, decrypt the packet, and send the packet to its destination inside the branch network. It is common to find that the appliance performing VPN is also the firewall and router. Firewalls today are sold with VPN software built in and licensed accordingly.

FIGURE 4.30   A typical site-to-site VPN

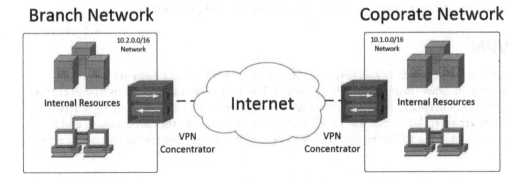

Client-to-Site VPN

Client-to-site VPN connectivity is a remote access strategy for mobile access. It can be used for *telecommuters*, salespeople, partners, and administrative access to the internal network resources. The key concept is that VPN access is granted on an individual or group basis for the mobile users. Using the example in Figure 4.31, you can allow salespeople to connect to the corporate network so they can update sales figures or process orders. This can all be done securely over the Internet while the users are mobile and have access to a network connection.

FIGURE 4.31   A typical host-to-site VPN

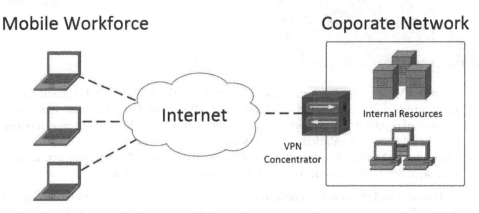

When a client computer establishes a VPN connection, it becomes part of the internal corporate network. This happens by assignment of an IP address from the internal corporate network. In Figure 4.32, you can see a mobile device such as a laptop with a VPN client installed in the operating system. When the connection is established with the VPN concentrator over the Internet, a pseudo network adapter is created by the VPN client. In this example, the pseudo network adapter is assigned an internal IP address of 10.2.2.8/16 from the VPN concentrator. The laptop also has its own IP address of 192.168.1.3/24, which it uses to access the Internet. A routing table entry is created in the operating system for the 10.2.0.0/16 network and through the pseudo network adapter. When traffic is generated for the corporate network, it is sent to the pseudo adapter where it is encrypted and then sent to the physical NIC and sent through the Internet to the VPN concentrator as data. When it arrives at the VPN concentrator, the IP header is stripped from the packet, the data is decrypted, and it is sent to its internal corporate network resource.

FIGURE 4.32   Client-to-site VPN connection

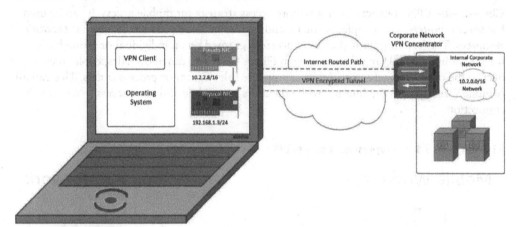

Clientless VPN   There are many different VPN solutions on the market. Each one of them traditionally requires the installation of a VPN client. However, there is a growing number of products that do not require the installation of a client; these products are called clientless VPN solutions. The VPN client is the web browser on the mobile device requiring connectivity back to the corporate network. The VPN appliance acts as a reverse proxy to the various resources internal to the organization.

Split tunnel vs. full tunnel   Traffic traveling across the VPN tunnel can be configured as two distinct ways: the client can be configured as a split tunnel or a full tunnel. A split tunnel allows for traffic destined to the corporate network to be directed over the tunnel. All other traffic is directed to the host's Internet configuration. A full tunnel requires all traffic to be tunneled back to the corporate network regardless if it is internal or external traffic. This configuration is common when an organization wants to filter content for the end users.

Remote Desktop Connection

The Remote Desktop Protocol (RDP) is used exclusively with Microsoft operating systems to provide a remote desktop connection. RDP is used as a remote access protocol and communicates over TCP 3389 to deliver the remote screen and connect the local mouse and keyboard to the RDP session. The protocol can also deliver local drives to the client via the RDP session. RDP uses TLS encryption by default.

Microsoft allows one remote user connection or a local connection on desktop operating systems via RDP, but not both. On server operating systems, Microsoft allows two administrative connections that can be a combination of local or remote access, but not to exceed two connections.

Microsoft also uses RDP to deliver user desktops via terminal services. When RDP is used in this fashion, a centralized gateway brokers the connections to each RDP client desktop session. Terminal services require terminal services licensing for either each user connecting or each desktop served. RDP can also be used to deliver applications to the end users via Microsoft *RemoteApp* on terminal services. When RemoteApp is used, the server still requires a terminal services license. However, just the application is delivered to the user host rather than the entire desktop.

Remote Desktop Gateway

The Remote Desktop Gateway is a Microsoft server role that allows centralized access to remote desktops, such as remote desktop workstations or remote desktop servers. The gateway usually sits between the users and the remote desktops and controls the access to the remote desktops. Although the term *remote desktop gateway* is a Microsoft role, every vendor for remote desktop services has a similar server or virtual appliance. The Remote Desktop Gateway is mainly responsible for the brokering of clients to their respective remote desktops.

The Remote Desktop Gateway is typically installed on the edge of the network, where it will border the external network it serves, such as the Internet. Because the gateway is installed on the edge of the network, it is also responsible for the security of the remote desktop sessions and users. The gateway provides TLS encryption via certificates, authentication for clients via Active Directory, and the authorization to the internal resources.

During the setup of the Remote Desktop Gateway, two policies must be configured for controlling authorization. The Connection Authorization Policy (CAP) specifies which group of users can access the Remote Desktop Gateway. The Resource Authorization Policy (RAP) then specifies which remote desktop or servers are allowed for each group of users. Between the CAP and RAP authentication policies, the Remote Desktop Gateway can be configured with granular security for both users and the remote hosts.

SSH

Secure Shell (SSH) is commonly used for remote access via a text console for Linux and Unix operating systems using TCP port 22. The SSH protocol encrypts all communications between the SSH client and SSH server, which is also called the SSH daemon. SSH uses a public-private keypair also called asymmetrical encryption to provide authentication between the SSH client and server. SSH can also use a keypair to authenticate users connecting to the SSH server for the session, or a simple username and password can be provided. It is important to understand that both the user and their host computer are authenticated when the user attempts to connect to the server. During the initial connection between the user's host computer and the SSH server, the encryption protocol is negotiated for the user's login.

Beyond logging into a Linux or Unix server for remote access, SSH can provide remote access for applications. Through the use of SSH port forwarding, the application can be directed across the SSH connection to the far end. This allows applications to tunnel through the SSH session. It also encrypts application traffic from the client to the server because it is carried over the SSH encrypted tunnel. SSH can behave similarly to a VPN connection, but it is more complex to set up than a VPN client.

Virtual Network Computing (VNC)

Virtual Network Computing (VNC) is a remote control tool for the sharing of desktops. The VNC client normally operates on TCP port 5900. VNC is similar to Microsoft RDP, with the exception that VNC is an open-source protocol and allows only one console session on a Microsoft operating system. It supports encryption via plug-ins but is not encrypted by default.

VNC operates in a client and server model. The server install for the host enables remote control of the host, and the client install allows for means to connect to the VNC server. It is normally configured with a simple shared password, but it can also be configured with Windows groups. Several clients can be used such as RealVNC, TightVNC, and many others, but all of the clients perform in a similar way.

Virtual Desktop

A virtual desktop is an end-user operating system that is installed inside of a virtualization platform. The collective system that maintains the virtual desktop is called the virtual desktop infrastructure (VDI), and it has become quite popular over the past decade. Organizations have embraced VDI as a remote access strategy for their employees, mainly because the organization can control the environment and where the organization's data is stored. This strategy can minimize an organization's data loss because the data never leaves the organization's data center.

There are many different VDI implementations on the market today, such as Citrix Virtual Desktop, VMware Horizon View, and Microsoft Windows Virtual Desktop, just to name a few. These products are normally installed and managed locally on the organization's private cloud. This requires an upfront capital cost similar to the cost of a physical PC, along with the same expected life cycle of five to seven years. The benefit is that all the management of the virtual desktops is concentrated in the data center. So, imaging is simplified, along with software rollouts, patching, and many other tasks such as these.

There is even a growing number of Desktop as a Service (DaaS) providers, such as VMware, Microsoft Azure, and HPE, just to name a few. These solutions are an ongoing cost to the organization, but the benefit is that the organization can scale without having to procure, install, and configure new servers. This solution also allows for downsizing when an organization needs to shrink. The downside is it's an operating cost, similar to the cost of electricity and other utilities.

Authentication and Authorization Considerations

Every plan has an unplanned consequence, in which we must consider the undesired outcomes. When an organization roles out remote access, the organization must consider authentication and authorization to minimize unscrupulous activities, data loss, and accidental destruction of data. Remote access gives the employees access remotely to the organization's data, which also relinquishes a bit of the organization's control in the process.

Implementing strong authentication of users is a key aspect for minimizing data loss or compromise by an attacker. By implementing two-factor authentication (2FA), also known as multifactor authentication (MFA), you can be assured that the user logged into the remote access technology is your trusted employee. Although, they are trusted, you should also audit activity and log when users log on and log off remote access technologies.

When authentication is coupled with machine learning, such as the Azure Active Directory Risky Sign-in feature, you can identify users that are performing risky activity. These activities might be impossible travel, such as login in two different locations within 5 minutes, like different continents. There also may be scripted logins or many other activities that the Azure AD Risky Sign-in feature can identify. When it is suspected that a user is compromised, the action can be to lock the user out or simply require the second factor of authentication again.

Authorization is another major consideration for remote access, because it allows remote access to the internals of an organization's network. Therefore, the principle of least privilege should be used. If the user does not require remote access to perform their job, then they should not be authorized to use it.

Just saying no to remote access doesn't always work, and therefore the consideration should be a blended strategy. When you allow remote access to internal resources, you should only allow the employee to access the resources their role needs. This is a great use of role-based access controls and management. Using role-based access controls ensures that you won't give more privileges than what is required.

In-Band vs. Out-of-Band Management

All enterprise networking devices have data, control, and management planes. The data and control planes service the data flowing through the device. The management plane allows for diagnostic and configuration of the device. Network devices are configured so that the *management plane* is accessible over the *data plane* that the device serves. For example, a router is accessible over the network for which it provides routing. This type of management is considered in-band management.

In-band management of the network device is great when the network device is running and functioning. However, when we have an equipment failure, we need to access the device to check configuration and diagnose the problem. Using the previous example, if an interface on the router goes down, you will lose the ability to manage the device since the management plane is served over the failed data plane. This is where out-of-band management is valuable. Out-of-band management is when the management plane is served out-of-band of the data plane. This allows us to access the equipment independently of the network connections the device is serving. Out-of-band management is also used for security purposes. This prevents a network intruder from accessing key management infrastructure by limiting connectivity to the management infrastructure with a physical connection. Out-of-band management can also be performed via a modem set up for the specific purpose of management.

Modem

Modems are legacy devices but still very valuable to the network administrator. When a WAN goes down, as shown in Figure 4.33, a modem gives console access to the device over the public switched telephone network (PSTN). This connection will have a top speed of 56 Kbps (54 Kbps in North America) on plain old telephone service (POTS) lines. If you are using VoIP lines, the usable speed is far less, but console access is normally 9600 bits per second, so speed is usually not a problem.

FIGURE 4.33   A modem for out-of-band management

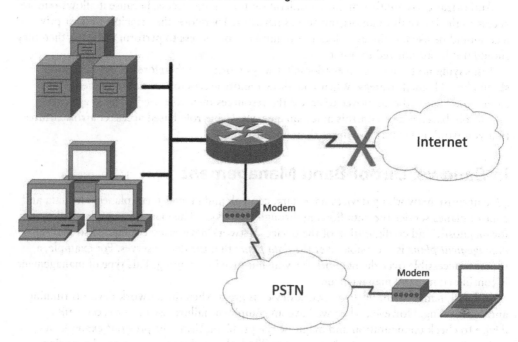

Console Router

The console port, as seen in Figure 4.34, is used to connect either a modem or a serial port for the technician's laptop. The console connection is often an RJ-45 connector terminated to a rollover cable, the other end is either a DB-9 (host) or DB-25 (modem) connector.

FIGURE 4.34   A router console connection

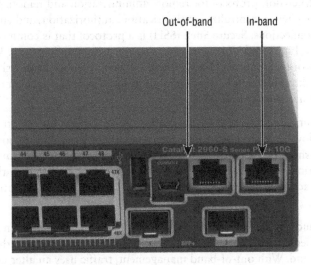

Console connections on routers are valuable to the network administrator because they allow console command-line interface (CLI) access. The console connection is used by the technician for either out-of-band configuration and diagnostics or initial setup. The switch in Figure 4.34 is equipped with both an RJ-45 console connection and a mini-USB connection. When the mini-USB connection is plugged into a laptop or computer, the operating system detects as a USB serial COM port.

It is common to ship a router with a modem to a remote site. A network administrator can then dial into the remote site router to set up the other end of a WAN connection. This allows the network administrator to be in two places at once!

Exam Essentials

Know the various types of VPN connectivity methods.   Site-to-site VPNs allow a remote office to connect to the main office over an Internet connection while protecting the data transmitted over the public Internet. Client-to-site VPNs allow for mobile workers to connect to a main site over the Internet for access to internal resources while protecting data transmitted over the public Internet. Clientless VPN is delivered via the web browser and the VPN acts as a reverse proxy to the application in the internal network. Split tunnel VPN allows communications directed to the private network to be delivered over the tunnel, and Internet activity uses the Internet connection. Full tunnel VPN requires all communication go through the VPN tunnel.

Know the various remote access protocols used for remote access.   Remote Desktop Protocol (RDP) is a Microsoft protocol for remote administration and remote desktop support. A remote desktop gateway centralizes authentication, authorization, and encryption for remote desktop connections. Secure Shell (SSH) is a protocol that is commonly used for test console sessions to Linux and Unix operating systems using public-private keypair encryption. Virtual Network Computing (VNC) is a remote-control tool for the sharing of a desktops. A virtual desktop is a virtualized workstation running in the data center where an employee will connect to the desktop.

Understand the authentication and authorization considerations for remote access. Remote access allows employees to access the organization's network remotely, therefore the network should be secured with two-factor authentication, also known as multi-factor authentication. Authorization for employees should be kept to only the employees that need remote access. Role-based access controls can help simplify authorization of employees access.

Understand in-band and out-of-band management concepts.   When the management traffic of a device is carried over the same network media that the device serves, the management is considered in-band. With out-of-band management, traffic uses an alternate media that is not served for data purposes by the network device. Modems are a typical out-of-band management device used for troubleshooting when a network link fails and in-band management cannot be used.

4.5 Explain the importance of physical security.

Physical security is often taken for granted by network administrators. However, physical security is directly related to network security. As an example, if you went to great lengths to secure your switches and routers with public and private keypairs but did not secure the network closets where they operate, a malicious actor could easily gain access to the switch or router by performing a password reset, which in most cases requires physical access to the device.

It is the network administrator's job to secure physical access for the network equipment. We can perform this duty by either detecting unauthorized access or preventing unauthorized access. Depending on how sensitive the information or system is, we sometimes need to both prevent and detect unauthorized access.

Detection Methods

Detection of physical access lets you know what happened, when it happened, and who did it. The last detail, *who*, is often the hardest piece of information to obtain when using detection methods. Detection methods help network administrators resolve and improve physical security problems. Detection can sometimes lead to intervention from the organization's security officers or the local authorities.

Camera

Video surveillance is the backbone of physical security. It is the only detection method that allows an investigator to identify what happened, when it happened, and, most important, who made it happen. Two types of cameras can be deployed: fixed and *pan-tilt-zoom (PTZ)*. Fixed cameras are the best choice when recording for surveillance activities. Pan-tilt-zoom (PTZ) cameras allow for 360-degree operations and zooming in on an area. PTZs are most commonly used for intervention, such as covering an area outside during an accident or medical emergency. PTZ cameras are usually deployed for the wrong reasons, mainly because they are cool! PTZs are often put into patrol mode to cover a larger area than a fixed camera can. However, when an incident occurs, they are never pointed in the area you need them! It is always best to use a fixed camera or multiple fixed cameras, unless you need a PTZ for a really good reason. They are usually more expensive and require more maintenance than fixed cameras.

Video surveillance can be deployed using two common media types, coaxial cable and Ethernet. Coaxial cable is used typically in areas where preexisting coaxial lines are in place or distances are too far for typical Ethernet. These systems are called *closed-circuit television (CCTV)*. Coaxial camera systems generally use appliance-like devices for recording of video. These CCTV recorders generally have a finite number of ports for cameras and a finite amount of storage in the form of direct attached storage (DAS).

Ethernet (otherwise known as IP) surveillance is becoming the standard for new installations. Anywhere an Ethernet connection can be installed, a camera can be mounted. Power over Ethernet (POE) allows power to be supplied to the camera, so the additional power supplies used with coaxial cameras are not needed. Ethernet also provides the flexibility of virtual local area networks (VLANs) for added security so that the camera network is isolated from operational traffic. IP surveillance uses *network video recorder (NVR)* software to record cameras. Because NVRs are server applications, we can use traditional storage such as network area storage (NAS) or storage area network (SAN) storage. This allows us to treat the video recordings like traditional data.

Coaxial camera networks can be converted to IP surveillance networks with the use of a device called a media converter. These devices look similar to a CCTV recorder. They have a limited number of ports for the coaxial cameras and are generally smaller than the CCTV recorder. This is because they do not have any DAS. The sole purpose of the media converter is to convert the coaxial camera to an Ethernet feed to the NVR.

The use of IP video surveillance allows for a number of higher-end features such as camera-based motion detection, *license plate recognition (LPR)*, and motion fencing.

Advanced NVR software allows cameras to send video only when motion is detected at the camera; this saves on storage for periods of nonactivity. LPR is a method of detecting and capturing license plates in which the software converts the plate to a searchable attribute for the event. With motion fencing, an electronic fence can be drawn on the image so that any activity within this region will trigger an alert. Among the many other features are facial recognition and object recognition.

Motion Detection

There are several different motion detection types that we can use to detect unauthorized access. *Passive infrared (PIR)* is the most common motion detection used today, mainly because of price. PIR sensors operate by monitoring the measurement of infrared radiation from several zones. In Figure 4.35, you can see the reflective panel that divides the infrared zones. A PIR sensor will always have this grid pattern on the sensor's face.

FIGURE 4.35   A typical PIR sensor

Microwave detectors also look like PIR sensors, but they do not have a reflective panel. Microwave detectors are common in areas where wide coverage is needed. Microwave detectors operate by sending pulses of microwaves out and measuring the microwaves received. These detectors are more expensive than PIR sensors and are susceptible to external interference, but they have a wider area of coverage.

Vibration sensors are another type of sensor used for motion detection. Although you may have seen them in the latest over-the-top heist movie, vibration sensors are really used in physical security systems. They are most often implemented as seismic sensors. They help protect from natural disasters and accidental drilling, or the occasional over-the-top heist.

Asset Tracking Tags

Asset tracking tags are used to track, secure, locate, and identify assets for your organization. Asset tracking is widely used in hospitals because tracking of medical equipment can be critical. In some hospitals, even doctor locations are tracked. Hospital settings are not the only use case for asset tracking; many companies have implemented asset tracking tags for increased productivity. Anyone who has taken on a weekend project and spent more time looking for the tools than performing the task can relate to the problem companies face on a daily basis.

Two main types of asset tracking tags exist: passive and active RFID. Passive asset tags require a high-powered transponder to activate the tag via radio frequency (RF) emitted signals. The passive asset tag will respond to the receiver with the unique ID of the tag that is tied to the asset. Passive asset tags are used to prevent shrinkage of inventory, but they are not practical for tracking and locating assets, mainly because of the limited number of receivers that can be deployed.

Active tracking tags contain a battery-powered transmitter. Active tracking tags come in a variety of deployments, such as traditional 802.11 wireless, Bluetooth, and RFID. Traditional 802.11 asset tracking tags require a powered wireless client with which a wireless LAN (WLAN) controller can track and triangulate the asset. Bluetooth operates on a frequency similar to 802.11, and many WLAN controllers can track and triangulate Bluetooth active tracking tags as well. Bluetooth is an expensive option for wireless asset tracking, and it requires very low power for operations. Triangulation for both traditional wireless and Bluetooth is normally a premium feature on WLAN controllers. RFID asset tracking tags are generally used by dedicated RFID tracking systems and software and require a separate infrastructure from wireless systems. Just like the WLAN controller, RFID systems can triangulate equipment. However, RFID systems can only be used for RFID tags and cannot serve traditional 802.11 wireless clients. Reasons for choosing an RFID tracking system over an 802.11 wireless tracking system can be driven by the need for isolation between the current 802.11 wireless system and the asset tracking requirement. Other reasons could be driven by internal politics in your company or the price of adding the functionality to the existing 802.11 wireless system. The reasons for choosing RFID are in isolation of services, chosen by either internal politics or price.

An obvious benefit of asset tracking is locating assets. However, an added benefit is the long-term data captured by these systems. This data can be analyzed for usage and mobility of the assets. From the analysis, an organization can shrink, expand, or redistribute the assets.

Tamper Detection

Tamper detection can indicate that a system is compromised in some way. There are two types of tamper detection: nonelectrical and electrical. Nonelectrical tamper detection consists of a label called a security strip that when peeled off displays a visible mark. Security strips are affixed on a portion of the equipment that would move if it was opened; therefore, the security tape would need to be peeled off or cut. This type of detection is effective and simple, but it requires intervention by a person to detect the tampering.

Electrical tamper detection is in the form of circuitry in the device and a micro switch. The micro switch is normally mounted on the case, where it makes contact with the case cover. If the case is removed, a tamper is detected on the device, and the operating system will create an SNMP alert. This type of detection is automated and can even generate an email or text message.

Tamper detection does not always need to include the network equipment. The simplest tamper detection is an alarm system. In remote offices where equipment is located, tamper detection can be installed on the door leading to the equipment. If an unauthorized person enters, the alarm can alert the appropriate person(s) to respond.

Prevention Methods

Detection can alert you to physical unauthorized entry into your systems. However, your main duty should be to deter and prevent unauthorized physical access. In the following sections I will discuss several tactics to protect physical access from unauthorized persons.

Employee Training

The best preventative measure that you can invest time in is to educate the employees, that is, employee training. The employees of an organization will be confronted with physical security risks and threats daily. It is up to the employee to identify that the threat exists and the potential risk of the threat being carried out. The employee might even be able to mitigate the risk without additional help. This is the product of good employee training on security as it relates to the organization.

For example, an organization might have just finished conducting training on secure areas. An employee might identify that people use a rear exit for a secure area when they go on break. This opens the threat to someone tailgating or piggybacking in the opposite direction in an attempt to enter the secure area. The risk for the threat is how often the other employees take breaks and if they prop the door to get back in. To mitigate the risk, training for all of the employees would stop this bad practice. However, if one employee perceives it as a risk, that person could raise the risk with a manager. The risk could then be mitigated by the manager instructing employees to enter and leave through the main entrance/exit.

Generally, people take pride in their jobs and take the organization's policies and procedures seriously. When an organization can empower employees to help secure the organization, they adopt an authoritarian attitude that benefits the organization's security. However, proper employee training is the key.

Access Control Hardware

Many organizations that require a level of physical security for an area or areas quickly realize they can't control access with simple lock and key security. Keys are often lent to other employees, and over time physical keys cannot be properly tracked. Physical keys can also be lost and stolen. In this section, I will cover access control measures that take multiple factors into consideration.

Access control systems allow us to conjoin physical-based security and electronic-based security together. Access control systems can grant users access to areas when their role in the organization changes, and access can also be revoked when the employee leaves the organization. These processes can even be automated with an enterprise resource planning (ERP) system.

Badges   *Identification badges* are used to provide proof of access to others. Proper processes and procedures must be in place for a successful implementation of this prevention tactic. Badges are only as good as the enforcement of the badges themselves. In many organizations that implement ID badges, all employees are required to display their ID badge at all times. If an employee is in an area where they are not recognized, other employees are trained to look for the ID badge and take appropriate action if it is not displayed. Many companies have implemented this policy as a personnel safety policy, but it ultimately serves as a physical security protocol.

Biometrics   *Biometrics* uses a metric related to a person's body to provide access to a system. Common metrics used are fingerprints, retina scans, and voice and facial recognition. In recent years biometrics has been implemented in access control of mobile devices. Several manufacturers have adopted fingerprint access control, and some have even adopted facial recognition with the forward-pointing camera.

Biometrics may sound like something out of your favorite spy movie, but it is a valuable tactic for preventing unauthorized access. Fingerprint recognition (Figure 4.36) is the most common biometric used for physical access control. If an electronic badge is used, it can be stolen and used by an unauthorized person for access. However, when biometrics are used, only your fingerprint can access the system. I'm sure that you can think of a scene in your favorite spy movie where a fingerprint is stolen and maliciously used, but in real life a passcode is also required.

FIGURE 4.36   A typical biometric reader

Locking Racks

Locking network racks is a good habit in any organization. Even if the network racks are kept in secured areas, they should always be locked. This can prevent someone from mistakenly powering down a server or piece of equipment by mistake. When racks are not located in a secure area, such as a wiring closet, it is even more important to make sure they are locked. Locking network racks can prevent someone from modifying existing wiring and prevent unauthorized access on the network.

Locking Cabinets

Locking cabinets where files are kept is another important physical security measure. Unlocked cabinets can invite an unauthorized person to peruse through the contents. Locking cabinets can even thwart an attacker from gaining unauthorized access to information or materials. Cabinets are not just used for files, there are other media and valuables that can be on hand and they should be locked up in cabinets as well.

Access Control Vestibule (Previously Known as a Mantrap)

The use of an access control vestibule, also known as a mantrap, helps prevent tailgating of nonauthorized users. The access control vestibule is a small room that has two access-controlled doors, as shown in Figure 4.37. When a person enters into the first door, they are trapped in the room until they have been authorized to enter the second controlled door. This close proximity between people in this confined space makes it uncomfortable for both the authorized user and the nonauthorized user attempting to tailgate, and it also completely prevents piggybacking. In this example, the doors are controlled by radio frequency identification (RFID) access controls and monitored by cameras. In high security areas the second door might also require positive identification of the person entering the area, such as photo identification and a passcode.

FIGURE 4.37   A common access control vestibule setup

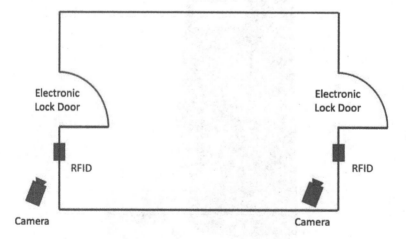

Smart Lockers

The smart locker is something that has been introduced with the explosive success of Amazon and its package delivery. Smart lockers are electronically controlled lockers that give you access to your package after you scan a delivery code. These lockers have revolutionized the safekeeping of deliveries.

Online retailers might use these smart lockers to lower the costs of delivery. However, smart lockers are not exclusive to online retailers. You can also find smart lockers dispensing laptops, cell phones, and other electronic devices. In many large tech-driven organizations, these smart lockers can dispense and track electronics for their employees. An employee simply has to scan their employee badge, and equipment is automatically checked out to them, and returning the devices requires a similar process.

Asset Disposal

When an asset is no longer functional to the organization, it needs to be disposed of. There are a couple of considerations when disposing of assets, such as accounting practices, environmental compliance, recycling, and most important, physical security. The asset should be checked against the organization's capital investment schedule as well as checked for leasing commitments. This can be achieved with the tracking of the asset's identification tag.

Outside of financial commitments, electronics that are improperly disposed of have a negative environmental effect. There are often regulations surrounding the proper disposal of electronics equipment, such as the federal Resource Conservation and Recovery Act (RCRA). The RCRA requires the proper disposal of electronics that are deemed e-waste, and it also prohibits the export to developing countries. Therefore, the disposal company should have the proper certification for disposal of e-waste, such as the Responsible Recycling (R2) and e-Stewards Standard for Responsible Recycling and Reuse of Electronic Equipment (e-Stewards). An alternative to disposing of the equipment is donating the equipment to another organization that has the proper certifications.

The importance of physical security is not exclusive to operational equipment. The physical security of the residual data on the equipment needs to be considered. When the equipment is donated or disposed of, the organization should be sure that none of its data resides on the equipment. This is to include any data specific to the organization, including configuration and software licensed to the organization. In the following sections, I will describe two methods that should be used when disposing of equipment to ensure that configuration of other important data is removed.

Factory Reset/Wipe Configuration

Equipment that doesn't contain stateful information such as switches and routers can be factory reset. Every vendor will have a procedure for factory resetting the equipment that will wipe the configuration. Be warned that a factory reset doesn't always mean that stateful information will be deleted or deleted to the point recovery is not possible. If a Windows 10 computer is factory reset, depending on the method, data may be recoverable. It is always best to consult the vendor's documentation on factory reset and the proper way to decommission a piece of equipment.

Sanitize Devices for Disposal

When a device is sanitized, the data contained in the storage area is deleted to a level of assurance that it cannot be recovered. Three types of devices contain data: magnetic, solid-state drive (SSD), and hybrid disk drives. Each one has a different method of sanitization:

Magnetic   Magnetic drives have spinning platters and drive arms that move back and forth on the platter and store data on the media with a magnetic field, hence the nickname. These types of drives have been in production since the late 1950s, although the 3.5″ drives we know today started becoming popular in the mid-1990s. The sanitization of these drives requires the overwriting of data because the data is stored magnetically on the platter and can technically be restored. Data is erased by writing 1s and 0s to each addressable cluster location in the filesystem.

Solid-State Drive (SSD)   Solid state drives don't have any moving parts; these drives contain non-volatile memory chips similar to flash drives. They also use proprietary algorithms to arrange the data in the memory. So, these drives cannot be sanitized by systematically writing of 1s and 0s to erase the underlying data. These devices typically require a vendor-specific tool that can erase the entire drive. Every vendor will have a proprietary tool to sanitize the data, and therefore you should always check with the vendor when preparing to sanitize an SSD.

Hybrid   A hybrid drive uses a conventional magnetic drive as the main media to store the data. These drives also contain a small amount of SSD flash to hold the most used blocks of data. Because of how data is stored on these drives, you must use a sanitization tool from the vendor and treat these drives like SSD media.

The DoD 5220.22-M standard has been used for years as a benchmark for data erasure for conventional magnetic media. The standard requires data to be written systematically, then read for verification; this is considered a pass. The standard requires three passes of overwriting to be done. The first pass requires 0s to be written and read, the second pass requires 1s to be written and read, and the last pass requires random data to be written and read. Only after all three passes is a device considered erased to this standard.

Outside of systematic overwriting of data and proprietary sanitization tools, there is another method of sanitizing devices. If the media is flexible media, such as a floppy disk, then a degaussing magnet can simply be used. There are even degaussing tools to erase hard drives as well. Physical destruction, such as shredding, is another extreme method of sanitization. Commercial data centers might use hydraulic presses to destroy the platters. There are even destruction services that will shred the drive.

Exam Essentials

Know the various tactics used for the detection of physical security violations.   Video surveillance can be deployed as a coaxial network called closed-circuit television (CCTV) or Ethernet. Motion detection uses passive infrared (PIR) to monitor differences in heat. Microwave motion detection sensors use pulses of microwaves and measure the microwaves that bounce back. Vibration sensors detect vibrations and are often deployed as seismic sensors. Asset tracking tags are used to track, secure, locate, and identify assets via software. Tamper detection for network equipment can be specific circuitry that monitors tamper detection or passive stickers that, when tampered with, display a visual indication that the equipment was tampered with.

Know the various tactics used for the prevention of physical security violations.   The best prevention method for physical security violations is employee training so the organization's employees can actively prevent violations. Badges are used for positive identification of authorized personnel. They can also contain a magstripe or RFID chip to electronically identify a person with the use of access control hardware. Biometrics uses a metric related to a person's body to provide access to an access control system. Locking racks prevent equipment from being affected by malicious intent or mistakenly being affected. Locking cabinets safeguard against snooping employees or attackers looking for files or equipment. An access control vestibule prevents tailgating and piggybacking by requiring a person to enter into a small room where a second access-controlled door is accessible. Smart lockers allow dispensing of equipment with the use of access-control systems.

Know common techniques used to dispose of assets.   Equipment that only holds configuration can be factory reset so that the configuration data is wiped. This method requires that no data is kept on the device. Sanitizing devices for disposal can require the overwriting of data if the device is a traditional magnetic drive. If the drive is a solid-state or hybrid drive, then you must use a vendor-specific tool to sanitize it. Other methods might include physical destruction of the device, such as using a hydraulic press or shredder.

Review Questions

1. Which security concept dictates that a user be given only the permission to perform their job?
   - **A.** Zero trust
   - **B.** Role-based access
   - **C.** Least privilege
   - **D.** Defense in depth

2. Which principle describes the process of verification of a user's identity?
   - **A.** Authentication
   - **B.** Authorization
   - **C.** Accounting
   - **D.** Auditing

3. Which authentication system is an open standard originally proposed by the Internet Engineering Task Force (IETF)?
   - **A.** RADIUS
   - **B.** TACACS+
   - **C.** Kerberos
   - **D.** LDAP

4. Which authentication system can use Advanced Encryption Standard (AES) encryption for encryption of user credentials?
   - **A.** RADIUS
   - **B.** TACACS+
   - **C.** Kerberos
   - **D.** LDAP

5. Which protocol is often used with single sign-on (SSO) to exchange credentials?
   - **A.** LDAP
   - **B.** SAML
   - **C.** ADFS
   - **D.** Kerberos

6. Which principle describes the process of verification of a user's permissions?
   - **A.** Authentication
   - **B.** Authorization
   - **C.** Accounting
   - **D.** Auditing

7. What protocol and port number does LDAP use for directory lookups?

    A. TCP/389

    B. TCP/1812

    C. UDP/389

    D. UDP/1812

8. Which option accurately describes an exploit?

    A. A known weakness in the operating system

    B. A configuration that weakens the security of the operating system

    C. A known operating system security flaw

    D. A technique to gain unauthorized access

9. Which attack involves the attacker impersonating both sides of a conversation between two hosts?

    A. On-path attack

    B. Deauthentication

    C. DoS

    D. Spoofing

10. Which type of attack will attempt to configure hosts with a malicious default gateway?

    A. DoS

    B. VLAN hopping

    C. Deauthentication

    D. Rogue DHCP

11. What attack vector can be used for an on-path attack?

    A. DHCP

    B. DNS

    C. Wireless

    D. All of the above

12. Which attack can be used on a native VLAN?

    A. Double-tagging

    B. VLAN traversal

    C. Trunk popping

    D. Denial-of-service

13. What type of filters can be placed over a monitor to prevent the data on the screen from being readable when viewed from the side?

    A. Security

    B. Privacy

    C. Degaussing

    D. Tempered

14. Which form of social engineering is nothing more than looking over someone's shoulder while they enter or view sensitive information?

    A. Shoulder surfing

    B. Phishing

    C. Tailgating

    D. Whaling

15. You need to protect your users from trojans, viruses, and phishing emails. What should you implement?

    A. Multifactor authentication

    B. Software firewalls

    C. Antimalware

    D. Antivirus

16. What can you use to protect against spoofing of internal IP addresses on the perimeter of your network?

    A. Access control lists

    B. Intrusion detection systems

    C. Transport Layer Security

    D. Host intrusion detection systems

17. You are implementing a public guest wireless network and require that users accept an acceptable use policy (AUP). What should you implement to accomplish the goal?

    A. ACLs

    B. MAC filtering

    C. Captive portal

    D. 802.1X

18. You are implementing a wireless network and need to make sure that only hosts that have up-to-date antivirus protection can join. Which technology should you implement?

    A. NAC

    B. 802.1X

    C. EAP-TLS

    D. ACLs

19. Which statement is correct about applying ACLs to an interface?

    A. An access control list can be applied in only one direction.

    B. An access control list can be applied only to a single protocol.

    C. An access control list can be applied only to a single port.

    D. All of the above.

20. Which console-based management protocol has built-in security?

    A. SSH

    B. SCP

    C. HTTPS

    D. FTP

21. You have several remote workers who enter patient information and require a high level of security. Which technology would best suit the connectivity for these workers?

    A. GRE tunnel

    B. Wireless WAN

    C. Client-to-site VPN

    D. Site-to-site VPN

22. On which network protocol and port does SSH operate?

    A. TCP port 3389

    B. TCP port 22

    C. TCP port 23

    D. TCP port 443

23. Which motion detection system has a reflective panel to create zones of detection?

    A. Microwave

    B. Vibration

    C. Passive infrared (PIR)

    D. Seismic

24. You require a physical security system that authenticates and authorizes employees into an area. Which system should you implement?

    A. Key fobs

    B. ID badges

    C. Biometrics

    D. Combination locks

25. What is a method for stopping tailgating?

    A. User authentication

    B. Access control vestibules

    C. Strong passwords

    D. Changing SSIDs

Chapter 5

Domain 5.0: Network Troubleshooting

THE FOLLOWING COMPTIA NETWORK+ OBJECTIVES ARE COVERED IN THIS CHAPTER:

✓ **5.1 Explain the network troubleshooting methodology.**

- Identify the problem
    - Gather information
    - Question users
    - Identify symptoms
    - Determine if anything has changed
    - Duplicate the problem, if possible
    - Approach multiple problems individually
- Establish a theory of probable cause
    - Question the obvious
    - Consider multiple approaches
        - Top-to-bottom/bottom-to-top OSI model
        - Divide and conquer
- Test the theory to determine the cause
    - If the theory is confirmed, determine the next steps to resolve the problem
    - If the theory is not confirmed, reestablish a new theory or escalate
- Establish a plan of action to resolve the problem and identify potential effects
- Implement the solution or escalate as necessary
- Verify full system functionality and, if applicable, implement preventive measures
- Document findings, actions, outcomes, and lessons learned

✓ **5.2 Given a scenario, troubleshoot common cable connectivity issues and select the appropriate tools.**

- Specifications and limitations
    - Throughput
    - Speed
    - Distance
- Cable considerations
    - Shielded and unshielded
    - Plenum and riser-rated
- Cable application
    - Rollover cable/console cable
    - Crossover cable
    - Power over Ethernet
- Common issues
    - Attenuation
    - Interference
    - Decibel (dB) loss
    - Incorrect pinout
    - Bad ports
    - Open/short
    - Light-emitting diode (LED) status indicators
    - Incorrect transceivers
    - Duplexing issues
    - Transmit and receive (TX/RX) reversed
    - Dirty optical cables
- Common tools
    - Cable crimper
    - Punchdown tool
    - Tone generator

- Loopback adapter
- Optical time-domain reflectometer (OTDR)
- Multimeter
- Cable tester
- Wire map
- Tap
- Fusion splicers
- Spectrum analyzers
- Snips/cutters
- Cable stripper
- Fiber light meter

✓ **5.3 Given a scenario, use the appropriate network software tools and commands.**

- Software tools
  - WiFi analyzer
  - Protocol analyzer/packet capture
  - Bandwidth speed tester
  - Port scanner
  - iperf
  - NetFlow analyzers
  - Trivial File Transfer Protocol (TFTP) server
  - Terminal emulator
  - IP scanner
- Command line tool
  - ping
  - ipconfig/ifconfig/ip
  - nslookup/dig
  - traceroute/tracert
  - arp

- netstat
- hostname
- route
- telnet
- tcpdump
- nmap
- Basic network platform commands
  - show interface
  - show config
  - show route

✓ **5.4 Given a scenario, troubleshoot common wireless connectivity issues.**

- Specifications and limitations
  - Throughput
  - Speed
  - Distance
  - Received signal strength indication (RSSI) signal strength
  - Effective isotropic radiated power (EIRP)/ power settings
- Considerations
  - Antennas
    - Placement
    - Type
    - Polarization
  - Channel utilization
  - AP association time
  - Site survey
- Common issues
  - Interference

- Channel overlap
- Antenna cable attenuation/signal loss
- RF attenuation/signal loss
- Wrong SSID
- Incorrect passphrase
- Encryption protocol mismatch
- Insufficient wireless coverage
- Captive portal issues
- Client disassociation issues

✓ **5.5 Given a scenario, troubleshoot general networking issues.**

- Considerations
    - Device configuration review
    - Routing tables
    - Interface status
    - VLAN assignment
    - Network performance baselines
- Common issues
    - Collisions
    - Broadcast storm
    - Duplicate MAC address
    - Duplicate IP address
    - Multicast flooding
    - Asymmetrical routing
    - Switching loops
    - Routing loops
    - Rogue DHCP server
    - DHCP scope exhaustion
    - IP setting issues
        - Incorrect gateway

- Incorrect subnet mask
- Incorrect IP address
- Incorrect DNS
- Missing route
- Low optical link budget
- Certificate issues
- Hardware failure
- Host-based/network-based firewall settings
- Blocked services, ports, or addresses
- Incorrect VLAN
- DNS issues
- NTP issues
- BYOD challenges
- Licensed feature issues
- Network performance issues

Understanding network concepts, infrastructure, operations, and security helps us design networks that are functional and secure. It is assumed that once a network is designed and implemented, it operates without any issues forever. Although this is the intended goal, we often run into issues that we must troubleshoot and rectify to regain proper network operations.

So far you've learned about the theories of networking concepts, infrastructure, operations, and security. In this chapter, you will learn how to troubleshoot network issues while applying those theories.

For more information on Domain 5's topics, please see *CompTIA Network+ Study Guide*, Fifth Edition (978-1-119-81163-3), and *CompTIA Network+ Practice Tests*, Second Edition (978-1-119-80730-8), both published by Sybex.

5.1 Explain the network troubleshooting methodology.

When a problem arises in the network, we must take an analytical approach to solving it. In this book you are examining the theory of networking, but overall you are learning computer science. Therefore, the scientific method of solving problems is applicable to networking issues you may encounter.

The scientific method for computer science is defined as follows:

- Asking a question or identifying the problem
- Researching the problem
- Creating a hypothesis
- Testing a solution
- Analyzing the solution
- Reaching a conclusion

In the following sections, I will cover network troubleshooting steps. Many of the steps involved will match up to the scientific method described here.

Identify the Problem

Identifying the problem is a crucial step. If the problem is not identified correctly, then hours, days, and even months can be wasted focusing on the wrong problem or researching the wrong criteria. Fortunately, some problems are evident and can be reproduced. However, some problems are elusive or intermittent, and these problems are the toughest to identify and solve.

Gather Information

A critical first step is the gathering of information related to the problem. Think of yourself as a detective; you must gather the information that helps reconstruct the problem. As you do, it is important to document your findings. The more complex the problem, the more important it is to document what you learn in this step.

Do not jump to a conclusion as you are gathering information. Jumping to a conclusion will not define the reasons for the problem, and such conclusions will only distract you from the problem. It is best to reserve judgment until the facts are gathered and you can develop a valid hypothesis.

Duplicate the Problem If Possible

Duplicating or reproducing the problem is a component of identifying the problem. Once you have gathered the information about the problem, you can begin reproducing the problem. The reproduction of the problem can either be live or in a test environment, depending on how disruptive the problem is. It is preferable to reproduce the problem in a test environment so that possible solutions can be tested without affecting others.

When reproducing the problem, be sure to document how the problem is reproduced. Going forward, when and if you need to consult technical support personnel, the documented steps will speed up a solution.

It is extremely efficient when you can reproduce a problem, but sometimes problems are not reproducible. Intermittent problems might not be reproducible and can be the most difficult to solve. Without a clear reproduction of the problem, you can only make a conclusion based on your judgment and not the facts related to the problem. Using judgment to solve the problem is an educated conclusion or guess. More importantly, if you make an incorrect judgment of the problem and implement a solution that is wrong, it could distract you from the proper solution or make the problem worse. Other problems are not reproducible because of the infrastructure or circumstances required to reproduce them.

Question Users

As part of your detective work in reconstructing the problem, you must interview users who are involved with the problem. The information from users will be biased, so you must be able to read between the lines and ask for exact information. During the interview, users will also try to self-diagnose their problem. Although this information is not always accurate or useful, it does provide their perspective.

Another pitfall when interviewing users is scope creep. The scope of the problem should be maintained during the entire interview process while still listening closely to the user. As an example, suppose you are diagnosing an application freezing up and a user veers from the scope of the problem to tell you that their mouse is also acting weird. The mouse issue might contribute to the perception that the application is freezing up and should be factored into the problem. However, if the user tells you that their CD-ROM drive is broken, this has nothing to do with the application freezing up and should be treated separately.

When dealing with problems that are either intermittent or not reproducible in a test environment, build a rapport with the users involved. These users will be instrumental in validating that a problem is fixed or that it has occurred again. You may also need to follow up with questions as you formulate a hypothesis of the problem.

Identify Symptoms

During the problem identity process, it is important to identify the symptoms that either cause the problem or are the result of the problem. You must define exactly what the problem affects and under which conditions the symptoms of the problem surface.

I will use the problem of a network slowdown that happens intermittently as an example. One of the symptoms might be that email slows down quite considerably. Another symptom might be that user cloud applications become unresponsive during these times as well. These symptoms might help you determine whether the problem is local to your network or external to your network. In this example, if Internet-connected systems are only affected, then it suggests the problem is outside your network.

Determine If Anything Has Changed

Sometimes problems are a direct result of a change in the network. The change does not need to be a recent one, since some problems only manifest themselves when the affected components are being used and their use may be infrequent. For example, suppose your firewall rules were cleaned up and a month later your human resources person complains that payroll cannot be uploaded. A firewall rule may have been removed that is creating the connectivity problem. Why a month later? Maybe payroll gets uploaded only once a month.

Some organizations require change management, as discussed in Chapter 3, "Domain 3.0: Network Operations." Change management documents might be the best starting point to determine whether anything has changed related to the current problem. Other organizations require logging changes to the network to a document called the change log. The change log details what exactly has been changed, when it has been changed, who has made the change, and why the change has been made. If these documents are not used by your organization, then talking among other administrators is advisable. This will help to identify if their changes could be the cause of the current problem.

Approach Multiple Problems Individually

We often get bombarded with problems all at once. When this happens, we often jump to the conclusion there is a central cause. However, problems are often not related to each other, and jumping to a conclusion is casting a judgment on the problem that will waste time. Therefore, each problem should be viewed as a separate problem with no commonality between them.

Each problem should be uniformly approached, and information should be gathered specific to the problem at hand. When interviewing users, focus on the current problem. If the same user has been a part of several problems, you should explain that you want to focus on one problem at a time. This prevents the Chicken Little syndrome of "the sky is falling" that users and network administrators suffer alike. When we look at problems individually, we can form better strategies to solve them individually.

Establish a Theory of Probable Cause

After a problem and its symptoms have been identified, the next step is to form a hypothesis and establish a theory of probable cause. This theory should be based on information gathered and supporting network theory. It is important to note that at this step of troubleshooting, the theory of probable cause could change based on new evidence. It is not uncommon for the first theory of probable cause to be incorrect, especially when all the problem's variables are not well defined.

Question the Obvious

When establishing a theory of probable cause, question everything related to the problem. The most obvious causes can sometimes be overlooked. Although the symptoms might be complex, they do not always describe how complex the cause of the problem is.

As an example, suppose a new VoIP phone system has been installed in your organization. The users complain that they are consistently receiving busy signals when calling others. The most obvious cause is that the other party is actually busy and the new system is leading users to believe the phone is the issue. A theory of probable cause in this example is that they are actually calling a busy phone.

Consider Multiple Approaches

When you establish a theory of probable cause, you shouldn't restrict yourself to one theory. You should practice pitching the symptoms, problem, and your theory to others. This serves two purposes: First, it allows you to articulate the elements of the problem to your peers. They will often ask more questions that you may have not thought of yet or simply overlooked. The second is that others may come up with alternate theories of probable cause to a problem. These alternate theories should be embraced and discussed further with your team.

Although pitching a problem to others is helpful, it is not always part of the diagnostic process. It is, however, important to keep an open mind and think of other approaches. The more time you invest in the problem, the more you will understand its causes.

Top-to-Bottom/Bottom-to-Top OSI Model

As you are considering different approaches to the problem, compare the OSI layers to the flow of information. Approaching the problem while considering what happens at each layer of the OSI model allows you to trace the process from the key click to the expected outcome. Although what happens in the upper layers, the Application, Presentation, and Session layers is usually unknown to network administrators, you can consult the programmers to validate that these layers are not the root cause of the problem. If the application has been unchanged, most problems will be isolated to the Transport, Network, Data Link, and Physical layers.

Tracing the information down the originating host's OSI stack, across the network, and up the destination host's OSI stack allows you to understand the flow of information. Problems should be analyzed at each layer down the originating stack and up the destination stack for the potential root cause.

Divide and Conquer

Although examining the data flow at each layer of the OSI is considered a technique to divide and conquer the problem, you should also separate out complex processes. Each separate subprocess should then be tested as a root cause of the problem.

For example, if the problem is a web form that emails from a web page and is not being received, several subprocesses can be divided out of the entire process—subprocesses such as form validation, form submission, server processing of the data, and then emailing of the data. Each one of these subprocesses can be examined individually; for example, "Is a simple email from the server being delivered?" Then you can progress to, "Is the form being submitted to email?" Each of these is a theory of probable cause that should be researched separately.

Test the Theory to Determine the Cause

After you have formulated a theory of probable cause, the next logical step is to test your hypothesis. Without a proper test of the theory, you cannot confirm the problem and determine its cause. Tests should be methodically planned out, and a list of their expected outcomes should be generated.

In the earlier example of a web form that emails the contents to a recipient, the theory of probable cause is the web server is not sending emails. A test to confirm this theory is to manually send an email from the web server to a recipient. If the recipient received the email, the problem is elsewhere; if the email is not received, then the cause of the problem is found, and your theory is validated.

Once the Theory Is Confirmed, Determine the Next Steps to Resolve the Problem

This task should be simple if you have a solid theory and understanding of the cause. When scientists conduct experiments with the use of the scientific method, there is a preconceived understanding of what the theory represents in relation to the problem. The test of the theory either confirms or negates the theory presented. Once the theory is confirmed, the resolution should be determined to resolve the problem.

In our example of an email *mail transfer agent (MTA)* not sending email to a recipient, we can plan more theories as to why and test them further. A possible resolution might be that the MTA service has stopped and needs to be restarted. The problem might also be more complex and require more testing, but the cause of the problem is now isolated to a system that can be diagnosed further.

If the Theory Is Not Confirmed, Reestablish a New Theory or Escalate

We hope that our theory of probable cause is sound and is confirmed during testing. However, if the test does not confirm the primary theory, then a new theory of probable cause must be established. We should use prior tests to conclude what the problem is *not* related to. This type of problem solving is known as the process of elimination. It is a relevant problem-solving technique, as long as adequate progress is made during each test.

In our example, if the MTA is operating properly and the test does not confirm the theory of probable cause, then a new theory needs to be established. A new theory might be that the web form is not being submitted to the email service. This theory can now be tested, and the MTA system has now been eliminated from the problem as being a possible cause.

At some point in the process, the progress of solving the problem will cease, and you will need to escalate the problem. Escalation might be in the form of consulting third-party experts or area experts in your organization. In the example, the web form is not submitting email to the email service. The next logical step might be to have a webmaster examine the code and verify that it is properly submitting the form to the email system. We can now state that we have eliminated the email system and provide proof as to why the code might be at fault.

Establish a Plan of Action to Resolve the Problem and Identify Potential Effects

The analysis of the solution can be simple or complex. Regardless of how simple the solution seems to be, you should identify its effects. It is frustrating to fix one problem and create several others.

In our example, we determine that DNS is the issue. During our tests, changing the DNS server for the server operating as the MTA fixes the problem. Implementing this change could have zero effect on anything else, or it could potentially disrupt all other email services. In this circumstance, further research of the potential problems should be identified and documented.

Implement the Solution or Escalate as Necessary

After we have determined the solution and identified the potential effects, we need to implement the solution. Implementing the solution might be as simple as changing a DNS entry, or it may be as complex as reinstallation of the system. Hopefully, in most cases the solution will be simple and within our control. However, in some instances we may need to escalate the implementation of the solution to a third-party expert or an area expert in our organization.

Verify Full System Functionality and, If Applicable, Implement Preventive Measures

The system functionality should be verified after the solution has been implemented. Outside of the initial system that was modified, all of the surrounding systems that interact with the modified system should be verified for full functionality.

In the event of a future system failure, preventive measures should be taken. In our example, such a measure might be to save the forms locally to a file or database before transmitting the data via email. This preventive measure would ensure that if the email was to fail again, we still have a copy of the data.

Document Findings, Actions, Outcomes, and Lessons Learned

The final step of problem solving is the documentation of the findings, actions, and outcomes. Proper documentation is often overlooked, which can be a detriment in the future if the same problem arises. Documentation allows us to reflect on the problem, so that if we or other technicians run into the same problem in the future we can save time. The documentation will detail which actions were performed to solve the problem and the specifics of the final solution to the problem.

Exam Essentials

Understand the various techniques for identifying network problems.   You should gather the information about a problem by facts and observation, and avoid jumping to conclusions. When the steps to reproduce a problem have been identified, reproduction of the problem is the next step. Reproduction can be in a test environment or live environment, depending on the requirements of the problem. Questioning users should be done in such a way as to avoid bias to a solution, and the questions should extract factual information. When questioning users, avoid the pitfalls of scope creep, stick to the problem, and build a rapport with the user for future questions. Identifying the symptoms of the problem will help you better understand when the problem is happening. You should review change log records for recent changes in the network as well as change requests to help identify the cause of the problem. As you encounter problems, they should be approached individually without assuming there is a commonality.

Understand the various techniques for establishing a theory of probable cause.   When establishing a theory of probable cause, question everything related to the problem.

Don't restrict yourself to one theory. Listen to what your peers think of the problem and consider multiple approaches. The OSI layers should be compared to the flow of information, and you should consider what happens at each layer of the model. The process that is possibly causing the problem should be separated into smaller subprocesses. Each subprocess should then be tested as a root cause of the problem.

Understand the techniques for testing a theory, implementing a solution, and documenting an outcome for a problem.   Tests should be methodically planned out, along with a list of their expected outcomes. The test of the theory either confirms or negates the theory presented. If the test does not confirm the primary theory, then a new theory of probable cause must be established and tested until a theory is confirmed. Following the successful test of a theory that establishes the root cause, the plan of action should be detailed. The plan of action should detail any potential adverse effects that will affect the problem system or supporting systems. After the solution is implemented, the primary system and surrounding systems should be tested for full functionality. Finally, a synopsis of the problem—all of the symptoms, causes, and fixes—should be documented so that future problems can be solved quickly.

5.2 Given a scenario, troubleshoot common cable connectivity issues and select the appropriate tools.

In the following sections, I will cover various scenarios that can cause issues in your wired network. I will also discuss how these issues can be detected and repaired with common tools of the trade. In addition, I will cover troubleshooting steps to determine the causes of these problems. At the end of the discussion of this exam objective, you should have a good understanding of troubleshooting cable connectivity and repair for day-to-day maintenance, operation, and troubleshooting of the network infrastructure.

Specifications and Limitations

As we learned in Chapter 1, "Domain 1.0: Networking Fundamentals," there are several different cabling standards that have been ratified jointly by the Telecommunications Industry Association (TIA) and the Electronic Industries Alliance (EIA). Each cabling standard has a different throughput, speed specification, and distance limitation. By choosing the proper cabling specification for the installation, you can future-proof the installation and satisfy the requirements of the installation.

Throughput   The throughput of the connection is the measured bandwidth utilized by the traffic over the connection. The sustained throughput of the connection is important, because if the speed is too low, the connection will be saturated with bandwidth and the problem will be manifested in the form of latency. Throughput and speed should be considered together when planning. For example, if you have a sustained throughput of 90 Mb/s and you are planning to cable a 100 Mb/s connection (speed), then you should probably plan a higher speed connection.

Speed   The speed of the connection is the top bandwidth that a connection can achieve. As a rule of thumb the sustained throughput should be no more than 50 percent of the connection speed. If the throughput exceeds the speed on the connection, planning should be done to raise the speed of the connection. As discussed, throughput and speed should be considered together during planning. If a port must carry time-sensitive traffic such as ISCSI traffic, then wire speed and non-blocking ports should be considered as they relate to the speed of the connection. Flow control sends blocking signals to the originating Ethernet device when the throughput reaches the wire speed of the connection.

Distance   Every cabling specification has a defined distance limitation that should not be exceeded. The specification is usually notated in the form of meters. The distance limitation is not an arbitrary number. The distance limit is usually based upon padding of Ethernet frames or the time a packet takes to traverse the connection before it is flushed from buffers. Problems with exceeding distance will manifest with latency and packet loss.

Throughout the years I've work with many installers that pride them-selves in their work and boast that exceeding the distance specification will be just fine. Although their tradecraft is excellent, they don't always understand why the specification is imposed. For example, with Fast Eth-ernet, 5 microseconds is the time it takes to transmit the first 64 bytes of data 100 meters in distance. It is also the time the transmitter keeps the transmitted data in its buffer for retransmitting in the event a problem is encountered in transmitting the first 64 bytes of data. If a problem is encountered after 5 microseconds (that is 101, 102, 103 meters), the data will already be flushed from the buffer and retransmit timers for upper later protocols will need to expire for retransmitting of data. This equates to latency! I've always taken the opportunity to educate the installer and insist the connection be kept within the maximum distance specification.

Cable Considerations

Cable installs should fall within the specifications for a successful installation, such as for speed and distance. However, the type of installation should also be considered when planning an installation of cabling. The cabling might require flexibility or strength running up a wall. If the cable is run in a ventilated space, there may also be fire code considerations. The following sections will discuss the common considerations for cable installation.

Shielded and Unshielded

Unshielded twisted-pair (UTP) is the most common cabling for Ethernet networks today due to its cost and ease of installation. However, it is unshielded from electromagnetic interference (EMI), which is why it's use can be problematic in areas where EMI exists. Therefore, UTP should be avoided in close proximity to heavy industrial equipment that can emit EMI. *Shielded twisted-pair (STP)* is not as common for Ethernet cabling as UTP, due to its cost and difficult installation. However, it is shielded for EMI and therefore it should be used in industrial settings where EMI is present. It is important to note that there are several different types of STP cable. Some STP cabling has a foil shielding around all four pairs of wires, some is foil shielded around each pair of wires with an overall foil shielding, and some cabling is shielded with a wire mesh. The consideration is more shielding and a heavier shield increases the cost and lowers the chance that EMI will affect data transfer.

When installing cable in an industrial setting such as a factory where cabling is exposed to vibrations, chemicals, temperature, and EMI, the MICE (Mechanical, Ingress, Climatic, Chemical, and Electromagnetic) classification should be followed. The standard is defined in an ISO/IEC (International Organization for Standardization/International Electrotechnical Commission) publication. It is best to engage an engineer to define the type of cabling to use when in doubt for an industrial setting because safety can be compromised.

Plenum and Riser-Rated

Riser-rated cable is used when cable is run between floors in a non-plenum area. The cable is made with a polyvinyl chloride (PVC) plastic–jacketed sheathing. However, if the PVC cabling catches fire, it emits a toxic black smoke and hydrochloric acid that irritates the lungs and eyes. Therefore, when installing cabling in circulated airspace such as HVAC ducting and air returns, also called plenum areas, the type of cabling should be considered. *Plenum cable* is made with Teflon-jacketed cable or fire retardant–jacketed cable. It does not emit toxic vapors when burned or heated, and it is more expensive than PVC cables. It is specified in the National Electric Code (NEC) that is published by the National Fire Protection Association (NFPA). Because a circulated airspace is highly subjective, when in doubt use plenum cabling. You will not want to be responsible for failing a code inspection because a code inspector defines a cabling passage as an airspace.

Cable Application

Cables can be used for many different applications. The most common are obviously Ethernet host connectivities. However, a Cat 5 cable can be used for a number of other purposes, as I will describe.

Rollover Cable/Console Cable

A rollover cable is typically flat stock cable that contains eight wires. A rollover cable is unmistakably different than an Ethernet cable, mainly because it is flat and each wire is a different color. A rollover cable is crimped with an RJ-45 end with pin 1 matched with wire 1 on one side. The other side is also crimped with an RJ-45; however, pin 1 is matched with wire 8. So pin 2 is connected to pin 7 on the other side, pin 3 is connected to pin 6, pin 4 is connected to pin 5, and so on. Eventually, pin 8 will be connected with pin 1 on the other side, as show in Table 5.1.

TABLE 5.1 Rollover cable pinouts

Side A	Side B
Pin 1	Pin 8
Pin 2	Pin 7
Pin 3	Pin 6
Pin 4	Pin 5
Pin 5	Pin 4
Pin 6	Pin 3
Pin 7	Pin 2
Pin 8	Pin 1

Rollover cables are used with EIA/TIA adapters that convert a DB-9 serial port to an RJ-45 end. The opposite end will plug directly into the router or switch for console access, as shown in Figure 5.1. Over the years I've seen variations on the cable used for a console connection. The EIA/TIA adapter can also be wired to use a standard Ethernet cable, so it is always best to read the manual before making any connections. It is also becoming very popular for routers and switches to furnish a mini-USB connection so that when they are plugged into a laptop or computer, the operating system detects as a USB serial COM port.

FIGURE 5.1   A router console connection

Crossover Cable

When connecting a switch to a switch, router to a router, or a host to a host, the cabling often needs to be crossed over. This means that the transmit pairs are crossed over to the receive pairs on the other side of the cable and vice versa. This is easily achieved with a crossover cable, which has the EIA/TIA 586A wiring specification crimped on one end and the EIA/TIA 568B wiring specification on the other end. The EIA/TIA 568A and 568B wiring specification is shown in Table 5.2.

TABLE 5.2   EIA/TIA 568 crossover cabling

RJ-45 Pins	568A	568B
Pin 1	White/green	White/orange
Pin 2	Green	Orange
Pin 3	White/orange	White/green
Pin 4	Blue	Blue
Pin 5	White/blue	White/blue
Pin 6	Orange	Green
Pin 7	White/brown	White/brown
Pin 8	Brown	Brown

Problems can arise when a straight-through cable is used to connect a switch to a switch, a router to a router, or a host to a host. You simply just won't get a link light, although, most newer routers and switches have medium dependent interface crossover (MDI-X) ports that sense a similar device is being plugged in and will automatically cross the signals over.

A valuable tool to have in your tool box is a small length of cable that acts as a crossover cable and a female-to-female RJ-45 adapter. If there is doubt that the connection requires a crossover cable, you can just pop this small crossover cable onto the existing cable and verify that the link light comes on.

Power over Ethernet

Power over Ethernet (PoE) allows for both the power and data to be transmitted on a standard Ethernet connection. This technology is what allows VoIP phones, WAPs, video cameras, clocks, and a number of other devices to be powered from the switching equipment without the need for power adapters.

There are two main standards for PoE: PoE (802.3af) and PoE+ (802.3at). The PoE (802.3af) standard is used to supply up to 15.4 watts of power and is commonly used with phone and video surveillance cameras. The PoE+ (802.3at) standard is used to supply up to 25.5 watts of power. PoE+ (802.3at) is sometimes required for the latest wireless standards on WAPs that require more power than PoE (802.3af).

A common problem you'll encounter with PoE is that the switch won't support the power required by the device. For example, you have a PoE+ device, but the switch only supports normal PoE (802.3af). In this circumstance you will need to upgrade the switch. Another common problem is exceeding the power budget of the device. This is usually caused by not using *Link Layer Discovery Protocol (LLDP)* or *Cisco Discovery Protocol (CDP)* to communicate power requirements to the switch. These power requirements conveyed to the switch lower the supply wattage of PoE and PoE+ at the switch. This allows for more efficient power usage of the end devices.

Common Issues

The proper cabling should always be used for the installation of any network and low-voltage or high-voltage application. In networks, if the wrong cabling is used, you may not be able to communicate at the required speeds. In extreme cases, you may not be able to communicate at all. In the following sections, I will cover the various common issues that you may encounter with cable connectivity. This discussion covers the most common cable connectivity issues as they pertain to Ethernet and common coaxial applications. You should be aware there are other types of cable installation and each type can be uniquely different, such as various telecommunications standards. Therefore, you should always check the specification for the cable installation and verify the common issues as they pertain to the type of cable installation you are diagnosing.

Attenuation

The term *attenuation* is often associated with the maximum distance of a network cable. However, the maximum distance of a network cable is normally not susceptible to attenuation. The distances network cables are defined by are related to the time an electrical signal takes to travel down the wire before the frame is removed from the originating host's send buffer.

Coaxial cables are susceptible to attenuation, because an RF signal is transmitted through the cable. As the RF signal resonates down the wire, it dissipates energy; this dissipation of energy is called attenuation. Attenuation in a coaxial cable can cause connectivity and speed issues because the amount of data is hindered by the error detection. Cable modems' coaxial connections are extremely susceptible to attenuation when cables have a poor signal entering the cable and the cable runs are too long.

EMI

Electrical magnetic interference (EMI) is an electrical disturbance in signal quality from a source of electrical or *radio frequency (RF)* signal. EMI is normally generated from outside sources, such as motors, transformers, radio equipment, and many others. However, the phenomenon of crosstalk is actually from EMI. It just happens to be from the electrical signals of the other pairs of wires in the cable.

If the proper category of cabling is used for network speed and transient signals still persist, then EMI could be the cause. EMI is generated by fluorescent lighting, high-voltage wiring that is run parallel with network cabling, or any source of high energy or RF. An amplified cable probe described in the section "Tone Generator" later in this chapter can often be used to identify EMI. However, sometimes you must use a spectrum analyzer to see the EMI. In high-EMI environments such as industrial settings, it is best to run shielded twisted-pair (STP) wiring to prevent EMI.

Crosstalk is a type of internal interference inside the cable. It is encountered when the signal of one wire induces a signal onto a parallel wire. The wires closely bundled together create induction, which in turn creates interference to each other. The induction effect, called crosstalk, can be mitigated by twisting the wires so that they are no longer parallel to each other. The tighter the twists per inch, the better the resistance to crosstalk the wires will have. The Telecommunications Industry Association (TIA) creates manufacturing specifications that define how many twists per inch are in each of the wire categories.

Decibel (dB) Loss

Decibels (dBs) are a relative measurement of signal strength. The measurement itself is a logarithm from a reference signal strength. Decibel loss is the measurable loss of signal in a cable. The loss of signal can be due to the distance of the cable installation or excessive splitting of the cable. Although decibel loss is commonly associated with the signaling in coaxial cable, the term can also be associated with fiber-optic cabling. Fiber-optic decibel loss in typically due to the loss around the insertion point of the fiber-optic connector; this is called insertion loss.

Cable vendors will have a published specification for the decibel (dB) loss over a specific distance of their cabling. Therefore, if you suspect decibel loss, the cable distance should be checked against the original signal strength. RF splitters such as the common cable splitter can significantly create decibel loss. Therefore you should minimize the use of cable splitters in any cable installation. Most cable splitters will advertise the decibel loss on the splitter itself so that total decibel loss can be easily calculated by a technician.

Incorrect Pinout

Incorrect pinout of connectors can also be troublesome for the administrator. A cable should always be tested after a cable end is crimped. The wires are very thin, and the person crimping the cable end must have a great deal of coordination. A cable tester will verify that the cabling has been crimped properly.

Network cables are not the only place that you can find the problem of incorrect pinout. Serial cables and other low-voltage cables can contain incorrect pinout problems. Specialized testers are made to check the various cables you may encounter. However, if you have an understanding of the cable pinout, a multimeter can be used to check continuity between the pins at each end of the cable.

Bad Port

As a network professional for the past 25 years, I have come across very few bad ports on switches and routers. You should inspect the configuration of the port first and compare it to a known good working port.

However, you may run across a bad port from time to time. When you do, the equipment on which the bad port resides should be replaced so that time is not wasted in the future if the port is used again. In the interim, while you are waiting for acquisition of new equipment, the host should be moved to a known good working port to regain operations.

Open/Short

An open connection refers to an open circuit, in which the circuit is not completed or connected. This can be a simple wire that is loose on a patch panel, or it can be a break in a wire. A cable tester is used to determine open connections in a patch cord, patch panel, or any network cabling between the tested points. A multimeter can be used for continuity checks on other wiring such as power cords and serial cables.

A short is just that: a short circuit between two connections. A cable tester can be used to identify shorts in network cabling. Although uncommon in network cabling, a short could be the source of a problem if the wire insulation has been scraped off during installation. A multimeter can also be used for checking shorts in other low-voltage cabling.

Network Connection LED Status Indicators

When an Ethernet link is turned up, the *light-emitting diode (LED)* indicator will light. There is also an activity LED on many Ethernet interfaces that will blink upon activity. Both of these LEDs provide a visual indication that the host is connected and communicating on the network, as shown in Figure 5.2. The link status LED is normally green, and the activity LED is normally yellow.

FIGURE 5.2   A typical Ethernet jack

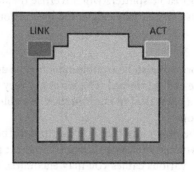

Some LED indicators may be next to the RJ-45 jack; this is common on many network interface card (NIC) expansion cards. In addition, some network indicators may not even be near the RJ-45 jack; they could be on the opposite side of the equipment, which is common on small office, home office (SOHO) switches. Many switch vendors group the indicators together above the ports, to the left of the ports, or to the right of the ports, as shown in Figure 5.3. No matter where the ports are located, every vendor includes a status LED for link status. It is uncommon to see a port without a status indicator.

FIGURE 5.3   A typical Ethernet switch

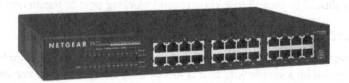

Incorrect Transceivers

Transceiver mismatch is not common with Ethernet transceivers because most transceivers autonegotiate speed and duplex. Also, most Ethernet transceivers are backward compatible with lower speeds. However, most 10 Gbps transceivers are not backward compatible with lower data rates, and some 1 Gbps transceivers are not compatible with lower data rates as well.

Fiber-optical transceivers must be identical on both sides of the fiber-optic cable. The wavelength of the light must match on the transmit side and the receive side or the link will not turn up. The wavelength of the transceiver is advertised in nanometers. Distance is also a factor; higher-powered transceivers should be matched or you run the risk of dropping a connection when the loss increases from vibrations of the mating surfaces.

Regardless of the type of transceiver, the specification of the transceivers should be checked against the requirements of the installation. The specifications of the cable should also be checked against the specifications of the transceivers to ensure a proper installation and trouble-free operations.

Duplexing Issues

A copper Ethernet connection is either half-duplex or full-duplex. Full-duplex describes that the connection can transmit and receive at the same time. A dedicated pair of wires is set aside for transmitting data to the host at the other end of the cable and receiving data from the other host at the other end of the cable. With half-duplex, the connection can transmit only if the other host is not transmitting. A single pair is used for both transmitting and receiving on both hosts, which can cause collisions and reduce the speed by up to 40 to 60 percent, depending on the amount of traffic.

Autonegotiation of IEEE 802.3u allows Ethernet 10BaseT and 100BaseT to autonegotiate speed and duplex. However, speed and duplex are often set statically on connections to routers and between switches. When this is done, both sides must match. If one side of the connection is set to full-duplex and the other side is set to half-duplex, you will see a high error rate on the full-duplex side and a high collision rate on the half-duplex side. The connection will still function but with severely degraded performance.

A speed mismatch can also occur when the autonegotiation of speed and duplex is turned off and statically set. However, unlike a duplex mismatch that causes errors and collisions, a speed mismatch will not allow the link to turn up. This is because Ethernet contains a carrier signal that is different between 10BaseT, 100BaseT, and 1000BaseT.

Transmit and Receive (TX/RX) Reverse

Ethernet cabling is standardized with the cable end specifications of EIA/TIA 568A/B. Transmit receive reversal is possible if a crossover cable is installed rather than a straight-through cable. Most transceivers will perform automatic medium dependent interface crossover (MDI-X). If a cable is suspected to be a crossover cable, you can test the cable with a cable tester to determine its configuration.

Fiber-optic cable is much more susceptible to TX/RX reversal, because each transceiver has a dedicated transmit optic on the left and a receive optic on the right. If the transmit and receive fiber-optic cable are reversed, the connection will not turn up. All fiber-optic connections must be crossed over on one side, allowing the transmit optic to feed to the receive optic on the other side, as shown in Figure 5.4. It is best practice to always cross the connection at a dedicated patch panel such as your main data frame (MDF). Then instruct the installer at the intermediate data frame (IDF) to connect the cabling as straight-through to the equipment.

If you are in doubt which cable is which, shine a simple flashlight through the cable. This should always be done from a distance because the cable could be wrong and you could directly look into a laser at the opposite end.

FIGURE 5.4 Fiber-optic transceivers

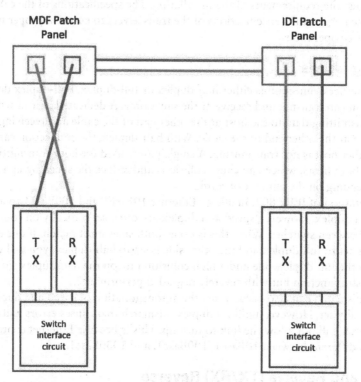

Dirty Optical Cables

Optical cables must be kept clean during storage and the optical ends should be thoroughly cleaned prior to use. When cleaning fiber-optic cables, it is best to use a simple glass cleaner and a microfiber cloth. The female end where the fiber-optic cable is inserted should be blown out with a short burst of air from canned air.

A dirty optical cable can create connectivity problems on an epic scale in your network. When an optical cable is dirty, it must use more power to compensate for the low signal strength at the opposite end. More power means more heat, which ultimately leads to failure. However, in some cases the dirt can be bad enough to intermittently hinder the connection all together. When this happens, the connection will drop and then come back; this is called a flap. In extreme cases a flapping port can create spanning tree problems, where spanning tree continues to recalculate and shut down normal working ports.

To avoid problems with dirty optical cables, always make sure the ends and mating surfaces are clean prior to installation. You should then check the decibel loss of the connection against nominal power settings; the optical transceiver will often have a nominal operating range detailed in the specifications sheet.

Common Tools

As network professionals we use hardware tools to repair and troubleshoot the physical connections in the network. The following sections cover the most common hardware tools that you will use when diagnosing copper and fiber-optic network cables. In addition, I will discuss testing equipment that is used by network professionals to verify operations.

Cable Crimpers

Cable crimpers, shown in Figure 5.5, are something that all network professionals should have in their toolbox. They are handy for fixing a bad cable end when the detent has broken off and won't stay inserted in the *network interface card (NIC)*. When using a cable crimper for the first time, you may find it a bit awkward, but with a little practice you can crimp a perfect end on the first shot.

FIGURE 5.5   A typical pair of cable crimpers

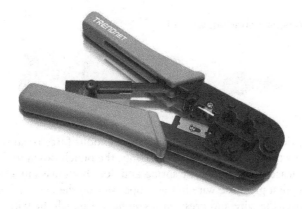

When you need to terminate an *RJ-45* on a network cable, you should first prepare your working area. Have an RJ-45 close by, the crimpers handy, and a wastepaper basket or waste receptacle. Start by cutting the sheath of the cable; give yourself about an inch. Some cable crimpers have a razor blade built in; I often find they cut either too much or too little, so it is best to have a special-purpose tool to score and cut the cable sheath. These tools often are spring loaded with an adjustable razor blade.

After cutting the sheath and pulling it off, fan out the pairs so the orange/white–orange wires are on the left and the brown/white–brown wires are on the right. Next, start untwisting the pairs. Once all of the pairs are untwisted, begin with the arrangement of wires starting left to right: white/orange and orange, then white/green, then blue, then white/blue, then green, and finally white/brown and brown. If you need a reminder, print out a wallet card of the EIA/TIA 568B wiring specification and keep it with you.

Next, holding the wire with one hand, wiggle the pairs with the other as you pull on them to straighten them out. Once they are straight, use the razor on the cable crimpers to cut the wires so there is a half inch of wire after the sheath. Then grab the RJ-45 with the connector window facing you (pin 1 is now to the left) and press the RJ-45 end on, making sure the wires are separated in the slot in the connector. Put the connector into the cable crimper, press on the wire until you see the wire cores in the connector end, and then crimp. Practice, practice, practice!

Punchdown Tool

When you think of a *punch-down tool*, you probably associate it with telephone work. However, in networks we use punch-down tools to punch down wires to patch panels. It is one of those tools right next to my cable crimpers. You can see a typical punch-down tool in Figure 5.6. Cabling on patch panels comes loose sometimes, such as when someone is installing a new network drop and accidentally bumps an existing one loose. Yes, it happens all the time.

FIGURE 5.6   A typical punch-down tool

Punching a wire down on a patch panel takes tremendous force because it clenches the wire and the tire cuts the excess wire off. Thankfully, the punch-down tool has a spring-loaded anvil that releases the force of the spring and does both tasks in a split second. To punch down a wire, first press the wire in the proper slot on the patch panel. Then, put the punch-down tool over the wire and press until you hear it punch the wire down. The die on a punch-down tool has a protruding angled blade on one side. Always make sure you have it pointed toward the excess wire; this is how the excess wire is trimmed, as shown in Figure 5.7.

Tone Generator

The *tone generator* is used in conjunction with a probe to trace network cables. A typical tone generator and *tracing probe* are shown in Figure 5.8. The tone generator is often integrated into the cable tester, but it can also be purchased as a separate tool. Tone generators can also be purchased for identifying telephone lines.

FIGURE 5.7   A punch-down tool punching a wire into a patch panel

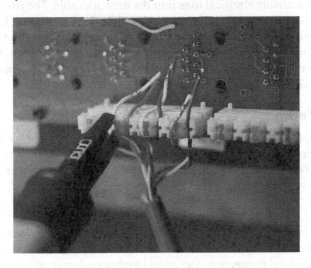

FIGURE 5.8   A tone generator and tracing probe

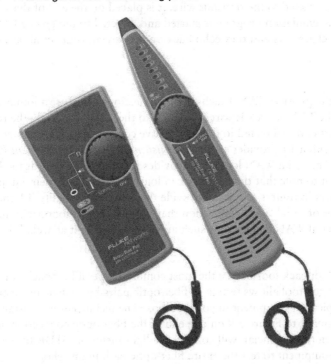

The tone generator is plugged into the cable connection that needs to be traced. It operates by injecting a warbling electrical tone into the network cable. The electrical tone is very weak, so it does not affect the network equipment it is plugged into. The probe then amplifies the electrical tone into an audible tone. The technique of identifying the wiring is to sweep over the cables with the probe until the faint tone is heard. Then, focus tracing in the area of the faint tone with the probe until the cable is identified by a much stronger tone. The cable tester can then be used to positively identify the cable.

Loopback Adapter

Several different types of loopback adapters are available that you can use in a network. The loopback adapter's job is to redirect transmissions so that the media or connection can be tested. In the following sections, I will cover the most common types of loopback adapters that you will use.

Serial

Serial loopback adapters are useful when you are trying to verify the connectivity of a serial adapter. When we plug into equipment and do not get a response back, we need to verify that we have a successful connection. The serial loopback adapter allows proper testing of the connection and lets us verify that we have the correct COM port configured.

The adapter is wired so that the transmit wire is redirected to the receive wire and the receive wire is redirected to the transmit wire. It is placed on the end of the serial adapter; then the terminal emulation program is started and directed to the proper COM port. If you are able to type characters and they echo back on the screen, your serial port configuration is correct.

Serial WAN

Serial wide area networks (WANs) such as T1 connections often use a loopback adapter to verify wiring. The T1 loopback is wired similarly to the serial loopback; the receive wires and transmit wires are redirected to their respective counterpart. The adapter is often used when working with a T1 provider so that the *customer premises equipment (CPE)* wiring can be verified. The serial WAN loopback provides testing wiring only at the Physical layer.

It is important to note that the provider can logically loop back their equipment, and newer transceivers in routers today can provide the same functionality. T1 connections are not the only type of serial WAN connection that use this type of loopback; there are several other types of serial WAN connections such as T3 that can use it as well.

Fiber-Optic

The fiber-optic loopback tool will be the most common type of loopback you will use. The fiber-optic loopback tool allows testing of fiber-optic pairs by a single technician and should be an essential piece of equipment in your toolbox. The technician will install the fiber-optic loopback tool similar to Figure 5.9 on one end of the fiber-optic connection, normally at the patch panel. Then the technician will connect the light meter or OTDR to the other end. This allows the test equipment to test the entire fiber-optic path in one shot.

When testing fiber-optic connections for WAN connectivity, the provider often loops the far-end side of the connection so that the entire path of the connection can be tested with a light meter. The provider often uses a device similar to the one shown in Figure 5.9.

FIGURE 5.9   An LC fiber-optic loopback plug

FIGURE 5.9   An LC fiber-optic loopback plug

OTDR

An *optical time-domain reflectometer (OTDR)* is used for diagnostic and testing of fiber-optic cable. A typical OTDR is shown in Figure 5.10. It has similar functionality to a TDR, but its functionality far surpasses a simple TDR. Fiber-optic cable spans much greater distances than copper Ethernet. It can find breaks in fiber just as a TDR can, so the technician can find the location of the fault sometimes spanning up to 75 miles. It does this by pulsing light in a fiber-optic cable and measuring the reflective return of light, which all fiber-optic cable has. It can also measure reflective loss, end-to-end loss, and points of high loss. Most high-end networking equipment today has fiber-optic analysis built in. The OTDR is mainly used by fiber-optic technicians to certify a fiber-optic installation, diagnose problems, and analyze expected loss.

FIGURE 5.10   An optical time-domain reflectometer

Multimeter

The *multimeter* is not typically used for testing network connections such as the previously covered equipment. It is used to provide testing of power sources with either the alternating current (AC) mode or the direct current (DC) mode. In Figure 5.11 you can see a typical multimeter.

FIGURE 5.11   A typical multimeter

The operation of the multimeter for testing of high-voltage power at the socket is performed on the AC mode. Multimeters must be set to a specific range for the voltage being tested, such as the range of 0 to 400 volts for normal AC sockets. This range will cover the typical voltages found in your data center of 120 v and 208 v. It is important to note that every meter will have a different range; 0 to 400 is only an example range. Some multimeters will range to 20 v, 200 v, and 1000 v; every multimeter is different. Newer multimeters will auto-range so that all you need to do is select the type of measurement. Use caution since high voltage can be fatal if proper precaution is not taken. The multimeter can also be used to test DC power supplies, although normally the voltage being measured is well under 27 volts and these voltages are typically classified as low voltage. Low-voltage DC testing is used with power supplies to confirm that they are supplying the proper voltage for the equipment.

Multimeters are called multimeters because they can also measure continuity and resistance. These functions are handy when you are determining whether a connection is faulty or determining the position of a pair of dry contacts on a relay. The multimeter used in these scenarios is often used with access control system (ACS) troubleshooting.

Cable Tester

The *cable tester* is another tool that network professionals should never be without. It is used to check a cable end that has been freshly crimped or to diagnose a patch cable that is suspected to be bad. Cable testers often come in pairs or transmitters and receivers, as shown in Figure 5.12.

FIGURE 5.12   A cable tester pair

If I were to explain how to terminate an RJ-45 on a network cable, I'm sure it would sound easy. However, terminating an RJ-45 takes plenty of practice to get it right the first time. The cable tester will test each individual wire for any faults or mis-wiring. Most cable testers will sequentially test each pair for the correct continuity and connectivity. Good pairs come back with a green light and a red light to depict a problem.

A *time-domain reflectometer (TDR)*, shown in Figure 5.13, is a sophisticated networking tool for troubleshooting wiring. It was once a tool that was out of reach of most networking professionals because of cost. Advanced cable testers now come with this TDR functionality built in for a little higher cost. A TDR allows you to find breaks in cables, bad patch cords, and bad connections, with the added benefit of the location of the problem.

All wires have a reflection of energy. For example, if two people hold a rope tight and you flick one end, the wave created will zip toward the other person and then back to you. Wires work the same way; when a pulse of electricity is introduced into them, it reflects back. The TDR operates by sending low-energy pulses of electricity down the wires and timing when the reflection is detected. Since speed multiplied by time equals distance, we can get an accurate distance of each wire. In a network cable, all eight wires should have the same timing.

If one wire is detected before the others, it is shorter than the other, and the problem is revealed. With a little estimating of cable lengths, you can even figure out where the problem is, because the TDR reports back the distances of each wire.

FIGURE 5.13   A time-domain reflectometer

A *cable certifier* does more than just test the cable end wiring; it is used for end-to-end certification of an installation. A cable certifier tests everything from the proper wiring of jacks, patch panels, and all cabling between for the required speed. It operates by sending a signal at the frequency designated by the EIA/TIA categories. For example, a 1 Gbps category 6a network designates the test frequency of 500 MHz. The signal is introduced to one end of the network and is measured at the other end for loss, accuracy of the signal, and crosstalk. If it passes this test at the designated frequency, then it is certified for 10 Gbps at 100 meters. Figure 5.14 details a typical cable certifier.

Wire Map

In my career, I've terminated thousands of cable ends and punched thousands of wires down. However, no matter how many I do I have the same dilemma when a cable fails. I don't know which cable end is bad or which punch down is wrong, it's always a 50/50 chance of getting it right a second time. The wire map test solves this dilemma by combining TDR functionality with cable testing functionality. A wire map can determine which end is actually bad and which wires are crossed, shorted, or open. Generally higher-end cable testers will come with this functionality.

FIGURE 5.14   A cable certifier

Tap

A tap is just as its name implies' it allows a technician to tap into a network connection. The tap enables the technician to listen to traffic between two endpoints of a network connection. Network taps can be purchased in two varieties; passive and active. A passive tap is nothing more than a simple slice for the technician's computer. However, active taps can be very expensive depending on the features and speeds it can handle. An active tap acts more like a switch with a monitored connection. In either case the technician can monitor the connection and capture network traffic for analysis.

Fusion Splicer

A fusion splicer is an amazing device that can control both power and precision. It is used to fuse two sections of a fiber-optic strand together to create a fiber-optic splice. The device must induce a temperature over 1,800 Celsius by discharging a precise spark to fuse the glass strands together. The glass must also be perfectly aligned to a thousandth of an inch. It performs these marvels all within the space of a 9-inch portable unit. However, the precision and power to fuse glass also come with a hefty price tag; some of these devices can be upward of $20,000 dollars depending on the features.

Spectrum Analyzer

The *spectrum analyzer* is specifically used with wireless communication troubleshooting. The spectrum analyzer allows us to see the radio frequency (RF) spectrum to identify noise and interference with wireless signaling. In Figure 5.15, a sample output from the NETSCOUT AirMagnet displays the 2.4 GHz RF band for 802.11 wireless.

FIGURE 5.15   NETSCOUT AirMagnet spectrum analyzer

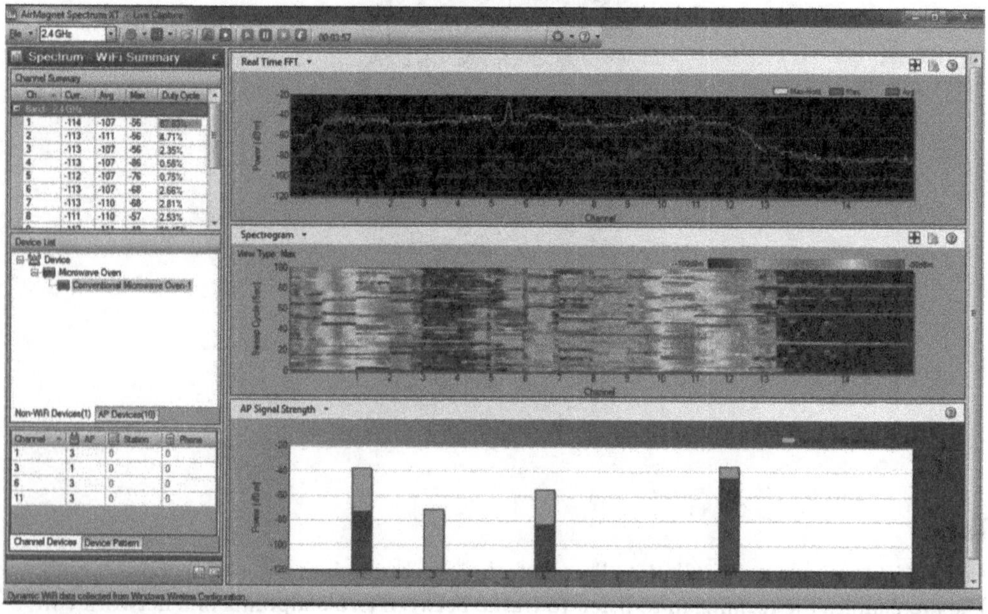

The spectrum analyzer software requires a specialized wireless dongle. This dongle is often connected to the technician's laptop via a USB connection. The dongle allows the software to capture the various RF airspace. Some network device vendors such as Cisco provide software that can connect to the wireless access point and turn it into a spectrum analyzer.

Snips/Cutters

Snips and wire cutters are the most underrated tools in the toolbox. When you're terminating wires, a sharp pair of wire cutters are just as important as the punch-down tool. I find that I need two types of wire cutting tools in my toolbox: the first is a pair of wire cutters that can easily and safely cut through a network cable. In Figure 5.16, you'll see a small pair of cable loppers and a typical wire cutter. The second wire cutting tool is a pair of really sharp scissors sometimes called snips. In Figure 5.17 you'll see a typical pair of snips. These are useful to the strength member inside riser cable or for just opening a package.

FIGURE 5.16   Wire cutters

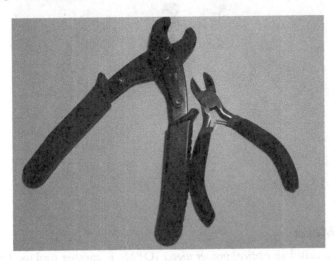

FIGURE 5.17   Wire snips

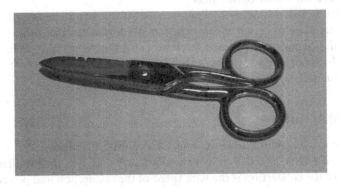

Cable Stripper

A cable stripper is another useful tool that is used to strip the sheath of a wire to expose the copper conductor. Or in the instance of network cable, they are used to expose the pairs of wires so that the network cable can be terminated to a patch panel or RJ-45.

In Figure 5.18, you'll see three different types of cable strippers. Some cable strippers can also look like a pair of cable snips with varying sized holes for each size conductor.

FIGURE 5.18   Typical cable strippers

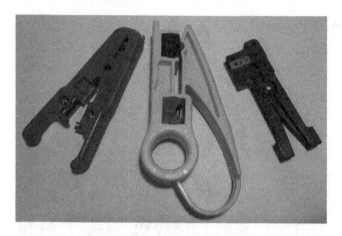

Fiber Light Meter

A light meter, also called an *optical power meter (OPM)*, is another tool used for diagnosis and testing of fiber-optic cable. The light meter measures the strength of the light from a reference light source that is paired with the light meter. The light meter also reports the amount of light loss for a fiber-optic cable.

The light meter function is normally built into an OTDR, but it can be purchased as a separate tool. It should also be noted that many small form-factor pluggable (SFP+) transceivers covered in Chapter 1, "Domain 1.0: Networking Fundamentals," have a built-in light meter function. In the operating system of the network device, signal strength can be verified with a simple command and without disrupting communications.

Exam Essentials

Understand how specifications and limitations affect a cable installation.
The throughput of a cable installation is the usable bandwidth that the installation will provide. The speed of the connection is the wire speed of the connection and potentially the speed a connection can burst up to. The distance of a cable installation is defined by the cable installation specifications and often noted in meters.

Know the various cable considerations.   The most common cables used in networks today are unshielded twisted-pair (UTP) and shielded twisted-pair (STP). UTP cabling is the most common cable used in networks today. STP cabling is used in networks that have high amounts of EMI from machinery. STP cabling is usually used in industrial Ethernet circum-stances and is more expensive than UTP. PVC jacketed cabling is also called riser-rated cable. PVC cable has a plastic that when burned can cause irritation in the lungs and eyes. There-fore, it is specified in the electrical and fire code that plenum-rated cable be used in airspace that provides ventilation or air-conditioning. Plenum cable is coated with a fire-retardant coating that is usually Teflon-based.

Know the various cable applications.   A rollover cable, also known as a console cable, is a flat stock telephone cable that is crimped on both ends with RJ-45 connectors. One side has an RJ-45 connector crimped starting at pin 1 and the opposite end has an RJ-45 connector crimped starting at pin 8. So, pin 1 maps to 8, pin 2 maps to 7, and so on. A crossover cable allows for the transmit pins of the cable to be crossed over to the receive pins on the opposite computer. Crossover cables are useful when connecting the same type devices together without the use of a switch or hub, such as computers. The PoE (802.3af) standard is used to supply up to 15.4 watts of power and is commonly used with phone and video surveillance cameras. The PoE+ (802.3at) standard is used to supply up to 25.5 watts of power.

Understand the common scenarios in which wired connectivity and performance issues can arise from physical factors.   Attenuation is common on RF cabling such as coaxial cabling; it is not common in Ethernet networks. Electrical magnetic interference (EMI) is generated by radio frequency (RF) devices, large motors, and high-voltage lines and can be counter-acted by using shielded twisted-pair (STP) wiring. Decibel (dB) loss is a measurable loss in signal on a cable. Incorrect pinout is generally associated with serial cables. The pinout can be checked with a multimeter. Bad ports on network switches should be identified and the equipment should be replaced so that time is not wasted in the future on diagnosing a bad port. Open conditions in a wire means that a wire is not making a connection, which can happen if a connector comes loose or a wire breaks. A short happens when two wires make a connection; this can happen if the insulation on the wires wears off or a foreign object is run into the wiring. Transceiver mismatch happens when the other transceiver does not offer backward support of the speed, or fiber-optic transceivers do not match the expected wave-length on both ends. Fiber-optic cables are also susceptible to the transmit and receive fiber-optic cable being reversed; when this happens, the link will not turn up.

Know the various hardware tools that you will encounter and use daily as a network admin-istrator.   Crimpers are used to crimp RJ-45 ends on network cabling. The punch-down tool is used to punch the wire of the network cable into a patch panel or female cable end. The tone generator is used for locating network cabling with a signal probe. The fiber-optic loop-back is used to loop one end of the fiber-optic cable so that testing can be done end to end. The optical time-domain reflectometer (OTDR) is used to measure the length of fiber-optic cable and identify breaks in it. The multimeter is commonly used to test power at outlets and power supplies and to test continuity in low-voltage wiring circuits. The cable tester is used to test patch cables and network cabling with male RJ-45 ends. A wire mapper is similar to a cable tester but also details which wire needs repaired in the event of a mis-wire.

A tap allows network equipment to tap into the signal so a tech can capture traffic. A fusion splicer is a device that fuses glass fiber together to splice fiber-optic cable together. The spectrum analyzer helps the administrator see the radio frequency (RF) spectrum and is often used to diagnose wireless interference problems. Snips and cutters are used to cut cabling and the components of a cable. Cable strippers allow the technician to remove the sheathing of the cable. The light meter allows the administrator to measure the amount of signal loss in a fiber-optic cable.

5.3 Given a scenario, use the appropriate network software tools and commands.

Now that you understand the considerations and how to provide a good solid cable installation, as well as the hardware used to troubleshoot cabling, we will focus on the software tools used to verify and identify logical problems with a cable installation. In the following sections, you will learn about the various software tools used to verify communications as well as troubleshoot problems.

Software Tools

Software tools are used to troubleshoot network problems and verify cause and validate effect. In the previous section, you learned about hardware tools that are used to repair network connections. You will now learn about the popular software tools that are used to detect the root cause of problems and troubleshoot networking issues.

Wi-Fi Analyzer

Wi-Fi analyzers help network administrators identify channel and wireless access point (WAP) problems. The functionality of Wi-Fi analyzers is generally incorporated into spectrum analyzers such as NETSCOUT AirMagnet, discussed earlier in this chapter. However, Wi-Fi analyzers can be used independently and are often free because of the basic functionality they provide. Spectrum analyzers will allow you to see non-Wi-Fi devices utilizing the RF airspace as well as interfering with electronics such as microwave ovens and wireless phones.

A Wi-Fi analyzer will provide power measurements of service set identifiers (SSIDs) and the encryption being used on each SSID. It will also display the channel the SSID is using and the MAC address of the WAP announcing the SSID. This information is useful because it shows the overall RF airspace as a device will see it. Figure 5.19 displays a popular Android phone application called Wifi Analyzer.

FIGURE 5.19　Android Wifi analyzer

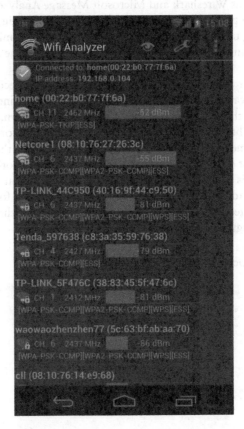

Protocol Analyzer/Packet Capture

Packet sniffers are software-based tools for capturing network traffic, also known as packet capturing. Packet sniffers can be used with wireless and wired network connections to capture packets. An example of a packet sniffer is the open-source *Wireshark* packet sniffer and analyzer. Microsoft also offers a free packet sniffer and analyzer called *Microsoft Message Analyzer* and *Microsoft Network Monitor*.

The packet sniffer by default will be able to capture broadcast, multicast, or direct traffic only on the host it is installed on. As discussed in Chapter 2, "Domain 2.0: Network Implementations," switches will forward frames only to ports that contain the destination host based on the MAC address table. We can configure port mirroring, also discussed in Chapter 2, "Domain 2.0: Network Implementations." Port mirroring will allow the port containing the packet sniffer to capture all network frames mirrored from the other port.

The packet sniffer's ability to capture network traffic is also directly dependent on the NIC. The NIC must support promiscuous mode, which allows the capture of frames with any destination MAC address. Although most newer NICs will allow promiscuous mode, the feature should be checked for the model of NIC with the vendor's specifications.

Protocol analyzers decipher frames of data that have been captured with a packet sniffer. Protocol analyzers such as Wireshark and Microsoft Message Analyzer also provide packet-sniffing capabilities. The protocol analyzer allows the network administrator to see the details of the data being transmitted or received. This allows the administrator to confirm that the data is being transmitted or received correctly or enables the administrator to focus on the problem area.

The protocol analyzer comes preloaded with parsers that help decipher the captured data. The parser is nothing more than a list of protocol numbers that define what protocols are being used from layer 2 through layer 7. Once the protocol is known, the data contained in the rest of the layer can be deciphered and displayed in a readable format.

For example, if a frame is captured with a Type field of 0x0806, then the frame is an ARP request and the rest of the data contained within is parsed according to an ARP frame layout. If the Type field is 0x0800, then the frame is an IPv4 frame and the data is parsed according to an IPv4 header layout. The data can be parsed further for the Transport and Application layers. In effect, the protocol analyzer de-encapsulates the data captured so it is readable, as shown in Figure 5.20.

FIGURE 5.20   Protocol analyzer of a TCP packet

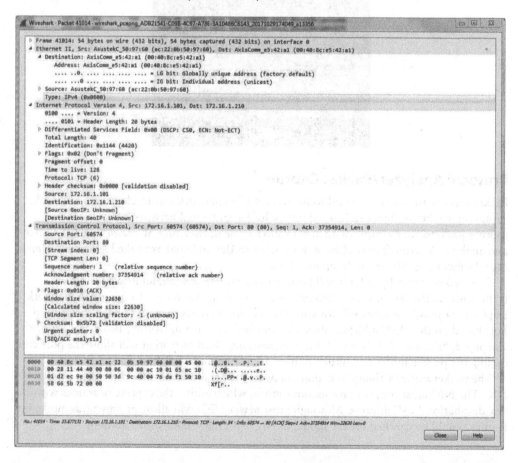

Bandwidth Speed Tester

Public bandwidth speed testers like `speedtest.net` are public Internet applets that communicate with dedicated Internet servers to determine your download and upload speeds. The inherent problem with these services is that they are being used by countless others and do not report an exact speed. They report the speed at which the server can communicate to you, which may not be the total speed of your connection. They are useful to validate that there is a problem with your Internet connectivity.

A more precise method of measuring bandwidth speed is the use of an open-source tool called iPerf. It requires a server to be set up to listen for an incoming request from the iPerf client. Many ISPs have an internal iPerf server so that you can test your WAN speed. When the iPerf tool is used, it saturates the entire line to report actual bandwidth speeds. It is also a useful tool for determining how well a firewall can perform under a high-bandwidth load as part of a stress test.

Port Scanner

Port scanners are used for troubleshooting connectivity issues and security assessments. When the port scanner is used for troubleshooting, the tool will scan the remote server to identify open ports that respond to the tool's requests. This is useful to validate that a server is serving information on the port and a firewall is not blocking the request.

We also use a port scanner to perform a security assessment of our servers. The port scanner verifies the open ports and the ports that are closed (firewalled). This helps reduce the risk that a firewall is misconfigured and allowing unauthorized access to services on the remote server.

There are several different port scanners that can be downloaded for free. The most popular open-source port scanner is Nmap. Originally it was compiled for Linux and Unix, but it has since been ported to the Windows platform. Microsoft also offers a free tool called PortQry, which is a command-line-based tool similar to Nmap.

iPerf

The iPerf tool is a software tool used to measure the performance of a network path. It measures the performance by sending traffic from one end to the other. The tool requires a client and a server: the server sits and waits for an incoming connection from the client and reports back the speed of the incoming packets. The most useful feature of this tool is that it's compiled for many different platforms such as firewalls, switches, Linux, and Windows, just to name a few. The tool also works in two different modes, TCP and UDP. In TCP mode the overhead of the acknowledgments and sequencing can be measured with overall traffic compared to UDP.

A typical application for iPerf is the measurement of bandwidth across a network path for Voice over IP (VoIP) applications. The iPerf tool acts as a stress test by sending large amounts of packets in an attempt to measure the overall throughput. Another application where iPerf is used is to benchmark the throughput for a router or firewall. In the following example, you will see the path across a network connection over an interval of 10 seconds.

```
C:\sys>iperf3.exe -c iperf.sybex.com
Connecting to host iperf.sybex.com, port 5201
[  4] local 172.16.1.181 port 58039 connected to 24.7.124.124 port 5201
[ ID] Interval           Transfer     Bandwidth
[  4]   0.00-1.00   sec  1.12 MBytes  9.43 Mbits/sec
[  4]   1.00-2.00   sec  1.38 MBytes  11.5 Mbits/sec
[  4]   2.00-3.00   sec   512 KBytes  4.19 Mbits/sec
[  4]   3.00-4.00   sec  1.38 MBytes  11.5 Mbits/sec
[  4]   4.00-5.00   sec  1.38 MBytes  11.5 Mbits/sec
[  4]   5.00-6.00   sec  1.38 MBytes  11.5 Mbits/sec
[  4]   6.00-7.00   sec  1.50 MBytes  12.6 Mbits/sec
[  4]   7.00-8.00   sec  1.38 MBytes  11.5 Mbits/sec
[  4]   8.00-9.00   sec  1.38 MBytes  11.5 Mbits/sec
[  4]   9.00-10.00  sec  1.38 MBytes  11.5 Mbits/sec
- - - - - - - - - - - - - - - - - - - - - - - - -
[ ID] Interval           Transfer     Bandwidth
[  4]   0.00-10.00  sec  12.8 MBytes  10.7 Mbits/sec                 sender
[  4]   0.00-10.00  sec  12.7 MBytes  10.6 Mbits/sec                 receiver

iperf Done.

C:\sys>
```

NetFlow Analyzer

A NetFlow-enabled device such as a router or firewall can be configured to export traffic to a NetFlow collector. The NetFlow collector serves as a centralized storage location for the NetFlow Analyzer. The NetFlow Analyzer will then read the collected NetFlow entries and create a visual report, such as one seen in Figure 5.21. There are many different NetFlow Analyzer software packages on the market today. There are free open-source NetFlow Analyzer software packages such as ntop, and then there are other premium software packages such as Paessler PRTG, ManageEngine, and SolarWinds, just to name a few.

NetFlow analyzers are extremely useful to visually see the flow of traffic through the network. This visualization allows the admin to look from a 10,000-mile view and slowly zone in on details. One common use of a NetFlow analyzer is to identify high traffic applications and users. An admin can quickly identify bandwidth hogs and restore normal consumption of bandwidth though the network.

FIGURE 5.21   A NetFlow analyzer

Trivial File Transfer Protocol (TFTP) Server

The Trivial File Transfer Protocol (TFTP) server is a software tool that allows a technician to upgrade or back up network devices. The TFTP software operates on UDP port 69 and does not require any authentication, which makes it perfect for impromptu use. Many vendor upgrade processes for switches and routers require the use of a TFTP server. The technician will start the TFTP server on their laptop, as shown in Figure 5.22. The technician will then use terminal emulator software to make a connection to the device, and then initiate an upgrade via the TFTP server. TFTP servers are not just for upgrades of a network operating system. It's also a popular option to back up configuration or to load new configurations to a router or switch.

Terminal Emulator

Terminal emulator software assists the technician with console-based access with a serial cable, a Telnet session, or an SSH session. Many network devices don't require a graphical user interface (GUI); they just need a way to communicate via their command-line interface (CLI) and this is where terminal emulator software comes in handy. Back in the day, terminal emulator software was performed via a serial line or Telnet, but today SSH has largely replaced these methods. However, a serial line is often needed when a device is first started and does not contain any initial configuration. A typical terminal emulator software can be seen in Figure 5.23.

FIGURE 5.22 A typical TFTP server

Tftpd32 by Ph. Jounin
Current Directory
C:\sys
Browse
Server interfaces
172.16.1.181
Show Dir
Tftp Server
Tftp Client
DHCP server
Syslog server
Log viewer
peer
file
start time
progress
bytes
About
Settings
Help

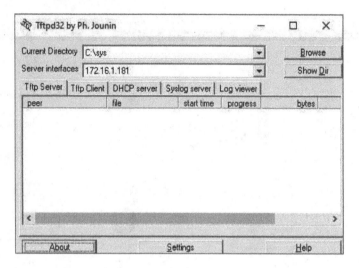

FIGURE 5.23 A typical terminal emulator

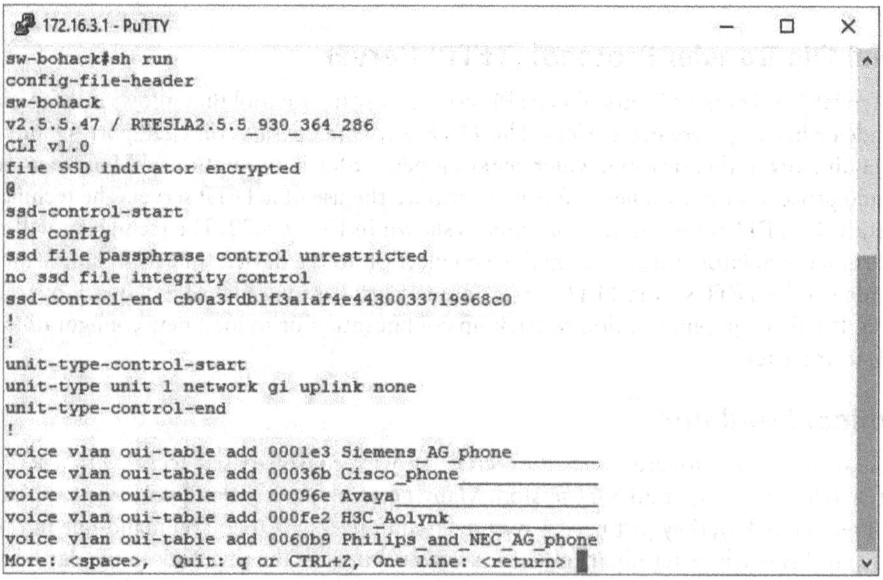

172.16.3.1 - PuTTY
sw-bohack#sh run
config-file-header
sw-bohack
v2.5.5.47 / RTESLA2.5.5_930_364_286
CLI v1.0
file SSD indicator encrypted
@
ssd-control-start
ssd config
ssd file passphrase control unrestricted
no ssd file integrity control
ssd-control-end cb0a3fdb1f3a1af4e4430033719968c0
!
!
unit-type-control-start
unit-type unit 1 network gi uplink none
unit-type-control-end
!
voice vlan oui-table add 0001e3 Siemens_AG_phone________
voice vlan oui-table add 00036b Cisco_phone____________
voice vlan oui-table add 00096e Avaya__________________
voice vlan oui-table add 000fe2 H3C_Aolynk_____________
voice vlan oui-table add 0060b9 Philips_and_NEC_AG_phone
More: <space>, Quit: q or CTRL+Z, One line: <return>

There are several different TFTP servers and terminal emulators on the market from various vendors. However, for the past two decades both Tftpd and PuTTY have been popular free open-source software (FOSS). The Tftpd application can be downloaded from https://pjo2.github .io/tftpd64/. The application acts as a server, client, DHCP server, and syslog server and contains a log viewer. The PuTTY application can be downloaded from www.putty.org and has a very rich feature interface.

IP Scanner

An IP scanner is used to scan a range of IP addresses, as shown in Figure 5.24. The IP scanner software tool is extremely useful for finding free IP addresses in a particular IP address range. The tool is also useful for locating a host within an IP address range. The tool will first scan the IP address space and report back if the IP address responds to an ICMP ping request. Most tools will then reverse the DNS address of the IP address to display the host's friendly DNS name.

FIGURE 5.24   A typical IP scanner

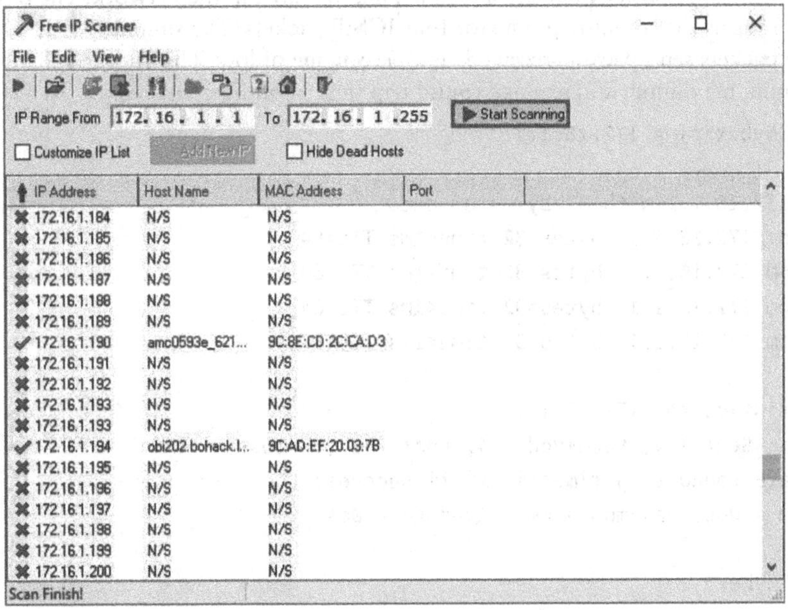

IP Address	Host Name	MAC Address	Port	
✖ 172.16.1.184	N/S	N/S		
✖ 172.16.1.185	N/S	N/S		
✖ 172.16.1.186	N/S	N/S		
✖ 172.16.1.187	N/S	N/S		
✖ 172.16.1.188	N/S	N/S		
✖ 172.16.1.189	N/S	N/S		
✔ 172.16.1.190	amc0593e_621...	9C:8E:CD:2C:CA:D3		
✖ 172.16.1.191	N/S	N/S		
✖ 172.16.1.192	N/S	N/S		
✖ 172.16.1.193	N/S	N/S		
✖ 172.16.1.193	N/S	N/S		
✔ 172.16.1.194	obi202.bohack.l..	9C:AD:EF:20:03:7B		
✖ 172.16.1.195	N/S	N/S		
✖ 172.16.1.196	N/S	N/S		
✖ 172.16.1.197	N/S	N/S		
✖ 172.16.1.198	N/S	N/S		
✖ 172.16.1.199	N/S	N/S		
✖ 172.16.1.200	N/S	N/S		

Although, this tool is useful for quickly finding out if an IP address is taken, many operating systems will not reply to a ping request by default. On many newer operating systems such as Windows 10 and Server 2019, the firewall is configured out of the box. So you should always use a more formal approach to IP address management (IPAM). With that being said, this tool does work in most situations.

Command-Line Tools

On any given day at work, you will always find a command prompt open on one of my many monitors. Using a command line is just faster than a bunch of clicking. Some tools can only be accessed via a command line, as you'll see in the following sections. These command-line tools allow us to diagnose and troubleshoot network issues.

ping

The ping command is the most basic troubleshooting command. It uses the Internet Control Message Protocol (ICMP) at layer 3 to verify that a server is reachable. It is also useful for displaying the round-trip response time to a specific IP address. It is the first command I use when trying to determine if a server is responding. It should be noted that if ICMP is being blocked on the host, it will still respond to application requests but will not respond to the ping command.

In the following example, you see a simple ping to a host in the network. The ping command returns the round-trip time for four ICMP packets. The summary that follows shows the packets sent, packets received, and percentage of loss. The output will also detail the minimum, maximum, and average round-trip time in milliseconds.

```
C:\Users\Sybex>ping 172.16.1.1

Pinging 172.16.1.1 with 32 bytes of data:
Reply from 172.16.1.1: bytes=32 time<1ms TTL=64
Reply from 172.16.1.1: bytes=32 time<1ms TTL=64
Reply from 172.16.1.1: bytes=32 time<1ms TTL=64
Reply from 172.16.1.1: bytes=32 time<1ms TTL=64

Ping statistics for 172.16.1.1:
    Packets: Sent = 4, Received = 4, Lost = 0 (0% loss),
Approximate round trip times in milli-seconds:
    Minimum = 0ms, Maximum = 0ms, Average = 0ms

C:\Users\Sybex>
```

ipconfig

The ipconfig command is a Windows command used to verify IP address configuration and its associated options. The command also allows control of the DHCP configuration of renewal and release as well as control of the local DNS cache.

When using the `ipconfig` command to display the current IP address configuration, you can use either the short or the long mode, as shown in the following code. If you enter the command by itself, the basic information of IP address, subnet mask, and default gateway is displayed. If you add the `/all` argument, it also displays the MAC address, DHCP status, lease times, DHCP server, and DNS server in addition to many other configuration options.

```
C:\Users\Sybex>ipconfig

Windows IP Configuration

Ethernet adapter Local Area Connection:

    Connection-specific DNS Suffix . : sybex.local
    Link-local IPv6 Address . . . . . : fe80::bc1e:1758:ba9a:ddf3%11
    IPv4 Address. . . . . . . . . . . : 172.16.1.101
    Subnet Mask . . . . . . . . . . . : 255.240.0.0
    Default Gateway . . . . . . . . . : 172.16.1.1

C:\Users\Sybex>ipconfig /all

Windows IP Configuration

    Host Name . . . . . . . . . . . . : ClientA
    Primary Dns Suffix . . . . . . . :
    Node Type . . . . . . . . . . . . : Hybrid
    IP Routing Enabled. . . . . . . . : No
    WINS Proxy Enabled. . . . . . . . : No
    DNS Suffix Search List. . . . . . : sybex.local

Ethernet adapter Local Area Connection:

    Connection-specific DNS Suffix . : sybex.local
    Description . . . . . . . . . . . : Intel(R) Gigabit Network Connection
    Physical Address. . . . . . . . . : AC-22-0B-50-97-60
    DHCP Enabled. . . . . . . . . . . : Yes
    Autoconfiguration Enabled . . . . : Yes
    Link-local IPv6 Address . . . . . : fe80::bc1e:1758:ba9a:ddf3%11(Preferred)
    IPv4 Address. . . . . . . . . . . : 172.16.1.101(Preferred)
    Subnet Mask . . . . . . . . . . . : 255.240.0.0
    Lease Obtained. . . . . . . . . . : Sunday, October 29, 2017 8:40:20 AM
```

```
Lease Expires . . . . . . . . . . : Sunday, October 29, 2017 11:40:20 PM
Default Gateway . . . . . . . . . : 172.16.1.1
DHCP Server . . . . . . . . . . . : 172.16.1.1
DHCPv6 IAID . . . . . . . . . . . : 246161931
DHCPv6 Client DUID. . . . . . . . : 00-01-00-01-1A-45-39-41-AC-22-0B-50-97
DNS Servers . . . . . . . . . . . : 172.16.1.1
NetBIOS over Tcpip. . . . . . . . : Enabled
```

`C:\Users\Sybex>`

Another common use for the ipconfig command is to release the current IP address and obtain a new IP address using the release and renew options. When a connection is unplugged and plugged back in, the operating system will automatically release and request a new IP address from the DHCP server. However, if the VLAN is changed, it will not register an unplugged/plugged connection, and ipconfig /release and ipconfig /renew will request a new IP address from the DHCP server.

The ipconfig command can also be used to view and control the local client DNS cache. When the operating system requests a query from the DNS server, the answer is cached locally in memory until the time to live (TTL) for the record expires. We can view the local DNS cache with the ipconfig /displaydns command, and we can dump the cache with the ipconfig /flushdns command. The second command is useful if we just change the IP address for a record and want the change to take effect immediately on the local machine. The ipconfig /registerdns command will force the local machine to register its dynamic DNS records with the DNS server.

ifconfig

The ifconfig command is similar to ipconfig, but it's strictly used on Linux and Unix operating systems. It is similar in that you can obtain IP address information from the operating system by using the command ifconfig -a:

```
root@sybex:~# ifconfig
eth0 Link encap:Ethernet HWaddr 00:0c:29:e9:08:92
     inet addr:172.16.1.161 Bcast:172.31.255.255 Mask:255.240.0.0
     inet6 addr: fe80::20c:29ff:fee9:892/64 Scope:Link
     UP BROADCAST RUNNING MULTICAST MTU:1500 Metric:1
     RX packets:141 errors:0 dropped:0 overruns:0 frame:0
     TX packets:92 errors:0 dropped:0 overruns:0 carrier:0
     collisions:0 txqueuelen:1000
     RX bytes:19193 (19.1 KB) TX bytes:11708 (11.7 KB)

lo   Link encap:Local Loopback
     inet addr:127.0.0.1 Mask:255.0.0.0
```

```
        inet6 addr: ::1/128 Scope:Host
        UP LOOPBACK RUNNING MTU:65536 Metric:1
        RX packets:0 errors:0 dropped:0 overruns:0 frame:0
        TX packets:0 errors:0 dropped:0 overruns:0 carrier:0
        collisions:0 txqueuelen:0
        RX bytes:0 (0.0 B) TX bytes:0 (0.0 B)
```

root@sybex:~#

The ifconfig command will allow you to do much more than just view the current IP address. Using the command, you can configure an IP address and subnet mask on any available interface. Setting a manual IP address with this command would look like the following. However, this IP address will not be persistent through a reboot. The IP address would need to be configured in the appropriate interface file for the Linux/Unix distribution.

```
root@sybex:~# ifconfig eth0 172.16.1.200 netmask 255.240.0.0
root@sybex:~# ifconfig -a
eth0 Link encap:Ethernet HWaddr 00:0c:29:e9:08:92
        inet addr:172.16.1.200 Bcast:172.31.255.255 Mask:255.240.0.0
        inet6 addr: fe80::20c:29ff:fee9:892/64 Scope:Link
        UP BROADCAST RUNNING MULTICAST MTU:1500 Metric:1
        RX packets:1076 errors:0 dropped:0 overruns:0 frame:0
        TX packets:264 errors:0 dropped:0 overruns:0 carrier:0
        collisions:0 txqueuelen:1000
        RX bytes:94756 (94.7 KB) TX bytes:40618 (40.6 KB)

lo    Link encap:Local Loopback
        inet addr:127.0.0.1 Mask:255.0.0.0
        inet6 addr: ::1/128 Scope:Host
        UP LOOPBACK RUNNING MTU:65536 Metric:1
        RX packets:0 errors:0 dropped:0 overruns:0 frame:0
        TX packets:0 errors:0 dropped:0 overruns:0 carrier:0
        collisions:0 txqueuelen:0
        RX bytes:0 (0.0 B) TX bytes:0 (0.0 B)
```

root@sybex:~#

In addition to setting an IP address and viewing the IP address configuration, ifconfig allows you to administer an interface to a down status or up status, set the interface into promiscuous mode if the hardware supports it, and change the maximum transmission unit (MTU). It is important to note that any configuration change made with ifconfig is temporary and not persistent, unless it is configured in the appropriate configuration file for the distribution.

ip

The ifconfig utility is slowly being replaced on certain distributions of Linux with the ip utility. Red Hat Enterprise Linux has adopted the ip utility and it's actually similar to the ifconfig utility. You can configure an address or show the configured IP addresses, similar to the ifconfig utility. You just need to memorize some of the commands, as shown in the following example. The output looks very similar to the ifconfig utility.

```
root@sybex:~# ip addr add 172.16.1.200/12 eth0
root@sybex:~# ip addr
eth0: <BROADCAST, MULTICAST, UP> mtu 1500 qlen 1000
 link/ether 00:0c:29:e9:08:92 brd ff:ff:ff:ff:ff:ff:ff:ff
 inet 172.16.1.200/12 scope global eth0
    valid_lft forever preferred_lft forever
 inet6 fe80::20c:29ff:fee9:892/64 scope link
    valid_lft forever preferred_lft forever
lo: <LOOPBACK,UP,LOWER_UP> mtu 65536 noqueue
 link/loopback 00:00:00:00:00:00:00:00 brd 00:00:00:00:00:00:00:00
 inet 127.0.0.1/8 scope host lo
    valid_lft forever preferred_lft forever
 inet6 ::1/128 scope host
    valid_lft forever preferred_lft forever

root@sybex:~#
```

nslookup

nslookup is a command that can be found on both Windows and Linux/Unix operating systems. However, Linux and Unix operating systems favor the dig command over nslookup. The nslookup command stands for *name-server lookup* and is used to resolve Domain Name Server (DNS) addresses. The command can be used to resolve any type of DNS resource record. It is useful in troubleshooting DNS resolution problems. You can point it to a specific server using the server= argument so that you can directly query a specific DNS server.

The command can also be used in either noninteractive command mode or interactive mode. In the next example, the nslookup command is used in noninteractive mode to retrieve the MX record for sybex.com. I then use it in interactive mode by entering just nslookup at a command prompt; then every command thereafter is interactive inside the nslookup command.

```
C:\Users\Sybex>nslookup -type=mx sybex.com
Server: pfSense.sybex.local
```

```
Address: 172.16.1.1

Non-authoritative answer:
sybex.com    MX preference = 20, mail exchanger = cluster1a.us.messagelabs.com
sybex.com    MX preference = 10, mail exchanger = cluster1.us.messagelabs.com

C:\Users\Sybex>nslookup
Default Server: pfSense.sybex.local
Address: 172.16.1.1

> set type=mx
> sybex.com
Server: pfSense.sybex.local
Address: 172.16.1.1

Non-authoritative answer:
sybex.com    MX preference = 10, mail exchanger = cluster1.us.messagelabs.com
sybex.com    MX preference = 20, mail exchanger = cluster1a.us.messagelabs.com
>
```

dig

The Domain Information Groper (dig) tool is almost identical to the `nslookup` tool and has become an adopted standard for name resolution testing on Linux/Unix operating systems. The tool allows us to resolve any resource record for a given host and direct the query to a specific server.

The command does not offer an interactive mode like the `nslookup` command. The command by default queries A records for a given host, and the output has debugging turned on by default.

In the following example, we see a query being performed on the DNS server of 8.8.8.8 for an MX record of sybex.com. The debugging output shows that one query was given, two answers were retrieved, and nothing was authoritative (not the primary servers). The output also details the query made and the answers returned.

```
root@Sybex:~# dig @8.8.8.8 mx sybex.com

; <<>> DiG 9.9.5-3ubuntu0.13-Ubuntu <<>> @8.8.8.8 mx sybex.com
; (1 server found)
;; global options: +cmd
;; Got answer:
;; ->>HEADER<<- opcode: QUERY, status: NOERROR, id: 49694
```

```
;; flags: qr rd ra; QUERY: 1, ANSWER: 2, AUTHORITY: 0, ADDITIONAL: 1

;; OPT PSEUDOSECTION:
; EDNS: version: 0, flags:; udp: 512
;; QUESTION SECTION:
;sybex.com.              IN   MX

;; ANSWER SECTION:
sybex.com.         899   IN   MX    10 cluster1.us.messagelabs.com.
sybex.com.         899   IN   MX    20 cluster1a.us.messagelabs.com.

;; Query time: 76 msec
;; SERVER: 8.8.8.8#53(8.8.8.8)
;; WHEN: Wed Nov 01 21:43:32 EDT 2017
;; MSG SIZE rcvd: 104


root@Sybex:~#
```

tracert/ traceroute

tracert is another useful ICMP-based command. In Windows, the command is tracert, and in Linux and Unix, the command is traceroute. Both commands perform the same function. For the remainder of this section I will refer to the command as tracert.

The tracert command performs a ping on each hop to a destination IP address. In the following example, it would take 12 hops to reach an IP address of 8.8.8.8 (Google DNS). The round-trip times for each hop are calculated and displayed next to the name resolution for each hop. In Windows, the name resolution can be turned off with the –d argument, and on Linux/Unix it can be turned off with the –n argument. Turning off name resolution will speed up the output from the command because no lookup is being performed. The tracert command is used to troubleshoot how packets are reaching the destination IP address by detailing the path the packets will take.

```
C:\Users\Sybex>tracert 8.8.8.8

Tracing route to google-public-dns-a.google.com [8.8.8.8]
over a maximum of 30 hops:

 1   <1 ms   <1 ms   <1 ms  pfSense.sybex.local [172.16.1.1]
 2   20 ms   12 ms   10 ms  96.120.62.213
 3   11 ms   11 ms   11 ms  te-0-4-0-13-c.pitt.pa.pitt.comcast.net [68.86.102.61]
 4   12 ms   12 ms   21 ms  te-8-3-ur01.wheeling.wv.pitt.comcast.net [68.86.100.26]
 5   14 ms   11 ms   19 ms  be-11-ar01.pa.pitt.comcast.net [68.86.147.109]
 6   18 ms   19 ms   19 ms  be-7016-cr02.ashburn.va.ibone.comcast.net [68.86.91.25]
```

```
7   17 ms   17 ms   18 ms  hu-0-11-0-2-pe07.ash.va.ibone.comcast.net [68.86.83.2]
8   22 ms   25 ms   17 ms  as4436-1-c.111.ny.ibone.comcast.net [173.167.57.162]
9   *       *       *      Request timed out.
10  18 ms   20 ms   19 ms  72.14.233.20
11  17 ms   18 ms   17 ms  209.85.247.207
12  18 ms   25 ms   16 ms  google-public-dns-a.google.com [8.8.8.8]
```

```
Trace complete.

C:\Users\Sybex>
```

arp

The arp tool can be found in every operating system, even network device operating systems. The tool allows the administrator to observe, delete, and change the *Address Resolution Protocol (ARP)* table in memory. The ARP table consists of the mapping for IP addresses to MAC addresses. The operating system keeps this information cached to speed up the communications process while limiting the number of ARP broadcasts in the network. If the operating system didn't keep this cache, it would need to perform an ARP request for the destination IP address it wants to communicate per frame.

The administrator can view the ARP table in memory for Windows by typing **arp -g** or **arp -a** in Linux/Unix. The arp tool also allows us to flush the table in Windows or Linux/Unix by typing **arp -d ***. We can also remove a specific entry by typing **arp -d 172.16.1.1**. In the following example, you will see the ARP table as well as the deletion of a specific entry:

```
C:\Users\Sybex>arp -g

Interface: 172.16.1.101 --- 0xb
  Internet Address      Physical Address      Type
  172.16.1.1            00-15-5d-01-12-0b    dynamic
  172.16.1.5            00-15-5d-01-12-07    dynamic
  172.16.1.10           74-d4-35-03-a6-b9    dynamic
  172.16.1.12           14-dd-a9-92-2f-1c    dynamic
  172.16.1.205          08-10-76-26-32-ec    dynamic
  172.16.1.210          00-40-8c-e5-42-a1    dynamic
  172.31.255.255        ff-ff-ff-ff-ff-ff    static
  224.0.0.22            01-00-5e-00-00-16    static
  224.0.0.251           01-00-5e-00-00-fb    static
  224.0.0.252           01-00-5e-00-00-fc    static
  239.255.255.250       01-00-5e-7f-ff-fa    static
  255.255.255.255       ff-ff-ff-ff-ff-ff    static

C:\Users\Sybex>arp -d 172.16.1.1
C:\Users\Sybex>
```

Notice that some entries have a static type and some have a dynamic type. The dynamic entries are removed from the ARP table after their TTL has expired. The TTL varies by operating system; the maximum TTL is around 2 minutes. The static entries will never be removed unless the host is rebooted or the ARP cache is manually flushed. The arp tool allows us to map a specific IP address with a specific MAC address. This is sometimes handy with older hardware during the setup process. The command to map an IP address to MAC address in both Windows and Linux/Unix is arp -s 172.16.1.1 00-15-5d-01-12-0b.

netstat

The netstat command can be found on both Windows and Linux/Unix operating systems. In Windows the command will display all of the current TCP and UDP connections as well as the state of the TCP connection. The command allows us to view the current bindings of layer 4 communications. This is useful for troubleshooting because it allows us to view the connection to an application. In the following example, we have several established states and one connection that is trying to complete a three-way handshake. The SYN-SENT state tells us that a SYN has been sent to the destination host of 172.16.1.55 but we have not received a response.

```
C:\Users\Sybex>netstat

Active Connections

  Proto  Local Address          Foreign Address        State
  TCP    127.0.0.1:443          Wiley:49755            ESTABLISHED
  TCP    127.0.0.1:49755        Wiley:https            ESTABLISHED
  TCP    127.0.0.1:49756        Wiley:49757            ESTABLISHED
  TCP    172.16.1.101:49237     iad23s61-in-f13:https  CLOSE_WAIT
  TCP    172.16.1.101:49238     iad23s60-in-f10:https  CLOSE_WAIT
  TCP    172.16.1.101:50703     172.16.1.161:ssh       ESTABLISHED
  TCP    172.16.1.101:50768     iad23s61-in-f14:https  ESTABLISHED
  TCP    172.16.1.101:50771     iad23s60-in-f14:https  ESTABLISHED
  TCP    172.16.1.101:50783     172.16.1.55:ssh        SYN_SENT
  TCP    [::1]:8307             Wiley:49762            ESTABLISHED
  TCP    [::1]:49762            Wiley:8307             ESTABLISHED

C:\Users\Sybex>
```

If we use the command netstat -a, we will get back all of the connections as well as any ports that are listening. This command helps us verify that the application has requested from the operating system a port to listen for requests on. Up until this point, I have focused on the output for the Windows operating system. Both the Windows and Linux/Unix versions of netstat operate the same to this point. In the next example, you see additional information about Unix sockets that is only relevant to Linux/Unix operating systems. A Unix socket is an interprocess communications (IPC) endpoint for the exchange of data on the same host.

```
root@sybex:~# netstat -a
Active Internet connections (servers and established)
Proto Recv-Q Send-Q Local Address        Foreign Address      State
tcp   0      0      localhost:6011       *:*                  LISTEN
tcp   0      0      localhost:mysql      *:*                  LISTEN
tcp   0      0      *:ssh                *:*                  LISTEN
tcp   0      64     172.16.1.161:ssh     172.16.1.101:50703   ESTABLISHED
tcp6  0      0      localhost:6011       [::]:*               LISTEN
tcp6  0      0      [::]:http            [::]:*               LISTEN
tcp6  0      0      [::]:ssh             [::]:*               LISTEN
udp   0      0      *:bootpc             *:*
udp   0      0      *:8398               *:*
udp6  0      0      [::]:12914           [::]:*
Active Unix domain sockets (servers and established)
Proto RefCnt Flags    Type    State      I-Node Path
unix  2      [ ACC ]  STREAM  LISTENING  11293  /var/run/acpid.socket
unix  2      [ ACC ]  STREAM  LISTENING  8495   /var/run/dbus/system_bus_socket
unix  8      [ ]      DGRAM              8539   /dev/log
unix  2      [ ACC ]  STREAM  LISTENING  1677   @/com/ubuntu/upstart
```

[Output cut]

The netstat -ab command in Windows can help us verify that an application is communicating by displaying the program that has created the binding. We can also use netstat -ab to show applications that are listening. In Linux/Unix, the command is netstat -ap.

```
C:\Users\Sybex>netstat -ab

Active Connections

  Proto Local Address        Foreign Address      State

  [svchost.exe]
  TCP   0.0.0.0:443          Wiley:0              LISTENING
  [wmpnetwk.exe]
  TCP   0.0.0.0:902          Wiley:0              LISTENING
  [svchost.exe]
```

```
TCP    0.0.0.0:5357        Wiley:0                LISTENING
[wininit.exe]
TCP    0.0.0.0:49153       Wiley:0                LISTENING
eventlog
[lsass.exe]
TCP    0.0.0.0:49155       Wiley:0                LISTENING
Schedule
[googledrivesync.exe]
TCP    172.16.1.101:49254  qu-in-f125:5222        ESTABLISHED
[googledrivesync.exe]
TCP    172.16.1.101:49256  iad23s58-in-f10:https  CLOSE_WAIT
[googledrivesync.exe]
TCP    172.16.1.101:49894  iad30s09-in-f10:https  CLOSE_WAIT
[googledrivesync.exe]
TCP    172.16.1.101:50625  qn-in-f188:5228        ESTABLISHED
[chrome.exe]
TCP    172.16.1.101:50632  209.11.111.11:https    ESTABLISHED
[chrome.exe]
TCP    172.16.1.101:50703  172.16.1.161:https     ESTABLISHED
[chrome.exe]
TCP    172.16.1.101:50803  iad23s61-in-f14:https  ESTABLISHED
[chrome.exe]
TCP    172.16.1.101:50804  iad23s61-in-f14:https  ESTABLISHED

[Output cut]
```

hostname

The hostname utility is a simple utility that returns the hostname of the operating system you are on. Although it is simple it is very useful when you have a number of remote sessions on your screen. It allows you to quicky know which system you are currently accessing, as shown in the following example. Thankfully the command is the same on Windows as it is on Linux.

```
Last login: Tue May 18 20:46:12 2021 from 24.7.124.124
# hostname
sybexsrv1.sybex.com
#
```

route

The route command is the Swiss Army knife of commands for viewing and changing the routing table on a host. The tool can be used to check the local host's routing table if it is suspected there is a routing issue. It is important to note that in Windows routing is not enabled, even if two or more network cards are installed. Routing requires the use of the Routing and Remote Access Service (RRAS). In Linux and Unix, the route command has similar features, such as the ability to view and configure the routing table.

In Windows, we can view the routing table by entering the command route print; in Linux or Unix, the command is route -n.

```
C:\Users\Sybex>route print
===========================================================================
Interface List
 11...ac 22 0b 50 96 60 ......Intel(R) 82583V Gigabit Network Connection
  1...........................Software Loopback Interface 1
===========================================================================

IPv4 Route Table
===========================================================================
Active Routes:
Network Destination        Netmask          Gateway       Interface  Metric
          0.0.0.0          0.0.0.0       172.16.1.1   172.16.1.101     10
        127.0.0.0        255.0.0.0        On-link        127.0.0.1    306
        127.0.0.1  255.255.255.255        On-link        127.0.0.1    306
  127.255.255.255  255.255.255.255        On-link        127.0.0.1    306
       172.16.0.0      255.240.0.0        On-link     172.16.1.101    266
     172.16.1.101  255.255.255.255        On-link     172.16.1.101    266
   172.31.255.255  255.255.255.255        On-link     172.16.1.101    266
        224.0.0.0        240.0.0.0        On-link        127.0.0.1    306
        224.0.0.0        240.0.0.0        On-link     172.16.1.101    266
  255.255.255.255  255.255.255.255        On-link        127.0.0.1    306
  255.255.255.255  255.255.255.255        On-link     172.16.1.101    266
===========================================================================
Persistent Routes:
 None

IPv6 Route Table
===========================================================================
Active Routes:
 If Metric        Network Destination            Gateway
  1    306                   ::1/128            On-link
```

```
11    266                    fe80::/64              On-link
11    266 fe80::bc1e:1758:ba9a:ddf3/128          On-link
 1    306                   ff00::/8               On-link
11    266                   ff00::/8               On-link
========================================================================
Persistent Routes:
 None
```

C:\Users\Sybex>

In Windows we can add a route with the command

```
route add 10.0.0.0 mask 255.0.0.0 172.16.1.5 metric 5 if 11
```

In the preceding command, the route add command is followed by the network 10.0.0.0 and the subnet mask 255.0.0.0. It is then followed by the gateway address 172.16.1.5, the metric 5, and the interface 11. We can also change and delete routes by specifying the following commands:

```
route change 10.0.0.0 mask 255.0.0.0 172.16.1.10 metric 5 if 11
route delete 10.0.0.0
```

Note that the route add command is not a persistent command. The route will not be preserved over a reboot. Therefore, the -p must be added between the route command and the add argument. The -p will preserve the route and make it persistent across a reboot.

telnet

The telnet command is a console-based terminal emulator that is installed by default on many Linux operating systems. Windows 10 has a telnet command, but the feature must be installed via the Programs and Features Control Panel applet. To start a Telnet session, you simply need to specify the command and the system you want to connect to, as shown in the following example.

```
root@sybex:~# telnet
telnet> open towel.blinkenlights.nl
Trying 2001:7b8:666:ffff::1:42...
Connected to towel.blinkenlights.nl.
Escape character is '^]'.
```

tcpdump

The tcpdump command is available on only Linux and Unix operating systems. The command is used to dump network data to a file or the console of the host you are connected to. It is useful when we want to see the network packets either entering or leaving a host.

The tcpdump command that follows will output all of the packets that match the port of SSH on interface eth0:

```
root@sybex:~# tcpdump -s 0 port ssh -i eth0
tcpdump: verbose output suppressed, use -v or -vv for full protocol decode
listening on eth0, link-type EN10MB (Ethernet), capture size 262144 bytes
22:17:59.829560 IP 172.16.1.161.ssh > 172.16.1.101.50703: Flags [P.], seq 32238
1889:322382097, ack 106937580, win 326, length 208
22:17:59.829719 IP 172.16.1.101.50703 > 172.16.1.161.ssh: Flags [.], ack 208, w
in 16121, length 0
22:17:59.831710 IP 172.16.1.161.ssh > 172.16.1.101.50703: Flags [P.], seq 208:4
96, ack 1, win 326, length 288
22:17:59.831782 IP 172.16.1.161.ssh > 172.16.1.101.50703: Flags [P.], seq 496:6
72, ack 1, win 326, length 176
22:17:59.831856 IP 172.16.1.101.50703 > 172.16.1.161.ssh: Flags [.], ack 672, w
in 16425, length 0
22:17:59.831863 IP 172.16.1.161.ssh > 172.16.1.101.50703: Flags [P.], seq 672:8
48, ack 1, win 326, length 176
22:17:59.831922 IP 172.16.1.161.ssh > 172.16.1.101.50703: Flags [P.], seq 848:1
120, ack 1, win 326, length 272
```

[Output cut]

The tcpdump command is so versatile that we can even capture traffic into a file and then pull the file up in Wireshark! The command
tcpdump -s 0 port ssh -i eth0 -w capture.pcap will save all the packets that match a port of SSH to the file called capture.pcap. We can also omit the filter for SSH and capture any traffic to and from the system. If we wanted to be really creative, we could use ifconfig eth0 promisc to turn on promiscuous mode for the interface and capture any traffic seen by the host.

nmap

The nmap tool allows us to scan open and closed ports on remote systems for audit purposes. It can be used to validate that the firewall is open to accept requests for an application. The nmap tool is a Linux/Unix-based tool that has been ported to Windows.

The nmap tool can scan all ports of a specific host or a range of hosts in the network. This allows for the discovery of a host that might not be known or protected with firewall rules. The nmap tool will also try to negotiate with Transport Layer Security (TLS) in an attempt to discover the encryption key strength being used. In addition to these features, it will try to predict the operating system the remote system is using.

In the following example, the nmap command was run with the -A argument that enables operating system detection, version detection, script scanning, and route tracing.

```
root@sybex:~# nmap -A scanme.nmap.org

Starting Nmap 6.40 ( http://nmap.org ) at 2017-10-31 21:34 EDT
Nmap scan report for scanme.nmap.org (45.33.32.156)
Host is up (0.094s latency).
Not shown: 993 closed ports
PORT    STATE  SERVICE    VERSION
22/tcp  open   ssh      (protocol 2.0)
| ssh-hostkey: 1024 ac:00:a0:1a:82:ff:cc:55:99:dc:67:2b:34:97:6b:75 (DSA)
| 2048 20:3d:2d:44:62:2a:b0:5a:9d:b5:b3:05:14:c2:a6:b2 (RSA)
|_256 96:02:bb:5e:57:54:1c:4e:45:2f:56:4c:4a:24:b2:57 (ECDSA)
25/tcp  filtered smtp
80/tcp  open   http     Apache httpd 2.4.7 ((Ubuntu))
|_http-title: Go ahead and ScanMe!
135/tcp  filtered msrpc
139/tcp  filtered netbios-ssn
445/tcp  filtered microsoft-ds
31337/tcp open   tcpwrapped
1 service unrecognized despite returning data. If you know the service/version,
please submit the following fingerprint at http://www.insecure.org/cgi-bin/ser
vicefp-submit.cgi :SF-Port22-TCP:V=6.40%I=7%D=10/31%Time=59F925EF%P=x86_64-pc-linux-
gnu%r(NUL SF:L,2B,"SSH-2\.0-OpenSSH_6\.6\.1p1\x20Ubuntu-2ubuntu2\.8\r\n");
Device type: general purpose|firewall|WAP|terminal
Running (JUST GUESSING): Linux 3.X|2.6.X|2.4.X (92%), IPFire Linux 2.6.X (88%),
IGEL Linux 2.6.X (85%) OS CPE: cpe:/o:linux:linux_kernel:3 cpe:/o:linux:linux_k
ernel:2.6 cpe:/o:ipfire:linux:2.6.32 cpe:/o:linux:linux_kernel:2.4 cpe:/o:igel:
linux_kernel:2.6 Aggressive OS guesses: Linux 3.2 - 3.6 (92%), Linux 2.6.32 - 2
.6.39 (90%), Linux 2.6.32 - 3.0 (89%), Linux 3.5 (88%), Linux 2.6.32 (88%), IPF
ire firewall 2.11 (Linux 2.6.32) (88%), Linux 2.6.15 - 2.6.26 (likely embedded)
(86%), Linux 2.6.32 - 2.6.33(86%), Linux 2.6.32 - 2.6.35(86%), Linux 2.6.18(86%)No
exact OS matches for host (test conditions non-ideal).
Network Distance: 12 hops

[Output cut]
```

If we add the -v argument, we will be able to see the progress of nmap as the scan progresses. The problem with scanning a remote host is that closed ports do not always respond as they should, and some operating systems do not respond at all. This lack of response makes it difficult to know whether the service is running, firewalled, or just dead. There are many other arguments that we can include to change the behavior of the scan:

- Use -sN for a NULL scan in which no flags are set in the Transport layer header. If the port is closed, then the destination operating system will send back an RST. If the port is open, then nothing is sent back.

- Use -sF for a FIN scan in which the FIN flag is set in an attempt to trick the operating system into responding to closed ports with an RST, similar to a NULL scan.

- Use -sX for an Xmas-Tree scan in which the URG, PSH, and FIN flags are set in an attempt to trick the operating system into sending an RST for closed ports.

Basic Network Platform Commands

In the following sections, I will cover a set of commands that are useful on any network operating system, such as Cisco IOS. You'll find that many other network operating systems from various vendors will have similar commands and some are verbatim. Once you know the basics, such as the following Cisco commands, you can adapt to any other vendor's network operating system.

show interface

The show interface command is most useful when you are trying to diagnose a problem with a connection. The output of the command will display the interface status, such as if it is connected or not. It will also display the duplex and speed that the interface negotiated with the connected equipment. The counters for the output of the command can also describe transmit and receive load for the interface, although these counters are on a scale of 1 to 255 and are proportional to the overall bandwidth. Some more advanced counters are packet input/output, errors, collisions, broadcast, and multicast traffic.

```
es-OAGR#show interfaces gig 1/24
GigabitEthernet1/24 is down, line protocol is down (notconnect)
  Hardware is Gigabit Ether Port, address is cc16.7557.1b47 (bia cc16.7557.1b47)
  Description: Oil and Gas Equipment Port - 110-17
  MTU 1500 bytes, BW 1000000 Kbit/sec, DLY 10 usec,
     reliability 255/255, txload 1/255, rxload 1/255
  Encapsulation ARPA, loopback not set
  Keepalive set (10 sec)
  Auto-duplex, Auto-speed, link type is auto, media type is 10/100/1000-TX
  input flow-control is off, output flow-control is off
  Auto-MDIX on (operational: on)
  ARP type: ARPA, ARP Timeout 04:00:00
  Last input never, output never, output hang never
  Last clearing of "show interface" counters never
```

```
      Input queue: 0/2000/0/0 (size/max/drops/flushes); Total output drops: 0
      Queueing strategy: fifo
      Output queue: 0/40 (size/max)
      5 minute input rate 0 bits/sec, 0 packets/sec
      5 minute output rate 0 bits/sec, 0 packets/sec
          0 packets input, 0 bytes, 0 no buffer
          Received 0 broadcasts (0 multicasts)
          0 runts, 0 giants, 0 throttles
          0 input errors, 0 CRC, 0 frame, 0 overrun, 0 ignored
          0 input packets with dribble condition detected
          0 packets output, 0 bytes, 0 underruns
          0 output errors, 0 collisions, 3 interface resets
          0 unknown protocol drops
          0 babbles, 0 late collision, 0 deferred
          0 lost carrier, 0 no carrier
          0 output buffer failures, 0 output buffers swapped out
es-OAGR#
```

This command is a wealth of information about an interface. Many a problem can be diagnosed with this command, especially when you are hundreds of miles away. It's important to realize that although CRC errors might be present, this will only identify a problem with wiring for incoming frames. It will not identify a problem at the far end of the connection. For that diagnosis, you will need to see the error rate on the remote device. The switch or router will only be able to detect CRC errors on incoming frames and not outgoing, since the CRC is the responsibility of the receiver.

show config

The ability to view the configuration of a router or switch is invaluable to diagnosing a problem. Fortunately, viewing the configuration is possible by using a common and easy command. When you want to view the configuration with Cisco network devices, you will issue the command show running-config; it is often abbreviated to sh run. This command will show the configuration that is resident in memory, as shown in the following example. This is the configuration from which the switch or router is currently running.

```
es-OAGR#show running-config
Building configuration...

Current configuration : 39849 bytes
!
! Last configuration change at 16:28:25 EDT Mon May 10 2021 by admin
! NVRAM config last updated at 16:28:26 EDT Mon May 10 2021 by admin
!
version 15.2
no service pad
```

```
service timestamps debug datetime msec localtime
service timestamps log datetime msec localtime
no service password-encryption
service compress-config
!
Hostname es-OAGR
!
boot-start-marker
boot system flash bootflash:cat4500e-universalk9.SPA.03.06.07.E.152-2.E7.bin
boot-end-marker
!
!
vrf definition mgmtVrf
 !
 address-family ipv4
```

[Output Cut]

The show startup-config command will show you the configuration that is stored in non-volatile RAM (NVRAM), which will be loaded into memory (running-config) when the device starts up. You can also use variations of the show running-config command by adding certain arguments. By default, certain configuration statements are hidden from the show running-config command since they are considered the norm. You can see these hidden configuration statements on most Cisco devices by adding the argument all, such as show running-config all. You can also just show the configuration for a specific interface by adding a few arguments, such as show running-config interface gigabitEthernet 1/4. This command will only display the configuration for the interface g1/4, as shown in the following example. This is particularly handy, if you want to focus on the configuration for a specific interface.

```
es-OAGR#show running-config interface gigabitEthernet 1/4
Building configuration...

Current configuration : 170 bytes
!
interface GigabitEthernet1/4
 description Rm103 MedLab Drop - 053-7
 switchport access vlan 11
 switchport mode access
 power inline never
 spanning-tree portfast
end

es-OAGR#
```

show route

To examine how traffic will be routed on a switch or router, the show ip route command will display the routing table. In the following example, we can see a routing table on a layer 3 switch. We can identify the default gateway of 10.1.1.1 for any traffic that doesn't specifically match the route statements that are explicitly defined. The default gateway is depicted by the S* at the beginning of the route. There is also a legend that appears with all of the possible routes. Examining the route table closer, we can see that there are two explicit routes for 10.1.0.0/16 and 10.2.0.0/16. Both routes are directly connected routes depicted by the C at the beginning of the route. Both VLAN 1 and VLAN 2 are directly connected because a local interface is configured with the IP addresses of 10.1.10.1 and 10.2.1.1, respectively. Both of these IP addresses can be derived from the statements that have the L as the beginning of the route. The IP addresses also have a subnet mask of /32 that identifies them as single IP addresses.

```
es-OAGR#show ip route
Codes: L - local, C - connected, S - static, R - RIP, M - mobile, B - BGP
       D - EIGRP, EX - EIGRP external, O - OSPF, IA - OSPF inter area
       N1 - OSPF NSSA external type 1, N2 - OSPF NSSA external type 2
       E1 - OSPF external type 1, E2 - OSPF external type 2
       i - IS-IS, su - IS-IS summary, L1 - IS-IS level-1, L2 - IS-IS level-2
       ia - IS-IS inter area, * - candidate default, U - per-user static route
       o - ODR, P - periodic downloaded static route, H - NHRP, l - LISP
       + - replicated route, % - next hop override

Gateway of last resort is 10.1.1.1 to network 0.0.0.0

S*     0.0.0.0/0 [1/0] via 10.1.1.1
       10.0.0.0/8 is variably subnetted, 4 subnets, 4 masks
C         10.1.0.0/16 is directly connected, Vlan1
L         10.1.10.1/32 is directly connected, Vlan1
C         10.2.0.0/16 is directly connected, Vlan2
L         10.2.1.1/32 is directly connected, Vlan2
es-OAGR#
```

Routers and switches are not the only network devices that have route tables. Every network device has a logical route table; this includes operating systems. You just need to know the command to view the route table; for example, in the Windows operating system the command is route print, as shown in the following example.

```
C:\Users\sybex>route print
===========================================================================
Interface List
  9...00 ff 75 54 25 1b ......TAP-Windows Adapter V9 for OpenVPN Connect
  8.......................NordLynx Tunnel
```

```
    3...24 4b fe 92 36 d3 ......Realtek Gaming GbE Family Controller
   16...00 ff d8 91 03 c8 ......NordLynx Tunnel
    1........................Software Loopback Interface 1
===========================================================================

IPv4 Route Table
===========================================================================
Active Routes:
Network Destination        Netmask          Gateway       Interface  Metric
          0.0.0.0          0.0.0.0       172.16.1.1    172.16.1.181     25
        127.0.0.0        255.0.0.0         On-link       127.0.0.1    331
        127.0.0.1  255.255.255.255         On-link       127.0.0.1    331
  127.255.255.255  255.255.255.255         On-link       127.0.0.1    331
       172.16.0.0      255.240.0.0         On-link    172.16.1.181    281
     172.16.1.181  255.255.255.255         On-link    172.16.1.181    281
   172.31.255.255  255.255.255.255         On-link    172.16.1.181    281
        224.0.0.0        240.0.0.0         On-link       127.0.0.1    331
        224.0.0.0        240.0.0.0         On-link    172.16.1.181    281
  255.255.255.255  255.255.255.255         On-link       127.0.0.1    331
  255.255.255.255  255.255.255.255         On-link    172.16.1.181    281
===========================================================================

Persistent Routes:
  None

[ Output Cut ]
```

Exam Essentials

Know the various software tools that you will encounter and use daily as a network administrator.   The Wi-Fi analyzer helps the administrator see the various wireless access points (WAPs), SSIDs, security issues, the MAC addresses of the WAPs, and the strength of the signal. Packet capture tools are used to collect network frames and packets for analysis and troubleshooting. The protocol analyzer provides an analysis of packet captures and allows the administrator to see the information contained inside the captured data. Bandwidth speed testers are used to view the maximum download speed and maximum upload speed for a given connection. Port scanners allow an administrator to verify that ports are not being firewalled and that they are open awaiting a request. The iPerf software tool allows you to measure the performance of a network path. A NetFlow analyzer will analyze exported NetFlow information into a visual representation so that you can identify problems. A Trivial File Transfer Protocol (TFTP) server is used for upgrading network devices and maintenance of configuration files. Terminal emulator software allows for console-based access via a serial port, Telnet, or SSH session. An IP scanner is a software tool that will scan a range of IP addresses and report back the IP addresses that respond.

Know the various command-line tools that you will use daily for troubleshooting.   The ping command is used to verify that a host is reachable via layer 3 connectivity. The ipconfig (Windows) or ifconfig (Linux/Unix) command allows us to verify the IP address configuration of the host. The Linux/Unix ifconfig command allows us to configure the IP address/subnet mask and promiscuous mode and turn the interface up and down. The nslookup command helps us test DNS resource records from a specific DNS server. The dig command is similar to the nslookup command; it allows us to verify name resolution for resource records. The tracert (Windows) or traceroute (Linux/Unix) command allows us see the path a packet will follow. The arp tool is used to view and configure the Address Resolution Protocol (ARP) table contained in the host's memory. The netstat command is used to see the port bindings and TCP states on both Windows and Linux/Unix systems. The hostname tool will return the hostname of the system. The route command is used to configure routes and view the current routing table of the host. The telnet tool is a console-based emulator that connect via the Telnet protocol. The tcpdump command is a packet sniffer and is used to capture packets from the local host. The nmap command is a port scanner and helps us determine whether firewall ports are open and the services awaiting request.

Know basic network platform commands.   The show interface command is used to view the status and statistics for a given interface. The command show running-config will display the configuration currently running in memory. The command show startup-config will display the configuration that will be loaded on startup of the device. The show ip route command on a Cisco router or switch will display the routing table. The route print command on a Windows operating system will display the routing table.

5.4 Given a scenario, troubleshoot common wireless connectivity issues.

In the following sections, I will cover various scenarios that can cause issues in your wireless network. I will discuss how these issues can be detected using the tools you learned about earlier. I will also cover troubleshooting steps to determine the causes.

Specifications and Limitations

As you learned in Chapter 2, "Domain 2.0: Network Implementations," there are several different wireless standards that have been ratified by the 802.11 IEEE working group.

Each wireless standard has a different throughput, speed, and distance limitation, depending on the frequency. By choosing the proper wireless standard for your organization, you can future-proof the solution, satisfy the requirements, and meet the expectations of the project budget.

Throughput The throughput of wireless will vary greatly, depending on the hardware and the wireless standards supported by the hardware. There are a number of factors for the variance in throughput. The most important factor is that wireless is shared media. When a host transmits and receives a signal on a radio frequency, also known as the channel, the host must share the channel with all other hosts connected to the same SSID. Therefore, this means that throughput is shared media. So, if we are using 802.11g at a top speed of 54 Mbps, our usable throughput is 54 divided by the number of hosts. To further impact this, if another access point is using the same channel as your access point and it has a different SSID, the hosts from the other network will time-share your bandwidth and can affect performance.

Over the past 15 years, as wireless networking became popular and the number of wireless devices quadrupled, newer wireless standards were engineered to allow for higher throughput sharing. Many of these wireless standards simply complemented the underlying wireless standards of 802.11. For example, multiuser multiple input, multiple output (MU-MIMO) allows for simultaneous transmitted and received signals by the 802.11ac protocol. In effect, we can share the bandwidth and achieve a higher throughput more efficiently. However, the physics remains the same. You are still time-sharing the radio space; you just have a higher throughput.

When a large number of devices are required and a nominal throughput needs to be achieved, the cell density must be increased. This is achieved by installing several access points in a very close proximity together and allow radio resource management (RRM) at the wireless LAN controller to vary their channels. The result is a single SSID spread across several wireless channels that work with each other.

Speed The speed of wireless is how fast you can theoretically move data from host to access point or host to host (ad hoc). Each wireless standard since the 802.11b IEEE working group has gotten faster and faster. The 802.11b standard was ratified at 11 Mbps and we are now up to theoretical speeds of 14 Gbps with 802.11ax. The speed of wireless data is largely dependent on the quality of the airspace around the host and access point. So, these theoretical speeds are only realistic in a lab or environment that is controlled.

Another interesting situation with wireless speed is the access layer switching equipment that supports today's network connections. The switching is normally purchased with 1 Gbps access links, but the new standards like 802.11ac require at least 2.5 Gbps access links or higher. This is why the IEEE created the specification of 802.3bz, also known as NBase-T or MGBaseT. This specification can supply 1 Gbps, 2.5 Gbps, or 5 Gbps bandwidth over a Cat 5e or Cat 6 cable.

Distance   In wired Ethernet networks, we can guarantee a maximum distance of 100 meters, or 330 feet. In wireless networks, distance is limited by several factors, such as the protocol used, frequency, power level, antenna gain, antenna type, antenna positioning, and building materials, among others. We can easily see that physical factors directly affect our distance from the AP. Each wireless technology released has effectively increased the distance of wireless access points.

Despite advancements in access point design and protocol development, as we move farther away from the signal source, our data rate is lowered to accommodate retransmits and the longer distance. When we approach the maximum limit, our client will experience disconnects. A wireless analyzer can help identify distance limitations by examining the received signal strength indicator (RSSI). Increasing the power on a WAP does not fix the problem because the client is still limited in size and power. However, purchasing antennas with higher gain can help with distance limitations.

Wireless distance is another subjective measurement, mainly because of the antenna and band you are using. However, other factors such as air quality also contribute to distance limitations. It is actually borderline impossible to find a published specification of distance for a wireless standard. This is why site surveys are so important to a proper wireless installation. As you move away from an access point, the data rate drops significantly, as show in Figure 5.25.

FIGURE 5.25   Distance vs. speed

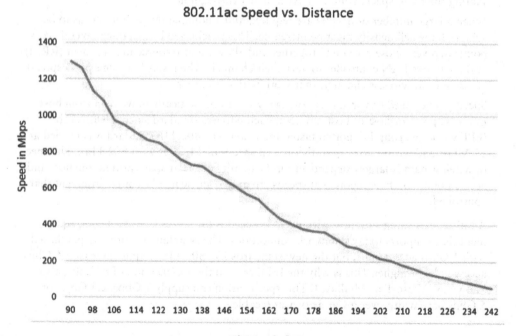

Distance in feet

The selection of band is also critical to the wireless signal distance. The higher the frequency, the lower the distance and higher speed. So, 5 GHz is great for speed in small cells (area). The lower the frequency, the higher the distance and lower speed. So, 2.4 GHz is great for outdoor use or a warehouse. However, 2.4 GHz has very few non-overlapping channels, therefore performance is impacted.

Received Signal Strength Indication (RSSI) Signal Strength   The received signal strength indication (RSSI) is the signal strength of the wireless signal. It is often found on your wireless device as a little grouping of bars. The more bars, the better your signal, also known as full bars. However, the RSSI is actually a measurement on a scale of 0 to 127 or 0 to 100. The chipset of the wireless device uses this signal strength to manage its own power back to the access point. The 802.11k-2008 standard is the mechanism the wireless device will use to limit power based upon the RSSI.

Effective Isotropic Radiated Power (EIRP)/Power Settings   The effective isotropic radiated power (EIRP) is the actual power radiated from a given antenna, based upon the antenna's gain and nominal power. Obviously, we have the option to transmit full power, but this decreases battery life of our wireless devices. We always want to pick an antenna that has a good gain, therefore we can dial back our power settings (EIRP). The short equation is the better the antenna, the less power we need to transmit the signal, which means less overall power used. Every antenna will be designed for a specific frequency; it is then tested at that frequency to derive its gain over the reference isotropic antenna. The result is an advertised value in decibels over isotropic (dBi), which is a logarithmic value. Therefore, an antenna with a 1 dBi rating is twice as good as the reference isotropic 0 dBi antenna.

Considerations

The definition of a consideration in this context is an undesirable outcome from the primary plan of action. Wireless is definitely a technology full of considerations. Most of the consideration might seem somewhat subjective, such as antenna placement or the type of antenna to be used, but these are definitely objective considerations. After reading the following sections, you should understand all of the considerations you will need to review for an optimal wireless network.

Antennas

A proper antenna choice and installation is the key to a successful wireless network. If the wrong antenna for the application is chosen or it is installed improperly, you will simply have problems. How these problems manifest themselves might be in the form of low throughput, or you may get drops, or no coverage in certain areas.

The access point antenna is critical because it serves two very important tasks: transmitting and receiving. Picking the right antenna for optimal transmitting of signal is important for optimal coverage. It is equally important for the receipt of signals from clients.

Keep in mind that an access point has far more power than a mobile device and the antenna on a mobile device is much smaller. So, the proper antenna on the access point becomes very important for overall coverage in the aspects of transmitting and receiving radio signals.

Placement   The placement of the antenna is a key consideration for security and coverage. You will want coverage internally within your organization's walls, but you will want to limit the signal that radiates outside of the organization's office space. An attacker can sit in a public place with a mobile device and attack the network if the antenna radiates too far. Coverage is equally important inside of the organization's office space. The proper placement might seem somewhat subjective. However, utilizing the specification sheets from the vendor and selecting the right antenna will objectively satisfy the installation. When the site survey is completed, it will validate your design.

Type   The placement of the antenna is dependent on the type of antenna used for the installation. There are two main types of antennas used for wireless networks, as covered in Chapter 2, "Domain 2.0: Network Implementations": directional and omnidirectional antennas. There are many different styles of antenna, such as Yagi, patch, dipole, just to name a few. However, their type will be either omnidirectional or directional, regardless of the style. An omnidirectional antenna will radiate the signal from the antenna in the shape of a doughnut, covering everything in a nondirectional pattern. An omnidirectional antenna is perfect for installation in the center of an office space. A directional antenna radiates the signal in the shape of a cone, as shown in Figure 5.26. These antennas are useful in areas where you want to shape the radiation pattern, such as the corner of a warehouse. If the wrong antenna is used to cover an area, the signal will not radiate in the expected pattern to where the clients will be located.

FIGURE 5.26   Omnidirectional vs. directional antennas

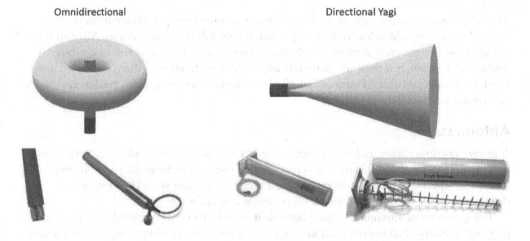

Omnidirectional   Directional Yagi

Polarization   All radio signals consist of a magnetic field and electromagnetic field. These fields are always perpendicular to each other and make up the signal's polarization. Signals are either vertically polarized or horizontally polarized. If the access point has its antennas pointing down from the ceiling, then the signal is considered to be vertically polarized. Clients such as laptops are normally horizontally polarized. The signal loss between a vertically polarized signal and a horizontally polarized client is about a 10 dB drop in signal.

Channel Utilization

When we think of wireless systems, we often think of how well they work at home. At home we have three to five clients maximum communicating on a WAP. However, in office settings we can easily stretch the capacity of the AP by having too many clients associated with or moving large amounts of data. When this occurs, we are considered at overcapacity on the wireless cell. The symptoms of high utilization are low bandwidth, high latency, and client disconnects.

The overutilization of channels is typically a problem when channels are bonded together. Each channel in the 5 GHz band is 20 MHz wide and there are 24 channels that can be bonded together. A total of 8 channels can be bonded together to form a 160 MHz wide data path. However, only 2 of these bonding can be made with the 5 GHz band, as shown in Figure 5.27. In a large building there will be overlap, which leads to channel utilization.

FIGURE 5.27   5 GHz channels

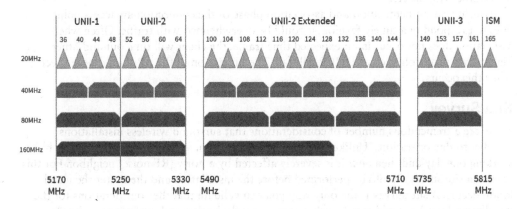

In the 2.4 GHz band channel, utilization is much worse since there are only 3 non-overlapping channels 22 MHz wide. It is not common to bond 2.4 GHz channels because of the small number of usable channels and the overlap, as shown in Figure 5.28. Channel utilization is very common on the 2.4 GHz band because you cannot control who uses a particular channel. A neighbor can overlap with your organization's functioning channels and create high channel utilization.

FIGURE 5.28   2.4 GHz channels

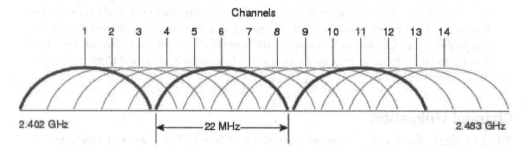

AP Association Time

An 802.11 access point can be in one of three states: not authenticated or associated, authenticated but not yet associated, or authenticated and associated. An access point must be in the last state of authenticated and associated to bridge traffic. Authentication must happen first and then association can occur by the access point. In Figure 5.29, we can see the exchange of 802.11 management frames between a mobile device and an access point. First the access point is sent a probe request; the access point then sends back a probe response. In the probe response the SSID, encryption, data rates, and capabilities of the AP are sent. The client then begins to authenticate with the AP. In this example the authentication is open, meaning that there is no passphrase or security. The client will then attempt to associate with the AP. If successful, the client then enters a state of authenticated and associated and can pass traffic with the AP.

If during the authentication and association phase of the connection an access point does not respond in a timely fashion, it could be overwhelmed with traffic. Often when association does not occur in an expected time frame, the client will time out and other higher-level protocols such as DHCP will fail. The utilization of the AP should be suspect when this occurs.

Site Survey

There are a tremendous number of considerations that surround wireless installations and day-to-day operations. Unlike with a wired installation, a wireless installation can be working one day and then next it is severely affected by a noisy (RF noise) neighbor. For this reason, a site survey should be performed before the installation and then after the installation occurs. A site survey is the only way you can validate that the considerations for the installation have been addressed, such as antenna polarization and antenna type, just to name a few.

The initial placement of the antenna might be correct for the coverage. However, office areas are often reconfigured and new obstacles for the wireless signal can be placed in its path. The wireless signal is often the last aspect of construction to be considered, and sometimes it's not even a thought until it becomes a problem. Wireless antenna placement should be documented during the installation and reviewed periodically.

FIGURE 5.29 802.11 Association process

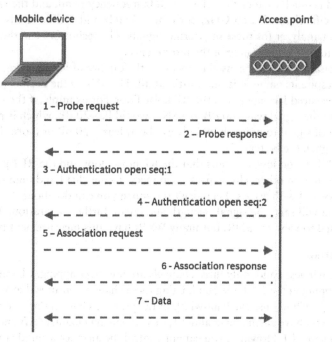

By performing a site survey after the installation, you can conclude a baseline of operation for your wireless network. Then, if a noisy neighbor moves in two doors down or a reconfiguration of an office space affects performance of the wireless installation, you can diagnose and adjust your network accordingly.

Common Issues

As you learned, there are numerous considerations with wireless vs. wired infrastructure. In addition, there are numerous common problems that we can experience with wireless networking. In the following sections, I will cover the most common issue you may experience.

Interference

Interference is caused by any signal that affects the reception of wireless. The source of interference can be anything, but often it is a device operating on the same frequency as the equipment. Sometimes the interference source doesn't even need to be operating on the primary frequency on which the interference is observed. The interference can even be caused by other wireless equipment. A spectrum analyzer helps identify interference sources by displaying the spectrum of frequency it is observing.

Common sources of 2.4 GHz interference are Bluetooth, non-Wi-Fi cameras, cordless phones, and microwave ovens. These devices operate closely on the 2.4 GHz frequency.

Common sources of 5 GHz interference are radar sources and cordless phones. The 5 GHz frequency band is much cleaner than the 2.4 GHz frequency band, and the radar sources are confined to specific channels of 5 GHz. Both the 2.4 GHz and 5 GHz bands can be checked with a spectrum analyzer for these interfering signals. The technician can then use the spectrum analyzer to locate the source of the interference.

Signal-to-noise ratio (SNR) is used to measure the quality of RF signal against the level of RF noise. Despite its name, it is not a ratio at all. The SNR is the decibel (dB) difference between the measured RF signal and the RF noise floor. For example, if the noise floor was –80 dB and the signal was –60 dB, the SNR would be –20 dB, which is pretty good. The separation of signal to noise should always be at least –20 dB or more. The SNR rule of thumb is the higher, the better.

When the SNR is too low, it means that the RF noise floor and the RF signal are indistinguishable from each other. This causes disconnects to the client and high retries because data will be received with errors. There isn't too much you can do about the noise floor, but a better antenna will raise the signal strength and create further separation. A spectrum analyzer can be used to view the SNR, but many WAPs have this measurement built in.

Channel Overlap

In the 2.4 GHz wireless band, only three channels are non-overlapping. Channels 1, 6, and 11 are non-overlapping in the 2.4 GHz band. Using these channels ensures that your clients on adjacent channels will not use the bandwidth of the primary channel they are connected on. For example, if you have clients on channel 1, then clients on channel 6 will not interfere with operations on channel 1. However, you cannot control the airspace around you. Other WAPs and clients you don't control can use channels between the non-overlapping channels, and your WAP will need to abide by the conversations. This in turn will diminish your effective bandwidth.

The good news is that the 5 GHz wireless band has 24 non-overlapping channels. Each 20 MHz channel is non-overlapping with the other 23 channels. This ensures that a conversation between a WAP and a client on one channel does not affect another channel. When single 5 GHz channels are used, there is no overlap. Channel bonding was introduced in 802.11n, which means that a WAP can use two adjacent channels and can overlap with a channel your WAP and client are using. 802.11ac introduced high bandwidths by allowing even more channels to be bonded, as discussed in Chapter 1, "Domain 1.0: Networking Fundamentals."

Channel overlap has become a problem that can no longer be avoided in wireless networks. Fortunately, Wi-Fi analyzers allow us to see the channels that are not being used by neighboring WAPs. We can switch our WAPs and clients to the unused channels. It doesn't ensure that channel overlap will not occur, but we do have 24 channels to choose from.

Antenna Cable Attenuation/Signal Loss

When installing an antenna, proper care should be taken to select an RF cable with low loss. The lower the loss means that you will have less attenuation of signal in the coaxial cable. The loss in coaxial cable is always measured in decibels (dB). It is also important to make sure that all connections are secure and crimped properly as these can contribute to loss.

On outdoor installations some vendors require the use of an RF insulating grease to keep moisture out of the connection. Another common issue with antenna cable attenuation is the radius bend of the cable. If the cable is bent past the vendor's recommendations, you could experience signal loss because the conductive core is closer to the shielding.

RF Attenuation/Signal Loss

Attenuation is also called free space loss; all RFs suffer from attenuation. Attenuation is the loss in the amplitude of a signal as the signal travels farther from its source. RF attenuates similarly to sound traveling through the air—as you move further from the source, the strength is diminished until you can no longer hear it. Both sound and RF are measured in decibels (dB).

Higher-frequency signals attenuate quicker than lower frequencies. The wireless 5 GHz band is an example of a higher frequency when compared to 2.4 GHz. The 2.4 GHz signals can travel farther than 5 GHz signals; thus the lower frequencies attenuate slower.

Wireless signals are measured in dB, and the reading is often labeled as the received signal strength indicator (RSSI). The RSSI is the level of the signal at the receiving point. 802.11 wireless will reduce the speed as the RSSI is reduced to accommodate adequate connectivity. A low RSSI at the AP means that the clients are too far away or that the antenna should be positioned to allow better sensitivity to the signal.

Absorption is the reaction of the RF signal being absorbed into the material upon contact. This is how a microwave oven operates, just with a lot more power. The RF energy is converted into heat and the signal is dissipated. Wireless signals run into the same problems with absorption. Table 5.3 lists common construction materials and their absorption rates. The absorption rate is displayed in *decibels (dB)*.

TABLE 5.3   RF absorption rates by common material

Material	Absorption rate
Drywall	3–5 dB
Glass wall and metal frame	6 dB
Metal door	6–10 dB
Window	3 dB
Concrete wall	6–15 dB
Block wall	4–6 dB

When designing a wireless network, these materials should be taken into account and reflected in your design. It is also important to note that materials can have multiple properties at the same time; for example, glass can both refract and absorb the signal. If the network is already designed and these materials may degrade signal and performance, moving the AP might mitigate the absorption rate and increase bandwidth.

Wrong SSID

When diagnosing wireless client problems, always check the SSID. Users can connect to the wrong SSID, and when this happens, they will be connected to a totally different network. Checking the IP address doesn't always guarantee you'll identify the problem. The other SSID might use an identical IP address scheme. A user doesn't need to intentionally connect to the wrong SSID; the operating system will often prefer an SSID and reconnect when within range.

Incorrect Passphrase

An incorrect passphrase is a very common problem when using an SSID that has been configured for *preshared key (PSK)* security. Entering a wrong passphrase will make a client exhibit this symptom during association.

When this occurs, there are some simple steps to troubleshooting. The first troubleshooting step is to verify the passphrase that the SSID is expecting. The second step is to verify that the keyboard is registering the characters properly. You can do so by entering the passphrase in Notepad, copying it, and then pasting it into the SSID passphrase dialog box. Passphrases are case sensitive, and this method allows us to verify the case of each character being typed before we paste it in the dialog box, which is often password masked.

Encryption Protocol Mismatch

A client will exhibit the same symptoms when a security type mismatch exists. The client will not be able to associate with the SSID because the security protocol does not match. Troubleshooting steps to avoid security type mismatch are straightforward. The first step is to verify the wireless security protocol. The next step involves clearing the failed wireless connection, sometimes called forgetting the connection. The last step is to manually set up the new SSID connection with the appropriate security protocol.

Insufficient Wireless Coverage

It is often thought that more is better, except for when it comes to wireless signal power levels. APs should be installed relatively close together to provide roaming of clients. When a client moves into the cell, it will connect to the strongest signal. If the power levels are too high on an adjacent AP, the client might connect to the wrong AP for its vicinity. Connecting over this perceived longer distance will create latency for the client and could promote disconnects.

The transmitter on an AP and the installed antennas will always be better than clients' transmit power and antennas. Clients generally choose their signal based on signal strength of the AP. However, just because the client can hear the AP doesn't mean they have the power to communicate with it. Therefore, power should always be turned down on the AP to the minimum level that still allows flawless roaming.

Captive Portal Issues

A captive portal is a mechanism that restricts Internet access until a requirement is met. It works when the user browses to a web page for the first time. The web browser will be redirected to the captive portal web page, in lieu of the page requested. The user will then have to satisfy the requirement on the page, such as logging in, agreeing to an acceptable use policy (AUP), or some variation. Once the requirement is satisfied, the user is then directed to the original page requested and is fully allowed to use the connection.

Unfortunately, the captive portal process is not without its issues. A common problem with captive portals is the original redirection of the web browser during the captive portal process. When the requested page is cached in the user's web browser, the web browser will never ask for the web page and the web browser will never get redirected. Subsequent pages should trigger this redirection, but if network connectivity is expected by other applications at this point, it could be a false flag to the user signaling to them that everything is fine.

The Windows operating system will display a yellow triangle on the icon for the network in the lower-right corner of the screen, when you have limited connectivity. If you hover over the network icon, it will display the No Internet Access error message. Clicking the icon will bring up the wireless connectivity settings, as shown in Figure 5.30. Here, a wireless icon is displayed, but limited connectivity such as this is not exclusive to wireless connections. Limited connectivity problems can also happen with wired Ethernet connections, although the icon will be different to reflect the connection.

FIGURE 5.30   Limited connectivity

Client Disassociation Issues

A client disassociation can happen for a number of reasons. The symptom is the client will suddenly disassociate from the access point, and it will need to authenticate and associate all over again. During this time the network connection is dropped, and network connectivity is lost. The two most common reasons are client signal strength and access point over utilization.

Client signal strength is always an issue, and it's one of the reasons a site survey is performed. Despite the best efforts of a site survey and a diligent install, clients can suffer from poor signal strength. This can cause a disassociation by the client.

Another common problem with signal strength happens when a client is roaming and the overlap between the cells is less than 20 percent. Authentication is passed between access points joined to a wireless LAN controller. So the client does not need to re-authenticate. The client simply needs to associate with the new access point and never loses connection during the roaming process. If the client does not have a signal to transition to and the original signal is lost, the client will disassociate from the first access point and will then wait to come into contact with the new access point. This will cause the client to probe, authenticate, and associate to the new access point.

Another common issue is overutilization of the access point. When an access point is overutilized, the client can miss the 802.11 maintenance frames because they are never sent in a timely fashion. This will trigger the client to disassociate from the access point and ultimately cause a disruption to the user's connection.

Exam Essentials

Understand how the specifications and limitations of wireless can limit performance.   The overall throughput is hindered by a number of considerations, starting with the speed for the hardware standard of 802.11 as well as the number of clients sharing the overall bandwidth. The speed of wireless is usually a theoretical speed, since there are many factors that can impede the advertised speed. The distance of wireless is a subjective limit as many wireless 802.11 standards do not advertise a distance. Distance and speed are closely related; as a client gets farther away, the data limit will be reduced.

Understand the common scenarios in which wireless connectivity and performance issues can arise from installation problems.   Using the incorrect antenna type in wireless installations can hinder performance and possibly damage the transmitting circuitry in the WAP. Incorrect antenna placement can cause problems such as high absorption, reflection, refraction, and overall poor coverage. Channel overlap diminishes effective bandwidth because the WAP and client must work around other channels overlapping with the primary channel being used. As a general rule of thumb, WAP capacity should be between 20 and 30 clients.

Understand the common issues associated with wireless connectivity.   Interference is a contributing factor to poor performance of wireless connectivity Interference does not necessarily need to be external; channel overlap can impede a wireless signal's performance as well. Attenuation is the reaction of RF waves being dissipated into various materials, which can reduce the signal strength. Attenuation is the loss in the amplitude of a signal as the signal travels farther from its source, so choosing a cable with high loss can affect signal quality. If the client connects to the wrong SSID, resources will be unavailable to the client. Using the wrong passphrase will cause the client to continually fail to connect to the SSID. A security type mismatch can also cause continuous failure when connecting to an SSID. Insufficient wireless coverage can lead to disconnects by the client. A site survey can avoid coverage gaps and can identify problem areas. A captive portal is a mechanism that directs a user to a splash page. The user then must complete an activity, such as signing in or acknowledging an acceptable use policy (AUP), before they can use the Internet. Browser cache is a leading cause of captive portal issues.

5.5 Given a scenario, troubleshoot general networking issues.

As a network administrator, you will need to identify and solve various problems. In the following sections, I will cover various scenarios that you will encounter. I will also cover the diagnostic steps used and troubleshooting with the tools discussed in the previous sections.

Considerations

There are several factors to be considered when you are troubleshooting a network issue. Although these considerations might not be evident, they are relevant and should always be checked to expedite the solution. In the following sections, you will learn about the most common considerations that can cause a networking issue.

Device Configuration Review

The configuration of the device in question should always be a consideration when troubleshooting a problem. Even if the problem is not directly considered to be caused by the configuration, the configuration should still be reviewed. In addition, the configuration on other devices along the path of the problem should also be reviewed. These devices can include switches, routers, and firewalls. For example, if an application is having issues communicating, the firewall rules should at least be reviewed for proper configuration.

Routing Tables

The path or route packets take to the destination is a key consideration when trying to troubleshoot a network connectivity problem. The routing table should be considered if there is a question as to how the packets are being delivered or if they are even being routed in the first place. The first step is to check the local routing table of the host to make sure that packets are being routed to the default gateway. The next step is to check the routing table at each hop along the way. Although at some point, the packets might be routed to the Internet and you'll have no way to see the routing table. If packets are routed on the Internet, you can see their path with the `tracert` command on the Windows operating system or `traceroute` on the Linux/Unix operating system.

Interface Status

Although the interface status of a device or the operating systems seems like a simple consideration, the speed and duplex can impact performance. The interface could possibly negotiate at a lower speed than the optimal speed required. The duplex for the interface can possibly negotiate at half-duplex vs. the optimal full-duplex. If the interface negotiates at half-duplex, the total throughput can be severely impacted by as much as 60 percent. That means that a 100 Mbps connection might only perform at 40 Mbps.

To prevent these problems, the interface status should be examined. If you find that the speed is lower than you anticipated, or the duplex is negotiating at half-duplex, then you should manually set the speed and/or duplex. Manually setting the speed and/or duplex will ensure that the connection is running optimally.

VLAN Assignment

The wrong VLAN assignment for a device or operating system can affect its overall access to the network or in some cases its performance. When the VLAN assignment is wrong, it means that the host is on the wrong network. If the host is on the wrong VLAN (network), it can experience network connectivity problems if access control lists (ACLs) or firewall rules are being applied to the network segment where the host resides. A host on the wrong VLAN can also experience performance problems if quality of service (QoS) is being applied to the VLAN. Therefore, the VLAN assignment for the affected host should always be considered when problems arise or performance of the application is affected.

Network Performance Baselines

A network performance baseline is a critical piece of information to have about your network. Without the network performance baseline, you cannot decipher between normal activity and abnormal activity that can be contributing to the problem you are trying to solve. Therefore, a network performance baseline should be collected periodically. The performance baseline should be collected over a week of normal network activity. One performance baseline is not enough. It should be collected quarterly or monthly depending on how often your network changes.

Once a network performance baseline is established, if a problem arises you'll be able to compare the current performance to the established performance. If the current performance is poor, you now have a metric for improvement. Once the problem is solved, you can compare the network performance again to the original network performance baseline. If it looks similar, then you can conclude the problem is solved. If it is still abnormal, then you could still have a problem. As you can see, network performance baselines are very useful to consider when you have a network performance problem.

Common Issues

Now that you understand the various considerations when you are troubleshooting network-related problems. we will focus on some of the most common problems you will encounter as an administrator. In the following sections, you will find the most common problems that CompTIA has identified.

Collisions

Collisions happen when the transmit pair of wires on one node is also the transmit wire for the other node. This is known as half-duplex Ethernet. A single pair of wires is used to transmit and receive for both nodes. This is similar to a one-lane road, where only one car can go down the road at a time. If two cars both go down the same road from opposite sides, a collision will happen. Ethernet frames are very similar to this analogy, although they are electrical pulses. When the electrical signals collide during simultaneous transmission, a collision occurs, and both hosts must transmit the data again. Collisions from half-duplex were common when 10 Mbps and 100 Mbps speeds were the norm, since 10BaseT or 100BastT could operate at half-duplex (one-lane road) or full-duplex. If we apply the analogy of cars on a road to full-duplex communication, it is similar to a two-lane road, with dedicated directions. A collision will not occur, since the electrical signals travel a single direction on a dedicated pair of wires to the other side.

Luckily, today switches normally operate at full-duplex, and it is very rare that a host will negotiate at half-duplex. However, it is something to check, and it's easy to fix; you just need to configure the switch to force full-duplex operations. Most switches will allow you to force speed and duplex. By default, both the host and the switch port are set to automatically negotiate, which can cause problems.

If you allow collisions to occur, the performance of the connected nodes will be severely degraded. Although, you might assume that a single road will allow the road to be shared one-half the time. When a collision occurs, back-off timers are set on both sides and the nodes will retry the communications after the timers expire. Consequently, you can see a 60 percent or more reduction in bandwidth if collisions are ignored. As shown in Figure 5.31, both node A and node B transmit at the same time, which results in a collision. The back-off timers are randomly set on both nodes. When the timers expire, the nodes can attempt to transmit again, but during the back-off period the hosts will send a jamming signal. This is how half-duplex carrier-sense multiple access with collision detection (CSMA/CD) operates.

FIGURE 5.31 Collisions

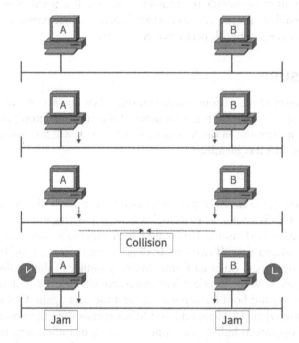

Broadcast Storm

A certain number of broadcasts are normal in an IPv4 network for supporting technologies such as DHCP and ARP traffic. When switches receive a broadcast, the switch forwards the broadcast to all active ports. As the number of nodes increases within the broadcast domain, the number of broadcasts will steadily increase as well. This is just how IPv4 works in networks; the number of broadcasts is just a cost of doing business with IPv4.

A broadcast storm is not normal in any network, and it happens when network loops are present, as shown in Figure 5.32. Because switches forward broadcast frames, when the switch receives the broadcast frame, it will forward the frame out of all the active ports. If the active port is part of a network loop, then the destination switch receives two copies of this broadcast frame, which then get duplicated and forwarded again and again. This avalanche effect can happen within milliseconds!

The effect of a broadcast storm is not just limited to increased traffic. It gets worse, because every node must process the broadcast frames. The node receives the broadcast frame and passes it up to the Network layer in its protocol stack. This processing uses CPU time as the node processes the broadcast. So, when broadcast storms happen, all the nodes in the network show a high utilization of CPU.

All of this can happen within a few moments and the consequences can be long lasting. MAC table thrashing can occur, and unless the problem is rectified, it can make it impossible to even diagnose. Therefore, you should always employ loop prevention techniques, such as Spanning Tree Protocol (STP), so that broadcast storms never have a chance to happen at all.

FIGURE 5.32   Broadcast storms

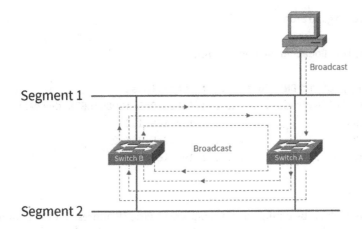

Duplicate MAC Addresses

MAC addresses should always be unique, because each vendor is assigned an organization-ally unique identifier (OUI) by the Institute of Electrical and Electronics Engineers (IEEE), and each card produced is given a unique ID. This standard has been adopted to ensure that MAC addresses are globally unique.

Despite these adopted standards, it is still possible to have a duplicate MAC address if the MAC address is statically set. Some NIC firmware allows for manual MAC address con-figuration. Virtualization platforms also allow for static MAC address assignment, although most virtualization software will not allow a duplicate MAC address to be configured on a virtual machine (VM).

Regardless of how the duplicate MAC address is configured, the symptoms are sim-ilar to a duplicate IP address. Sporadic loss of network communication will be observed. These problems are difficult to identify as a duplicate MAC address. Identifying the actual duplicate MAC address is easier than finding a duplicate IP address because you have the MAC address already. You just need to connect to the switch and find the port that the duplicate MAC address is located on. If it is a VM, the virtualization software will most likely notify you by displaying an error next to the VM, stating that a duplicate MAC address is configured.

Duplicate IP Addresses

Starting with Windows Vista, when the operating system starts up, it will send an ARP request for its configured IP address. If an ARP reply is received, then a message stating a duplicate IP address has been detected will appear on the screen. The symptoms of a duplicate IP address on the network will be a loss of connectivity for both hosts sporadically.

Fortunately, with the skills you've learned in this chapter, you can identify a host with the duplicate IP address on the network. You must first record the configured IP address using `ipconfig`.

```
C:\Users\Sybex>ipconfig

Windows IP Configuration

Ethernet adapter Local Area Connection:

   Connection-specific DNS Suffix . : sybex.local
   Link-local IPv6 Address . . . . . : fe80::9e8e:2086:b678:dee3%11
   IPv4 Address. . . . . . . . . . . : 192.168.1.2
   Subnet Mask . . . . . . . . . . . : 255.255.255.0
   Default Gateway . . . . . . . . . : 192.168.1.1

C:\Users\Sybex>
```

Then locate the host by configuring a temporary static IP address on the computer that is not duplicated with any other host and still within the intended network range. You then ping the original IP address; the ping may fail if the firewall is enabled on the remote system. However, this process will allow you to obtain the MAC address via the ARP process. You then use the arp command to obtain the MAC associated with the problematic IP address.

```
C:\Users\Sybex>ping 192.168.1.2

Pinging 192.168.1.2 with 32 bytes of data:
Reply from 192.168.1.2: bytes=32 time<1ms TTL=64
Reply from 192.168.1.2: bytes=32 time<1ms TTL=64
Reply from 192.168.1.2: bytes=32 time<1ms TTL=64
Reply from 192.168.1.2: bytes=32 time<1ms TTL=64

Ping statistics for 192.168.1.2:
   Packets: Sent = 4, Received = 4, Lost = 0 (0% loss),
Approximate round trip times in milli-seconds:
   Minimum = 0ms, Maximum = 0ms, Average = 0ms

C:\Users\Sybex>arp -g

Interface: 192.168.1.5 --- 0xb
  Internet Address      Physical Address      Type
  192.168.1.2           00-15-5d-01-12-0d     dynamic
  192.168.1.255         ff-ff-ff-ff-ff-ff     static
  224.0.0.22            01-00-5e-00-00-16     static
  224.0.0.251           01-00-5e-00-00-fb     static
```

```
224.0.0.252        01-00-5e-00-00-fc    static
239.255.255.250    01-00-5e-7f-ff-fa    static
255.255.255.255    ff-ff-ff-ff-ff-ff    static
```

```
C:\Users\Sybex>
```

The last step is to connect to the switching equipment and locate the port associated with the MAC address of 00-15-5d-01-12-0d as discovered in the previous step. Most switch operating systems will allow you to show the content addressable memory (CAM) table that is used for forward filter decisions. This allows us to identify the port number the duplicate IP address is occupying by the MAC address recorded in the previous step. If your switch does not support this function, then you will need to visit each computer until you have identified the duplicate IP address.

Multicast Flooding

Multicast is a sort of smart directed broadcast. A great analogy is that a broadcast is like being in an auditorium where the speaker is broadcast to the people in attendance. You are going to hear the speaker, whether you like it or not, because the speaker will be broadcast to you. A multicast is sort of like a radio station; you won't hear the radio until you tune in to the station. Once you've tuned in, you have no control over the content unless you turn off the radio.

Multicast requires the feature of port snooping on switches. When a client joins a multicast group via the Internet Group Messaging Protocol (IGMP), the switch registers the client with the port the IGMP message was seen upon. Now any multicast packets transmitted and destined for the specific multicast group are forwarded to the port joined to the group. All other ports never see any of the traffic from the multicast session. This is similar to the radio in your car being tuned to a specific channel. All the other cars on the road have no idea of what you are listening to, unless they are tuned to the same channel.

Multicast works great because it restricts other ports that are not part of the multicast group from receiving the traffic. However, multicast is very complicated to properly set up for some applications. Therefore, it is a common issue to have multicast flooding occur on ports that are not joined to the multicast group. The symptom is the non-multicast client will experience poor network performance and potentially higher CPU utilization during a multicast transmission. There is no real cure for multicast flooding for a specific port other than to properly configure the multicast-enabled switch. You can verify that the port is being improperly flooded with packet capture analysis.

Asymmetrical Routing

Asymmetrical routing is an exotic problem to have on a network. It is typically only seen when an organization has more than one path back to the source network. In the example shown in Figure 5.33, path A and path B both lead to router D. As packets leave router A via path A, they finally make it to the destination of router D. However, when packets leave router D, they come back on path B. This is a classic example of asymmetrical routing.

FIGURE 5.33   Asymmetrical routing example

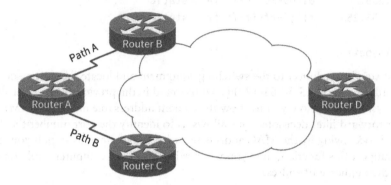

Some networks have asymmetrical routing and the administrator never knows. However, it creates multiple failure points. For example, if either path A or path B goes down, routing stops and that negates why you have redundant routes in the first place. The other issue is if path A has a lower bandwidth than path B, then performance on the network will suffer. Unfortunately, there is no cure-all solution for asymmetrical routing. Each network will have a different fix. The objective is to understand the symptoms and effect on the network.

Switching Loops

Networks should have redundant paths between switches in the event that a link fails or an entire switch fails. Redundant switching paths are good for the continued operation of the network. As shown in Figure 5.34, switch A and switch B are configured with two adjoining segments: segment 1 and segment 2. If any link on segment 1 fails, then segment 2 will switch the packets, and if segment 2 fails, then segment 1 will switch packets.

FIGURE 5.34   Redundant switch paths

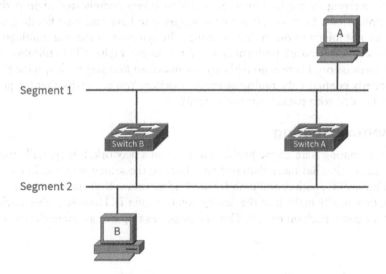

However, both segment 1 and segment 2 cannot forward packets simultaneously or switching loops will occur. The Spanning Tree Protocol (STP) is used to prevent switching loops while retaining redundant links. STP will calculate the redundant path and block frames from being forwarded to the redundant port. If something were to happen to the original port that is designated to forward frames, the backup port would take over.

When STP is improperly configured and switches are connected together with redundant links, duplicate frames are forwarded and broadcast storms are created. The effects can be seen immediately on the network, as performance is degraded swiftly.

Routing Loops

When routing loops happen, they completely prevent network connectivity from end to end. Routing loops can happen for a number of reasons unrelated to this objective. It is important to be able to diagnose and understand how routing loops impact network communications.

As shown in Figure 5.35, we see three networks, A, B, and C, along with their corresponding routers A, B, and C. Each router has a routing table that directs the packets to the next network hop. Routers B and C both have a path to network A routing through each other: router B believes that the path to network A is through router C. Router C believes that the path to network A is through router B. So packets will route in a loop between these two routers until the packets' time to live (TTL) reaches 0 and the packets are no longer considered routable.

FIGURE 5.35   Routing loop example

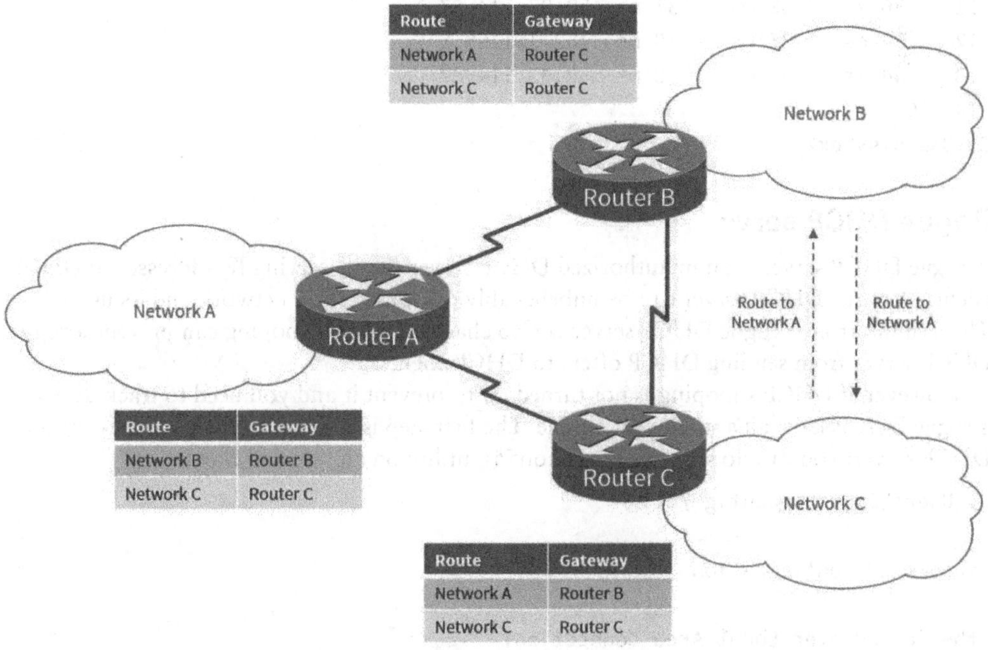

You can diagnose routing loops by using the tracert command on the Windows operating system or the traceroute command on the Linux/Unix operating system. In the following output, you can see that after hop number 6, the packets bounced between 52.93.114.87 and 162.151.65.5. Finally, Ctrl+C was pressed to exit the tracert routing loop. If you were to discover this issue, you could most likely get some answers or confirmation from your Internet service provider (ISP). Ultimately, the provider involved would need to fix this issue since it was so far outside of your network.

```
C:\Users\sybex>tracert www.wiley.com

Tracing route to d1x6jqndp2gdqp.cloudfront.net [99.84.98.57]
over a maximum of 30 hops:

  1    <1 ms    <1 ms    <1 ms   172.16.1.1
  2    14 ms    13 ms    11 ms   96.120.62.213
  3    11 ms     9 ms    11 ms   96.110.215.113
  4     8 ms    22 ms    15 ms   96.110.48.166
  5    10 ms    15 ms     8 ms   52.93.114.87
  6    11 ms    13 ms    13 ms   162.151.65.5
  7    34 ms    36 ms    34 ms   52.93.114.87
  8    23 ms    21 ms    23 ms   162.151.65.5
  9    34 ms    35 ms    34 ms   52.93.114.87
 10    25 ms    29 ms    27 ms   162.151.65.5
 11    36 ms    39 ms    37 ms   52.93.114.87
 12    34 ms    36 ms    38 ms   162.151.65.5
 13    44 ms    48 ms    48 ms   52.93.114.87
 14    ^C
C:\Users\sybex>
```

Rogue DHCP server

A rogue DHCP server is an unauthorized DHCP server that is serving IP addresses to DHCP clients. A rogue DHCP server can be unbelievably disruptive for a network and its users. The cleanup from a rogue DHCP server is also chaotic. DHCP snooping can prevent a rogue DHCP server from sending DHCP offers to DHCP clients.

However, if DHCP snooping is not turned on to prevent it and you need to track down a rogue DHCP server, it's somewhat simple. The first step is to identify the IP address of the DHCP server; you can do so with the ipconfig utility on an affected client.

```
C:\Users\Sybex>ipconfig /all

Windows IP Configuration

Ethernet adapter Local Area Connection:

  Connection-specific DNS Suffix . : sybex.local
```

```
Description . . . . . . . . . . . : Intel(R) Gigabit Network Connection
Physical Address. . . . . . . . . : AC-22-0B-50-97-60
DHCP Enabled. . . . . . . . . . . : Yes
Autoconfiguration Enabled . . . . : Yes
Link-local IPv6 Address . . . . . : fe80::bc1e:1758:ba9a:ddf3%11(Preferred)
IPv4 Address. . . . . . . . . . . : 172.16.1.80
Subnet Mask . . . . . . . . . . . : 255.255.255.0
Lease Obtained. . . . . . . . . . : Saturday, November 11, 2021 9:30:20 AM
Lease Expires . . . . . . . . . . : Saturday, November 11, 2021 2:30:20 PM
Default Gateway . . . . . . . . . : 172.16.1.2
DHCP Server . . . . . . . . . . . : 172.16.1.50
DHCPv6 IAID . . . . . . . . . . . : 246161931
DHCPv6 Client DUID. . . . . . . . : 00-01-00-01-1A-45-39-41-AC-22-0B-50-97
DNS Servers . . . . . . . . . . . : 172.16.1.50
NetBIOS over Tcpip. . . . . . . . : Enabled

C:\Users\Sybex>
```

The DHCP server that has sent the DHCP offer and DHCP acknowledgment is detailed in the output of the `ipconfig /all` command. To track it down, we need to cache its MAC address. This is done with `ipconfig /release` and `ipconfig /renew`. The process of releasing the IP addresses and requesting a renewal will generate traffic to the DHCP server. We now have a MAC address in the ARP cache that we can use to track down the rogue DHCP. Now we head to the switch and look at the CAM table. This will show which port on the switch is associated with the MAC address.

```
C:\Users\Sybex>arp -g

Interface: 172.16.1.101 --- 0xb
  Internet Address      Physical Address      Type
  172.16.1.1            00-15-5d-01-12-0d     dynamic
  172.16.1.50           74-d4-35-03-a6-b9     dynamic
  172.31.255.255        ff-ff-ff-ff-ff-ff     static
  224.0.0.22            01-00-5e-00-00-16     static
  224.0.0.251           01-00-5e-00-00-fb     static
  224.0.0.252           01-00-5e-00-00-fc     static
  239.255.255.250       01-00-5e-7f-ff-fa     static
  255.255.255.255       ff-ff-ff-ff-ff-ff     static

C:\Users\Sybex>
```

It is important to note that you can also use a packet capture and analysis to obtain the rogue DHCP server IP address. However, using the ipconfig command is much quicker.

DHCP Scope Exhaustion

A symptom of an exhausted DHCP scope is that clients will not attain their IP address from the DHCP server. Clients will instead autoconfigure a link-local address of 169.254.x.x, also called Automatic Private IP Addressing (APIPA).

The first step of diagnosing is with the client. The ipconfig utility will display the APIPA address and state that it was configured through autoconfiguration. The client should be checked for the correct VLAN and port configuration.

```
C:\Users\Sybex>ipconfig

Windows IP Configuration


Ethernet adapter Local Area Connection:

   Connection-specific DNS Suffix .  :
   Link-local IPv6 Address . . . . . : fe80::bc82:6ccb:a1e1:32f6%11
   Autoconfiguration IPv4 Address. . : 169.254.50.246
   Subnet Mask . . . . . . . . . . . : 255.255.0.0
   Default Gateway . . . . . . . . . :


C:\Users\Sybex>
```

A packet capture and analysis tool can be used to diagnose the problem as well. DCHP discover messages will be seen in the analysis but no DHCP offers from the server. When you determine the problem to be a DHCP server problem and discover the scope is exhausted, you will need to add IP addresses to the range in the DHCP server or release client leases from the clients. Never delete the leases from the server—you will create the problem of duplicate IP addresses if you do so.

IP Setting Issues

There are several IP setting issues that you can encounter in an IP network. The setting issues you will encounter are generally related to static configuration. However, these issues can also happen with DHCP if you make a mistake. It will affect a lot more people if you make the mistake with DHCP vs. a single static configuration. In either case, the following sections cover the most common IP setting issues you may see.

Incorrect Gateway

The default gateway in your network is the way out of your immediate network through a router. The gateway is important because it allows you to communicate with other networks, such as other VLANs or the Internet. Think of the gateway as the door that leads out of a room you are in. The door in this analogy is the router, and the room is the immediate network. It is not common to have more than one gateway in a LAN, but you will see this from time to time in networks. It is common to have multiple gateways to the Internet, because this allows for the redundancy of the Internet connection.

If a host is set to the wrong gateway or to a gateway that does not exist, communications to remote networks or the Internet will fail. These problems can be diagnosed with `tracert` on Windows or `traceroute` on Linux/Unix. As shown in the following output, we can see the path the ICMP packets have taken to the destination IP address of 192.168.1.80.

```
C:\Users\Sybex>tracert 192.168.1.80

Tracing route to hostb.Sybex.local [192.168.1.80]
over a maximum of 30 hops:

  1   <1 ms   <1 ms   <1 ms pfsense.Sybex.local [172.16.1.1]
  2    2 ms    3 ms    2 ms int-router.Sybex.local [172.16.2.1]
  3    3 ms    3 ms    2 ms ext-router.Sybex.local [192.168.5.1]
  4    5 ms    7 ms    7 ms hostb.Sybex.local [192.168.1.80]

Trace complete.


C:\Users\Sybex>
```

If an incorrect gateway was configured on any node in the path, we could quickly identify the problem, as shown in the following output. We would then need to check the routing table on the last node that successfully responded, which is 172.16.2.1. You may also see the packet take a path out the wrong gateway, which will also be detailed in the output. The last router that you expected to see in the output should always be checked for the proper route statements to the destination network.

```
C:\Users\Sybex>tracert 192.168.1.80

Tracing route to hostb.Sybex.local [192.168.1.80]
over a maximum of 30 hops:

  1   <1 ms   <1 ms   <1 ms pfsense.Sybex.local [172.16.1.1]
  2    2 ms    3 ms    2 ms int-router.Sybex.local [172.16.2.1]
  3    *       *       *     Request timed out.
  4    *       *       *     Request timed out.
  5    *       *       *     Request timed out.

[Output cut]
Trace complete.


C:\Users\Sybex>
```

Incorrect Subnet Mask

The importance of the network mask was covered in Chapter 1, "Domain 1.0: Networking Fundamentals." The network mask defines the local host's network ID. The local host also uses its network ID to decide if a packet needs to be routed or locally switched to the destination IP address. An incorrect network mask can create connectivity or performance problems.

In Figure 5.36 you see two /24 networks: 10.1.0.0/24 and 10.1.1.0/24. Each host inside the two networks has a /24 network mask. However, host A is configured with an incorrect network mask of /16. Everything will work as normal when host A communicates with hosts on its immediate network. However, when host A communicates with host B on the other subnet, host A will match its network ID with the destination network ID and will determine that the host is local; consequently, the information will never make it off the immediate network. The local network ID is derived from the logical ANDing process of the host's IP address and the network mask, which will be 10.1.0.0. The destination IP address will also be ANDed against the host's network mask, which will produce a value of 10.1.0.0. When the two are compared, they will be identical, so the local host will try to deliver it directly via an ARP request, which will never be heard by the remote host B.

FIGURE 5.36   Incorrect /16 netmask in a /24 network

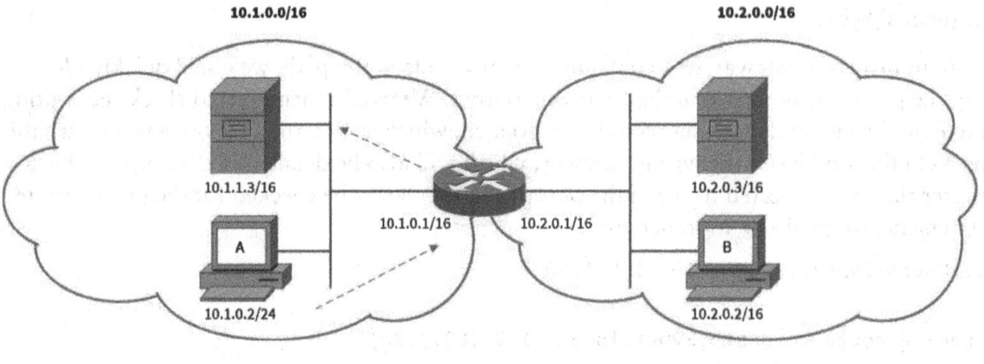

In Figure 5.37 you see two /16 networks: 10.1.0.0/16 and 10.2.0.0/16. In this example, host A is configured with an incorrect network mask of /24. Everything will work normally when host A communicates with host B; the frame will be sent to the router from host A and routed to the remote host B. However, when host A attempts to communicate with the destination server IP address of 10.1.1.3, the frames will first be forwarded to the router, then to the host, and this creates a performance problem. Because host A calculates its immediate network ID as 10.1.0.0 and the destination network of 10.1.1.0, host A will determine that the host is remote and forward the frame to the router. When the router receives the frame, it will then attempt to deliver the frame itself. In certain circumstances, the frame might not be delivered at all.

FIGURE 5.37   Incorrect /24 netmask in a /16 network

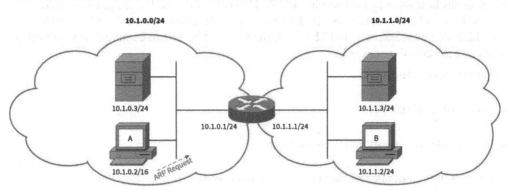

The problems mentioned here can be identified and remedied by using the skills learned in the previous sections. First, we need to diagram the network, as shown in Figure 5.36 and Figure 5.37. Then we should obtain the IP addresses associated with the hosts, along with their subnet mask. We can then identify the problem. The `ipconfig` command can be used on Windows hosts to obtain the current IP address and subnet mask. In Linux and Unix, the `ifconfig` command will perform the same function.

```
C:\Users\Sybex>ipconfig

Windows IP Configuration

Ethernet adapter Local Area Connection:

   Connection-specific DNS Suffix . : sybex.local
   Link-local IPv6 Address . . . . . : fe80::bc1e:1758:ba9a:ddf3%11
   IPv4 Address. . . . . . . . . . . : 172.16.1.101
   Subnet Mask . . . . . . . . . . . : 255.240.0.0
   Default Gateway . . . . . . . . . : 172.16.1.1

C:\Users\Sybex>
```

Incorrect IP Address

An incorrect IP address will directly affect the host on which it's incorrectly configured. That is unless it is wrongly configured on a router that serves an entire network. In that case, you will know that the problem exists right away. If an incorrect IP address is configured on a host, it can affect how it communicates with other hosts or the host may not be able to communicate outside of the host's immediate network.

In the following example, the host is configured with an IP address of 172.17.1.24, a subnet mask of 255.240.0.0, and a default gateway of 172.16.1.1. In this example the host will not be able to communicate with the gateway or any other host in the network. This is because this host is configured within the 172.17.0.0/12 network, but the gateway is configured in the 172.16.0.0/12 network. By changing the IP address to an IP address in the 172.16.0.0/12 network, such as 172.16.2.1, the host will be able to communicate with other hosts and the default gateway.

```
C:\Users\Sybex>ipconfig

Windows IP Configuration

Ethernet adapter Local Area Connection:

   Connection-specific DNS Suffix .  : sybex.local
   Link-local IPv6 Address . . . . . : fe80::bc1e:1758:ba9a:ddf3%11
   IPv4 Address. . . . . . . . . . . : 172.17.1.24
   Subnet Mask . . . . . . . . . . . : 255.240.0.0
   Default Gateway . . . . . . . . . : 172.16.1.1

C:\Users\Sybex>
```

Incorrect DNS

Incorrect DNS settings will create name resolution problems with the client. If the client is pointed to a public DNS server, it will even prevent the client from joining a Windows domain. It is typical to point clients to an internal DNS server that is forwarded to an external DNS server such as the Internet service provider (ISP).

You can troubleshoot where the client is configured by using the ipconfig /all command, as shown in the following example. The command's output will display the configured DNS server or servers if more than one is configured. If more than one server is configured, make sure that both have the same local zones configured and they are both configured for forwarding to the same upstream DNS servers. If they are not configured the same, then you can have intermittent issues with name resolution.

```
C:\Users\Sybex>ipconfig /all

Windows IP Configuration

Ethernet adapter Local Area Connection:

   Connection-specific DNS Suffix .  : sybex.local
   Description . . . . . . . . . . . : Intel(R) Gigabit Network Connection
   Physical Address. . . . . . . . . : AC-22-0B-50-97-60
   DHCP Enabled. . . . . . . . . . . : Yes
```

```
Autoconfiguration Enabled . . . . : Yes
Link-local IPv6 Address . . . . . : fe80::bc1e:1758:ba9a:ddf3%11(Preferred)
IPv4 Address. . . . . . . . . . . : 172.16.1.80
Subnet Mask . . . . . . . . . . . : 255.255.255.0
Lease Obtained. . . . . . . . . . : Saturday, November 11, 2021 9:30:20 AM
Lease Expires . . . . . . . . . . : Saturday, November 11, 2021 2:30:20 PM
Default Gateway . . . . . . . . . : 172.16.1.2
DHCP Server . . . . . . . . . . . : 172.16.1.50
DHCPv6 IAID . . . . . . . . . . . : 246161931
DHCPv6 Client DUID. . . . . . . . : 00-01-00-01-1A-45-39-41-AC-22-0B-50-97
DNS Servers . . . . . . . . . . . : 172.16.1.50
NetBIOS over Tcpip. . . . . . . . : Enabled


C:\Users\Sybex>
```

Missing Route

A missing route is pretty easy to diagnose because traffic will drop after the missing route. A missing route can be caused by a number of problems, most of which will be out of your control if it is on the Internet. However, your Internet service provider (ISP) can verify the routing issue and open a ticket with their upstream service provider. A missing route on your own network can be caused by a number of factors, but here we'll focus only on the diagnosis of a missing route.

To diagnose a missing route, you can use the `tracert` command on the Windows operating system, or the `traceroute` command on the Linux/Unix operating system. In the following output, you can see that after hop number 6, the packets drop with a request timed out status. Finally, Ctrl+C was pressed to exit the `tracert` command.

```
C:\Users\sybex>tracert www.wiley.com

Tracing route to d1x6jqndp2gdqp.cloudfront.net [99.84.98.57]
over a maximum of 30 hops:

  1    <1 ms    <1 ms    <1 ms   172.16.1.1
  2    14 ms    13 ms    11 ms   96.120.62.213
  3    11 ms     9 ms    11 ms   96.110.215.113
  4     8 ms    22 ms    15 ms   96.110.48.166
  5    10 ms    15 ms     8 ms   52.93.114.87
  6    11 ms    13 ms    13 ms   162.151.65.5
  7     *        *        *      Request timed out.
  8     *        *        *      Request timed out.
```

```
 9     *       *       *      Request timed out.
10     *       *       *      Request timed out.
11     *       *       *      Request timed out.
12     *       *       *      Request timed out.
13     *       *       *      Request timed out.
14  ^C
C:\Users\sybex>
```

Although using the `tracert` or `traceroute` command is useful in diagnosis of a missing route, you should be aware that many providers block Internet Control Message Protocol (ICMP) packets. So, it is always best to escalate to the ISP or the application provider once you diagnose a problem; they can confirm that there is an outage.

Low Optical Link Budget

The term *power budget* refers to the total amount of power that an optical transceiver can function within. There is often a minimum and maximum power level that is notated in decibels (dBs). The power budget is often a calculation between the output power of the transmitter and the minimal input power for the receiver.

The loss budget is a bit more involved because it takes the fiber installation into account. The loss budget is a calculation of the estimated loss of the cable (according to length), connectors, and splices and how clean the optics are. To calculate the loss budget, we can use some rule-of-thumb numbers, such as each connector will attribute to 0.75 dB. If we had four connectors, two for each patch cable, then 4 × 0.75 dB = 3 dB of connector loss. We also need to know the wavelength we are going to operate at and the loss of the cable at the wavelength. For example, the vendor might have a loss of 1.5 dB per km at 1500 nm. If we were going to have a run of 500 meters, the equation is .5 km × 1.5 dB = 0.75 dB of cable loss. We then add the connector loss of 3 dB and the cable loss of 0.75 dB for a total loss of 3.75 dB.

With an average power budget of 5 to 6 dB from the transceivers, we are 1.25 dB away from problems. So, cleanliness of the optics becomes an important factor for optimal operation.

Many SPF+ transceivers allow the administrator to view power budget and optical loss. In the following output, we can see the adjusted values for two 10 Gbps transceivers. Assuming the switch on the other end is sending similar values, this fiber-optic link is optimal.

```
es-4thfl#sh interfaces transceiver module 1
If device is externally calibrated, only calibrated values are printed.
++ : high alarm, +  : high warning, -  : low warning, -- : low alarm.
NA or N/A: not applicable, Tx: transmit, Rx: receive.
```

```
mA: milliamperes, dBm: decibels (milliwatts).

                                   Optical   Optical
           Temperature  Voltage   Tx Power  Rx Power
Port       (Celsius)    (Volts)   (dBm)     (dBm)
---------  -----------  -------   --------  --------
Tel/1         34.9       3.23      -1.9      -2.1
Tel/2         37.1       3.23      -2.0      -1.4

es-4thfl#
```

Certificate Issues

There are several problems that plague certificates. Of the two major problems, one is related to the proper setting of time and date and the other is trust-related. The time on the host should always be checked along with the expiration of the SSL certificate. If the certificate is expired, this will cause problems.

On the other hand, when an untrusted SSL certificate is encountered, the web browser will alert you that the SSL certificate is not valid, as shown in Figure 5.38. Every web browser comes with a list of trusted certificate publishers. If a certificate is issued to a website or is not trusted, a warning box will come up preventing you from visiting the site. You can click through the warning prompt and visit the site anyway, but the address bar will still read "Not secure" or display an unlocked lock icon during your visit.

FIGURE 5.38   An untrusted SSL certificate warning

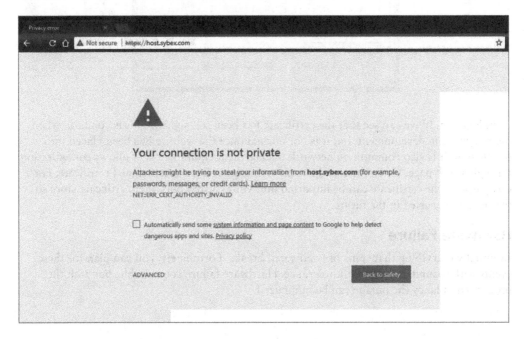

The problem should always be investigated further since information entered in the site could be intercepted if the site was hacked. The first step to diagnose is checking the hostname in the URL. All certificates must match the hostname in the URL that they are issued for. If you tried accessing the site by the IP address, this warning is benign and can be disregarded. However, if you entered the correct hostname, then the certificate should be inspected. Every web browser is different, but every web browser will let you view the certificate, as shown in Figure 5.39.

FIGURE 5.39   A self-signed certificate

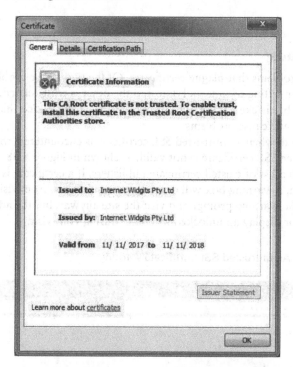

In Figure 5.39 we can see that the certificate has been self-signed. This is common when the website is in development, but it is not normal once the website has been placed into production. It is also common on network management equipment that allows configuration through a web page. Often the management web page will use a self-signed certificate. For this purpose, the certificate can be imported into your trusted publisher certificate store so that it can be trusted in the future.

Hardware Failure

Eventually everything that spins or is powered breaks. Fortunately, you can plan for these events with redundancy and fault tolerance. Hardware failure is inevitable, but with the proper redundancy the outage can be minimized.

Service contracts on equipment ensure that hardware failures minimize the impact to the network. Contract response time is directly related to the cost of the service contract. Some contracts are designed for a 4-hour turnaround on parts, which is the critical care plan. A 4-hour response time is generally reserved for critical components because of the price. Next business day is the norm for equipment that has redundancy built into it. If one of your dual-power supplies fails, the next business day is more than sufficient.

Host-Based/Network-Based Firewall Settings

When the host-based firewall is incorrectly set, it can affect applications and services the host provides. Similar to perimeter firewalls, host-based firewalls must be set up to allow both inbound and outbound ports for the application. When the host-based firewall is incorrectly set, it can affect all clients, if the service or application is accessed by all the clients.

To diagnose incorrect host-based settings, use a port scanner, which will indicate which ports are accessible and which ports are blocked. A packet capture and analysis tool can also be useful to see the incoming requests for an application. If a problem is detected, it is best to consult the vendor's firewall documentation; most application vendors will describe the host-based firewall configuration for their application.

Blocked Service, Ports, or Addresses

When TCP and UDP ports are blocked, the symptom can be an unresponsive application. Another symptom might be that features of the application do not function correctly or at all. I have even seen applications crash because the ports are blocked. This can be very frustrating for the network administrator or the people supporting the application.

Most organizations block outbound port connections. This is done to limit the abuse of the Internet, but it's mainly for security reasons. When a new application is installed, the appropriate firewall rules will be configured. The vendor of the application should furnish a document detailing the firewall rule considerations or specifications.

Blocked outbound ports or IP addresses can be diagnosed by using a port scanner like Nmap to check the destination host ports. This will allow you to see the blocked and permitted ports for a particular IP address. A packet capture and analysis tool like Wireshark is also useful to verify that the application is initiating the connection outbound to the destination host. Once the problem is diagnosed as a blocked port, the firewall rules should be checked against the vendor's documentation.

Incorrect VLAN

If a host is configured on an incorrect VLAN, the host might not be able to communicate with other hosts or the Internet, or the host could have elevated privileges. The only way to diagnosis the possibility of an incorrect VLAN is to view the running configuration for the interface. As we see in the following example, interface GigabitEthernet 2/8 is configured for VLAN 15. If the client was incorrectly configured for a particular VLAN, then entering global configuration mode and switching the VLAN would be the remedy. After the VLAN is configured, the shutdown and no shutdown commands should be used on the port to allow the client to realize the VLAN has been switched. When the `shutdown` command is entered, the interface on the client will drop, then when the `no shutdown` command is issued, the interface will come back online. When the client sees the interface is back online, the operating system will attempt to configure a new DHCP address.

```
es-4thfl#show running-config interface GigabitEthernet 2/8
Building configuration...

Current configuration : 341 bytes
!
interface GigabitEthernet2/8
 description FSTA232003 - R232-1
 switchport access vlan 15
 switchport mode access
 spanning-tree portfast
end

es-4thfl#
```

DNS Issues

We rely heavily on fully qualified domain names (FQDNs) and Domain Name System (DNS) for network communications. FQDNs and DNS also allow for easy reconfiguration of an IP address, and they are easier to remember. www.sybex.com resolves to 208.215.179.132, and www.sybex.com is a lot easier to remember than the IP address. We can also swap out the IP address and you can still reference www.sybex.com to get to it. When an FQDN does not resolve, we simply cannot connect to the destination host. Fortunately, name resolution is simple to diagnose.

To understand the diagnostic process, you need to understand the name resolution process end to end. In Figure 5.40 you see a typical DNS process. On the left we have the client that requires resolution, and at the top we have the Internet DNS servers that contain the authoritative copy of the zone file. All network clients contain a DNS resolver service that is pointed to a DNS server for queries. The DNS resolver also contains a local DNS cache to cache DNS query results. When the DNS resolver does not have the answer for a DNS query, the query will be forwarded to the configured DNS server. In most corporate networks, you will find an internal DNS server to which all of the clients are pointed for name resolution. This internal DNS server may contain internal DNS zones or caches that take precedence over queries directed to it. If the internal DNS server cannot resolve the answer, it may be configured to query the Internet DNS servers directly using the root zone, or it may forward the request to your ISP's DNS servers. The ISP DNS servers will have a cache and may have local zones configured as well that will take precedence over the query. Ultimately, if the ISP DNS servers cannot answer the query, they will recursively query the Internet DNS servers for the answer.

FIGURE 5.40   The DNS query process

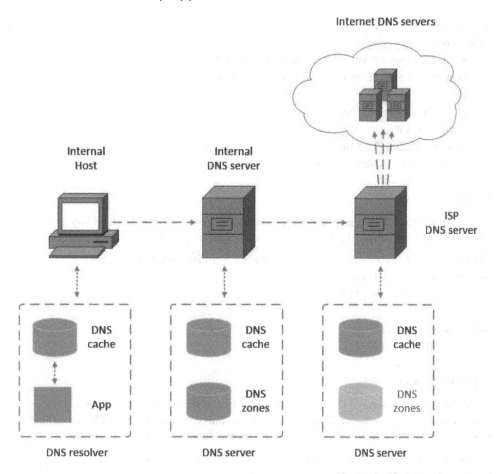

When diagnosing name resolution problems, always verify that the source of your name resolution is returning the proper resource record value and work your way back. You can use nslookup or dig to help verify DNS resolution. Suppose we are having trouble resolving www.sybex.com to the IP address of 208.215.179.132 on the internal host. The sybex.com zone is hosted on an Internet DNS server. Therefore, we will start at the source and check the name servers hosting the sybex.com zone file. We will start by obtaining the SOA record for sybex.com using the nslookup command and querying a public DNS server.

```
C:\Users\Sybex>nslookup -type=soa sybex.com 8.8.8.8
Server: google-public-dns-a.google.com
```

```
Address: 8.8.8.8

Non-authoritative answer:
sybex.com
    primary name server = jws-edcp.wiley.com
    responsible mail addr = istech.wiley.com
    serial = 70794
    refresh = 3600 (1 hour)
    retry  = 900 (15 mins)
    expire = 1209600 (14 days)
    default TTL = 3600 (1 hour)


C:\Users\Sybex>
```

We can see that the primary DNS (authoritative) server is jws-edcp.wiley.com, so we will check that next to verify that the resource record is correct.

```
C:\Users\Sybex>nslookup -type=a www.sybex.com jws-edcp.wiley.com
Server: jws-edcp.wiley.com
Address: 208.215.179.100


Name:  www.sybex.com
Address: 208.215.179.132


C:\Users\Sybex>
```

We have now confirmed the primary DNS (authoritative) server of jws-edcp.wiley .com is returning the correct IP address for the resource record. We now check our ISP's DNS server to which our internal servers are forwarding requests for resolution.

```
C:\Users\Sybex>nslookup -type=a www.sybex.com 75.75.75.75
Server: cdns01.comcast.net
Address: 75.75.75.75


Non-authoritative answer:
Name:  www.sybex.com
Address: 208.215.179.132


C:\Users\Sybex>
```

We have now confirmed that the ISP servers are resolving the record correctly. If we didn't expect the value that was returned, the record could have been recently changed and still in the ISP's DNS cache. The SOA will define the default TTL that you should wait for before checking again. It is also possible for the resource record to have an explicit TTL set. This can be checked by adding -debug to the command string:

nslookup -type=a -debug www.sybex.com 75.75.75.75.

Next we check our internal DNS server for the proper name resolution for the resource record.

```
C:\Users\Sybex>nslookup -type=a www.sybex.com 172.16.1.1
Server: pfsense.Sybex.local
Address: 172.16.1.1

Non-authoritative answer:
Name: www.sybex.com
Address: 208.215.179.132

C:\Users\Sybex>
```

We have now confirmed that our internal servers are resolving the record correctly. If a different value from the one we expected was returned, the record could be cached, or a zone file matching sybex.com could be hosted locally. The SOA from the server would verify where the name resolution was answered from. This will guarantee that we are obtaining resolution from the source.

```
C:\Users\Sybex>nslookup -type=soa sybex.com 172.16.1.1
Server: pfsense.Sybex.local
Address: 172.16.1.1

Non-authoritative answer:
sybex.com
    primary name server = jws-edcp.wiley.com
    responsible mail addr = istech.wiley.com
    serial = 70794
    refresh = 3600 (1 hour)
    retry  = 900 (15 mins)
    expire = 1209600 (14 days)
    default TTL = 3600 (1 hour)

C:\Users\Sybex>
```

If the problem is not identified, it must be the client cache or perhaps the DNS server for which the client is configured for name resolution. The ipconfig command can be used to check both the resolver configuration and the cache.

```
C:\Users\Sybex>ipconfig /all
[Output cut]

Ethernet adapter Local Area Connection:

  Connection-specific DNS Suffix . : Sybex.local
```

```
Description . . . . . . . . . . . . : Intel(R) Gigabit Network Connection
Physical Address. . . . . . . . . : AC-22-0B-50-97-60
DHCP Enabled. . . . . . . . . . . : Yes
Autoconfiguration Enabled . . . . : Yes
Link-local IPv6 Address . . . . . : fe80::bc1e:1758:ba9a:ddf3%11(Preferred)
IPv4 Address. . . . . . . . . . . : 172.16.1.101(Preferred)
Subnet Mask . . . . . . . . . . . : 255.240.0.0
Lease Obtained. . . . . . . . . . : Friday, November 10, 2021 7:28:56 AM
Lease Expires . . . . . . . . . . : Friday, November 10, 2021 11:28:56 AM
Default Gateway . . . . . . . . . : 172.16.1.1
DHCP Server . . . . . . . . . . . : 172.16.1.1
DHCPv6 IAID . . . . . . . . . . . : 246161931
DHCPv6 Client DUID. . . . . . . . : 00-01-00-01-1A-45-39-41-AC-22-0B-50-97
DNS Servers . . . . . . . . . . . : 172.16.1.1
NetBIOS over Tcpip. . . . . . . . : Enabled

C:\Users\Sybex>ipconfig /displaydns

Windows IP Configuration

[Output cut]

    www.sybex.com
    ----------------------------------------
    Record Name . . . . . : www.sybex.com
    Record Type . . . . . : 1
    Time To Live . . . . : 895
    Data Length . . . . . : 4
    Section . . . . . . . : Answer
    A (Host) Record . . . : 208.215.179.144

[Output cut]

C:\Users\Sybex>
```

We can see that the wrong IP address is cached on the client. The command
`ipconfig /flushdns` will purge all resolver caches on the client. Then the connection
should be attempted again, and the command `ipconfig /displaydns` should be used to
check for proper resolution of the resource record.

NTP Issues

There are many issues that can be resolved by just setting the correct time. When client PCs get old, their BIOS battery that keeps the real time clock (RTC) goes dead or no longer keeps time. When this happens, the date can often get set to January 1, 1900, or a date that isn't in this decade. This will invalidate certificates because certificates have a valid from and to date. Every SSL-enabled site will display a security warning.

There are also many protocols that are time-dependent and will not function if the time is off by even 5 minutes. The Microsoft-adopted protocol of Kerberos is one of them. If the time is off by 5 minutes, you will not be able to authenticate a user account on a domain and get logged in. Normally time is synced via the Network Time Protocol (NTP) from the domain controllers, so the entire network is on the same clock.

You can verify a Windows client for proper NTP time configuration and synchronization with the w32tm command. However, on non-domain-joined computers, the w32time service must manually be started, as shown in the following example. You can then query the status with the command w32tm /query /status. You can check the configuration window by using the command w32tm /query /configuration. In the following example, after we start the service, it has not synchronized. However, after the second status query you will see that it has synchronized with the source IP address of 13.86.101.172. This objective is not specific to the Windows NTP provider or client. The objective is all about troubleshooting NTP. In the output of the w32tm /query /status command, you can clearly see the status of synchronization. Every operating system has a different utility for checking the NTP status, but they are all similar in output.

```
C:\Users\sybex>net start w32time
The Windows Time service is starting.
The Windows Time service was started successfully.


C:\Users\sybex>w32tm /query /status
Leap Indicator: 3(not synchronized)
Stratum: 0 (unspecified)
Precision: -23 (119.209ns per tick)
Root Delay: 0.0000000s
Root Dispersion: 0.0000000s
ReferenceId: 0x00000000 (unspecified)
Last Successful Sync Time: unspecified
Source: Local CMOS Clock
Poll Interval: 10 (1024s)


C:\Users\sybex>w32tm /query /configuration
```

[Configuration]

EventLogFlags: 2 (Local)
AnnounceFlags: 10 (Local)
TimeJumpAuditOffset: 28800 (Local)
MinPollInterval: 10 (Local)
MaxPollInterval: 15 (Local)
MaxNegPhaseCorrection: 54000 (Local)
MaxPosPhaseCorrection: 54000 (Local)
MaxAllowedPhaseOffset: 1 (Local)

FrequencyCorrectRate: 4 (Local)
PollAdjustFactor: 5 (Local)
LargePhaseOffset: 50000000 (Local)
SpikeWatchPeriod: 900 (Local)
LocalClockDispersion: 10 (Local)
HoldPeriod: 5 (Local)
PhaseCorrectRate: 1 (Local)
UpdateInterval: 360000 (Local)

[TimeProviders]

NtpClient (Local)
DllName: C:\Windows\system32\w32time.dll (Local)
Enabled: 1 (Local)
InputProvider: 1 (Local)
AllowNonstandardModeCombinations: 1 (Local)
ResolvePeerBackoffMinutes: 15 (Local)
ResolvePeerBackoffMaxTimes: 7 (Local)
CompatibilityFlags: 2147483648 (Local)
EventLogFlags: 1 (Local)
LargeSampleSkew: 3 (Local)
SpecialPollInterval: 32768 (Local)
Type: NTP (Local)
NtpServer: time.windows.com,0x9 (Local)

NtpServer (Local)
DllName: C:\Windows\system32\w32time.dll (Local)
Enabled: 0 (Local)

```
InputProvider: 0 (Local)

C:\Users\sybex>w32tm /query /status
Leap Indicator: 0(no warning)
Stratum: 4 (secondary reference - syncd by (S)NTP)
Precision: -23 (119.209ns per tick)
Root Delay: 0.0403872s
Root Dispersion: 8.2870061s
ReferenceId: 0x0D5665AC (source IP:  13.86.101.172)
Last Successful Sync Time: 5/31/2021 3:17:20 PM
Source: time.windows.com,0x9
Poll Interval: 10 (1024s)

C:\Users\sybex>
```

BYOD Challenges

There are a number of challenges your organization can face with a rollout of a bring your own device (BYOD) strategy. The most common challenges are related to the diversity of devices to be supported, network coverage, and, most importantly, security.

Device Diversity   The majority of devices you will encounter in a BYOD strategy are Apple devices, Android devices, and Windows devices. Although this seems like a short list of devices, the software versions for these devices will vary significantly. After rolling out a BYOD strategy, you will quickly find out that in different Apple IOS versions, settings are in different places depending on how you are trying to help the user. The Android operating system interface is also usually highly customized by the hardware vendor. Each hardware vendor, such as Samsung, LG, and Motorola, just to name a few, will have settings in different spots in the Android operating system. Windows 10 devices will follow a similar pattern as Android devices, but Microsoft has made tremendous efforts to keep the setting for the Windows 10 operating system similar between vendors.

There is a small percentage of devices that won't fit into the mainline coverage of your BYOD strategy. You may encounter a tablet device with an unsupported Android operating system, in which a required download is unavailable. You could also encounter a totally unsupported operating system, like the OS on an antique Apple laptop. Of course, an antique Apple laptop is an extreme example, but an unsupported operating system is very commonly encountered. The problem with unsupported operating systems is that certificates are not kept current and the operating system is usually a security risk due to the lack of patches.

When planning a BYOD strategy, you should plan for these considerations. A good start is creating a document that details the minimum supported operating system. Other strategies might include using mobile device management (MDM) software, which will dictate the supported devices that can be used.

Network Coverage   Network coverage is a challenge that coincides with the features of the device to be supported. Because an organization will not have control over which BYOD devices are selected, some devices will have sub-par wireless capabilities. A device that behaves fine on a person's home wireless might act erratically on the organization's wireless. This directly affects the user experience and your network is usually blamed. Having the proper network coverage is important to exonerate your network from being the problem with someone's wireless device.

In order to be assured network coverage is not to blame for a bad user experience, two things should be done: survey it and set expectations. The network should be surveyed for coverage, and it should be clearly communicated where service is not expected, such as a bathroom, closet, or parking lot. You would be surprised where people expect to work. Another expectation that should be communicated is the minimum wireless specification for optimal service. Currently the norm is 802.11ac (5 GHz), but there is a tremendous amount of 802.11g (2.4 GHz) devices still out there. Whichever specification becomes your minimum recommended, the network should be surveyed and covered for the wireless specification.

Security   Security is the biggest concern as it applies to BYOD devices. The biggest reason is that the organization has less control over BYOD devices than over devices it issues and owns. BYOD devices come with two inherent risks: data leakage and data portability. Data leakage happens when a device is lost or compromised in some way. There are tactics to mitigate this, such as full device encryption. However, the user's device is then forcefully encrypted by the organization and there could be legal ramifications. Another common tactic is to use mobile device management (MDM) software that creates a partition for company data. This would allow the company to encrypt their data and not affect the user's data.

Data portability means that the user can cart away organizational data when they leave. Although most of the time this is not a risk, an unscrupulous salesperson may be a big risk to the organization. A line of business (LOB) application should be selected that only displays the data on a mobile device and does not allow data storage. Another tactic is to employ MDM software that allows remote wiping of the organization's data. When an employee leaves, the wipe is executed and the organization's data is gone. This type of functionality is also useful if a device is lost, so it also mitigates the risk of data leakage.

This is in no way a complete list of all of the BYOD challenges. Every organization will have different challenges. This section, however, covers the most common BYOD challenges encountered.

Licensed Feature Issues

A licensed feature refers to functionality that requires additional licensing over and above the base requirements of the product. Licensed feature issues are some of the hardest to troubleshoot because the assumption is that you have a license for the feature already. One example of this is Windows 10 Home edition. The Home edition does not allow joining the operating system to a Windows Active Directory (AD) domain, and this restriction is pretty well known. However, this also means that the device cannot be joined to an Azure AD domain. This functionality is not highly well known and troubleshooting it could cost you serious time until you figure it out.

Many of these style problems can be attributed to the user not knowing what features they have and what the limitations of the current features are. There are other more advanced licensed features that might only apply to administrator needs. The Windows operating system is not the only operating system that has licensing concerns. Routers and switches have licensed features that might work on a trial basis. These are concerning because the trial period might be six months, and that is a long time to remember a renewal of a license and the consequences of forgetting are usually disruptive.

When in doubt, if a licensed feature is affecting operation, check with the vendor. The vendor will clearly state the requirements for a certain feature, and licensing is usually at the top of the list.

Network Performance Issues

Network performance issues are some of the most elusive issues to rectify. This is usually due to the fact that most network performance problems are intermittent. Persistent network performance issues are much easier to solve, but both are difficult to diagnose. The importance of a network performance baseline becomes very apparent when you are trying to decipher what is normal and what is abnormal. This is the very reason that baselines are captured. A network performance baseline allows you to establish a normal pattern of traffic and performance for your network.

Historical performance charting and statistics help to view traffic patterns and identify problems. As shown in Figure 5.41, a utility called SmokePing monitors Google DNS and a gateway to the Internet with ICMP echo requests. By monitoring these two destinations, you can judge where and when a performance problem happens. It's best to monitor several different points in your network so that you can identify where in the network a performance problem is happening.

FIGURE 5.41   Historical performance charting

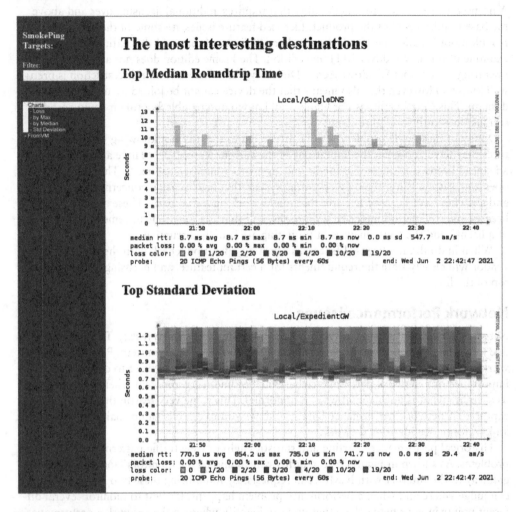

Exam Essentials

Know the various considerations for general troubleshooting.   You should always review the configuration for a device to determine if the problem is a fault configuration or if the issue is attributed to configuration. The routing table of both the device and routers should be checked for proper route statements. The tracert/traceroute commands are used to diagnose routing problems. The interface status should be checked for proper negotiation with the adjoining host. The host should also be checked for proper VLAN assignment since improper VLAN assignment can cause issues. Network performance baselines can help identify performance problems because they establish a level of normalcy for the network.

Understand the scenarios and diagnostic process for the common network issues.   Collisions can cause significant reductions of bandwidth. By statically setting speed and duplex, you can avoid half-duplex communication issues. Loop avoidance should be used to assure that the network is loop free to avoid broadcast storms. A duplicate MAC or IP address on the network can create intermittent problems for the clients with the duplicate addresses. Multicast flooding is usually caused by incorrect multicast configuration. Asymmetrical routing happens when the route out of the network is not the same as the route back into the network. Switching loops can be avoided with the Spanning Tree Protocol (STP). Routing loops can be diagnosed with the `tracert`/`traceroute` command. A rogue DHCP server can be identified by IP address and looking at the client's lease. When the DHCP scope has been exhausted and contains no more leases, the client will autoconfigure an APIPA address. There are several different IP address issues you can encounter and most of them can be diagnosed with the `ipconfig /all` command. A missing route can be diagnosed with the `tracert`/`traceroute` command. Hardware failures can be minimized with fault-tolerant systems. Hostnames that do not resolve should be tested from the source to the host having the trouble using the `nslookup` command. A blocked TCP or UDP port can make an application nonresponsive. Incorrect host-based firewall settings can make services unavailable for clients. Incorrect VLAN configuration can prevent applications and services from being reached; they can also prevent security from being properly applied. Expired IP addresses are a direct result of a DHCP down or not responding. An untrusted SSL certificate should always be investigated since it may be malicious in nature or the host's time is misconfigured. BYOD challenges are commonly based on device diversity, network coverage, and security. To diagnosis license issues, it is always best to contact the vendor.

Review Questions

1. Which should you do during the process of identifying a problem? (Choose all answers that apply.)
   A. Duplicate the problem.
   B. Establish a plan of action.
   C. Question users.
   D. Create a hypothesis.

2. Which technique used to determine the root cause of a problem involves splitting a system into smaller subprocesses for examination?
   A. Top-to-bottom OSI analysis
   B. Divide and conquer analysis
   C. Bottom-to-top OSI analysis
   D. Process analysis

3. What is the next step in problem solving once a theory is confirmed?
   A. Create a hypothesis.
   B. Consider multiple approaches.
   C. Establish a plan of action.
   D. Approach multiple problems individually.

4. What is the final step in resolving a problem?
   A. Implement a solution.
   B. Validate a theory.
   C. Establish a plan of action.
   D. Document.

5. Which tool is used to troubleshoot wiring breaks in network cabling?
   A. OTDR
   B. Tone generator
   C. TDR
   D. Multimeter

6. You need to find a network cable that is not labeled on a wiring panel; which tool should you use to identify the cable?
   A. Cable tester
   B. Tone generator
   C. TDR
   D. Multimeter

7. You are working alone and want to test a fiber-optic cable. Which tool will help you test the fiber-optic cable quickly?

A. OTDR

B. TDR

C. Light meter

D. Loopback adapter

8. Which software tool will allow you to check if a web application running on a server is online?

A. `ping`

B. `nslookup`

C. `tracert/traceroute`

D. Port scanner

9. Which commands can be used to retrieve the A record for `www.wiley.com`? (Choose two.)

A. `tracert/traceroute`

B. `ipconfig`

C. `nslookup`

D. `dig`

10. Which tool allows examination at the packet level for traffic from an application?

A. Protocol analyzer

B. `dig`

C. Spectrum analyzer

D. `nslookup`

11. You need to check the configured MTU on the interface of a Linux host; which command should you use?

A. `ipconfig`

B. `ifconfig`

C. `mtuconfig`

D. `iptables`

12. You need to check the port an application is listening on; which command should you use to view the information?

A. `portqry`

B. `ifconfig`

C. `netstat`

D. `iptables`

13. You need to analyze whether an application is responding to a client request; which command will allow you to capture the traffic?

- **A.** `tcpdump`
- **B.** `nmap`
- **C.** `portqry`
- **D.** `netstat`

14. Which command will allow you to clear the cached MAC addresses on a host?

- **A.** `arp -g *`
- **B.** `ipconfig /flushdns`
- **C.** `arp -d *`
- **D.** `iptables -f`

15. Which describes what happens to a wireless signal as it moves farther away from the source?

- **A.** Increased latency
- **B.** Increased jitter
- **C.** Increased attenuation
- **D.** Decreased reflection

16. You believe there is a break in a fiber-optic cable that spans 5 miles; which tool will help you determine where the cable break is?

- **A.** TDR
- **B.** OTDR
- **C.** Cable tester
- **D.** Cable certifier

17. Which Nmap scan will send an URG, PSH, and FIN flag to trick the operating system to respond with an RST?

- **A.** Xmas-tree scan
- **B.** Fin scan
- **C.** Null scan
- **D.** UDP scan

18. Which type of antenna is directional?

- **A.** Yagi
- **B.** Omnidirectional
- **C.** Isotropic
- **D.** Decibel

19. Which term describes the phenomenon of a wireless signal diminishing as it passes through different materials?

A. Reflection

B. Absorption

C. Attenuation

D. Refraction

20. You find that a workstation has no connectivity to the network. When you use `ipconfig`, the IP address reports as 169.254.34.22 with a subnet mask of 255.255.0.0. What is the possible problem?

A. The subnet mask is incorrect.

B. The IP address is on the wrong subnet.

C. The gateway address is on the wrong network.

D. The original IP address has expired.

21. You believe that packets are being routed via the wrong gateway; which tool will allow you to verify the route a packet takes to the destination IP address?

A. `route print`

B. `tracert`

C. `ipconfig`

D. `dig`

22. You are diagnosing a wireless issue and you believe that the problem is related to RF noise. Which measurement should you focus on to prove your theory?

A. RSSI

B. SNR

C. dB strength

D. EMI

23. What is the outcome if you have a speed mismatch on a network connection?

A. Degraded performance

B. High collision rate

C. High error rate

D. No link status

24. You have a high error rate on an interface and believe that crosstalk is to blame. What should be checked to prove your theory?

A. Network cable specifications

B. Duplex

C. Speed

D. EMI

25. Which command is used to verify NTP configuration on the Windows operating system?

    A. `nmap`

    B. `w32tm`

    C. `ipconfig`

    D. `portqry`

Appendix

Answers to Review Questions

Chapter 1: Domain 1.0: Networking Fundamentals

1. B. The Presentation layer is responsible for encryption and decryption services. The Presentation layer is also responsible for compression and decompression and translation services. The Application layer is where APIs exist, and it also serves as the layer that communicates with the user. The Session layer provides dialogue control for applications. The Transport layer is where TCP and UDP protocols segment data for transmission.

2. D. The Data Link layer provides the framing of data for transmission on the physical media. The Application layer is where APIs exist, and it also serves as the layer that communicates with the user. The Physical layer is where the framed data is transmitted in light, air, or electrical media. The logic link control (LLC) layer is a portion of the Data Link layer that communicates with upper protocols.

3. C. The proper protocol data unit (PDU) for data at the Application layer is user datagrams. The bits PDU is used to describe data at the Physical layer. The segments PDU is used to describe data at the Transport layer. The frames PDU is used to describe data at the Data Link layer.

4. B. A campus area network (CAN) is a connectivity method that is locally owned and managed by an organization to connect multiple LANs together. A metropolitan area network (MAN) is a connectivity method used in a metropolitan area but is owned and managed by someone other than the organization. A wide area network (WAN) is a connectivity method that is used for connectivity in a wide area and is owned and managed by someone other than the organization. A wireless local area network (WLAN) is usually owned and managed by the organization it is serving, but it is not normally used to connect multiple LANs together.

5. A. A star topology has a centralized switch connecting all of the devices outward like a star. A full mesh topology allows for a decentralized switching design, where any link failure will not affect switching. A partial mesh topology is normally performed between the layers of core, distribution, and access to allow for a single link failure while maintaining switching services. A hybrid topology is where several different topologies are employed, such as star and mesh.

6. B. Increased redundancy of connections is a direct benefit of a full mesh topology. Although bandwidth will increase because of multiple paths, additional dynamic routing protocols will need to be implemented to achieve this. A full mesh topology will not decrease the switch count and can even require more switching equipment because of the number of connections. When a full mesh topology is employed, it increases complexity, but this is not considered a benefit.

7. D. The core of a single-mode fiber-optic cable is normally 9 microns in diameter. It may be found in smaller sizes such as 8.6, but it is considered 9 microns in diameter. A core diameter of 50 microns describes a multimode fiber-optic cable. The size of 125 microns is normally the size of the jacket on most fiber-optic patch cables. A core diameter of 62.5 microns describes a multimode fiber-optic cable.

8. C. A Quad Small Form-factor Pluggable+ (QSPF+) can connect up to four different devices from one transceiver with the use of a breakout style cable. A Small Form-factor Pluggable (SPF) and Small Form-factor Pluggable+ (SPF+) both only allow one connection per transceiver. A Gigabit Interface Converter (GBIC) is legacy hardware, but it could only connect one device per transceiver.

9. D. An angled physical contact (APC) fiber-optic connection end is used to minimize reflection loss of the original light signal. Vendor interoperability is a non-issue as the APC fiber-optic connection end is found on the SC connection standard. An APC fiber-optic connection end will not increase the speed of the connection. An extremely polished surface is found on ultra-physical contact (UPC) and not APC type cabling.

10. C. The category 6 cabling standard was the first to support 10 Gbps at a maximum length of 55 meters. The category 5 and 5e cabling standard introduced 1 Gbps at a maximum length of 100 meters. Category 7 was never ratified as a standard and therefore it is not a correct answer.

11. C. Network address translation (NAT) was created to slow the depletion of Internet addresses. It does this by translating RFC 1918 privatized addresses to one or many public IP addresses. It allows a packet to masquerade as the public IP address on the Internet until it is translated back to the private IP address. Classless Inter-Domain Routing (CIDR) is a notation used to express the network for a host. Classful addressing is the original addressing scheme for the Internet. Virtual private networks (VPNs) are used for remote access.

12. B. IPv4 allows for 2^{32} = 4.3 billion addresses. However, only 3.7 billion are usable because of reservations and classful addressing. The current IPv4 address space is exhausted, and IPv6 allows for 2^{128} = 3.4 × 10^{38} addresses. IPv6 still requires NAT for backward compatibility with IPv4. Although IPv4 is slowly being replaced with IPv6, IPv4 is still dominant in networks and the Internet. IPv6 does not need to be subnetted like IPv4 by borrowing bits from the network mask; there are 16 bits dedicated for subnets. However, that functionality does not create the need for an entirely new address scheme.

13. B. The IP address 135.20.255.255 is a Class B broadcast address. It is not a Class A address, nor is it the default gateway address. The default mask of a Class B address is 255.255.0.0.

14. A. The mask you will need to use is 255.255.255.252. This will allow for two hosts per network for a total of 64 networks. The formula for solving for hosts is 2^x – 2 equal to or greater than 2(hosts), which in this case is $(2^2 - 2) = (4 - 2) = 2$. So 2 bits are used for the host side, leaving 6 bits for the subnet side. 6 bits + 24 bits (original subnet mask) = /30, or 255.255.255.252. All of the other options are incorrect.

15. D. The IPv6 address 2001:0db8:45::102::12 is not a valid IPv6 address. The double colon cannot be used twice in the IPv6 address. All other answers are valid IPv6 addresses.

16. C. Secure Shell (SSH) is a cryptographic protocol that provides encrypted text console–based access over an IP network. It is commonly used to securely administer Linux servers. Telnet provides text-based access, but it is in clear text. Remote Desktop Protocol (RDP) provides remote access to Microsoft servers for administration of the operating system. SFTP is a protocol that uses SSH to transfer files.

17. D. Remote Desktop Protocol (RDP) provides remote access to Microsoft servers for administration of the operating system. RDP redirects the keyboard, mouse, and monitor to the administrator's computer. Simple Network Management Protocol (SNMP) is used to transmit information and metrics about the operating system. Light Directory Access Protocol (LDAP) is lightweight database query protocol that is commonly used with Microsoft Active Directory (AD). Telnet provides text-based access, but it is in clear text.

18. D. The Transmission Control Protocol (TCP) provides sequenced and acknowledged segments. Because each segment is sequenced and acknowledged by the receiving computer, any segments lost in the delivery process will be rerequested at this layer. Internet Control Message Protocol (ICMP) is an IP layer helper protocol. User Datagram Protocol (UDP) is a connectionless protocol that is not provided with assured delivery of segments. Internet Protocol (IP) is used for logical addressing of IP addresses.

19. C. A DHCP reservation will allow for the printer to obtain the same IP address every time it is turned on. The DHCP server will serve the same IP address to the printer based on the printer's MAC address in the reservation. Configuring an A record will not achieve the goal. Configuring a DHCP exclusion for the printer would only work if you had already set it to a static IP address and didn't want that IP address assigned to another host. Configuring an PTR record will not achieve the goal.

20. C. The PTR, or pointer record, is used to look up IP addresses and return FQDNs that are mapped to them. This is helpful to identify an IP address, and in the case of SSH, it is used to positively identify the host you are connecting to. The A record is used to look up an IP address for a given hostname. The CName record is used to look up the alias for a given hostname. The AAAA record is used to look up an IPv6 address for a given hostname.

21. D. Only switching between campus (distribution) switches should be performed at the core layer. Nothing should be done to slow down forwarding of traffic, such as using ACLs, supporting clients, or routing between VLANs. Routing of data should be performed at the distribution layer of the Cisco three-tier model. Supporting clients should be done at the access layer of the Cisco three-tier model. The configuration of access control lists (ACLs) should be performed at the distribution layer of the Cisco three-tier model.

22. C. The hybrid topology is most often seen at the access layer. The devices are connected in a star topology and the access layer switches are partially meshed to the distribution layer switches. The distribution layer is normally connected with a full mesh topology. Routing layer is not terminology used to describe one of the three layers in the Cisco three-tier design model.

23. B. Distribution layer switches are fully meshed for redundancy. The number of links can be calculated with the formula of $N(N-1)$. So if you had four distribution switches, the ports required for a full mesh would be $4(4-1) = 4 \times 3 = 12$ ports among the four switches. The formula of $N(N-1)/2$ would give you the number of links (connected ports): $4(4-1)/2 = 4 \times 3/2 = 6$ links. The core layer is normally implemented with a star topology. The access layer is normally implemented with a partial mesh topology or hybrid topology. Routing layer is not a valid term in the Cisco three-tier design model.

24. A. The National Institute of Standards and Technology (NIST) defines three cloud types: Platform as a Service (PaaS), Software as a Service (SaaS), and Infrastructure as a Service (IaaS). A DR site hosting at a cloud provider is an example of IaaS. Although DRaaS can be used as a term to advertise a type of cloud service, it is not defined by NIST as a type of service.

25. C. A hosted medical records service is an example of the SaaS, or Software as a Service, model. The customer cannot choose variables such as vCPU or RAM. The cloud provider is responsible for the delivery of the software, maintenance of the OS, and maintenance of the hardware. An example of Platform as a Service (PaaS) would be Google App Engine or Microsoft Azure, where code could be executed on a virtual stack of equipment (programming platform). An example of Infrastructure as a Service (IaaS) is Amazon Web Services (AWS) Elastic Compute (EC2), where a VM can be started up with virtual network services with only a credit card and you are billed periodically. An example of Backup as a Service (BaaS) is Microsoft Azure cloud backup or Google Drive, just to name a couple.

Chapter 2: Domain 2.0: Network Implementations

1. B. Switches provide the lowest latency with the use of application-specific integrated circuits (ASICs). Hubs are multiport repeaters and diminish usable bandwidth. Bridges are software-based switches and provide higher latency than switches. Routers introduce latency because of decapsulation, routing, and encapsulation of the packets.

2. B. Intrusion detection systems and intrusion prevention systems (IDSs/IPSs) offer detection and prevention of network intrusion of malicious activity. Firewalls will normally prevent but will not detect malicious network activity. Proxy servers will only proxy requests and therefore do not prevent or detect. Content filters will filter content that users request.

3. A. A hub will act as a multiport repeater by repeating the physical bits on an incoming port to all the other connected ports. A switch or bridge will only forward the frame to the port it is destined for. Even when broadcasts are received, the frame is still processed and not blindly repeated. A WAP acts similarly to a switch and will only forward frames to the connected wireless or wired network.

4. D. Switches learn MAC addresses based upon incoming ports and examination of the source MAC address. It will build a MAC address table for future lookups. It then determines forwarding interfaces based upon the destination MAC address contained in the frame. Forwarding of data is based upon MAC addresses, which are physical addresses "burned" into the network interface card (NIC) called MAC addresses. Repeating electrical signals to all ports describes how a dumb hub would operate. MAC addresses are learned by the source MAC address on incoming frames to the switch, not the destination frames.

5. B. Pan tilt zoom (PTZ) cameras allow for intervention of a situation. In situations where you must track and record equipment as it is moved, such as in casino environments, PTZ cameras should be used. Closed-circuit television (CCTV) defines an installation type and does not satisfy the requirement. Coaxial cable is normally used with CCTV installations. Power over Ethernet (PoE) is a way to power an IP-based camera, but it alone will not satisfy the requirement.

6. C. You should implement a next-generation firewall (NGFW) to protect against application-level threats, such as access to a particular URL. An intrusion detection system (IDS) will alert you to a potential security issue, but it will not prevent it. A proxy server will only proxy requests for web pages. Although an NGFW can function as a proxy server and block content, a proxy server alone cannot satisfy the requirement. A router will only route requests at layer 3.

7. A. The human machine interface (HMI) is a common component for SCADA systems. The HMI allows a plant operator to observe the production line for potential problems. An access control panel and a security console are both used with access controls systems. A smart speaker is an Internet of Things (IoT) device and not commonly found in a SCADA system.

8. A. Default routing is best implemented in stub networks because all networks other than the immediate one are accessed through the default gateway. RIP routing should be used in more complex scenarios where the network has many different routes. Static and dynamic routing are types of routing that dictate either an entry is created for each route or a dynamic routing protocol is used.

9. D. Border Gateway Protocol is used as an external routing protocol for the Internet. When two providers are connected to a single site using BGP, the connection can fail over in the case of one provider suffering an outage. Routing Information Protocol version 2 (RIPv2) is an interior routing protocol normally used in small networks with fewer than 15 hops. Enhanced Interior Gateway Routing Protocol (EIGRP) is an interior routing protocol that is proprietary to Cisco. Open Shortest Path First (OSPF) is an interior routing protocol that has the ability to scale.

10. D. The Class of Service (CoS) marking is a 3-bit field in the 802.1Q trunk frame. This 3-bit field contains eight possible queues for QoS at layer 2. Although the 802.1Q protocol supports quality of service (QoS) via the CoS field, 802.1Q is a trunking protocol. Type of Services (ToS) and Diffserv are layer 3 methods for QoS.

11. A. Border Gateway Protocol is a path-vector routing protocol. Routing Information Protocol (RIP) is a distance-vector routing protocol. Open Shortest First Path (OSPF) is a link-state protocol. Enhanced Interior Gateway Routing Protocol (EIGRP) is considered a hybrid protocol, incorporating distance-vector and link-state mechanisms.

12. D. The administrative distance (AD) is always used to choose the routing protocol's route over another routing protocol with the same destination route. Round robin is not a valid answer. Hop count is only used by distance-vector routing protocols. Congestion is typically used by hybrid routing protocols, such as Enhanced Interior Gateway Routing Protocol (EIGRP).

13. B. The backbone 0.0.0.0, also known as area 0, must always be configured first for Open Shortest Path First (OSPF). Configuration of area 1 is a secondary task if another area is required. An area border router (ABR) is a router that borders two areas. Link-state announcements (LSAs) are messages between routers to update OSPF routing tables.

14. A. The Differentiated Services Code Point (DSCP), also known as DiffServ, is a 6-bit value contained in the 8-bit Type of Services (ToS) field in the IP header. The Class of Service (CoS) is a 3-bit value in an 802.1Q frame. Quality of service (QoS) defines both layer 2 and layer 3 priority queuing of frames and packets.

15. C. The addition of the clients to the immediate network most likely raised the number of broadcasts in the network. Although you could assign static IP addresses to all computers to reduce DHCP, ARP is still broadcast-based. The recommended remedy is to create several broadcast domains with network segmentation. All other answers are incorrect.

16. A. The normal MTU for Ethernet is 1500 bytes, or 1518 bytes if you are including the source MAC address, destination MAC address, type field, and frame check sequence (FCS). All other answers are incorrect.

17. B. When a broadcast is sent, the destination MAC address will be ff:ff:ff:ff:ff:ff:ff:ff. This destination MAC address tells the switch to forward the traffic to all active ports. Internet Control Message Protocol (ICMP) traffic will not contain a destination MAC address of ff:ff:ff:ff:ff:ff:ff:ff. Multicast traffic will have a destination MAC address that is calculated for the multicast group. Internet Group Management Protocol (IGMP) is a protocol used to create multicast groups.

18. C. The 802.1Q protocol is an open standard trunking protocol. Inter-Switch Link (ISL) is another trunking protocol, but it can only be used on Cisco devices. Because your switches are from two different vendors, they are not both Cisco devices; therefore, 802.1Q must be used. The 802.1D protocol is Spanning Tree Protocol (STP), used to prevent loops in networks. The 802.1w protocol is Rapid Spanning Tree Protocol (RSTP), which is also used to prevent loops in networks.

19. D. When calculating Spanning Tree Protocol (STP), the switch with the lowest MAC address will become the root bridge if all of the priorities are set to the default. However, if the priority on a particular switch is lower than the others, it will always become the root bridge. All other answers are incorrect.

20. D. Port security can restrict a switch port to a specific number of ports configured by the administrator. The specific MAC addresses can be preconfigured or learned dynamically. The use of jumbo frames will allow 9000 bytes to be framed, in lieu of 1500 bytes normally in a frame. The use of 802.1x will restrict users from communicating on a switch, but it does not limit the number of devices communicating on a switchport. Access control lists are used to restrict traffic based upon IP address and destination port, among other attributes.

21. D. Link Layer Discovery Protocol (LLDP) and Cisco Discovery Protocol (CDP) communicate with neighboring devices and exchange power operating conditions. Turning on LLDP will quickly rectify the problem by adjusting power consumption. All other answers are incorrect.

22. A. The 802.11n wireless standard introduced channel bonding. The 802.11n standard allows for the bonding of up to two channels to provide a 40 MHz channel. All other answers are incorrect.

23. C. The Global System for Mobile Communications (GSM) was developed by the European Telecommunications Standards Institute (ETSI) and is now used globally. All other answers are incorrect.

24. C. The 2.4 GHz wireless band has three non-overlapping channels: 1, 6, and 11. Although they overlap with other channels, these three channels do not overlap between themselves. All other answers are incorrect.

25. A. Lightweight Extensible Authentication Protocol (LEAP) is a Cisco proprietary protocol that was developed and is used by Cisco devices for authentication via 802.1x. Extensible Authentication Protocol (EAP) allows for multiple methods of authentication to be added to existing security. Protected Extensible Authentication Protocol (PEAP) is an open standard commonly used with wireless for authentication via 802.1x. Network Admission Control (NAC) is a captive portal device that checks a client's health to a specific standard before allowing the client to connect to the network.

Chapter 3: Domain 3.0: Network Operations

1. D. Performance baselines gathered over time help create a historical representation of activity and normal operations. When a server is performing poorly, the baseline can validate both the problem and implemented solution.

2. B. Before an NMS can collect SNMP statistics, the management information base (MIB) from the manufacturer must be loaded. The object ID (OID) is the hierarchal notation of the counter. An SNMP trap command is a message from the SNMP agent to the NMS when a threshold for a counter is exceeded. An SNMP get command is a request message from the NMS to the SNMP agent for the value of a counter.

3. C. When humidity falls below 20 percent, there is a huge potential for electrostatic discharge (ESD). Although lower temperatures create lower humidity levels, they do not directly attribute to ESD. Electrical factors are related to power surges, sags and spikes. Flooding will not cause electrostatic discard, but it will cause electrical shorts.

4. D. The giants interface counter will increment when jumbo frames (9000 bytes) are received on an interface configured with the default maximum transmission unit (MTU) of 1500 bytes. Runts are frames smaller than 64 bytes that are received on an interface. Encapsulation errors happen when there is a mismatch of encapsulation protocols. Cyclic redundancy check (CRC) errors happen when a frame is damaged in transfer and the 4 byte frame check sequence (FCS) does not checksum against the data.

5. D. SNMP version 3 introduced message integrity, authentication, and encryption to the SNMP suite. SNMP version 1 was the first release of SNMP and it is considered deprecated. SNMP version 2e is not a valid version of SNMP. SNMP version 2c is an amendment of SNMP version 2 that added the set command and other improvements.

6.   A. The NetFlow collector is responsible for collecting NetFlow statistics and collating them into a visual representation of the traffic. The NetFlow cache is a temporary place in memory in which the traffic information is held until it is sent to the NetFlow collector. The NetFlow packet is the vehicle in which the NetFlow data is sent over the network. The NetFlow router is the device in which NetFlow is actively exporting the NetFlow information to the NetFlow collector.

7.   B. The network management station (NMS) is a server to which SNMP is polled back or in which SNMP information is trapped. The NMS can escalate problems via email, text message, or even visual indicators. Examples of NMS systems are Solarwinds Orion and OpenNMS. The syslog is a logging file where system messages are sent. The object identifier (OID) is used to describe the SNMP counter being requested. The management information base (MIB) is a sort of database of counters that SNMP can use for a specific device.

8.   B. Jitter is the variation of latency between the source and destination, and it is measured in milliseconds. Latency is the time it takes for a packet or frame to travel from source to destination. Bandwidth is the speed of a connection and throughput is the utilization of the connection.

9.   C. A logical diagram depicts how a network operates by representing the flow of information. A physical diagram details how everything is connected and why it works. A local area network (LAN) diagram shows the placement of LAN components. A network schematic or network diagram is a physical diagram detailing how everything is connected.

10.   B. The standard operating procedure (SOP) document details the step-by-step instructions necessary to decommission a server. An ISO document is not a valid answer; ISO is a certification of standard practices. A server policy is a technical policy that is applied to a server. Asset destruction is an incorrect answer.

11.   D. The change advisory board reviews changes proposed for the network so that they do not affect day-to-day operations. Network operations personnel keep the network operating consistently. The executive committee is often a high-level group of people in an organization. The stakeholders are the people that are directly responsible for key actions, and some of them are part of the change advisory board.

12.   B. Labels should depict the least specific location, such as a building, to the most specific location, such as the outlet number. Workstation names and purposes can change over time. The location information should be from the least specific to the most specific location because it is read from left to right. The host purpose can change over time and does not depict the host's location.

13.   B. Life-cycle management software assists in tracking IT inventory from the cradle to the grave for an organization. Mobile device management software (MDM) is used to manage mobile devices. Accounting software is used by organizations to keep track of assets and the net worth of the company in addition to costs. System upgrade software is used for the explicit purpose of upgrading software.

14.   C. A bring your own device (BYOD) policy defines the minimum specifications for an employee's device used for work-related access. The mobile device management (MDM) software would usually dictate these specifications. The acceptable use policy (AUP) defines acceptable usage on the network. The network disclosure agreement (NDA) is an agreement that includes specifics that are not disclosed outside of an organization.

15. C. An SLA of 4 nines is 52.56 minutes per year of expected downtime. This equates to 4.38 minutes per month that the service can be down. All other answers are incorrect.

16. A. Configuring a group of disks with RAID level 5 striping with parity is an example of fault tolerance because redundancy of resources is used to ensure operations in the event of failure. High availability is what RAID level 5 will create via fault tolerance. Clustering is when two or more hosts operate to create high availability. Load balancing spreads the demand of an application across multiple hosts.

17. D. Load balancing should be implemented with two or more web servers to scale out the servers and lower demand on any one single web server. Clustering creates high availability for an application or operating system. Port aggregation combines two or more connections to aggregate their combined bandwidth. Fault tolerance is the ability of a system to remain running after a component failure.

18. A. A cold site is the least expensive to maintain over time because very little or no hardware is at the site. If a disaster occurs, it will take time to acquire hardware and configure it. A warm site contains equipment but requires intervention to bring it online. A host site or cloud site contains a replica of the organization's servers and is probably the most expensive. The difference between a hot and cloud site is where the servers are running.

19. B. The recovery time objective (RTO) is a measurement of how quickly you can recover from data loss using backup. The recovery point objective (RPO) is the point in time to which you can recover in the event of a disaster. The grandfather, father, son (GFS) rotation is a systematic way to archive backup media. The backup window is the window of time in which a backup can be performed.

20. B. Disk-to-disk backups will speed up any backup since the backup is coming off disks and being backed up to disks. A disk-to-tape backup is the traditional method to back up networks and is considered slower than disk-to-disk. A full backup is generally done once a week and consists of a full backup of the network servers. Although GFS rotations may speed up end-of-week and end-of-month backups, it is considered a rotation strategy rather than a backup method.

21. D. An incremental backup will only back up files that have the archive bit set. After the files are backed up, the archive bit is reset for the next backup. The archive backup is not a real backup option. The differential backup does not reset the archive bit and backups consistently get bigger each day until the next full backup. The full backup is a complete backup of all files and the archive bit is reset.

22. C. An online UPS uses the AC power for the rectifier/charging circuit that maintains a charge for the batteries. The batteries then supply the inverter with a constant DC power source. The inverter converts the DC power source back into an AC power circuit again that supplies the load. A line interactive UPS starts inverting power when the power is lost. A standby UPS shifts the load to a separate inverter circuit. There is no such thing as a failover UPS.

23. B. A full backup is used for grandfather, father, son (GFS) rotations. GFS rotations help to maintain a lengthy RPO by keeping fewer backups using daily, weekly, and monthly backups. All other answers are incorrect.

24. D. Virtual Router Redundancy Protocol (VRRP) is an open standard protocol that is used for high availability of default gateways. Network Load Balancing (NLB) is a Windows service that allows for load balancing of network services. Hot Standby Router Protocol (HSRP) is a Cisco proprietary high availability protocol. New Technology File System (NTFS) is a file system that is used with the Windows operating system.

25. B. Clean agent systems are normally found in data centers because the suppression agent is in the form of a gas and will not hurt electronics. A deluge system dumps water out of all the fire suppression nozzles. A preaction system requires a detector to pre-charge the system before water is released. A dry pipe system doesn't contain water in the pipes. When the pressure drops, the water will be released from the nozzles.

Chapter 4: Domain 4.0: Network Security

1. C. The principle of least privilege dictates that a user be given the least permission to perform their job. Zero trust is a method of requiring the user to authenticate for each resource they access, regardless of where the asset is located. Role-based access is a method of granting permissions based upon a role in the organization. The defense in depth security concept is a layered approach to security, where several layers are used to protect the organization.

2. A. Authentication is the process of verification of a user's identify. It can be performed with various factors such as something you know, something you are, or something you have, in addition to other factors. Authorization is the process of checking the permission of the authenticated user for the resource. Accounting and auditing are used to log the actions of a user or computer, such as authentication and access to resources.

3. A. Remote Authentication Dial-In User Service (RADIUS) was originally proposed by the IETF and became an open standard for authentication, often used with 802.1X. TACACS+ is a Cisco technology that became an open standard. Kerberos is exclusively used by Microsoft for authentication of users. Lightweight Directory Access Protocol (LDAP) is a protocol that is also exclusively used by Microsoft for lookup of objects in Active Directory.

4. C. Kerberos is an authentication system that used Data Encryption Standard (3DES) and uses Advanced Encryption Standard (AES) encryption for encryption of user credentials. It is exclusively used by Microsoft Active Directory as an authentication protocol. Remote Authentication Dial-In User Service (RADIUS) is a protocol used to authenticate users and computers and supports TLS security. TACACS+ is an authentication protocol that does not support AES encryption. Lightweight Directory Access Protocol (LDAP) is not an authentication protocol.

5. B. Security Assertion Markup Language (SAML) is an open-standard XML-based framework used for transmitting authentication and authorization information of users and computers. Lightweight Directory Access Protocol (LDAP) is a protocol that is exclusively used by Microsoft for lookup of objects in Active Directory. Active Directory Federation Services (ADFS) is Microsoft's single sign-on platform. Kerberos is exclusively used by Microsoft for authentication of users with Active Directory.

6. B. Authorization is the process of verifying whether a user has permission for a specific action; it is followed by the authentication of the user. Authentication is the process of verification of the user's identify. It can be performed with various factors such as something you know, are, or have, in addition to other factors. Accounting and auditing are used to log the actions of a user or computer, such as authentication and access to resources.

7. A. The protocol TCP and the port number 389 are used for LDAP lookups. All of the other answers are incorrect.

8. D. An exploit is a script, code, application, or technique used to gain unauthorized access to an operating system through a vulnerability. A weakness in the operating system and a known operating system security flaw are considered vulnerabilities. A configuration that weakens the security of the operating system is considered a threat.

9. A. An on-path attack, also known as a man-in-the-middle MiTM attack, allows the attacker to impersonate both parties involved in a network conversation. A deauthentication attack is a method of deauthenticating all of the wireless users in an attempt to hijack the access point. A denial-of-service (DoS) is an attack that attempts to run a service out of resources, thereby denying valid service requests. Spoofing is the act of impersonating a user or computer.

10. D. A rouge DHCP is an attack in which another DHCP serves out IP addresses along with a malicious default gateway. User traffic is then redirected through the malicious gateway in an attempt to steal information. A denial-of-service (DoS) is an attempt to deny legitimate service requests, by overutilizing resources. VLAN hopping is an attack in which malicious traffic is double-tagged in an attempt to hop to another VLAN. Deauthentication is an attack that attempts to deauthenticate 802.11 traffic and hijack a wireless SSID.

11. D. Any service that allows the user to create a connection or access to information can be used as an attack vector. In the case of DHCP, the attacker will set the gateway to their IP address. In the case of DNS, the attacker could spoof a request to redirect the traffic. In the case of wireless, the attacker can spoof the secure set identifier (SSID).

12. A. Double-tagging is an attack that can be used against the native VLAN. The attacker will tag the native VLAN on a frame and then tag another inside that frame for the VLAN that the attacker intends to compromise. When the switch receives the first frame, it removes the default VLAN tag and forwards it to other switches via a trunk port. When the other switch receives the frame with the second VLAN tag, it forwards it to the VLAN upon which the attacker is targeting the attack. VLAN traversal is not an attack; it is a term to describe a VLAN traversing a trunk link between two switches. Trunk popping is not a valid attack; it is not a term used in networking, and therefore, it is an invalid answer. A denial-of-service (DoS) attack is an attack in which an attempt to exhaust a service's resources is launched to knock the service offline.

13. B. Privacy filters are either film or glass add-ons that are placed over a monitor. They prevent the data on the screen from being readable when viewed from the sides. Security is the overall goal and not the correct answer. Degaussing is associated with magnetic media erasure. Tempered glass is a type of glass and does not prevent side viewing.

14. A. Shoulder surfing involves looking over someone's shoulder as they enter information. Phishing is the act of attempting to steal credentials by sending an email that takes the recipient to a fraudulent login. Tailgating is the act of following a person through an access control point using their credentials. Whaling is a form of phishing that targets high-profile individuals.

15. C. Antimalware covers a wide array or of security threats to users, including trojans, viruses, and phishing emails. Multifactor authentication combines two or more single-factor authentication methods to create very secure authentication for users. Software firewalls will not prevent threats such as trojans, viruses, and phishing emails. Antivirus software protects you only from viruses and trojans, not phishing emails.

16. A. Access control lists (ACLs) are an effective way to mitigate spoofing of internal IPs from outside the trusted network. ACLs are used to control traffic by allowing, denying, or logging traffic depending on specific conditions. An intrusion detection system (IDS) can be used to notify you if it detects an attack, but it will not prevent an attack. Transport Layer Security (TLS) communications offer both encryption and authentication of the data via certificate signing. This would prevent tampering of the data end to end, but it will not prevent spoofing. A host intrusion detection system (HIDS) is an application that runs on a host to detect intrusions. A HIDS is similar to an IDS, but it is all software-based and resides on the host it is to protect.

17. C. A captive portal will capture the users' first web page request and redirect them to either a login page or an AUP. Access control lists (ACLs) and MAC filtering restrict specific traffic. The 802.1X protocol is used to authenticate users and devices to control a layer 2 switchport.

18. A. Network access control (NAC) is used in conjunction with 802.1X and can restrict clients if specific security policies are not met, such as current antivirus and software updates. The 802.1X protocol is used to authenticate users and devices to control a layer 2 switchport. EAP-TLS is a protocol used to authenticate users and computers. Access control lists (ACLs) are used to restrict specific traffic.

19. D. Access lists can be applied to a port, to a protocol, and in a direction. For example, you could apply only one ACL to the interface Fa0/1, to the protocol IP in the inbound direction.

20. A. Secure Shell (SSH) negotiates encryption when a connection is made. SSH is used as a replacement for the unencrypted Telnet protocol. Secure Copy (SCP) is used to securely copy files. Hypertext Transfer Protocol Secure (HTTPS) uses TLS encryption to securely transmit web-based content. File Transfer Protocol (FTP) is an unencrypted file transfer protocol.

21. C. Since you have several remote workers who telecommute, the best connectivity option is a client-to-site VPN. A GRE tunnel is unencrypted and will not provide any security. A wireless WAN can be used to connect clients to the Internet, but the client-to-site connection would be the private connection to the organization's network. Site-to-site VPN connections are intended for connecting sites to each other via an encrypted tunnel over the Internet.

22. B. The SSH protocol operates on TCP port 22. The Remote Desktop Protocol operates on TCP port 3389. The Telnet service operates on TCP port 23. HTTPS operates on TCP port 443.

23. C. Passive infrared (PIR) contains a reflective panel that creates different zones of detection. The reflective panel is distinctive to PIR sensors. Microwave sensors work with radio waves. Vibration sensor and seismic sensors work off of vibrations and not infrared.

24. C. Key fobs, ID badges, and combination locks do not provide authentication of employees. Only biometrics will provide a factor of authentication.

25. B. Using access control vestibules, also called mantraps (small rooms that limit access to one or a few individuals) is a great way to stop tailgating. User authentication will not prevent or stop tailgating. Strong passwords will not prevent tailgating because tailgating is a physical security problem. Changing SSIDs will not stop tailgating because tailgating does not pertain to wireless.

Chapter 5: Domain 5.0: Network Troubleshooting

1. A, C. During the identification of a problem, you should question users and try to duplicate the problem. Establishing a plan of action is done after you have created a hypothesis, both of which happen after you identify the problem.

2. B. The divide and conquer analysis technique is used to divide complex processes into small subprocesses that are easier to analyze. The top-to-bottom OSI analysis is a method of understanding what happens from the application down to the physical layer to identify the problem. The Bottom-to-top OSI analysis method is similar to the top-to-bottom, except it is from the physical to the application layers. Process analysis is not a valid answer.

3. C. After a theory or hypothesis is confirmed, you should establish a plan of action to resolve the problem. The creation of a hypothesis is a step in the establishment of a probable cause. Considering multiple approaches is done during the establishment of a theory. Approaching multiple problems individually is done in the initial identification of the problem.

4. D. The documentation of the findings, actions, and outcomes is the final step in the resolution of a problem. It allows us to solve future problems more quickly. Implementing a solution, validating a theory, and establishing a plan of action all precede the final steps in resolving a problem.

5. C. A time domain reflectometer is a tool that sends electronic pulses of energy down a wire and reads the time it takes for their reflection to come back. A calculation is made to determine the length of the cable. An optical time domain reflectometer is a tool used to find breaks in fiber-optic cable. A tone generator is used in conjunction with a tracing probe to identify network cables. It operates by injecting a warbling tone into the cable so that the tracing probe can amplify the signal audibly. A multimeter is used to test for voltage and continuity in wiring.

6. B. A tone generator is used in conjunction with a tracing probe to identify network cables. It operates by injecting a warbling tone into the cable so that the tracing probe can amplify the signal audibly. A cable tester is used to test the proper wiring of a network connection. A time domain reflectometer is a tool that sends electronic pulses of energy down a wire and reads the time it takes for their reflection to come back. A calculation is made to determine the length of the cable. A multimeter is to test for voltage and continuity in wiring.

7. D. Although you could use a light meter to test the fiber-optic cable, you would need to move the source over to the other fiber strand. A loopback adapter will allow you to test the cable with one test of both strands. An optical time-domain reflectometer is a tool used to find breaks in fiber-optic cable. A time-domain reflectometer is a tool that sends electronic pulses of energy down a wire and reads the time it takes their reflection comes back. A calculation is made to determine the length of the cable.

8. D. A port scanner will allow you to check if an application is accepting connections. The port will return an open status, and most port scanners will check for an HTTP response. The `ping` utility will only check if the server is online. The `nslookup` utility will allow you to resolve a domain name to an IP address and vice versa. The `tracert/traceroute` command will allow you to watch a packet as it traverse a network path to its destination.

9. C, D. The `nslookup` and `dig` commands can be used to retrieve the A record for a domain name, such as www.wiley.com. The `tracert/traceroute` command is used to find problems in the routing path for a destination. The `ipconfig` command is used to view the IP address information on the Windows operating system.

10. A. A protocol analyzer will allow us to inspect packet levels of traffic that is captured from an application. The `dig` and `nslookup` commands are used to perform DNS name resolution. A spectrum analyzer is used to view the RF spectrum and it is not a valid answer.

11. B. The `ifconfig` command will allow you to inspect the MTU on the interface of a Linux host. It will also allow you to change the MTU temporarily. The `ipconfig` command is a Windows operating system command. The command of `mtuconfig` is not a real command. The `iptables` command is an incorrect answer for this question.

12. C. The `netstat` command will allow you to see layer 4 binding between applications and the TCP/UDP ports. On Windows, the `netstat -ab` command will display listening ports. On Linux/Unix, the `netstat -ap` command will perform the same function. The `portqry` and `iptables` commands are not valid answers. The `ifconfig` command is used to view the interface configuration for Linux and Unix operating systems.

13. A. The `tcpdump` command will allow packet capture of an interface. When run on the server on which the application is responding, `tcpdump` can capture the response of the application for further analysis. The `nmap` tool is used to verify that an application is listening for an incoming request. The `portqry` command is similar to `nmap`, but it is not the correct answer. The `netstat` command will allow you to see the active connections in use on the operating system.

14. C. The `arp` command allows you to manipulate the MAC address cache of a host. When you issue the `arp -d *` command, you will clear all MAC address entries in the ARP cache. Therefore, the `arp -g *` command is not the correct answer. The command `ipconfig / flushdns` will flush the DNS cache for the Windows operating system. The command `iptables -f` is not the correct answer to this question, since it is used with the iptables Linux firewall.

15. C. The attenuation of the signal increases as the signal moves farther away from the source. Attenuation is the gradual absorption of a signal's energy in the air. Latency is a delay in time that the signal takes to reach its destination. Jitter is the difference between the latency periods. Reflection is the bounce-back signal off of solid objects.

16. B. An optical time-domain reflectometer (OTDR) sends a pulse of light down the fiber-optic cable and measures the time and reflection strength. This measurement will determine where a break occurs in the fiber-optic cable. A time-domain reflectometer is used to diagnose electrically conductive cables. Cable testers and certifiers are used to verify proper cable wiring.

17. A. The Xmas-tree scan will send the URG, PSH, and FIN flags in the TCP header to trick the operating system into sending back an RST for closed ports. All other answers are incorrect.

18. A. A Yagi antenna is a directional antenna used for wireless coverage of an RF signal in a specific direction. An omnidirectional antenna radiates the signal in all directions in the shape of a doughnut. An isotropic antenna is a theoretical point in which the RF signal radiates, similar to an omnidirectional. A decibel (dB) is a measurement used for radio signals.

19. B. As a wireless signal passes through different materials, the signal will suffer from absorption. Reflection happens when a signal bounces off of a hard surface and is reflected back. Attenuation happens as a signal passes through the air. Refraction is an invalid answer.

20. D. The 169.254.x.x prefix is an Automatic Private IP Addressing (APIPA) IP address, also called a link-local address. The presence of this address means that either the original DHCP address has expired or the DHCP server is unavailable. All other answers are incorrect.

21. B. The `tracert` command will allow you to see the path an IP packet takes to the destination. The Linux/Unix command is `traceroute`. The `route print` command will display the device's routing table. The `ipconfig` command will allow you to verify the IP address information on the Windows operating system. The `dig` command will allow you to verify name resolution.

22. B. Wireless access point (WAP) diagnostics and spectrum analyzers will display RSSI and SNR. The signal-to-noise ratio is the separation of signal to floor noise measured in decibels (dB). The SNR will prove the theory of excess RF noise compared to the originating signal. All other answers are incorrect.

23. D. If there is a speed mismatch between two connection devices, you will have no link status because the carrier signal is different. All other answers are incorrect.

24. A. Crosstalk happens when the electrical signals on one wire induce erroneous signals on another wire. The correct category cable specifications are defined by the Telecommunications Industry Association (TIA).

25. B. The `w32tm` command is used to verify NTP configuration on the Windows operating system. The `nmap` command is used to audit open ports on a remote operating system. The `ipconfig` command is used to verify IP address configuration on the Windows operating system. The `portqry` command is an invalid answer.

Index

2.4 GHz, 238–239
5 GHz, 239
5G (fifth generation), 253–254
802.11a, 236
802.11ac, 237
802.11ax, 237–238
802.11b, 235–236
802.11g, 236
802.11n, 236–237
802.1X protocol, 362–363

A

ABRs (area border routers), 209
access control, 193–194
  access control panel, 195
  ACSs (access control servers), 194–195
  door locks, 196
  hardware, 410
    biometrics, 411
    ERP (enterprise resource planning),
      411–412
    identification badges, 411
  readers, 196
  security console, 194
  tailgating, 196
access control panel, 195
access control vestibule (mantrap), 412
access port, 230
ACLs (access control lists), network
  hardening, 388–389
ACSs (access control servers), 194–195
addresses. See also IP addresses
agreements
  MOU (memorandum of understanding), 316
  NDA (nondisclosure agreement), 315
  SLA (service-level agreement), 315–316
ANDing, 99
answers to review questions
  fundamentals (chapter 1), 538–541
  implementation (chapter 2), 541–544
  operations (chapter 3), 544–547

  security (chapter 4), 547–550
  troubleshooting (chapter 5), 550–552
antennas, 243–244
  network troubleshooting and, 489–491
  placement, 391
anycast, 86
API (application programming interface), 13
APIPA (Automatic Private IP Addressing), 97
Application layer (OSI model), 13
  API and, 13
  events, 13–14
  GUI and, 13
architecture
  core layer, 139
  host locations, 144–145
  SDN (software-defined networking), 140–141
  spine and leaf, 142–143
  three-tiered model, 139–140
  traffic flows, 143–144
arp, 473–474
ARP (Address Resolution Protocol), 177, 218
  network hardening, 383
  spoofing, 372
ASBRs (autonomous system boundary routers), 209
ASCII (American Standard Code for Information
  Interchange), 14
ASDL (Asymmetrical Digital Subscriber Line),
  45–46
ASICs (application-specific integrated circuits), 175
ASN (autonomous system number), 212
assessments
  penetration testing, 364–365
  posture assessment, 365
  risk assessment, 365
  SIEM (security information and event
    management), 366
  vulnerability assessments, 364
asset disposal
  factory reset/wipe, 413–414
  sanitization for disposal, 414
asset tracking tags, 409
attacks
  human and environmental, 378–379
  social engineering, 378–379

technology-based
    ARP spoofing, 372
    deauthentication, 378
    DNS poisoning, 371
    DoS (denial of service), 368–370
    evil twin, 374
    IP spoofing, 377
    MAC spoofing, 376–377
    malware, 378
    on-path, 370–371
    password attacks, 375–376
    ransomware, 374–375
    rogue access point, 374
    rogue DHCP, 372–373
    VLAN hopping, 371–372
attenuation, 439–440
audit and assessment report, 313–315
    Cybersecurity Risk Assessment,
        313
audit logs, 276–277
AUP (acceptable use policy), 303–304
authentication, 357–358
    802.1X protocol, 362–363
    deauthentication, 378
    EAP (Extensible Authentication Protocol),
        250, 363–364
    EAP-FAST (Extensible Authentication
        Protocol-Flexible Authentication via
        Secure Tunneling), 251
    EAP-TLS (Extensible Authentication
        Protocol - Transport Layer Security),
        251
    Kerberos, 362
    LDAP (Lightweight Directory Access
        Protocol), 361–362
    local authentication, 362
    multifactor, 358–359
    PEAP (Protected Extensible Authentication
        Protocol), 251
    RADIUS (Remote Authentication Dial-In User
        Service), 360–361
    remote access and, 403
    SSO (single sign-on), 359–360
    TACACS+, 359
authorization
    open security, 251
    PSK (preshared keys), 251
    remote access and, 403
    shared passphrases, 251
    WEP (Wired Equivalent Privacy),
        251
auto MDI-X (Medium Dependent Interface
    Crossover), 233
AWS (Amazon Web Services), 156
azimuth plane, antennas, 243

B

backups
    differential, 335
    disk-to-cloud, 335
    disk-to-disk, 334–335
    disk-to-tape, 334
    FIFO (first-in, first-out), 334
    full, 335
    GFS (grandfather, father, son), 334
    incremental, 335
    LTO (Linear Tape Open), 334
    network devices, 336
    RPO (recovery point objective), 334
    RTO (recovery time objective), 334
    snapshots, 336
bandwidth
    CoS (Class of Service), 215
    DiffServ, 213–214
    DSCP (Differentiated Services Code
        Point), 213–214
    network metrics, 268
    QoS (quality of service), 213
    traffic shaping, 212–213
baseline configurations, 315
BGP (Border Gateway Protocol), 37, 208, 211–212
    ASN number, 212
    CIDR notation, 212
    eBGP (External Border Gateway Protocol), 212
    iBGP (Internal Border Gateway Protocol), 212
bidirectional transceivers, 64
biometrics, 411
Bitcoin, ransomware and, 374–375
blocking port, 223
BPDUs (Bridge Protocol Data Units), 222
bridge ID, 223
bridges, 176–177
Broadband Cable, 46–47
broadcast domains, 216–217
broadcasts, 84–85
bus topology, 31–32
business continuity plan, 300–302
BYOD (bring your own device), 304
byte counts, 284–285

C

cabling
    applications
        console cable, 437–438
        crossover cable, 438–439
        PoE (power over Ethernet), 439
        rollover cable, 437–438

attenuation, 439–440
bad ports, 441
camera deployment, 197
connectors
   copper, 55–57
   fiber, 58–60
copper
   Cat 3, 71
   Cat 5, 71
   Cat 6, 71
   Cat 6a, 71
   Cat 7, 71–72
   Cat 8, 72
   categories, 70
   coaxial cable, 52–53
   connectors, 55–57
   RG-59, 73
   RG-6, 73
   solid core, 53
   speed, 70
   STP (shielded twisted-pair), 51–52
   stranded, 53
   Twinax, 73
   UTP (unshielded twisted-pair), 51
dB (decibel) loss, 440–441
duplexing issues, 443
EIA (Electronic Industries Alliance), 434
EIA/TIA 586A, 438
EMI (electrical magnetic interference), 440
fiber-optic, 53–54
   dirty, 444
   MMF (multimode fiber-optic cable), 55
   SMF (single-mode fiber-optic cable), 54
incorrect pin-out, 441
labeling, 312
LED status indicators, 441–442
open circuit, 441
plenum, 436
riser-rated, 436
RJ-45 end, 437
short circuit, 441
STP (shielded twisted-pair), 436
TIA (Telecommunications Industry Association), 434
tools
   cable stripper, 455–456
   cable testers, 451–452
   crimpers, 445–446
   cutters, 454–455
   fiber light meter, 456
   fusion splicer, 453–454
   loopback adapter, 448–449
   multimeter, 450
   OPM (optical power meter), 456
   OTDR (optical time-domain reflectometer), 449
   punchdown tool, 446, 447
   snips, 454–455
   spectrum analyzer, 454
   tap, 453
   tone generator, 446–448
   tracing probe, 446–447
   wire map, 452–453
   transceivers, incorrect, 442–443
   TX/RX (transmit/receive) reverse, 443–444
   UTP (unshielded twisted-pair), 436
cameras
   CCTV (closed-circuit television), 197, 407
   LPR (license plate recognition), 197
   NVR (network video recorder), 197, 407
   PTZ (pan-tilt-zoom), 197, 407
CAN (campus area network), 36
CAP (Connection Authorization Policy), 401
captive portal, 394–395
Cat 3 cable, 71
Cat 5 cable, 71
Cat 6 cable, 71
Cat 6a cable, 71
Cat 7 cable, 71–72
Cat 8 cable, 72
CCMP-AES, 250
CCTV (closed-circuit television), 197, 407
CDMA (code division multiple access), 252
CDP (Cisco Discovery Protocol), 234
cellular connectivity
   5G (fifth generation), 253–254
   CDMA (code division multiple access), 252
   GSM (Global System for Mobile Communications), 253
   LTE/4G (Long-Term Evolution), 253
   TDMA (time-division multiple access), 252
change advisory board, 298
change management, documentation, 297–298
channels, 491–492
CIA (confidentiality, integrity, availability), 348–349
CIDR (Classless Inter-Domain Routing), 106
   BGP routers, 212
   calculator, 107
CIRT (computer incident response team), 298
client-server networks, 33
cloud computing
   access, 151
   cloud resources, 163
   connectivity
      Private-Direct Connection, 160
      VPNs (virtual private networks), 160
   elasticity, 152, 161–162
   IaC (Infrastructure as Code), 157–159

local resources, 163
measured service, 152
mesh topology, 30
multitenancy, 161
on-demand self-service, 151
resource pooling, 151
scalability, 162
security, 162–163
services, 155
    DaaS (Desktop as a Service), 157
    IaaS (Infrastructure as a Service), 156–157
    PaaS (Platform as a Service), 156
    SaaS (Software as a Service), 156
cloud delivery
    community cloud model, 154–155
    hybrid cloud model, 154
    private cloud model, 152–153
    public cloud model, 153–154
cloud sites, 331
CNA (converged network adapter), 148
CNAME (canonical name), 125
collision domains, 216
command-line tools
    arp, 473–474
    dig (Domain Information Groper), 471–472
    hostname, 476
    ifconfig, 468–469
    ip, 470
    ipconfig, 466–468
    netstat, 474–476
    nmap, 479–481
    nslookup, 470–471
    ping, 466
    route, 477–478
    tcpdump, 478–479
    telnet, 478
    tracert/traceroute, 472–473
commands, troubleshooting and, 484–485
community cloud model, 154–155
connection-oriented protocols, 121–122
connectionless protocols, 121–122
connections. See also cabling
    distance, 435
    speed, 435
    throughput, 435
connectivity
    Private-Direct Connection, 160
    VPNs (virtual private networks), 160
connectors
    BNC connector, 57
    F-connector, 57
    pin-out, incorrect, 441
    RJ-11, 56
    RJ-45, 55–56, 437
    termination standards, 73

    crossover cables, 75–76
    straight-through cables, 74–75
    TIA/EIA 568A/B, 74
console cable, 437–438
console router, 405
CoPP (control plane policing), network
    hardening, 383–384
CoS (Class of Service), 215
CPE (customer premises equipment), 39, 40
CPU (central processing unit), 40
    utilization, 266
CRC (cyclic redundancy check), 19
    errors, 286
    interface statistics and, 285
crossover cable, 438–439
crossover cables, connectors, 75–76
CSMA/CD (Carrier Sense Multiple Access with
    Collision Detection), 219–220
CSUs/DSUs (channel services units/digital service
    units), 39–40, 50
CWDM (coarse wavelength division
    multiplexing), 63
Cybersecurity Risk Assessment, 313

D

DaaS (Desktop as a Service), 157
DAD (Duplicate Address Detection), 218
DAS (direct attached storage), 145
Data Link layer (OSI model), 13
    Ethernet II frame, 19
    LLC (logical link layer), 18–20
    MAC (media access control) layer, 18–20
    switches, 175–176
data loss prevention, 306–307
datagrams, 21
DCE (data communication equipment), 40
deauthentication, 378
decapsulation, 22–23
decibel (dB) loss, 440–441
default credentials, network hardening, 386
default routing, 206
defense in depth, 353–354
    honeypot/honeynet, 357
    NAC (network access control),
        356–357
    screened subnet, 354–355
    segmentation, 354
    separation of duties, 355–356
demarcation point, 39
detection methods
    asset tracking tags, 409
    cameras, 407–408

motion detectors, 408
  tamper detection, 409–410
devices, 173
  bridges, 176–177
  cameras, 197
  firewalls, 187–188
    NGFW (next-generation firewalls), 188–189
  hubs, 174
  HVAC (heating, ventilation, air conditioning)
    systems, 198–199
  IDS (intrusion detection system), 186–187
  industrial control systems, 201–203
  IoT (Internet of Things), 199
    smart doorbell, 200–201
    smart speakers, 200
    smart thermostat, 200
  IPS (intrusion prevention system), 187
  layer 3 switches, 178
  load balancer, 182
  logs, 274–276
    audit logs, 276–277
    Event Viewer, 275
    logging levels, 278–279
    severity levels, 278–279
    Syslog, 277–278
    traffic logs, 276
  media converters, 175
  metrics, 266–267
  modems, 183–184
  physical access control, 193–194
    access control panel, 195
    ACSs (access control servers), 194–195
    door locks, 196
    readers, 196
    security console, 194
    tailgating, 196
  printers, 191–193
  proxy servers, 182–183
  repeaters, 175
  routers, 177
  SCADA (supervisory control and data
    acquisition), 201–203
  switches, 175–176
  VoIP gateway, 185–186
  VoIP PBX, 184–185
  VoIP phones, 189–191
  VPN headend, 189
  WAP (wireless access point), 178–179
  wireless LAN controller (WLC or WLAN
    controller), 179–181
  wireless range extender, 181
DevOps, 158
DHCP (Dynamic Host Configuration Protocol), 88,
  93–94, 112–113, 132–133

DHCPv6, 96
DORA (Discover, Offer, Request,
  Acknowledgement), 93–94
  IP exclusions, 134
  IP helper, 135–137
  lease time, 134–135
  MAC address reservations, 133
  relay agent, 135–137
  rogue DHCP servers, 373–374
  scope, 133–134
  snooping, network hardening, 386
  TTL (time-to-live), 134–135
  Windows DHCP/static IP dialog box, 97
dial-up service, 47
dig (Domain Information Groper), 471–472
disaster recovery, 318
  active-active, 331–334
  active-passive, 331–334
  backups
    differential, 335
    disk-to-cloud, 335
    disk-to-disk, 334–335
    disk-to-tape, 334
    FIFO (first-in, first-out), 334
    full, 335
    GFS (grandfather, father, son), 334
    incremental, 335
    LTO (Linear Tape Open), 334
    network devices, 336
    RPO (recovery point objective), 334
    RTO (recovery time objective), 334
    snapshots, 336
  cloud sites, 331
  cold sites, 331
  hot sites, 331
  MTBF (mean time between failures), 334
  MTTR (mean time to repair), 333
  plan, 300–302
  warm sites, 331
distance-vector routing protocols, 208–209
DKIM (Domain Keys Identified Mail), 124
DLP (data loss prevention), 306–307
DMZ (demilitarized zone). *See* screened subnet
DNAT (dynamic network address translation), 82
DNS (Domain Name System), 110
  cloud-hosted, 127
  DNS poisoning, 371
  external DNS, 126
  forward zone, 130–132
  hierarchy, 127–128
    caching DNS server, 129
    forwarding DNS server, 129
    iterative lookups, 129–130
    primary DNS server, 128

recursive lookups, 129–130
secondary DNS server, 128
TTL (Time to Live), 129
zones, 129
internal DNS, 126
record types
A (address record), 123
AAAA (quad a record), 124
CNAME (canonical name), 125
DKIM (Domain Keys Identified Mail)
records, 124
Dynamic DNS, 126
MX (Mail Exchanger), 124–125
NS (Name Server), 125
PTR (Pointer Record), 126
SOA (Start of Authority), 125–126
SPF (Sender Policy Framework) records, 124
SRV (Service Locator Records), 124
TXT records, 124
reverse zone, 130–132
split-brain model, 126
third-party, 127
DNSSEC (Domain Name System Security
Extensions), 371
DOCSIS (Data Over Cable Service Interface
Specification), 46
documentation, 307–308
agreements
MOU (memorandum of understanding),
316
NDA (nondisclosure agreement), 315
SLA (service-level agreement), 315–316
audit and assessment report, 313–315
baseline configurations, 315
business continuity plan, 300–302
cable labeling, 312
change management, 297–298
disaster recovery plan, 300–302
floor plan, 309
IDF/MDF, 311
incident response plan, 298–299
CIRT (computer incident response
team), 298
incident documentation, 299–300
logical diagrams, 307–308
physical diagrams, 307–308
rack diagrams, 309–310
site survey report, 313, 314
wiring diagrams, 311–313
door locks, 196
DoS (denial of service) attacks, 368–369
amplified, 369
DDoS (distributed denial of service) attack,
370
reflective, 369

DPI (deep packet inspection), 188
DR (designated routers), 209
DSCP (Differentiated Services Code
Point), 213–214
DSL (Digital Subscriber Line)
ASDL (Asymmetrical Digital Subscriber
Line), 45–46
SDSL (Symmetrical Digital Subscriber Line), 46
VDSL (Very-high-bitrate Digital
Subscriber Line), 46
DSSS (direct-sequence spread spectrum)
modulation, 235
DTE (data terminal equipment), 40
DTP (Dynamic Trunking Protocol), 372
duplex connections, 63, 443
DWDM (dense wavelength division
multiplexing), 63
Dynamic DNS, 126
dynamic routing, 206

E

E1/E3 lines, 44
EAP (Extensible Authentication Protocol),
363–364, 392–393
LEAP (Lightweight Extensible Authentication
Protocol), 363
PEAP (Protected Extensible Authentication
Protocol), 393
EAP-FAST (Extensible Authentication Protocol-
Flexible Authentication via Secure
Tunneling), 393
EAP-TLS (Extensible Authentication Protocol-
Transport Layer Security), 393–394
EBCDIC (Extended Binary Coded Decimal
Interchange Code), 14
EIA (Electronic Industries Alliance), 70, 434
straight-through cables, 74–75
EIGRP (Enhanced Interior Gateway Routing
Protocol), 210–211
EIRP (effective isotropic radiated power), 489
elasticity, cloud computing, 161–162
Elastisearch, 275
electrical, 290–291
elevation plane, 243
EMI (electromagnetic interference), 51, 440
encapsulation, 22–23
errors, 288–289
environment
electrical, 290–291
flooding, 291
humidity, 289–290
temperature, 289
ephemeral port numbers, 15

Ethernet
  1000BaseLX, 78
  1000BaseSX, 78
  1000BaseT, 76–77
  100BaseFX, 77
  100BaseSX, 78
  100BaseTX, 76
  10BaseT, 76
  10GBaseLR, 78
  10GBaseSR, 78
  10GBaseT, 77
  40GBaseT, 77
  standards
    copper, 76–77
    fiber optic, 77–78
  switching
    auto MDI-X (Medium Dependent Interface
      Crossover), 233
    broadcast domains, 216–217
    collision domains, 216
    CSMA/CD (Carrier Sense Multiple Access
      with Collision Detection), 219–220
    flow control, 219
    helper protocols, 218
    interface properties, 227–231
    ISL (Inter-Switch Link), 229
    jumbo frames, 233
    loops, 221–226
    MAC addresses, 220–221
    PoE (Power over Ethernet), 234
    port aggregation and, 233
    port mirroring and, 232
    port security and, 232–233
    segmentation, 227–231
    ST (Spanning Tree Protocol), 221–226
    switchports, 219
EUI-64 (Extended Unique Identifier 64), 95
EVCs (Ethernet virtual connections), 46
evil twin attack, 374
exploits, 351

F

facilities
  fire suppression, 329–330
  HA (high availability concepts), 330–336
  HVAC, 328–329
  infrastructure support, 326–327
  PDUs (power distribution units), 328
  power generators, 328
  redundancy and, 330–336
  UPS (uninterruptable power supply), 327
FCoE (Fibre Channel over Ethernet), 148
FDDI (Fiber Distributed Data Interface) rings, 29

FHRPs (first-hop redundancy protocols), 325, 333
fiber connectors
  APC (angled physical contact), 59–60
  LC (local connector), 58
  MTRJ (mechanical transfer registered jack), 60
  SC (standard connector), 59
  ST (straight tip), 58
  UPC (ultra-physical contact), 59–60
fiber-optic cable, 53–54
  dirty, 444
  Ethernet standards, 77–78
  MMF (multimode fiber-optic cable), 55
  SMF (single-mode fiber-optic cable), 54
Fibre Channel, 147–148
fire suppression
  clean agents, 330
  deluge pipe system, 330
  dry pipe system, 330
  preaction pipe system, 330
  wet pipe system, 329
firewalls
  high availability and, 325–326
  network hardening, 390
firmware, upgrades, network hardening, 387
flooding, 291
flow control, 219
forwarding port, 223
FTP (File Transfer Protocol), 111

G

GARP (Gratuitous Address Resolution
  Protocol), 373
Geofencing, 252, 394
giant frames, 286–287
GRE (Generic Routing Encapsulation),
  38, 118–120
GSM (Global System for Mobile
  Communications), 253
Gto4 tunneling, 91
GUI (grapical user interface), 13

H

H.323, 116
HA (high availability) concepts
  clusters, 320, 323–324
  firewalls, 325–326
  hosts, 324
  load balancing, 318
  multipathing, 318–319
  NIC (network interface card) teaming, 320

RAID (Redundant Array of Independent
Disks), 320–321
RAID-1, 321–322
RAID-5, 322
RAID-6, 322–323
routers, 325
SANs (storage area networks), 324
STP blocks, 324
switches, 324–325
hard changes, 297
hardening policies
AUP (acceptable use policy), 303–304
BYOD (bring your own device), 304
off-boarding procedures, 305
onboarding procedures, 305
passwords, 303
remote access policies, 304
hardening techniques
ACLs (access control lists), 388–389
ARP (Address Resolution Protocol)
inspection, 383
common passwords, 386
CoPP (control plane policing), 383–384
default credential changes, 386
DHCP snooping, 386
firewall rules, 390
firmware upgrades, 387
patching, 387
port security, 382–383
RA (Router Advertisement) Guard, 382
role-based access, 389–390
services, disabling, 385
SNMP security, 381–382
switchports, disabling, 385
updates, 387
VLANs
native, 386–387
private, 384–385
HBA (host bus adapter), 146, 319
helper protocols, 218
HIPS (host-based intrusion prevention system), 187
HMI (Human Machine Interface), SCADA
system, 202
hold-downs, 209
host locations
colocation, 145
company-owned data center, 144
public cloud, 144
ROBOs (remote offices/branch offices), 145
hostname, 476
hot sites, 331
HSRP (Hot Standby Router Protocol), 107, 325
HTTP (Hypertext Transfer Protocol), 113
HTTPS (Hypertext Transfer Protocol Transport
Layer Security), 113

hubs, 174
humidity, 289–290
HVAC (heating, ventilation, air conditioning)
systems, 198–199, 289–291, 328–329
hybrid cloud model, 154
hybrid drives, sanitizing, 414
hybrid routing protocols, 210–211
hybrid topology, 32
hypervisor, 42
Type 1, 43
Type 2, 43

I

I/G (Individual Group) bit, 20
IaaS (Infrastructure as a Service), 156–157
IaC (Infrastructure as Code), 157–160
IANA (Internet Assignment Numbers
Authority), 80, 89–90
ICMP (Internet Control Message
Protocol), 117–118
ICMP protocol, 17
SLAAC and, 94
identification badges, 411
IDF/MDF (intermediate distribution frame/main
distribution frame), 311
IDS (intrusion detection system), 186–188
IETF (Internet Engineering Task Force), 360
ifconfig, 468–469
IGMP (Internet Group Management Protocol), 85
IMAP (Internet Message Access Protocol), 115–116
IMAP over SSL, 116
incident response plan
CIRT (computer incident response team), 298
incident documentation, 299–300
industrial control systems, 201–203. See also
SCADA (supervisory control and data
acquisition)
interface errors/alerts
CRC errors, 286
encapsulation errors, 288–289
giants and, 286–287
runts and, 287
interface statistics, 279–281
byte counts, 284–285
CRCs (cyclic redundancy checks), 285
link state, 281
PowerShell commands, 279–280
protocol packets, 284–285
send/receive traffic, 283–284
speed/duplex, 282–283
IoT (Internet of Things), 28, 199
security considerations, 395

smart doorbell, 200–201
smart speakers, 200
smart thermostat, 200
ip, 470
IP addresses. *See also* VIP (Virtual IP)
    APIPA (Automatic Private IP Addressing), 97
    assignments, 93–98
    CIDR (Classless Inter-Domain Routing), 106
    classful, 103–105
    classless, 105
    default gateway, 87
    DHCP (Dynamic Host Configuration Protocol), 93–94
    DHCPv6, 96
    EUI-64 (Extended Unique Identifier 64), 95
    IPv4, 84–87
    IPv6, 88–93
    NAT (network address translation)
        DNAT (dynamic network address translation), 82
        PAT (port address translation), 82–83
        port forwarding, 84
        SNAT (static network address translation), 81–82
    options, 88
    private, *versus* public, 80–81
    protocol types
        GRE (Generic Routing Encapsulation), 118–120
        ICMP (Internet Control Message Protocol), 117–118
        IPSec (Internet Protocol Security), 120–121
        TCP (Transmission Control Protocol), 118
        UDP (User Datagram Protocol), 118
    reservations, 98
    SLAAC (Stateless Address Autoconfiguration), 94–95
    static, 96–97
    subinterfaces, 98
    subnet mask, 87–88
    subnetting, 99–103
    VLSM (variable-length subnet mask), 105–106
IP headers
    DiffServ, 213–214
    ToS (Type of Services) field, 213
IP protocol, 17, 25–26
IP spoofing, 377
ipconfig, 466–468
IPS (intrusion prevention system), 187
    firewalls, 187–188
    HIPS (host-based intrusion prevention system), 187
    NIPS (network-based intrusion prevention system), 187

IPSec (Internet Protocol Security), 38, 120–121, 189
IPv4, 206–212
    addresses, RIR, 81
    anycast, 86
    broadcasts, 84–85
    loopback, 86–87
    multicasts, 85
    reserved, 86–87
    unicast, 86
IPv6, 206–212
    addressing, 88–91
    anycast addresses, 91
    APIPA (Automatic Private IP Addressing), 90
    dual stack, 92
    global unicast address, 90
    link-local addresses, 90
    multicast addresses, 91
    NDP (Neighbor Discovery Protocol), 93
    router advertisements, 92
    tunneling
        Gto4, 91
        ISATAP, 91
        Toredo, 92
    unicast, 90
    unique local addresses, 91
ISATAP (Intra-Site Automatic Tunnel Addressing Protocol), 91
iSCSI (Internet Small Computer System Interface), 146, 148
ISDN (Integrated Services Digital Network), 39, 43, 50
ISL (Inter-Switch Link), 229
ISM (industrial, scientific, and medical) radio bands, 238
ISO (International Organization for Standardization), 12
    documents and, 296
ISPs (Internet Service Providers), multiple, 332
IVR (interactive voice response), 185

J

jitter, network metrics, 269

K

Kerberos, 362
keypad readers, 196
Kibana, 275

L

L2TP (Layer 2 Tunneling Protocol), 189
LACP (Link Aggregation Control Protocol), 233
LAN (local area network), 28, 34, 50
latency, network metrics, 268–269
layer 3 switches, 178
LDAP (Lightweight Directory Access Protocol),
    116, 361–362
LDAPS (Lightweight Directory Access Protocol
    of SSL), 116
leased lines
    E1/E3 lines, 44
    ISDN (Integrated Services Digital Network), 43
    OC3-OC1920, 44–45
    PRI (Primary Rate Interface), 44
    T1/T3 lines, 44
least privilege principle, 351–352
LED (light-emitting diode) link status, 441–442
link state, 281
    routing protocols, 209–210
LLC (logical link layer), 18–20
LLDP (Link Layer Discovery Protocol), 234
LLMNR (Link-Local Multicast Name
    Resolution), 33–34
load balancing, 182, 318
local authentication, 362
logging levels, 278–279
loopback addresses, 86–87
LPR (license plate recognition), 407
LTE/4G (Long-Term Evolution), 253
LUN (logical unit number), 146

M

MAC (media access control) layer, 18–20
    Ethernet switching, 220–221
MAC addresses, 17–18
MAC filtering, 252
MAC spoofing, MAB (MAC Authentication
    Bypass) protocol, 376–377
magnetic drives, sanitizing, 414
malware, 378
MAN (metropolitan area network), 36
mantrap, 412
MDI-X (Medium Dependent Interface
    Crossover), 76
media converters, 62–63, 175
media types
    copper cabling, 51–53
    fiber-optic, 53–55

memory, device metrics, 266–267
mesh topology, 30–31, 247–248
Metropolitan Ethernet, 46
mGRE (Multipoint Generic Routing
    Encapsulation) protocol, 38
MICE (Mechanical, Ingress, Climatic, Chemical,
    Electromagnetic), 436
microwave detectors, 408
MIMO (multiple input, multiple output), 237, 242
MitM (man-in-the-middle) attacks, 162–163. *See
    also* on-path attacks
MMF (multimode fiber-optic cable), 55, 77
modems, 183
    cable modems, 184
    DSL modems, 184
    POTS (plain old telephone service), 184
motion detection
    microwave detectors, 408
    PIR (passive infrared) sensors, 408
    vibration detectors, 408
MOU (memorandum of understanding), 316
MPIO (multipath IO), 318–319
MPLS (Multiprotocol Label Switching), 37
MRTG (Multi Router Traffic Grapher), 292
MSDCs (massively scalable data centers), 143
MTU (maximum transmission unit), 26
    giant frames, 286–287
MU-MIMO (multiuser multiple-input, multiple-
    output), 242
multicasts, 85
multifactor authentication, 358–359
multipathing, 318–319
multitenancy, cloud computing, 161
MX (Mail Exchanger), 124–125
MySQL, 117

N

NA (Neighbor Advertisement), 93
NAS (network attached storage), 145, 146
NAT (network address translation)
    DNAT (dynamic network address
        translation), 82
    SNAT (static network address
        translation), 81–82
NBI (northbound interface), 140
NDA (nondisclosure agreement), 315
NDP (Neighbor Discovery Protocol), 93, 218
Netflow Data, 292–293
netstat, 474–476
Network layer (OSI model), 13
    ICMP protocol, 17

IP protocol, 17
routing, 17
network metrics, 267–270
   bandwidth, 268
   jitter, 269
   latency, 268–269
network troubleshooting
   addresses, blocked, 519
   antennas, 489–491
      cable attenuation, 494–495
   AP association time, 492
   asymmetrical routing, 505–506
   broadcast storm, 502–503
   BYOD issues, 527–528
   certificates, 517–518
   channels, 491–492
   collisions, 501–502
   common issues, 493–498
   considerations, 489–493
   device configuration review, 499
   DHCP
      rogue server, 508–510
      scope exhaustion, 510
   distance, 488
   DNS, incorrect, 514–515
   DNS issues, 520–524
   EIRP (effective isotropic radiated power), 489
   encryption protocols, 496
   firewall settings, 519
   gateway, incorrect, 510–511
   hardware failure, 518–519
   interface status, 500
   interference, 493–494
   IP addresses, duplicate, 503–505
   IP addresses, incorrect, 513–514
   IP settings, 510–515
   licensed features, 529
   limitations, 486–489
   MAC addresses, duplicate, 503
   missing route, 515–516
   multicast flooding, 505
   NTP issues, 525–527
   passphrases, 496
   performance baselines, 500–501
   performance issues, 529–530
   portals
      captive, 497
      client disassociation issues, 498
   ports, blocked, 519
   power budget, 516–517
   RF attenuation, 495–496
   routing loops, 507–508
   routing tables, 499–500

   RSSI (Received Signal Strength Indication), 489
   signal strength, 489
   site survey, 492–493
   specifications, 486–489
   speed, 487
   SSID, 496
   subnet mask, incorrect, 512–513
   switching loops, 506–507
   throughput, 487
   VLAN, incorrect, 519–520
   VLAN assignment, 500
   wireless coverage, 496–497
networking models, three-tiered, 139–140
networks. *See also* virtualization
   architecture (*See* architecture)
   cabling
      copper, 49
      fiber-optic, 49
   CAN (campus area network), 36
   client-server, 33
   CSUs/DSUs, 39–40
   demarcation point, 39
   LAN (local area network), 34
   MAN (metropolitan area network), 36
   media converters, 62–63
   MPLS (Multiprotocol Label Switching), 37
   PAN (personal area network), 37
   peer-to-peer, 33–34
   SAN (storage area network), 36
   SDWAN (software-defined wide area network), 37–38
   service delivery, 48–49
   service types
      Broadband Cable, 46–47
      dial-up, 47
      DSL (Digital Subscriber Line), 45–46
      leased lines, 43–45
      Metropolitan Ethernet, 46
      satellite, 47–48
   service-related entry point, 39
   smart jacks, 40
   transceivers, fiber-optic, 60–64
   WAN (wide area network), 34, 35
   wireless, 49
   WLAN (wireless local area network), 34, 35
NFV (network function virtualization), 41–43
NICs (network interface cards), 17
NIPS (network-based intrusion prevention system), 187
NLB (Network Load Balancing), 318
nmap, 479–481
NMS (network management station), 270
   uptime/downtime, 293–294

non-root bridges, 222
NS (Name Server), 125
NS (Neighbor Solicitation), 93
nslookup, 470–471
NTP (Network Time Protocol), 114, 137
NVR (network video recorder), 197, 407

O

OC3-OC1920, 44–45
OFDM (orthogonal frequency-division
    multiplexing), 236
on-path attacks, 370–371
onboarding/offboard procedures, 305
open connections, 441
orchestration software
    Ansible, 160
    Chef, 159
    Puppet, 160
OSI (Open Systems Interconnection) model,
    12–13
    Application layer, 13–14
    Data Link layer, 13, 17–20
    datagrams, 21
    decapsulation and, 22–23
    encapsulation and, 22–23
    hubs and, 174
    IP protocol, 25–26
    Layer 3 switches, 178
    layer protocol numbers, 18
    Network layer, 13, 17
    NGFW (next-generation firewalls), 188
    PDUs (protocol data units), 21
    peer-layer communication, 16
    Physical layer, 13, 20–21
    Presentation layer, 13, 14
    routers, 177–178
    Session layer, 13, 14–15
    Transport layer, 13, 15–16
    WAP (wireless access point), 179
OSPF (Open Shortest Path First), 37,
    209–210
OUI (organizationally unique identifier), 20
OWA (Outlook Web Access), 188

P

PaaS (Platform as a Service), 156
PAgP (Port Aggregation Protocol), 233
PAN (personal area network), 37
password attacks, 375–376

password policies, 303
passwords, network hardening, 386
PAT (port address translation), 82–84
patches, network hardening, 387
path-vector routing protocols, 211–212
PDUs (power distribution units), 328
PDUs (protocol data units), 21, 23
PEAP (Protected Extensible Authentication
    Protocol), 393
peer-layer communication, OSI, 16
peer-to-peer networks, 33–34
penetration testing, 364–365
performance metrics, 265–266
    baselines, 291–292
    device logs, 274–279
phishing, 379
phones. See VoIP (Voice over IP)
physical access control, 193–194
    access control panel, 195
    ACSs (access control servers), 194–195
    door locks, 196
    readers, 196
    security console, 194
    tailgating, 196
Physical layer (OSI model), 13, 20–21
physical security, 406
    asset disposal
        factory reset/wipe, 413–414
        sanitization for disposal, 414
    detection methods
        asset tracking tags, 409
        cameras, 407–408
        motion detectors, 408
        tamper detection, 409–410
    prevention methods
        access control hardware, 410–413
        access control vestibule, 412
        employee training, 410
        locking cabinets, 412
        locking racks, 412
        smart lockers, 413
piggybacking, 379
pin-out, incorrect, 441
ping, 466
PIR (passive infrared) sensors, 408
plans, 296
    business continuity plan, 300–302
    disaster recovery plan, 300–302
    incident response plan
        CIRT (computer incident response
            team), 298
        incident documentation, 299–300
PLC (programmable Logic Controller), SCADA
    system, 202

plenum cable, 436
PoE (Power over Ethernet), 234
    cabling, 439
poison reverse, 209
policies, 296
    DLP (data loss prevention), 306–307
    hardening
        AUP (acceptable use policy), 303–304
        BYOD (bring your own device), 304
        off-boarding procedures, 305
        onboarding procedures, 305
        passwords, 303
        remote access policies, 304
    security, 305–306
POP (Post Office Protocol), 115
POP3 over SSL, 115
port cost, 223
ports, 15
    access port, 230
    aggregation, 233
    bad, 441
    blocking port, 223
    duplexes, 219
    ephemeral port numbers, 15
    forwarding port, 223
    mirroring, 232
    network hardening, 382–383
    security, 232–233
    trunk port, 230
    well-known port numbers, 15
posture assessment, 365
power generators, 328
PowerShell, interface statistics, 279–280
PPTP (Point-to-Point Tunneling Protocol),
    189
Presentation layer (OSI model), 13, 14
prevention methods
    access control hardware, 410–413
    access control vestibule (mantrap), 412
    employee training, 410
    locking cabinets, 412
    locking racks, 412
    smart lockers, 413
PRI (Primary Rate Interface), 44
printers
    centralized printing, 193
    decentralized printing, 192
    EMF (Enhanced Meta File), 191
    GDI (graphic display interface), 191
    network print process, 191
    PCL (Printer Control Language), 191
    peer-to-peer printing, 192–193
private cloud model, 152–153
Private-Direct Connection, 160

procedures, 296
    system life cycle, 302
processes, 296, 297
protocol packets, 284–285
protocols
    BGP (Border Gateway Protocol), 37
    connection-oriented, 121–122
    connectionless, 121–122
    DHCP (Dynamic Host Configuration
        Protocol), 112–113
    DNS (Domain Name System), 110
    FTP (File Transfer Protocol), 111
    GRE (Generic Routing Encapsulation), 38
    H.323, 116
    helper protocols, 218
    HTTP (Hypertext Transfer Protocol), 113
    HTTPS (Hypertext Transfer Protocol Transport
        Layer Security), 113
    IMAP (Internet Message Access
        Protocol), 115–116
    IMAP over SSL, 116
    IPSec, 189
    L2TP (Layer 2 Tunneling Protocol), 189
    LDAP (Lightweight Directory Access
        Protocol), 116
    LDAPS (Lightweight Directory Access Protocol
        of SSL), 116
    mGRE (Multipoint Generic Routing
        Encapsulation), 38
    MySQL, 117
    NTP (Network Time Protocol), 114, 137
    OSPF (Open Shortest Path First), 37
    POP (Post Office Protocol), 115
    POP3 over SSL, 115
    PPTP (Point-to-Point Tunneling Protocol), 189
    RDP (Remote Desktop Protocol), 114
    SFTP (Secure File Transfer Protocol), 111
    SIP (Session Initiation Protocol), 114–115
    SMB (Server Message Block), 115
    SMTP (Simple Mail Transport Protocol), 111
    SMTP TLS (Simple Mail Transport Protocol
        Transport Layer Security), 111
    SNMP (Simple Network Management
        Protocol), 113–114
    SQL (Structured Query Language), 117
    SQLnet, 117
    SSH (Secure Shell), 110
    Syslog, 117
    Telnet, 112
    TFTP (Trivial File Transfer Protocol), 112
proxy servers, 182–183
PSKs (preshared keys), 251, 392
PSTN (public switched telephone network), 185
PTR (Pointer Record), 126

PTZ (pan-tilt-zoom), cameras, 197, 407
public cloud model, 153–154

Q

QMS (quality management system), 296
    processes, 297
QoS (quality of service), 26

R

RA (Router Advertisement), 218
RA (Router Advertisement) Guard, network
    hardening and, 382
RADIUS (Remote Authentication Dial-In User
    Service), 304, 360–361
RAID (Redundant Array of Independent Disks)
    RAID-1, 321–322
    RAID-5, 322
    RAID-6, 322–323
RAM (random access memory), 40
    device metrics, 266–267
ransomware, 374–375
RDP (Remote Desktop Protocol), 114, 400–401
readers, 196
redundancy
    FHRPs (first-hop redundancy protocols),
        333
    VRRP (Virtual Router Redundancy
        Protocol), 333
remediation, incident response, 300
remote access
    authentication considerations, 403
    authorization considerations, 403
    console router, 405
    data plane, 403
    in-band management, 403–405
    modems, 404
    policies, 304
    RDP (Remote Desktop Protocol), 400–401
    Remote Desktop Gateway, 401
    security, 397–405
    SSH (Secure Shell), 401–402
    VDI (virtual desktop infrastructure), 402
    VNC (Virtual Network Computing), 402
    VPNs (virtual private networks), 397–400
Remote Desktop Gateway, 401
repeaters, 175
reports. See documentation
reserved addresses, 86–87

REX (request to exit), 196
RFID (radio-frequency identification), cards, 196
RG-59 cable, 73
RG-6 cable, 73
RID (router ID), 209
ring topology, 29–30
RIP (Routing Information Protocol), 208–209
RIR (Regional Internet Registry), 80–81
    ASNs (autonomous system numbers), 212
riser-rated cable, 436
risk assessment, 365
ROBOs (remote offices/branch offices), 145
rogue access point, 374
rogue DHCP, 372–373
role-based access, 352
    network hardening, 389–390
rollover cable, 437–438
root bridge, 222
root cause, incident response, 300
route, 477–478
routers, 177
    ABRs (area border routers), 209
    ASBRs (autonomous system boundary
        routers), 209
    broadcast domains, 217
    console router, 405
    DR (designated routers), 209
    FHRPs (first-hop redundancy protocols), 325
    HSRP (Hot Standby Router Protocol), 325
    IPv6, 92
    RID (router ID), 209
    VRRP (Virtual Router Redundancy
        Protocol), 325
routing, 204–206
routing loops, 208–209
routing protocols
    AD (administrative distances), 207
    BGP (Border Gateway Protocol), 208
    distance-vector, 208–209
    hybrid, 210–211
    IPv4, 206–212
    IPv6, 206–212
    link-state, 209–210
    path-vector, 211–212
    RTP (Reliable Transport Protocol), 211
RPO (Recover Point Objective), 301
RS (Router Solicitation), 94, 218
RSSI (Received Signal Strength Indication), 489
RSTP (Rapid Spanning Tree Protocol), 225–226
RTO (Recovery Time Objective), 301
RTP (Reliable Transport Protocol), 211
RTU (Remote Terminal Unit), SCADA system, 202
runt frames, 287

S

SaaS (Software as a Service), 156
SAN (storage area network), 36
    FC (Fibre Channel), 146
sanitization
    hybrid drives, 414
    magnetic drives, 414
    SSD (solid-state drive), 414
SANs (storage area networks), 145, 146–147
    connection types
        FCoE (Fibre Channel over Ethernet),
            148
        Fibre Channel, 147–148
        IB (InfiniBand), 149
        iSCSI (Internet Small Computer System
            Interface), 148
satellite service, 47–48
SBI (southbound interface), 140
SCADA (supervisory control and data
    acquisition), 201
    communications infrastructure, 202–203
    HMI (Human Machine Interface), 202
    PLC (programmable Logic Controller), 202
    RTU (Remote Terminal Unit), 202
    supervisory system, 202
scalability, cloud computing, 162
SDN (software-defined networking), 140–141
SDSL (Symmetrical Digital Subscriber Line), 46
SDWAN (software-defined wide area
    network), 37–38
security
    assessments
        penetration testing, 364–365
        posture assessment, 365
        risk assessment, 365
        SIEM (security information and event
            management), 366
        vulnerability assessments, 364
    authentication, 357–358
        802.1X protocol, 362–363
        EAP (Extensible Authentication
            Protocol), 363–364
        Kerberos, 362
        LDAP (Lightweight Directory Access
            Protocol), 361–362
        local authentication, 362
        multifactor, 358–359
        RADIUS (Remote Authentication Dial-In
            User Service), 360–361
        SSO (single sign-on), 359–360
        TACACS+, 359
    CIA (confidentiality, integrity,
        availability), 348–349
    defense in depth, 353–354

        honeypot/honeynet, 357
        NAC (network access control), 356–357
        screened subnet, 354–355
        segmentation, 354
        separation of duties, 355–356
    exploits, 351
    IoT considerations, 395
    least privilege principle, 351–352
    physical, 406
        asset disposal, 413–414
        detection methods, 407–410
        prevention methods, 410–413
    policies, 305–306
    remote access methods and, 397–405
    role-based access, 352
    threats, 349–350
    vulnerabilities
        CVE (Common Vulnerabilities and
            Exposures), 350
        zero-day, 351
    wireless
        antenna placement, 391
        capitive portal, 394–395
        client isolation, 391–392
        EAP (Extensible Authentication
            Protocol), 392–394
        Geofencing, 394
        guest network isolation, 392
        MAC filtering and, 390–391
        power levels, 391
        PSKs (preshared keys), 392
    zero trust, 352–353
security console, 194
segmentation, VLANs (virtual local area
    networks), 227–228
    ports, tagging/untagging, 230
    trunking, 228–230
    voice VLAN, 230–231
send/receive traffic, 283–284
service-related entry point, 39
services, disabling, network hardening, 385
Session layer (OSI model), 13, 14–15
    full-duplex communication, 14
    half-duplex communication, 14
    simplex communication, 15
severity levels, 278–279
SFTP (Secure File Transfer Protocol), 111
short circuit, 441
shoulder surfing, 379
show config operating system command, 482–483
show interface operating system
    command, 481–482
show route operating system command, 484–485
SIEM (security information and event
    management), 366

SIP (Session Initiation Protocol), 114–115
site survey, network troubleshooting, 492–493
site survey report, 313, 314
SLA (service-level agreement), 315–316
SLAAC (Stateless Address Autoconfiguration), 94–95, 218
smart devices, 200–201
smart jacks, 40
smart lockers, 413
SMB (Server Message Block), 115
SMF (single-mode fiber-optic cable), 54, 77
SMTP (Simple Mail Transport Protocol), 111
SMTP TLS (Simple Mail Transport Protocol Transport Layer Security), 111
SNAT (static network address translation), 81–82
SNMP (Simple Network Management Protocol), 113–114, 270, 292
    agent, 271
    commands, 271–273
    community name, 273
    components, 270
    MIB (management information base), 274
    network hardening and, 381–382
    NMS (network management station), 270, 271
    OIDs (object identifiers), 273–274
    versions, 273
SOA (Start of Authority), 125–126
social engineering
    phishing, 379
    piggybacking, 379
    shoulder surfing, 379
    tailgating, 379
sockets, 15
soft changes, 297
software troubleshooting tools
    bandwidth speed tester, 461
    IP scanner, 465–466
    iPerf, 461–462
    NetFlow Analyzer, 462–463
    packet sniffers, 459–460
    port scanner, 461
    protocol analyzer, 459–460
    terminal emulator, 463–465
    TFTP (Trivial File Transfer Protocol) server, 463
    Wi-Fi analyzer, 458–459
SOPs (standard operating procedures), 296, 297
SPAN (Switched Port Analyzer), 232
speed/duplex, connections, 282–283
SPF (Sender Policy Framework), 124
spine and leaf architecture, 142–143
split horizons, 208
SQL (Structured Query Language), 117
SQLnet, 117
SRV (Service Locator Records), 124

SSD (solid-state drive), sanitizing, 414
SSH (Secure Shell), 110, 401–402
SSL (Secure Sockets Layer), 14
    firewalls, 188
SSO (single sign-on), 162–163, 359–360
STA (Spanning Tree Algorithm), 223
star topology, 28–29
static routing, 205–206
storage, device metrics, 267
storage types
    DAS (direct attached storage), 145
    NAS (network attached storage), 145, 146
    SANs (storage area networks), 145, 146–147
STP (shielded twisted-pair) cabling, 436
STP (Spanning Tree Protocol), 175, 221
    convergence, 225
    operations, 223
    port states, 224–225
    RSTP (Rapid Spanning Tree Protocol), 225–226
    STA (Spanning Tree Algorithm), 223
    STP (802.1D), 222–223
straight-through cables, connectors, 74–75
subnetting, 99–103
switches, 175–176
switchports, 219
    disabling, network hardening, 385
    duplex, 282
    speed, 282
Syslog, 117, 277–278
system life cycle, 302

T

T1/T3 lines, 44
TACACS+ (Terminal Access Controller Access Control System+), 359
tailgating, 196, 379
tamper detection, 409–410
TCP (Transmission Control Protocol), 23–24, 118
    sliding window, 25
tcpdump, 478–479
TDM (time-division multiplexing), 184
TDMA (time-division multiple access), 252
telnet, 478
Telnet, 112
temperature, 289
tenants, cloud computing, 161
termination points
    cable management panels, 69–70
    fiber distribution panels, 68–69
    patch panels, 68
    punchdown blocks

110 block, 65, 66
66 block, 65, 66
BIX (Building Industry Cross-connect), 68
Krone block, 65, 67
TFTP (Trivial File Transfer Protocol), 112
threats, 349–350
three-tiered networking model, 139–140
three-way handshake, TCP, 24
TIA (Telecommunications Industry
    Association), 70, 434
    straight-through cables, 74–75
TKIP-RC4, 249
TLS (Transport Layer Security), 14
topologies, 28, 50
    bush, 31–32
    hybrid, 32
    logical *vs.* physical, 28
    mesh, 30–31
    ring, 29–30
    star, 28–29
Toredo tunneling, 92
tracert/traceroute, 472–473
traffic flows, 143–144
    send/receive, 283–284
traffic logs, 276
transceivers, fiber-optic
    bidirectional, 64
    incorrect, 442
    QSFP (quad small form-factor
        pluggable), 61–62
    QSFP+ (quad small form-factor pluggable+), 62
    SFP (small form-factor pluggable), 61
    SFP+ (small form-factor pluggable+), 61
    unidirectional, 63–64
Transport layer (OSI model), 13, 15–16
troubleshooting, 427
    cabling
        attenuation, 439–440
        bad ports, 441
        dB (decibel) loss, 440–441
        duplexing issues, 443
        EMI (electrical magnetic interference), 440
        incorrect pin-out, 441
        LED status indicators, 441–442
        open circuit, 441
        optical, dirty, 444
        short circuit, 441
        tools, 445–456
        transceivers, incorrect, 442–443
        TX/RX (transmit/receive) reverse, 443–444
    command-line tools
        arp, 473–474
        dig (Domain Information Groper), 471–472
        hostname, 476

ifconfig, 468–469
ip, 470
ipconfig, 466–468
netstat, 474–476
nmap, 479–481
nslookup, 470–471
ping, 466
route, 477–478
tcpdump, 478–479
telnet, 478
tracert/traceroute, 472–473
connections, 435
documentation, 433
establish plan of action, 429
establish probable cause theory, 430–432
identify the problem, 428–430
implement solution or escalate, 432–433
network issues
    addresses, blocked, 519
    asymmetrical routing, 505–506
    broadcast storm, 502–503
    BYOD issues, 527–528
    certificates, 517–518
    collisions, 501–502
    common issues, 493–498
    considerations, 489–493
    device configuration review, 499
    DHCP rogue server, 508–510
    DHCP scope exhaustion, 510
    DNS, incorrect, 514–515
    DNS issues, 520–524
    firewall settings, 519
    gateway, incorrect, 510–511
    hardware failure, 518–519
    interface status, 500
    IP addresses, duplicate, 503–505
    IP addresses, incorrect, 513–514
    IP settings, 510–515
    licensed features, 529
    limitations, 486–489
    MAC addresses, duplicate, 503
    missing route, 515–516
    multicast flooding, 505
    NTP issues, 525–527
    performance baselines, 500–501
    performance issues, 529–530
    ports, blocked, 519
    power budget, 516–517
    routing loops, 507–508
    routing tables, 499–500
    specifications, 486–489
    subnet mask, incorrect, 512–513
    switching loops, 506–507
    VLAN assignment, 500

VLAN, incorrect, 519–520
operating system commands, 481–485
software tools and
    bandwidth speed tester, 461
    IP scanner, 465–466
    iPerf, 461–462
    NetFlow Analyzer, 462–463
    packet sniffers, 459–460
    port scanner, 461
    protocol analyzer, 459–460
    terminal emulator, 463–465
    TFTP (Trivial File Transfer Protocol)
        server, 463
    Wi-Fi analyzer, 458–459
test theory, 431–432
trunk port, 230
TTL (time to live), 26
Twinax cable, 73
TWT (Target Wake Time), 238
TX/RX (transmit and receive) reverse, 443

U

U-NII (Unlicensed National Information
    Infrastructure), 236
UC (Unified Communications), 185
UDP (User Datagram Protocol), 15, 23, 118
unicast, 86, 90
unidirectional transceivers, 63–64
updates, network hardening, 387
UPS (uninterruptable power supply), 327
uptime/downtime, 293–294
USOC (universal service order code), 40
UTP (unshielded twisted-pair) cabling, 436

V

VDI (virtual desktop infrastructure), 402
VDSL (Very-high-bitrate Digital
    Subscriber Line), 46
vibration detectors, 408
video surveillance, 197
VIP (virtual IP), 106
    FHRP (first-hop redundancy protocol), 106
    HSRP (Hot Standby Router Protocol), 107
    VRRP (Virtual Router Redundancy
        Protocol), 107
virtualization, 40
    virtual networking components

NFV (network function
    virtualization), 41–43
vNIC (virtual network interface card),
    41
vSwitch (virtual switch), 41
VLANs (virtual local area networks), 227–228
    benefits, 228
    ISL (Inter-Switch Link), 229
    native, network hardening, 386–387
    ports, tagging/untagging, 230
    private, network hardening, 384–385
    troubleshooting, 500
    trunking, 228–230
    VLAN hopping, 371–372
    voice VLAN, 230–231
VM (virtual machine), 40
VNC (Virtual Network Computing), 402
vNIC (virtual network interface card), 41
voice VLANs, 230–231
VoIP (Voice over IP), 38
    PBX (private branch exchange), 184–185
    phones, 189–191
    PSTN (public switched telephone network), 185
VoIP gateway, 185–186
    PSTN (public switched telephone network), 185
VoIP PBX, 184
    TDM (time-division multiplexing) phones, 184
    UC (Unified Communications), 185
VPNs (virtual private networks), 160, 397–398
    client-to-site VPN, 399–400
    headend, 189
    protocols
        IPSec, 189
        L2TP (Layer 2 Tunneling Protocol), 189
        PPTP (Point-to-Point Tunneling
            Protocol), 189
    security, 397–400
    site-to-site VPN, 398
    tunneling, 189
VRRP (Virtual Router Redundancy Protocol),
    107, 325, 333
VSAT (very small aperture terminal), 48
VSLM (variable-length subnet mask),
    105–106, 107
vSwitch (virtual switch), 41
vulnerabilities
    CVE (Common Vulnerabilities and
        Exposures), 350
    zero-day, 351
vulnerability assessments, 364
VXLAN (virtual extensible local area
    network), 143

W

WAN (wide area network), 28, 34, 35, 50
WAP (wireless access point), 178–179
  CAPWAP (Control and Provisioning of Wireless Access Points), 180
  LWAP (lightweight access point), 180
  rogue access points, 374
warm sites, 331
well-known port numbers, 15
WEP (Wired Equivalent Privacy), 251
WiMAX (Worldwide Interoperability for Microwave Access), 49
Winsock, 15
wired topologies
  bus, 31–32
  hybrid, 32
  logical *vs.* physical, 28
  mesh, 30–31
  ring, 29–30
  star, 28–29
wireless antennas, 243–244
wireless multipath interference, 240
wireless networks, security
  antenna placement, 391
  captive portal, 394–395
  client isolation, 391–392
  EAP (Extensible Authentication Protocol), 392–394
  Geofencing, 394
  guest network isolation, 392
  power levels, 391
  PSKs (preshared keys), 392
wireless range extender, 181
wireless standards, 235–238
wiring diagrams, 311–313
WLAN (wireless LAN)
  802.11 standards, 235–238
  antennas, 243–244
  cellular connectivity
    5G, 253–254
    CDMA, 252
    GSM, 253
    LTE/4G, 253
    TDMA, 252

channel bandwidth, 240
channel bonding, 240–241
controller, 179–181
distance requirements, 240
frequencies
  2.4 GHz, 238–239
  5 GHz, 239
MIMO (multiple input, multiple output), 242
MU-MIMO (multiuser multiple-input, multiple-output), 242
security
  authentication, 250–252
  authorization, 250–252
  CCMP-AES, 250
  geofencing, 252
  MAC filtering, 252
  open, 251
  TKIP-RC4, 249
  WPA (Wi-Fi Protected Access), 249
  WPA2 (Wi-Fi Protected Access II), 249
site surveys, 244–245
speed requirements, 240
topologies
  ad hoc operation, 245–246
  ESS (extended service set), 247
  infrastructure, 246–247
  mesh networks, 247–248
  SSID (service set identifier), 245
WEP (Wired Equivalent Privacy), 251
WLC (wireless LAN controller), 247
WLAN (wireless local area network), 34, 35
WLC (wireless LAN controller), 179–181, 247
  MAC filtering, 391
WPA (Wi-Fi Protected Access), 249
WPA2 (Wi-Fi Protected Access II), 249
WWAN (wireless wide area network), 190
WWN (worldwide name), 147

X–Y–Z

Yagi antenna, 243
zero trust, 352–353

Online Test Bank

Register to gain one year of FREE access after activation to the online interactive test bank to help you study for your CompTIA Network+ certification exam—included with your purchase of this book! All of the chapter review questions and the practice tests in this book are included in the online test bank so you can practice in a timed and graded setting.

Register and Access the Online Test Bank

To register your book and get access to the online test bank, follow these steps:

1. Go to www.wiley.com/go/sybextestprep (this address is case sensitive)!
2. Select your book from the list.
3. Complete the required registration information, including answering the security verification to prove book ownership. You will be emailed a pin code.
4. Follow the directions in the email or go to www.wiley.com/go/sybextestprep.
5. Find your book on that page and click the "Register or Login" link with it. Then enter the pin code you received and click the "Activate PIN" button.
6. On the Create an Account or Login page, enter your username and password, and click Login or, if you don't have an account already, create a new account.
7. At this point, you should be in the test bank site with your new test bank listed at the top of the page. If you do not see it there, please refresh the page or log out and log back in.